PUBLIC POLIC

Perspectives & Choices

Second Edition

PUBLIC POLICY
Perspectives & Choices

Charles L. Cochran
U.S. Naval Academy

Eloise F. Malone
U.S. Naval Academy

McGraw-Hill
College

Boston   Burr Ridge, IL   Dubuque, IA   Madison, WI
New York   San Francisco   St. Louis
Bangkok   Bogotá   Caracas   Lisbon   London   Madrid   Mexico City
Milan   New Delhi   Seoul   Singapore   Sydney   Taipei   Toronto

McGraw-Hill College

A Division of The **McGraw-Hill** *Companies*

PUBLIC POLICY
Perspectives & Choices, Second Edition

This book is printed on acid-free paper.

1 2 3 4 5 6 7 8 9 0 DOC/DOC 9 3 2 1 0 9 8

ISBN 0–07–290896–3

Editorial director: *Jane E. Vaicunas*
Sponsoring editor: *Monica Eckman*
Senior marketing manager: *Suzanne Daghlian*
Project manager: *Vicki Krug*
Production supervisor: *Sandy Ludovissy*
Freelance design coordinator: *Mary L. Christianson*
Senior photo research coordinator: *Carrie K. Burger*
Supplement coordinator: *Rita L. Hingtgen*
Compositor: *GAC-Indianapolis*
Typeface: *10/12 Times Roman*
Printer: *R. R. Donnelley & Sons Company/Crawfordsville, IN*

Freelance cover designer: *Kristyn A. Kalnes*
Cover photograph: © *Diana Ong/SuperStock*

Library of Congress Cataloging-in-Publication Data

Cochran, Charles L.
    Public policy : perspectives & choices / Charles L. Cochran.
Eloise R. Malone — 2nd ed.
      p.   cm.
    Includes bibliographical references and index.
    ISBN 0–07–290896–3
    1. Policy sciences.   I. Malone, Eloise F.   II. Title.
H97.C6   1999
320'.6—dc21   98–42232
                                       CIP

www.mhhe.com

ABOUT THE AUTHORS

CHARLES L. COCHRAN is a professor of political science and past chairperson of the department at the U.S. Naval Academy. He holds a B.S. degree from Mount St. Mary's College and a Ph.D. from Tuft's University. He has authored numerous articles, contributed several chapters to books, and edited and coauthored a book on civil-military relations. He has served as a consultant to the Department of Energy, Commerce, and Transportation. He has also worked at the Defense Intelligence Agency. He has served on the editorial board of scholarly journals. Professor Cochran is married and has four adult-aged children.

ELOISE F. MALONE is an associate professor of political science at the U.S. Naval Academy. She received her B.A. from the Pennsylvania State University and her Ph.D. from American University. Professor Malone previously worked at the U.S. Department of State where she analyzed public opinion. Professor Malone's primary fields of teaching and research are political philosophy, quantitative methods and policy analysis, the use of computer applications in political science, and French Canadian politics. She is the author or coauthor of numerous articles ranging from public opinion analysis to ethics, and psychological preferences.

For Mimi and Our Children,
Christy, Collie, Cassie, and Chip
and my parents,
Leo and Mary Cochran
C.L.C.

For Dave and Our Children,
Jim, Mike, and Katherine
and my parents,
Richard and Margaret Forgette
E.F.M.

CONTENTS

PREFACE

The primary purpose of the second edition is to tell the story of public policy in a clear, scholarly, balanced, and interesting manner. It is a narrative of great importance—one that sharpens and clarifies our understanding of present day public policy and provides a unique perspective not found in other fields of political science or economics.

The study of public policy continues to grow as the discipline of political science matures. Just as important perhaps is the erosion of barriers between disciplines. New perspectives, new evidence, new policy problems, and new and changing values invite a reconsideration of basic disputes and past approaches to policy.

Although the basic characteristics and aspects of the first edition are retained, the second edition has been substantially updated and revised.

Why *Public Policy: Perspectives and Choices*

In this edition we present the theoretical foundations and practical realities of public policy. We present the most recent contribution to policy theory from the field of economics known as public choice theory. Public choice theory applies the economic model of the market to politics and has had a major impact on policy analysis and decision-making. In this edition we analyze the theory and make clear both its strengths and weaknesses in the realm of public philosophy.

Understanding the implications of public policy choices is essential for every educated citizen. For over two centuries, the United States has been an inspiring example to the rest of the world representing what an informed and involved citizenry could achieve. The potential for Democratic government to be regarded as a positive instrument in promoting the general welfare appeared victorious after the Great Depression. This has prompted many nations with nondemocratic pasts to turn to participatory government along with the harnessing of market solutions to resolve many policy dilemmas.

At the same time, political realities have encouraged many conservative politicians to attack positive government policies as a threat to American freedoms and to propose a minimalist role for government. As the new millennium approaches, many Americans have become increasingly detached from public life. Attacks on the institutions of

American government as *the problem* make it extraordinarily difficult to craft compromises needed to produce effective policies. Unfortunately this tactic is increasingly used by well-financed special interest groups to block policies inimical to their interests. Politicians, pundits, and the media often focus on symbols leading to polarization and paralysis, rather than on the substantive issues that might lead to consensus and real problem solving. The ability to assess the perspectives of liberal and conservative ideologies that sometimes work against collective responsibility and to assess proposed policy alternatives is enhanced if one has a grounding in policy theory.

Public policy, as a discipline, is optimistic. It is based on the profoundly significant belief that the citizenry in a democratic society can take responsible actions to improve the national well-being.

The Plan of This Text. How It Is Different and How It Has Changed in the Second Edition.

Introductory public policy textbooks often ignore basic concepts used by policy analysts and social scientists. Some begin by encouraging students to discuss controversial substantive issues without any development of theory, while others study public policy primarily as process, or encourage the use of basic model(s) with which to examine policy. Although political scientists have long used these approaches, interdisciplinary techniques in recent decades have contributed important new understandings. We believe it is important for students to be thoroughly grounded in the application of such concepts as opportunity costs, production possibilities, market failures, the median voter, and market externalities among others. The first five chapters provide a tour of the basic elements of a "political scientist's way of thinking" about policy issues, while always keeping in mind that politicians pay more attention to the need to raise money and to win votes than to policy analysts.

These chapters deal with fundamental aspects of issues including scarcity, rational self-interest, the tragedy of the commons, the free rider problem, market and government failures, and other issues relating to the political, economic, and philosophical basis of public policy. Although the leading professional journals in public policy now routinely deal with these topics, they are frequently ignored in public policy texts. We believe that these topics should be presented as an essential part of the "core" of public policy that students will remember long after the course is over. We develop the difference between the idealism often presented and the reality of the environment in which public policy is hammered out. We often hear that the people rule in our "democracy" and we would like to think it were true. However candidates for political office must raise large sums of money from private benefactors while pretending that their views of policy are not influenced by major donors. The general interests of ordinary citizens are drowned out by financial elites and special-interest groups. Growing cynicism leads to an ironic alliance between the average citizen who comes to believe that the democratic process is largely a mockery, and therefore agrees with the financial elite that it is best to entrust as little to government policymaking as possible.

In economic markets practically everything is for sale. In a political society, many things should be beyond price. This edition emphasizes that an overreliance on markets produces suboptimal political outcomes. In fact market solutions only provide a new set of rules in determining winners and losers.

Understanding the principles are important because they are fundamentally very logical, but often misunderstood by intelligent laypersons. Almost every idea in public policy can be explained clearly in language understandable to the average reader. We have done our utmost to accomplish this task. At the same time we try to avoid over-simplification of the complexities of many policy issues. We try to elevate the policy problems by highlighting political, philosophical, or economic problems that underlie the issue. We find that policy issues that are interwoven with theoretical perspectives and choices work well.

In this edition we have increased the boxed areas that contain further explanations of concepts, contain case studies, or connect problems with other ideas addressed elsewhere in the text. The boxed areas serve at least two purposes. First, they illustrate the application of ideas or concepts in policymaking. Secondly, they serve as a medium for introducing or developing important ideas and issues that may be tangential to the main flow of the chapter, and are therefore best treated separately.

Even more than in the first edition, we have compared U.S. approaches to public policymaking with those of other advanced countries of the world. Today what goes on in the rest of the world has a far greater impact on a variety of policy issues in the United States than was the case fifty years ago. Other countries have faced the same policy dilemmas as the United States and frequently they have made different policy choices that can inform U.S. policy choices.

Finally we have tried to emphasize that, although capitalism appeals to the individual's self-interest, public policy goes beyond the narrow appeal to individual self interest, to the larger purpose to "promote the general welfare." All capitalist societies recognize that market failures contribute to outcomes that are unacceptable. Individual welfare is inextricably bound up with the general welfare of others. Policy studies must inevitably raise issues about the ethical relationship between man and his fellowman. The study of public policy involves the thoughtful use of interdisciplinary insights and empirical evidence in pursuit of "social justice." Government involvement is inevitable. The goal is for wise policymaking to provide for a humane society and an efficient economy.

ACKNOWLEDGMENTS

We are indebted to so many people for their help in writing this book that it is difficult to know where to begin thanking them. Our parents imparted a strong sense of social justice and fairness to us. We were also encouraged by them to be informed about political issues and to be open to new ways of seeing things. This debt cannot be repaid, only acknowledged.

Second, our spouses, Mimi and Dave, have continued to encourage us in the undertaking of the second edition. Others have helped in numerous ways from checking footnotes to tracking down sources. Among them we owe special thanks to Barbara Breeden, Dr. Katherine Dickson, William McQuade, Barbara Yoakum, and Florence Todd. Ann Scotti helped with word processing. Many of our colleagues helped by providing information, sources, articles, and frequently unknowingly, through conversations that stimulated new ideas, or resulted in the modification of our own.

Throughout the entire process there were many reviewers who read and reread our drafts and made many helpful comments: Dr. Denis J. Woods, Shepherd College; Dr. Anne M. Gurnack, University of Wisconsin at Parkside; Dr. Michael T. Corgan, Boston University; Dr. Don F. MaCabe, Southern Illinois University at Edwardsville; Dr. Lilliard Richardson, The University of Tennessee, Knoxville; Dr. Gary Klass, Illinois State University; William Arp, III, Louisiana State University; Robert Bartlett, Purdue University; Dennis Daley, North Carolina State University; David Davis, University of Toledo; John Hird, University of Massachusetts–Amherst; Michele Hoyman, University of Missouri–St. Louis; Karen Hult, VPI; Susan Hunter, West Virginia University; Eugene McGregor, Indiana University; Mark Peterson, University of New Mexico; Terrel Rhodes, University of North Carolina; Evan Ringquist, Texas Tech University; David Robertson, University of Missouri–St. Louis; Susan Tenenbaum, Baruch College; and R. Lawson Veasey, University of Central Arkansas.

Several revisions were classroom tested by midshipmen at the United States Naval Academy, students at The Johns Hopkins University, and at Central Michigan University. These students made helpful comments which we have tried to incorporate in the final draft of the manuscript.

Particular acknowledgment must be made to those at McGraw-Hill who have been extremely helpful throughout the entire process of producing this text. Rose Arlia, as always, was extremely supportive and enthusiastic. We especially appreciate the attention and interest provided by Monica Eckman, the political science editor, and Vicki Krug, the project manager, who guided the project through each step and took a special interest in this work. Hannah Glover was also very helpful with information, responding to questions, and pressuring us to make deadlines. Heartfelt thanks goes to Rose Kramer whose vigilant copyediting has saved us from public ridicule. For any errors that remain, the authors blame each other.

Charles L. Cochran

Eloise F. Malone

1

BASIC CONCEPTS IN PUBLIC POLICY

We begin this book by introducing you to the vocabulary of public policy. The following pages define concepts students need to know to understand the policy process. The driving forces pushing public policies are scarcity and rational self-interest. In a diverse society embracing different values and points of view, interests collide and compromises are unavoidable. The policy analyst must deal with practical questions of who will gain and who will lose by any given policy. Will government intervention improve upon a market solution? The analyst must also be aware of the need to examine the ideas regarding normative values of what is good for society as a whole.

WHAT IS PUBLIC POLICY?

Public policy emerged as a prominent subfield within the discipline of political science in the mid-1960s. In a broad sense, the analysis of public policy dates back to the beginning of civilization. **Public policy is the study of government decisions and actions designed to deal with a matter of public concern.** **Policy analysis** describes the investigations that produce accurate and useful information for decision makers.

Policy Analysis as a Subfield of Political Science

The social sciences emerged from the humanities and the natural sciences during the latter part of the nineteenth century. The commitment to the methods of the natural sciences, with its concern for methodological and analytical rigor in the study of human behavior, has been critical to the development of social science. The social sciences developed from the historic cultural values and condition of the social community with the conviction that rational scientific methods could be used to improve the human condition. The scientific method began to be applied to a wide range of social activity ranging from the efforts of Frederick A. Taylor's studies on scientific management to the politics of the Progressives. Legislation in the Progressive era delegated to "experts" in such new and presumably independent, shielded from political pressure, regulatory agencies as the Federal Trade Commission and the Federal Reserve Commission.

Positive Policy Analysis and Value Neutrality   Although the social sciences emerged in an environment of social reform, by the early twentieth century there was a general retreat from any sort of policy advocacy. The social sciences in general adopted a value neutral position under the guise of scientific objectivity. Scientific thought is probably one of the most prestigious activities in modern life. And those engaged in policy studies from a variety of social science disciplines were attracted to the idea that their studies would be more scientific if they eliminated values and merely focused on social behavior. The result was to confine many policy studies to empirical descriptions. Such studies may prove useful in a variety of ways.

Positive Policy Analysis   Emphasis on value-free policy analysis is referred to as **positive policy analysis** and is concerned with understanding how the **policy process** works. This aspect strives to understand public policy **as it is.** It also endeavors to explain how various social and political forces would change policy. Positive policy analysis tries to pursue truth through the process of testing hypotheses by measuring them against the standard of real-world experiences. Positive policy analysis usually deals with assertions of cause and effect. A disagreement over such analysis can usually be resolved by examining the facts. For instance, the following is a positive statement: "If the U.S. government raises interest rates, then consumers will borrow less." We can check the validity of this statement by measuring it against real-world observations. Other positive policy statements such as "If long-term welfare recipients were required to finish their high school education as a condition of continuing to receive their welfare checks, a high percentage would develop employable skills and become self-sufficient," may be tested by setting up an experiment within a state. The results may confirm or refute the statement.

The attempt to become more scientific by excluding values had several major effects. First, by narrowing their focus it reduced the relevance of policy analysts for policymakers who must be concerned with preferred end-states such as "reduced ethnic antagonisms." Secondly, it reduced the importance of values in policy debates by shifting the discussion to cost-benefit analysis or the appropriate way to test a hypothesis. Finally, by glossing over the normative issues, the field of values was abandoned to business interests and social conservatives. Applying models based on market efficiency while ignoring issues of "justice and fairness" played into the hands of business interests and social conservatives who never stopped touting the values of right to property, and the virtues of self-reliance, independence, thrift, and hard work.

Normative Analysis   The Great Depression and Franklin Roosevelt contributed to a major change in policy approaches. The Roosevelt revolution swept aside any suggestion that promoting the general welfare could be divorced from normative goals. Nevertheless there were many in the New Deal who preferred to think of themselves as a rather elite group of experts engaged in administering programs remaining above petty partisan bickering. Until the Depression, in which 25 percent of the labor force was unemployed, it was thought that unemployment was a personal problem, not a matter for government action. The Roosevelt administration changed that perception by opposing excessive unemployment through a variety of government policies. Government planning during the New Deal gave great impetus to operations research, systems analysis, and cost-benefit analysis as techniques for efficient management. After WWII, debates within the social sciences forced a search for more inclusive policy models. During the Kennedy administration new techniques such as the Planning, Programming, and Budgeting System (PPBS) were used by the "whiz kids" brought into government service by Robert McNamara in the Pentagon.

The applied orientation of these techniques in the Department of Defense earned public recognition and acceptance of policy analysis while it encouraged debate within the social sciences to become more active contributors to policy analysis and policymaking.[1] The techniques noted above, along with survey research, had wide applicability not only in public policy, but also in private industry. The result was increased debate between those in the social sciences who wished to maintain a more theoretical approach of positive analysis and those who wished to see the policy sciences applied to society's problems. In 1966, Hans J. Morgenthau, a well-known political scientist, summed up the views of those in favor of applying quantitative techniques to achieve practical outcomes in a statement that could just as well apply to all the policy sciences when he wrote:

> A political science that is neither hated nor respected, but treated with indifference as an innocuous pastime, is likely to have retreated into a sphere that lies beyond the positive or negative interests of society. The retreat into the trivial, the formal, the methodological, the purely theoretical, the remotely historical—in short, the politically irrelevant—is the unmistakable sign of a "noncontroversial" political science which has neither friends nor enemies because it has no relevance for the great political issues in which society has a stake.[2]

David Easton, in his presidential address to the American Political Science Association in 1969, signaled this momentum when he called for a "post-behavioral" approach that used techniques, methods, and insights of all relevant disciplines in dealing with social issues.[3]

This analysis performed by **policy analysts** with a view toward resolving public issues is **prescriptive** rather than **descriptive** in that it recommends action to be taken rather than merely describe policy processes. This is referred to as normative policy analysis. **Normative policy analysis is directed toward studying what public policy ought to be to improve the general welfare.**

---

[1]Robert A. Heineman, et al. *The World of the Policy Analyst: Rationality, Values, & Politics.* (Chatham, NJ: Chatham House Publishers, Inc., 1990), p. 17.

[2]Hans J. Morgenthau, "The Purpose of Political Science," in James C. Charlesworth (ed.), *A Design for Political Science: Scope, Objectives, and Methods,* Monograph 6 (Philadelphia: The American Academy of Political and Social Science, 1966), pp. 67–68.

[3]David Easton, "The New Revolution in Political Science," *The American Political Science Review* 63 (December 1969): pp. 1051–61.

Normative analysis deals with statements involving value judgments about what **should be.** For example, the assertion that "the cost of health care in the United States is too high" is a normative statement. This statement cannot be confirmed by referring to data. Whether the cost is too high or is appropriate is based on a given criterion. Its validity depends upon one's values and ethical views. Individuals may agree on the facts of health care costs but disagree over their ethical judgments regarding the implications of "the cost of health care."

It is important to be aware of the distinction between positive and normative policy analysis, and not to substitute the goals or methods of one for those of the other. That is because the value of policy analysis is determined by the accurate observation of the critical variables in the external environment. Only an accurate rendering of factual relationships can indicate how best to achieve normative goals. For example, a normative view that we should improve the educational system in the United States does not indicate how to achieve that goal most effectively or most efficiently. If we have limited resources to add to the education budget, how should we spend the funds? Would higher salaries attract more capable teachers? Should we extend the school year? Should we improve the teacher-to-pupil ratio by hiring more teachers? Should we add alternative educational programs? Only a rigorous study of the costs and benefits of various alternatives can indicate a preferred solution. In a republican form of government such as our own, such questions are settled by voting and through decisions made by those elected to run the institutions of government.

Frequently, however, normative statements can be used to develop positive hypotheses. Generally, most people do not feel strongly about the value of a capital gains tax cut. Their support or opposition to such a change in the tax law depends on a prescriptive belief about a valued end state. Many politicians press to reduce the federal tax on capital gains. They argue that a reduction in the capital gains tax would increase incentives to invest in the economy and thus fuel economic growth. However, computer estimates have shown that this change in the tax structure would reduce government revenues after several years and raise the federal deficit. Estimates also showed that upper-income groups would receive a larger per capita benefit by far than other income groups. The result of these estimates, when publicized, was an increased popular perception that the tax cut would be "unfair." Despite a modest capital gains cut, Republicans have had difficulty in aggressively pressing the issue.

In the decision to study public policy, there is an implicit ethical view that people and their welfare are important. We must try to learn about all the forces that affect the well-being of individuals and of society in the aggregate. The desire to improve the current system is the basis for public policy. To achieve that goal, students of public policy must first understand how the current system works.

The analysis of public policy conveys the importance of the use of rigorous methodological tools and rational argument. In democratic societies, the decision-making authority is characterized by varying degrees of decentralization. When decision-making authority is distributed between different power centers, such as the different branches of government—executive, legislative, and judicial, as well as local, state, or national levels and including various interest groups, and the general public—no single group's will is totally dominant. **Policy analysts** therefore study **how the actors in the policy**

process make decisions: how issues get on the agenda, what goals are developed by the various groups, and how are they pursued. Political elites must share power. They often differ concerning not only which problems must be addressed, but how they should be addressed. The policy that results is often the result of different powerful groups pulling in different directions. The outcome often differs from what anyone intended. Policy analysts therefore study how individuals and groups in the policy process interact with each other.

Policy analysts also attempt to apply rational analysis to the effort to produce better policy decisions. Thus by empirical and rational analysis, a body of research findings opens up the possibility for policy analysts to provide valuable input to "promote the general welfare."

DECISIONS AND POLICY MAKING

Public opinion polls confirm that people worry about their economic well-being more than any other concern. People worry about educating their children and meeting mortgage payments. They worry about the high cost of health care, the needs of an elderly parent, and the threat of unemployment. These concerns cut across age groups. Students worry about finding a job when they graduate, paying their rent, and making insurance payments. Many people express concern for economic problems like federal budget deficits, taxes, and inflation. Many are increasingly aware that personal well-being is somehow related to broader social trends. This relationship is the domain of public policy, though few really understand how the public policy process works or how it affects them personally.

Public policy consists of political decisions for implementing programs to achieve societal goals. These decisions hopefully represent a consensus of values. When analyzed, **public policy consists of a plan of action or program and a statement of objectives,** in other words, a map and a destination. The objectives statement, the destination, tells us **what we want to achieve with policy.** Objectives also describe **who** will be affected by policy. Public policy program statements, the map, outline the process or the necessary steps to achieve the policy objectives. They tell us how to do it. For example, a newly proposed public policy for national health care would include an objective statement explaining why a health care policy matters along with a detailed health care program or procedure. The program might be "managed competition," or perhaps a "Canadian single-payer" program. Usually, the program stage is when the rubber hits the road and people are forced to face up to the values and principles they espouse.

Ultimately public policy is about people, their values and needs, their options and choices. The basic challenge confronting public policy is the fact of **scarcity**. We cannot have everything we want. Unfortunately available resources are limited, while for practical purposes human wants are limitless. **Scarcity is an ever present attribute of the human condition.** The combination of limited resources and unlimited wants, requires that we choose among the goods and services to be produced and in what quantities. Because of scarcity, government may intervene to ration the distribution of certain goods and services thought to be in the public interest. Thus, because of scarcity, there is a need for governmental organizations (such as the Departments of Education,

Energy, Defense, Health and Human Services, Treasury, and so forth) to allocate resources among competing potential users. Conversely, if there were no scarcity, we would not have to make choices between which goods or services to produce.

Poverty and scarcity are not synonymous. Scarcity exists because there are insufficient resources to satisfy all human wants. If poverty were eliminated, scarcity would remain because even though everyone might have a minimally acceptable standard of living, society still would not have adequate resources to produce everything people desired.

Opportunity Costs

Public policy focuses on the **choices** individuals and governments make. Because of scarcity, people and societies are forced to make choices. **Whenever we make a choice, opportunity costs are incurred**. When individual, or society's unlimited wants press against our limited resources, some wants must go unsatisfied. To achieve one goal, we usually have to forego another. Policy choices determine which wants we will satisfy and which will go unsatisfied. The most highly valued opportunity forfeited by a choice is known as the **opportunity cost.** This cost equals the value of the most desired goods or services forgone. In other words, to choose one alternative means that we sacrifice the opportunity to choose a different alternative. For example, when you decide to enroll in college rather than get a job, the opportunity cost of college includes not only the cost of tuition and other expenses, but also the forgone salary.

People grouped in societies face different kinds of choices. **The opportunity cost of any government program is determined by the most valuable alternative use.** One tradeoff society faces is between national defense (guns) and social goods (butter). A fixed amount of money, say $100 billion, can be used to buy military goods, or an equivalent amount of social goods (education or health care), but it cannot be used to purchase both goods simultaneously. A decision to have more of one good is also a decision to have less of other goods. Another policy tradeoff society faces is between a cleaner environment and income. Laws requiring reduced pollution result in higher production costs, which simultaneously squeeze profits, put a downward pressure on wages, and an upward pressure on prices. Laws to reduce pollution may give us a cleaner, healthier environment, but at the cost of reducing corporate profits and workers' wages while raising costs for consumers.

The saying that **there is no such thing as a free lunch** indicates that, because of scarcity, choices must be made which preclude other alternatives.[4] This may seem an obvious point, but many often assume that there is a free lunch. For instance many people speak of "free public schools," or the need for "free medical care," or "free highways." The problem is that "free" suggests no opportunities forfeited and no sacrifice. This is not the case, however, as the resources that provide education, health care, or

---

[4]The statement is accurate when referring to the market in the long run. However, it is not necessarily true in the polity in the short run. There are many public policies in which taxes paid by some people are redistributed to provide benefits for others. For example middle-income taxpayers may provide funds for food stamps for the poor. Those providing the largesse for others usually want spending reductions, while the recipients of the benefits favor more resources.

FIGURE 1-1
PRODUCTION POSSIBILITIES CURVE.

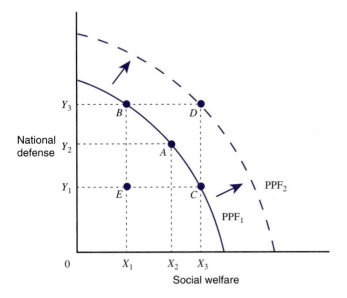

highways could have been used to produce other goods. Recognizing that we face choices with tradeoffs as individuals, and collectively in society, does not tell us what decisions we will or should make. But it is important to recognize the tradeoffs in our choices because we can make astute decisions only if we clearly understand the options.

The opportunity cost principle can be illustrated. Figure 1-1 summarizes the hypothetical choices in what political economists call a **production possibilities curve (PPC).** This production possibilities curve or **production possibilities frontier (PPF)** provides a menu of output choices between any two alternatives. **Think of it as a curve representing tradeoffs.** It illustrates the hard choices we must make when resources are scarce, or the opportunity costs associated with the output of any desired quantity of a good. It also illustrates the indirect effect of **factors of production** defined as land, labor, and capital. Our ability to alter the mix of output depends on the ease with which the factors of production can be shifted from one area to another. For example, with the collapse of communism the government shifted some production from the defense industry to the civilian sector.

In figure 1-1 the economy is at point A but conservatives want to pull it to point B while liberals prefer point C, resulting in a political struggle. Both could get the quantity they want through economic growth (point D). Even at point D both soon find that their wants are greater than the scarce resources available. And the tug-of-war would soon begin on the new PPF. Keep in mind that points on (not inside) the production possibilities frontier indicate efficient levels of production. When the economy is producing at point A, for example, there is no way to produce more of one good without producing less of the other. If we want more of one good we must get less of the other. When a policy decision moves the production from point A to point B, for instance, society produces more national defense but at the expense of producing less social welfare.

The economy cannot operate outside its production frontier with current resources and technology. It is not desirable to operate inside the frontier. Note that point E is a feasible output combination but not a desirable one. Why? Because by moving to B, for instance, the economy could produce as much social welfare as at E but it could also produce considerably more national defense. Or by moving to C more social welfare could be produced without sacrificing the production of defense. Production at point E means that the economy's resources are not being used efficiently.

As we move more factors of production from the production of national defense toward social welfare, we must give up ever-increasing quantities of defense in order to get more social welfare and vice versa. **This is a phenomenon so universal that it is referred to as the principle of increasing costs.** It states that the opportunity costs of producing additional units of one good increases as more resources are used to produce that good. Or, stated differently, in order to get more of one good in a given period, the production of other goods must fall by ever-increasing amounts.

Production potential is not fixed for all time. As more resources or better technology become available, production possibilities increase. As population increases, the number of potential workers increases production possibilities. An improvement in the quality of the labor force, such as through improved education, or investment in new plants and equipment, can also increase production possibilities. The outward shift of the PPF is at the heart of an expanding economy. This also means a reduction of opportunity costs and a potential increase in an overall standard of living.

The points along the production possibility curve or frontier indicate that many bundles of goods can be produced with the same resources. Consequently, movement along the PPF demonstrates that most changes in public policy are modest or **incremental** shifts. Policy changes are usually, but not always, relatively small, and are typically made with **current conditions** in mind. Hence the best predictor of what the federal budget will be next year is the current budget. The decision to change the budget is made at the **margin.** Essentially, **decisions at the margin** mean that we focus on the effects of small changes in particular activities. Policy makers usually consider marginal factors, not total benefits and costs, and, as a result, we are not faced with all-or-nothing choices. An important principle for anyone studying public policy is the significance of **marginal analysis. Marginal analysis** is a decision-making process that is concerned with the additional benefits that a plan of action will provide and the additional costs that will be incurred. A policy analyst would recommend that a proposed action be taken if and only if the marginal benefit of the action exceeds the marginal cost.

Studying the PPF helps us see that choosing what mix of goods and services to produce is the essence of public policy considerations. A nation may face a guns-versus-butter choice in a period of high threat to national security, and environmental protection versus health care might come to the fore in peacetime. Shifts outward in the PPF represent growth; however the production possibilities curve says nothing about the desirability of any particular combination of goods and services. To understand this, we have to know more than what choices have been made. **We must also know why and how individuals and groups make choices and who benefits.**

SOCIAL CHOICE

Resource scarcity sets up the conditions for social choice. It is important to emphasize that choices are ultimately made by individuals. The press may report that "Congress passed a bill," or that "a divided Supreme Court decided . . . ," but these are summary expressions of a group decision-making process. Actually a majority of the **individual members** of Congress voted for a bill, or a majority of the **individual members** of the Court decided a case before it. The mechanism for aggregating individual choices to arrive at collective decisions is democratic majority rule. The democratic process translates the private interests of individual human beings into group decisions. Interested individuals freely express their preferences and decide, in the aggregate, what the public policy decision will be. However, as we shall examine later, public opinion and the voting process may provide very weak guidance to political elites.

While individual choice is the basic unit of public policy analysis, there are often situations in which we treat an organization such as a government agency, a lobbying group, or even a family as a black box. A black box is a gadget whose output is known even though its internal workings are not completely known. Mechanisms such as television sets or computers are, for most, black boxes. In the public policy realm, in some instances we will open the black box to examine exactly how and why certain individual and group decisions are made. It is of crucial importance that as students of public policy we understand what goes on within the black box of the "political system." We need to know how policy is produced within the institutional processes of the political environment and how voters, interest groups, and political parties behave.

More importantly, public policy originates in our understanding of the public interest. Appealing to that public interest is difficult because it mirrors the disagreement among competing concepts of social morality and justice. In many situations there may be no conflict between acting in one's self-interest **and** the interest of others, or the common good, simultaneously. More frequently, however, if people act in their narrow self-interest, it becomes impossible to achieve the common good. A healthy public spirit, the social form of altruism, sometimes referred to as social responsibility, is essential for a healthy democracy. A willingness to accept the general interest as one's own is what President Kennedy referred to when he said, "Ask not what your country can do for you, but what you can do for your country."

SOCIAL JUSTICE

Public policy analysis is by its very nature **normative.** Normative analysis raises questions about what policy **should be.** Questions are raised about what "ought" to shape the dissatisfaction felt over current policy, as well as the proposals for a "preferred" policy in the future. Normative policy analysis is concerned with how the individual justifies the use of state authority to pursue one purpose rather than another.

Because self-interest inevitably conflicts with the interest of others, it is impossible to achieve an absolute moral consensus about appropriate government policy. A fundamental problem is that the American polity lacks a practical agreement on the meaning of justice. The result is that conflict and not consensus is at the center of modern politics and public policy.

To illustrate the problem, consider a controversy between two individuals. One individual, Joan, is concerned with what she believes is the arbitrary nature of the distribution of wealth and income. She is particularly distressed over the accompanying inequality of power between those with considerable wealth and those without. She concludes that the poor are virtually powerless to improve their condition, while the wealthy are able to increase their wealth and power with ease. The great inequalities in wealth and power are considered **unjust** by Joan. She concludes that government efforts to redistribute wealth in the direction of the poor through taxes is demanded by simple justice. This help by government activity will lead to greater individual freedom and justice. Joan therefore decides to vote for political candidates who support such taxes and her notion of justice.

The second individual, Robert, has worked hard to achieve certain goals in life. These include financial independence that permits him to purchase a house, to travel, to send his children to college, and sufficient investments to permit a comfortable retirement. He now finds his goals jeopardized by proposals to raise taxes to reduce the deficit and to provide housing for the indigent. He regards these policies that threaten his goals as **unjust** because they deprive him of his financial resources against his will. He believes that justice demands the full entitlement of each person to the fruits of his or her own labor, and that each individual should have the complete rights to use and control them.

If the economy is growing rapidly enough, Joan's projects may be implemented without threatening Robert's goals. In that case they may both vote for the same political candidates. But if the economy is stagnant, and either Joan's or Robert's policies must be sacrificed to the other, it becomes clear that each has a view of justice that is logically incompatible with the other. In such cases each will use their competing concepts of justice to promote incompatible social goals.

John Rawls has received considerable attention for his treatise *A Theory of Justice,*[5] in which he addresses the question of what constitutes a just distribution of goods in society, what kinds and how much. He holds that principles of just distribution may limit legitimate acquisition. If applying principles of just distribution requires a redistributive tax or the taking of property through eminent domain, that acceptance of the taking of property is the price that must be paid to achieve a broader justice in the community.

Robert Nozick argues in his book *Anarchy, State, and Utopia* in response to Rawls that each individual has a right in justice to the product of his or her labor unless or until that individual chooses to give some part of it to another person (or to a central authority for redistribution).[6] If the result of individual acquisition is a gross inequality between individuals, justice requires that the disparity be accepted.

The price to be paid for justice in each definition must be paid by another group. Neither of these contending principles of justice is socially neutral.[7] American culture

[5]John Rawls, *A Theory of Justice* (Cambridge, MA: Harvard University Press, 1971).

[6]Robert Nozick, *Anarchy, State, and Utopia* (New York: Basic Books, 1974). This work is primarily a response to John Rawls. The extension of Nozick's thought leads to a view that the only form of economic life compatible with individualism is laissez faire capitalism.

Nozick's position is in the tradition of writers in the anarcho-capitalist tradition. His response to Rawls has attracted more comment than the writings of others with similar views.

[7]See Alasdair MacIntyre, *After Virtue: A Study in Moral Theory,* 2d ed. (Notre Dame, IN: University of Notre Dame Press, 1984), especially Chapter 17, "Justice as a Virtue: Changing Conceptions," for an excellent comparison of the theory of John Rawls and Nozick's countering view.

has no accepted rational criterion for deciding between rights based on lawful entitlement versus claims based on need. However, Rawls and Nozick both suggest rational principles to appeal to the contending parties. Some, like Rawls, define justice in relation to an equitable distribution in society. For them, justice is based upon a consideration of the present-day distribution. Justice should have priority over economic efficiency. This leads them to an appeal against absolute entitlement. Others, like Nozick, argue legal acquisition of wealth and income in the past alone is relevant; present-day distribution is irrelevant.[8] They appeal against distributive rules to a justice based upon entitlement.

Neither Rawls nor Nozick refer to what is **deserved** based upon justice. But concepts of what is **deserved** or **merited** are implied. Nozick argues that **individuals are entitled in justice to their wealth and property**, and **not that they deserve that wealth and property.** However, groups supporting this position invariably argue that they are entitled to what they have acquired through their efforts, or the efforts of others who have legally passed title to them. Rawls protests on behalf of the poor that their poverty is undeserved and therefore unwarranted. The child born to the migrant worker is no less deserving than the child born to a family of wealth and privilege. Rawls called this the "natural lottery." Both complain about perceived injustice.

The debate over taxes further illustrates this difference in values between distributive justice and entitlement theory. The modern opposition to any tax increases or government expenditure policies originates in the strongly negative attitude toward taxation among those who must pay them. Taxes, they argue, are paid primarily by the haves, while benefits accrue primarily to the have nots. Many of the more fortunate members of society oppose all taxation, but their opposition to the redistribution of wealth through tax policy is not put so crudely.

A concern for liberty, the requirements of justice, efficiency, or the virtues of laissez-faire capitalism are the most frequently cited justifications. Indeed it is perhaps naive to expect the privileged to respond sympathetically to policies that transfer resources from themselves to others, particularly since there is no community consensus on virtue. The affluent attack government as an arbitrary, profligate liability that is only held in check by relentless attention to its defects and efforts to hold it in check. Those with the temerity to promise increased services for the needy are promptly labeled "big spenders."

The Rawls-Nozick philosophical debate is an extension of the economic and political rift between different groups in society. Not only is there no value consensus in public policy, but modern political competition is a less violent form of civil war.

POLITICS AND ECONOMICS

How societies decide to utilize their scarce resources is determined by a variety of factors, along with values including the history, culture, socioeconomic development, and forms of government and economic organization of those societies. The classic definition of

---

[8]Nozick's critics point out that his thesis assumes that legitimate entitlements can be traced back to rightful acts of earliest acquisition. Based upon that criterion, however, there are few legitimate entitlements as most property has been inherited from those who originally used force or theft to steal the common lands of the first inhabitants.

political science is that it is a study of **"Who gets what, when, and how in and through government."**[9] Consequently, politics involves the struggle over the allocation of resources based on the values of the society. **Public policy is the outcome of the struggle in government over who gets what.**[10] Economics has been defined as **"the science of how individuals and societies deal with the fact that wants are greater than the limited resources available to satisfy those wants."**[11]

These definitions of the two disciplines of political science and economics have a great deal in common. Both are concerned with studying human behavior in competition for scarce resources. Public policy exists at the confluence of these disciplines (see chap. 2). As such, any definition of public policy will reflect these origins. Most definitions of public policy are rather imprecise and we will offer only a working definition. For our purposes **public policy includes actions of government to convert competing private objectives into public commitments as well as decisions not to take action**. **Public policies are purposeful decisions made by authoritative actors in a political system recognized because of their formal position as having the responsibility for making binding choices among goals and alternatives for the society.**[12] Public policy is a form of government control usually expressed in a law, a regulation, or an order. Since it reflects an intent of government, it is backed by an authorized reward or incentive or a penalty. The laws reflect the expedients of policy in the struggle as politicians respond to the articulated will of the voters.

The assumption voiced in the Declaration of Independence that individuals create government to secure their rights poses a paradox in contemporary American public policy. Men and women can advance their individual freedom only by giving up the anarchistic freedom of no government. **Government policy must be coercive and constrain the individual in order to promote the general welfare and secure order and predictability**. People organize out of a dread fear of uncertainty.

PUBLIC POLICY TYPOLOGY

One practical means of categorizing policies is based upon the technique of control used by policy makers. Three categories of control are **patronage, regulatory, and redistributive policies.**[13]

Patronage (or promotional) policies include those government actions that provide incentives for individuals or corporations to undertake activities they would only reluctantly undertake without the promise of a reward. As distinct from policies that threaten punishment for noncompliance, this kind of policy motivates people to act by using

[9]Harold Lasswell, *Politics: Who Gets What, When, How* (Cleveland: Meridian Books, 1958).

[10]Thomas R. Dye, Harmon Zeigler, and S. Robert Lichter, *American Politics in the Media Age,* 4th ed. (Pacific Grove, CA: Brooks/Cole, 1992), p. 2.

[11]Roger A. Arnold, *Macroeconomics* (St. Paul, MN: West Publishing Co., 1996), p. 6.

[12]See Larry N. Gerston, *Making Public Policy: From Conflict to Resolution* (Glenville, IL: Scott, Foresman and Co., 1979), pp. 4–6. See also Jay M. Shafritz, *Dictionary of American Government and Politics* (Chicago: The Dorsey Press, 1988), p. 456.

[13]See Theodore Lowi, "American Business, Public Policy, Case Studies and Political Theory," *World Politics* (July 1964), pp. 677–715. See also by the same author, *The End of Liberalism: The Second Republic of the United States* (New York: Norton, 1979).

"carrots." Not surprisingly, it is the recipients of the rewards who often convince the government to subsidize individuals or corporations to act. **These promotional techniques can be classified into three types: subsidies, contracts, and licenses.**

The use of subsidies has played a central role in the history of the United States. Alexander Hamilton wrote in his *Report on Manufactures,* one of the first policy planning documents in the administration of George Washington, that subsidies for American business should be provided by "pecuniary bounties" supplied by the government. Subsidies to business quickly became commonplace in America, ranging from land grants given to railroad companies to cash subsidies for the merchant marine fleet, for shipbuilders, and for the airline industry. Other subsidies to businesses have included loans to specific companies like the Chrysler Corporation or the more recent broader savings-and-loan "bailout" which will end up costing taxpayers over $150 billion.

Subsidies have also been provided to individuals through such policies as land grants to farmers in the nineteenth century, or the current tax deductions allowed for interest on home mortgage payments.

Subsidies are typically made possible through the largesse of the American taxpayer. Since the cost is spread out among all the population, each person bears only a minuscule portion of the whole cost. There is little opposition to these kinds of subsidies. The threat of their removal can arouse intense reactions from their recipients, for whom their loss could entail significant financial hardship. However, subsidies are often attacked as "pork-barrel" programs, so every effort is made to tie such projects to some "high national purpose" (such as military defense) to avoid that label.

Contracting is also an important means of promoting particular policies. It can be used to encourage corporations to adopt certain behaviors, such as equal employment opportunity, which they might otherwise find burdensome.

In the same way, governments can grant through licensing the privilege of carrying on a particular activity. Licensing allows corporations or individuals to conduct a business or engage in a profession (e.g., a licensed pilot) that without the license is illegal. The government is therefore also able to regulate various sectors of the population and the economy through this process.

Regulatory policies allow the government to exert control over the conduct of certain activities. If patronage policies involve positive motivation (the use of carrots), then regulatory policies involve negative forms of control (the use of "sticks"). The most obvious examples of regulation techniques include civil and criminal penalties for certain behaviors. The immediate example that comes to mind is regulating criminal behavior. Other forms of regulated conduct are not necessarily criminal or immoral by themselves, but may have negative side effects. These activities are regulated not to eliminate the conduct, but to deal with the negative side effects. For example, a public utility may provide a community with the "desired good" of electricity, but there is a strong probability it will seek monopoly profits. The conduct of the utility is "regulated" rather than "policed" in a criminal sense in that the company is given an exclusive license to provide electrical energy to a given geographical area but in return the government holds the right to regulate the quality of service and the rates charged.

Other forms of regulatory policies that generate more controversy include environmental pollution, consumer protection, or employee health and safety concerns. Tax policy often may have as its primary purpose not raising revenue but regulating a certain type of behavior by making that behavior too expensive for most individuals or companies to engage in. By taxing a substance like gasoline, tobacco, or alcohol, the government encourages a reduction in the consumption of these products. Likewise, "effluent taxes" may raise the price of goods and services that pollute, which encourages companies to reduce their pollution to reduce or avoid the tax.[14]

Some environmentalists are critical of the use of market mechanisms to control pollution even though they may reduce pollution efficiently. They feel that pollution is morally wrong and a stigma should be attached to the deed. If market mechanisms alone are used to reduce pollution, it is increasingly perceived as morally indifferent, a good to be bought or sold in the market like any other good. Environmental policy is thereby transformed from an expression of the current generation's trusteeship responsibility over the environment for future generations to an area where economic self-interest is the guiding standard.

Regulatory decisions frequently reallocate costs for those affected. Unlike promotional policies that appear to provide only benefits and thus to have only winners, regulatory policies are usually thought of in terms of winners and losers because the losses they cause are as obvious as their benefits.

Redistributive policies control people by managing the economy as a whole. The techniques of control involve fiscal (tax) and monetary (supply of money) policies. They tend to benefit one group at the expense of other groups through the reallocation of wealth. Changing the income tax laws in the 1980s, for example, significantly reduced the taxes of upper-income groups compared to other income groups in the society, although lower-income groups were taken off the tax roles altogether. The result was a decline in the middle class.[15] Since those who have power and wealth are usually reluctant to share those privileges, redistribution policies tend to be the most contentious. Many past policies aimed at redistributing wealth more equitably, even when initially successful, faced severe obstacles in their long-term viability. The 1960s' Great Society and War on Poverty programs are the most obvious examples. Programs with widely distributed benefits such as Social Security have enjoyed more success because of the larger number of people with a stake in their continuation.

Fiscal policy uses tax rates and government spending to affect total or aggregate demand. Each particular approach to taxing or spending can have a different impact on

---

[14]Taxation for the purpose of discouraging certain conduct or eliminating certain activities is often opposed on the grounds that the affluent can buy the right to behave in a manner that is prohibitive to the less wealthy. The charge is correct in that the affluent may be less deterred by the higher price of gasoline, alcohol, tobacco, or other products that cause pollution, than will the poor who may be eliminated from the market by the repressive features of the tax. However, exercising the right to buy the products will make the wealthy poorer. It should also be pointed out that, by discouraging the purchase of certain products, public health should improve and the environment become cleaner. The repressive nature of the tax may also be beside the point if the extra amount that the affluent pay exceeds the value we place on the harm caused by alcohol or tobacco consumption, or if a cleaner environment caused by less consumption of gas or other products that cause pollution results in the transference of real income to the population as a whole.

[15]See Richard Morin, "America's Middle-Class Meltdown," *The Washington Post,* December 1, 1991, p. C1. Reporting on several studies, Morin stated that "the boom years of the 1980s were a bust for fully half of all Americans. At the same time, the safety net of social programs for the nation's poor was replaced by a safety net for the rich, speeding the decline of the middle class."

the overall economy, so political entrepreneurs often propose or initiate policies with the goal of achieving specific impacts. For example, President George Bush, faced with a sluggish economy in an election year, proposed a policy of stimulating the economy by cutting taxes to increase demand (and thereby employment). He also proposed cutting taxes on capital gains, a policy that would have benefitted primarily higher-income people, with the claim that it would encourage real investment.[16]

Monetary techniques used by the Federal Reserve Board (the "Fed") also try to regulate the economy through policies directed at changing the rate of growth of the money supply or at manipulating interest rates. The Federal Reserve System's control over the money supply is the key aspect of U.S. monetary policy. The Fed has three primary levers of power. The first concerns the reserve requirement. The Fed requires private banks to keep some fraction of their deposits in reserve. The reserves are held in the form of cash or as credits in the bank's reserve account at its regional Federal Reserve Bank. By changing the reserve requirement, the Fed can directly affect the ability of the banking system to lend money. The second lever concerns the Fed's discount rate. The Fed changes the cost of money for banks and the incentive and ability to borrow. The third and most important lever involves the Fed's open market operations, which directly alter the reserves of the banking system. When the Fed buys bonds, it increases the deposits (reserves) available in the banking system. If the Fed sells bonds, it reduces the reserves and restricts the amount of money available for lending. (For more on this see chap. 6.)

BASIC ECONOMIC SYSTEMS

If political science is the study of who gets what, when, and how, then public policy may begin by examining the current state of affairs of who already has what, and how it was obtained. There are three basic types of economic organization. The oldest form of economic organization with only a few examples still remaining throughout the world is the traditional economy. **Traditional economies** are those in which economic decisions are based on customs and beliefs handed down from previous generations. In these societies the three basic questions of *what, how,* and *for whom* to produce are answered according to how things have been done in the past. Today, in countries like Bolivia, the peasant economy, except in a city like La Paz, is predominantly traditional.

Command (or planned) economies are characterized by government ownership of nonhuman factors of production. Since the government allocates most resources, it also makes most of the decisions regarding economic activities. In socialist economies for example, the government may own most resources other than labor. Governments then decide *what, how,* and *for whom* goods are to be produced. Such governments generally follow policies resulting in wages being more evenly distributed than in capitalist economies.

Pure market (or capitalistic) economies are characterized by private ownership of the nonhuman factors of production. Decision making is decentralized and most

---

[16]**Capital gains** is the realized increase in the value of an asset. **Real** investment refers to the accumulation of real capital such as machinery or buildings rather than to financial investment (which refers to the acquisition of such paper instruments as bonds).

economic activities take place in the private sector. In a market economy *what* to produce is left up to entrepreneurs responding to consumer demand. *How* to produce is determined by entrepreneurs seeking the most efficient means of production. And *for whom* the goods are produced is determined by consumer demand—if you have the money you can buy it. How goods are produced is answered by the available technology and the entrepreneurs' profit-motivated desire to produce most efficiently. Prices are the signals in a market economy for what and how to produce goods.

Finally, in command economies the government determines to whom the goods will be distributed. In theory this occurs according "to one's needs." In practice it has often been charged that what is produced is distributed according to political or party loyalty. In a market economy, on the other hand, to whom the goods are to be distributed is again ignored by the government and public policy. The goods are distributed to those having what can be labeled as "rationing coupons." **Dollar bills serve as rationing coupons.** If you have sufficient dollar bills, you can purchase whatever you demand in the marketplace: food, cars, health care, education, or homes. If you do not have these rationing coupons, the system will not recognize your needs, since entrepreneurs respond only to those having the means to demand (i.e., those willing and able to pay for the good in question). Thus, members of a **pure market system** with no government intervention would have to be willing to watch people starve to death in the streets, unless those starving could prevail upon some private charity to provide minimum support.

Of course the real world is much more complex than these simple definitions indicate; there are simply no examples of pure capitalism or pure command economic systems. While there are some examples that are closer to the definitions than others, it is not possible to draw a line between pure capitalism and pure command (or socialist) economies and place countries squarely on either side.

Mixed capitalism combines some features of both types of economic organization. Mixed capitalism is a system in which most economic decisions are made by the private sector, but the government also plays a substantial economic and regulatory role.

Clearly economic systems that rely on command are significantly less efficient than those that rely primarily on the market. Most noteworthy in this regard are the former Soviet Union and Eastern European countries, who became notorious for their shoddy goods, shortages and surpluses in the market, absenteeism among the labor force, and an overall lack of innovation in products and production techniques. Mikhail Gorbachev finally proclaimed that he supported the dismantling of the command economy in favor of "mixed capitalism." Today most countries that had planned economies have abandoned this system in favor of mixed capitalism.

While command systems are very inefficient, pure market systems do not allocate resources in a way that most people are willing to tolerate. Hence mixed capitalism in the United States, and increasingly in the rest of the world, is the basis for an increasing number of politico-economic organizations. John Maynard Keynes, as chapter 6 develops, was the theoretician of a partnership between government and private enterprise. In Keynesian economics, government is responsible for initiating policies that lead to full employment, while ownership of the means of production and profits remain in private hands.

The perceived legitimate public policy role for government is much greater in those countries emerging from command economies, or other varieties of socialism, than in countries living under mixed capitalism that evolved from more libertarian origins such as the United States. The American political and economic system begins with a bias in favor of a **laissez-faire** attitude, which has come to mean a minimal role for government in private lives and distributional policies.

This is significant because, as we shall see, the existence of certain public policies that are taken for granted in many nations (such as a system of national health care) may be challenged by many people in the United States as not even legitimate for government to consider undertaking.

WHY GOVERNMENTS INTERVENE

While markets are usually the most efficient way to organize economic activity to provide goods and services, there are some exceptions to the rule. Sometimes market forces do not work as the theory would suggest. Policy analysts use the term **market failure** to refer to those situations where the market does not allocate resources efficiently.

The market mechanism works well as long as an exchange between a buyer and seller does not affect a bystander, or third party. But all too often a third party is affected. Examples are everywhere: people who drive cars do not pay the full cost of pollution created by their car. A farmer who sprays his crops with pesticides does not pay for the degradation of streams caused by the runoff. Factory owners may not pay the full cost of their smokestack emissions into the atmosphere that destroy the ozone layer. Such social costs are referred to as **externalities** because they are borne by individuals external to the transaction that caused them. In these cases, the government may improve the outcome through regulation.

Markets also fail in the face of excessive power through oligopolies or monopoly power. In such instances the invisible hand of the market does not allocate resources efficiently because there is little or no price competition. For example, if everyone in a town needs water, but only one homeowner has a well with potable water, the owner of the well has a monopoly and is not subject to competition from any other source of drinking water. Government regulation in such cases may actually increase efficiency.

The market mechanism does not distribute income or wealth fairly. The market system certainly does not guarantee equality. To the contrary, the market ensures inequality, since one source of its efficiency is to be found in the way that it distributes rewards and penalties. Many believe that the market is overly generous to those who are successful and too ruthless in penalizing those who fail in market competition. Thus, capitalist markets provide for great opulence to exist next to abject poverty and may reduce overall economic efficiency. The goal of many public policies is to provide a system that is closer to our ideas of social justice than capitalism provides (see chap. 7).

A final area in which the market fails to perform adequately is in the provision of what policy analysts call **public goods.** Consumers in the marketplace express their collective answer to the question of *what* to produce by offering to pay higher or lower prices for certain goods, thus signaling their demand for those goods. The market mechanism works efficiently because the benefits of consuming a specific good or service are available only to those who purchase the product. A **private good** is a good or service whose benefits are confined to a single consumer and whose consumption excludes consumption by others. If it is shared, more for one must mean less for another. For example, the purchase of a hamburger by one individual effectively excludes others from consuming it. If the purchaser shares the hamburger with someone else, the portion shared cannot be consumed by the purchaser.

Certain other products in our society do not have the characteristic of private goods because they never enter the market system, so the market does not distribute them. These **public goods are indivisible and nonexclusive**—that is, their consumption by one individual does not interfere with their consumption by another. The air from a pollution-free environment can be inhaled by many people simultaneously, unlike a hamburger which cannot be consumed simultaneously by many individuals. No one can be excluded from the use of a public good. You can be denied the use of your neighbor's swimming pool, but you cannot be denied the protection provided by the nation's national defense network. If the national defense system works, it defends everyone under its umbrella whether they have contributed to its purchase or not.

Another characteristic of public goods is that policy can be provided only by collective decisions. The purchase of private goods depends on an individual decision as to whether to spend one's income on hamburgers or swimming pools. But it is not possible for one person to decide to purchase national defense, dams, or weather services. The decision or agreement to buy a public good and the quantity of it to buy is made collectively. There are few examples of pure public goods, but air pollution control and national defense come as close to meeting the characteristics that define public goods as anything can. Other examples that do not meet the criteria as clearly, but nevertheless have enough of the characteristics to qualify as public goods in need of collective, governmental provision on grounds of economic efficiency, include police protection and education. Police protection generally provides a safer environment for everyone living in an area even if one does not contribute to the purchase of that protection. Education is a similar good. The primary beneficiary of an education is the person educated. However, there are secondary benefits to society of a better-educated workforce. Moreover, the amount of education allotted to one person does affect the amount left over for others. The same could be said for highway space or the administration of justice.

The communal nature of public goods leads to a major problem in public policy known as the free rider. **A free rider is someone who enjoys the benefits of someone else's purchase of a public good while bearing none of the costs of providing it.** If we both will benefit from national defense, good public education, or pure air, the question arises as to who should pay for it. Each individual has an incentive to avoid payment, hoping to take a free ride on other people's "purchase." As a result, all parties will profess little interest in purchasing the good, hoping others will step forward, demand the good, and pay for it. This is a rational response for individuals with limited resources. Everyone will benefit from the good by more than their proportionate cost, but they would benefit even more if others paid the entire cost. Thus, the good will not be purchased unless the government makes the purchase and requires everyone to pay his or her fair share through mandatory taxes.

How do we determine how many and what mix of public goods the government should purchase? By relying on a specific means of public decision making: voting. Because voting is a very imprecise mechanism that limits us to a "Yes" or a "No" for candidates, it does not make any distinctions regarding the myriad of issues that must be acted on collectively. Nor does it register the intensity of preferences by various individuals or groups. Therefore, we sometimes find ourselves with an oversupply and sometimes with an undersupply of public goods. But it is clear that the market mechanism cannot determine a desirable level of the output of public goods, and some kind of political technique of making public policy decisions must be used.

Some **conservatives** tend to believe that **some public goods could be treated as private goods and brought into the market system while reducing the role of government.** For example, tolls could be charged on all roads and bridges for their maintenance. This would limit the building and repair of highways to the amount of demand expressed by those paying the tolls. We might charge an admission fee sufficient to pay for the services provided in public parks, thereby reducing the number of those needing those services.[17] Public libraries could charge fees for their services to provide the budgets needed for salaries and the purchase of books and materials. Public transportation in cities could be required either to charge the fees necessary to operate profitably or to reduce their service, producing only that amount of service demanded by those paying the fares. According to conservatives, other areas of government operations could also be reduced through privatization. For example, the operation and maintenance of prisons could be contracted out to private companies rather than being staffed by public employees.

The privatization of public goods and services in this manner would certainly produce them more or less as if they were private goods. However there are many difficulties associated with this approach. First, there are the technical difficulties of making some public goods private. How do you make national defense a private good? Also, this approach offends our sense of justice and **equity.** Do we really think that national or state parks should exist to be enjoyed only by those with sufficient income to pay for their upkeep?

Imperfect Information

As noted, the market system is built on the assumption that individuals are **rational** and do not act capriciously, and that they have roughly accurate information about the market. Without adequate correct information, people cannot make decisions in their **rational self-interest.** In fact, most people do not have adequate information to make rational decisions. Developing or finding the information has a significant opportunity cost associated with it. Very few people have the resources or time to do a complete research job.

Information, then, can be considered a public good, or a good with positive external effects. Once the information is provided, it can be shared by any number of people.

---

[17]See, for example, Dan Bechter, "Congested Parks—A Pricing Dilemma," *Monthly Review,* Federal Reserve Bank of Kansas City (June 1971). Overcrowding at public parks may reflect a distortion in the recreation market by charging too little for their use. It is suggested that such low pricing amounts to a misallocation of resources. Raising the price would help "clear" the market and relieve congestion. If the price of visiting national parks were increased, more people would substitute other leisure activities.

Once in the public domain, it is impossible to exclude anyone from using it. Information is a positive externality.

Manufacturers of consumer products, such as cigarettes, do not have an interest in advertising the health hazards associated with the use of their products. But ignorance about those hazards can be reduced by informing consumers, through mandatory labels on cigarette packages, that smoking is dangerous. The manufacturers may still advertise their cigarettes. But the mandatory labels attempt to mend omissions in the market system by introducing information so that individuals can make better choices.

Many people believe the government has a role in researching and disseminating various kinds of information relevant to consumer choices. For instance, the government might investigate and publicize information about the safety of different consumer products such as cars, ingredients in drugs, food additives, microwave ovens, and other potentially dangerous products.

There is a debate regarding how this remedy for market failure should be applied. **If you accept the proposition that the individual is the best judge of his/her own welfare,** then many argue that governmental actions should be limited to the **provision of information. The government,** having produced the information, **should not regulate the behavior of individuals,** according to this view. Once people have been supplied with all the relevant information, they should be permitted to make their own choices—to consume dangerous substances (e.g., to purchase tobacco products), or to purchase potentially dangerous products. Only if the risks extend beyond the user—meaning negative externalities exist involving third parties—may there be an argument for expanding the role of government beyond providing information. For example, those in favor of the right to a smoke-free work environment argue that the spillover effect of inhaling secondary smoke is hazardous to nonsmokers' health.

This view of the informational role of government is not followed consistently in practice. For example, the Pure Food and Drug Act prohibits the sale of certain harmful products but does not provide the option of informing consumers of the product's harmful effects.

Equity and Security

Public goods, externalities, and ignorance all cause resource misallocation. They result in the market mechanism failing to produce the optimal mix of output. Beyond a failure of **what to produce,** we may also find that **for whom the output is produced** violates our sense of fairness.

These are situations, however, when markets fail to achieve the ideal economic **efficiency.** In a very literal sense, in fact, markets always "fail" because economic efficiency is a fabricated definition based upon a normative model of how the world **should** be. Market failure indicates that supply and demand forces have resulted in a mix of output that is different from the one society is willing to accept. It signifies that we are at a less-than-satisfactory point on the production possibilities curve. Some cases of market failure are so extreme, and the potential for corrective public policy action sufficiently unavailable, that most people would support some form of governmental intervention to achieve a better output mix. Because of these limitations, no country relies exclusively on the free market to make all of its socioeconomic policy decisions.

Not everyone agrees that turning the decision making over to the public policy mechanism of government constitutes a good solution. Many people believe that governmental processes to alter production choices or to redistribute goods and services do not promote efficiency. Therefore, in their view, whatever the deficiencies of market mechanisms, the market is still to be preferred over government intervention in matters of distribution.

In general, the market mechanism answers the question of *for whom* to produce by distributing a larger share of output to those with the most rationing coupons (dollars). While this method is efficient, it may not be in accordance with our view of what is socially acceptable. Individuals who are unemployed, disabled, aged, or very young may be unable to earn income and need to be protected from such risks inherent in life in a market economy. Government intervention may be sought for income redistribution through taxes and programs like unemployment compensation, Social Security, Medicare, and Aid to Families with Dependent Children (AFDC), which shift those risks to taxpayers as a whole.

Redistribution of income to reduce inequities also falls under the theory of public goods because it adds to public security. Without some redistribution, we could expect more muggings and thefts to occur as people sought to escape the consequences of poverty. Moreover, leaving inequalities of wealth solely to market mechanisms would produce the phenomenon of the free rider again. Some individuals would no doubt contribute to charities aimed at reducing poverty, and everyone would benefit from somewhat safer streets. But those who did not so contribute would be taking a free ride on those who did.

Society is therefore forced to confront tradeoffs between the efficiencies of the market system and our views of justice and equity. For example, it is true that current policies of unemployment compensation and welfare benefits may be structured in ways that prolong unemployment by a high benefit-reduction rate that decreases incentives to find employment, but those policies are solving other problems. Programs like Social Security reduce the incentive to save money, which provides capital formation for greater economic growth, but they too answer social needs we have been unable to provide for in other ways.

Every society has to deal with the question of what constitutes an equitable distribution of income. It is clear that no government policy is neutral on the question. Income distribution tends to reflect the biases of governments ranging from traditional laissez faire economics to theories of planned economies. The political process by which any society governs itself must ultimately decide what constitutes an acceptable inequality of wealth and income.

Although government *can* improve on market outcomes, it is by no means certain that it always *will*. Public policy is the result of a very imperfect political process. Unfortunately policies are sometimes designed as a quid pro quo for campaign contributions. At other times they merely reward society's elites or otherwise politically powerful individuals. Frequently they are made by well-intentioned political leaders forced into so many compromises that the resulting policy bears little resemblance to the original proposal.

A major goal of the study of public policy is to help you judge when government action is justifiable to promote specific ends such as efficiency or equity, and which policies can reasonably be expected to achieve those goals and which ones cannot.

CONCLUSION

1 The crux of all of our public policy problems is to be found in the hard reality of limited (scarce) resources. The free market has proved a superb device for efficiently producing goods and services, based upon individual rational self-interest. Problems of scarcity, which are universal, require intervention. This suggests that solutions, whether left to market forces or government intervention, reflect values. There are a variety of possible solutions reflecting the biases and choices of the individuals proposing them.

2 People face tradeoffs when they make choices. The cost of any action, whether individual or collective, is measured in terms of what must be given up. People as well as societies tend to make decisions by comparing their marginal costs against their marginal benefits. People and societies will adjust their behavior whenever incentives change.

3 It is important to keep in mind that although markets are a good way to organize many of society's activities, there are several areas where markets fail or produce outcomes unacceptable to society's collective values. In those cases, government can improve on market outcomes. Government efforts to relieve market imperfections (failures) by public policy may also be flawed, however. The question is whether government, which was created to "promote the general welfare," will provide solutions that will be less imperfect than market mechanisms.

4 Government may be the only actor that can improve market efficiency or alter economic and social costs, risks, and income distribution in a positive way. Some argue that these problems can be solved, but that most solutions mean someone must accept significant economic losses. No one willingly accepts a loss. So people struggle to veto any solution that would impact negatively on them, or at minimum have the cost transferred to someone else, or another group. The effect is to produce "veto groups" waiting to aggressively fight any proposed public policy that would result in a loss to their position. Often, the political struggle that results causes a larger cost than gain for those attempting to effect the change. The result is often political and economic paralysis.

5 Not all public policy solutions must be **zero-sum solutions**, where one group's net gains must be offset by another group's losses. There are **nonzero-sum solutions**. Achieving those usually involves increasing economic growth so there is more for everyone. But even this solution requires the intervention of government in the form of industrial policies, and many people see this as just another effort to have government provide a remedy no more promising than any the market itself can provide. The major economic competitors of the United States, including both Japan and Germany, have incorporated industrial policy as a key component of their public policies, but it is a controversial issue in the United States.

QUESTIONS FOR DISCUSSION

1 If society desires health care and a clean environment for everyone, why does the free market not provide it?

2 Explain the difference between self-interest and selfishness.

3 Explain how scarcity, choice, and opportunity costs are related and make public policy inevitable.

4 Give several examples of significant tradeoffs that you face in your life. What are the major considerations in your decision making?

5 Should you consciously think about your values and goals when analyzing important tradeoffs and choices that you face? Why?

6 How is it possible for some self-interested behavior to be selfish while other self-interested behavior may be altruistic?

7 Explain why policymakers should consider the importance of incentives.

8 Is reliance upon the market to resolve policy issues inherently conservative, or is it inherently progressive?

9 Explain the different types of economic organization and how they answer the questions of what, how, and for whom to produce.

KEY CONCEPTS

efficiency

equity

externalities

free rider

incremental

laissez faire

margin

market failure

mixed capitalism

nonzero-sum solution

opportunity cost

patronage policies

private goods

production possibilities curve (PPC)

public goods

pure market economies

rational self-interest

redistributive policies

regulatory policies

scarcity

zero-sum solution

SUGGESTED READINGS

Henry J. Aaron, Thomas E. Mann, and Timothy Taylor (eds.), *Values and Public Policy* (Washington, DC: The Brookings Institution, 1994).

James E. Anderson, *Public Policymaking,* 3d ed. (New York: Houghton Mifflin Co., 1997).

David R. Berman, *American Government, Politics and Policy Making*, 3d ed. (Englewood Cliffs, NJ: Prentice-Hall, 1988).

Henry Demmert, *Economics: Understanding the Market Process* (New York: Harcourt Brace Jovanovich, 1991).

E. J. Dionne, Jr., *Why Americans Hate Politics* (New York: A Touchstone Book, Simon & Schuster, 1991).

Robert Heilbroner, "The Embarrassment of Economics," in *Challenge* (Armonk, NY: M. E. Sharpe, 1996), pp. 46–49.

Robert A. Heineman, William T. Bluhm, Steven A. Peterson, and Edward N. Kearny. *The World of the Policy Analyst: Rationality, Values, & Politics* (Chatham, NJ: Chatham House Publishers, Inc. 1990).

Lawrence J. R. Herson, *The Politics of Ideas: Political Theory and American Public Policy* (Prospect Heights, IL: Waveland Press, 1984).

Stuart Nagle, *Public Policy: Goals, Means and Methods* (New York: St. Martin's Press, 1984).

Robert B. Reich, *The Resurgent Liberal and Other Unfashionable Prophecies* (New York: Vintage Books, 1989).

Steven E. Rhoads, *The Economist's View of the World: Government, Markets, and Public Policy* (New York: Cambridge University Press, 1990).

Mark E. Rushefsky, *Public Policy in the United States: Toward the Twenty-First Century* (Belmont, CA: Wadsworth Publishing Company, 1996).

Andrew Shonfield, *In Defense of the Mixed Economy* (New York: Oxford University Press, 1984).

Lester C. Thurow, *The Zero-Sum Society: Distribution and the Possibilities for Economic Change* (New York: Basic Books, 1980).

Jim Tomlinson, *Public Policy and the Economy Since 1900* (New York: Oxford University Press, 1990).

2

METHODS AND MODELS FOR POLICY ANALYSIS

Although public policy has been recognized as a subfield of political science for only a few decades, the study of ways to "promote the general welfare" goes back centuries. Policy is made in the present, based upon the past, with the purpose of improving the well-being of society's future. It utilizes both normative and scientific methodologies to achieve this. Public policy is action-oriented. The purpose of studying public problems is to provide insight into a range of policy options in order to take some control over the future.

POLICY ANALYSIS AS A SUBFIELD OF POLITICAL SCIENCE

Every academic discipline has its own language and its own specialized way of thinking based upon its specific subject matter and goals. Physicists analyze matter and energy and their interactions. Economists talk about inflation, unemployment, comparative advantage, and income distribution. Chemists examine the composition and chemical properties and processes of substances. Psychologists talk about personality development, cognitive dissonance, and perception. Sociologists focus on the collective behavior and interaction of organized groups of human beings in social institutions and social relationships.

Political science is no different. Political scientists focus on people with conflicting interests competing for governmental power. As previously noted, political science is about who gets what, when, and how. In other words, it focuses on what decisions are made by those in authority and why those decisions were made. Political scientists are concerned with the exercise of *political power.* Many observers of humankind's condition see human nature as one dimensional. Aristotle put forward a biological explanation for political power when he said: "It is evident that the state is a creation of nature, and that man is by nature a political animal."[1] To Aristotlean thinkers the state and political power are as natural and innate as the instinctual behaviors among herd animals. Still, refusal to accept prevailing authority, or even any governmental authority has always been prevalent.

A number of political scientists have developed sociological explanations for the transmission of cultural values that hold a political society together through child rearing, religious education, and socioeconomic class. These scholars see people in plastic terms. People are pliable and are molded by their social environment. Political authority and even legitimacy is threatened when those in authority lose touch with the cultural values the masses have been taught to accept. It is frequently a calculated strategy therefore, of one group competing for power to claim that the struggle is a war over the very culture of the society, and that the other side would destroy the cultural values on which the society was built. Some theorists would hold that since all behavior is learned, we could teach, or condition, members of society to adopt "good" behavior patterns and unlearn negative behaviors. B. F. Skinner was a radical behaviorist whose theories ignore internal psychic processes. For him, behavior is the result of its consequences in the external environment. Skinner held that through *operant conditioning*—providing positive rewards for individuals engaging in behavior society deems good, and negative rewards for behavior deemed undesirable by society—we could improve society. Freudian theory suggests that culture is transmitted by the interactions between parents and children. Karl Marx and other political economists argue that the economic foundations of society determine the culture and what the law recognizes as legitimate. However, Marx's view has been challenged by the fact that some countries with very similar cultures have developed very different political systems, conversely countries with very different cultures have similar political systems and values. Finally, some Darwinian biologists see all human behavior as driven by genes.

Political philosophers such as John Locke have argued that human beings are rational. Individuals use their mental faculties and try to rise above mere conditioned behaviors or emotional attachment to past practices. Locke certainly agreed that the human mind is shaped as individuals grow and mature. Experiences develop the human capacity for reasoning. Ideas stem from experiences which act on our senses. Subsequent behavior flows from the rational ideas thus developed. Locke was aware that most rulers, if not checked, would favor their own selfish interests over that of the general welfare. Since everyone is equal and self-interested, and most are rational, a social contract may be agreed upon to limit power and ensure the general welfare. A government is formed to protect individuals and their property. Power resides with the citizenry who can dissolve the contract if the government abuses its authority. Locke's theory does not deny the power of psychological, cultural, or other influences on behavior and may even incorporate parts of them.

It was only a small step from the political theory of human nature as being rational and acting to promote the general welfare, to the theory of modern economic man, which describes human nature in terms of rational self-interest. This economic theory is now

[1]From Aristotle, *Politics,* in William Ebenstein and Alan Ebenstein, *Great Political Thinkers,* 5th ed. (New York: Harcourt Brace, 1991), p. 93.

frequently applied in many areas other than economic transactions, such as political, sociological, and psychological models.

Policy analysts recognize the complexity of human nature and avoid any attempt to analyze humans using just one or two of these theories. For example, to reduce human beings, as some economists do, to material self-interest, or as some sociologists might, to a being completely defined by culture is a mistake. A single theory of the individual, whether based in biology, sociology, economics, or psychology, results in a misleading oversimplification of complex human beings, although each may have an element of truth.

The purpose of this text is to introduce you to the political scientist's way of thinking. In particular, this book is about the political scientist as a **policy analyst. Policy analysis** describes investigations that produce accurate and useful information for decision makers. Learning to approach political problems as an analyst is a developmental process and does not occur quickly. This text will provide a combination of social science theory, case studies, and examples of current public policy issues in the news to help you to develop these skills.

Before developing the issues of public policy, this chapter provides an overview of why the field of public policy is interdisciplinary, and why policy analysts must be eclectic in their methodology.

In the Middle Ages all study was under the rubric of philosophy, which means "to seek wisdom." Philosophy in medieval times was divided into two parts: moral philosophy and natural philosophy. Moral philosophy focused on human existence and has come down to us as the **humanities.** The subject matter of the humanities is our social world, or in other words, the human condition and human values. Because the social world is a projection of human nature, individuals can no more completely understand or control it than they can completely understand and control themselves. Indeed, it is the very intimacy of the human involvement with the social world that inhibits both the comprehension of and authority over it.[2]

Natural philosophy has evolved into the natural sciences. Since it is focused on the outside world that can be observed, weighed, and measured, it is viewed as being **value-free.** It is a paradox that the natural world, which humans did not create, is much more susceptible to human understanding than is the social world, which is created by humans themselves. Through the discovery of the laws by which the universe is ordered, people can look back into the past and project into the future. Through this understanding, they can control and even harness the forces of nature as they wish.

More recently, a new set of disciplines existing between the humanities and the natural sciences, the social sciences, have matured and have made significant contributions to our understanding of human society through the systematic study of various aspects of the human condition.

The social sciences have a split personality. They not only exist between the humanities and the natural sciences, but they borrow freely from both. The social sciences

---

[2]Hans J. Morgenthau, "The Purpose of Political Science," in James C. Charlesworth (ed.), *A Design for Political Science: Scope, Objectives, and Methods* (Monograph 6) (Philadelphia: The American Academy of Political and Social Science, 1966), pp. 67–68.

developed from the historic cultural values and conditions of the social community. At the same time, they borrow the methods of the natural sciences. Many believe that political science, of which the study of public policy is a subfield, exists at the confluence of the social sciences. It is not an independent discipline within the social sciences. In their view, a political scientist focuses on the political ramifications of the other social sciences.

As a consequence, political scientists use methods of investigation that span the range of intellectual and scientific disciplines. The criterion for using a particular method is whether the tools of inquiry from the other disciplines match the particular problems the political scientist is addressing. It should be noted in passing that political science is not the only social science that uses a borrowed toolbox, and this practice of utilizing a toolbox of methodologies borrowed primarily from the physical sciences has caused considerable concern.[3] Since the social sciences, especially political science, economics, sociology, and to a lesser extent, psychology, are generally moving toward greater involvement in policy making, it may be appropriate to think of them more generally as "policy sciences." This is most frequently said about economics. In the view of policy makers, John Maynard Keynes' theories in the 1930s moved economics well ahead of the other social sciences as a source of relevant ideas for public policy.

Statistical inference is widely used in public policy, as is historical inquiry. Many statistical procedures have been adjusted to fit the data. Likewise, the use of historical investigation is somewhat different when undertaken by those interested in public policy than when carried out by a historian. Students of public policy must study the present with an understanding of the past for the purpose of guiding the future. In this regard, no part of humanity or civilization is beyond their concern.

Policy analysis owes its birth to the development of the social sciences, but the physical sciences are an increasingly important part of the policy agenda. There are increasing concerns in all levels of government for science policy. Issues regarding such questions as the environment—including the ozone layer, pollution, earth warming, nuclear energy, and population issues, to name just a few—require the policy analyst to not only be cognizant of, but to take part in scientific studies. Policy analysts today must have more than an appreciation of prevailing interpretations of scientific theory relevant to policy issues. This means that the political scientist in the role of policy analyst must be increasingly prepared to work with specialists in the natural as well as the social sciences.

The political scientist's perspective, scholarly interests, and manner of thought are heavily influenced by the society of which he or she is a member. Every society has biases that encourage an acceptance of and conformity to its political culture. However, the political scientist's obligation to seek the truth about the world of politics will necessarily result in messages that society will not want to hear.

---

[3]The concern is that humans are the makers of tools that shape their environment, guide their vision, and help make their destiny. When people use these tools on themselves and other people, it is important to ask how these tools affect their vision of humanity. Charles Hampden-Turner in *Radical Man: The Process of Psycho-Social Development* (New York: Anchor Books, 1971) argues that the scientific method has a very conservative bias when applied to the human environment.

A civilization's prevailing socioeconomic culture and the political institutions that grow out of that culture contain an elaborate articulation of the culture's ideals which are pursued through the political system. Existing political systems are usually defended by conceding that they have problems, but that those problems can best be dealt with in terms of the existing system. Consequently, a society that styles itself Marxist, like the People's Republic of China, cannot allow a searching investigation into the assumptions upon which communist theory is based. Conversely, societies whose economies are basically capitalist in nature are biased against inquiries regarding the goal of equal distribution of property. A society based upon a caste system, or some other type of ethnic or racial discrimination, cannot accept such issues as proper subjects for scientific inquiry. Likewise, in republican forms of government, it is taken for granted that the voting mechanism of the nation reflects fairly the "will of the people."

Since every society fosters support for the premises upon which the community is based, a commitment to truth in studying a society leads to questioning and controversy regarding the values and institutions of that society. Thus, the influence of political scientists and economists on policy makers goes beyond their role as policy analysts. As John Maynard Keynes has written:

> The ideas of *economists* and *political philosophers,* both when they are right and when they are wrong, are more powerful than is commonly understood. Indeed the world is ruled by little else. Practical men, who believe themselves to be quite exempt from intellectual influences, are usually slaves of some defunct economist. Madmen in authority who hear voices in the air, are distilling their frenzy from some academic scribbler of a few years back.[4]

The Political Scientist as Scientist

The scientific method was developed in the natural sciences as a way to help explain phenomena by developing theories[5] to explain and predict how things happen; the same is true in the social sciences, of which political science and policy studies are a part. To those outside the social sciences it may seem unnatural and even a bit pretentious to claim that political science is a science. After all, political scientists do not utilize the equipment and other trappings of science. The essential element of science, however, is found in the method of investigation. It requires the impartial construction and testing of hypotheses regarding the social world. The method of developing theories and testing them with regard to the effect of gravity on embryo development is just as applicable to studying the impact of a proposed tax subsidy for home construction to create additional housing.

Why Theory Development Requires Simplification   While policy scientists use theories and observation like natural scientists do, they face a complication that makes their effort especially difficult: experiments are sometimes impossible in the policy sciences.

---

[4]John Maynard Keynes, *The General Theory of Employment, Interest, and Money.* (New York: Harcourt Brace Jovanovich, 1966), orig. published 1936, p. 383.

[5]For our purposes we can use the terms "theory" and "model" interchangeably.

Biochemists testing a theory of the effect of pollutants on fish embryos can obtain many fish eggs to generate data to test their theories. Policy analysts usually do not have the luxury many natural scientists possess of being able to freely conduct experiments. At best, many social science experiments are difficult to carry out. People do not willingly let themselves become the laboratory subjects for someone else's experiment. For example, if policy scientists wanted to study the relationship of imports to total employment, they would not be allowed to control imports to generate data. The risks and cost to society would be deemed too great. In this sense, policy scientists are not unlike astronomers in that their observations of distant galaxies may provide them with data for analysis, although their ability to conduct controlled experiments will be very limited.

The difficulty in conducting controlled experiments in political science and public policy means that these social scientists will pay very close attention to the events of history as a type of informal spontaneous experiment. For example, the turbulence in several Asian economies once vaunted as models of economic development to be emulated causes concern in financial markets throughout the world. In affected Asian countries it depresses living standards. For policy analysts it poses difficult policy problems of how to respond to contain the problem and reverse the economic decline. But it also provides policy scientists with an opportunity to study the relationships between banking policy, barriers, and subsidies to international trade, currency speculation, and domestic savings and consumption policies. The lessons learned from this episode will continue long after this particular crisis is past. Such events provide important case studies because they improve our theoretical understanding of these critical variables and suggest ways to monitor and evaluate current economic policies.

PUBLIC POLICY AND THEORY

The first step in the scientific method is to recognize, or identify, the problem to be addressed. Isaac Newton, a seventeenth century mathematician, observed an apple fall from a tree. Newton's thinking over the problem of explaining "why" the apple fell, led him to develop a theory of gravity that applies not only to apples but to other objects in the universe. Policy analysts must likewise identify the problem to be addressed. It may be a problem such as how to improve the labor skills of the average worker.

Scientists must make **assumptions** to cut away any unnecessary detail. Assumptions are made to help us get to the heart of the problem by reducing its complexity. Assumptions help make a problem easier to understand. In chapter 1, for example, we looked at a production possibilities frontier which assumed there were only two types of goods in an economy, when in fact there might be dozens or even thousands of types of goods. By assuming only two types of goods we can concentrate on the relationship between those goods. Once the relationship is understood between military goods and social welfare goods we are in a better position to understand the greater complexity of a world with other goods.

A critical skill for anyone engaged in scientific inquiry is in deciding which assumptions to make. For example, suppose that we want to study what happens to the quality of health care provided to the indigent if Medicaid funding were increased. A key factor in the analysis would be how prices respond to increased funding. Since many Medicaid fee schedules are set by the government, we might assume prices would not change in the short run. But in the longer run, we would expect physicians and other health care providers to demand higher prices or payments for their services covered under Medicaid. Thus, in the longer run we would have to assume price increases. Just as a physicist may assume away the effect of friction when dropping a feather and a baseball in a vacuum (different assumptions would be necessary in calculating the effect of friction in the atmosphere when dropping a feather and a baseball over the side of a building), policy scientists must modify their assumptions when conditions change. Models and theories are similar to assumptions in that they also simplify reality by omitting many details so that by refining our concentration we can better understand reality.

If we wished to provide policy makers with a complete description of "income distribution," we could go out and collect all the facts we could find and present the data to decision makers and "let the facts speak for themselves." But a complete description, including information gathered from thousands of researchers gathering data from millions of households, thousands of separate federal, state, and local governments, and thousands of firms, is unworkable and would be ineffective as a guide to public policy.

Theories help make sense of the millions of facts. Theories help explain how the political and economic aspects of society work by identifying how basic underlying causal relationships fit together. **A theory in a scientific sense is a set of logically related, empirically testable hypotheses.** Theories are a deliberate simplification of related generalizations used to describe and explain how certain facts are related. Their usefulness derives from their ability to simplify otherwise complex phenomena. Thus a theory is not a mirror image of reality.[6] A theory will usually contain at least one **hypothesis** about how a specific set of facts is related. The theory should explain the phenomena in an abstract manner. The inclination to abstract from nonessential details of the world around us is necessary because of the awesome complexity of reality. **Abstraction** is the process of disregarding needless details in order to focus on a limited number of factors to explain a phenomenon. As an abstraction, a theory is useful not because it is true or false, but because it helps analysts understand the interactions between variables and predict how change in one or more variables will affect other dependent variables.

Theories attempt to do the same thing—bring order and meaning to data which without the theory, would remain unrelated and unintelligible. For example, a policy analyst might wish to explain why some people have very high incomes while others barely survive economically. To do so, the analyst must try to separate or abstract the meaningful data from the insignificant data. Thus, variables such as gender, age, education, and occupation may be considered meaningful. Other variables such as the educational level or parents' income may be considered important but less significant. Still other variables such as eye color, height, or weight may be considered unimportant and not be included among the explanatory variables. The theory developed by the analyst is built on all these assumptions and makes up a simplified, logical account of income inequality and its causes.

---

[6]A model is a simplified representation of how the real world works. Its usefulness is judged by how well it represents reality. Models may be depicted by mathematical equations, charts, and graphs, or may be descriptively stated.

FIGURE 2-1
STEPS IN THE SCIENTIFIC METHOD.

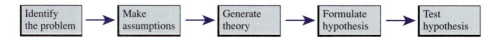

A theory must be consistent with the facts that it draws together. And the facts, in turn, must lend themselves to the interpretation that the theory puts upon them. Finally, the conclusions derived from the theory must flow logically from the theory's premises or assumptions.

The policy analyst, therefore, must determine which variables to include and which to ignore when conducting social analysis. Events and forces in a socioeconomic setting reflect all the intrinsic ambiguity of human nature in motion. But it should also be kept in mind that under comparable circumstances, events and forces will appear in a similar manner. As Michel de Montaigne said:

> As no event and no shape is entirely like another, so also is there none entirely different from another. . . . If there were no similarity in our faces, we could not distinguish man from beast; if there were no dissimilarity, we could not distinguish one man from another. All things hold together by some similarity; every example is halting, and the comparison that is derived from experience is always defective and imperfect.[7]

From the interpretations of variables (known as theories), we are able to formulate hypotheses. **A hypothesis is a tentative assumption or generalization that has not yet been tested.** Because hypotheses, like theories, are abstractions, it is necessary to test them. The hypothesis must be stated as an affirmative proposition (i.e., not as a question) that is capable of being tested against empirical evidence. Accordingly, a hypothesis is most useful when it relates two or more variables in terms of a comparison. For example, we might develop a hypothesis like the following: "Cost-control incentives in health care proposed by the private sector are more effective than those imposed by government agencies." The analyst will include only those variables in the hypothesis that are critical in explaining the particular event.

Hypotheses contain variables that can take on different values. **Values refer to the measurable characteristics of a variable (such as strong, neutral, or weak).** We might hypothesize: "Strong support (value) for a president will vary positively with low (value) inflation and low (value) unemployment." In this hypothesis, presidential support is the dependent variable. Inflation and unemployment rates are independent variables. The variables or values selected depend on the questions being asked or the problems to be resolved. Variables are the most basic elements in theories. **A variable is a term in a hypothesis that can assume different values.** In the hypothesis above we could have substituted the variables "support for a member of the Senate" or "support for a member of Congress" for "support for a president."

All this is part of the scientific method applied to the social sciences, as shown in figure 2-1.

---

[7]Michel de Montaigne, *The Essays of Michel de Montaigne,* edited and translated by Jacob Zeitlin (New York: Alfred A. Knopf, 1936), Vol. III, p. 270 (emphasis by Montaigne).

FIGURE 2-2
DEDUCTION AND MEASUREMENT IN THEORY BUILDING.

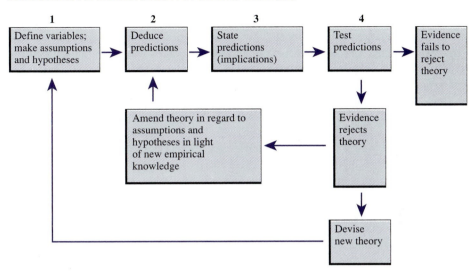

(From *Macroeconomics* by Roger A. Arnold. Copyright 1989 West Publishing. Reprinted by permission of South-Western College Publishing, a division of International Thomson Publishing Inc., Cincinnati, Ohio 45227.)

The Scientific Method in the Social Sciences

The scientific method, as applied in the social sciences to develop theories, progresses along the pathway of theory and observation suggested in figure 2-2. The variables are defined, assumptions noted, and hypotheses framed. Various implications and predictions are deduced from the hypotheses. This deductive process moves from the general to the particular, from a general theory to implications for a particular case. Predictions are then stated. These three steps comprise the building of a theory. In the fourth step, the theory is tested. The data either reject the theory or fail to reject the theory. If the data fail to reject the theory, this still does not prove it true. It merely fails to disprove it. This can increase one's confidence in the theory, but it must continue to be monitored by seeking additional tests. If, on the other hand, the evidence rejects the theory, there are two possibilities. Either the theory can be amended based on the evidence obtained from the test, or it can be abandoned altogether, in which case those who formulated the theory must return to step 1 and start developing a new one. Usually political scientists prefer simple theories to complicated ones. The preference for the simplest of competing theories over more complicated theories when both are consistent with the data is known as **Ockham's razor,** after a fourteenth century philosopher who urged its use to "shave away" superfluous theoretical complexities.

When a theory cannot predict the consequences of the actions being studied better than alternative explanations, it must be modified or replaced. The scientific method requires setting up a theory to explain some phenomenon and then ascertaining if that theory can be disproven by evidence. The danger in this approach is that the world is so complicated that *some confirming evidence* can be found for almost any theory—which is why conspiracy theories abound in American politics.

The Role of Theory in Policy Science

One of the most humbling aspects of the study of public policy is how complex it actually is. Dividing the policymaking process into the stages of agenda setting, selection of an alternative, adoption, implementation, and evaluation simplifies policy making into workable segments for inquiry. Most researchers feel forced to concentrate their efforts on just one stage of the process to reduce their studies to manageable size. In the last two decades process studies have contributed to understanding what goes on in policy making, but by themselves do not show the causal relationships between the policy-making stages. There has been a considerable effort by those in the rational public choice school to develop a theory of policy making within that tradition.[8]

It is important to bear in mind that **theories are abstractions based on assumptions.** This means the resulting predictions are **theoretical** predictions, and will hold true only as long as the basic assumptions of the theory are valid. Public policy makers are not so much interested in theoretical predictions as they are in broader factual forecasts. That is, they are more likely to be interested in cosmopolitan views rather than narrower political or economic theories in a given situation. For example, theory can correctly claim that a competitive labor market erodes wage discrimination based upon gender. But that is clearly not an accurate description of events in the markets where gender discrimination is institutionalized, making it difficult for the erosion of wage discrimination predicted by competitive labor theory to make itself felt. Policy research shows that gender discrimination acts as an intervening variable. For the maker of public policy, then, economic forces that are offset by social forces are only of **theoretical** and not of **actual** value in making predictions.[9] The policy maker must understand social reality as well as economic theory to develop appropriate policy. In the case of wage discrimination based on gender, the policy maker must have a broad knowledge of the institutional arrangements and cultural aspects involved in order to find a viable solution. Policy theory has developed a disreputable public image—partly because of its inability to predict future outcomes with the same precision as the natural sciences, partly because of some theorizing that is irrelevant or trivial, and partly because many politicians have found it expedient to ridicule theory in policy analysis.

[8]See for example, Larry Kiser and Elinor Ostrom, "The Three Worlds of Action," in E. Ostrom (ed.), *Strategies of Political Inquiry* (Beverly Hills: Sage, 1982), pp. 179–222.

[9]Theories require modification when masked variables are detected. A typical example of price discrimination that has been frequently used is doctors' pricing of health care services. A patient with fewer alternative providers, the theory postulates, can be charged a higher price for medical care. However, masked variables have caused trouble for this theory. Take the issue of race. Suppose that black patients have lower average incomes than whites. Some physicians might be less willing to accept black patients because of racism and/or a fear that black patients will be less able to pay for medical services. If that were true, according to the above theory, then those physicians willing to treat black patients could charge higher prices and be less likely to lose black patients to other physicians. Some studies in the 1970s found support for that hypothesis. More recent studies, using more extensive data, have found no evidence of physician price discrimination on the basis of race. Earlier studies had not included region of the country, which masked cost of living and fee differentials, and misattributed those effects to the racial composition of a physician's patients. The point is that this example illustrates the importance of not ending analysis at the theoretical level. The question must be pursued in the real world to determine if the theoretical argument is an accurate explanation of what is really happening. Accordingly, basing our understanding of the world and public policy on empirically empty theory is dangerous. See Alvin E. Headen, Jr., "Price Discrimination in Physician Services Markets Based on Race: New Test of an Old Implicit Hypothesis," *The Review of Black Political Economy,* vol. 15, no. 4 (Spring 1987), pp. 5–20.

We must distinguish between policy theory and public policy. **Policy theory** can develop rules and principles of policy that can serve as a guide for action in a given set of circumstances. **Public policy refers to the actual action taken.** In an ideal world public policy would always be consistent with policy theory put forward. Policy problems and issues by definition have political ramifications. The result is that policy theory is modified by political realities. For instance, theory might indicate that we should raise taxes to reduce inflation, but during an election year the theory may yield to political realities resulting in reduced taxes to win votes.

But it is exactly the importance of public policy that makes policy theory so critical. If there were no possibility of changing the general social welfare through public policy, political science and economics might both be disciplines asking merely historical questions such as "How did the U.S. government react to the stagnant economy during the Great Depression of the 1930s?" or "How have health or education policies changed since the mid-1970s?"

Policy analysis is a natural development of the social sciences. World War II and its aftermath encouraged several developments in technique, such as operations research, cost-benefit analysis, and linear programming. These developments moved political science from the purely theoretical, and brought it closer to becoming a contributor to policy input. Leaders in the American Political Science Association such as David Easton and Harold Lasswell actively tried to move the profession toward more policy involvement.

The joining together of theory and applied analysis took shape during the administrations of John F. Kennedy and Lyndon Johnson. It fell especially to Johnson's Great Society programs to improve the effectiveness of the disadvantaged through greater organization and management techniques. But faith in the ability of social science to provide answers to societal problems was not guaranteed by applying theory to real world issues.

Analytical techniques provide a more powerful method of analysis, but they are not theoretical perspectives. The liberal and conservative perspectives previously examined represent *normative* theories—those analytical perspectives based upon values which lead to value judgments. Techniques of policy analysis are indifferent to values and merely clarify relationships between cause and effect. Thus, conservatives attacked the Great Society programs using the same analytical techniques used by the Great Society's supporters.

Theories and concepts guide the study of public policy, and provide guidelines to focus research and to give structure to our inquiry.

Human Behavior and Predictability

The policy sciences deal with the behavior of people, which is not so neatly categorized as other phenomena. How do you find order with so many variables that cannot be isolated? A variation of this view holds that human beings are the least controllable or predictable of subjects for scientific inquiry.[10] However, even if one accepts the argument of the great

---

[10]Russell Kirk, a critic of the scientific study of politics, has argued that "Human beings are the least controllable, verifiable, law-obeying and predictable of subjects." See Russell Kirk, "Is Social Science Scientific?" in Nelson W. Polsby, Robert Dentler, and Paul Smith (eds.), *Politics and Social Life* (Boston: Houghton Mifflin, 1963), p. 63.

complexity of the social sciences, one cannot conclude that the discovery of relationships is impossible, only that **there are more variables making it more difficult to discover the critical ones.**

Another argument runs that, while the natural sciences deal with inanimate matter subject to natural laws, the social sciences focus on humans with free will and passions not subject to such laws. Consequently, generalizations formulated in the social sciences lack predictive power. It is true that free will and passions like love, hate, pride, envy, ambition, and altruism are more unpredictable in their effects on human behavior than natural causes are on the behavior of atoms. All of these influences, which are extremely difficult to understand, interact within individual humans, and affect human behavior. Nevertheless, having free will and passions does not mean that individuals do not act rationally on the basis of their values, disposition, character, and external restraints, and that these actions cannot be understood.[11]

As an example of the difference between the natural and social sciences, **if** hydrogen and oxygen are mixed under specific conditions, **then** water will result. However, if the government decides for budgetary reasons to reduce welfare payments (and incidentally support the self-help work ethic), it finds that some individuals will adopt the desired behavior pattern and others will not. Some people, faced with reduced benefits, will work very hard to find a job and become self-sufficient. Others, seeing few options, may adopt a life of crime as their avenue of escape. And the same individuals may react differently at different points in time.

The social sciences have developed ways to predict group behavior even though how individuals will behave is not known. For example, social scientists cannot predict which particular individuals will be killed by handguns or automobile accidents on a given weekend, but they can predict with surprising accuracy the total number that will be killed. Pollsters are likewise able, through sampling techniques, to learn the major concerns of voters. Political candidates can use this knowledge to place themselves in a favorable position to gain the support of potential voters. The ability to predict is of course crucial for makers of public policy who wish to know how people will react to a policy change in, for example, the capital gains tax. One's reaction to a capital gains tax cut will depend upon several factors, such as income level, expectations regarding how one's own position will be helped or hurt by the proposed tax change, and awareness of the law and its effect. Some individuals will react in surprising ways, but the overall response will be predictable within a small margin of error.

Public policy analysis bases its predictive efforts on the assumption that individuals act so consistently in their rational self-interest that they can be said to obey "laws" of behavior. Several such generalizations about human behavior provide a logical matrix for understanding human behavior similar to the laws used to account for events in the

---

[11]For example: Democratic society is based upon the assumption that rational people acting "freely" may decide to violate the law. The cost of such action is determined by the probability of being punished. The sanction of the law makes sense in part because it presumes that most people will "freely decide" to obey the law. In fact it is only because we can act freely that we can be held responsible. For example, deranged individuals are less accountable precisely because they do not "freely" choose their actions. These, then, are research problems, not unbeatable methodological barriers.

material world. Human beings bent on maximizing their self-interest may behave in a number of different ways, depending upon their understanding of their situation. All of this is in the way of saying that one must be aware of the limitations of social scientific generalizations.

Nevertheless, the unpredicted or random movements—the error—of individuals tend to offset each other. Knowledge of this fact makes possible **the statistical law of large numbers** that is based on the **normal curve of error.** It states that **the average error of all individuals combined will approach zero.** Since the irregularities (errors) of individual behavior will tend to cancel each other out, the regularities will tend to show up in replicated observations.

The Policy Analyst as Policy Maker

Policy experts are often asked to **explain the causes** of certain events. Why, for example, has violent crime declined in almost every American city in the last few years? At other times, policy analysts are asked to **recommend policies** to reduce crime. When social scientists are asked to explain why violent crime has declined they are acting in their role as scientists. When they are proposing policies to reduce criminal activity, they are acting in their role as a policy maker.

It may be useful to point out once again as we did in Chapter 1, the difference between positive and normative analysis. Positive analysis tries to explain the world as it exists. While policy makers may value scientific analysis, they have an additional goal. Someone involved in normative analysis is trying to bring about a different and presumably better end-state. For example, two individuals might be involved in a discussion of drug usage in the United States. The following exchange might be heard:

Jim: Current drug laws contribute to urban decay.
Colleen: Most drug laws should be rescinded.

The important distinction between the two statements is that the first is *descriptive* of a social condition, at least as perceived by Jim. The second is *prescriptive* in that it describes the legal order as it *should be* (i.e., the law ought to be changed). We can gather evidence to support or counter Jim's statement. Colleen's *normative* statement about what the policy ought to be cannot be confirmed or refuted by merely gathering evidence. Deciding on the appropriate policy will involve our philosophical views and personal values. This is not to deny that our evaluation of the evidence about drug laws and urban decay will influence our value judgments about what the policy ought to be. Specialists in public policy spend a great deal of time trying to determine what the critical relationships are and exactly how society works. But the whole purpose of government and public policy is to improve society by promoting the general welfare.

Why Policy Analysts Disagree

The fact that policy is dependent upon values results in the community of policy scholars being no more unified in outlook than is the political community. Policy scholars generally agree on various analytical aspects of policy, yet they hold different views about what is best for society. Since public policy analysts, like everyone else, come from across the political spectrum, they hold different opinions about the "best" or "right" solution to public policy problems. One example may illustrate why the analysis of public policy problems may not lead to agreement on a policy decision.

In the mid-1990s, some policy makers were determined to reduce the federal deficit. Some public policy analysts disagreed about the accuracy of the different theories regarding the impact of the deficit and the importance of balancing the budget. Analysts also disagreed on what the policy goals should be. Some believed that a full employment deficit would help create jobs which ought to be a major goal of public policy. Other analysts believed that the greatest threat of deficits is found in rising inflationary pressures. And they believed that the primary responsibility of government is to reduce inflation. Some policy makers in Congress and in the executive branch of government found political advantage on either side of the question and staked out their position largely along the lines of appealing to their traditional constituents. As the deficit fell faster than most had anticipated, the disagreement shifted to the issue of whether there should be a tax cut and a further reduction in the role of government, or a reduction in the national debt. Once again many analysts honestly disagreed on which policy should be adopted based upon the theories and data available. Their disagreements were undoubtedly influenced by their individual values and vice versa.

Another perennial issue is tax policy. Are Americans taxed too much? Would individual saving and spending be a better stimulus for the economy than government spending in the long run? Public policy analysts are no better at answering this question than are physicians when determining whether the right to abortion is justifiable. Such judgments in the United States are determined by the people through the democratic process of voting those with specific policy goals into office.

Increasingly there are cases in which policy experts agree, but the role of special interest groups and frauds obscures the consensus. For example, for years the tobacco companies funded research that downplayed the significance of the risks to health from smoking, even though scholars, not dependent upon tobacco companies for their funding, were unanimous in their findings about health risks of smoking. Similarly, studies were funded as the result of the Civil Rights Act of 1964 to assess the extent to which individuals were being denied educational opportunities because of race or other attributes. The research was not politically neutral. It was limited to questions that provided information helpful to one side of the issue. Studies are vulnerable to manipulation by the choice of alternatives considered, or the interpretation of the findings.

The result is that much policy analysis research is used in the U.S. political process in an advocacy fashion. The research is not examined by political entrepreneurs or special interest groups for its utility in improving policy so much as it is used selectively to undercut an adversary's position or to strengthen one's own. Politicians and lobbyists often look for support for preformed political and ideological positions rather than information to help shape and guide policy. Administrations are distressed to find that the results of policy analyses hinder the pursuit of policies on which they have already embarked. The more ideologically motivated the administration or bureaucracy, the more policy is made on the basis of ideological inputs rather than policy analysis. In recent years, for example, conservatives backed and buttressed their aims by funding policy analysis groups such as The Heritage Foundation, or the American Enterprise Institute as an alternative to institutes perceived as having a more liberal orientation.[12]

THE POLICY MAKING PROCESS

Public policy did not appear as a subfield of political science until the mid-1960s. The effort to provide an abstract framework for the entire policy process was presented by David Easton.[13] Since that time effort has concentrated on the analysis of specific substantive areas of public policy research. Research has focused on topics such as health care, education, the environment, welfare, and national security. Many of these studies have provided very detailed descriptive historical case studies of the development and evolution of policy. More recently there have been greater efforts to apply theoretical models to these case studies, focusing on the factors that affect policy formulation and implementation. This evaluation research judges the formulation of the policy proposal, the process of policy adoption, and the operation of the policy program.

Public policy analysis has not progressed in developing scientifically law-like propositions. Similarly, the current understanding of the policy process is really a heuristic model, not a theory that allows explanation and prediction. As noted earlier, this model separates the policy making process into five stages: problem identification and agenda setting, policy formulation, adoption, implementation, and evaluation (see fig. 2-3). The model contains no clear and consistent postulates about what drives the process from one stage to the next. Its primary value has been that it divides the policymaking process into manageable units of analysis. Thus the model has resulted in research projects which focus almost exclusively on a single stage without tying individual results into the results of other projects that have focused on other stages. So little theoretical coherence exists from one stage to the next.[14]

Problem Identification and Agenda Setting

Step 1 in figure 2-3 simply indicates that public policy begins when a problem is perceived and gets on the **policy agenda.** There are many problems in society that are not part of the policy agenda because they have not gotten the attention of the authoritative actors in the government and therefore do not cause any policy response.[15] The desire for policies to provide for individual needs is insatiable, while room on the agenda is scarce. This raises the question as to why some issues get on the agenda while others do not. The

---

[12]In addition to institutes funded to conduct policy research such as the American Enterprise Institute or The Brookings Institution, Congress employs thousands of staff members who also do such research. There are several thousand more analysts who work for other government support agencies, such as the General Accounting Office (GAO), the Office of Technology Assessment (OTA), the Congressional Research Service (CRS), and the Congressional Budget Office (CBO). These agencies generally respond to requests by congressional representatives and their staffs for specific studies. They also may engage in studies on their own initiative. As such, they are a significant source of policy agenda items.

[13]David Easton, *A Systems Analysis of Political Life* (New York: John Wiley and Sons, 1965).

[14]Paul A. Sabatier, "Political Science and Public Policy," *PS Political Science and Politics,* vol. 24 (June 1991), p. 145.

[15]For a sophisticated and sound theoretical treatment of agenda setting, see John Kingdon, *Agendas, Alternatives, and Public Policies* (Boston: Little, Brown and Co., 1984). See also Barbara Nelson, *Making an Issue of Child Abuse* (Chicago: University of Chicago Press, 1984).

FIGURE 2-3
FIVE KEY ELEMENTS AND PATHWAYS BETWEEN ANALYSIS AND THE POLICY-MAKING
PROCESS.

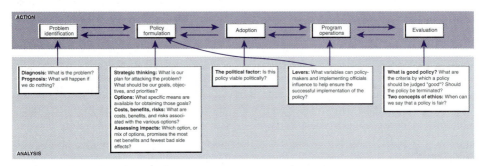

(*Source:* Grover Starling, *Strategies for Policymaking* [Chicago: Dorsey Press, 1988] p. 10.)

dynamics of a changing political environment, new political players, policy entrepreneurs, and new windows of opportunity are major elements in new issues gaining a place on the agenda. For instance the Great Depression provided the opportunity for legislation which ushered in various policies such as Social Security and minimum wage laws. More recently, the conservative reaction that swept Ronald Reagan to the presidency provided a window of opportunity for the reduction of social welfare legislation and the introduction of supply-side economics on the policy agenda.[16]

But in truth, success in getting on the policy agenda does not ensure a policy response. Some issues manage to get on the agenda yet drift along for years without getting beyond step 1. For example, health care reform has been accepted as a policy item because of the strength of voter attitudes on the issue. However, both political parties are in disarray as to how to proceed in implementing any reforms. The two major alternatives proposed are a universal plan administered by the government, or a plan that would require coverage but use existing structures of private insurance. Neither political party has coalesced around any firm proposals. Intense lobbying by special interest groups, ideological biases, and questions regarding costs have made it difficult to get beyond the agreement that something should be done. The lack of consensus on how to proceed has resulted mostly in considerable debate and posturing by political entrepreneurs.

Other items may get on the policy agenda only to disappear into a black hole by the crush of other issues, then resurface later in slightly modified forms. Thus the question as to whether the United States should develop an **industrial policy** to promote a resurgence of U.S. business growth was placed on the agenda in the early 1980s. The idea was brushed aside by the Reagan White House, which viewed industrial policy as inappropriate interference with an unfettered free market, one of the goals of his administration. More recently, the administration of Bill Clinton has quietly instituted an industrial policy designed to strengthen business and U.S. exports as part of his overall economic program.

The first step in the policy making process is a prerequisite for all the steps that follow. So even though getting on the policy agenda provides no assurance that an issue will go any further, failure to get on the agenda guarantees it will not go anywhere at all.

---

[16]See Kingdon, *Agendas, Alternatives, and Public Policies,* pp. 183–84.

For that reason, getting on the policy agenda is the most critical step, and also the most nebulous and amorphous in the entire process.

Some researchers suggest that the policy agenda should be thought of as consisting of a **systemic** and an **institutional agenda.** The **systemic agenda** is made up of those issues perceived by the political community as meriting public attention and resolution.[17] However, the systemic agendas of national and state governments are largely symbolic in nature. The issues they contain are often controversial, and some items may be on one systemic agenda but not another. For example, some believe that the "right to bear arms" is guaranteed by the Constitution, and that it should be beyond the authority of Congress or the states to regulate in any way. Therefore, the issue of gun control has until very recently remained on the systemic agendas of the federal government and most state governments, with many gun control opponents urging its removal altogether. Another subset of items on the systemic agenda are those subject to nothing more than discussion; these are termed "pseudo-agenda items."

The **institutional agenda** consists of those items that receive the powerful and earnest attention of decision makers. These items are not always easily identified or agreed upon either. They do include those issues that are actively pursued through the various institutions of government.

Items may shift from the systemic to the institutional agenda as a result of a variety of events. For example, Congress may prefer to keep an item such as a bill on abortion on the systemic agenda because it may be perceived as a no-win situation for members to take a stand by voting. However, a decision by the Supreme Court, such as *Roe v. Wade,* may force the issue back to the national legislature and require some action. Policy issues typically move from private decision making to the public agenda when they progress from the systemic to the institutional agenda.

The Scope of the Conflict   If policy is not made through public decisions by the government, it will be made through private decisions, primarily by businesses or financial elites. Traditionally, the principle of laissez faire meant that government should not interfere with business. As a practical matter, it meant that government supported business decision making through legislation and court decisions that legitimized and reinforced corporate interests. Thus corporations made policy that provided pervasive control over the lives of individuals unhindered by government interference. Businesses were given a free hand to set the terms of employment, wages, hours, and working conditions for employees, and those terms were supported by government stipulations regarding the rights to private property and freedom of contract.

Under laissez-faire doctrine, business provided for individual economic needs through free enterprise, and was loosely supervised by lower levels of government. But with the rise of giant corporations in the late nineteenth century, the power of business organizations over the lives of individuals grew correspondingly. The result was an overwhelming popular demand for government action to correct the perceived abuses of power by corporate interests.

This demand for reform expanded the scope of the conflict from the private arena of management versus labor to the public arena of government versus business. For example, the

---

[17]See Roger W. Cobb and Charles D. Elder, *Participation in American Politics: The Dynamics of Agenda Building,* 2d ed. (Baltimore: Johns Hopkins University Press, 1983), p. 85.

national government took the lead in legislating workmen's compensation and child labor laws. With the Great Depression came even more pressure for the government to take an active role in managing the economy and business.

Despite this expansion of governmental regulation, businesses still have a "privileged position" in American politics even today. They can often make major decisions with only a minimum of government control. In arguing for corporate autonomy from government regulation, executives point out that business must submit first of all to the discipline of the marketplace if it is to be successful. When an issue affecting business does get on the public policy agenda, business organizations are well represented in the public and governmental debates. Corporate leaders are effective proponents for their companies and for the interests of capitalism in general. They also provide many people for government positions, which encourages a probusiness bias in government policy making.

As long as decisions are made in the private sector they are outside the realm of politics even though those decisions may affect many people and the allocation of vast resources. Indeed (as noted in chap. 4), private conflicts are taken into the public arena precisely because someone or some group wants to make certain that the power ratio among the private interests shall not prevail in the final decision making.[18] In fact **politics may be defined as the socialization of conflict:**

> The political process is a sequence: conflicts are initiated by highly motivated, high-tension groups so directly and immediately involved that it is difficult for them to see the justice of competing claims. As long as the conflicts remain **private** . . . no political process is initiated. Conflicts become political only when an attempt is made to involve the wider public. Pressure politics might be described as a stage in the socialization of conflict.[19]

Enlarging the Scope   As noted earlier, democracies provide the political means for private controversies to spill over into the public arena. An issue or condition must attract sufficient attention and interest to expand the scope of the conflict into the public arena if there is to be any hope of changing its current disposition or status.

Some of those involved in the issue will prefer the status quo, and attempt to limit the scope of the conflict to keep it off the public policy agenda. And those with interests already on the public policy agenda will not welcome new items that threaten to displace their own. Since only a finite number of items can be considered at any given time. There is always tension when new issues erupt into public consciousness. Those items already on the agenda have a public legitimacy by virtue of having been accepted onto it. New items have not yet established their public legitimacy. For all of these reasons, **the political system has a bias in favor of the status quo and will resist the addition of new issues to the policy agenda.**

Who Sets the Public Policy Agenda?   Determining which issues move from the systemic to the institutional agenda is an extremely important part of the entire policymaking process. The policy agenda is overburdened with a wide assortment of foreign policy

---

[18]E. E. Schattschneider, *The Semi-Sovereign People: A Realist's View of Democracy in America* (New York: Holt, Rinehart and Winston, 1960) p. 38.
[19]Schattschneider, *The Semi-Sovereign People,* p. 39.

issues, national security affairs, economic questions, and domestic concerns. For a problem to become a salient agenda item, it is important that it have an influential advocate, most especially the president. Another route for an issue to move onto the institutional agenda is for it to be regarded as a crisis. The perception of a problem as being serious may even be more important than its actual seriousness. A triggering event, for example, the single act of a terrorist, may focus attention on an issue like terrorism even though the overall threat of terrorism is receding.

Increasingly, policy agendas are determined by tightly knit groups that dominate policy making in particular subject areas. **Iron triangles** refer to the reciprocal bonds that evolve between congressional committees and their staffs, special interest groups, and bureaucratic agencies in the executive branch.[20]

Members of Congress have incentives to serve on committees that deal with special interest constituencies from their districts. Senators and representatives will bargain for such appointments. And over time, committees in Congress tend to be dominated by members who are highly motivated to provide generous support for the agencies they oversee. This translates into an expansion of the programs of those agencies in the districts of the members of Congress overseeing them. These congressional committees make up one side of the iron triangle; they tend to be insulated from many party pressures and to develop committee member alliances that cross party lines.

The special interest groups form a second part of the triangle. These lobbyists and political action committees provide specialists, or experts in the special interest area. They provide committees with resources for public relations and media coverage, and supply campaign financing to committee members. Finally, the bureaucracies of federal agencies in the executive branch are the third side of the triangle, with their own entrenched interests in particular issues or programs. Congressional hearings provide excellent opportunities for government agency representatives and lobbyists to build imposing cases for their positions.[21]

Iron triangles exemplify disturbing problems in public policy. Policy alternatives that challenge the established interests of the triangle may never receive serious attention. Also, congressional and bureaucratic agency oversight of a congenial special interest group is not vigorously pursued.

Responses to the situation created by iron triangles have been based mainly on two different approaches to understanding the nature and functioning of government: elite theory and pluralism or group theory. Those espousing elite theory are critical of iron triangles, pointing to their power as proof of the victory of greedy special interest groups over the general welfare. Pluralists, on the other hand, are more likely to conclude that

---

[20]See Jeffrey M. Berry, "Subgovernments, Issue Networks, and Political Conflict," in Richard Harris and Signey Milkis (eds.), *Remaking American Politics* (Boulder, CO: Westview Press, 1990), pp. 239–69.

[21]The lobbying on behalf of the B-1 bomber is an excellent example of an iron triangle at work. Although various studies over thirty years recommended against its production, the U.S. Air Force formed an alliance with various defense contractors to build the B-1. They were able to rouse political support for the program, valued in excess of $28 billion, in part because of the jobs it was anticipated it would create across the country in forty-eight states. The Air Force and defense contractors lobbied many members of Congress not on any of the armed services committees, emphasizing the jobs and the money that would flow into each Congress member's state. See Nick Kotz, *Wild Blue Yonder: Money, Politics, and the B-1 Bomber* (Princeton, NJ: Princeton University Press, 1988).

THE ISSUE-ATTENTION CYCLE

Anthony Downs contends that many issues appear on the policy agenda in a standardized process that comprises an **"issue-attention cycle."** In his view, key domestic problems leap into prominence and remain the center of public attention for a short time, then fade from concern even though they remain largely unresolved. It is in part the length that public attention stays focused upon any given issue that determines whether enough political pressure will be brought to bear to effect a change. This cycle is rooted in the nature of many domestic problems and the way the communications media interact with the public. The cycle has five stages each of variable duration that usually occur in the following sequence:

1 *The preproblem stage.* Some major problem arises, and although policy experts and special interest groups may be alarmed by the situation, the general public is generally not aware of the problem or its magnitude. The general press has given it prominent coverage. It is not unusual for problems, such as racism or malnutrition, to be worse during the preproblem stage than they are by the time the public's interest is aroused.

2 *Alarmed discovery and euphoric enthusiasm.* Often as a result of some dramatic events (like riots or demonstrations), the public becomes aware of the problem. Authoritative decision makers then make speeches, which are enthusiastically received by the public, regarding the politicians' determination to resolve the problem. This optimism is embedded in American culture, which tends to view any problem as *outside* the structure of society, and naively believes that every problem can be resolved *without any basic reordering of society itself.* American optimism in the past has clung to the view that we as a nation could accomplish anything. Since the late 1960s, a more realistic awareness that some problems may be beyond a complete "solution" has begun to develop.

3 *Realization of the cost of significant progress.* A realization that the cost of solving the problem is extremely high sets in. The solution would not only take a great deal of money, but would also require that some groups give up some economic security (through taxes or some other redistribution of resources in favor of

such triangles simply reflect strategies developed to promote policies in a diverse nation whose subgroups have different interests.

Getting from the Systemic to the Institutional Agenda   According to elite theory, elites who are powerful in their own right have relatively little trouble getting their issues before the public. Those who own the media can publish stories or air television shows.[22] A member of Congress or the president, including their respective bureaucracies, can propose a policy. Special interest groups also frequently approach the government with their perceptions of problems and proposed solutions.

Ordinarily an individual must enlarge the scope of the conflict by mobilizing public opinion. This might be done by enlisting the aid of experts who are knowledgeable about the issue and how to publicize it. Frequently, the simplest solution is to seek out an interest group that already deals with a related topic. For example, if one is

---

[22]A number of works make the point that the media, popular opinion to the contrary, tend to be conservative and supportive of the conservative bias of elites. See, for example, W. Lance Bennett, *News: The Politics of Illusion,* 2d ed. (New York: Longman, 1988).

others). The public begins to realize the structural nature of the problem, and a human inconsistency regarding public policy makes itself felt: We favor collective coercion to raise our personal standard of living, and oppose it when it is used to limit our own actions and raise someone else's income.

Many social problems involve the exploitation, whether deliberately or unconsciously, of one group by another, or people being prevented from benefitting from something that others want to keep for themselves. For example, most upper-middle-income (usually white) people have a high regard for geographic separation from poor people (frequently nonwhite). Consequently equality of access to the advantages of suburban living for the poor cannot be achieved without some sacrifice by the upper middle class of the "benefits" of that separation. The recognition of the relationship between the problem and its "solution" is a key part of the third stage.

4 *Gradual decline of intense public interest.* As more people realize how difficult and

costly to themselves a solution would be, their enthusiasm for finding a "solution" diminishes rapidly. Some come to feel that solving the problem threatens them; others merely get bored or discouraged with the perceived futility of grappling with the issue. Also by this time another issue has usually been discovered by the media and is entering stage 2, and it claims the public's attention.

5 *The postproblem stage.* Having been replaced by successive issues at the center of public interest, the issue moves into a stage of reduced attention, although there may be a recurrence of interest from time to time. This stage differs from the preproblem stage in that some programs and policies have been put in place to deal with the issue. A government bureaucracy may have been given the task of administering a program and monitoring the situation. Special interest groups may have developed a symbiotic relationship with the bureaucracy and have had a successful impact even though the "action" has shifted to other issues.

Source: Anthony Downs, "The 'Issue-Attention Cycle,'" *The Public Interest,* no. 28 (1972), 38–50; also Anthony Downs, "Up and Down with Ecology: The Issue-Attention Cycle," *Public Interest,* no. 32 (1973): 39–53.

---

concerned that local public school students appear to be falling below national standards in testing, one might approach the local Parent Teachers Association (PTA) regarding remedial steps that might be taken. Getting the local newspaper to write an article might elicit support for new school policies designed to improve the quality of education in the local schools.

The number of people affected by an issue, the intensity of the effect an issue has on the community, and the degree to which everyone's self-interest can be aroused to confront the problems are all factors to be considered when trying to get an issue on the institutional agenda. An analysis of what will happen if nothing is done about a problem, in terms of who will be affected and in what ways, can be a powerful inducement to action.

Symbols and Getting on the Agenda   Ultimately the need to attract broad support to get an issue on the political agenda, and to try to move it to the institutional agenda, encourages the use of symbols. Symbols legitimize issues and attract support for the proposed policy goals. Symbols help people to order and interpret their reality, and even create the reality to which they give their attention. A major attribute of successful symbols is ambiguity. A **symbol** may be a slogan, an event, a person, or anything to which people attach meaning or value. Symbols can mean different things to different people. They permit the translation of private and personal intentions into wider collective goals by appealing to people with diverse motivations and values.[23] Ambiguity permits maneuvering room to reduce opposition to a policy. For instance, in the 1980s "welfare" came under increasing attack in a period of tight budgets and declining support for egalitarian policies. Calling the programs "work-fare" rather than "welfare" reduced some of the opposition to them since the new term implied welfare recipients would not be getting "a free ride."

Civil rights efforts in the 1960s were initially known primarily for their use of slogans and symbolic marches rather than for any solid achievements. When marchers appealing to "equal rights," the "constitution," and "justice and equality" were shown on television being attacked by police using dogs and fire hoses, the news reports had a powerful impact on the nation. After a relatively brief period, several effective pieces of legislation passed Congress. It is doubtful that the legislation could have passed without the powerful symbols that preceded it.

Policy Formulation and Proposal

Success in getting a problem accepted onto the policy agenda may depend in part on the ability to convince others that it is amenable to some governmental solution. Once the problem is on the agenda, however, specific plans for attacking it must be addressed. The problem has been clearly identified, and the need to do something about it accepted; **policy formulation** is then concerned with the **"what"** questions associated with generating alternatives. What is the plan for dealing with the problem? What are the goals and priorities? What options are available to achieve those goals? What are the costs and benefits of each of the options? What externalities, positive or negative, are associated with each alternative?

The first option after looking at the proposed solutions may well be **to do nothing.** Most, but not all, public policy proposals cost money. Currently there are severe economic constraints on new policy initiatives at the state level and particularly at the national level. The **economic costs** of new programs at the national level have made it extremely difficult to add any new programs.

The result of these huge federal deficits has been that since the mid-1980s, budgetary problems have dwarfed all others as the president and Congress have wrestled with the gap between revenues and demand. The result has been few new policies being added to the public agenda, and old programs being reauthorized at the same or even reduced spending levels.

Increasingly programs are expected to be financed by their recipients. For example, the Medicare Catastrophic Coverage Act that was passed with bipartisan support prior to the 1988 election provided insurance against catastrophic illnesses for those on Medicare by imposing a ceiling on medical bills and paying 100 percent of the costs

---

[23]Charles D. Elder and Roger W. Cobb, *The Political Uses of Symbols* (New York: Longman, 1983), pp. 28–29.

CASE STUDY

THE DILEMMA OF TAX CUTS, DEFICITS, AND SOCIAL WELFARE

The huge budget deficits that started in the 1980s have been a continuous problem for policy makers. When President Reagan took office in 1981 he was committed to a reduction in tax rates especially for the affluent. He found reducing government expenditures more difficult politically than cutting taxes. The result was a period of massive budget deficits that continued through the Reagan and Bush administrations and well into Bill Clinton's.

The government ran budget deficits through most of the years from the 1950s through the 1970s. The deficits were modest however and the overall economy grew faster than the deficits. The fact that the national debt was actually declining when measured against the Gross Domestic Product (GDP) during this period meant there was no cause for alarm as the government was living within its means. When the Reagan tax cuts were not accompanied by cuts in government spending, the growth in government debt relative to the GDP began rising. The government had to finance the growing deficit by borrowing the money (selling bonds). This had the effect of pulling money away from investment in new capital equipment, which slows economic growth and depresses the living standards of Americans in the future. Policy makers, of whatever political persuasion, accept this basic theory and see persistent deficits growing as a percentage of the GDP as a significant policy problem. They disagree on the question of how to reduce the deficit.

There are three ways to reduce the deficit: raise taxes, cut spending, or promote a more rapid growth in the GDP than in government spending. When Bill Clinton took office in 1993 deficit reduction was his major goal. In fact Bill Clinton boasts that the deficit has declined in each year he has been in office. His first action was to raise taxes among upper income groups while reducing the rate of growth of the budget. When the Republicans took control of Congress in 1995, they opposed any further tax increases, and pressed for more tax cuts to encourage private sector savings (which might be translated into capital investment). The result has been a reduction in spending for many welfare programs as Clinton proposed to "end welfare as we know it." Modest cuts in military spending and a long steady growth in the economy has reduced the size of the deficit, and the debt relative to the GDP.

More recently Clinton has proposed using the surge in tax receipts as the deficit gap decreases, for a modest tax cut and an increase in spending for education and other social welfare programs. Republicans in Congress propose greater tax cuts and are committed to a smaller government.

Like many policy issues, the debate over budget deficits has several facets. Policy makers agree on the general theory, but disagree on the best solution. The result is incremental changes at the margins resulting from compromise. It should also be noted that it took several years before the issue got on the agenda for serious debate and action. Budgets and economic policy will be discussed more fully in later chapters.

through Medicare. The goal was to relieve worry among the elderly that they would be impoverished by the high costs of medical care, especially hospitalization. This insurance was to be paid through a surtax on the income taxes of the elderly. The wealthiest elderly would pay most—a maximum surtax of $800 per year in 1989, rising to $1,050 in 1993. The poorest among the elderly would pay $4 per month. The theory was that the elderly as the program's beneficiaries should bear the cost.[24]

Another major concern for political entrepreneurs are the **political costs** associated with taking action. Since many policies will alter the distribution of income, it can be expected that those whose incomes will be adversely affected will generally oppose them, while those who will be helped will generally be favorably disposed toward them. Political entrepreneurs sometimes find themselves caught between doing what they think is right and choosing the alternative that is the least costly from a political perspective.

Selecting Alternatives   The formulation of a policy proposal ordinarily includes not only a statement of the goals of the policy, but various alternatives (or programs) for achieving the goals. How the problem is formulated will often suggest how the alternatives are proposed.

Some policy theorists promote **rational analysis** as a plan for achieving government efficiency through a comprehensive review of all the policy options and an examination of their consequences. Rational analysis selects the option that **maximizes utility.**

Much of the animosity surrounding the budgetary process is claimed to result from its *lack* of rationality. Everyone from the person-in-the-street, to bureaucrats, to special interest groups, to Congress, to the president believes that he or she can produce a better, more rational budget. However, **rational analysis of the budgetary process implies that each option be considered,** and no analyst can do this nor can any analysis of the budget be completely comprehensive.[25] Some things are inevitably left out of every analysis. There is not even a basis for constructing a satisfactory list of criteria to determine which goals or alternatives are the most reasonable and which could be left out.

A model of all social problems that included their ranking by importance would be very expensive and difficult to keep up to date. People's and society's concerns change constantly. For instance, until about 1980, most Americans outside the medical profession were unaware of Alzheimer's disease. It is now generally known to be a relatively common form of dementia that afflicts a significant percentage of the elderly population. It causes memory loss, personality disorders, and a decrease in other mental capabilities. After research helped to define Alzheimer's as a particular pathology, an organization was formed by people who had family members diagnosed with the disease. The Alzheimer's Association has since opened an office in Washington to lobby Congress to double the amount of federal funds currently dedicated to Alzheimer's research. However, a complete analysis of the appropriate amount of federal money to spend for Alzheimer's research would have to include an analysis of **all other possible ways to spend the money.** That is, every other

---

[24]It may be surprising to some that an administration committed to tax reduction would propose such a program. It was put forth in part to secure the support of the elderly, whose backing of the Republicans had been weak. The pay-as-you-go plan flopped, however. Retirees who had procured insurance benefits in the private sector led an effort to repeal the bill. The wealthier elderly did not want to trade some of their economic independence to help less-well-off retirees reach an equal plane regarding health care. They resented subsidizing the less wealthy. Those leading the opposition, however, appealed to the less wealthy retirees by arguing that the medical costs of the elderly should be the responsibility of younger Americans as well. They argued successfully that to make the elderly alone pay more, regardless of economic circumstances, was unfair, and the beginning of a reduction in benefits for all retirees was to be firmly resisted.

[25]See Charles E. Linblom, "The Science of 'Muddling Through,'" *Public Administration Review,* vol. 19 (1959), pp. 79–88.

item in the budget such as aid to education, the space program, cancer research, environmental protection, even deficit reduction and lowering taxes would have to be considered.[26]

Only the political process can do this. **Budgetary decision making is a political process regarding choices about values.** The suggestion that this process could be replaced with an apolitical rationality is ingenuous. Several presidents have argued in favor of Congress giving the president a **line-item veto,** as though this would take politics out of the process. But the budget is inherently a political document. To suggest taking politics out of the budgetary process is rather like saying one should take doctors out of medicine or teachers out of teaching. In 1996 Congress handed the president additional power to cut the budget by providing a limited line item veto. The first time President Clinton used this power in the fall of 1997, the Supreme Court held that the Line Item Veto Act was an unconstitutional delegation of power to the executive.[27]

Other policy theorists therefore contend that an incremental approach is actually much more rational. **Incrementalism is an approach to decision making in which policy makers change policy at the margins.** That is, they begin with the current set of circumstances and consider changing things in only a small way. Particularly in budgeting, this is the typical approach. Just note that **the best predictor of what next year's federal budget allocations will be is this year's allocations.** Incrementalism assumes that public policy decisions will usually involve only modest changes to the status quo and not require a thorough inspection of all the available options.

Incrementalism assumes the rational self-interest approach of individuals and groups. Since individual and group interests usually conflict, compromise will be required in which everyone will have to settle for less than they hoped for. This results in relatively small changes in existing policy. The budgetary process is thus simplified into a task that assumes each existing program will continue to be funded at its existing level because this level is perceived as fair. If the budget is growing, each program gets approximately the same percentage increase, with those programs having unusually strong support getting a slightly larger increase and those whose support or visibility are waning receiving slightly less. These new funding levels become the bases for the next year's budget.

Aaron Wildavsky maintains that incrementalism is the best technique for reaching budgetary decisions, because it reduces the decision-making process to manageable size. It focuses only on the **changes** to existing programs rather than requiring a complete justification of the entire program annually. The result is also an allocation of money according to each program's political strength. Since the selection of programs is a normative decision, according to Wildavsky, it is about as good a measure as we have regarding which programs are most deserving.[28]

---

[26]Other supporters of the rational model agree that it is impossible to find the best of all possible courses of action. They would instead reduce the number of courses of action to a reasonable set of contenders. Then statistical decision-making models might be used to decide on a final rational allocation of budgetary resources. However, critics point out that the initial selection of contenders is a political decision and arbitrary.

[27]Clinton v. City of New York, 118 S.Ct. 2091 (1998).

Arguably a president using a line-item veto would merely be substituting one individual's judgment for the collective will of Congress—and a judgment presumably based just as much upon ideology, special interest group pressure, partisan concerns, and personal views about the nature of the general welfare as that of any senator or congressional representative.

[28]Aaron Wildavsky, *The Politics of the Budgetary Process* (Boston: Little, Brown, 1964; rev. 4th ed., 1984).

The result of incrementalism is **satisficing,** or adopting a policy acceptable from all viewpoints rather than seeking the best solution possible. The "best" solution might prove unacceptable to so many decision makers that it would be voted down if proposed. For example, many public policy experts have recommended a significant tax increase on gasoline at the pump as the "best" way to reduce gas consumption and U.S. reliance on imported oil. Fear of consumer reaction and Republican opposition forced President Clinton to reduce a proposed gasoline tax increase from 20 cents to 5 cents a gallon. When the tax kicked in during the fall of 1993, few even noticed. In the fall of 1994, after inflation, gasoline prices were actually lower than before the tax increase. Since politics is the art of the possible, a negotiated compromise that wins some, if not all, support is preferred to defeat.

Incrementalism works, then, because it is in some ways the most rational approach to policy making. Time and resources are too limited to permit an examination of all the alternatives. There is a legitimacy in previous policies and programs, while the feasibility of new ones is less predictable. Incrementalism also permits quicker political settlements, particularly when disputes are at the margins regarding the modification of programs.

Adoption

Getting a proposed policy from the institutional agenda through the adoption process is crucial to effecting a change. In the late 1960s many public policy scholars focused on the question of how a bill becomes a law and the many veto points in the process. The process of proposing a bill and getting it passed is very straightforward in that it must follow a standardized procedure. However, the pitfalls that can befall a bill in the process are well known.

The definition of an issue and its impact on different portions of the population usually changes in the debate during the policy process. Political entrepreneurs try to redraw the dimensions of the dispute in an effort to reconfigure political coalitions and gain a winning edge. Party leaders and senior members of the Congressional committee considering the issue often bide their time, waiting for other members of the committee or of Congress to become familiar with the issue. They generally then move when they sense the time is ripe for action, based upon their experience in dealing with such matters.

The separation of powers in government allows each branch to judge the legitimacy, and if necessary to take action to check the moves, of the other branches. The actors involved here are clearly political elites and must be persuaded not of the wisdom of the proposed policy, but of its chances of success politically. For this reason the major concern at this point is the following: "Is the proposed policy politically viable?" The broadest support for the program must be in evidence here to convince political entrepreneurs that it is in their own interests to promote the policy through their votes.

Implementation and Operation

In the policy process, once a problem has been identified, alternatives examined, and a policy selected and legitimated through the adoption of legislation, one part of the policy making process has been completed. But this is also the beginning of another part of the process—implementing the policy. **Implementation** means carrying out the policy or program operations. Or as Robert Lineberry asserts, implementation is "a continuation of policy making by other means."[29] Implementation has attracted a significant amount of research because policies often do not accomplish what they were designed to achieve.[30] There are a series of decisions and actions that are necessary to put a policy into effect, and as in chess, miscalculation in the original design strategy or in implementation may bring the entire effort to naught.

Policy advocates have come to realize that **the time to plan for the implementation phase is during the formulation and policy selection stage.** All the earlier phases, if done well, will reach this state where the proposal is to be translated into action. Several factors in the design phase will facilitate the implementation stage. Perhaps most critical is the question of **policy design.** That is, has the problem been accurately defined? Only if the problem is accurately understood do the causal relationships become evident and allow the policy analyst to correctly perceive the connections between a particular policy's operation and its intent. For example, the Americans with Disabilities Act of 1990, prohibited discrimination against people with disabilities. The Equal Employment Opportunity commission and other federal agencies held lengthy hearings to create the regulations spelling out the standards of compliance.[31]

Congress can reduce the discretion of administrators by providing very detailed legislation. For example, Social Security legislation provides very precise terms for eligibility and levels of benefits and formulas for additional earnings. Even so, eligibility for benefits under the Social Security Disability Insurance cannot be set forth with such precision. The general definition of disability states that an individual is unable to engage in significant gainful employment by reason of a medically diagnosable mental or physical impairment expected to last at least twelve months or result in death. This definition, of necessity, leaves much room for subjective judgments and interpretation.[32] Implementation of SSDI benefits has resulted in significant controversy and thousands of cases of litigation.

It is usually much easier to implement a policy if it is **clearly stated and consistent with other policy objectives.** Vague and ambiguous language will be received by the state officials handling the implementation quite differently than crisp lucid legislation. Vaguely worded laws may be subject to varying interpretations by bureaucrats or state officials tasked with implementing a program. Vagueness may even permit opponents to effectively sabotage the policy. On the other hand, there are times when vagueness may be preferred to clarity, if the alternative would be no program at all. An excellent example of this is the Constitution, which as the basic framework of the U.S. government is also a policy statement. When the Founding Fathers were unable to agree on

[29]Robert Lineberry, *American Public Policy* (New York: Harper & Row, 1977), p. 71.

[30]See Paul Sabatier, "Top-Down and Bottom-Up Models of Policy Implementation: A Critical Analysis and Suggested Synthesis," *Journal of Public Policy,* vol. 6 (January 1986), pp. 21–48. See also Laurence O'Toole, "Policy Recommendations for Multi-Actor Implementation: An Assessment of the Field," *Journal of Public Policy,* vol. 6 (April 1986), pp. 181–210.

[31]See Peter C. Bishop and Augustus J. Jones, "Implementing the Americans with Disabilities Act of 1990: Assessing the Variables of Success," *Public Administration Review,* vol. 53 (March–April 1993), pp. 121–28.

[32]See Martha Derrick, *Agency Under Stress: The Social Security Administration in American Government,* (Washington: Brookings Institution, 1990).

clear statements on several issues, they compromised on vague, broad statements and agreed to let later practice determine the outcome. The "necessary and proper" clause is an obvious instance.

Another factor that facilitates the implementation of a policy is its perceived legitimacy. For instance, a program that passes both houses of Congress with large majorities or a decision by the Supreme Court that is unanimous or nearly so will generally also have the support of those tasked with its implementation. Even those who have misgivings will be more inclined to go along with the perceived mandate.

Implementation is the most important part of the policy making process for students of public administration. Much of the important work of implementing policy is done by the "street-level" bureaucrats, including judges, public health workers, school teachers, social workers, and other federal, state, and local government employees.

Evaluation

The last stage of the policymaking process is **evaluation.** Every state involves a purposeful effort to bring about some change in the political environment. But in particular the process of formulating a proposal and choosing among alternatives to achieve the policy's objectives suggests the need for some criteria or standard to determine if the implemented policy has achieved its objectives.

Evaluation is the assessment of how a program achieves its intended goals. All the earlier stages of the policy process look toward a future goal to be achieved; evaluation looks backward. It is a tool whose primary purpose is to appraise the operation of a program and provide feedback to those involved in the earlier stages. This feedback permits modifications in the policy to improve its efficiency and effectiveness. Evaluation also pinpoints unintended effects of a policy and allows adjustment in the implementation process to avoid those that are undesirable. In addition, it can be used to monitor the expenditure of funds to see that they were spent according to the terms of the law or grant. Thus, such assessments focus on the implementation of a program and how it has met the goals and objectives spelled out in the selection and adoption phases of the policy process.

Evaluation of public policy programs came into its own during the 1960s. Under Great Society legislation, there was a surge in government programs to deal with a variety of social ills. At the same time critics charged that these programs resulted in many **government failures,** and at a significant cost to taxpayers. The media reported cases of waste and inefficiency, as well as programs that were not achieving their intended goals. Congress began requiring more vigorous evaluations of programs by agencies like the General Accounting Office (GAO).

It is useful to make a distinction between policy making and policy analysis. This course is primarily concerned with the policymaking process. Policy analysts, however, emphasize the evaluation process and use a variety of different methods to assess policy. Those include laboratory studies, simulations, case studies, sample surveys, and cost-benefit analyses, to name just a few. The process often also involves the use of analytical techniques, such as applied statistical analysis, to measure program effectiveness in meeting goals.

CONCLUSION

1 Public policy has developed as a subfield within the discipline of political science since the mid-1960s. As a social science, it draws upon the humanities, and history in particular, for its data. It also utilizes the scientific method in an effort to explain and predict underlying causal relationships in policy making and uses empirical methodology to test the validity of causal relationships. Existing at the confluence of the social sciences, public policy draws upon theoretical developments in the various social sciences.

2 Policy analysts utilize the scientific method in order to understand the social world in which they work. Like other scientists, they must make assumptions and construct models to simplify a very complex world to provide greater understanding. Policy scientists study all the issues that are of interest to policy makers, which is to say that it is wide ranging and interdisciplinary.

3 When policy analysts are engaged in positive analysis they are concerned with understanding the world as it *is*. When policy analysts are concerned with normative issues (how the world *ought* to be), they are acting more in the role of policy maker. An objective understanding of how the world *is* will influence one's values.

4 Specialists in public policy issues may not always agree because they have different scientific judgments regarding theories developed from studies. They also disagree because they have different value systems about what *ought to be* to improve society. Sometimes there may be wide agreement among policy scientists, but there is a public perception of a lack of consensus because special interest groups often provide studies and spokespersons claiming expertise to support almost any position imaginable.

5 The complexity of the problems in policy analysis has made the development of public policy theory difficult. Predictions that may be valid solely in terms of the underlying assumptions of a discipline such as economics or political science are often not based on data broad enough in scope to assure their accuracy in the larger policy scheme. Such predictions fail to take into account all the significant phenomena that influence the politico-economic variables related to a problem. This means that any effective theory development must begin at the micro level and take into account individual rational actors and their decision-making preferences, then move toward the macro-level aspects of institutional constraints and the societal effects of policy.

6 Scholarship over the last twenty years has resulted in a significant accumulation of knowledge regarding the public policy making process. Dividing the process into stages beginning with getting an issue on the public agenda, formulating the policy proposal, achieving its adoption, implementing the policy as a program, and evaluating the program's effectiveness in achieving the original policy goals has been the standard analytical approach. This has resulted in uncovering phenomena, such as "critical actors," that were previously overlooked.

7 The political system transfers private disagreements into public disagreements. Getting an issue on the public policy agenda is a critical procedural process. Elites in the society have far more influence than the average citizen.

QUESTIONS FOR DISCUSSION

1 Discuss the role of theory in understanding phenomena from the natural sciences. Does it differ from the role of theory in the social sciences? Why?
2 Why is the development of theory in the social sciences more difficult than in the natural sciences?
3 What are the special problems in developing theory in the policy sciences?
4 Should theories and models be a completely accurate reflection of reality?
5 Why are the contributions of policy analysts often not held in high regard by policy makers?
6 What if anything can be done to strengthen the role of policy analysts?
7 Why is it so difficult to get a proposed policy adopted and implemented? How would you suggest streamlining the process?

KEY CONCEPTS

abstraction
assumption
evaluation
hypothesis
implementation
incrementalism
institutional agenda
iron-triangle
issue-attention cycle
line-item veto

normal curve of error
policy agenda
policy formulation
rational analysis
satisficing
symbols
systemic agenda
theory
values
variables

SUGGESTED READINGS

Bruce Adams, "The Limitations of Muddling Through: Does Anyone in Washington Really Think Anymore?" *Public Administration Review,* vol. 39 (November/December 1979).
John J. Bailey and Robert J. O'Connor, "Operationizing Incrementalism: Measuring the Muddles," *Public Administration Review,* 35 (January/February 1975).
William E. Connally (ed.), *The Bias of Pluralism* (New York: Atherton, 1971).
Robert Dahl, *Who Governs?* (New Haven, CT: Yale University Press, 1961).
Thomas R. Dye, *Who's Running America? The Bush Era,* 5th ed. (Englewood Cliffs, NJ: Prentice-Hall, 1990).
John S. Furnival, *Colonial Policy and Practice* (New York: New York University Press, 1956).
John W. Kingdon, *Agendas, Alternatives, and Public Policies* (Boston: Little, Brown, 1984).
Charles E. Linblom, "The Science of 'Muddling Through,'" *Public Administration Review,* vol. 19 (Spring 1959).
C. Wright Mills, *The Power Elite* (New York: Oxford University Press, 1956).
Morley Segal, *Points of Influence: A Guide to Using Personality Theory at Work* (San Francisco: Jossey-Bass Inc, 1997).
David B. Truman, *The Governmental Process* (New York: Knopf, 1971).

3

RATIONAL PUBLIC CHOICE

This chapter is concerned with the theory of **rational choice** which was originally developed by economists but was quickly adapted to other policy science disciplines. Indeed there is nothing especially economic about rational behavior. There are several differences between the economic marketplace and political markets. In most economic markets, firms compete to sell products to the consumer who makes the final choice. Theoretically at least, the consumer is sovereign. Production matches itself to the demand of consumers based on their willingness and ability to pay. Political markets are typically decided by a one-time choice at the ballot box in which a majority wins. Interested parties may continue to pressure an elected official for the duration of the term of office following the election, but all consumers get the same political goods whether it is health care, public schools, or national defense.

This chapter is concerned with how individuals and elected policy makers make decisions. Can we develop a set of assumptions regarding individual preferences, and from these derive principles of political behavior for individuals as well as those seeking election? Do elected officials' decisions reflect the will of the voters? Is the competition in the political marketplace as responsive to consumer's wishes as it is in the economic marketplace?

RATIONAL CHOICE

Rational choice theory, sometimes called public choice, is the study of the collective decisions made by groups of individuals through the political process to maximize their own self-interest. Public choice assumes that individuals are just as rational and self-interested in the political sector as they are in the economic marketplace.[1] According

---

[1]The adaptation of this theory from economics to political science began with William Riker at the University of Rochester. But it has developed most broadly in the Virginia state university system, especially at George Mason University, VPI, and the University of Virginia, and is sometimes referred to as the Virginia school. James Buchanan, an economist from George Mason University, won a Nobel Prize for his work in this area.

FIGURE 3-1
MASLOW'S NEED HIERARCHY.

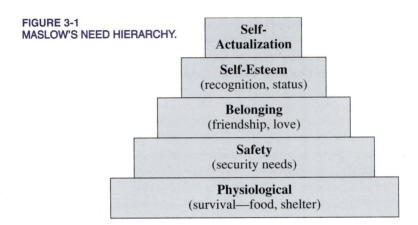

to public choice theory, when people behave differently in the political sector than in the marketplace it is because the institutional arrangements are different and not because of a lack of self-interest.

Many political scientists defend public choice as being wholly value-free and scientific.[2] **Rational public choice attempts to provide an analysis and an explanation of the society as it is and not necessarily as it should be.** That is, it explains actual social behavior. It explains why individuals with high incomes are more likely to vote than those with low incomes, and why they are more likely to be active members of special interest groups. The theory also suggests why there are built-in social and political supports for the status quo, because despite the claim of many of its practitioners that the theory is value free, positive science, the conclusions of public choice have a definite modern day conservative cast.

Personal Decision Making

In chapter 2 we pointed out that human beings are multifaceted creatures. Human nature is too complex to be explained in one or two dimensions. But we do assume that people are *motivated* to engage in goal-directed actions to satisfy their needs. Each individual has a unique set of needs that is influenced by his or her own history including: gender, age, ethnic background, intellectual abilities, family situation, and financial status to name just a few. Motivation theories tell us that we all are motivated to fulfill a variety of needs. Abraham Maslow proposed that there is a hierarchy of needs that is common to mentally healthy adults. Any of the five needs are capable of motivating behavior (fig. 3-1).[3] He believed that these needs arranged themselves in a distinct order. According to his theory, as long as a lower-level need was unsatisfied, an individual will be highly motivated to choose actions calculated to satisfy that need.

[2]See William H. Riker. *Liberalism Against Populism: A Confrontation Between the Theory of Democracy and the Theory of Social Choice.* (San Francisco: Freeman). 1982. See also William C. Mitchell. *Government as It Is* (London: Institute of Economic Affairs, 1988).
[3]Abraham Maslow, "A Theory of Human Motivation," *Psychological Review,* 50 (1943), pp. 370–96.

According to this theory, once a lower need, like the physiological needs are satisfied a person will direct his/her attention toward satisfying safety needs and so on. Research on Maslow's model has resulted in several criticisms, although none of the criticisms have been fatal. First, a person's needs may change over time. The needs of a young adult embarking on a new career and starting a family will differ from those of a veteran employee preparing for retirement. And changes in society may result in changes in the significance of different needs. For example: an economy falling into recession with rising unemployment may cause one to shift his or her attention from esteem needs to safety and physiological needs. A second criticism suggested by research is that people often work to satisfy several needs at the same time. For example, a person's employment may satisfy the physiological need to acquire money to provide for the survival needs, while simultaneously providing for safety needs through insurance and pension programs. One's peers at work may also satisfy esteem and self-actualization needs through friendship and the mutual participation in creative work endeavors. Despite these criticisms, Maslow's theory retains a certain popularity because of its intuitive appeal and because understanding how individual needs appear is critical in understanding what motivates individual behavior.

The conventional view of policy making in America is that people act on the basis of self-interest in public and private affairs. The "public interest" may be understood as the entirety of these individual preferences expressed as choices. **Society is improved when some people's preferences can be satisfied without making other people worse off.** Usually we assume the economic market will serve best to improve society. Public policies are needed when a policy makes improvements more efficiently than the market.[4] This is not a statement of how public policies are actually made, but how they are justified.[5]

Public policy is interested in purposeful rational choice. In this sense, **rational behavior simply means making choices the consumer believes will maximize personal satisfaction or utility.** Adam Smith described this as "the desire of bettering our condition" which begins at birth and never leaves until we go to our graves.

Since the concept of **rational self-interest** is often a source of misunderstanding, it is important to clarify its meaning.[6] **Rational self-interest means that individuals have preferences**. People **intend** to act in such a way to achieve those preferences when the expected benefits exceed the costs of available choices. Since people try to make decisions by comparing costs and benefits, their behavior may change if the costs or benefits they face change. Rational choice follows the basic rule of logic that holds that **behavior is rational as long as its marginal benefit is equal to its marginal cost.** A rational actor is expected to choose the action that will *maximize* expected benefits. This simple rule of logic is central to rational choice thinking. The marginal benefit from taking a certain action is the increase in total benefit from doing it once more. While the marginal cost is the increase in total costs from doing it once more. Behavior is maximized by making decisions until the net benefit equals the net cost.

---

[4]As an economic term, efficiency is defined as maximizing output with given resources (costs). It implies the impossibility of gains in one area without losses in another.

[5]Robert B. Reich, *The Resurgent Liberal and Other Unfashionable Prophecies* (New York: Vintage Books, 1989), p. 259.

[6]For an excellent summary of rational self-interest, see Henry Demmert, *Economics: Understanding the Market Process* (New York: Harcourt Brace Jovanovich, 1991), pp. 4–6.

Some rational choices may seem irrational. For example, a rational choice made by an individual with limited information, may not appear rational to someone with more information. A consumer may pay a high price for a product when the identical item may be for sale at a much lower price at another store nearby. But the consumer may not be aware that the other store carries the product let alone at a lower price. Decisions are often made with less than perfect information. Information has a cost in time, and sometimes money.

Rational self-interest does not mean that people make the best decisions. Mistakes will still be made. Decisions are usually made under conditions of limited information. The costs associated with acquiring all the relevant information may be too high, or the information required for utility-maximizing behavior may not be available. For example, the government spends close to 30 billion dollars a year to acquire the best information available regarding other countries' capabilities and intentions. Much of the information is gathered despite the attempts of other countries to maintain its secrecy. The government may formulate foreign policy based on intelligence findings which is the best information available. Failures of foreign policy occur when there is an incorrect assessment of the intelligence information, or when there is a failure to uncover all critical information.

Even if the full range of information needed to make a truly rational, self-interested choice is unavailable or too great for a person to adequately assimilate, the **process of choice** rather than the outcome of the process can still be considered rational. Behavior may be procedurally rational when it is the outcome of appropriate consideration based on incomplete information.

Rational behavior does not mean that individuals never make a bad decision. Still, only a self-destructive individual will knowingly choose an inferior alternative to a more preferred one. People may make irrational decisions, for example, by ignoring opportunity costs. An individual who squanders his money gambling and is then unable to pay his rent or mortgage has acted irresponsibly, and to a public choice theorist, irrationally. There is evidence that people learn from their experience and when faced with a repeated situation learn to consider opportunity costs. The concept of rational self-interest only holds that an individual would never knowingly choose a higher-cost means of achieving a given end when a lower-cost alternative is available.

The notion that people will respond to incentives in predictable ways is central to rational choice and to public policy. If the cost of health care rises in real terms (adjusted for changes in inflation), less will be demanded. Drivers will buckle their seat belts if the perceived benefits (reduced risk of injury) outweigh the cost (the time spent buckling and the discomfort of the restraint). But, if the cost of their use is viewed as exceeding the benefit, seat belts will remain unbuckled. People will try to reduce costs and increase benefits to themselves.

Rational self-interest arouses ambivalence in many people. It evokes images of reason and informed decision on the one hand, but on the other hand suggests a sophisticated self-centered behavior. **Rational self-interest is not the same as selfishness or greed.** An individual who is injured in an accident and seeks medical attention is acting in his or her self-interest, but we would not accuse the individual of being selfish because of that action. By the same token, obeying the law may be in one's self-interest, but it is not selfish conduct. Selfish conduct is behavior that disregards the interest of others in situations in which their interests should not be ignored. For example, to take an ample supply of

ALTRUISM AND SELF-INTEREST

Opinions regarding what motivates individual choices are often raised in public policy discussions. There is an often heard contention that there are no truly altruistic acts. **Unselfish** acts, such as volunteering to work in a soup kitchen to feed the hungry, make people **feel morally correct** by giving them a clear conscience. Thus actions are altruistic only at a superficial level. Upon closer examination, the motivation to act "altruistically" is really to achieve the self-satisfaction of thinking of one's self as being a good person.

To derive satisfaction from helping others does not make one selfish. The unselfish person **does** derive satisfaction from helping others, while the selfish person does not. The truly selfish person is unconcerned about the suffering of others. It is sophistry to conclude that, because an individual finds satisfaction in helping to feed the poor, she or he is selfish. If we ask **why** someone gains satisfaction from volunteering to work in a soup kitchen, it is because the individual cares about other people, even if they are strangers; the volunteer does not want them to go hungry, and is willing to take action to help them. If the individual were not this kind of person, he or she would receive no satisfaction in helping others; this feeling of satisfaction is a mark of unselfishness, not of selfishness.

Source: James Rachels, *The Elements of Moral Philosophy* (New York: McGraw-Hill, 1986), pp. 56–60.

food and water on a camping trip is not selfish, but to refuse to share some of one's excess food to a hiker who has been lost and without food would be selfish.

Rational self-interest does not deny altruism. Individuals may act out of altruism in working in soup kitchens or in homeless shelters. However, rational self-interest does suggest that the altruistic behavior of individuals will be affected by changing perceptions of costs and benefits. For example, if tax deductions for charitable contributions are reduced or eliminated, such contributions will decline. Conversely increasing the tax benefit for charitable contributions will result in their increase. The corollary to the point that rational self-interest does not coincide with selfishness is the observation that rational self-interest does not mean individuals are motivated solely by the pursuit of material goods. Individuals may be motivated by love, justice, power, and other abstract influences. It is still true, however, that economic welfare may often be the basis for achieving even many nonmaterial goals.

None of the foregoing is meant to suggest that individuals consciously calculate benefits and costs before selecting an alternative. Rational self-interest describes **behavior** not **thought processes**.[7] A physicist would describe the forces involved in achieving balance in riding a bicycle quite differently than the average adolescent riding one. However, the child riding a bike will act as if he or she has a physicist's understanding when, in fact, he or she does not.

Rational self-interest is an assumption about the way people do behave, and is not a judgment about how they should behave. The term "rational" does not indicate approval or disapproval of the goal itself.

[7]Rachels, *The Elements of Moral Philosophy,* pp. 5–6.

Calvin and Hobbes

by Bill Watterson

The Tragedy of the Commons

Any discussion of rational self-interested behavior should point out that individual rationality and group rationality are not identical and may even be opposed. To understand this dilemma, we consider a metaphorical story written by biologist Garrett Hardin. Hardin asks us to assume that several farmers use a common pasture to graze their sheep. As the common meadow is owned by everyone, it is the responsibility of no one. The total number of sheep grazing this pasture is at the maximum sustainable amount of grass the pasture can yield to maintain the sheep. It is in the farmers' collective interest not to allow any additional sheep to graze in this pasture and to try to secure an agreement among themselves to that effect.

But, since the sheep are the sole means of livelihood for each farmer, the number of sheep each farmer has directly relates to the income his family has. For each farmer, therefore, the rational strategy is to sneak additional sheep into his flock to graze in the common meadow. The point is that it is always in the individual's self-interest to exploit the commons to the maximum (whether it is public grazing land, the environment and pollution, or fisheries) because the individual will receive all the benefits of his/her action, while the cost will be shared by all members of the community. The triumph of rational egoism through market capitalism has the effect of aggravating the tragedy of the commons. It may also serve to reduce trust and the feeling of community between the members of society.

Each farmer has an incentive to act according to a short time horizon to improve his or her personal well-being. But at some point in the future this behavior, though individually rational, will result in the disintegration of the entire common from overgrazing. The individual farmer is seeking immediate large gains over what appear to be smaller losses in the remote future. The **tragedy of the commons** is found in the conflict between individual interests and the well-being of the collective. If the meadow were privately owned, the farmer with title to the property would have an incentive not to overgraze his or her meadow. **The moral of the metaphor is that individual rational self-interested behavior to maximize private gain may be suboptimal in the long run.**

The story concerns what policy analysts call "the public interest" and what economists call "collective goods." The ideas revealed in the "Tragedy of the Commons"

CASE STUDY

THE TRAGEDY OF THE COMMONS AND COMMON RESOURCES

As the tragedy of the commons illustrates, when people own resources in common, they have little incentive to use them efficiently. Private decision makers have an incentive to overuse the common resource. Governments' policy response is to impose a cost for the use of the resource to reduce its overuse.

Fisheries are the classic example of the overuse of a common resource. Fish and whales have commercial value, which every fisherman has an economic incentive to exploit. But no one has an economic incentive to manage or protect these fisheries. Fish and mammals in the ocean are often considered a common resource. Cod, tuna, mackerel and many other species are being seriously depleted by overfishing. The natural tendency is for every fishing vessel to take as many fish as possible from the oceans.

The United Nations has found it extremely difficult to develop a global system to manage the common fishery and repropagate depleted species. The difficulty in reaching an agreement on how a treaty regulating fishing rights would be policed and enforced, especially among newly independent states that are very sensitive to issues of national sovereignty, makes it difficult to reach a negotiated settlement. Within a country's internal waters, governments may pass laws with relative ease placing limits on the size or total catch of fish, charging a fee for a license to catch fish, and limiting fishing seasons. Some entrepreneurs have tried to control their exclusive access to privatized stocks by developing "fish farms."

Note that many animals with commercial value have been threatened with extinction when they are viewed as a common resource (buffalo and elephants, for example). Many other animals with commercial value, (cattle, chickens, and cows) are not threatened with extinction. In fact their commercial value provides a sufficient incentive for private ownership. And it provides the owners with an incentive to conserve these resources for future generations.

Pollution of the environment is another example of market failure in dealing with a common resource. An environment with clean water and clean air is a common resource for all to enjoy. Excessive pollution that degrades the environment beyond its ability to naturally replenish itself is another instance of the tendency to overuse a common resource to the detriment of all.

Question: Why must policy makers be concerned with the use of common resources? How can policy makers best regulate the usage?

---

undermine Adam Smith's laissez-faire assumption that self-interested behavior will maximize social benefit. Many of those who identify themselves as libertarian in the 1990s were drawn from conservative circles and the "New Left" of the 1960s and 1970s, both of which applied the same laissez-faire logic to politics that others applied to economics.

FROM INDIVIDUAL TO GROUP CHOICE

We have looked at the behavior of individuals when they act to maximize their utility. Now we turn our attention to consider how the model might be applied to explain or predict the behavior of government. Rational choice theory when applied to government or public policy decision making is often referred to as public choice theory. For our purposes we can use rational choice and public choice interchangeably.

A basic premise of rational public choice is that "political man" or "woman" (political entrepreneurs, voters, and members of special interest groups) and "economic man" or "woman" (producers and consumers) are one and the same person. The person who votes or runs for political office is also the consumer of economic goods and concerned with opportunity costs. In both roles people decide on their preferences based upon their rational self-interest and act purposefully to bring about outcomes that are desirable to them. Again this is not to deny that people may also have social consciences or value altruism. But it suggests why it may be difficult to develop a broad commitment in society to transfer benefits from contributors to noncontributors (i.e., from the privileged to the poor). It also suggests why the "haves" acquire more power with which to further their self-interest than the "have-nots."

It is based upon the premise that competition takes place in the political arena. Although the coercive power of government is imposing, it is still limited by several factors. It is constrained, first of all, by the resources that it can command. The government relies on its taxing and spending powers in many instances to conduct public policy. **The function of taxes is to transfer control over capital from the private sector to the public sector.** By using that purchasing power to buy goods and services for the public, the government is altering the mix of goods and services that would be demanded if everything were left to the private sector. This inevitably means a move to a different point on the production possibilities curve (see chap. 1).

The government is also constrained by the political landscape. For example, there are only two major political parties in the United States, which constrains the selection of alternatives by the voters. In the private sector, if there were only two firms producing a good, we would define the market as a shared monopoly with no competition to give consumers a choice.

The public choice theory of government stresses that government actions result from the effort of politicians and government workers attempting to maximize their own interests rather than the public interest. To understand how and why the government operates as it does it is necessary to understand the complex network of individuals each attempting to maximize their own objectives.

We often think of government officials as motivated by the desire to follow policies that promote the general welfare. The government is made up of a collection of individuals, most of whom are sincerely dedicated to promoting the perceived general welfare. They may have different views about what constitutes the general welfare. And their own views on the subject may change. Dedicated officials may have conflicting goals. For example, an elected official's views may clash with the majority that elected her which may create a dilemma with the desire to be reelected. Similar conflicts may arise when a candidate for office has an opportunity to receive a campaign contribution from an organization that favors certain policies different from his own. The problem is made more difficult if a much needed contribution will go to an opponent if he will not support the contributing organization's policies. The final decision will be based on cost and benefit calculations.

Since every elected official will be subjected to his or her own conflicting pressures, it is not accurate to think of the government as a single entity having a well-defined set of objectives. The U.S. government acts through a distinctive assortment of institutional arrangements to develop public policy. Our representative democracy is based upon majority voting, frequently focused through special interest groups, and its policies and programs are implemented by a government bureaucracy. Rational public choice theory makes it clear that government policy making, like market allocation, may not result in the best attainable outcome. A society may be faced with the dilemma of choosing between a market solution that is imperfect and a government policy that is also not perfect. Simplistic notions demanding that we should return to basics and "let the market do it" or that we should abandon the market and "let government do it" must themselves be abandoned. Instead the costs and benefits of market solutions to social problems, government solutions, or a combination of the two must be examined in order to select policies that will be the most effective in meeting society's needs.

Whenever market performance is judged to be defective, we speak of **market failure**. Market failure does not mean that nothing good has happened, but only that the best attainable outcome has not been produced. There are two senses of "the best attainable outcome has not been produced." One relates to the inability of the market to achieve efficiency in the distribution of the community's resources. The other sense has to do with the failure of the market to further social goals, such as achieving the desired distribution of income or providing adequate health care for everyone. Consequently, a private market that functions without government intervention may lead to consequences a society is unwilling to accept.

COST-BENEFIT ANALYSIS

Public policy is the political decision by a state to take action. The increasing use of cost-benefit analysis to gauge the appropriateness of a policy decision typifies the application of market-based criteria to gauge the appropriateness of state action. Cost-benefit analysis is one of the most widely used tools of policy analysts. Cost-benefit analysis finds and compares the total costs and benefits to society of providing a public good. When several options are being considered for adoption, the one with the greatest benefit after considering the costs should be selected.

The need for public goods compels government intervention to provide a variety of goods and services that the market will not produce on its own in an optimal quantity for the society. The government must then decide not only what kinds of goods to provide but also what quantity to provide. However, the government cannot easily obtain the required information to decide which public goods to provide or the correct quantities. Since consumers of public goods or services have incentives not to disclose their true preferences and to downplay their willingness to pay in the hopes that others will be taxed, how is the government to decide how much to provide? Moreover, when government moves to use resources to alter the mix of goods and services produced, there will inevitably be conflicting goals and constituencies between which political choices must be made. Government finds itself in the middle of the adversarial relationship between those private-sector forces that stand to lose as a result of government action and those that stand to gain.

CASE STUDY

THE DIFFICULTY IN APPLYING
COST-BENEFIT ANALYSIS

The most efficient use of public resources would be to rank proposed programs from highest to lowest in terms of their benefit-cost ratios, and proceed to implement those programs in priority order beginning with those having the highest ratios. This would meet one goal of cost-benefit analysis: determining the most efficient ways of using public funds. But cost-benefit analysis has a second goal: determining the merit of specific government policies such as discouraging the use of disposable containers, encouraging higher average miles-per-gallon standards for use of gasoline by automobiles, promoting transportation safety, and establishing honesty in product labeling. "Merit" is different from "efficiency," but it also has economic consequences.

In dealing with private market goods, the demand for a particular good determines the benefits of its production. But in regard to some public goods, the benefits generated by its "output" are less clear. For example, government control over air quality usually involves political tradeoffs between a healthy

and aesthetic environment and the loss of production of other economic goods. Reducing air pollution from automobiles increases the price of cars, which results in the decreased production of automobiles and therefore fewer jobs. In this case, the losers from this government policy are those whose jobs are lost or who cannot afford to buy a higher-priced car. The winners are those who advocate environmental protection, and those who will suffer fewer illnesses (or perhaps will not die) because of a cleaner atmosphere.

The objective of public policy is to promote the welfare of society. The welfare of society must depend on the welfare of individuals. It is people that count.

Cost-benefit analysis emphasizes measurement and tangible factors. Its insistence on quantifying measures almost invariably stresses costs over benefits. The main reason for this is that in areas such as education, environment and health policies produce benefits that can not be quantified, while the costs are much more easily calculated. How does one put a value on human life for example? To the individual or a spouse or one's child, human life is priceless in that no amount of money would be accepted for those lives. However lives are not priceless

In theory, determining the optimal mix of output is uncomplicated: More government-sector endeavors are advisable only if the gains from those activities exceed their opportunity costs. So **cost-benefit analysis (CBA) as applied to government activities is used to calculate and compare the difference between the costs and the benefits of a program or project.** Basically, the benefits of a proposed public project are compared to the value of the private goods given up (through taxes) to produce it. But while the notion that the benefits or utility of a project should exceed its costs is uncomplicated enough in principle, it is exceedingly difficult to determine this ratio in practice.

In theory, all the costs and benefits of a program should be identified and converted into monetary units covering the life of the proposed project. Ideally an attempt is made to consider the negative externalities resulting from the program, such as the roadside businesses that will be lost due to the construction of a new limited-access highway. In theory also, with benefits and costs measured in the same units, the benefits and costs of alternative policies can be determined not just within a policy sector, but across diverse sectors. For example, cost-benefit analysis could be used to determine policy

or we would provide everyone with unlimited health care, require cars to be much safer, require much lower speed limits. Some courts have determined the value of a life by estimating what the individual might have earned if they had had a normal life expectancy. But this leads to the absurd conclusion that a disabled or retired person's life has no value. Another method is to examine the risks people voluntarily take in their jobs and how much they must be paid to agree to take them. Or how does one put a value on the survival of the spotted owl, which has little or no economic value, against the value of harvesting the trees in the state of Washington—the value of which can be easily assessed?

Citizens may be aware of the costs of programs in terms of their taxes paid, but may not be aware of noticeable benefits for a recession averted, a healthier environment, or a flood averted. In some cases then, leaders may be punished for their planning and judgment.

Another defect of CBA is that it does not consider the distributional question of "who" should pay the cost and "who" should receive the benefits. It may be that a new highway will displace residents in a low-income housing project, while it will benefit affluent business investors who own commercially zoned land along a proposed highway route.

The most serious defect of cost-benefit analysis, however, is that it seeks to maximize only the value of efficiency when other values such as equity, justice, or even the environment might deserve inclusion in the consideration of public policy decisions. Since it is not possible to reduce moral or ethical concerns to the requirements of cost-benefit analysis, this means the analysts who use this approach must go beyond it in making their policy recommendations; not to do so will have the effect of **positively excluding normative concerns.** In a period of tight federal budgets, government officials often defend their reliance on CBA by claiming that they should not be involved in controversial "ideological" debates, but rather only with the most efficient policy. They may even assert a moral obligation to apply CBA in order to save taxpayers money. CBA is useful for clarifying approaches to problems, but it is not without methodological difficulties and it is certainly not "value free."

alternatives in health care such as whether funds would be more efficiently spent on prenatal care for pregnant women who are indigent, for AIDS research, or for a screening and preventive medicine program to reduce mortality from cardiovascular disease. Such analysis then could also be used to determine if the funds to be allocated to the highest benefit-to-cost ratio program in the health care sector would be more efficiently spent if allocated to the construction of a dam.

POLITICAL ENTREPRENEURS

Politicians play a role similar to business entrepreneurs when seeking votes for political office and in making collective political decisions. In markets, consumers register their opinions about the value of a product by the simple decision of whether to buy it or not. Consumers register their votes with dollar bills. In political markets, politicians demand votes supplied by citizens. Votes cannot be technically bought and sold in electoral markets. Instead politicians must accumulate, or purchase (bribe?) voters for their votes by carefully positioning themselves on a variety of policy issues to correspond to the views of more voters than opposing candidates. Positioning includes conveying impressions of greater talent, higher moral character, and a preferred vision of the nation's future. Politicians with strong policy views on some issues may try to win votes by persuading voters to change their views, by putting the issue in a new context and suggesting new arguments that voters may find appealing. Persuading voters may be more successful with new issues about which many voters have not yet formed strong opinions.

An elected official also is expected to reflect the views of his or her constituents, not merely his or her own personal views. But unlike business where consumers clearly "vote" on products by buying or not buying them, in politics the voting mechanism is not well suited to determining how constituents want to be represented on any given issue. Take education as an example. In theory, one votes for more education by electing the candidate committed to initiating new programs or putting more resources into education. Nonetheless, in practice it is much more complicated than that since every candidate campaigns on a whole series of issues of which education is only one, and the winning candidate may have been elected on the basis of issues other than his or her position on education or even despite it. This makes constituent views on any issue difficult to discern, nor is there any reliable way to assign weights to the different views of voters.

Furthermore, fewer than half of those eligible to vote usually participate in any given election. Voter turnout peaked at 63 percent of persons over 21 years of age in 1960, but has declined since then. In 1992 voter turnout increased to 55 percent due in part to the high level of interest sparked by a strong third party candidate, but declined to 49 percent of the eligible voters in 1996. In 1996, Bill Clinton was elected with 49.2 percent of the votes cast for President. Of 196.5 million eligible voters, 151.7 million (about 77 percent) were actually registered to vote. Of those registered, 95.8 million actually turned out on election day to cast their ballots. The participation rate was just 63 percent of registered voters and less than half (48.8 percent) of eligible voters. Clinton won with 49.2 percent of the popular vote. Thus he was elected by about 23 percent of the eligible voters. Presidential elections show the highest voter turnout. For off-year congressional and state elections, the turnout rarely exceeds 40 percent of those registered to vote.[8]

Therefore, since the first task of political entrepreneurs is to get elected and the second to get reelected,[9] and since they are expected to reflect the views of their constituents, this means they are likely to reflect the views of constituents who actually vote or who make their views known to their political representatives in other ways (writing letters, lobbying, etc.).

[8]Usually about two-thirds of those eligible to vote are registered in local elections. Thus a political entrepreneur may win an election with only about 20 percent of those eligible to vote, which reduces any legitimate claim to a mandate. See Norman R. Luttbeg, "Differential Voting Turnout in the American States, 1960–82," *Social Science Quarterly,* vol. 65 (March 1984), pp. 60–73. See also, "Elections," *Statistical Abstract, 1996,* pp. 267–92.

[9]There is little disagreement with Richard Fenno's statement that candidate goals include reelection, influence within the Congress, and good public policy. See Richard Fenno, Jr., *Congressmen in Committees* (Boston: Little, Brown Co., 1973). This is not to suggest that politicians seeking election or reelection are motivated by greed. Politicians may seek power, not as an end in itself, but as the means for implementing their visions of good public policy. But election is a prerequisite to the achievement of good policy, and therefore must be an immediate goal.

CASE STUDY

VOTING AND CHOICE

Do people vote based on rational choice? There are three major factors, which often overlap, that go into the voting choice. **Party identification** is the sense of an affiliation with a perspective on politics and an evaluation of policy issues. Party identification is often acquired during childhood from the family. It is reinforced or subverted by the socialization process in college and subsequently within one's career and peer groups. **Candidate appeal** has grown in importance during this century with media coverage and the ability to package and market a candidate. The ability to focus on a candidate's strengths (or an opponent's weaknesses) through the press is extraordinary. Television sound-bites can be used to emphasize the positive elements of one candidate's character and the negative elements in an opponent's background. Personal qualities may be more easily assessed than the candidates' positions on complicated issues. This is especially so since candidates frequently deliberately obscure their position on issues so they cannot be easily attacked. The impact of **issues** as assessed by voters is also significant. Voters typically do not vote based on one specific policy issue such as national health care or education. During the Cold War, Republicans were able to capitalize on such issues as foreign policy and fear of the Soviet Union. By 1992, with the collapse of the Soviet Union, George Bush was vulnerable for his handling of the economy which most described in negative terms. Bill Clinton emphasized the state of the economy and the deficit in his campaign. To maintain the campaign's focus, a sign at Clinton's campaign headquarters reminded the staff that, "It's the economy, stupid!"

Many voters cast *retrospective votes,* that is, judging the incumbent on how he *has* performed, rather than voting *prospectively* on what he promises to do if elected.

As table 3-1 suggests, the higher a person's socioeconomic status as measured by income, education, employment, and other demographic characteristics, the more likely the person will be to register and vote. These same characteristics also influence *how* they vote. Age is a significant factor affecting voter turnout. Older voters may be more settled in their lives, and have experienced voting as an expected activity and are more likely to vote than the young. Ethnic background is also important in determining the level of voter turnout. Whites are most likely to vote, followed by blacks and then Hispanics. Women have recently been more likely to vote than men. Generally speaking too, the more education one has the more likely one is to vote. Differences in income levels also lead to differences in voter turnout. Wealthier voters are overrepresented among those who actually vote. Low-income and less-educated people are less likely to vote. Of course the foregoing demographic characteristics may reinforce each other. White voters are more likely to have a higher income and (closely related) to have more education.

Nonvoting is also a choice. The most frequently cited reason for nonvoting is that people think that their vote does not count or that they do not know enough about the candidates or the issues. About a fourth of the nonvoters indicate that they are disgusted with the government or the choice of the candidates. Can the decision not to vote be a result of cost-benefit calculations? Can a decision to remain ignorant of the candidates and the issues really be considered *rational ignorance?*

TABLE 3-1
A DEMOGRAPHIC PORTRAIT OF VOTERS, 1996 (%)

Characteristic	All voters	Clinton	Dole	Perot
National		49	41	8
Men	48	43	44	10
Women	52	54	38	7
White	83	43	46	9
Black	10	84	12	4
Hispanic	5	72	21	6
18–29 yrs old	17	53	34	10
30–44 yrs old	33	48	41	9
45–59 yrs old	26	48	41	9
60 and older	24	48	44	7
No high school diploma	6	59	28	11
High school grad	24	51	35	13
Some college	27	48	40	10
College grad	26	44	46	8
Post grad education	17	52	40	5
White Protestant	46	36	53	10
Catholic	29	53	37	9
Jewish	3	78	16	3
Republicans	35	13	80	6
Independents	26	43	35	17
Democrats	39	84	10	5
Family income is:				
Under $15,000	11	59	28	11
$15,000–$29,999	23	53	36	9
$30,000–$49,999	27	48	40	10
Over $50,000	39	44	48	7
Over $75,000	18	41	51	7
Over $100,000	9	38	54	6

The voting records of congressional representatives, senators, and even presidents reflect a heightened awareness of constituent interests as elections draw nearer. Conversely, their voting records show more independence immediately after they are safely voted back into office. Senators show the most independence after an election, since they are safely in office for six years. Members of the House of Representatives, who run for reelection every two years, are the most closely attuned to the views of the constituents who voted for them. Their high return rate to Congress may reflect that to some extent. Presidents also respond to the political market pressures exerted by the not so invisible hands of voters at the ballot box. The late H. R. Haldeman, Richard Nixon's chief of staff, noted how political self-interest dominated that administration's policy making when he wrote the following in his diary dated December 15, 1970:

K [Henry Kissinger] came in and the discussion covered some of the general thinking about Vietnam and the P's [President Nixon's] big peace plan for next year, which K later told me he does not favor. He thinks that any pullout next year would be a serious mistake because the adverse reaction to it could set in well before the '72 elections. He favors, instead, a continued winding down and then a pullout right at the fall of '72 so that if any bad results follow they will be too late to affect the election.[10]

President Nixon understood that the United States could not win in Vietnam and that after an American pullout, the South Vietnamese army would disintegrate. In the end he agreed with Kissinger, and delayed that outcome for political reasons. After the election in 1972, an agreement was signed in January 1973 on terms that led quickly to the inevitable North Vietnamese victory. In the private marketplace, communications between consumers and producers are much more direct and time-sensitive.

BALLOTS AND DECISION MAKING

Political discussions often make references to the "will of the people." But ascertaining what that will is when people make conflicting demands is not an easy task. Different voting rules have been suggested, including unanimity voting, simple majority voting, and two-thirds majority voting.

Unanimity

In an ideal world, there would be no conflict. Public choice would result from the unanimity of views from the population. The great advantage of the **unanimity rule** is that no one is misused, since every voter must approve each proposition. The difficulty with a unanimity rule is that each voter has a veto power. Anyone likely to be made worse off by the proposal would veto it. Thus, a government's public policies would have to meet the condition of a **Pareto improvement, which occurs when a reallocation of resources causes at least one person to be better off without making anyone else worse off.**[11] Unanimity is at the base of any policy agreement between two individuals in that, when two people agree on a policy, they do so because it makes both of them better off. That is, they are unanimous in agreeing to the exchange or they would not have agreed upon it. But in the world of public policy matters, unanimity is not likely to lead to useful outcomes.

---

[10]H. R. Haldeman, *The Haldeman Diaries: Inside the Nixon White House* (New York: G. P. Putnam's Sons, 1994), p. 221.

Other presidents have also made military decisions with an awareness of potential voter reaction. President Lincoln was willing to shift troop deployments during the Civil War in a way that strengthened his chances for reelection. Troop units from states in which his reelection chances were close were either moved to the rear of battlefronts or out of the fighting altogether to reduce their casualties and the reasons that families and friends from those states would have to oppose Lincoln. Troops from states where his reelection chances were either very high or very low were moved to areas where the fighting was heaviest and the likelihood of casualties the greatest. See Gore Vidal, *Lincoln* (New York: Ballantine Books, 1984). Robert Tollison's research supports Gore Vidal's position. See Robert Tollison, "Dead Men Don't Vote" (Fairfax, VA: Public Choice Center, George Mason University, 1989).

[11]This is distinguished from a Pareto optimum, which is a situation in which it is impossible to make any Pareto improvement, that is, when it is impossible to make any person better off without making someone else worse off. Under unanimity rules, the individual being made worse off would veto any change.

Suppose, for example, that a remote community is considering the construction of a community satellite dish to receive otherwise inaccessible television programming. Suppose also that the dish is to be financed by dividing the cost equally among the members of the community. Sensing how much the project means to everyone else, one villager who greatly desires access to satellite television may nevertheless profess a preference for keeping the intrusions of the outside world out of the community's peaceful valley. He or she may then demand a large bribe not to veto the project. A unanimity rule is an invitation to bribery because it offers individuals an incentive to hide their true preferences regarding public goods in order to reduce personal costs or to gain something at the expense of others. The costs of reaching a decision under such conditions are prohibitive, and government paralysis results with no practical decisions able to be made. Therefore it is necessary to accept some principle for public decision making short of unanimity.

Majority Voting

The excessively high cost of decision making associated with unanimity voting leads to a search for lower-cost alternatives. **The majority voting rule provides that in the choice between alternatives, an action or decision is approved if it receives a majority of the votes.** Majority rule is a basic principle of decision making in democratic societies.

Unfortunately, majority rule also has serious problems. For example, under it, a bare majority may get some benefit no matter how slight, while a ponderous sacrifice is exacted from the minority. Thus majority rule may result in a situation in which a society is worse off in that the benefit to the majority may fall far short of the total costs imposed on the minority.

For example, suppose there are 100 villagers in the remote community we mentioned earlier considering the investment in the satellite dish. Each would require a line from the dish to their cottage to receive the benefit of the cost to the community. Suppose under majority rule 51 villagers vote to invest in the satellite dish and connect their cottages by cable to it, and also to assess every villager an equal amount to pay for the dish and the hookups. The minority 49 villagers who voted against the measure must pay the tax but will get no benefit and thus will suffer significantly, while the majority 51 villagers may well receive a benefit that barely exceeds their assessment. Consequently, there is an overall loss to this community because of majority rule.

Majority rule can be inefficient also because a policy that may benefit a minority a great deal may be defeated if it makes the majority slightly worse off. For instance, most people will not contract AIDS. But for the minority that do, the cost of treatment is extremely high. The majority may resist paying a relatively small tax to cover the cost of health care for those so afflicted however.

This last example points up the major weakness of majority rule, and one long recognized: *It places minority rights at risk.* Thus most democratic forms of government that employ majority rule try to protect the rights of minorities against "overbearing" majorities by constitutional means.[12]

---

[12]Another obvious dilemma that arises with majority rule is that minorities have an incentive to break majority coalitions in order to become a part of new majority coalitions. Accordingly, in the satellite dish example, the 49 villagers excluded from the winning coalition might try to reform the coalition by persuading at least two members of the majority to join them in return for a side payment. Under majority rule, the search for new coalitions always continues while existing coalitions try to firm up their support.

TABLE 3-2
THE VOTER'S PARADOX

Program	Colleen	Mike	Cassie
Education	1st choice	3rd choice	2nd choice
Health care	2nd choice	1st choice	3rd choice
Housing	3rd choice	2nd choice	1st choice

The Voting Paradox

Majority rule does not generate such manifestly unfair results if voters act rationally in their decisions. But for rational behavior to occur, transitivity is necessary.[13] **Majority rule, to be rational, should produce a transitive group decision. However, majority rule may not necessarily generate a transitive group decision, even though each individual chooses rationally.**

Table 3-2 shows an example of what happens when transitivity is violated. In this example, the figure is perfectly symmetrical in that all three voters rank their preferences for three different issues. Every policy is one person's first choice, another person's second choice, and yet another's third choice. But if two policy issues are voted on at a time, it will result in an intransitive ranking. Each person presumably ranks the issues in order of their importance to themselves.

As shown in table 3-2, if education is paired against health care, education wins as it is Colleen's first choice and Cassie prefers it to health care. If health care is opposed to housing, health care wins as it is Mike's first choice and Colleen's second choice. If housing is paired against education, housing wins because Mike prefers it to education and joins Cassie in a winning coalition. Here majority rule has resulted in incompatible results. It is this inconsistency that is **the voting paradox. The voting paradox is that majority rule can produce inconsistent social choices even if all voters make consistent choices.** If the second and third choices of one of the voters were reversed in table 3-2, the paradox would disappear. Nonetheless, majority rule may result in no clear winner.

When majority rule does not result in transitive preferences, any policy choice is somewhat arbitrary. The final choice will be determined by the political process.

The majority party in the legislature usually can determine the agenda and the order of voting, and thereby control the outcome. Regardless of the option selected, a political entrepreneur can argue that he or she followed the popular mandate. This inconsistency leads to incongruous policies in which the government provides agricultural subsidies that raise the prices of food items and then provides food stamps to assist poor people to purchase the higher-priced foodstuffs.

In the example shown in tables 3-2 and 3-3, if limited funds mean only one or two programs can be funded, which is funded will depend entirely on the arbitrary order in which they are taken up. The result highlights the importance of how the voting agenda

---

[13]The transitivity axiom states that if preferences are transitive, then all the alternatives can be placed in order whenever there are more than two choices. Therefore if **a** is preferred to **b**, and **b** is preferred to **c**, then **a** is preferred to **c**. This permits ranking alternatives from the most to the least preferred.

TABLE 3-3
OPPOSING CHOICES AND OUTCOMES

Opposing Choices	Outcome
Education versus health care	Education
Health care versus housing	Health care
Housing versus education	Housing

is set.[14] The outcome of voting between several alternatives will often depend on the order in which the choices are considered.

Logrolling—Rolling Along or Getting Rolled

Majority voting rules allow voters to only vote yes or no on an issue. The vote disregards the intensity of the views held by the voters. The votes of those who are fervently in support of a bill count the same as the votes of those only mildly in favor. And while ordinary voters seldom trade their votes, it is not unusual for legislators to trade votes. This form of vote trading is often used to organize compromises that include several policy issues in one informal understanding. **Logrolling is vote trading by representatives who care more intensely about one issue with representatives who care more intensely about another issue.** Legislator A may agree to vote for a bill that Legislator B feels strongly about in return for B's promise to vote for a bill that is very important to A. This vote trading (or logrolling) provides a way for a minority group on one issue to win the vote and become a majority in return for changing a vote on another issue that the minority finds less important.

With single issues, the intensity of preference in voting is not important. However, in the political process the issues being considered are always multiple, and each involves varying degrees of support by minorities. Some people are very concerned about some issues, while other people are indifferent regarding those particular policies. By trading votes, representatives can register just how strongly they feel about various issues. Suppose Katherine and Chip tend to be slightly negatively inclined toward more defense spending. Christy, however, strongly feels the need for more defense spending. In a system that permits logrolling, Christy may be able to convince Katherine to vote for more defense spending if Christy promises to vote for a health care bill sponsored by Katherine.

Logrolling can increase or decrease government program efficiency depending upon the circumstances. But the practice has its defenders. They contend that logrolling can potentially lead to public policies of benefit to society that otherwise would not be produced. Such vote trading also has the advantage of revealing the intensity of preferences. And finally, compromises, such as those implicit in logrolling, are necessary for a democratic system to function.

---

[14]Kenneth Arrow, who won a Nobel Prize in economics in 1972, produced an exceptional proof of the impossibility of formulating a democratic process for reaching a majority decision that ensures transitive and nonarbitrary group choices in his work *Social Choice and Individual Values* (New York: John Wiley, 1951).

TABLE 3-4
LOGROLLING—POSITIVE OUTCOME*

	Christy	Katherine	Chip	Net benefit to society's welfare
Health care	+20	−5	−3	+12
Defense	−5	+20	−3	+12

*Logrolling can produce an efficient outcome when the benefits (+) exceed the costs (−) to each individual or society. Each project would lose with simple majority voting. Yet with logrolling each project can pass, improving the general welfare.

Table 3-4 illustrates the advantages of logrolling. If both policies—health care and defense—were put to a simple majority vote, both would lose. But passing them is a Pareto improvement in that everyone is better off relative to not passing them. In this case, logrolling can overcome the problem of an "oppressive majority."

Logrolling can just as easily lead to negative outcomes for society. Table 3-5 illustrates the same programs as those shown in table 3-4. However, Chip opposes both more intensely. The sum of the preferences indicates that Chip's intense opposition will count for more than the combined support by Christy and Katherine. Thus logrolling among the three will hurt the chances of both programs being passed. If neither program passes, there will be a net loss to society's welfare, even if Christy and Katherine logroll as before because the net benefit to them individually is greater.

Tying two bills together can be very convenient for legislators, who can then claim they do not support policies opposed by their constituents even though they voted for them. They defend themselves by arguing that they did not want the health care bill, for example, but had to vote for it to get the defense bill they and their constituents do want.

In general, logrolling has a negative reputation. Called "pork-barrel" legislation, it may lead to policies that are not only inefficient, but also opposed by the majority of voters. For example, the United States maintains many military bases that do not contribute significantly to national security. Unneeded military bases are notoriously difficult to close down, however, because congressional representatives in effect become lobbyists for special interest legislation to keep the bases in their districts open. Many military bases continue to exist because votes are traded to keep them in congressional districts to maintain certain levels of economic activity and numbers of jobs in those districts. On the other hand, the Pentagon has lobbied occasionally **for** the closing of bases so that

TABLE 3-5
LOGROLLING—INEFFICIENT RESULT*

	Christy	Katherine	Chip	Net loss to society's welfare
Health care	+20	−5	−17	−2
Defense	−5	+20	−17	−2

*If the costs (−) exceed the benefits (+), logrolling can lead to an inefficient outcome.

TABLE 3-6
THE MEDIAN VOTER

Voter	Most preferred annual tax increase for added police, $
Christy	$ 0.00
Collie	25.00
Cassie	75.00
Chip	125.00
Jim	300.00

the savings could be used for higher military salaries and more weapons systems.[15] It is apparent then that **logrolling may lead to an improvement in the results of simple majority voting, but it may as frequently lead to inefficient outcomes.**

The Median Voter—In the Eye of the Storm

We have noted that political entrepreneurs have a particular incentive to be responsive to voters rather than to nonvoters. One way to accomplish this is by identifying and paying attention to the median voter. The median voter is the voter whose preferences lie in the middle of an issue, with half the voters preferring more and half preferring less. The median voter theory merely predicts that **under majority rule the median voter will determine the decision.**[16]

To illustrate the principle of the median voter, suppose that five people must vote on a tax increase to provide more police protection for their community, as shown in table 3-6. Since each voter's preference has a single peak, the closer another voter's position is to one's own, the more the second voter prefers it. Christy does not perceive a need to increase expenditures for police protection at all and would prefer no tax increase for that purpose.

An increase to $25.00 would be approved by Collie, Cassie, Chip, and Jim, however. And an increase to $75.00 would be approved by Cassie, Chip, and Jim. A movement to $125.00 would be thwarted by a coalition consisting of Christy, Collie, and Cassie. A preference for either extreme will be outvoted by four votes, and a preference for the second or fourth position will be blocked by three votes. But a majority will vote for an assessment of $75.00, which is the median voter's preference. Notice that the median voter in this example does not prefer the average amount of the proposed expenditures, but is merely the voter in the middle. **In majority rule voting, the outcome reflects the preferences of the median voter.**

Since each voter will vote for the candidate who is closest to his or her own position, the candidate who is closest to the median position will win the election. This is not lost upon candidates for public office. Politicians need to get elected, so they are inclined to

---

[15]It is not clear that the net benefit to society would be greater by transferring the funds from closed bases to higher salaries and weapons systems. See Richard Halloran, "Pentagon Fights for Budget Cut (Yes)," *The New York Times*, Apr. 30, 1989, Sec. E, p. 5.

[16]This assumes that the voters have **single-peaked preferences,** so that as they move away from their most preferred position in any direction their utility of outcome consistently falls.

CASE STUDY

A SINGLE-PEAKED
IDEOLOGICAL SPECTRUM

Let us assume that political competition mobilizes public opinion along a political spectrum from the far left to the far right, as shown in figure 3-2. In a normal distribution of opinions, there is a split right down the middle by **M** indicating the "middle-of-the-roaders." The voter right at **M** is the **median** voter. Each candidate will try to get to the middle of the spectrum to increase his or her chances of winning. If either party's candidate moves away from the median and adopts an extreme such as the liberal (**L**) position, that office seeker will get less than half the vote. As voters will vote for political candidates closest to their own positions, less than half the voters will be closer to **L** than to a candidate positioned at **M**. If one candidate is at **L** and one is at **M**, the candidate at **L** will receive all votes to the left of **L**, while the candidate at **M** will receive all votes to the right of the median and the larger percentage of the votes under the curve between **M** and **L**. Clearly, each candidate will move toward the center.

If a third candidate enters the race, the possibilities change dramatically. If the latest candidate adopts a position just to the right of **M** and the other candidates are at **M**, he or she will get all the votes to the right of **M** and defeat the two centrist candidates. However, the entry of the third candidate will probably encourage the more liberal of the two centrist candidates to move toward **L**. The candidate still at **M** will be boxed in with a small portion of the vote between **L** and **C**. That candidate then has an incentive to move just outside the **LC** portion, thereby trapping one of the other candidates. In a three-party contest in which all three start at the center, there will be an incentive for one to move away. There are limits, however. As long as the voter distribution is single-peaked with its center at **M**, an office seeker can increase his or her portion of the vote by moving toward **M**. And with three candidates at **L, M,** and **C**, additional political contestants can increase their votes by shifting toward the center.

take positions that will increase their vote. If both political parties want to maximize their vote, they will try to take positions close to the median voter. The theory of the median voter also helps to explain why many voters feel that elections do not provide them with a real choice: both political parties try to capture the middle to avoid defeat.

The threat of H. Ross Perot in the 1992 presidential election encouraged George Bush to move from the centrist position. To strengthen his support on the right, he stressed opposition to abortion and gay rights, and support for traditional family values. This permitted Bill Clinton to grab the strategic center, which is often difficult for a challenger to do. When Perot dropped out of the race, it became impossible for Bush to regain the center by credibly portraying Clinton as being out of the mainstream.

Median positions maximize the vote-getting potential. The disruptive potential of major third party candidates to challenge the centrist political party's control of government provides the major parties with an incentive to make it difficult for third parties to get on the ballot either by erecting election-rule barriers, or by incorporating variations of the third parties' positions into a more moderate setting.

Now consider a situation in which there are just two candidates a Republican (R) and a Democrat (D). The Republican is concerned with keeping taxes low and wants to increase per capita expenditures by $25.00 a year. The Democrat wants to increase per

FIGURE 3-2
SINGLE-PEAKED IDEOLOGICAL SPECTRUM.

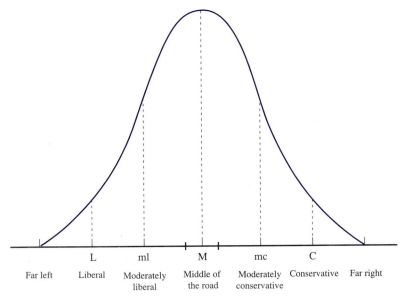

	L	ml	M	mc	C	
Far left	Liberal	Moderately liberal	Middle of the road	Moderately conservative	Conservative	Far right

capita spending by $125.00 per year. With an eye on public opinion polls and sensing the potential to gain the necessary majority, candidate D proposes a $120.00 per capita increase. Candidate R, not to be outdone proposes a $35.00 increase. In short, both candidates will try to move toward the middle in order to attract the median voter. In truth, they will try to move to the center sooner rather than later to preempt their opponents from seizing the middle ground. Figure 3-3 illustrates how candidates move toward the middle as campaigns progress toward election day.

What does the model of the median voter predict? There are several conclusions that follow from the principle of the median voter.

1 Public choices selected may not reflect individual desires. The system will result in many frustrated voters who feel that their views are not being considered. Many, perhaps 49 percent, of the voters in the minority will not have their views accepted.

The principle of the median voter will permit, and perhaps even require, that the views of those on the extreme left or right be neglected at least to the extent that no political entrepreneurs can overtly court those views beyond listening sympathetically and pointing out that they themselves are closer to those on the far right (or left) than their opponents who are "dangerously out of touch" (i.e., at the other end of the spectrum).

Since the median voter determines the outcome, the intensity of the views of the other voters is irrelevant. Only the intensity of the median voter's view is significant. Thus, the most dissatisfied voters will likely be those on the far right or left. This is in distinct contrast to the market in private goods, where demand counted in terms of "dollar votes" clearly records the intensity of preferences.

FIGURE 3-3
POLITICAL ENTREPRENEURS MOVE TOWARD THE MIDDLE.

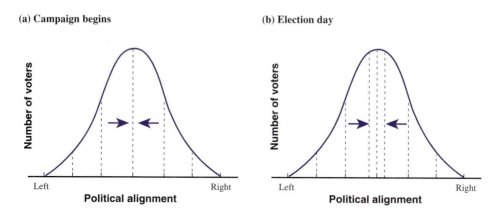

(a) Campaign begins

(b) Election day

2 Candidates for office will try to seize the middle ground first, and claim to be moderate, while labeling their opponents as "out of the mainstream" on the right or left. In their effort to command the vital middle, candidates will portray themselves as moderates. Some conservative Republicans, believing the spectrum had shifted in 1996, boldly proclaimed themselves in favor of a "conservative agenda." This sent the wrong message to many voters who identified as being more moderate.

It also offers an explanation as to why the nonincumbent party is often put in the position of running a "me-too" campaign—"We can do the *same* job as the incumbents, only better."

This is not to suggest that all candidates are actually alike. Candidates as political activists usually do have political philosophies and positions that can be labeled as more or less conservative, or more or less liberal. But as political entrepreneurs, they are forced to mask them during campaigns to seize the middle. Once elected, they may try to support their philosophical inclinations so long as they can still position themselves to maintain their majority support in the next election.

President Clinton's extraordinarily high favorable rating after six years in office is attributed to his having taken control of the political center by, among other policies, reforming federal welfare programs (made easier by a booming economy), supporting the death penalty, and providing additional funds for police protection. While many liberals in the Democratic party feel he has betrayed basic party commitments going back to the New Deal, they have no alternative. Republicans feel many of their issues have been taken away from them, but cannot criticize him too harshly without sounding "too far right."

3 Candidates will constantly monitor public opinion through polling. They will make slight modifications in the direction of their opponents' positions on those issues in which the opposing candidates are preferred in the polls. When polls tell a candidate that they would lose the race if the election were held today, they cannot afford to do nothing. They must change their position to attract more voters. In order to successfully sell themselves in the political market, political entrepreneurs try to make position adjustments as subtly as possible to avoid the charge of "political opportunism." Political opponents are always quick to seize on shifts of position to question the integrity of each other. That is, they question whether those they are running against are just "waffling" or, in a more sinister fashion, are not being honest regarding their positions until after the election. Position adjustments also tend to blur the distinction between candidates, which presumably no one wants.

The positions of parties will not be identical. In part this is because political entrepreneurs are not able to identify the median positions perfectly since public opinion, and the median voter, are moving targets. Also since there are many nonvoters, candidates may stake out positions that they believe will appeal to the median of the population he or she expects will vote. In some instances, a candidate may stake out a position to appeal to the median of a group including a set of nonvoters precisely because he or she hopes to increase voting turnout by appealing to that group.

4 Political candidates will prefer to speak in general rather than specific terms. Voters (and candidates for public office) are inclined to agree on the **ends** much more than on the **means** to achieve those ends, or in some cases the **feasibility** of reaching the ends. For instance, voters across the political spectrum agree that an expanding economy is preferable to a contracting economy. They agree that low unemployment rates are preferable to high unemployment. There is also a consensus that lower taxes are preferable to higher taxes, and that a good education system is preferable to a bad educational system. However, there are great differences between how those we might label conservative and those we might label liberal think these goals might be accomplished. Conservatives tend to prefer pursuing them through less government intervention and private means, while liberals are more likely to perceive a positive role for government in seeking what they perceive as public goods. Candidates will therefore be more likely to talk about the ends, on which there is more of a consensus, than the means on which there is wide disagreement.

VOTING AND THE POLITICAL MARKETPLACE

If politicians are the entrepreneurs of the political marketplace, voters are the consumers looking out for their best interests by voting for the candidates promising them the most benefits. As noted earlier, many people who are eligible to vote do not. The key question is: What motivates a person to vote? There is a cost to voting and the probability of a single voter determining the outcome of an election is extremely small. Therefore the marginal costs of learning about the issues and the candidates' positions, registering to vote, and going to the polls may exceed the marginal benefit of voting. If however, the candidates have staked out contrasting positions on certain issues and there are indications the election will be close, the marginal benefit of voting increases and voter turnout also rises.[17] In essence, it appears that individuals do make a cost-benefit analysis of their interests in resolving to vote. And in addition to the benefits hoped for from a candidate's promises, voters also receive the psychological "benefit" of knowing they have performed their civic duty.

---

[17]See Yoram Barzel and Eugene Silberberg, "Is the Act of Voting Rational?" *Public Choice*, vol. 16 (Fall 1973), pp. 51–58.

A concern in the formation of public policy is whether people make informed choices when they vote. We can expect voters to gather information about candidates that will influence their decisions about whom to vote for as long as the benefits of gathering additional information exceed the costs. Often, though, voters decide that it is not cost-effective to gather information. Anthony Downs labels the shortage of information gathered on the part of the public that does vote **"rational ignorance," which is the decision not to actively seek additional information because people find the marginal cost of its acquisition exceeds the marginal benefit of possessing it.** This feeling of excessive marginal cost in turn can arise because information gathering is more complicated for public choices than for private choices. There are several reasons for this.

In the political market, voters must evaluate and select a package deal. This is unlike the commercial marketplace, where in buying apples or shirts you can decide to buy one item more or one item less; that is, you can engage in making decisions at the margin. When you place an additional item in your shopping basket, you register a clear plebiscite for its production. However, when you vote in a political election your vote is registered not for a single item supported by the political entrepreneur, but for the entire package of issues the candidate or party supports. Like many voters, you may vote for a candidate because of his or her support for a particular issue that is of intense interest to you, such as defense spending. You are likely to find several other items in the candidate's bundle that you really do not want.

Voting occurs infrequently and irregularly, in contrast to the buying in the commercial marketplace where consumer choices are registered frequently and repetitively. In the commercial market, consumers communicate very effectively when they cast millions of votes every day to producers by deciding to buy or not to buy the products offered. But the electorate does not have the opportunity, or perhaps the inclination, to vote frequently enough to send a clear signal to political entrepreneurs regarding its political desires. Voters typically get to vote for candidates only every 2, 4, or 6 years. This makes it difficult to find candidates who will support public wants reliably for their entire term and over a range of issues that often emerge after the election. It is impossible to know in advance whether a candidate will support a particular position on issues that were not foreseen at the time of the election. It is also impossible to know the final shape of future bills to be voted on by representatives.

This means political entrepreneurs are relatively free of control by the electorate. The main control voters have is in elections in which an incumbent is running for reelection, where they can retrospectively sanction or reject the candidate's record in the voting booth. Voters can use indicators providing clues about how someone might vote on unanticipated issues such as claims by a candidate that he or she is "conservative," or "moderate," or "Republican." But picking someone based on a label is a very inexact system.

The infrequency of elections also requires that many different choices be made at the same time. The many candidates and the many different issues at the local, state, and national levels inevitably lead to great complexity for voters trying to make informed choices.

There is little incentive for voters to be informed. The political realities noted above make it difficult for the best intentioned voter to evaluate candidates and issues with confidence. The cost of acquiring useful information is very high. For example, suppose the government suggests it is necessary both to spend billions of dollars on the savings and loan bailout to protect confidence in the U.S. banking system and to provide aid to the Soviet government to provide assistance for Yeltsin's continued leadership there, and that those expenditures will require a cutback in unemployment compensation for U.S. workers laid off from their jobs. How can the average voter obtain information to make a rational choice in such a situation?

Some voters will decide to remain rationally uninformed because they decide that the costs exceed the benefits of being fully informed on these issues. Others may choose to become **free riders** not only by refusing to gather any information but by not even voting. If the choices of those who vote are beneficial to the nonvoters, the nonvoting free riders will benefit without incurring any costs. More likely, the political entrepreneurs will soon discover who the nonvoters are and ignore those items in the package that would most benefit them.

Many voters reduce the cost of gathering information for themselves by relying on the "brand names" in the political marketplace of Republican and Democrat. Brand names are at least as important in the political market as in private markets. They provide information regarding general public philosophies. The packaging of a candidate as well as factors like incumbency also provide brand-name information regarding quality. An incumbent has a track record that can be evaluated and has a brand-name identification usually not found among challengers. Voters tend to support incumbent reelection bids just as consumers tend to develop brand-name loyalty to products they buy in stores.

In conclusion, there are important differences between the political and the private marketplaces. Communicating demands in the political marketplace through the process of infrequent voting is more problematic than communicating them on a daily basis through the process of buying and selling. In this area the political marketplace is less efficient than the private marketplace, due in part to the way the political marketplace is designed.

Since any one person's vote is unlikely to affect the outcome of an election, there is less of an incentive for the average person to stay informed than if his or her vote would likely affect the outcome. This increases the power of special interest groups because unorganized voters have more diffuse interests and are less likely to become informed.

INTEREST GROUPS—ADDED MUSCLE IN THE POLICY MARKET

Interest groups are collections of individuals with intensely held preferences who attempt to influence government policies to benefit their own members. Because their interests are strongly affected by public policies in a particular area, their members keep themselves well-informed regarding legislation in that area. This contrasts with the general voter, who is often uninformed on many issues because the cost of acquiring information is deemed too high relative to its benefit. And if a proposed policy will confer benefits on one group while imposing costs on another, both affected groups will probably organize, one to support and the other to oppose the policy. For example, teachers will be well-informed about tax laws and programs that support public education or hurt it. Members of the teaching profession usually know much more about the laws affecting education than the general public, so as individuals they make informed voting decisions and through teachers' organizations they lobby for or against specific laws.

The existence and importance of special interest groups have to do with the principle of rational ignorance. Individuals, and members of groups, are more likely to have incentives to seek information concerning candidates' stands on issues affecting them personally. They are more likely to try to influence other people to adopt their positions, to take an active part in campaigning for candidates supporting their interests, and to vote. Political entrepreneurs seeking election thus try to court special interest groups at the expense of the general welfare. Thus special interest groups are likely to have significant effects on policy decisions in areas where they think they have the most to gain or lose by the outcomes.

The high costs of running modern campaigns necessitated by television advertising and so forth, makes political candidates more eager for offers of campaign contributions from special interest groups. The more the general public is uninformed, the more likely the cost to a politician for supporting special interest group policies, related to the benefit of the campaign contribution diminishes.

There are limits on the influence of special interests, though. Politicians seeking election or reelection typically take money from interests groups in return for supporting positions favorable to those groups. Although they need contributions to mount successful campaigns, they may be wary of accepting money from groups whose positions may be unacceptable to **unorganized voters.** Interest groups themselves are aware that it may be best not to press legislators in causes to which the unorganized voters are hostile. Thus legislators often vote as the unorganized, but interested, voters want, and congressional decision making often takes into account the wishes of voters who are not members of interest groups. This can even diminish the possible number of special interest groups since by not antagonizing unorganized voters it encourages them to remain unorganized.[18]

Special interest groups propose and support legislation they perceive as important to their interests; in general, voters who are not members of such groups are not likely to oppose such legislation or to lobby politicians against it if they do not think it will affect them adversely or at all. As an example, assume that a state proposes to reduce the budget for its state-supported university system because of a shortfall of tax receipts. The state may propose a reduction in the faculty and staff, to be accompanied by an increase in tuition for the students. Since the faculty, staff, and students will bear the brunt of this decision, they may form an interest group to propose an increase in taxes within the state to be used not just to avoid layoffs, but to maintain low tuition and even increase faculty and staff salaries. In other words, this interest group is petitioning the state to raise the wealth of its members at the expense of general taxpayers. They are demanders of a transfer of wealth from the state.

---

[18]See Arthur T. Denzau and Michael C. Munger, "Legislators and Interest Groups: How Unorganized Interests Get Represented," *American Political Science Review,* vol. 80 (March 1986), pp. 89–106.

The suppliers of this wealth transfer are the taxpayers, who probably will not find it worthwhile to organize to oppose having their wealth taken away by the state university system. General taxpayers probably will be less well-informed about this legislation than members of the special interest group. But even if they are well-informed, they will have to calculate the costs and benefits of opposing the legislation. Say that if the tax increase passed, the average taxpayer would have to pay out approximately $2. But he or she might have to spend $10 to defeat the proposal. Thus even those knowing of the legislation and aware its passage would cost them money would probably conclude it was not worth the cost of opposing it.

The role of special interest groups in the making of public policy cannot be overemphasized. In a large and complex economy such as that of the United States, a high number of interest groups is to be expected. Many of the interest groups overlap. There are, for example, women's rights groups, minority rights groups, religious groups, physician groups, lawyer groups, farmer groups, and so forth. And special interest groups are responsible for much of the misallocation of public resources. However, legislation by special interest groups is not necessarily bad. Much of it may even benefit the general public. In the example used, education is a public good and the citizens of the state may be well served by having a good state university system for the general population. The point to be stressed is that **the costs and benefits of being informed on certain issues and the marginal costs and marginal benefits for lobbying for or against those issues are different for members of a special interest group and the general public. It is this difference in the allocation of costs and benefits of being informed and taking an active political stance that usually influences the type of legislation proposed and implemented.**

James Madison denounced interest groups ("factions," he called them) as being the cause of instability, injustice, and confusion in democratic politics. He defined factions as "a number of citizens . . . who are united and actuated by some common impulse of passion, or of interest, adverse to the rights of other citizens, or to the permanent and aggregate interests of the community."[19] Since that time, every interest group has claimed to represent *the national interest* rather than a parochial interest. And each group has looked suspiciously at every other interest group as aggregations of conniving, self-seeking individuals.

The late Mancur Olson accepts the Madisonian standard model of human nature that **individuals know their self-interests and act rationally to further them.**[20] He concluded that **collective goals** are seldom rationally pursued. If, as we noted above, broadly dispersed interests find it difficult to organize for political action, then in all likelihood small, narrow interest groups will engineer a redistribution of benefits toward themselves and away from the dispersed interests. However, since individuals discover the benefits of group organization for themselves, a stable society gradually accumulates an increasing number of special interest groups. Each will have a disproportionate political influence on the areas of its needs. The implications for society are ominous, in that **special interest groups redistribute national wealth to themselves, which reduces society's**

---

[19]James Madison, *The Federalist,* #10.
[20]Mancur Olson, *The Rise and Decline of Nations* (New London: Yale University Press, 1982).

overall efficiency. In other words, special interest groups seek to preserve their benefits at the cost of general economic stagnation.[21]

For example, neither Herbert Hoover nor George Bush wanted a depressed economy, but there were many in their constituencies who were financially secure and not threatened with unemployment. Many in this more affluent element preferred those conditions to taxing and spending policies to reduce unemployment and stimulate economic activity, which they feared might reduce their status.

THE BUREAUCRATIZATION OF THE POLITY

The legislative branch of government passes laws and approves specific levels of public policy spending. The actual implementation of the laws and the actual distribution of funds is delegated to various agencies and bureaus of the executive branch. Bureaucrats, like politicians and the average voter, have a variety of interests.

In reality, bureaucrats are often attacked for being unresponsive to the public they serve. Still other critics complain that politicians make their bureaucracies too responsive to special interest groups instead of allowing them to impartially administer the programs for which they were created.

Bureaucrats are the unelected U.S. government officials tasked with carrying out the program approved by Congress and the president. Many laws are passed that are more symbolic than substantive insofar as they indicate the "intent" to ensure automotive safety, guarantee safe working conditions, or protect the environment without specifying exactly how to accomplish these goals. Bureaucrats must use their administrative authority to give meaning to vague platitudinous legislation and determine how the law will actually be applied.

Those working in bureaus tend to be supportive of the legislature's goals. They also prefer a growing budget, which usually correlates with opportunities for promotion and higher salaries for themselves. In public bureaucracies there are no incentives to minimize budgets. Instead bureaucrats try to maximize the sizes of their agencies through high salaries and the perquisites of office, power, and patronage. Within these organizations, in fact, a person's prestige and authority is measured by the number of personnel under his or her authority. (Even if bureaucrats did operate very efficiently, the general voter would be unaware of that due to the principle of rational ignorance).

---

[21]By intensifying distributional struggles and encouraging the primacy of political competition, special interest groups siphon a society's talents and energies away from the production of goods and focus them instead on winning the distributional contest. Olson claims that the postwar economic miracles in Germany and Japan were due in part to the purging of all special interest groups as a result of the war, which opened the way to rapid growth. Countries like the United States and England found their special interest groups still viable at the end of the war and experienced slower growth in the postwar era as a result.

Olson's solution would be to save democracy from its own excesses by reducing special interest groups' influence on the political process. He hopes that schools and mass media will create a widespread antipathy to special interest groups and bring about a cultural change. Perhaps society could then achieve the ideal of a state devoid of special interest politics and continually remain adaptive and innovative.

But the proposed system, lacking interest group mediation, would effectively cripple democratic institutions. Without interest groups, which are the breeding grounds for democratic opposition independent of state power, the strength of representative democracy would be weakened. Special interest groups shape social values. Group morality is defined and refined through their workings.

Therefore bureaucrats **compete** with other bureaucrats for a larger share of the available funds. Bureaus typically do not end each fiscal year with budget surpluses, but rather spend all their revenues before the end for fear of appearing not to need as much money in the future. Bureaucrats try to increase the size of their agency by influencing politicians who provide their budget. This leads them to typically exaggerate their claim of a mismatch between their responsibilities and their limited resources.

They may indeed be providing efficient services to the special interest groups that were responsible for the legislation creating the bureaus, and they may even be serving the public that is their clientele efficiently. But they must also answer to the legislature that funds and oversees them. It should be noted that in doing this, bureaucracies have significant information advantages over the typical legislator, who must be concerned with literally hundreds of different programs. And bureaucracies themselves provide the information the legislators need to oversee the bureaus.

Those who criticize bureaucracies for being less efficient than private firms miss a fundamental point of the purpose of a bureaucracy. Typically its existence is the result of some market failure—of a situation in which market competition could not resolve some issue or issues. Consequently it cannot be measured by normal market criteria. Many government bureaucracies provide services for which there is no competition. For example, there is only one place to go to get a driver's license, or a zoning permit.

Public bureaucracies associated with high national purposes of the state such as the military, the Central Intelligence Agency, or the Federal Bureau of Investigation are generally held in high regard as patriotic public servants. Ironically, the members of the largest governmental bureaucracy, the military, often do not even consider themselves bureaucrats. Bureaucracies associated with domestic regulatory or redistributional programs adversely affecting the more privileged members of society are generally condemned as being wasteful and inefficient, while the individual bureaucrats tasked with enforcing those policies are usually held in contempt as incompetent bumblers.

A CRITIQUE OF RATIONAL CHOICE

Rational choice theory began as an explanation of how a rationally self-interested person behaves in the marketplace. To the extent that individuals choose what they most prefer among potential choices in the market, they are engaging in rational behavior. It claims a scientific objectivity in alleging that it is descriptive of how people actually behave in markets without making any value judgment about that behavior. As a model of decision making, the logic of rational choice has widespread application throughout the social sciences and has found increasing applicability in the policy sciences. Its strength is to be found in its illustration of how to make efficient choices and in the model's ability to explain individual as well as group behavior.

Rational egoism, as a general rule may be perfectly acceptable in the market. There is no reason for the individual contemplating a choice between purchases to be committed to any particular political philosophy. Democratic forms of government require that rational man be concerned not just with his or her own personal well-being, but to concern him or herself with the general welfare of the community of citizens. The invasion

of narrowly self-interested economic rationality into the political thought and behavior of individuals overwhelms and ravages democratic politics.

Universal rational egoism assumes that individuals will act just as rationally, and just as self-interested in political arenas as in economic markets. In economic thinking there is a strong bias in favor of free markets with a great concern that any government intervention will reduce efficiency. This same bias against government is evident in the thought of many policy scientists who have adopted rational choice thinking. Supporters of the rational choice model claim the analysis describes government and political behavior *as they are*—free from any wishful notions about how they *should be*.[22] Nevertheless, the conclusions of public choice have a clear bias in favor of free market principles and limited government. Critics point out that rational choice disregards the role that culture plays in modifying and restricting decision making. Rationality can mean different things in different cultures.[23]

Social choice theory shows that if individuals actually behave the way the theory describes, all collective voting mechanisms are subject to manipulation in which the

---

[22]See James Buchanan, "Politics Without Romance: A Sketch of Positive Public Choice and Its Normative Implications." In *Contemporary Political Theory,* ed. Alan Hamlin and Philip Pettit, (New York: Macmillan, 1991), pp. 216–28. See also William C. Mitchell, *Government As It Is* (London: Institute of Economic Affairs, 1988).

[23]Ellen Coughlin, "How Rational Is Rational Choice?" *The Chronicle of Higher Education,* 7 December 1994, A16.

popular will may be thwarted. Or whoever controls the voting order can determine the results. Even bureaucracy is interpreted as being rationally concerned primarily with increasing its budget and power. The conclusion is that most government agencies are not in the public interest. The obvious implication for anyone suspicious of government is that all bureaucratic organizations and budgets are too large so budgets may be cut without fear that the affected agencies cannot still carry out their responsibilities. The main problem for "responsible" government then is little more than to reign in out-of-control agencies.

The average citizen has a modest interest in policy issues, but the costs are too high relative to the benefits to become well versed on either the specific issues or the policy positions of their elected officials. Politicians have a positive incentive not to inform the voters on specific policy proposals but only to speak in general of the goals of "peace and prosperity." Rather than speaking to the public about policy issues, they can be expected to espouse ethical principles and humbly acknowledge their own moral rectitude while castigating that of their opponent. Citizens are usually rationally ignorant and not well positioned to monitor public policies in a manner assumed by democratic theory. Political elites formulate policies in a way that maximizes their benefits in the theory.

In the rational choice model, which is descriptive of what is, without passing judgment, politics is little more than a game in which all participants seek to maximize their benefits while treating the cost as a negative externality to be transferred to the commons (all taxpayers).

The world of politics as viewed through the lens of rational choice is almost unrecognizable to the student of liberal democratic thought. There is no doubt that the economic calculus of public choice (rational egoism) explains one facet of the human psyche. This explanation has grown, and is accepted, to the point that it threatens to crowd out other approaches.

Rational choice theory has a difficult time explaining altruistic behavior. Why do individuals who perceive no benefit to themselves for helping others nevertheless do so? Rational choice theory would not predict that individuals would engage in "good Samaritan behavior." Nor do rational choice theorists have an easy explanation for collective action for the general welfare. For example, even though the cost of collecting information and going to the polls to vote outweighs the likelihood that the vote will have any influence on the outcome of the election, millions of people do go to the polls.

Finally, many cognitive psychologists argue that individuals usually do not have complete information and therefore cannot ascertain the "best" choice from a rational perspective. As a result individuals are more likely to seek a minimum level (rather than the maximum) of satisfaction from their decisions. This is referred to as satisficing.

On the positive side, one contribution of the theory has been to suggest to policymakers one avenue to develop public policies. We agree that a competitive market can allocate resources efficiently and without any guidance from government. At the same time we recognize that the market has several weaknesses. The market is unable by itself to cope with business cycles and unemployment, income inequality, or the consequences of a concentration of market power and money. A market does not protect the commons. The market is incapable of providing public goods. Many of society's most urgent public policy issues—urban decay, pollution, the social unrest that is attributable to poverty is to some degree the result of some market shortcoming.

Many market imperfections can be treated by policies that make use of the market mechanisms. Policy makers increasingly attempt to take the incentives of the free market into account when designing public policy. Privatizing government operations is one such effort to use the profit motive to increase efficiency. Deregulation of some industries such as the airline and trucking industry are examples. The effort to use market mechanisms to control pollution is another example. As noted earlier, many critics of this approach feel that to permit businesses to pay a fee to pollute removes the moral stigma from the act. The right to pollute is reduced to any other market good that can be bought or sold. In the case of the tragedy of the commons each individual acts rationally in his/her self-interest with the result being collective irrationality. The basic consequence of public choice is that of "rational man, irrational society."[24]

Adam Smith, writing in an earlier age, thought of economics as a part of moral philosophy. It never occurred to him that economics might be thought of as value free (see chap. 5). On the contrary, his theory was based on the desire to improve the situation of the masses. As he wrote in *The Wealth of Nations:*

> Consumption is the sole end and purpose of all production; and the interest of the producer ought to be attended to, only so far as it may be necessary for promoting that of the consumer.

Robert Heilbroner has pointed out that economists today claim to be engaged in value free scientific thinking because of the prestige associated with pursuing a science resembles the grandeur of religious pursuits in an earlier age. He holds that all "economic analysis is shot through with ideological considerations whose function is to mask the fullest possible grasp of some of the properties of a capitalist social order."[25] The social sciences cannot achieve the rigor (or objectivity) of the natural sciences as long as the worth of the individual is valued. Normative values regarding the values of life, health, and human dignity permeate public issues. In fact as members of a social order, it is impossible to describe these orders without using the feelings of attachment and identification that make us a part of the fabric of society. A nonideological being could not exist as a sentient member of society.

This is as it should be especially in public policy since its purpose is to promote the general welfare. The next two chapters explore the relationship between the individual and society.

CONCLUSION

1 Markets fail to produce ideal outcomes in the best attainable allocation of goods and services. Democratic governments are asked to intervene to correct the deficiencies of market outcomes, but must do so through the institutions of representative democracy, with voting procedures, political entrepreneurs, and interest groups serving as intermediaries.

---

[24]See Brian Barry and Russell Hardin (eds.), *Rational Man and Irrational Society?* (Beverly Hills, CA: Sage Publications, 1982).

[25]Robert Heilbroner, "The Embarrassment of Economics," *Challenge,* (Armonk, NY: M. E. Sharpe, Inc, 1996), p. 49.

2 The process is one in which individuals in politics act, as people are assumed to do in the marketplace, on the basis of their preferences based on their views of their rational self-interest. Rational public choice theory offers an explanation regarding how individuals act in the political marketplace. It should be seen as a view about how the system actually works and not how the system *should* work.

3 In some ways the government is even less efficient than the private marketplace. This is particularly true in limiting voters to infrequent elections and in requiring the political "package deals" achieved through logrolling.

4 The principle of the median voter results in the "middle ground" of the electorate being critical in any election. Since both candidates in a two-way race must compete for the median voter's position and portray their opponent as being an extremist and "out of touch with the mainstream," campaigns usually fail to produce any bold initiatives for change. Rather they eschew substance in favor of efforts by candidates to tar their opponents with negative symbols.

5 The voting paradox also allows political entrepreneurs to take almost any position on an issue and claim that this was supported by a majority. Consequently, whoever controls the voting agenda on several related items will have a powerful influence on the voting outcome.

6 Special interest groups are organized voters who see their self-interest bound up with a specific issue, are informed about it, and are therefore inclined to vote based upon that issue. The general population of potential voters, following the principle of rational ignorance, is likely to be uninformed about and indifferent to most political issues. Special interest groups, then, have a political influence out of proportion to their numbers, although politicians are reluctant to antagonize the general voter needlessly because they too have the potential to mobilize and retaliate through their own interest groups.

7 The accumulation over time of special interest group legislation redirects public resources toward those groups at the expense of the unorganized and less-likely-to-vote general public and particularly the poor. This may result in further movements away from the ideal of government correction for market failures.

8 Rational choice thinking is a valuable tool for policy scientists. An overemphasis on the model can legitimize an approach to public policy that treats all issues and positions as of equal value. In such a scenario the role of policy scientists is reduced to tabulating wins and losses for different groups.

QUESTIONS FOR DISCUSSION

1 What is public choice theory? How does it help in analyzing public behavior and policy?
2 How can democratic voting behavior lead to undemocratic results? How can that be squared with the idea of justice? Is there a solution to this problem?
3 Why do political candidates move to the center in a single-peaked two-party system? Why are parties more likely to have more fixed ideological points in multiparty systems?
4 Why do candidates prefer to campaign on general terms rather than specific issues? Conversely, why do candidates reduce an opponent's general stands into specific positions?
5 What is the idea of rational ignorance? How can this be squared with the democratic ideal of an informed citizenry?

6 The democratic ideal also contains the concept of each citizen having an equal voice in government. How then can special interest legislation be justified?

7 Are there ways to make government bureaucracies more concerned about the efficiency of their programs?

KEY CONCEPTS

cost-benefit analysis	public choice theory
interest groups	rational ignorance
logrolling	rational public choice
majority voting rule	tragedy of the commons
market failure	transitive preferences
median voter	unanimity rule
Pareto improvement	voting paradox

SUGGESTED READINGS

Kenneth Arrow, *Social Choice and Individual Values* (New York: John Wiley, 1951).

David Austen-Smith and Jeffrey Banks, "Elections, Coalitions, and Legislative Outcomes," *American Political Science Review,* vol. 82 (June 1988), pp. 405–22.

John S. Dryzek, "Democracy in Capitalist Times: Ideals, Limits, and Struggles" (New York: Oxford University Press, 1996).

Harold D. Lasswell, *A Pre-View of Policy Sciences* (New York: American Elsevier, 1971).

Nicholas P. Lovrich and Max Neiman, *Public Choice Theory in Public Administration: An Annotated Bibliography* (New York: Garland, 1982).

Dennis C. Mueller, *Public Choice* (New York: Cambridge University Press, 1979).

Kenneth A. Shepsle and Mark S. Bonchek, *Analyzing Politics: Rationality, Behavior and Institutions.* (New York: W. W. Norton, 1997).

Kenneth Shepsle and Barry R. Weingast, "Political Preferences for the Porkbarrel: A Generalization," *American Journal of Political Science,* vol. 25 (February 1981), pp. 96–111.

Kaare Strom, *Minority Government and Majority Rule* (Cambridge, England: Cambridge University Press, 1990).

Laurence H. Tribe, "Policy Science: Analysis or Ideology?" *Philosophy and Public Affairs* 2 (Fall 1972).

Gordon Tullock, *Private Wants, Public Means: An Economic Analysis of the Desirable Scope of Government* (New York: Basic Books, 1970).

Louis F. Weschler, "Public Choice: Methodological Individualism in Politics," *Public Administration Review,* vol. 42 (May/June 1982), pp. 288–94.

Viktor Vanberg and James M. Buchanan, "Rational Choice and Moral Order," in James H. Nichols, Jr., and Colin Wright (eds.), *From Political Economy to Economics and Back?* (San Francisco, Institute for Contemporary Studies, 1990), pp. 175–91.

4

IDEOLOGIES AND INSTITUTIONAL CONSTRAINTS: PUBLIC POLICY IN AMERICA

Public policy in the United States must be considered in the context of the peculiarities of its political institutions and its culture. If politics is the art of the possible, it is also a truism that the problems that get on the agenda and the viable policy options will be determined by the culture and institutions of the society. The framers of the Constitution fragmented power rather than concentrating it. The system of checks and balances, separation of powers, and federalism was the result of choice and the political realities of the time. By providing for a limited government and guaranteeing certain individual liberties, the framers also provided a channel through which public opinion may constrain policy.

National crises, such as the Civil War, the Great Depression, and World War II have changed the parameters of the struggle over policy. More recently, opinion is divided over whether the system created in 1787 can still provide for *effective* government in the twenty-first century. Many critics of the system propose schemes to streamline institutions, and encourage a concentration of power. Others praise the work of the framers and the virtues of inefficient government as extolled by James Madison in *The Federalist #10*. The chapter examines the origins of this debate and how the conservative bias among the delegates to the Constitutional Convention was reflected in the Constitution. It examines the role of Federalism and its impact on policy making. It also examines the American political culture and public philosophy and its impact on public policy formulation. Finally it looks at how the public philosophy is related to political attitudes and peculiarly "American" values.

IDEOLOGY AND PUBLIC POLICY

An ideology refers to a structure of interrelated values, ideas, and beliefs about the nature of people and society. It includes a set of ideas about the best way to live and about the most appropriate institutional arrangements for society. As such it invariably includes a belief that society could be improved. Ideologies include an image of the good society and the means for achieving it. Therefore supporters of an ideology believe that if their plan is followed and the appropriate policies adopted, the society will be improved. Ideologies thus provide a perceptual lens through which to view politics by helping to organize thoughts and evaluate policies, programs, political parties, and politicians. Ideologies are a device to simplify the complexities of political reality and therefore are never completely accurate or inaccurate descriptions of political reality.

The term **ideology** was first used during the French Revolution to describe a view of how society should be organized that was separate from religious views that were becoming increasingly controversial. Today, the term often is used to refer to the outlook of individuals with rigidly held beliefs. In fact, the mainstream of American politics has never been rigidly ideological; only the far right and far left are concerned with a correct set of values and behaviors for their members. Those passionately committed to an ideology are not likely to make good policy scientists, as they often cannot dispassionately examine a problem without confusing it with their ideological goals. Ideologues find it difficult to compromise because an ideology carries with it a commitment to try to change the society in the direction of their ideology. Policy making becomes more difficult when issues are cast in ideological terms because the policy problem becomes transformed into a "conservative" or "liberal" *principle* which cannot be compromised.

In the United States more people have consistently identified themselves as "conservative" rather than "liberal" over the last twenty years.[1] People in America often describe themselves as liberal or conservative even while they prefer to think of themselves as pragmatic, political moderates, who decide issues on their merits rather than through any ideological set of values or beliefs. Many people who call themselves liberal or conservative only accept a certain part of that ideology. Many Americans who accept the conservative view that the role of government in the economy should be reduced, want greater government involvement in the regulation of social issues, such as gays in the military. Conversely, others who view themselves as accepting a liberal position of more government intervention in the economy, feel the government should have a smaller role in the area of personal morality. Many who are conservative on social issues may be liberal on economic issues and vice versa. This is not necessarily logically inconsistent. It suggests that political ideology in the United States is rather fluid. It also suggests that an ideology is somewhat malleable to the political environment in which it exists.

A liberal or conservative orientation does not determine political postures for most people, but it is a useful means for self-identification and articulation of policy positions. The more informed people are the more likely they are to have policy positions consistent with their ideological orientation. Since the 1980 election, the Republican Party has strengthened its identification with a conservative ideology. Ideological awareness has grown in the United States in recent presidential elections with a stronger association between ideological self-identification and voting patterns.

---

[1]See Center for Political Studies, University of Michigan, National Election Study Cumulative Data File, 1952–1992, *1994 National Election Study,* and *1996 National Election Study.* Those identifying as conservative or extremely conservative have averaged just over 20 percent of the population, while those identifying as liberal or extremely liberal average about 18 percent.

Most Americans, in fact, do not organize their thoughts systematically or consistently. For example, a voter may want tax cuts but would like the government to increase funding for Medicare. Many Americans view their position on one issue, such as tax cuts, in isolation from their view on another issue, such as their desire for more defense spending. Some attentive voters have difficulty finding candidates who reflect their view on a wide variety of issues because the government is involved in an ever-wider variety of public policies.

Political entrepreneurs, including legislators, lobbyists, special interest groups, and party activists are more likely to be ideologically committed. They often try to mobilize public opinion toward their ideology, but find that more voters may react negatively when such appeals seem too far out of the mainstream. For example, the Republican leadership turned back an attempt to make opposition to late term abortions for party candidates a prerequisite to receive campaign financial assistance. The conservative leadership learned the hard way that they drove many voters, especially women, out of their party by appearing to oppose any dissenting views. Political parties must make some accommodations with voters and ad hoc coalitions to maintain viability. This stands in stark contrast to many countries whose political parties are organized around competing political philosophies and ideologies. In those countries political parties are more disciplined and political struggles take on the form of a protracted conflict.

Nevertheless most voters are not on the "dead center" of a political spectrum. Rather they have a tendency to be "a little more conservative" or a "little more liberal." Political entrepreneurs therefore try to use ideology as an organizing strategy. Ideology is important. Therefore it is imperative to understand the main ideologies in the United States and how they influence public policy.

Today, ideological controversy is a part of the debate on the whole variety of public policy issues from whether gay marriages should be recognized by law, to how to reduce the flow of drugs into the country, what the nation's international trade policy should be, or how to improve the nation's educational system.

Should the government be less involved in our lives? Would it be better if people were forced to rely more upon themselves and the market for their well-being? How should the government provide for economic growth and price stability? Should the government adopt a more restrictive immigration policy? How can we stop urban decay? Ideological controversy and debate are very much a part of our political process.

TWO MAJOR IDEOLOGIES

There are several different theories that try to describe how governments should behave (normative theories) or how they actually do behave (positive theories). These ideologies are actually theories or perspectives from which to judge government policies.

Liberalism

Liberalism is an ideology committed to a set of policies that have as their common goal greater freedom for individual men. The term "liberal" first acquired its modern political connotation from the Liberales, a Spanish party that supported a version of the French constitution of 1791 for Spain.[2] Liberal thought has two central ideas. The first is the opposition to arbitrary authority and its replacement with more democratic forms of authority. The second idea is a desire for greater overall freedom for the individual. Early liberalism emphasized freedom *from* arbitrary authority. It began with support of freedom of conscience and a demand for religious tolerance.

The spirit of this rational liberalism can be traced back to John Locke and his *Two Treatises of Government* (1690). Locke's philosophical rationalism, common sense, and liberal spirit is reflected in the work which stresses individual "natural rights," labor, property, and reason. Locke's treatises contain the basic doctrine of liberalism. Later economic liberals stressed the observation made by Locke that the first requisite for national economic growth was the protection of private property. Unless people had a right to property, the incentive to work dissolved and production would fall.

Adam Smith, the founder of modern economics is often considered to be the greatest of the economic liberals. Smith published *The Wealth of Nations* in 1776 in an effort to refute the mercantilists, who argued that the true wealth, or power, of nations was not determined by the amount of gold that a nation acquired, but by the amount of goods and services produced by the society. Rather than focusing on the role of the state as the mercantilists did, Smith focused on the role of the individual. Smith argued that interference with market forces by the government must lead to inefficiencies and reduced growth. The government, by directing economic resources toward one industry, must necessarily draw those resources from other areas that are then underfunded.

There was concern that permitting everyone to follow his or her own self-interest would lead to chaos throughout society. Smith argued that the discipline of market forces would lead not to lower production resulting from the zero-sum relationships perceived by the mercantilists, but to benefits for both parties to a trade, or they would not consummate the agreement. The most efficient manufacturers will survive and the inefficient will go under. The invisible hand of market forces can regulate the market far better than the government.

The idea that society should be free from government interference was summed up by Thomas Jefferson, a classical liberal, with his famous phrase, "That government governs best which governs least." This view was well suited to the new country that had just thrown off the shackles of arbitrary interference in political and economic decisions of the American settlers by George III. A young, vigorous nation with resources and room to expand provided an excellent foundation for an ideology of freedom from economic or political control. Because of their experience with monarchial government, both Smith and Jefferson saw government as a threat to individual well-being. Jefferson said, "The care of human life and happiness, and not their destruction, is the first and only legitimate object of good government." Classical liberals were fearful of the heavy hand of government and sought to "free" the individual from state oppression.

Classical liberals had greater faith in the influence of the markets than of governments. Both thought that their theories would lead to an improvement in the well-being of the nation's citizens. Liberalism emphasizes man's reasonable nature that leads to

---

[2]David Smith, *Liberalism,* "The International Encyclopedia of the Social Sciences," (New York: The Macmillan Company & The Free Press, 1972), vol. 9. p. 276.

cooperation (such as in the social contract), and to competition in a constructive way. If society is set up correctly, we may all gain from competition. Conversely, classical liberals focused on abusive uses of power by the state. Jefferson's Declaration of Independence catalogued a list of abuses of the British government. Unlike the mercantilist who viewed competition as zero-sum, liberals saw competition as constructive and positive-sum or one that is mutually advantageous. If two individuals meet in the market and one has brought grapes but prefers apples, and another has brought apples but prefers grapes, then both can benefit through an exchange.

The classical liberal view had a strong bias in support of the market whenever a choice was to be made between the two. Classical liberalism also became associated with a preference for democratic forms of government. Democracies were preferred because by weakening centralized power, individual freedom was made more secure. Democratic forms of government with separation of powers and checks and balances can be more easily thwarted in any policy that requires decisive centralized decision making.

The Industrial Revolution resulted in the rapid urbanization of Europe, rapid population growth as a result of better living and health standards, and the destruction of the landed aristocracy and the petty nobility who were made irrelevant by the changes. The aristocracy was replaced by new elites made up of manufacturers, financiers, merchants, and government officials. **Jeremy Bentham** (1748–1832) was an observer of the changing conditions and the principal commentator of **utilitarianism.** Bentham joined the two threads of liberalism together by applying the concept of utility and the marketplace to politics and the tasks of democratic government. He is well-known for his observation that "nature has placed mankind under the governance of two sovereign masters, *pain* and *pleasure*" and his utility principle of the greatest good of the greatest number. However Bentham did not identify utility with selfishness, for he says that the "first law of nature is to wish our own happiness; and the united voices of prudence and efficient benevolence add,—Seek the happiness of others,— seek your own happiness in the happiness of others."[3]

Jeremy Bentham proposed that politics and law should provide for a maximum of free choice and liberty for all. He believed that education, free speech, inclusive representation and an expanded suffrage, and the regular accountability of the governors to the governed, that is, politics patterned after the model of the free economy, were necessary to provide good government. His theory first combined economic liberalism with positive political action.

In the mid-1800s more challenges were raised about this anti-state view of liberalism. The goal of liberalism was individual freedom. But it was becoming increasingly clear that economic progression had brought about situations that could reduce individual freedom. For example, although political power was decentralized and pushed out of the marketplace, market power was becoming increasingly centralized. Liberals had expressed great faith in *freedom of contracts* (agreements between two consenting parties without government interference). If one party does not like the agreement, one does not sign the contract. This might not be a viable option when the bargaining power between the two parties is highly unequal. What if a powerful corporation offered a

---

[3]Ebenstein, p. 596. The quote is from Bentham's *Deontology, or Science of Morality,* published in 1834.

contract with a very low wage to a poor person desperate for a job to provide for his family? The contract might require a twelve-hour workday and even carry a clause in which the individual agreed never to join a union as a condition of employment. Does the person in urgent need of a job really have a choice? Corporations also claimed the right under laissez faire to share lists of troublesome workers who might have agitated for higher wages, thus blacklisting anyone who objected to low wages. Classical liberals believed that wages would find their own natural level even if it was at a Malthusian subsistence level.

The growth of the modern corporation and industrial technology transformed the world of Adam Smith who had not conceived of the organizational power of large corporations. Great inequalities in the employment market made one man's economic freedom another man's oppression. The market in commodities such as child labor, impure or adulterated foods, and slum housing led some to conclude that government regulation could expand the freedom especially of the poor. Some "modern liberal" political and economic writers began to suggest that in such a circumstance it was time for the government to be brought back into the marketplace to protect people from the inequities in the system. Modern liberals began to support wage and hour legislation, the right to unionize, and workman's compensation. Other economic liberals defended the tenets of laissez faire transforming the means of liberalism into ends and transforming their liberalism into conservative ideology.

John Stuart Mill inherited the liberalism of Adam Smith and Thomas Jefferson as taught by his father, James Mill, a noted political economist (and friend of Bentham's). John Stuart wrote a treatise on the *Principles of Political Economy* in 1848 which gave liberalism a new meaning.[4] He argued that liberalism had been an important force in the destruction of arbitrary centralized power. It provided the very foundation for democratic revolutions and reforms while invigorating individual liberty in Europe and America. But liberty that merely sanctioned the amassing of wealth was insufficient, according to Mill, who also wanted moral and spiritual progress. He thought that the state should take some action to correct market failures and to nudge social progress along. For example, the state should allow for individual freedom in most cases. Parents ordinarily should be free to raise their children as they see fit. However, there is a parental duty and a moral obligation for parents to educate their children. This moral obligation is to the children and also to society. This obligation of the parents to educate their children takes priority over their rights to raise their children as they see fit. The state has a right to use its coercive authority to require the education of the children. However, since some parents cannot afford the cost of educating their children, the government is obligated to provide grants to make the education of poor children possible. Mill's views on education were similar to his views in other areas of social welfare.

In his later years, Mill became increasingly willing to tolerate, or even require, government involvement in a number of social issues. The question was always *when* to permit government intervention, and how far should the intervention be tolerated. The Progressive period in the American experience (roughly 1890–1920) signaled the willingness to use government and social institutions to improve the human condition.

---

[4]John Stuart Mill, *Principles of Political Economy,* 2 vols., (London, 1848, 7th ed. 1871).

John Maynard Keynes further contributed to the willingness of liberals to regulate the economy for the general welfare. His analysis showed that laissez-faire principles could lead to economic chaos and that government intervention could provide much needed order. Keynes believed that the state needed to be active to provide an improvement in society's condition (see chap. 5 for a further explanation of his views).

Vaclav Havel, president of the Czech and Slovak republics is often quoted as a modern liberal theoretician. He has worried that there is a danger in placing too great a dependence on the market, which can result in tragic social consequences for the market and the individual. Moving from too powerful a state (communism) to too weak a state can risk creating a backlash that could usher in authoritarian rule. He advises moderation:

> The market economy is as natural and matter-of-fact to me as air. After all, it is a system of human activity that has been tried and found to work over centuries. . . . It is the system that best corresponds to human nature. But precisely because it is so down-to-earth, it is not, and cannot constitute, a world view, a philosophy, or an ideology. Even less does it contain the meaning of life. It seems both ridiculous and dangerous when . . . the market economy suddenly becomes a cult, a collection of dogmas, uncompromisingly defended and more important, even, than *what the economic system is intended to serve— that is, life itself.*[5]

The philosophy of John Rawls fits the modern liberal view of the proper relationship between liberty and equality. His first principle is that each person is to have an equal right to the most extensive total system of basic liberties compatible with a similar system of liberty for all. His second principle is that social and economic policies should be arranged so that they help the least advantaged at least as much as the most advantaged.

What can one conclude about liberalism today? First, modern liberalism keeps the same end of the free individual that has always guided this ideology. The means to the end have changed, but the goal of increasing human freedom remains the same. Liberalism asserts that the individual is more important than the state. But though economic man is based upon rational egoism, political man must be concerned with the broader welfare. The state is created to serve the individual and his or her well-being. Modern liberalism does call upon the power of the state, but it is the interest of expanding freedom for all, although it may mean that some have less freedom to do as they please. The market is useful as an efficient and peaceful process to bring people together in mutually advantageous trade. However, there are some things the market does not do well. In those cases, government must step in to promote societal goals. Whenever possible the government may try to use market incentives to achieve societal goals.

Conservatism

The term **conservativism** may be used in a couple of different ways by social scientists. Temperamental conservatism describes a cluster of attributes that most people exhibit in all societies. The major elements in the conservative temperament include habit, inertia, fear of the unexpected, the need to be accepted, and fear of being alone. These traits

---

[5]Vaclav Havel, "What I Believe," in *Summer Meditations,* trans. Paul Wilson (New York: Knopf, 1992), p. 73.

are often found among some of the more marginal groups in society such as the poor, the elderly, or the ignorant.[6] A conservative temperament is given a high "value" in the gathering of knowledge and transmitting the culture from generation to generation. The maintenance of law and order would not be possible without this conservative inclination. This sentiment is also necessary for individuals to accept the division of labor and the system in which people accept the wage structure as being better than any other system devised.

Closely related to temperamental conservatism is situational conservatism which is the natural and culturally determined disposition to resist dislocating changes in the traditional pattern of living. Basically, situational conservatism is a general opposition to changes in the social, economic, political, or cultural order. The fear of change is the distinguishing characteristic of conservatism. In the politico-economic arena it becomes a fear of those who would plan to change the world or to "improve" it by sacrificing the accepted societal values, institutions, and habits of living. Although the more affluent are prime candidates to be content with the established order in the society, persons at all socioeconomic levels may lament change in the *status quo*. For reasons that range from the instinctive to the pragmatic, many will find the security of the established order preferable to the unknown of change. The maxim, "Better the devil that you know, than the one you don't" sums up this view.

Political and economic conservatism is the result of conservatives of temperament and situation being thrust into political issues. The most general meaning of the term conservatism refers to political conservatism (or the "Right"). Politico-economic conservatism refers to the attitudes that venerate the inherited patterns of morality and existing institutions, and are distrustful of the competence of popular government to provide change that will improve on the status quo. Politico-economic conservatives can be counted on to oppose liberal proposals for reform. Not surprisingly, such conservatism draws its major support from those with the greatest interest in the existing order.

Like liberalism, modern conservatism has undergone an evolution from "classical conservatism." Edmund Burke, a contemporary of Adam Smith, was the epitome of conservative thinking in the late eighteenth century. Burke agreed with Smith that a free market was the best economic system. He was in sympathy with the American colonies and opposed sending British troops to put down the rebellion.

The liberalism of the American Revolution was a seminal event in Europe. Liberal ideas appeared to be sweeping Europe and were influenced by philosopher Jean-Jacques Rousseau and Thomas Paine. The application of liberalism in America was not difficult once the British withdrew since there was no embedded aristocracy to contend with. Democratic government fell easily into place. But in France, the revolution based on "liberty, equality, and fraternity" met with fierce resistance from the aristocracy and the Roman Catholic Church which received state support. The revolutionaries dealt with the intransigence by means of the guillotine in an effort to sweep aside all institutions.

Edmund Burke watched in horror. His *Reflections on the Revolution in France* (1790) began as a discussion of the French Revolution but expanded into an examination of the

---

[6]Clinton Rossiter, *Conservatism,* "The International Encyclopedia of the Social Sciences," vol. 3, (New York: The Macmillan Company & The Free Press, 1972).

nature of reform and revolution and was to become the standard work of modern conservatism. Underlying Burke's philosophy was a deep pessimism that is visible throughout his writing. Burke realized that the French Revolution was not merely a French affair, it was a revolution in beliefs and theory. He called for a European crusade to crush this new wild, enthusiastic revolutionary spirit by force of arms. He believed that no monarchy would be safe before the tyranny of the multitude.

Burke opposed the *individualism* represented by the new philosophy. He saw society not in terms of equal individuals but of unequal groups with long-standing interests. People are not basically rational as Locke had written, they are only partly rational and are generally guided by their emotions and passions. It was to contain men's irrational passions that society has evolved institutions, traditions, and moral standards, such as the aristocracy, churches, and rules of morality. If these were swept aside the resulting chaos and tyranny of the masses would be far worse than any injustice suffered before the revolution. Therefore these institutions should be *conserved* even if they are not perfect. They have evolved over hundreds of years of trial and error and people have adapted to them. He was not opposed to change however, it was just that change should occur gradually, allowing time for people to adapt. A state without the ability to change would not have the ability to "conserve" itself. The historic mission of conservatism has not been to defeat revolutions but to avert them.

Burke believed that the characteristic essence of all property "formed out of the combined principles of its acquisition and conservation, is to be *unequal.*"[7] The touchstone of modern conservatism is that its outlook is more pessimistic regarding the rational side of man's nature than liberals, whether classical or modern. Their view emphasizes the limits of rationality and the view that for most people, their intellect is subordinate to their emotions and passions. They tend to emphasize human inequality as a given and that the unequal distribution of property naturally follows from that fact.

The political and economic conservative is typically the prisoner of the pressures for change in the social process. Those proposing change keep the social process in motion while the conservative reacts. When the pace of change is pushed by market forces through multinational corporations, computers, and automation, the conservative position illustrates that support of a social revolution can coexist with opposition to political reform.

The first principle of government for the conservative is to protect property and maintain order. They retain the view of classical liberals that after it performs that function, government should have little regulatory authority that would impede the acquisition of property. Government should have an increased role however to encourage respect for tradition. For example, conservatives would like to see government take action to get prayer into schools, restrict abortion, and limit gay and lesbian rights. Modern conservatives are also traditional concerning questions of women in the military and affirmative action: they oppose them.

Milton Friedman, a modern conservative and Nobel prize–winning economist, argues in favor of Adam Smith's principle of laissez faire. President Ronald Reagan in the United States, and Margaret Thatcher in Britain attempted to apply this aspect of classic liberalism, now frequently called *neoconservatism.* They advocated free markets at home

---

[7]Alan O. Ebenstein, *Great Political Thinkers,* 5th ed. (New York: Harcourt Brace Publishers, 1991), p. 578.

and in international trade and minimal state interference otherwise except in the area of national security. Reagan complained that a progressive income tax was improper and denounced policies designed to reduce inequalities as "social engineering." The top tax rate in the United States was reduced from 70 percent in 1980 to 33 percent in 1986. Critics denounced that rolling back government regulations resulted in giving away natural resources and relaxing environmental protection standards contributed to the growing inequality in the distribution of income and wealth in the nation (see chap. 6). For modern conservatives individual liberty is to be overwhelmingly preferred to equality. Modern conservatism continues today as a combination of the ideas of Edmund Burke and Adam Smith's idea of laissez faire, although the problems of where the balance between individual freedom in the market and state interests remain.

By the late nineteenth century it became apparent that the free market had several problems identified earlier by Smith. The market system produced oligopolies and monopolies which reduced competition. Individual consumers did not benefit, as Smith had hoped, when sellers could collect monopolistic rents. Inequalities in the marketplace produced great inequalities in the distribution of wealth. Left to market forces, stratified class positions were increasingly inherited. Affluent parents provided their children with the advantages that come with class: excellent educational opportunities, connections to jobs, and inheritances to provide succeeding generations with appropriate privileges. At the lower end of the socioeconomic ladder, it became difficult for those at the bottom to acquire the means necessary to achieve upward mobility. Recurring sharp fluctuations in the business cycle hit the poor and working class the hardest.

Conservatism as Philosophy   As a philosophy, committed to the defense of the status quo and the leadership of certain groups within the society, conservatism is an important ideology in the United States. Conservatism is thriving in the realm of ideas with a certain set of core principals. Clinton Rossiter has noted that the persistent themes of the philosophers of modern conservatism include the following:

> The existence of a universal moral order sanctioned and supported by organized religion.
> The obstinately imperfect nature of men, in which unreason and sinfulness lurk always behind the curtain of civilized behavior.
> The natural inequality of men in most qualities of mind, body, and character.
> The necessity of social classes and orders, and the consequent folly of attempts at leveling by force of law.
> The primary role of private property in the pursuit of personal liberty and defense of the social order.
> The uncertainty of progress and the recognition that prescription is the chief method of such progress as a society may achieve.
> The need for a ruling and serving aristocracy.
> The limited reach of human reason, and the consequent importance of traditions, institutions, symbols, rituals, and even prejudices.
> The fallibility and potential tyranny of majority rule, and the consequent desirability of diffusing, limiting, and balancing political power.[8]

[8]Clinton Rossiter, *Conservatism,* "The International Encyclopedia of the Social Sciences," vol. 3, (New York: The Macmillan Company & The Free Press, 1972). p. 293.

Rossiter also notes that there is a conservative preference for liberty over equality as reflected in Burke's philosophy. Conservatism in America is a jumble of disparate answers to persistent questions about where to draw the line between the rights of the individual and the demands of the community. Conservatives generally support government action to protect the status quo or promote the interests of those who tend to be among the more affluent. Conservatives also are inclined to favor a decentralization of power.

COMPETING PERSPECTIVES OF ANALYSIS

The ideological perspectives provide an indication of how individuals holding particular views would try to work to change society. The social sciences also suggest competing theoretical viewpoints that prove useful in analyzing public policy. The pluralist and elite models, and variations on them, offer a myriad of insights into individual and collective political action and the deep-seated tensions within society. The two theories examined here adopt different units of analysis and logic of social action, along with different interpretations of data. They are often put forward as discordant approaches to analysis. However there are so many compatible elements in both approaches that a synthesis of the approaches combining several aspects of both can strengthen our analytic efforts.

Pluralism (Group) Theory

Pluralism is a theory of government that attempts to reaffirm the democratic character of American society by asserting that public policy is the product of competition and negotiation between groups in society. It begins with the view that individuals acting in their self-interest engage in political action in an effort to obtain some benefit from the government. The individual must compete with others in the effort to shape policy outcomes. Pluralism accepts that there are shortcomings in traditional democratic theory, which emphasizes individual responsibility and control. Pluralism itself emphasizes the tendency of individuals with common interests ("factions" in James Madison's term) to form groups to push their demands upon government. Competing groups make demands upon government through political institutions. Individuals are important to the extent that they act on behalf of group interests.

The pluralist view of the world is one in which multiple centers of power compete to shape policy outcomes. Power in America is fluid and diffused among many groups. The decentralized nature of politics guarantees group access to power. Competition between interest groups helps to protect individual interests by placing checks on the power groups can accumulate and preventing them from abusing the power they do achieve. Public policy at any given time results from the equilibrium achieved among the competing groups. The legislature, in this theory, acts as a referee of the group competition and records the victories of different groups in the form of statutes.[9] If the competing interest groups are

---

[9]Earl Latham, "The Group Basis of Politics," in Heinz Eulau et al., *Political Behavior* (New York: Free Press, 1956), p. 239.

roughly balanced, the policy that results roughly approximates the preferences of society in general. Overlapping group membership helps maintain the balance by preventing any single group from moving too far from societal values. Public policy tends to move in the direction of groups whose influence is growing and away from those whose influence is waning.

From the pluralist perspective, the state has no role other than to reflect and respond to the demands of participants in the political system. The government provides the representative mechanism through which groups press their demands for policy outputs. Although pluralism does not require a small state, many suggest that a minimal amount of government intervention is most compatible with the model. The government's role is primarily to be an umpire between the competing groups, to interpret and enforce the rules agreed upon. As Milton Friedman says, "the role of the government . . . is to do something that the market cannot do for itself, namely, to determine, arbitrate, and enforce the rules of the game."[10]

Group theory does not deny that individuals by themselves have little power or influence. Individuals play only a limited role by voting, or working in interest groups. And even though the right to participate is open to everyone, active participation is heavily biased toward the most affluent members of society, who are also the better educated with higher-status occupations.[11] The poor make up a much smaller part of the activist population and their perceptions are not communicated with the clarity or urgency of the more affluent.

Neopluralists challenge the earlier pluralist idea that power is decentralized and that no single interest dominates the government.[12] Charles Lindblom holds that corporate officials, in reality, are a set of policy makers parallel to elected officials who act without the restraints of legislators. Elected officials are in fact very solicitous of corporate officials and their desires because failure to accommodate them may lead to consequences such as unemployment that government officials are unwilling to accept. The result is that the bias within the system and the special status of business is decidedly in favor of the affluent. The neopluralists provide a bridge to the elite theory.

Elite Theory

Elite theory is based on the straightforward empirical observation that despite the pluralist vision of diffuse and fluid power centers with open access, the reality is very different. Power is concentrated in elites drawn from business and financial centers of the society. The basic unit of analysis is not the individual or an organized interest group, but the small layer of elites who control powerful institutions: primarily financial, but it may also include governmental and military organizations. Elites, being rational and self-interested, use the resources to maintain order in society by managing a consensus that represents their interests—which is to say, the status quo. The elites in government

---

[10]Milton Friedman, *Capitalism and Freedom* (Chicago: University of Chicago Press, 1962), p. 27.

[11]Sidney Verba and Norman H. Nie, *Participation in America: Political Democracy and Social Equality* (New York: Harper & Row, 1972), p. 336.

[12]See for example, Theodore Lowi, *The End of Liberalism* (New York: W. W. Norton, 1972), especially chap. 2. Also Charles E. Linblom, *Politics and Markets,* (New York: Basic Books, 1977).

CASE STUDY

ELITES, INTERESTS, AND THE TENSION
BETWEEN CAPITALISM AND DEMOCRACY

A standard argument against *democracy* that has concerned conservatives of all stripes as well as elites is that in a true democracy there would be nothing to prevent the masses from using their democratic majority to take away the property of the relatively few *haves* and redistribute it to the *have nots*. The concern was that the tyranny of the majority would incite unscrupulous politicians to sell out to the mob's rage for economic equality by using the tax system to confiscate the property of those who have more.

The framers of the Constitution were determined that this would not happen in America. They put together a system of separation of powers and checks and balances and federalism to safeguard individual liberty and property rights. Many of the Constitution's other key provisions, such as the indirect election of the president and senators (prior to the Seventeenth Amendment), and the appointment of judges for life were a determined effort to limit democracy. Adam Smith had gone so far as to charge that governments were really instituted to defend the rich against the poor.

The transfer of power away from more democratic forms can also occur through bureaucratic shifts. One mechanism of government that can manage the tension between democracy and capitalism is to create boards that are part of the national government yet insulated from the electoral process and even largely from the control of politicians. In fact, the structure can even be justified on the notion that it should be immune from the pressures of competing self-interested pressure groups, especially since many lack the "expertise" to be involved. However the Chairman of the Board is nominated only after extensive consultation with the elite members of the financial community which primarily is made up of CEO's of major American banks.

The Federal Reserve Board (the Fed) is the prime example of this variation on the principle of popular control over government which reflects the fear of too much democracy and the need to protect one of the primary government functions from too much democracy. The U.S. Federal Reserve is largely insulated from democratic control. It should be noted that comparable mechanisms occur in many central banks in Europe. The Federal Reserve controls monetary policy, that is, the money supply, and through it determines some of the most important questions of the political economy. Its policies have a tremendous influence on economic growth, price stabilization, and levels of employment. Access that an individual has to the legislature is completely lacking with regard to the Fed. The Federal Reserve is shielded from public control in part by its own official secrecy.

The Federal Reserve was created in 1913 as an independent agency. It is integrated into the group of over 5,000 Federal Reserve member banks with national charters and twelve district Federal Reserve Banks. Major state banks are also members. The Federal Reserve Banks are private, for-profit, institutions. Its seven member Board of Governors serve staggered fourteen-year terms as presidential appointees with the advice and consent of the Senate. The Chairman of the Board is appointed by the president, with Senate approval, serving a four-year term.

try to structure the debate to quash any problem that would threaten their hold on power or that would significantly redistribute power. This model does not perceive the state as the neutral umpire of the pluralists' view.

This view accepts the idea of interest group competition that results in legislation. But the issues involved in such instances are not central to the welfare of society. The elite model holds that most election issues deal with a middle level of power. Pluralist politics, by focusing on the competition at the middle level tends to miss the critical issues at the top, and neglects the issues at the bottom. Middle-level politics is often symbolic, while the critical issues are not open to electoral challenge but are agreed upon through elite collaboration.

Every political system has inherent biases concerning who has access to it. The American Founding Fathers supposedly produced a system based on the notion that "all men are created equal." But according to elite theorists, the machinery of government was (and is) not open to all men (and certainly not to all women). There were built-in mechanisms designed to make it difficult for most groups to gain access to the government or to make changes in the way it functioned. Therefore, the idea that American government reflects "the will of the people," as popularly understood, is inaccurate in the view of elite theory.

Elite theory holds that most government decisions are made by a minority elite that has enormous power. Elites derive their power from the control of key financial, communications, industrial, and governmental institutions. Power flows not from the elite individuals themselves, but from the positions of authority they have in large institutions. Their power and "privileged positions" originate from the immense wealth of large corporations and the significance of those corporations for the overall national economy.[13]

Supporters of this view that elites and not the masses govern America make a strong case that it is the elites who have access to and largely determine the public policy agenda, because they have the real authority over the major institutions that shape the lives of the masses. **Elite theory holds that elites govern all societies,** not just America. Alexander Hamilton explained the existence of elites in the following way:

> All communities divide themselves into the few and the many. The first are the rich and well-born, the other the masses of people. The voice of the people has been said to be the voice of God; and however generally this maxim has been quoted and believed, it is not true in fact. The people are turbulent and changing, they seldom judge or determine right.[14]

The privileged aristocracy in preindustrial Europe has been generally superceded by wealthy capitalists of the present time. The common thread is that elites in every era tend to believe that what is good for themselves must be good for all.

Elite theory accepts upward social mobility that permits nonelites to become elites because this openness provides stability by reducing the potential of revolution from below. Individuals who might supply the revolutionary leadership become part of the

---

[13]Elite theory has been developed in many works. C. Wright Mills, *The Power Elite* (New York: Oxford University Press, 1956), is certainly a classic work. See also, Michael Parenti, *Democracy for the Few,* 5th ed. (New York: St. Martin's Press, 1988). Also see Thomas R. Dye and Harmon Zeigler, *The Irony of Democracy,* 7th ed. (Monterey, CA: Brooks/Cole, 1987). Charles Lindblom, *Politics and Markets* (New York: Basic Books, 1977), is another who argues that business has a privileged position in the American political system (see especially pp. 170–85).

[14]Alexander Hamilton, *Records of the Federal Convention of 1787,* as quoted in Thomas R. Dye, *Who's Running America: The Bush Era* (Englewood Cliffs, NJ: Prentice-Hall, 1990), p. 3. This discussion of elite theory relies heavily on this work by Dye, and on Dye and Zeigler, *The Irony of Democracy,* pp. 3–11.

elite, and in the process assimilate the values of the ruling class they are joining. Privileged elites have a vital interest in the perpetuation of the system upon which their entitlements rest. Upward social mobility means that even potential members of the elite share a consensus on the need to preserve the system by discouraging changes that would jeopardize the elite's position.[15] Competition thus occurs over a rather narrow range of issues and usually concerns **means** rather than **ends.**[16]

Consensus among American elites is built around the sanctity of private property, limitations on government authority, and the economic virtues of a capitalist culture. In this view, public policy does not result from the popular will so much as it mirrors the concerns and values of the elite. Public policy changes and innovations result from shifts in elite positions. Since elites tend to be very conservative because of their overriding interest in preserving the system, changes tend to be incremental rather than radical. Major changes take place only when the security of the basic system is jeopardized. Then elites may move swiftly to institute the reforms required to preserve the system and their privileged position within it. Elite theory does not argue that elites are unconcerned about the welfare of the masses, only that the general welfare of the masses depends upon the actions of the elites. The masses rarely decide issues but accept the symbolic "democratic" institutions of voting and party membership, which gives them a means to identify with the system.[17] Thus public policy decision making is limited to issues that do not imperil the elites. They organize the policy agenda so that certain kinds of decisions are eliminated from it.[18]

The theory holds that the masses are largely submissive, and indifferent to and poorly informed regarding policy issues. Elites, having more at stake, and holding their positions of power, are more active and well informed. Elites generally control the communications process, which means that information generally flows from the elites to the masses. **Elites will more frequently influence the masses than the masses will influence the elites.**

Elites find some issues more acceptable than others, based upon how the issues are perceived and presented to those with the real power. The net effect of this, according to two analysts, "is that new demands, particularly those of disadvantaged or deprived groups, are the least likely to receive attention on either the systemic agenda of controversy or the

---

[15]Richard Hofferbert has developed a conceptual framework of public policy making that emphasizes elite influences. The policy process in his model is developed with governmental decisions being the dependent variable. The policy output is dependent upon historical-geographic conditions, socioeconomic conditions, mass political behavior, governmental institutions, and, most immediately the behavior of the members of the elite itself. The model has been criticized for dealing in aggregate rather than individual choices. It also presumes that policy decisions are driven by socioeconomic conditions and mass political behavior filtered through governmental institutions and elite behavior. Other researchers noted earlier, however, suggest that it is the elites who drive the policy decisions rather than merely filtering them. See Richard Hofferbert, *The Study of Public Policy* (Indianapolis: Bobbs-Merrill, 1974).

[16]Dye and Zeigler, *The Irony of Democracy,* p. 6.

[17]Dye and Zeigler, *The Irony of Democracy,* pp. 6–7.

[18]Dye and Zeigler point out that it is critical to understand **what elite theory is *not* as well as what it *is*.** Elite theory does not assume that those in power are constantly at odds with the masses, or that they always achieve their goals at the expense of the public welfare. Nor does it hold that elites are involved in a conspiracy to suppress the masses. The theory does not suggest that members of the elite are always in agreement with each other, and it does not even hold that they always get their way.

institutional agenda."[19] Elite theory as a tool of analysis would seem to closely conform to the conservative ideology.

Plural Elites

Both the elite and pluralist models have merit. Elite theory recognizes that the power of elites is not inherent in the people themselves, but flows from their positions of authority in large institutions. Different groups in society may have interests that diverge from each other as the pluralists claim. But the leaders (elites) of these groups, whether in politics, banking, manufacturing, insurance, construction, and so on, will typically have more in common with each other than with the organizations from which they derive their power. They may cooperate or be in conflict with other groups. Stratified interaction will take place primarily between the elite members of the organizations who speak and negotiate on behalf of their members and are expected to keep them in line. Elites in turn must deliver at least enough to their followers to maintain their acquiescence.[20]

AMERICAN GOVERNMENT: THE DECLINE IN CONFIDENCE

Confidence in the political institutions responsible for the formulation and implementation of public policy has declined. In 1964, 78 percent of the American public indicated that they could "trust the government in Washington to do what is right always or most of the time." Today, only about one in four Americans express such trust.[21] Trust in all government institutions has declined, including the presidency, Congress, the judiciary, and the military. But government is not alone. Public confidence has declined for many institutions of American society during the last twenty-five years: business 30 to 21 percent; medicine 58 to 40; schools 58 to 40 percent.[22]

Nor is this merely an American phenomenon. Many countries, including Canada, United Kingdom, Belgium, Denmark, Italy, Japan, Spain, and Ireland have also experienced a decline in confidence.[23] If the growing distrust was a peculiarly American phenomenon, the search for the cause would be easier. However, since many other countries have been similarly affected it suggests the problem is more complex.

The United States was born in a revolution against oppressive and arbitrary elitist monarchial power. The major issue that divided the Founding Fathers was clearly drawn between those who wanted a strong government and those who were wary lest we exchange foreign royal oppression for local elitist oppression, and therefore believed that the less government the better. Alexander Hamilton believed, along with many of the

---

[19]Roger W. Cobb and Charles D. Elder, "The Politics of Agenda Building," *Journal of Politics,* vol. 33, no. 4 (November 1971), p. 910.

[20]Robert Dahl has referred to this theory of plural elites as "polyarchy." See Robert A. Dahl, *Polyarchy: Participation and Opposition* (New Haven, CT: Yale University Press, 1971).

[21]George Gallup, Jr. *The Gallup Poll: Public Opinion 1996* (Wilmington, DE: Scholarly Resources, Inc. 1997), p. 172.

[22]*The Gallup Poll: Public Opinion 1996,* pp. 170–73.

[23]See Elizabeth Hann Hastings and Philip K. Hastings, (eds.), *Index to International Public Opinion, 1987–1996* (5 vols.), (Westport, CT: Greenwood Press, 1997). See also, Hans-Dieter Klingemann and Dieter Fuchs (eds.), *Citizens and the State* (New York: Oxford University Press, 1995).

more affluent, that we needed a strong central government to support fledgling American commerce. The Constitution provided a decided break from European monarchies and cast it in a progressive political direction based upon broad-based institutions and active popular participation. The compromise was a government of institutions that would sacrifice efficiency and speed of decision making in favor of a more deliberative democracy to protect the liberty of a beleaguered minority. As James Madison wrote in *The Federalist #10*, extensive debate would be necessary before government could move. Public opinion polls are not easily translated into government policy making.

It is in this context that polls showing a decline in confidence in American government must be placed. First, there are inconsistencies. For example, although confidence has declined in some institutions like Congress (from 42 to 21 percent between 1973 and 1995), respondents believe their own members of Congress deserve reelection by 62 to 19 percent.[24] Support has declined for medicine and schools, but people are satisfied with their own physician and local school. The majority of citizens want the federal budget balanced but oppose cutting programs like Social Security or Medicare.[25] Some of the dissatisfaction is clearly related to how distant people feel they are from government. This results in a higher level of satisfaction with local government over the national government.

Another factor in the satisfaction with American government may be related to when the polls were taken. Government increased its scope of activity as a direct result of the Great Depression, World War II, and the attendant rise of the welfare state. After the government dealt successfully with issues like the Great Depression, World War II, protecting the welfare of its citizens through taking on the responsibility of providing jobs, a minimum wage, and Social Security, confidence in American government reached its zenith. Since polling began in earnest after World War II, confidence in American government reached its highest point in 1964 when 78 percent of the people indicated that one could "trust the government in Washington to do what is right always or most of the time."

Part of the blame for the growing cynicism can be laid at the door of negative campaigning that constantly attacks the character and integrity of political opponents. Despite a pervasive condemnation of negative advertising in campaigns, it is used increasingly because it has been found to be very effective in influencing perceptions regarding the political opposition. Members of Congress are often portrayed and perceived as cynical, self-promoting, and concerned primarily with their own reelections rather than with the welfare of the polity. The lower the regard in which politicians and politics are held by the public, in part as a result of negative campaign ads, the more voters respond to attack themes in those ads. However, because of a backlash against negative campaigns, candidates try to disguise their attacks as issue-related campaign advertising. The backlash against politicians produced by a politics that

[24]Gallup, op. cit.

[25]See Hastings and Hastings, op. cit., 1997, p. 124. Ninety-two percent agreed "Strongly" or "Somewhat" that the federal government should guarantee a Social Security pension to help provide for retirement. And 86 percent agreed "Strongly" or "Somewhat" that the federal government should provide some minimal level of health care. Another 84 percent supported nursing home care for the elderly as well as subsidized prescription drugs.

depicts government as the root of the problem illustrates that such methods cannot help but damage faith in and the effectiveness of political institutions. This is not to suggest that candidates should not attack their opponents' positions on such issues. Campaigns must try to simplify politics to focus voters' minds and distinguish between the various candidates' positions on such issues as health care, education, or energy and the environment. Consequently, campaigns must be loud and raucous (and expensive) to capture the attention of voters and stimulate them to vote. Low-key, low-budget decorous campaigns do not arouse people out of their lethargy to vote.

The staging of politically inspired spectacles for photo opportunities or scripted interviews, especially by the president, may get air time on the evening news, but a lack of substance where it exists is not lost on the public. Symbolic politics rather than serious policy have become the standard fare of partisan politics. The growing perception that money from special interest groups heavily influences political decisions has increased the gap between the politicians and the public. The numbers of those voting in presidential elections has declined from 64 percent of the adults in 1960 to 49 percent in 1996. The staging of photo opportunities by candidates and negative campaigning reflect the increasing importance of the media in American politics. Politicians have learned that the media are critical in getting elected, and in getting reelected. Endorsement by a political party is not as important as favorable press coverage for oneself and negative coverage of an opponent.

The rising importance of the mass media has an almost inverse relationship to the decline in the influence of political parties. By the use of investigative reporting, politicians have become more vulnerable to critical media coverage.

Political struggles are increasingly carried on outside the electoral process, which discourages popular participation in elections. Through the technique of investigations and leaks of potentially damaging information intended to negate election results, political power is splintered, denying elected officials a secure political base to effectively pursue policy initiatives. Those dissatisfied with the electoral results increasingly attempt to make public any negative information regarding elected or appointed government officials by leaks to the media. The subsequent investigation often arouses hostile attitudes toward the individual or the political party being investigated. Supporters become passive under the attack, lest they be viewed as favoring the alleged misconduct. Embattled supporters are strongly tempted to abandon a beleaguered politician, especially if the charges appear to be substantive. These tactics prevent an electoral winner from the fruits of their victory. The result is weakened government.

The break-in at the Democratic national headquarters known as Watergate is sometimes pointed out as the first example of a steady leaking of revelations of misconduct leading to further investigations and the indictment of several federal officials, ultimately forcing President Nixon's resignation. In this case, however, there was evidence not only of a burglary, but the payment of large sums of money from the White House to buy the silence of those who carried out the break-in. Subsequently, the Iran-Contra conflict revealed violations of the Boland amendment which prohibited the selling of arms to Iran. Arms were sold in secret to Iran from the military inventory and the funds received for those arms, rather than being returned to the Treasury, were diverted to fund the Nicaraguan Contras against the specific instructions of Congress. Several high-ranking members of the Bush administration were the subject of criminal prosecutions for their role in Iran-Contra. President Bush pardoned several administration officials before leaving office, charging that the Democrats were trying to criminalize policy differences.

Members of both political parties subsequently attacked prominent members of the opposite party in an effort to weaken their opponents. Republicans drove House Speaker Jim Wright, Democratic Whip Tony Coehlo, and Dan Rostenkowski from office for financial misdeeds. Republican forces also scuttled the nomination of Lani Guiner as Assistant Attorney General for Civil Rights by characterizing her as a radical liberal. Those who orchestrated the attack readily acknowledged their effort and indicated that they had a score to settle with the Democrats for their opposition to the nomination of Robert Bork and Clarence Thomas to the Supreme Court.

After the Republican takeover of both houses of Congress in 1994, Republicans such as Senator Alphonse D'Amato of New York made clear their intention to embarrass President Clinton by drawn out hearings on possible wrongdoing over investments known as Whitewater. Republicans charged that an earlier independent counsel appointed to look into Whitewater had not been aggressive enough. A new independent counsel, a well-known Republican activist was appointed to pursue the allegations more aggressively. There was daily coverage of the investigation which focused on charges leveled against First Lady Hillary Clinton. The official investigations were aided by unofficial legal, political, and journalistic attacks funded by Richard Mellon Scaife, heir to the Mellon banking fortune, who gave millions to conservative foundations to challenge the Clinton White House.

There is no reason to believe that the level of political corruption is greater today than before 1970; however, the increasing use of negative campaigning and attack politics, and damaging press leaks contributes to voter anger towards government. These tactics undermine the legitimacy of government, fuel anti-government sentiment, and reduce the ability of the government to govern. Voter alienation also reduces turnout.

The Scope of Government Activity

A partial explanation for the decline in confidence in government since 1964 is that the string of successes from the Great Depression through World War II and the commitment of the government to maintain full employment led to a level of confidence that was unrealistic to maintain. Confidence may decline even though performance remains the same if the government is engaged in more controversial policy making such as environmental conditions, health and safety, or racial and gender issues. Even if the public generally approves of public policy making in this area, there is likely to be a greater sense of government trespass into areas best left to private choice.

The framers of the Constitution were products of the Enlightenment with the result that individuals were given control over various aspects of decision making, such as religious questions. Government was to be more limited. The preamble superbly states the purpose and *raison d'etre* of democratic government when it states its purpose is to form a more perfect union and to: (a) establish justice, (b) insure domestic tranquility, (c) provide for the common defense, (d) promote the general welfare, and (e) secure the blessings of liberty for themselves and for posterity. This list has been used to justify government public policy making. "To promote the general welfare" is the one that has the greatest potential to expand and justify any government policy.

Today, however, the American government's effort to "promote the general welfare" lags behind that of many other governments in providing a basic level of education, health care, housing, or income. Clearly there is less consensus on what it means to "promote the general welfare" in the United States than in many other advanced countries.

Voters make many inconsistent demands upon their political representatives. Candidates, taking the pulse of the American electorate through polling, assess what will have the greatest appeal and then offer a package deal of policies to the voters in which the inconsistencies are muted. And voters are inclined to respond without scrutinizing the incompatible nature of their demands. For example, polls indicate that in the late 1990s most Americans support increased government spending on health care, while they oppose any tax increase to pay for it; in fact, they are inclined to vote for candidates favoring tax cuts, which makes it more difficult to eliminate budget deficits. In a like manner, Americans have reacted enthusiastically to the declining price of gasoline by consuming more of it, while at the same time they indicate a desire for reduced dependence on oil from the Middle East. Yet they oppose any increase in taxes on gas consumption that would reduce demand for oil from the Middle East and could be used for research on alternative fuels.

THE IMPACT OF INSTITUTIONS ON THE PRESENT AND FUTURE

The Founding Fathers were aware of the above-mentioned contradictions in voter preferences which discouraged political candidates as entrepreneurs from considering long range goals when seeking election. They also desired to protect the citizenry from the arbitrariness of dictatorial authority, with which they were all too familiar from dealings with the British monarchy. The institutional design of government put in place by the framers of the Constitution provides important pathways for policy development. Key institutions provide focal points for examining public policy in America. The most conspicuous feature of the American political system is the **institutional fragmentation** and decentralized sources of power.

A major reason for frustration in dealing effectively with society's problems is the basic design and evolution of the Constitution. **The Constitution was purposely designed to make governing difficult—not to simplify political choices but to complicate them.** Rather than entrusting political leaders with sufficient control, it hinders them with insufficient authority.

The members of the Constitutional Convention agreed that the Continental Congress had erred in the direction of being too weak and powerless when it wrote the Articles of Confederation, which unified the executive and legislative powers; individual liberty had not been threatened, but the national government was totally dependent on the states to validate and ratify all its actions, and could not control the competitive impulses of the states that worked against the common national interest. It had also become apparent that the European powers sought to exploit the competition between states regarding overlapping claims on western territories and trade and tariff policies in order to weaken the new nation.

The failure of government under the Articles of Confederation to meet these and other challenges was the reason for the 1787 convention held in Philadelphia. The delegates agreed on the need to develop a new form of national government that could act with more vigor and dispatch. And while there were disagreements on many features of the proposed government, there was no disagreement on the principle of **separation of powers—the notion that the powers of government must be separated into legislative, judicial, and executive branches.** They believed that this separation—"fragmentation" is probably a better description—would make a tyrannical concentration of power inconceivable. The forced *sharing* of powers would make the concentration of power difficult. James Madison also expressed concern that a legislature could not be counted upon to act for the common good when competing issues were presented.[26] Ultimately, **checks and balances** were introduced, designed to prevent any power from becoming the undisputed dominant force by being balanced against, or checked by, another power source within the government. Thus governmental power was divided among the three branches, and each branch was to be given authority to prevent encroachments on its power by the others. As Madison said in his famous maxim, "ambition must be made to counter ambition."[27]

At the time of the Constitutional Convention, every state, with the exception of Pennsylvania, had a bicameral legislature, so the compromise, although barely adopted, was a well-known concept throughout the states. The Senate was intended to be more independent of public control than the House, so members were given longer terms. Also, Senators were to be appointed by the state governments rather than elected directly by the people in an effort to restrain too much democracy. As a compromise, to enhance the status of the House of Representatives, it was given exclusive power to originate revenue bills. The compromise conciliated the small states by allowing them to dominate in the Senate and the large states by allowing them to dominate in the House.

The executive branch that was to administer and execute the laws adopted by the legislature was treated in a rather cursory manner, but there were fears here too. Benjamin Franklin worried that a unified executive had the potential to drift toward monarchy because of a natural human tendency to prefer strong government. The Constitution says little about the powers of the presidency. Chief Executives have relied upon the clause that declares "the executive power shall be vested in a president" to expand their authority. The Constitution does not even define "executive power" which has allowed presidents to claim that their actions fell within the realm of inherent executive powers not precisely spelled out in the Constitution. **The framers of the Constitution clearly intended to design the institutions of government to slow the policy process through the system of checks and balances in the belief that it would help reason to triumph over passion.**

---

[26]In *The Federalist #10* Madison stated: "No man is allowed to be a judge in his own cause because his interest would certainly bias his judgment, and, not improbably, corrupt his integrity. . . . Yet what are many of the most important acts of legislature but so many judicial determinations, not indeed concerning the rights of single persons, but concerning the rights of large bodies of citizens? And what are the different classes of legislators but advocates and parties to the causes which they determine? . . . It is in vain to say that enlightened statesmen will be able to adjust these clashing interests and render them all subservient to the public good. Enlightened statesmen will not always be at the helm."

[27]James Madison, *The Federalist, #51.*

Over time presidential power has expanded. Congress has responded to a more assertive presidency by defending and extending its own authority through more specific instructions on how public monies can be spent. Indeed, it is Congress that has created and authorized the funding of various important agencies of the government such as the Securities and Exchange Commission, the Federal Reserve Board, the Interstate Commerce Commission, and other regulatory bodies. Presidents have consistently sought greater autonomy in dealing with these agencies. But every grant of additional authority to the president has been accompanied by protections assuring congressional ability to shape the actions of the agency involved.

Because the Founding Fathers wrote obscurely about the nature of the federal court system, some argue that they did not want a strong judicial branch. However the Constitution makes explicit the authority of the judicial branch to resolve disputes between state and federal laws. The federal courts' responsibility is to determine which power is exclusive to the federal government, which is exclusive to the states, and which is shared by both. The Constitution also directs the federal courts to resolve disputes between citizens of the different states. This authority grew over time because, as the U.S. national economy developed, citizens turned to the federal court system to resolve many disputes. Judicial review, or the authority to declare a law unconstitutional, is not directly mentioned in the Constitution but it is implied. Although the court system is structured in a loose hierarchy with lower courts subject to Supreme Court decisions, it often does not work that way in reality. Differing and conflicting decisions often emerge from parallel courts. Litigants therefore "district shop" to find courts that may be more favorably disposed to their concerns. Lower courts are frequently accused of deliber-ately misapplying or misinterpreting higher court rulings. And the Supreme Court hears a smaller portion of the rising tide of cases addressed at the lower levels.

The American government has expanded in ways that would have astounded the Founding Fathers. However the survival of the key features of their design—decentral-ization, separation of powers, checks and balances, and limited government—affirms the permanence of their effort. The fragmentation defies the effort to bring more orderly and empirical approaches to the policy process.

Federalism and Fragmentation

One of the greatest obstacles faced by the framers of the Constitution was the knowl-edge that, regardless of the design of the document, they had to obtain ratification from the state legislatures for it to go into effect. Consequently, it was understood that the states would have to retain significant autonomy regardless of other governing arrange-ments. The difficulty then was to strengthen the national government so that it could carry out its will in certain necessary areas while reassuring the states that they would retain all their essential powers. The delegates crafted a federal system because that was the most they could hope to get accepted by the states. It was recognized that under the Articles of Confederation the states had ultimate authority, leaving the national govern-ment bereft of energy for meaningful policy making. As in other areas of constitutional debate the Federalists were not able to agree on a precise relationship between the national and state governments.

A major concern of the delegates in Philadelphia was to design a national government with enough power to protect private property and provide economic stability.[28] Although they accepted the principle that government has a responsibility to protect everyone's right to life, liberty, and property, it is clear that property held a preferred position. On the one hand, they wanted to place the protection of property and commerce in the hands of the national government to protect them from state legislatures. But on the other, they wanted to ensure that the national government would not itself jeopardize commerce or private property. The delegates also specifically forbade the states to tax imports or exports, to coin money, to enter into treaties, or to impair obligations and contracts.

The Federalists were also concerned about the possibility of power being fragmented between the national government and states in a system of federalism since they had observed the threats to property and to national unity that could occur when authority was too decentralized. See figure 4.1.

While they feared the tyrannical rule of despots, they had also experienced the difficulties of a government that lacked the ability to act because it had insufficient power under the Articles of Confederation. State governments ran up huge debts to finance the Revolutionary War. In the aftermath, the states raised taxes to repay the debt, which threatened many farmers with bankruptcy and farm foreclosures. Farmers frequently faced jail for their inability to pay their debts. The threat of armed rebellion over issues of debts and taxes led to Shays' Rebellion. The rebellion by Daniel Shays, a Revolutionary War veteran, on behalf of beleaguered farmers never seriously threatened the government, but raised alarm over the inadequacy of the Articles of Confederation to maintain internal order. Madison expressed his concern over the threat from those who would nullify debts, contracts, or taxes in *The Federalist #10*, when he decried "a rage for paper money, for an abolition of debts, for an equal division of property, or for any other improper or wicked project." Therefore Article VI of the Constitution was added which contained the **supremacy clause** stating that the Constitution and the laws of the national government made in pursuance of its provisions are the supreme law of the land. The authority of the national government was expanded at the expense of the states when the federal government began to deal with interstate commerce, economic development and recessions, and successive crises caused by wars and military activity.

The distribution of political power in the Constitution between the national government and the states would make it difficult for government at either level to threaten property rights. The fragmentation of authority would make it very difficult for any political interest to gain control of sufficient levers of power to produce any public policy adverse to the interests of the propertied class. By definition, a federal arrangement would make any unified policy very burdensome to achieve. But the actual balance of power between

---

[28]The concern of the delegates to the convention about protecting private property has been well documented. See Calvin C. Jillson and Cecil L. Eubanks, "The Political Structure of Constitution Making: The Federal Convention of 1787," *American Journal of Political Science,* vol. 28, no. 3 (August 1984), pp. 435–58. The view that the delegates' economic self-interest was the basis for private property and economic concerns was popularized by Charles Beard, *An Economic Interpretation of the Constitution* (New York: Free Press, 1913, reprinted in 1965). On economic stability see also John P. Roche, "The Founding Fathers: A Reform Caucus in Action," *American Political Science Review,* vol. 55, no. 4 (December 1961), pp. 799–816.

FIGURE 4-1
THE FRAGMENTATION OF POWER IN THE U.S. GOVERNMENT.

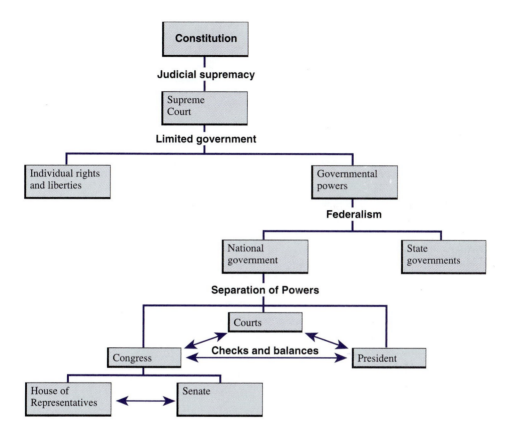

the national government and the states has been determined by political realities rather than through law or political theory. For the first seventy years of government under the Constitution, the national government was very tentative in exerting its authority. There were sectional differences between the South, which opposed effective national government, and the industrial North, which wanted greater national control of trade and tariff policies. Thus, American economic development resulted in regional economies with competing and diverse interests. Different regions have competed with each other to shape national policy regarding taxes, tariffs, and regulatory policies.

States have not retreated from the competition for power however. Many federal policies rely on states to implement the programs. States have power through the dual banking system and many regulations imposed by states. They have become more active in passing environmental legislation, consumer protection, and occupational health and safety laws. States also often compete with each other to attract business and investment to their jurisdiction by offering tax exemptions to business, suspending state regulations of business, providing loan guarantees, and even direct tax subsidies.

CASE STUDY

THE U.S. SENATE: UNDEMOCRATIC AND
BECOMING MORE SO

The U.S. Senate is one of the least representative legislative bodies in the western world and will become more so in the next century. A basic principle of democratic representation is that each person's vote should be equal. The Senate is designed to provide equal representation of states rather than on the size of the constituency. The result is that an ever smaller minority of the electorate elects a majority of the senators. California has 66 times as many people as Wyoming. Texas, with more than 19 million people, has only two senators—like Montana, which has a population of less than 1 million.

From the eighteenth century to the present, the ratio of large to small state populations has grown from 19 to 1 to 66 to 1. Today, half of the Senate can be elected by only 15 percent of the American population. And the problem will get worse because almost all of the population growth in the foreseeable future is projected to be concentrated in a few already populous states (especially California). Right now just 10 percent of the population elects 40 percent of the Senate. Thus, Senators representing about 10 percent of the population can block reforms through the filibuster. The result is minority rule. For example:

- The Republicans controlled the Senate from 1980–1986. During that period Republican senators as a group received fewer votes nationwide than did Democratic senatorial candidates. If the Senate were elected based on population, the Democratic Party would have controlled the Senate through Reagan's eight years in office.

- In order to pass his 1993 budget package, President Clinton had to cave in to demands by senators from Montana, Arkansas, and Louisiana to lower the gasoline tax.
- Clinton's 1993 domestic stimulus program, which was targeted at metropolitan areas in large states like California, was killed by conservative Republican and Democratic senators from underpopulated states like Oklahoma.

The Senate exaggerates the power of rural, mostly white, conservatives.

The Senate was created at the Constitutional Convention to satisfy small states like Rhode Island, that demanded equal representation. In the *Federalist #22*, Alexander Hamilton criticized the equal representation of the states under the Articles of Confederation as one of the worst defects of that system. Allotting representation on the basis of statehood rather than population, he wrote, "contradicts the fundamental maxim of republican government, which requires that the sense of the majority should prevail."

In the 1960s, the Supreme Court struck down malapportioned state legislatures as unconstitutional, arguing that they violated the principle of one person, one vote. In 1963, the Supreme Court rejected state arguments that they could mimic the structure of the federal legislature and have one house not based on population. The Court declared in *Gray v. Sanders* that "the conception of political equality from the Declaration of Independence to Lincoln's Gettysburg Address to the 15th, 17th, and 19th Amendments can mean only one thing—one person, one vote." Thus the Supreme Court ruled that the structural principle underlying state senates was unjust and unconstitutional.

Michael Lind, "75 Stars" *Mother Jones,* January–February 1998, pp. 44–49.

Political Parties

Political parties play a critical role in modern democratic society. In fact mass political parties first developed in the United States with the election of 1800. Even before that, Alexander Hamilton wanted support for a national bank and tried to forge a coalition across the Constitutionally separated branches of the executive and Congress. The checks and balances between the branches of government made competition an inherent part of the Constitutional order. Hamilton's effort to join together what the Constitutional Convention had separated provided the foundation of the Federalist party, the first political party in America. The political party developed into an "indispensable instrument that brought cohesion and unity, and hence effectiveness, to the government as a whole by linking the executive and legislative branches in a bond of common interest."[29] In point of fact however, "What the Constitution separates our political parties do not combine. The parties are themselves composed of separated organizations sharing public authority."[30] A unified national government, in which the executive and the Congress are controlled by the same political party, has not always guaranteed cooperation, but it has given a strong impetus toward building a coalition to bridge the gap between those institutions and provide an effective vehicle for policy adoption and implementation.

The emergence of the Federalist party brought into being a countervailing coalition of political interests. Thomas Jefferson led this **coalition** composed primarily of agrarian interests to oppose the merchant/financial interests of Hamilton and the Federalists. Jefferson was the champion of those opposed to a strong national government. They became known as the Jeffersonian-Republicans to indicate their opposition to the Federalists led by Alexander Hamilton, who supported the moneyed interests and wanted a strong national government to protect them from the "excesses of democracy." The Federalists referred to Jefferson's emerging political party as the Democratic-Republicans in an effort to link them pejoratively with the excesses of democracy. The Jeffersonians accepted the term as an indication of their faith in the ability of rational people to manage their own affairs without government intervention. They dropped the "Republican" part of the label and began calling themselves "Democrats." This is the oldest political party in the United States still in existence. The Federalists went out of existence by 1820.

In early America, because of the extension of suffrage to a large and relatively unorganized electorate, parties became the vehicle to mobilize voters to go to the polls. But in order to mobilize the electorate to get the vote out, party elites have had to make concessions on a routine basis.

In fact, as E. E., Schattschneider notes, "Decentralization of power is by all odds the important single characteristic of the American major party; more than anything else this trait distinguishes it from all others. Indeed, once this truth is understood, nearly everything about American parties is illuminated."[31] Nonetheless, he states that "The rise of political parties is indubitably one of the principal distinguishing marks of

---

[29]James L. Sundquist, "Needed: A Political Theory for the New Era of Coalition Government in the United States," *Political Science Quarterly,* vol. 103 (Winter 1988–89), p. 614.

[30]Richard E. Neustadt, *Presidential Power: The Politics of Leadership from FDR to Carter* (New York: John Wiley & Sons, 1980), p. 26.

[31]E. E. Schattschneider, *Party Government* (New York: Holt, Rinehart and Winston, 1942), p. 129.

modern government. Political parties created democracy; modern democracy is unthinkable save in terms of parties."[32]

A political party's main goal is to elect governmental officeholders united under a given label. The party serves to link the elites in governmental institutions and harmonize their views to the broad outlines of a public policy agenda. Parties also serve to link individuals to government and at minimum give people the feeling that they can affect policy decisions and that they are not completely powerless. Of particular importance is the political party's effort to provide an antidote to the rational ignorance of many potential voters. Party labels evoke powerful messages about the general posture parties might take on many issues thereby reducing the amount of specific information required of voters.

Political parties also serve as a collection place for different interest groups. Parties must represent overarching values and goals that are widely shared across the nation. By aggregating separate interest groups into one party, each group must moderate its demands to hold the coalition together to win elections. By cooperating, such groups can hope to get some of their demands met. The best known example of providing a coalition of different interest groups that together commanded a majority was the Democratic Party coalition constructed by Franklin D. Roosevelt in 1932. It consisted of many groups, several of which overlapped: Catholics, Jews, organized labor, blacks, Irish, Italians, Poles, and farmers. As long as it held together the Democratic coalition was unbeatable. It was responsible for most of the progressive legislation of the twentieth century including labor legislation, social welfare legislation (Social Security), and progressive economic policies. More recently, the coalition began to erode.

The Republican party, beginning with President Ronald Reagan, formed a coalition of several economic and noneconomic conservative groups, such as the Christian Coalition, southerners, the gun-lobby, and anti-abortion groups. The Republicans have had difficulty in maintaining this coalition because of the strong ideological fervor of some of the groups who resist compromising with other coalition members. For example, the anti-abortion activists and many from the Christian Coalition want to require pledges of support and insert platform planks to provide a litmus test for candidates on the abortion issue as a requirement for receiving campaign finance assistance. The issue continues to roil through party membership.

The single-member, simple-plurality, winner-take-all electoral system of the United States is tremendously significant for the political process. The single-member plurality system means that the candidate with the most votes wins the election and the winning margin is immaterial. This system encourages political parties to appeal to as broad a spectrum as possible to win a plurality of the votes. Parties with broad appeal squeeze out narrowly focused parties. Ultimately the system encourages as few parties as possible (the minimum number being two) to compete for the vital center. More recently, as noted above, conservative elites in the Republican Party have tried to mobilize public opinion in favor of a distinctly more conservative stance, instead of shifting the party to a more centrist position.

[32]E. E. Schattschneider, ibid., p. 1.

At different times in American history, critical elections in response to some pronounced set of issues such as war or economic crises, resulted in new coalitions under the banners of the two political parties. These new ruling coalitions permitted a party to pursue a coherent set of policy agendas for a period. But as the crisis faded, the coalitions tended to decay as well. While coalitions last, they may significantly influence the roles that elites play within those coalitions.

Outside the parties, interest groups mobilize to advance their interests, and at minimum to protect them. Corporations may use their resources to contribute to electoral candidates directly as well as through professional or trade associations. They may additionally be represented by professional lobbyists who represent several different corporations or businesses in general such as the National Association of Manufacturers. Over 3,000 corporations have representatives in Washington, with over 500 professional associations and over 400 additional groups representing foreign business interests.[33] While there are approximately 100 labor organizations represented, labor has not been a credible threat to business interests in the United States.

The overrepresentation of some groups compared to others is clearly a matter of economic resources. For example, a study in the mid-1980s noted that while individuals occupying managerial and administrative positions make up only about 7 percent of the population, business associations with representatives in Washington accounted for over 70 percent of the interest groups. Conversely, nonfarm workers made up slightly over 40 percent of the population but comprise only about 4 percent of the interest groups.[34]

The QWERTY Phenomenon

In Professor Krugman's work, *Peddling Prosperity,* he points out that the layout of the keyboard on your personal computer has the same arrangement as those of old-fashioned typewriters from the nineteenth century.[35] Why do we still have this keyboard arrangement? It is not the most efficient arrangement of keys in terms of finger movement. The QWERTY arrangement was designed for early mechanical typewriters. It was an advantage to have typists type more slowly to reduce the tendency of keys to jam. Improved designs, electric typewriters, and eventually electronic keyboards made the problem of jamming keys a thing of the past. It would make sense to shift to other keyboards with a more efficient design. But it is too late! Typists learn on QWERTY keyboards and manufacturers make QWERTY typewriters because that is what typists know. The keyboard, the state of the art with the invention of typewriters, became "locked in" despite the advances in technology. Paul Krugman and other economists found that stories like that of the typewriter keyboard are pervasive in the economy. Many technology choices have a striking resemblance to the QWERTY tale. For example, Bill Gates and his associates

[33]Marc Allan Eisner, *The State in the American Political Economy* (Englewood Cliffs, NJ: Prentice Hall, 1995), p. 24.

[34]Robert Salisbury, "Interest Representation—The Dominance of Institutions." *American Political Science Review,* vol. 78, 1 (1984); pp. 64–76.

[35]This discussion of the QWERTY phenomenon is taken from Paul Krugman's discussion of this idea as it pertains to economics. We use it here because its application to politics is readily apparent. See Paul Krugman, *Peddling Prosperity: Economic Sense and Nonsense in the Age of Diminished Expectations* (New York: W. W. Norton, 1994), chap. 9.

developed the DOS software system and sold it to IBM. Since IBM was the major manufacturer of computers, all other systems had an incentive to be "IBM compatible." Although there were other operating systems with similar capabilities, the DOS system became "locked in."

This led many economists to adopt a whole new way of thinking about economics. This approach led many to reject the idea that markets invariably lead the economy to a unique best solution. Rather the outcome of market competition may depend on historical accidents. Such accidents of history force us down pathways created by earlier events. This "path dependence" limits our freedom to choose, and where we end up depends on what happened along the way.

What does this have to do with public policy? Probably a great deal. The Founding Fathers designed a Constitution which, despite flaws observable with 20/20 hindsight, is the oldest written constitution continuously in force. On the one hand, the document attests to the benefits and effectiveness of such a well-crafted document that represents the collective political will of the American people to maintain a republican form of government.

On the other hand, there is great frustration in dealing effectively with society's problems that stem from the basic design and evolution of the Constitution. By decentralizing power and authority, the Founding Fathers designed the Constitution to make governing difficult. The result has left political leaders weak and unable to make binding decisions. Popular participation in the American system is encouraged by means of picking candidates through petition drives, primary elections, and party caucuses. Since money is essential to running campaigns, and political parties cannot provide it in significant amounts, candidates must develop independent fundraising capabilities. In this system, "all politics is local" in that individuals must organize and run campaigns on local levels. This permits politicians to ignore or even oppose their party's positions on the national level.

In Europe, parliamentary democracies function much differently. The constitutional systems of Europe centralize power. In the United States, the judiciary is a powerful check on presidential and congressional actions. In Europe, courts cannot overturn acts of Parliament. In Europe, candidates for office are chosen by party leaders, which makes successful candidates accountable to their parties.

At the heart of the low esteem in which the government is held in the United States is its inability to deal effectively with issues in which there is a clear national consensus. For example, public opinion polls have indicated for the last twenty years that a clear preponderance of public opinion is supportive of stricter gun control laws, but only recently has any progress been made in this area. Also for the last decade a significant majority of the American people has felt that the government is not sufficiently supportive of affordable housing, health care, high-quality education, or protecting the environment, although leaders of both parties solemnly profess their grave concern with these problems.

The potential veto points found in the separation of powers, checks and balances, and federalism among others make it extremely difficult to respond to many felt needs of the public. Once the basic Constitutional parameters are set down, the state is resistant to further change.

However, democracy is not a static political order. Rather it is an ideal that we must constantly pursue. Anthony Downs stated it in the following terms:

> Democracy is a dynamic process of governance and even of living in general, not a static institutional construct. Supporters of democracy must continue to change its specific meaning and forms, without destroying its fundamental nature.[36]

Democracy is something we must strive for, although, like perfection, it will never be finally achieved. A democratic society that does not constantly explore new possibilities for further democratization will tend to solidify the existing power relationships of the society. The elites will try to "freeze" the power relationships by manipulating voters through campaign contributions and opportunistic politicians.

Democratic governments vary greatly from each other because each system reflects its own unique political, social, economic, and cultural values and has evolved through its own distinct historical experience. However, despite the differences, all have been forced to address the changing interpretation of three core values central to democratic government: (1) the right to vote and participate in a meaningful way in government, (2) individual liberty, and (3) equality.

We have a democratic form of government and a capitalist economic system. The evolution of a democracy joined with a capitalist political economy can evolve in many different ways. A capitalist economy, like a democracy, can never stand still. It must constantly grow through processes of creative destruction, or stagnate and decay. Historically, capitalism and democracies have been thought to mutually reinforce each other since liberal democracies have originated only within capitalist economies. The state is required to carry out the minimalist functions of enforcing contracts, maintaining civil order, protecting private property rights, and issuing and controlling money, all of which are essential for market capitalism to function well. Otherwise the state should remain aloof and neutral in the competition between individuals in their own self-interest. Market capitalism does not require a particular form of a political system to carry out these functions. Accordingly, authoritarian political systems such as those found in Singapore or Chile, may also exist in a capitalist framework.

VOTING AND CITIZEN PARTICIPATION

Although Thomas Jefferson, writing in the Declaration of Independence, stated that it was self-evident "that all men are created equal" and that governments derive "their just powers from the consent of the governed," the framers did not go so far as to permit all adult citizens to vote. That right was restricted to citizens who were also male property holders. In the debates at the Constitutional Convention, proposals to explicitly broaden the franchise were firmly resisted based on the notion that if the less deserving intruded their needs on the political process it would descend to mob rule. If the conflict is limited to the more "gentlemanly" disagreements among the more fortunate, proper order and decorum are maintained.

---

[36]Anthony Downs, "The Evolution of Democracy," *Daedalus,* 1987, vol. 116 (3), pp. 119–48.

The members of the political community most benefitting from this arrangement were eager to lock in these state functions as an essential requirement of "democratic government." Privileged individuals and groups attempted to defend themselves and the state from further democratization. They maintained that extending the franchise to new individuals and groups would undermine good government.[37] The rising tide of democratization with the principle of citizen participation drowned the opposition. One barrier after another was swept away before the onrushing tide: property qualifications, slavery, poll taxes, and gender restrictions. Removing legal barriers to the franchise left informal constraints in place until the last quarter of the twentieth century.

Liberty versus Equality

The sixteenth-century Enlightenment left a legacy which held that all individuals by virtue of their membership in the human community possess natural rights. These rights include the individual's **right to liberty, which refers to the individual's right to freedom from government interference with private actions.** A second natural right developed by political philosophers during the Enlightenment was the individual's **right to equality, which emphasized a disposition toward the political and social equality of all citizens.** Thomas Jefferson held that liberty and equality were not incompatible rights for those pursuing egalitarian or libertarian goals.

However it is widely held today that there is an inescapable trade-off between these two democratic principles.[38] An example illustrates the trade-off. In the United States, where liberty is achieved at the cost of significant economic inequalities, the ratio of the pay of CEOs to that of the lowest paid full-time worker in their company is over 125 to 1. In Japan, a country with more egalitarian governmental policies, it is 25 to 1.

The Impact of Increased Voting Rights on the Equality Principle

The increase in voting rights has influenced the interpretation of the principle of equality. **Democratic governments are agents by which private conflicts are transferred to the political arena and are made into public conflicts.**[39] The democratic method consists of an institutional arrangement for political decisions in which individuals are given the power to decide by winning a competitive struggle for the people's vote.[40] In

---

[37]Various conservative voices have been raised in defense of the lack of participation in democratic processes by many citizens. For example, Michel Crozier, Samuel P. Huntington, and Joji Watanuki wrote in *The Crisis of Democracy: Report of the Governability of Democracies to the Trilateral Commission* (New York: New York University Press, 1975), on the need to protect government functions from too much democracy.

[38]Social Darwinists such as William Graham Sumner argued explicitly that Darwinism justified the free and unregulated capitalist competition and the extreme social inequality that would result. He wrote: "We cannot go outside of this alternative: liberty, inequality, survival of the fittest; not—liberty, equality, survival of the unfittest." See William Graham Sumner, "The Challenge of Facts," in *The Challenge of Facts and Other Essays,* Albert Galloway Keller (ed.), (New Haven: Yale University Press, 1914), p. 25.

[39]See E. E. Schattschneider, *The Semisovereign People* (New York: Holt, Rinehart and Winston, 1960), for a fuller explanation of the thesis regarding the significance of the scope of the conflict for the outcome of political struggles.

[40]See Joseph A. Schumpeter, *Capitalism, Socialism, and Democracy*, 3d ed. (New York: Harper Torchbacks 1962), p. 269.

this theory, the political process is an agent of socialization of disputes between special interests. When voting was limited to adult male property holders, most Americans were merely bystanders observing the debates between the elite political contenders. Political struggles between elites could ignore the disenfranchised who were unable to affect the outcome. With each enlargement of the franchise, successive groups of bystanders were eligible to get involved in political quarrels. In fact, the bystanders had the power through their votes to determine the outcome of political disputes.

In any conflict, those who are winning would like to limit the scope of the conflict to the participants already involved to assure a favorable outcome. It is in the interest of those who are losing to enlarge the scope to involve the bystanders on their behalf. In fact, the franchise was first enlarged when Thomas Jefferson, as a leader of a group of elites, found it necessary to push for the expansion of the franchise in the name of a fuller liberty and equality for all. Had the Federalists been successful in maintaining a limited franchise, it is very doubtful that Jefferson would have been elected.

Since the inclusion of bystanders can change the outcome, the best time to limit the scope of the conflict is at the very beginning of the struggle, by mobilizing one's own forces to get a quick resolution before the opposition has time to mobilize new forces favoring its position. Throughout American history there has been a continuing battle between the effort to privatize or limit, and the struggle to socialize or expand, the scope of political and social conflict. Many arguments are used to try to limit the scope of conflicts or even to keep the nonpropertied or poor out of the political arena altogether: the right to privacy, individual freedom, private enterprise, limited government, states' rights, and individual liberty.

As the franchise was expanded to include the poorer members of society, they gained potential political influence. Political elites were forced to compete for their votes to gain a legislative majority. To form winning coalitions, political parties had to take into consideration the interests of the less affluent and support their "general welfare." In time, a series of programs emerged beginning with Franklin Roosevelt's New Deal and continuing to the present, all of which taken together constitute the "welfare state." **A welfare state is a governing principle in which the public policy of the government is to provide economic and social benefits for each of its citizens.** The welfare state provides public assistance to those without the ability to relieve their problems of unemployment, income insecurity, health care, physical and mental disabilities, old age, and property losses due to natural disasters.

In fact, **the welfare state is a natural result of extending the franchise and democracy's equality principle.** Once lower-income people also had the power to vote, they possessed at least one tool, previously an exclusive privilege of wealth, that gave them political influence to benefit themselves. The effect has been to reduce the large income inequalities that result from unregulated markets. This is accomplished primarily through a redistribution that takes place though taxes and income transfers toward lower income individuals. The overall effect is to increase economic equality slightly.

The welfare state has not resulted so much from the pursuit of philosophical principles of social justice as it is a natural consequence of the universal right of suffrage and the economic vagaries of market capitalism. Providing citizens with individual liberty to pursue their economic self-interest necessarily reduces economic equality. And in a capitalist political economy, economic differences breed political inequalities. Once there is economic inequality, those with more are in a stronger position to further reinforce their preferred position in relation to those who are less well off.

However, policy decisions to increase economic equality through welfare state policies must by necessity constrain certain liberties. Taxes reduce the amount of money available for consumption and transfer that authority to the government. Regulation of working conditions, health and pension programs, environmental pollution, and minimum wage rates constrain the liberty of business owners.

Prior to giving the vote to ever larger shares of the citizens, the affluent property holders had a great deal of liberty, while the disenfranchised had very little. Laws in the eighteenth century permitted business owners to collude to hold wages down, while worker associations were outlawed. Labor laws in England prohibited a worker from moving from one parish to another to take advantage of higher wage rates.

Thus the poor, also being politically powerless, had a very qualified form of liberty. Those with money and property were not surprisingly the first to attain the ballot. The affluent have viewed with apprehension the broadening of political inclusion as weakening their power. An increase in liberty for the poor by encouraging their political participation may come at some expense of the heretofore unregulated liberties of the wealthy even though total freedom is increased. However the distribution of income and wealth in the United States and other countries shows that the top and bottom quintiles remain surprisingly steady in their share of economic resources. That is, the regulatory interference with individual liberties has not significantly reduced economic inequality. Indeed, economic inequality has been increasing at least since the early 1980s (see chap. 7).

There are many notions used to legitimize and encourage expanding the scope of political conflict: "whistle blowing," unions, political alliances, civil rights, equality, and justice. These tend to socialize conflict and invite outside intervention on behalf of those engaged in such struggles. A whistle blower by definition is someone who witnesses illegal or unethical behavior by superiors within an organization and therefore finds it necessary to go outside the organization for support to stop the behavior.

The Principle of Liberty

To illustrate the point, the Constitution was a democratic document by the standards of the time. But today, few would maintain that a system that permitted barriers to voting based on property ownership, racial, or gender considerations was a democratic system. Central to the idea of a democracy is a nation's commitment to the values of equality and tolerance. No one would concede in the year 2000, that any nation that permitted slavery, or did not guarantee the right to vote was democratic. That issue was notably settled by a military conflict because the Constitution was not able to provide a peaceful resolution of the issue. A nation approaches the democratic ideal to the extent that the people have control over the government in what *The Federalist* calls "a dependence on the people."[41] The ability of the people to change the government through elections is the ultimate power of the people. However, without an intelligent and well-informed

[41]*The Federalist #51.*

public this power cannot be exercised wisely. This is Jefferson's implication when he wrote: "If a nation expects to be ignorant and free, in a state of civilization, it expects what never was and never shall be." Therefore the democratic ideal is more closely approached to the extent that public control is meaningful, informed, and skillfully engaged rather than symbolic or manipulated.

We would also point out that unemployment in the United States was considered primarily a personal problem (the more affluent usually judged unemployment the natural result of a debilitating character weakness, laziness, or other immorality). Under the best of circumstances it was a personal tragedy. However since government was presumed to have no control over personal morality it was not in either case a social problem over which the government was thought to have responsibility.

The Great Depression and the election of Franklin D. Roosevelt (FDR) did much to change those views. The response of the New Deal included public works programs to create jobs, provide unemployment insurance, and a bewildering variety of other government programs. As a result, unemployment came to be considered a social problem and the responsibility of the government to resolve. The "Employment Act of 1946" states clearly that it is the obligation of the national government to try to create the conditions that will result in full employment. All democratic governments accept the obligation to conduct business-friendly policies to aid an expanding economy and full employment. Likewise, a government would not be considered democratic today, if it did not accept responsibility for the economic well-being of its citizens.

The traditional capitalist economic system survived in the United States as a result of the alleviation of those problems that capitalism handles poorly by the intervention of the Keynesian welfare state. Capitalism cannot resolve the problems of poverty, unemployment, income insecurity, and environmental pollution. Welfare state spending increased employment during periods of economic downturns. The "welfare state" legitimizes the capitalist system among those at the bottom of the ladder by softening the rough edges of the system.

CONCLUSION

1 An ideology is a set of beliefs about values and the role of government. In America today, liberalism and conservatism dominate the dichotomy of political views and values. Other ideologies such as communism or libertarianism exist on the fringes and do not exert significant influence. Although most people do not identify strongly with an ideology, they do nonetheless indicate a general tendency to view politics from a slightly more liberal or conservative perspective. Strongly held ideological convictions make it more difficult to objectively evaluate policy issues or to reach a compromise.

2 Classical liberals were concerned primarily with the notion that the best way to increase individual freedom was by protecting the individual *from* government. Classical conservatives were more concerned with preserving those institutions, such as the family and religion, that had grown over time and had a certain legitimacy. In the liberal view, governments should contract while the private sphere should grow. By the mid-1800s it became clear that although government authority had receded in many areas, corporate influence grew to replace the vacuum left by the state. As large corporations grew they influenced many aspects of social and economic welfare of individuals. As a result, modern liberals began to reject laissez-faire capitalism and concluded that the government could protect and enlarge individual freedom by regulating business and engaging in social welfare programs. Conservatives remained distrustful of government intervention in the economy and worried that too much government intervention would reduce the disciplines of the marketplace.

3 Two perspectives often utilized by policy scientists to analyze the world of public policy are the pluralist and elite models. The pluralist model assumes that multiple centers of power compete to influence public policy. Power in pluralist groups is wielded by those who occupy the top positions in those organizations. The elite perspective maintains that elites hold the critical positions of power in society. They manage conflict to ensure that the political debate and the policy changes do not threaten their elite positions.

4 Government failure to provide a clear direction in policy formulation and implementation has caused an increase in frustration and dissatisfaction among the electorate. Politicians have exploited the lack of direction by campaigning on anti-government platforms, which further reduces the credibility of government institutions.

5 American public policy has been profoundly influenced by the institutions of government created by the Founding Fathers. The separation of power, checks and balances, federalism, and limited government are a testimonial to the success of the framers' efforts to make government cumbersome and difficult to control. These barriers also contribute to the inefficiencies in policy making that many find so frustrating. The barriers to the formulation and implementation of new policy options reflect a bias against change.

6 Political parties were developed to overcome the separation of powers and checks and balances put in place by the framers. The American decentralized winner-take-all pluralistic system forces political parties to fight to position themselves in the center of the political spectrum.

7 Democracy in the American political system is something that we must seek although we never fully achieve it. The major tension in the political debate in America is between liberty and equality.

QUESTIONS FOR DISCUSSION

1 What are the shared values of American political culture?
2 Explain why many classical liberals are called conservative today.
3 Thomas Jefferson was a classical liberal and would be considered a liberal today. Why?
4 What political institutions are most responsible for defeating coherent public policy today?
5 Why were decentralized parties a natural outgrowth of the impact of the framers' design?
6 Why is democracy something that must be forever pursued?
7 Is there a natural tension between liberty and equality? Why?

KEY CONCEPTS

Jeremy Bentham

checks and balances

coalition

conservatism

elite theory

ideology

liberalism

John Stuart Mill

pluralism

utilitarianism

SUGGESTED READINGS

Peter Bachrach, *The Theory of Democratic Elitism: A Critique* (Boston: Little, Brown and Company, 1967).

Karl Dietrich Bracher, *The Age of Ideologies: A History of Political Thought in the Twentieth Century* (New York: St. Martin's, 1984).

Karen S. Cook, and Margaret Levi, (eds.) *The Limits of Rationality* (Chicago: The University of Chicago Press, 1990).

John S. Dryzek, *Democracy in Capitalist Times: Ideals, Limits, and Struggles* (New York: Oxford University Press, 1996).

Marc Allan Eisner, *The State in the American Political Economy* (Englewood Cliffs, NJ: Prentice Hall, Inc., 1995).

Francis Fukuyama, *The End of History and the Last Man* (New York: Free Press, 1992).

William Greider, *Who Will Tell the People: The Betrayal of American Democracy* (New York: Touchstone Book, 1992).

Alonzo Hamby, *Liberalism and Its Challengers,* 2d ed. (New York: Oxford University Press, 1992).

James Davison Hunter, *Culture Wars: The Struggle to Define America* (New York: Basic Books, 1992).

Robert Skidelsky, *The World After Communism: A Polemic for Our Times* (London: Macmillan, 1995).

5

ECONOMIC THEORY AS A
BASIS OF PUBLIC POLICY

Some knowledge of the nature of economic forces and economic theory is a prerequisite for thoughtful public policy analysis. The purpose of this chapter is to address the implications of economic theory for public policy. It is impossible to comprehend the significance of policy choices without some understanding of the economic theory underlying market capitalism. Adam Smith's *Wealth of Nations* is based upon the concept that the nation-state is a collection of people bound together in a shared responsibility for each other's mutual well-being. But the idea of a "national purpose" to promote the general welfare has come under increasing strain in recent years.

Political and economic theories that seek to explain the conditions of social and economic existence have moral as well as explanatory implications, while those who have prospered within a given economic system usually look for explanations that will support the moral legitimacy of their success. Those favored by the status quo derive an ideology from such theories to justify the continuance of the policies that brought them their good fortune. Those favored by the system are also dominant in the political and economic life of their societies. Thus, it is important to be aware of how theories can be adapted to the service of policies not originally foreseen when those theories were developed.

INTRODUCTION

Though not every public policy of the government involves questions of resource allocation, many do. In chapter 1 we saw that micro failures in the economy bring about situations that force government intervention to prevent free riders and to produce certain public goods. Individuals organize to distribute the costs of public goods among those people who receive the benefits. Cost sharing is necessary through government purchases to realize an ideal supply of a public good. Other failures, such as externalities, force government intervention to influence production or to determine who pays for certain goods. Members of society on occasion may decide that they are unhappy with the market determination of what, how, or for whom that society's goods are being produced. Government is also asked to intervene when real markets deviate from the ideal markets envisioned in classical economic theory.

The failures of the market provide specific justifications for government intervention through public policy. The trend of government growth and involvement in the public sector has increased dramatically in the United States since the 1930s. Until then the government was limited primarily to the basic functions of providing for defense, administering the system of justice, and providing a postal service. Since the Depression, and largely because of it, the federal government has become involved in a whole range of new activities including public works, environmental regulation, education, health care, income redistribution through income transfer programs like Social Security, and Medicare. Significant growth in government does not just mean at the federal level. State and local governments are even more important than the federal government as sources of employment and production.

Does economic theory have anything to say about what role the government should have in policies that affect the public sector? Can economic theory suggest what effect public versus private spending will have on the economy, job creation, and social well-being? Is it supportive or negative? Can it suggest what kind of policies should be used in certain situations? This chapter will explore these questions.

ADAM SMITH AND CLASSICAL OPTIMISM

Adam Smith (1723–1790) saw economics as a branch of moral philosophy with a mission to improve the condition of humanity, especially that of the poor. Writing in the latter half of the eighteenth century, he recommended a system of natural liberty in which the individual would be free to pursue his or her own interests. By pursuing one's self-interest, each person maximizes benefits for herself or himself or for other individuals and for society as a whole. The supporters of **mercantilism,** with whom Smith took issue, advocated government regulation because they believed that the selfish pursuit of one's own self-interest would lead to less wealth for everyone. The mercantilists viewed competition as a zero-sum scenario where more for one, by necessity, meant less for others. In 1776 Smith challenged that notion.

The year 1776 was pivotal for the Declaration of Independence and also for the publication of Adam Smith's *Wealth of Nations.* Both were basic manifestations of the movement away from authoritarian monarchical forms of governmental control, and toward individual liberty. The American Revolution attacked not only the political control of the American colonies by England, but also the system of economic authority which made that control inevitable. The colonists—and English entrepreneurs—had already experienced what Adam Smith argued: State domination of the economy inhibited new opportunities for increasing production and profits.

He maintained that if I want something from you that I cannot produce myself, I must make something you want and then agree upon an exchange. Both of us benefit because we agree to give up something that has less value to us personally than the products we receive. Thus the total welfare has been enhanced. As Smith stated in a famous passage: "It is not from the benevolence of the butcher, the brewer, or the baker, that we expect our dinner, but from their regard to their own interest."[1] According to his theory, self-interest and competition will eliminate two kinds of waste: unrealized trades and inefficient production. Conversely it will encourage mutually beneficial trades and efficient production.

Smith had none of the illusions of later classical economists that associated wealth with morality. He noted that people of the same trade seldom are in each other's company even on social occasions "but the conversation ends in a conspiracy against the public, or in some contrivance to raise prices."[2] He pointed out the concern of merchants only for their own self-interest:

> Our merchants and master-manufacturers complain much of the bad effects of high wages in raising the price, and thereby lessening the sale of their goods both at home and abroad. They say nothing concerning the bad effects of high profits. They are silent with regard to the pernicious effects of their own gains. They complain only of those of other people.[3]

Smith said that greed and competition are the driving forces of production.[4] Further, all goods have two prices: a **natural price** (today referred to as normal price) and a **market price.** He defined a natural price as the price that would have to be realized to cover the costs of production, with a small amount left over for a profit. He defined the market price as the price the product actually brings in the marketplace. Whenever the market price deviates from the natural price, it will be driven back in the direction of the natural price as if by an invisible hand. Every entrepreneur attempting to accumulate profits is held in check by other competitors who are also trying to attain a profit. This competition drives down the price of goods and reduces the revenue earned by each seller. In a market unrestrained by government, the competition between entrepreneurs erases excessive profits, employers are forced to compete for the best workers, workers

---

[1]Adam Smith, *An Inquiry into the Nature and Causes of the Wealth of Nations,* edited by Edwin Cannan (New York: G. P. Putnam's Sons, 1877; originally published in 1776), p. 27. Further on Smith said that there is an invisible hand which channels behavior to improve social welfare. He stated: "Every individual necessarily labours to render the annual revenue of the society as great as he can. He generally, indeed, neither intends to promote the public interest nor knows how much he is promoting it . . . he intends only his own gain and he is in this, as in many other cases, led by an invisible hand to promote an end which was no part of his intention. Nor is it always the worse for the society that it was no part of it. By pursuing his own interest he frequently promotes that of the society more effectually than when he really intends to promote it. I have never known much good done by those who affected to trade for the public good. It is an affectation, indeed, not very common among merchants, and very few words need be employed in dissuading them from it." (p. 354).

[2]Adam Smith, *The Wealth of Nations,* 6th ed. (London: Metheun & Co., Ltd., 1950), vol. 1, p. 144.

[3]Ibid., 110.

[4]Smith was against the government meddling with the market mechanism. As Robert Heilbroner has pointed out: "Smith never faced the problem . . . of whether the government is weakening or strengthening the market mechanism when it steps in with welfare legislation. . . . There was virtually no welfare legislation in Smith's day—the government was the unabashed ally of the governing classes. . . . The question of whether the working class should have a voice in the direction of economic affairs simply did not enter any respectable person's mind . . . by a strange injustice the man who warned that the grasping eighteenth-century industrialists 'generally have an interest to deceive and even to oppress the public' came to be regarded as their economic patron saint. Even today—in blithe disregard of his actual philosophy—Smith is generally regarded as a *conservative* economist, whereas in fact, he was more avowedly hostile to the *motives* of businessmen than most New Deal economists." See Robert Heilbroner, *The Worldly Philosophers,* 3d ed., rev. (New York: Simon and Schuster, 1967), pp. 63–64.

compete for the best jobs (usually defined in terms of wages and working conditions), and consumers compete to consume products. Consequently, producers are forced to search for the lowest-cost production methods. Finally, resources are distributed to their most highly valued use, and economic efficiency prevails.

According to Smith, the owners of business tend to reinvest their profits, thereby consuming little more than the workers. The entrepreneurs inadvertently share the produce of all their improvements with the workers, though they intend only "the gratification of their own vain and insatiable desires."[5] He continued this thought with the following:

> [Business owners] . . . are led by an invisible hand to make nearly the same distribution of the necessaries of life which would have been made had the earth been divided into *equal portions among all its inhabitants*. . . . (Emphasis added)

Because reality deviates from the market ideal, society experiences significant inequality and waste. Adam Smith conceived of the idea that order, stability, and growth are intrinsic characteristics of capitalism. **In the classical view, the economy will "self-adjust" to any departure from its long-term growth trend.** The market is self-regulating in that, if anyone's profits, prices, or wages depart from the levels set by market forces, competition will quickly force them back. Thus the market, which is the apex of economic freedom, is also an uncompromising taskmaster.[6]

Smith opposed government intervention as a hindrance to the unfettered workings of self-interest and competition. Therefore, he has become identified with a laissez-faire economic philosophy. This is the fundamental philosophy of conservative-minded individuals today. His commitment to freeing individuals from the heavy hand of monarchial rule through a commitment to liberty as benefiting the general public was a very liberal position to take in his day. Smith opposed many conservative views of his time and endorsed the working class against the "manufacturing class." He opposed the low-wage doctrine of the mercantilists and supported the higher wages that accompanied economic development:

> Is this improvement in the circumstances of the lower ranks of the people to be regarded as an advantage or as an inconveniency to the society? The answer seems at first sign abundantly plain. Servants, labourers and workmen of different kinds, make up the far greater part of every great political society. But what improves the circumstances of the greater part can never be regarded as an inconvenience to the whole. No society can surely

---

[5]Adam Smith, *The Theory of Moral Sentiments,* edited by D. D. Raphael and A. L. Macfie (Oxford, England: Clarendon Press, 1976; originally published in 1759), p. 386.

[6]Smith's writings in *The Wealth of Nations* were at least in part an effort to refute the mercantilists' contention that the economy should be regulated by the monarchy to provide support for merchants, which would ultimately increase the nation's power.

In Smith's view, the English king felt free to intervene in the most arbitrary and capricious ways as an exercise of "sovereign right." Smith supported private rights when he wrote: "England, however, has never been blessed with a very parsimonious government, so parsimony has at no time been the characteristic virtue of its inhabitants. It is the highest impertinence and presumption, therefore, in kings and ministers, to pretend to watch over the economy of private people, and to restrain their expence, either by sumptuary laws, or by prohibiting the importation of foreign luxuries. They are themselves always, and without exception, the greatest spendthrifts in the society. Let them look well after their own expence, and they may safely trust private people with theirs. If their own extravagance does not ruin the state, that of their subjects never will." See Smith, *An Inquiry into the Nature and Causes of the Wealth of Nations,* 1877 ed., pp. 227–78.

be flourishing and happy, of which the far greater part of the members are poor and miserable.[7]

Smith is a classical liberal because he tried to free the individual from the heavy hand of monarchial oppression and mercantilist policies to control the economy. This liberalism was in contrast to the mercantilism of the day which felt that government should control the economy for the interest of the state. Appalled by the arbitrary abuses of monarchial rule the classical liberals saw emancipation in individual freedom. Liberals today see the possibility in democratic governments to provide active leadership to increase freedom in the society by solving social problems and helping the needy. By that definition, Smith would be a liberal in today's political environment, because his support of laissez-faire policies was at that time not value neutral, but designed to help those who were less well off.

Smith did see a significant, although limited, role for the state. He advocated three principal uses of government, including (1) the establishment and maintenance of national defense, (2) the administration of justice, and (3) the maintenance of public works and other institutions that private entrepreneurs cannot undertake profitably in a market economy.

Smith's classical economic view was optimistic. According to its principles, the economy would continue to expand through growing production based upon increased investment in machinery. Machinery strengthened the division of labor that was so beneficial in expanding economic output and improving the productivity of the workers. It saw the market system as an enormous power for the buildup of capital primarily in the form of machinery and equipment, which would provide jobs and result in self-sufficiency for all. It predicted any slowdown in the economy would be only temporary and self-correcting.

Smith was confident that the system would generate economic growth. The purpose of this growth was to improve society's welfare by extending consumption opportunities "to the lowest ranks of the people." Smith believed that free market forces would bring about an agreeable, mutually acceptable solution to the problem of individual self-interest within society as long as individuals were free to pursue their self-interest in a political and moral environment where everyone had equal basic rights that were acknowledged by all. This aspect of Smith's views is not usually emphasized, but in fact **he was explicit in his judgment that self-interest could be destructive if it was not moderated with justice.** He condemned capitalist "rapacity." He noted that civil **government is in reality instituted for the defense of the rich against the poor, or of those who have some property against those who have none at all."**[8] He wrote: **"All for ourselves, and nothing for other people, seems, in every age of the world, to have been the vile maxim of the masters of mankind."**[9]

It should also be noted that Smith did not endorse the view that the unequal distribution of income was inherently just. He clearly indicated that coercion influences wages agreed upon between capitalists and workers. Capitalists want to pay as little as possible and possess a stronger bargaining position when dealing with workers. The legal

---

[7]Adam Smith, *The Wealth of Nations,* Edwin Cannan (ed.), (New York: Modern Library, 1937), p. 79.
[8]Smith, *The Wealth of Nations,* 1937 ed., p. 674.
[9]Smith, *The Wealth of Nations,* 1937 ed., p. 389.

system during Smith's time also favored capitalists by permitting cooperation among manufacturers to hold wages down while prohibiting unions. Smith clearly broke with mercantilist views favoring a large working class that would be paid as little as possible to provide an incentive for hard work.

Smith also disagreed with the view that traits associated with individuals in different social classes were inherent in people's makeup but attributed them instead to their positions in society. He held that **"the very different genius which appears to distinguish men of different professions, when grown to maturity, is not upon many occasions so much the cause as the effect of the division of labor."**[10] He believed that the poor were victims of the capitalist economic system and argued that high wages would be more fair. He said:

> It is but equity, besides, that they who feed, cloathe and lodge the whole body of the people, should have such a share of the produce of their own labour as to be themselves tolerably well fed, cloathed and lodged.[11]

Smith argued against policies that worked against the poor. For instance, he criticized the Settlement Act, which prevented workers from moving from one parish to another to take advantage of employment opportunities. His writings support the conclusion that **he favored the workings of market forces and laissez-faire policies as preferable to government support of mercantilist policies which oppressed the poor. He left the door open for government policies to reduce economic inequalities.**

CLASSICAL MALTHUSIAN MELANCHOLY

Despite Smith's vision of how the natural forces of a self-regulating market would lead to a constant improvement in the living conditions of the labor force, there was a nagging concern about the numbers of workers whose conditions were not improved by a market economy. The problem concerned the nature of what Smith termed "effectual demand" and its association with the distribution of income. In a nutshell, the problem is that since capitalists produce only for consumers with the money to buy, production will mirror their demand. Businesses will produce everything for those with money, and nothing for those without. It is one thing to argue that the market process is efficient. It is quite another to defend a system that produces nothing or almost nothing for the many, which after all make up the bulk of the population. The pure free market system ignored those in poverty, and indeed made it difficult for the poor to share in the benefits of an expanding market economy.

This anxiety was soon raised by the socialists, who perceived that things were not as universally rosy as Smith believed. Karl Marx was among the most famous of those to analyze the problem and offer a solution along socialist lines. But others tried to defend the market approach, with less than satisfactory results. Among these was **Thomas Robert Malthus** (1766–1834), who was the first to suggest a resolution within a market economy framework. A minister by vocation, the Reverend Malthus found the problem of poverty to be essentially moral in nature and therefore not susceptible to resolution

---

[10]Smith, *The Wealth of Nations,* 1937 ed., pp. 15–16.
[11]Smith, *The Wealth of Nations,* 1937 ed., p. 79.

by government policy. In his view, natural forces were at work and capitalists need not feel any pangs of conscience regarding wages that maintained their employees at subsistence levels of existence.

According to Malthus, there is a natural law of wages that tends toward the subsistence level. This occurs on the one hand because any increase in wages above subsistence results in workers procreating, and more mouths to feed means their wages in effect fall back to a subsistence level. On the other hand, say the price of food rises; workers then will force their wage rates up to pay for the necessities of their existence, thus maintaining a subsistence level. Either way, there is a natural wage rate that always tends toward the level of subsistence, which Malthus termed the **"Iron Law of Wages."**

The conclusion for Malthus was inescapable. Assisting the poor only transfers more resources to them and enables them to have more children. The resulting increase in population means there is no overall improvement of the living conditions of the population. Therefore it is futile to look for social causes and cures for poverty. In fact, giving assistance to the poor only transfers wealth from the productive wealthy to the poor, generating ever more poor people. According to Malthus, if the "lower classes" do not want to be poor, all they have to do is to have fewer children. The burdens associated with poverty are a natural punishment for the failure of the lower classes to restrain their urges to procreation. Their only salvation is literally dependent upon their moral reform, not government assistance.

A very important public policy implication of the Malthusian analysis is that no government assistance should be provided to the poor. On the contrary, a Malthusian view sees tragedies such as the miseries of poverty, famine, plague, and war as natural means of punishing and increasing the death rates of those who do not practice moral temperance. If it were not for these "natural" checks on population growth, the increasing numbers of poor would soon outstrip food production, which in turn would lead to their starvation. Malthus wrote that we should encourage the operations of nature in producing this mortality:

> . . . and if we dread the too frequent visitation of the horrid form of famine, we should sedulously encourage the other forms of destruction, which we compel nature to use. Instead of recommending cleanliness to the poor, we should encourage contrary habits. In our towns we should make the streets narrower, crowd more people into the houses, and court the return of the plague. In the country, we should build our villages near stagnant pools, and particularly encourage settlements in all marshy and unwholesome situations. But above all, we should reprobate specific remedies for ravaging diseases; and those benevolent, but much mistaken men, who have thought they were doing a service to mankind by projecting schemes for the total extirpation of particular disorders. If by these and similar means the annual mortality were increased . . . we might probably every one of us marry at the age of puberty, and yet few be absolutely starved.[12]

Not surprisingly, Malthus recommended the abolition of the poor-laws that provided meager relief in England at the time. Thomas Carlyle, after reading Malthus's pessimistic analysis, called political economy "the dismal science!" He was only partially correct since Malthus's analysis was dismal—but only for the poor.

---

[12]Thomas Robert Malthus, *An Essay on the Principle of Population,* 6th ed., in E. A. Wrigley and D. Souden (eds.), *The Works of Thomas Robert Malthus* (London: William Pickering, 1986), vol. 3, p. 493.

Malthusian analysis proved to be incredibly reassuring to the economically privileged members of society. It calmed their doubts and fears by asserting that the chase after wealth primarily served the interests of society. Perhaps more importantly, it claimed that the affluent need not concern themselves with an undue sense of social responsibility for the conditions of the poor, since workers caused their own miserable fates by relentlessly reproducing themselves into poverty. By inference, the converse was also true—the affluent were morally superior to the poor. Social virtue was attributed to those possessing wealth since the market system was solemnly held to provide rewards in proportion to one's economic contribution. The doctrine of laissez faire holds that the free market system has within itself the capacity to best resolve economic problems on the basis of justice and fairness for all participants. By reinforcing the commitment to a doctrine of laissez faire, Malthus devised a superb justification for the affluent to deny any responsibility for a serious economic problem. The effects of this immensely reassuring and convenient theory on the affluent made Malthus one of the most influential economic thinkers of his century. The fact that his theory was based upon his personal pondering and was not subject to empirical verification did not cause any serious objections at the time. But subsequently it led to the scathing attack on market economics by Karl Marx.

THE HAUNTING SPECTER OF KARL MARX

The writings of **Karl Marx** (1818–1883) posed a different view of market economics than those of either Adam Smith or Thomas Malthus, and led to a radically different proposed solution for society's problems. He disagreed with the capitalist assumption that politics and economics could be separated. To the mercantilists, the state was a powerful force to direct the economy. To the classical liberals, the state was a threat to economic freedom. To Marx the state was not independent of the economic structure. The real purpose of the state is to serve the interests of the wealthy owners of capital.

Marx was impressed with the ability of a capitalist economy to automatically allocate resources efficiently with no direction from the government, and to be extraordinarily efficient in producing goods and services. As Marx and his colleague Friedrich Engels commented, "The bourgeoisie, during the rule of scarce 100 years, has created more massive and more colossal productive forces than have all preceding generations together."[13] Capitalism transformed the world:

> The bourgeoisie, by the rapid improvement of all instruments of production, by the immensely facilitated means of communication, draws all nations, even the most barbarian, into civilization. . . . It compels all nations, on pain of extinction, to adopt the bourgeois mode of production; it compels them to introduce what it calls civilization into their midst, i.e., to become bourgeois themselves. In a word, it creates a world after its own image.[14]

---

[13]Robert C. Tucker (ed.), *The Marx-Engels Reader,* 2d ed. (New York: W. W. Norton & Company, 1978), p. 477.

[14]Karl Marx and Friedrich Engels, *The Communist Manifesto*, Samuel Beer (ed.), (New York: Appleton-Century-Crofts, 1955), p. 9.

Capitalism swept aside all former relationships and "left no other bond between man and man than naked self-interest."[15]

Marx viewed history as a continuing struggle between elites and the masses. He thought that the class struggle between capitalists and workers over profits and wages would ultimately lead to the end of capitalism. Marx, unlike Adam Smith, saw the potential for instability and chaos in the laissez-faire market economy. His intricate analysis held that capitalists are able to increase their profits and wealth only at the expense of the workers. In his theory of **surplus value,** he argued that exploited labor generates profits which are squeezed out through the capitalist ownership of machinery.

The significance of Marx for our purpose is that he was among the most influential thinkers to focus upon the weaknesses of the market system. He emphasized the importance of the economic and social instability resulting from the tension between the opposing demands of capital and labor. In his view, the rapaciousness of business results in ever larger business firms because small firms go under and their holdings are bought up by surviving firms. This trend toward a few large firms and the resulting concentration of wealth intensifies the struggle between labor and capital, and will eventually lead to a small group of wealthy capitalists and a mass of impoverished workers. In the end, the imbalance will be too great, resulting in the collapse of the market system. The means of production will then be centralized, that is, taken over by the government. Great inequalities and exploitation will cease.

Marxist theory has generated controversy regarding whether a pure market economy would collapse from its internal tensions. Critics of Karl Marx point out that, despite difficulties in market economies, they have not collapsed. On the contrary, those systems that ostensibly have tried to model themselves upon Marx's precepts have shown the most internal tension and in most instances have come unraveled.

Marx's contribution primarily rests on his pointing out the dynamic tensions in the market system. While market capitalism has not collapsed, it has survived in part because it has been willing to move away from a laissez-faire mode. In particular, government public policy programs have moved into many areas to ameliorate the living conditions of middle- and lower-income workers.

The Uneasy Relationship Between Politics and Economics

For more than a century following the political and economic revolution represented by the American War for Independence and Smith's writings, the state shrank as the dominant and controlling force in the economy of the United States and much of Europe. **Economies grew largely with government support, but without political interference.** It was widely believed that a society would prosper best when left to the free play of market forces. The basic policy principle of "non-interference" or **laissez faire** logically flowed from that belief. Market forces would determine the flow of goods and capital. But economic policy, in the sense of a government's commitment to certain objectives for the economy, such as full employment, stable prices, or a satisfactory economic growth rate, did not exist. Governments were required to raise taxes to provide

[15]Ibid., p. 12.

for national defense, administer justice, and provide for other incidental governmental functions. But there was no attempt to influence the volume of economic activity. There was no monetary policy because the amount of currency in circulation was automatically controlled by the amount of gold or silver possessed by the government. The business cycle seemed beyond the purview of government. Unemployment rose and fell with the "business cycle" while government looked on from the sidelines making no attempt to prevent or alleviate its effects. The market was supposed to take care of any temporary dislocations. There was little inclination to tamper with a system that brought a growing economy and prosperity to the nation into the early twentieth century. Although progress was uneven and subject to periodic spasms, laissez faire was validated by the upward trajectory of the American economy. The idea that the economy could or should be "managed" to achieve economic growth or reduce unemployment would have seemed incomprehensible a century ago. Such perspectives on the relationship between politics and economics prevented the development of economic policy.

In spite of the diminished role of government in economic matters, however, it was recognized that markets are dependent upon governments for their existence. Democratic societies are based upon a *social contract* in which the government is given monopoly power on the legitimate use of force in return for the state's agreement to use that power to protect people's lives and property, and to enforce contracts. Smith wrote about the mutual self-interest among parties to trades in a market system. However, such a system cannot function unless there is some instrument that is entrusted to interpret and protect individual and corporate property rights. Without such a guarantor, agreed-upon trades cannot be enforced and dishonest parties can steal back the items traded, or otherwise not live up to their part of business bargains, with impunity. This would lead to mutual distrust, a radical reduction in trade, and the collapse of the system itself. Thus the need for government as economic guarantor to establish an environment in which markets can function was recognized.

The classical view just described, identified with Adam Smith, emphasized that individuals following their own self-interest will lead to economic order, not chaos. Karl Marx, writing approximately three-quarters of a century later, saw economic trials and troubles everywhere and predicted the collapse of capitalism. John Maynard Keynes, writing still later, was also critical of the problems created by an unfettered market system, but aimed his theories not at the collapse of capitalism but its reform.

THE REALIST CRITIQUE OF KEYNES

The economist who did the most to challenge Karl Marx's pessimistic conclusions regarding the inevitable collapse of the market system was **John Maynard Keynes** (1883–1946). Keynesian theory represents his effort to deal with the chaotic conditions produced by the Great Depression of the 1930s.[16] From the outset, Keynes rejected

---

[16]There is far more to the Keynesian analysis than the few points made here. In addition to Keynes's own *General Theory of Employment, Interest, and Money* (New York: Harcourt, Brace & World, 1936), recommended works for further reading include: Dudley Dillard, *The Economics of John Maynard Keynes* (New York: Prentice-Hall, 1948); also G. C. Harcourt (ed.), *Keynes and His Contemporaries* (New York: St. Martin's Press, 1985).

communism as a religion with a certain mass appeal, but it was not a profound theory of political economy. Russia's repressive communist regime and its contempt for human rights was unpardonable. And he agreed with Adam Smith's preference for free market alternatives. But even before the Great Depression he complained that some people alleged virtues in a laissez-faire economy that went beyond what the theory actually claimed when he wrote:

> It is *not* true that individuals possess a prescriptive "Natural liberty" in their economic activities. There is *no* "compact" conferring perpetual rights on those who Have or on those who Acquire. The world is *not* so governed from above that private and social interest always coincide. It is *not* so managed here below that in practice they coincide. It is *not* a correct deduction from the Principles of Economics that enlightened self-interest always operates in the public interest. Nor is it true that self-interest generally *is* enlightened; more often individuals acting separately to promote their own ends are too ignorant or too weak to attain even these. Experience does *not* show that individuals, when they make up a social unit, are always less clear-sighted than when they act separately.[17]

The severe disturbances of the economies throughout Europe and North America shook the very foundation of those economic and political organizations. It is difficult for anyone who did not live through the **Great Depression** to grasp the dimensions of the catastrophe. But the statistics are staggering. The Depression wiped out one-half of the value of all goods and services produced in the United States. Twenty-five percent of the labor force lost their jobs; another 25 percent had their jobs reduced from full to part time or had their wages reduced. Over 9 million savings accounts disappeared when banks failed and more than a million mortgages were foreclosed.

The level of despair and discontent raised doubts about whether the market system could survive. Many of the more affluent who had not been seriously hurt by the Depression viewed the crisis with calm detachment. They opposed the reforms proposed by Franklin Roosevelt in the New Deal as a threat to their favored status. Roosevelt linked the political machines of urban areas, organized labor, farmers, and ethnic minorities to the federal executive branch through programs that benefitted these constituencies. The federal government entered the economic life of the nation through the New Deal to assume responsibility for the nation's economic well-being. There is a general consensus that the policies of the Roosevelt revolution not only changed the character of the national government, but also rescued the traditional capitalist economic system in America.

Keynes's *The General Theory of Employment, Interest, and Money*, published in 1936, was a much more complex analysis of the market economy than Adam Smith's. Undertaking a macroeconomic analysis which Smith had not concerned himself with, led him to conclude that laissez faire was not the appropriate policy for a stagnant economy like that of the 1930s. Keynes stated his profound disagreement with the classical tradition in his one-paragraph first chapter:

> I have called this book the *General Theory of Employment, Interest and Money,* placing the emphasis on the prefix *general.* The object of such a title is to contrast the character

---

[17]John Maynard Keynes, "The End of Laissez-Faire," in *Essays in Persuasion* (New York: W. W. Norton, 1963), p. 312.

of my arguments and conclusions with those of the *classical* theory of the subject . . . which dominates the economic thought, both practical and theoretical, of the governing and academic classes of this generation, as it has for a hundred years past. I shall argue that the postulates of the classical theory are applicable to a special case only and not to the general case. . . . Moreover, the characteristics of the special case assumed by the classical theory happen not to be those of the economic society in which we actually live, with the result that its teaching is misleading and disastrous if we attempt to apply it to the facts of experience.[18]

The classical school of economics offered no solution to the problems facing the nation during the 1930s. But obviously the optimistic view that the economic problems were temporary, requiring only belt-tightening and waiting for the economy to grow, was not acceptable to most of the population. Keynes asserted that classical economists:

were apparently unmoved by the lack of correspondence between the results of their theory and the facts of observation—a discrepancy which the ordinary man has not failed to observe. . . . The celebrated optimism of traditional economic theory . . . is . . . to be traced, I think, to their having neglected to take account of the drag on prosperity which can be exercised by an insufficiency of effective demand. For there would obviously be a natural tendency towards the optimum employment of resources in a Society which was functioning after the manner of the classical postulates. It may well be that *the classical theory represents the way in which we should like our Economy to behave. But to assume that it actually does so is to assume our difficulties away.*[19] (Emphasis added)

Keynes believed that the psychological and organizational conditions of the nineteenth century that permitted laissez-faire notions to work as a policy were in fact a special case that was shattered by World War I. The convoluted and contrived system depended upon free imports of goods and export of capital made possible by peace. It depended also on a delicate class balance between capital and labor, and a moral balance between capital and spending. In the 1920s, price instability led to the unjustified enrichment of some and impoverishment of others which cut the moral link between effort and reward. Worker acceptance of modest wages depended on the dominant business class producing job opportunities. There was also a psychological balance between saving and consumption in which savings was a great virtue. But increasingly, consumption and material outcomes were the measures of success—and failure. And increasingly, capitalism's driving force was a "vice" Keynes called "love of money."[20]

It was also no longer possible to contend that people pushed into uncompensated unemployment were simply too lazy to get a job, or that they could find work if they would only lower their wage demands. Marxists of the day felt vindicated, believing that the Depression was the death knell of the market system. **At the core of his disagreement with the classical view was his argument that a market economy is inherently unstable.** The market system could reach a "position of underemployment equilibrium" in which the economy could have a high level of

---

[18]See Keynes, *General Theory*, p. 3 (emphasis in original).

[19]Keynes, *General Theory*, pp. 33–34.

[20]Robert Skidelsky, *J. Maynard Keynes: The Economist as Saviour, 1920–1937* (New York: Viking Penguin, 1992). See especially chapter 7, "Keynes Middle Way."

unemployment and idle industrial equipment.[21] The basic characteristic of a recession
or depression is a decline in aggregate demand or purchasing power by consumers, business, and government. The result is an economic downturn caused by a reduction in production and the consequent increase in unemployment as employers react to reduce their
costs. The significance of his theory in relation to classical theory was that it claimed
**there is no self-correcting property in the market system to return a stagnant econ-
omy to growth and full employment.** If his analysis was correct, the classical nostrum
of tightening your belt and riding out the storm was disastrous. It meant that if demand
was established at levels so low that unemployment would remain high and businesses
would not be willing to invest in new capital investments the situation would remain
indefinitely in that depressed state, unless some variable in the economic equation was
changed. According to Keynes, political management of the economy was the solution.
**Government spending might well be a necessary public policy to help a depressed
market economy regain its vigor.** According to Keynes, to the extent that there were
market failures leading to insufficient demand, government should intervene through
fiscal and monetary policies to promote full employment, stable prices, and economic
growth. Useful government action against recessions come down to fiscal and monetary measures designed to expand consumer and investment spending. This would simultaneously improve the general social welfare by improving the position of those who are
the most vulnerable in periods of economic stagnation: the unemployed.

   **Fiscal policy involves the use of government taxing and spending to stimulate or
slow the economy.** The bottom line is that the government can increase or decrease
aggregate demand by increasing or decreasing its share of taxing and spending. Keynes
argued that fiscal policy could reduce unemployment by increasing government spending while taxes remained the same or were reduced. The increased spending would result
in increased employment to meet those demands. Conversely, by increasing taxes (the
least popular of all fiscal policies) or reducing government spending, fiscal policy could
reduce the flow of spending and slow an inflationary economy.

   **Monetary policy refers to actions taken by a central bank (the Federal Reserve
in the United States) to control the money supply.** Those actions in turn control the
volume of lending and borrowing by commercial banks and ultimately by investors and
consumers. In a depression, the government should increase the money supply to keep

---

[21]Keynes stressed the significance of aggregate demand as the immediate determinant of national income,
output, and employment. Demand is the sum of consumption, investment, government expenditures, and net
exports. Effective demand establishes the economy's equilibrium level of actual output. A problem frequently
occurs when the equilibrium level of actual output is less than the level that would exist to maintain full
employment.

   Keynes held that investment spending is inconstant. Investment spending is determined by the rate of interest and the expected rate of return on investments. The interest rate, in turn, depends on people's preferences
for liquidity and the quantity of money. Investments are made only on the expectation of future profits and
the cost of capital.

   He also challenged the classical notion that wages and prices are flexible downward. Implicit understandings between employers and workers that wages will not be cut in temporary downturns are common.
Union contracts and minimum wage laws may also prevent employers from reducing costs by lowering wages.
Employers tend to respond to lowered demand by reducing production and laying off workers. Businesses are
also reluctant to reduce prices. Declining demand usually results in reductions in output and employment
rather than reduced prices.

interest rates down. That policy might also be matched by reducing taxes for workers to increase demand and by increasing government spending to stimulate business investments, employment, and demand.

Monetary and fiscal policies are the mechanisms by which the government can achieve the objective of economic growth. To increase the total number of jobs in the economy, the government makes more money available, lowers interest rates, buys more output, and even becomes the employer of last resort.

Conservative critics of Keynes, opposing a larger role for government, charged that his views were too radical and threatened the very foundations of capitalism. Many denounced him as a socialist. Keynes, however, viewed himself as a conservative trying to defend capitalism against the growing attractions of communism. Even before the Depression, Keynes had observed that **market capitalism had imperfections** which, if corrected, would strengthen capitalism. In a book titled *The End of Laissez-Faire,* he noted aspects of the unfettered market that lead to reduced efficiency and production and suggested how governments might exercise "directive intelligence" over the problem while leaving "private initiative unhindered." He wrote:

> Contrariwise, devotees of Capitalism are often unduly conservative, and reject reforms in its technique, **which might really strengthen and preserve it,** for fear that they may prove to be first steps away from Capitalism itself. . . . For my part, I think that Capitalism, wisely managed, can probably be made more efficient for attaining economic ends than any alternative system yet in sight, but that in itself it is in many ways extremely objectionable. Our problem is to work out a social organisation which shall be efficient as possible without offending our notions of a satisfactory way of life.[22] (emphasis added)

Keynes never faltered in his admiration of capitalism. Keynesian theory was dedicated to the preservation of the capitalist economic system and the position of those who were most favored by it. Yet his theory required some tinkering with the system by the government. The affluent were highly suspicious of any proposal that permitted government control over their interests. And they deeply resented the improved status he gave to the "working class" as an essential ingredient in the overall health of the economy. They found especially irritating his suggestion that their own privileges might actually contribute to economic instability.

If Keynes was right in his analysis and prescriptions for curing the ills of capitalism, then the attraction of a planned economy as represented by communism would atrophy because people prefer to be employed and self-sufficient rather than dependent upon the government for everything. His public policy solution was one in which business and government would act as partners in running the economy. The government would engage in public policies that would create a sufficient demand to maintain full employment, and profits would go to business as they had in the past. Government was the only party of this arrangement that could pull it off, however, since it alone could act in the role of a non-self-interested party. He saw government acting as a positive instrument for individual freedom by, for example, funding programs such as education that would help individuals as well as society, and for economic freedom by protecting a system

---

[22]John Maynard Keynes, *The End of Laissez-Faire* (New York: W. W. Norton, 1926), p. 321.

THE APPEAL OF CONVENIENT LOGIC

The effort to understand the world through rigorous analysis is essential if we are to achieve social progress. Unfortunately, there is considerable evidence that what is passed off as objective analysis is often largely an exercise in seizing upon those parts of a theory most in harmony with our financial and political self-interest. Human beings have a remarkable tendency to believe those things most in accordance with their self-interest. We resist the intrusion of reality that might suggest otherwise.

Problem-solving techniques taught in academic settings usually move from cause to effect. A diagnosis of a problem leads us to appropriate corrective action. In real-life situations, though, what often happens when our interests are involved is that we choose the remedy in which we incur the least cost and which will require the least amount of reorganization of our other self-interested beliefs. We then reason back to a cause for which our lowest-cost remedy provides the greatest congruence. In some cases, this may require significant mental gymnastics.

By way of illustration, this chapter has pointed out the problem of poverty in a market economy. Adam Smith wrote hopefully that natural forces would lead to a nearly equal distribution of income between capitalists and workers in a market economy. And he heartily approved of higher wages for workers.

The failure of the equalization to occur was worrisome because it raised fundamental questions about the soundness of Smith's model. Malthus's view that the poor are immoral and responsible for their own fate was a most welcome and gratifying reasoning from the effect (poverty) back to the cause (immorality) for the affluent because it relieved them of any burden of conscience concerning subsistence wages. And it provided them with a basis for righteous indignation at any suggestion of an unwelcome obligation to transfer financial resources to the poor. Subsequently, "Social Darwinism" was invoked as a self-explanatory justification through adaptation of Darwin's law of the "survival of the fittest": Wealth should not be passed from the wealthy (or "fit") to the poor (or "unfit") as doing so would violate a natural law.

More recently, Keynesian analysis showed that the causes of unemployment and poverty can be found in impersonal market forces such as inadequate demand, and in economic policies that tolerate unemployment to keep a downward pressure on prices. Other studies make it clear that economic deprivation in childhood,

whose entrepreneurs could flourish, albeit in a regulated way. **Keynes maintained that economic prosperity is the only certain guarantee of a liberal political system.**

Keynesian theory was a clear advancement in our understanding of market capitalism. Part of his success was also based upon the fact that he addressed not only pressing problems of the moment—economic depression and unemployment—but enduring policy concerns like growth and stability. And, like Adam Smith before him, he developed a theory that rationalized what was already being done out of necessity. Without the Great Depression, Keynes would never have written his *General Theory,* but already by the time of its publication Franklin D. Roosevelt had been elected and was implementing his New Deal, which was Keynesian in practice.

Conservative critics of Franklin Roosevelt argue that his efforts to stimulate the economy by running deficits did not get the United States out of the Great Depression. Rather,

racial and gender discrimination, and inadequate education among other factors are also causes of poverty.

It can no longer be claimed that poverty is caused primarily by personal immorality (or that the wealthy are more moral than the poor—recall the recent savings-and-loan scandals). And one might reasonably expect solutions to be proposed related to the new diagnosis of the causes of poverty—for example, economic policies that do not rely on accepting high unemployment to reduce inflation, strict enforcement of equal opportunity laws, and greater efforts to provide educational opportunities to the disadvantaged. Unfortunately all these remedies require the affluent to incur a cost, which they find deeply disturbing. So less painful alternatives are suggested, based on a view of the causes of poverty more in keeping with the solutions they wish to see implemented. Poverty can no longer be explained as the result of immorality, but instead is blamed on government policy: The poor are "victims" of the well-intentioned but misguided Great Society programs of the 1960s aimed at helping them. This view alleges that the poor have no incentive to work because they are the beneficiaries of the welfare programs that been lavished upon them. In other words, **the poor have too much!** So the true solution of poverty, according to this view, is a reduction in public expenditures for the poor so they will be motivated to work harder.

Obviously this is a most agreeable policy proposal for the more affluent. And its logic is carried a disconcerting step further: Just as the poor have too much and need to feel the misery of deprivation to spur them to work, the wealthy have not been working because they have too little. High taxes are identified as the reason for a lack of incentive for performance by the wealthy. A reduction in taxes, especially a cut in the capital gains tax (along with a corresponding increase in income) would be an excellent motivation for the wealthy. And, it is claimed, this proposal favoring the affluent is motivated by compassion for the poor. It is primarily in the interest of the poor because it is alleged to create useful employment for them. **Thus, in this logic, the poor have too much to be motivated. The wealthy have too little. Therefore benefits should be reduced for the poor and increased for the affluent.**

This is loosely adapted from a graduation address by John Kenneth Galbraith titled "Reverse Logic" and reprinted in J. K. Galbraith, *A View from the Stands* (New York: Houghton Mifflin, 1987), pp. 34–38.

they argue, that WW II ended the Depression. This misses the point however. Roosevelt's New Deal deficits were not large enough to offset the reduction in private expenditures by businesses, households, and state governments. It is true that it was not until the Second World War that the economy began to come out of the Depression. But this expansion was caused by the vast increase in government purchases associated with the war that stimulated employment and aggregate demand. This actually reinforced Keynes's theory of the role of government as employer of last resort and purchaser of goods to stimulate the economy.

Keynesian theory supplanted the classical school not only because of its more penetrating analysis, but also because the essentials of the classical school supported a basic posture of passivity regarding government public policy. Especially in crisis situations such as depressions or wars, it is not a realistic option for governments to "do nothing."

A major part of the legacy of Keynes is an understanding that government does bear a major responsibility for the overall performance of the economy. The questions of economic stability, employment, growth, and inflation require government leadership and cannot be left to laissez-faire inaction and faith that the system will resolve all economic problems in its own time.

Keynesian thinking was almost the opposite of Adam Smith's views. Disturbances in employment, output, or prices are likely to be magnified by the invisible hand of the marketplace. A catastrophe like the Great Depression is not a rare occurrence but rather a disaster that will return if we depend on the market to self-adjust. Thus when the economy stumbles we cannot wait for an invisible hand to provide the needed adjustments. The government must intervene to safeguard jobs and income. The total number of jobs in the economy is determined by macroeconomic variables including the levels of consumption, investment, and imports and exports. His analysis also made short work of Malthusian perspectives. The poor, he made clear, were not poor because they were less moral than the affluent, they were poor because of their position in society and impersonal economic forces.

A critical factor in determining the total number of jobs in the economy, or the "employment pie," is the relationship between employment and inflation, which constrains the number of jobs that decision makers can or should create. Liberal Keynesians are more concerned about high rates of unemployment than inflation. They are opposed to high interest rates, and prefer fiscal—as opposed to monetary—policy to pursue broad economic goals. Conservative Keynesians are more concerned about inflation, and therefore accept higher unemployment to reduce it, and are less willing to use fiscal policy (especially deficits) to provide full employment.

From the mid-1930s on in the United States, a consensus emerged on government fiscal policies that accepted mild deficits. The principal goal was the achievement of "full employment," which was defined as an unemployment rate of about 4 percent. At 4 percent, existing unemployment was thought to be "frictional" or "structural" rather than "cyclical."[23]

Political leaders of both parties in the United States have long held an overwhelming presumption that in regard to election and reelection prospects few things are more foolhardy than a tax increase or more helpful than a tax cut. **The temptation to run big deficits when the economy is not in recession was reined in by Keynesian theory, which held that large deficits would result in higher inflation,** requiring high interest rates to stop rising prices, bringing about a recession, which would spell disaster in elections. The perceived close connection between short-term economic trends and politics produced an arrangement that permitted deficits but kept them within a narrow range.

Keynes's analysis provided the rationale for governments to adopt public policies to keep inflation and unemployment low while encouraging economic growth.

---

[23]Frictional unemployment refers to the temporary unemployment of new entrants into the labor force or those who have quit one job while they look for a better one. It is not considered a serious problem. Structural unemployment refers to unemployment due to a mismatch between the skills of the labor force and the jobs available. Cyclical unemployment refers to unemployment caused by a lack of jobs in the economy due to a general economic downturn.

Governments would have a major macroeconomic role with their state, but there should be free trade between states. These policies were embodied in the *Full Employment Act of 1946*, which committed the government to an activist policy to stimulate enough growth to keep unemployment low. Among the more affluent it continued to be viewed with as much alarm as Roosevelt's policies, since federal intervention in the economy was seen as interfering with "natural processes."

Stagflation

In the early 1960s, John F. Kennedy became the first president to avowedly follow the Keynesian approach to shaping public policies. For nearly eight years this interventionist approach to policy was so successful in producing an uninterrupted expansion of the economy that economics was declared to be a science. The decision to extend the Nobel Prize to include an annual award in the area of economics capped this newfound prestige. But ironically, Keynesian economics was about to suffer an erosion in confidence at the moment of its greatest triumph.

Keynes's concern was with an economy with high unemployment and low demand in which the economy would be running well below capacity. Inflation would not be a problem with such excess capacity. But in the late 1960s inflation began to rise as unemployment declined.

The idea that unemployment could be too low to be consistent with stable inflation is of recent origin. A. William Phillips (1914–1976) analyzed data concerning the relationship between unemployment and inflation going back almost a century in the United Kingdom.[24] He discovered a trade-off between unemployment and inflation which became known as the **Phillips curve.** He found an inverse relationship between inflation and unemployment. The explanation for the relationship is implied in Keynesian theory and is intuitively obvious. Labor does respond to the market forces of supply and demand. When unemployment is high, the competition for jobs by unemployed workers allows management to fill their labor needs at relatively low wage rates. As the economy expands and unemployment declines, management must lure workers with higher wage rates. Higher wages for labor will result in higher costs of production and ultimately in higher prices. The significance of this discovery was that it suggested a tool that could be used by government to regulate the economy. Policy makers could reduce unemployment by inflating the economy. The "cost" of reducing unemployment for the policy maker was the necessity of accepting higher inflation.

This view of the relationship between unemployment and inflation broke down in the 1970s with the occurrence of **stagflation, or the concurrent increase in both unemployment and inflation.** One explanation for this anomaly was that constant attempts to reduce unemployment by expansionary fiscal and monetary policies created higher inflation without reducing unemployment. Other Keynesians argued that the full employment of the 1960s created expectations of continuous growth that would result in higher income levels. Businesses and individuals made wage, price, and consumer

---

[24]A. William Phillips, "The Relation Between Unemployment and the Rate of Change of Money Wage Rates in the United Kingdom, 1861–1957." *Economica* 25 (November 1958), pp. 283–99.

decisions based on the expectation of continued growth and inflation, thus creating a self-fulfilling prophesy of continued inflation.

Supply-Side Revelries

In the late 1970s, a new approach to economic problems began to take shape. It did not displace the Keynesian emphasis on government intervention, but did suggest different ways for public policy to deal with economic stability and growth. This variation on classical economics was the **supply-side approach, which stresses the need to increase productivity by increasing incentives for working, saving, and investing.**

The stagflation that began during the Nixon administration continued through the Ford and Carter administrations. The doubling of the price of OPEC oil helped inject a shock of inflation into the American economy accompanied by an increase in unemployment from 6.3 to 7.6 percent in the spring and early summer of 1980 where it remained through the rest of the year. The economy sliding into recession with high unemployment and a large budget deficit was perfectly timed for the advantage of the challenger, Ronald Reagan. Reagan ran a campaign in 1980, as Carter had in 1976, against stagflation. Reagan's message was clear and simple, he proposed to roll back the welfare state, reduce government regulatory burdens on business, and provide across-the-board tax reductions which he argued would stimulate economic expansion. He claimed that this would reduce inflation while providing major increases in defense spending.

He placed the blame for most of America's problems on the public policies that resulted in a major role for the government in the economy, "The most important cause of our economic problems has been the government itself."[25] One of the assumptions underlying Reagan's economic program was that big government was the cause of economic decline because of the inefficiencies that it imposed. Although this argument was made often by the administration, the evidence does not support the claim. For example in 1980 the U.S. government claimed 30.8 percent of the GDP, compared with 40.1 percent in the United Kingdom, 44.5 percent in France, and 44.7 percent in West Germany. Yet those nations with larger public sectors performed better than the United States in unemployment, inflation, and productivity gains.[26] The second assumption of the Reagan policy was that significant tax cuts without corresponding cuts in spending could be reconciled with a balanced budget. Many observers at the time found it reassuring to be told that cutting spending was not necessary, just cutting taxes would be sufficient. After all, Kennedy's tax cut stimulated economic activity. Since it had been shown that some taxes *can* stimulate economic activity, some jumped to the conclusion that any tax cut *will* increase government tax receipts.

Reagan's fiscal 1982 budget proposed a $7.2 billion increase in military spending and a $41 billion reduction in nondefense spending. Succumbing to political pressure, Congress limited the nondefense cuts to $35 billion. Popular middle class programs like Social Security were left largely unscathed. However, means tested entitlements such

---

[25]"Program for Economic Recovery, White House Report, February 18, 1981." *Weekly Compilation of Presidential Documents* 17, 8 (1981), p. 141.

[26]Marc Allan Eisner, *The State in the American Political Economy* (Englewood Cliffs, NJ: Prentice-Hall, Inc., 1995), p. 288. See also OECD, *Historical Statistics, 1960–1988* (Paris: OECD 1990), pp. 48, 51, 68.

as Medicaid, Aid to Families with Dependent Children (AFDC), Food Stamps, and Supplemental Security Income were cut significantly. Congress limited some of the cuts. For example, a requested AFDC reduction of 28.6 percent was reduced to a 14.3 percent cut. A requested 51.3 percent reduction in Food Stamp funds was limited to a 13.8 percent cut. But because these cuts were implemented during the deepest recession since the Great Depression, the impact on the poor was intensified.[27]

This period also saw the greatest peacetime buildup of the military in the nation's history. By 1985, the defense budget authority, after adjusting for inflation had increased by 53 percent. By the end of the Reagan administration, defense spending was larger than it had been at the height of the Vietnam War. Most of the increase was in procurement and research and development (R&D) rather than in personnel which provided a major stimulus to the economy and great profits in the defense industry.[28]

Reaganomics and Monetary Policy

These policies led to an upward pressure on prices and rising inflation. The Reagan administration relied upon the Federal Reserve Board under Paul Volcker to deal with the problem of inflation. The Federal Reserve Board's policy to control inflation was simply to limit the money supply which reduced the amount of money that banks had to lend. The result was that interest rates soared which led to the greatest recession since the 1930s. High interest rates contributed to high unemployment and reduced demand and declining inflation. In addition to the action of the Fed, the collapse of OPEC resulted in a steep decline in oil prices which also put a downward pressure on prices.

The determination to wring inflation out of the economy by driving up interest rates came at a very high price. The intentional slamming on of the monetary brakes resulted in the loss of over 1.8 million manufacturing and mining jobs during the Reagan administration. The real cost to American families is striking. Median family income fell from $33,454 (in 1989 dollars) in 1979 to $30,111 in 1983 and did not reach the 1979 level again until 1987. Only those in the top 20 percent of the income scale finished the 1980s with real incomes well above their earnings in the late 1970s. Stopping inflation by creating an economic slow-down does not affect everyone equally:

> Recessions are not equal opportunity disemployers. The odds of being drafted into the fight against inflation increase steadily the lower an individual's earnings and family income to begin with. The relative income losses suffered by the working heads of poor families, for example, are four to five times as great as the losses for those heading high-income families, even after adjusting for the cushioning effect of taxes and transfers; and the 1981–1982 recession drove 4.3 million more people into poverty. At every income level, male heads of families experience greater income losses than female heads of families, and black men suffer the most of all.[29]

[27]Eisner, op. cit., p. 292.

[28]Phil Williams, "The Reagan Administration and Defense Policy," In *The Reagan Presidency: An Incomplete Revolution?* Dilys M. Hill, Raymond A. Moore, and Phil Williams (eds.), (New York: St. Martin's Press, 1990), pp. 203–5.

[29]Isabel V. Sawhill and Charles F. Stone, "The Economy: The Key to Success." In *The Reagan Record: An Assessment of America's Changing Domestic Priorities* (Cambridge, MA: Ballinger, 1984), p. 80.

MONETARISM: ANOTHER ALTERNATIVE

Monetarism as a school of thought has its roots in the classical tradition of economic theory and, like the supply-side approach, rejects much of the Keynesian school. Just as the more affluent found a great appeal in the convenient logic of supply-side thinking, they also found an appeal in monetarism because it promises a way to achieve steady economic growth without inflation. For the affluent, inflation is a great economic evil because it redistributes income in an arbitrary manner. The usual way to halt inflation is to lower aggregate demand, either by raising taxes or raising interest rates. Among the more affluent, raising interest rates rather than taxes is the preferred method of curing inflation. Tax rates may not be reduced again once raised but higher interest rates reward those with money to lend even while they reduce inflation by reducing aggregate demand. But having to deal with inflation after it occurs is not ideal either, and monetarism proposes an alternative.

The central tenet of monetarism is simplicity itself. **Monetarism holds that the most important determinant of aggregate demand is the quantity of money in circulation. It claims that, if the quantity of money in circulation is allowed to expand at a steady rate based upon the long-term growth of the economy, prices will be stable and the economy will be encouraged to continue its growth.**[30] Monetarists believe, like the classical economists, that the economy is self-regulating and that it tends to equilibrium at full-employment output. Further, they argue, it is monetary—not fiscal—policy that has the greatest short-term effect on the business cycle. Given this view, monetarists support a limited "laissez-faire" role for government. Actually, the wing of monetarism led by Milton Friedman proposes that the government limit its own activities so they will not interfere and prevent the economic system's self-regulating tendencies from asserting themselves.

Friedman argues that allowing the Federal Reserve System to exercise discretionary policy regarding the money supply, credit, and interest rates actually destabilizes the economy. He describes this approach as being like a driver alternately hitting the brakes and flooring the acceler-

[30]Monetarism must be distinguished from **monetary policy,** which refers to Federal Reserve policies directed at changing the money supply or changing interest rates or both.

Inflationary fears are a very real concern to policy makers, whose choice of policy ultimately determines the course of the economy. Yet many observers feel that the risk of inflation inherent in an active monetary policy to stimulate economic growth and employment is worth taking since the costs of recessions are not shared equally throughout society. Lower- and middle-income workers are much more likely to become unemployed than the more affluent members of the labor force. Inflation, however, appears to impact the more affluent. As economist Alan Blinder of Princeton University wrote:

> Sometimes inflation is piously attacked as the "cruelest tax," meaning that it weighs most heavily on the poor. . . . On close examination, the "cruelest tax" battle cry is seen for what it is: a subterfuge for protecting inflation's real victims, the rich. . . . [E]very bit of evidence I know of points in the same direction: inflation does no special harm to the poor.

ator. He argues that, if the money supply were increased at a steady, predictable rate of between 3 and 4 percent, the economy would grow at a constant rate and without inflation.[31]

The monetarist position is largely based upon the principle of rational expectations. It holds that inflation is fueled by expectations of future inflation and that it can be cured quickly if a commitment not to accommodate inflation by increasing the money supply can be made credible to the public. Monetarism has always been understood as more effective in pulling inflation down by tightening the money supply than in stimulating the economy by increasing it.

An effort to rigorously control the money supply in the early 1980s contributed to the most severe recession since the Great Depression with unemployment rising above 10 percent of the labor force. The disastrous policy was halted midway through Reagan's first four years when the Fed announced it was abandoning the effort to achieve strict monetary growth targets. In several short years, monetary policy had

been tried and was found to be incapable by itself of providing economic stability.

President Reagan nonetheless remained faithful to the constituency of satisfied voters who supported him by employing economic theories supportive of laissez faire. Both supply-side economics and monetarism view the state as an unnecessary burden at best since according to their tenets the economy will return to full employment by itself if one is sufficiently patient. (Patience of course is much easier to feel in this case if one is fully employed.) President Bush continued in this tradition by insisting on the need to "get the government off the back of the American people." His supporters never faltered in their free market beliefs, which permit government support for but not regulation of business, as offering the best hope for long-term economic growth. In their view, the low growth of the 1980s and 1990s has been part of the self-correcting adjustments necessary in the economy and should not result in a misguided panic response of intervention by the government.

[31]This theory had acquired such intellectual respectability among conservatives that by the early 1980s there were serious discussions about whether to enforce a tight control over the money supply by returning the country to the gold standard.

. . . The meager costs that inflation poses on the poor are dwarfed by the heavy price the poor are forced to pay whenever the nation embarks on an anti-inflation campaign. . . .[32]

Activists believe that the small costs inflation inflicts on the poor are overshadowed by the high price paid by those in the lower-income brackets when policy makers begin an anti-inflation campaign.

Supply-side policies include a reduction in taxes, particularly for upper-income groups. Supply-side proponents see greater after-tax income as a key ingredient to stimulate economic investments. Another major supply-side lever is the deregulation of business to remove "impediments" to profits. The suggestion that large reductions in

[32]Alan Blinder, *Hard Minds, Soft Hearts: Tough-Minded Economics for a Just Society* (Reading, MA: Addison-Wesley, 1987), p. 54.

marginal tax rates would stimulate enough economic growth to produce sufficiently increased tax revenues to balance the budget, without spending cuts, was novel. If correct, it would permit government to cut taxes and spend more at the same time—the politicians' equivalent of the medieval alchemists' assertions that they could turn lead into gold.

The major difference between supply-side and classical economists is that the former support an **activist** approach. Classical economists favor a laissez-faire policy, fearing that government activism, however well intentioned, will usually make things worse. Supply-siders differ from Keynesians in that they believe government should actively intervene only to promote a pro-market agenda. Keynesians believe government should intervene to regulate as well as stimulate the market, and favor policies that focus on demand forces.

Paul Peterson argues forcefully that the Reagan-Bush deficits cannot be understood apart from the breakdown of the economic consensus that permitted only mild government budget shortfalls.[33] Reagan needed an economic theory that would provide an acceptable policy doctrine as the intellectual basis for a dramatic departure from previous practice.

The supply-side approach, largely identified with the Reagan administration, reopened a debate many thought had been settled by the Great Depression when it boldly admitted its intention to widen the gap between economic "winners" and "losers" as an incentive to work hard, save, and invest. Many observers felt that the distribution of income in the United States was already so unequal as to be unjust. And cynics labeled supply-side programs a return to the "trickle-down" economics of a bygone era. Nevertheless President Reagan was swept into office in a tremendous victory in 1980, partly on the basis of a "supply-side" campaign: He promised to cut income taxes, particularly for those in the upper-income brackets, pass investment tax credits for firms, and increase defense spending. He argued that the latter step would increase productivity growth and expand the tax base sufficiently to more than make up for revenues lost from the tax cuts.

In fact, tax cuts in a global economy cannot stimulate sufficient income growth to pay for themselves. The reasons are clear: while it is true that reduced taxes increase the money available to consumers, part of the money (especially for affluent taxpayers) will go into savings, and at least 16 percent would go abroad immediately to import goods and services produced abroad. Public sector spending would have the same effect in the long run, but the first round of spending would be at home, so that imports would only go up after the first round of spending to improve the economic infrastructure was paid out as wages. The supply-side tax cuts raised the national debt while an increased demand for imports expanded the trade deficit fourfold.

Critics of this policy point out that productivity growth actually declined in the 1980s (to less than 2 percent per year) from levels in the 1970s (3.2 percent per year). Savings and investment rates also declined significantly in the 1980s. The tax cuts contributed to unprecedented budget deficits throughout the decade. Finally, these policies contributed to the increase in inequality that occurred in the 1980s.

---

[33]Paul E. Peterson, "The New Politics of Deficits," in John E. Chubb and Paul E. Peterson (eds.), *The New Direction in American Politics* (Washington, DC: The Brookings Institution, 1985), p. 393.

Reagan's economic policy was premised on the rejection of Keynesian theories. However, the high levels of spending and record peacetime deficits resulted in one of the largest stimulative Keynesian economic policies in the history of the nation. Reagan's Keynesian policy was focused differently than that of earlier presidents. Earlier tax reductions were not targeted on the wealthy. And rather than increasing spending throughout the economy, Reagan concentrated on the defense industry. Wealth was transferred to the defense industry, while financing the redistribution was spread among all taxpayers.

For all of these reasons, supply-side economics is no longer touted as a viable alternative to Keynesian economics.[34] However, a major cut in taxes targeting the wealthy was deeply appreciated by those so favored. Even if the theory did not hold up, many cynical neoconservative politicians saw supporting more tax cuts for the rich could be a forceful instrument for campaign financing.

George Bush, muffled his early criticism of supply-side economics, and pledged "no new taxes" in the campaign of 1988. Bush abandoned a strict reliance on supply-side arguments in favor of a call for a "kinder, gentler nation." In his inaugural address, however, he noted that "we have more will than wallet," indicating that he did not envision a larger role for government in securing that kindness and gentleness. However, within two years, with deficits climbing at a dizzying pace, the economy slipped into a recession. Threats of forced spending cuts mandated by Gramm-Rudman legislation, caused George Bush to raise income tax rates on the affluent and also to raise the gasoline tax rate. Outraged conservatives felt betrayed and claimed that the taxes brought on the recession that set the stage for his defeat in 1992. The economy actually began to recover in March of 1992. But economic growth was so weak that unemployment continued to grow through the end of 1992 to 7.4 percent which was higher than it had been at the depth of the recession. What was most surprising was that unemployment rose to 7.4 percent with the stimulus of a budget deficit of $290 billion (well above the previous record set by Reagan of $221 billion).

The state of the economy at the end of the Bush administration provided a significant boost to Clinton's campaign. Unemployment was at 7.4 percent and per capita income was falling. There was a record budget deficit that year of $340 billion and a federal debt that had risen to 68.2 percent of GDP. U.S. trade deficits were growing and had fluctuated between $465 billion and $109 billion during the Bush administration. The Reagan and Bush administrations criticized Carter and the Democratic Party's support for big government which claimed 21.4 percent of the GDP during Carter's term. Gleeful Democrats pointed out that after twelve years of Republican administrations, the role of the federal government had grown to 23.5 percent of GDP after several years of growth. In 1980, the federal government spent $613 billion which grew to $1.5 trillion in 1992.[35]

Although these conditions helped Clinton win the election, he was now forced to govern under these unfavorable conditions which had led to the defeat of his predecessor.

---

[34]Three Nobel Prize–winning economists, James Buchanan, Milton Friedman, and George Stigler, with impeccable conservative credentials, scorn supply-side thinking. Alan Greenspan, chairman of the Federal Reserve under both Bush and Clinton, clearly a conservative, is also disdainful of supply-side thinking.

[35]*Economic Report of the President, 1993* (Washington, D.C.: Government Printing Office, 1993), Tables B-37, 59, 74, 76, and 77.

The size of the deficit and the national debt were the key economic problems to face Clinton. Failure to make progress on this front would crush every other policy initiative. The deficit required action because as interest payments approached $200 billion, the government was competing with business in money markets driving up interest rates. This made it more expensive for American firms to borrow funds for capital investments to improve growth. The cost of financing the debt would also prevent the administration from pursuing any other social welfare goals requiring funding. No significant programs to improve conditions in education, health care, housing, or the environment could be initiated under such conditions. With fiscal policy makers paralyzed, the power to make economic policy would be transferred to the Federal Reserve. However the president and the Fed serve different constituencies. The president's primary concern is with encouraging economic growth and full employment, while the Fed has very limited power in this area and is more concerned with maintaining price stability.

Clinton's campaign set two basic goals for his first term: to cut the federal budget deficit in half and to create an economic environment that would create 11 million new jobs. In his campaign for a second term Clinton could boast that the economy had created 14 million jobs, with two-thirds of those jobs paying wages above the median, and an unemployment rate that had dropped from 7.5 percent to 5.4 percent. The core inflation rate fell from 3.7 percent in 1992 to 2.7 percent in 1996.[36] And by early 1998 Federal revenues as a percentage of total GDP declined to 19.9 percent. The administration's most important economic policy accomplishment was the reduction in the deficit from $290 billion in 1992 to $107 billion in 1996. It was cut by more than half (63 percent). In 1992, the U.S. general deficit (the total deficit for all levels of government) was larger in relation to the GDP than in either Japan or Germany. By 1996 the deficit was a smaller fraction of GDP than in any other major industrialized country and showed a small surplus in FY1998.

In 1996, the voters rewarded Clinton by making him the first Democrat reelected to office since Franklin D. Roosevelt. The Republican Party found it difficult to attack Clinton's economic record, so they touted the symbolic issues of the "character and integrity" of their candidate, Senator Dole.

Clinton's success was the result of many factors. The most important were the fiscal policy changes adopted in the Omnibus Budget Reconciliation Act of 1993 (OBRA93). The act raised taxes on upper income Americans while it reduced spending. The other budget savings resulted from the higher tax revenues resulting from increased employment and lower spending brought about by a stronger economy. The effect of deficit reduction on business confidence is difficult to measure, but is important nevertheless.

Looking Forward

A balanced budget that seemed almost impossible a few years ago became a reality in 1998. President Clinton and Congress have three basic policy options regarding what to do with any budget surplus.

---

[36]*The Economic Report of the President,* February 1997 (Washington, D.C.: Government Printing Office, 1997), p. 23.

First, they can begin paying down some of the national debt that has accumulated. At the end of World War II the national debt stood at $204 billion. By 1975 the debt doubled. It doubled again to over $800 billion between 1975 and 1982. In the last fifteen years it has more than quadrupled so that the national debt is now over $5 trillion. Rather than raising taxes, the government financed the debt by issuing more Treasury bonds. Interest payments on the debt were about $244 billion dollars, or about 15 percent of the national budget.

Eliminating annual budget deficits means that the total debt is no longer increasing. Paying down the debt would give policy makers room to maneuver in the future in dealing with the increasing costs for Social Security and Medicare when the baby boom generation begins to retire by 2010. Paying down the debt has some voter appeal in terms of demonstrating "responsible" government. Other policy analysts think that the benefits of paying down the debt would be very modest. They point out that as the economy continues to grow while the debt does not, the debt load and the interest payments will become a smaller part of the total budget. Total interest payments that equal about 3 percent of GDP in 1998, will decline to less than 1.5 percent by 2010.

The second alternative, cutting taxes, has more voter appeal then reducing the debt, especially among conservatives. This is so despite the fact that Americans pay fewer taxes than nationals of almost any other state. Opponents point out that the supply-side argument that tax cuts would stimulate economic growth and more than pay for themselves does not necessarily work. Yet, using the surplus to cut taxes has an ideological appeal to conservatives who would like to reduce the size of the national government anyway. Also, by cutting taxes, the surpluses disappear and are not available for other social welfare programs.

Third, the government could use the money surplus to provide funding for a variety of initiatives. Some have pointed out that the infrastructure of bridges, federal highways, and mass transit systems are in need of repair and upgrading. Supporters of spending in this area point out that such spending strengthens the nation economically by providing jobs and improving commerce. President Clinton, for example, has proposed making Medicare available to people starting at age 55. Another proposal is to increase spending on education and training. Supporters of this proposal point out that this spending will make people more productive citizens, keep them off welfare, and out of jail.

The surplus may be too small to permit any significant initiatives. And the political process of making policy will probably result in a compromise in which something is selected from each alternative. These policies will be explored more fully in later chapters.

The Decline and Renewal of Keynes

Parts of Keynes's theories were inconvenient to the accepted orthodoxy of the affluent. Among other things, his analysis suggested that the poor and the unemployed are not less moral than the affluent, but rather too frequently fall victims to economic forces beyond their control. In fact, he insisted that insufficient demand leading to unemployment can be caused by low wages, as well as by a tendency of the affluent to save rather than to consume and invest. Such analysis legitimized policies that included increased government intervention and a progressive tax policy aimed at taking wealth from the

CASE STUDY

WHO SHOULD GET THE CREDIT FOR
BALANCING THE BUDGET?

After the Bay of Pigs disaster, President
John F. Kennedy observed that successful
policies have "a thousand fathers" while a
policy failure "is an orphan." It is no surprise that self-interested politicians want to
take credit for a successful policy and distance themselves from any failure. So
despite the rush to take credit for the possible balanced budget, how would policy
analysts assess who should be credited?

George Bush is entitled to take some
credit. Bush made his pledge of "no new
taxes" a centerpiece in his 1988 campaign.
By 1990, Mr. Bush recognized that the
deficit was literally out of control and that
there would have to be tax increases.
Alarmed Democrats in Congress talked
publicly of a tax increase and were immediately pilloried as "tax and spend liberals."
Democrats made it clear that they would
not support raising taxes unless Mr. Bush
was willing to take the lead. Bush broke his
no new tax pledge and negotiated an agreement with the Democratic majority in
Congress. The bill which was signed into
law in November 1990, raised taxes and cut
spending. The law contained a "pay as you
go" requirement that obliged Congress to
pay for any tax cuts by reducing spending
and conversely, to either raise taxes or cut
spending elsewhere in the budget if they
increased spending in any program. This
discouraged Congress from expanding or

creating any new entitlements. The 1990
bill was passed with the Democrats in
Congress, as a substantial majority of congressional Republicans voted against the
legislation. Initially the recession that
began in July 1990 and ended in the spring
of 1991 wiped out any savings from the
bill. Many conservatives were unable to
forgive Mr. Bush for breaking faith with
Reaganomics. George Bush himself later
recanted and said the tax increase was a
major blunder.

Presidential candidate Ross Perot, a
third party candidate in the 1992 campaign,
also deserves some credit because he forced
the two major party candidates to address
an issue that they would have preferred
avoiding.

When Bill Clinton became president
in 1993, he worked skillfully on the legislation to reduce the deficit primarily
through tax increases that affected people
with high incomes. Newt Gingrich, who
later became Speaker of the House, charged
that the bill would lead to a "job-killing
recession." Republican Dick Armey, now
the House majority leader described the
measure as a "recipe for disaster." The bill
passed by the narrowest of margins: 218 to
216 in the House and 51 to 50 in the Senate,
where Vice President Al Gore broke a tie.
In an impressive display of party discipline
no Republican in either chamber voted
for the measure. In 1994 Republicans
campaigned heavily against Democrats as
reckless tax and spenders citing the
1993 bill as an example. As affluent

affluent and returning it to the circular flow of the economy through, among other things,
increased public expenditures that would benefit the poor. The anger of the affluent over
both the analysis and the resulting policies is well known.

However, it is clear that Keynes, like Smith, was too optimistic in his economic views.
He assumed that a better understanding of the relationship between economic variables
would permit government to enter the market system to maximize social welfare. He
implicitly accepted the notion that government would be neutral and benign and would
intervene only to increase demand and provide employment, thus increasing output and

Americans reduced their contributions to the Democratic Party, Bill Clinton lamented that perhaps he had raised taxes too much. But that bill did lay a foundation for subsequent economic growth. Clinton's commitment to reducing the deficit has been a factor in restoring confidence and a "better-than-expected" economic performance. When the government borrows less, interest rates are lower allowing industry to borrow more easily. Declining deficits contribute to a growing economy which generates more tax revenues, which reduce the deficit further.

Mikhail Gorbachev also deserves credit by helping to bring about the end of the Cold War. It was the collapse of the Soviet Union that allowed significant cuts in the defense budget that was essential for the United States government to make sizable cuts in military spending.

As does Alan Greenspan, the chairman of the Federal Reserve, who has made it clear that progress on deficit reduction is essential to keep interest rates low. Monetary policy has been exercised skillfully in recent years.

The political parties have played a role, though their record is somewhat mixed. Republicans have campaigned tirelessly on balancing the budget and shrinking the deficit, but have been quick to vote for tax cuts which increases deficits. Democrats have typically preferred to reduce the deficit by raising taxes, but have also agreed to reduce spending as well. Interestingly, while politicians want to take credit for reducing the deficit, they do not want to brag about the steps they took to achieve it. Democrats do not want to boast about raising taxes, however necessary the increases were. No politician wants to claim credit for having cut farm subsidies, Medicare payments to doctors or hospitals, or curbing the growth of veterans' benefits.

Reducing the deficits has helped strengthen the economy which has raised tax revenues while reducing the demand for food stamps. The strong economy has literally produced millions of jobs. The number of people on welfare dropped below 10 million in 1998, less than 4 percent of the population, which is the smallest proportion since 1970. Both administration officials and congressional Republicans are quick to each claim credit for the decline, though it is not clear what has happened to all the people no longer receiving welfare. Fewer welfare recipients mean lower government outlays.

Finally, a good deal of luck must be acknowledged. There have been no recent shocks to the economy. A serious problem in one of the world's trouble spots, or an oil shock, for example, could raise deficits and unravel a carefully orchestrated effort.

Robert Pear, "Budget Heroes Include Bush and Gorbachev," *The New York Times,* Jan. 19, 1998, p. A12. Robert Pear, "Number on Welfare Dips Below 10 Million," *The New York Times,* Jan. 21, 1998, p. A12.

---

improving income distribution. He assumed that an understanding of the shortcomings of market economics would lead to agreement about solutions. He seems not to have been aware of the degree to which governments are penetrated by self-interested groups who lobby for their own special interests rather than the general welfare of society.

Despite flaws in his analysis or in his optimism about the impartiality of government, in one sense Keynes has won the debate with the classical school regarding whether or not governments should intervene in the natural processes of the market to achieve societal goals in economic and other policy matters. Several factors that cannot be ignored compel government involvement in a wide range of public policy issues and will prevent its withdrawal in the future. Among these factors are the following:

1 Democratization. Around the world democratic forms of government are increasingly displacing authoritarian forms. One element of democracy is greater access to government by interest groups demanding that their needs be placed on the policy agenda.

2 Demands for economic security. As nations have become more prosperous, demands have increased for governments to provide protection from the vagaries of market forces. Tolerance of economic disruption declined at the very time when the expansion of industrialization and modernization was increasing competition. This trend began before the Great Depression, but was legitimized by that crisis of enormous proportions. More recently, major businesses have demanded that government not let them fail, citing the potential damaging effects on the overall national economy (to say nothing of the effects on company executives). Government has been pressured to undertake measures ranging from protective legislation, to favorable tax treatment, to business loans, and to outright bailouts in the cases of Chrysler Corporation and the savings-and-loan industry.

It is not surprising that, if corporations can successfully plead their special right to subsidies to remain in business, ordinary citizens will plead their right for aid to alleviate the vicissitudes of poverty through assistance in unemployment compensation, health care, education, Food Stamps, and Temporary Assistance to Needy Families (TANF), among other programs.

3 Demands for social justice. The demand for equal treatment before the law in the United States and throughout the world reflects the demand that gender, ethnic, racial, and religious discrimination come to an end. There is an unwillingness to endure humiliating and degrading treatment at the hands of an elite. Not infrequently the discriminatory practices are protected by the state at the expense of victims and in favor of those not discriminated against.

4 Urbanization. Increased urbanization has enlarged the public sector of the economy in areas such as public health, police protection, sanitation, and education that in a more rural society were left to individuals or private groups.

5 War. Two world wars and a Cold War in this century have resulted in a quantum increase in government spending on national defense. Even with the collapse of the major military threat represented by the Soviet Union and Eastern Europe, military spending in the United States will still remain at levels high enough to be a pivotal influence on the national economy.

6 Technology. Governments have been forced to respond to problems created by new technologies that require national regulation in communications (radio, telephone, and television), aviation, legal and illicit drugs, and automobiles, just to name a few.

7 Policies in other countries. Governments in developing countries have resorted to economic planning in an effort to modernize and achieve living standards comparable with those of the Western World. Governments elsewhere engage in a variety of policies such as education to improve the quality and productivity of their labor forces. Many countries such as Japan and Germany have industrial policies, in which the government acts as a partner with business firms in charting national economic development. These policies are designed to improve the economic competitiveness of the countries' firms internationally, thereby improving the national economic and social welfare. The U.S. government is, however reluctantly, being pushed in this direction just to compete with these countries in international trade.

Moreover, the view popularized during the 1980s that government intervention is unneeded and that it is actually likely to be harmful has come increasingly under question. Social problems such as homelessness, the need to improve education standards, and the need to deal with public health problems such as AIDS have contributed to this. At the same time, scandals in the banking and the securities industries have led to calls for greater government regulatory powers.

ADVANTAGES OF GOVERNMENT INTERVENTION TO CORRECT MARKET FAILURES

Government by definition has a universal membership made up of all its citizens; it also has the power to compel obedience to its laws. Together these give it distinct advantages in attempting to correct failures in the marketplace:

1 It can avoid **free rider problems** in providing a public good precisely because of its universal membership. Individuals may not easily opt out of the system.

2 It has the power to **prohibit** certain activities—what we might call public "bads." For example, by law or through regulatory processes it may prevent the opening of a bank, the selling of certain drugs, or the practice of medicine by particular individuals.

3 It has the power to **punish.** The government can exercise a range of punishments for violations of its laws far more severe than any that could be carried out through private arrangements.

4 It has the power to **tax**—perhaps its most important advantage. Individual insurance firms may recognize that certain behaviors increase the risks against which they provide insurance. Those firms would like to discourage smoking, for example, since it increases the incidence of health problems. Insurance companies can run ads against smoking, but the government can actively discourage the practice by raising the prices of tobacco products through taxes on them.

5 Government can improve **markets having imperfect information.** Business can provide information on products in ways aimed at preventing consumers from comparing differences in quality and price. The government can require that such information be provided in a standardized, easy-to-understand manner.

CONCLUSION

1 The classical school of economics associated with Adam Smith promotes an economic model that claims full employment of workers and capital can be maintained without any government intervention. Deviations from the ideal resulting in economic slowdowns, reduced output, or unemployment will self-adjust as if an invisible hand intervened, thus eliminating the need for government involvement. This school concludes that government should not intervene in the economy because any economic problem is only temporary. From this perspective, government's role should be limited as much as possible. Although there is much in Smith's analysis supportive of government intervention into the economy, today's conservatives are inclined to ignore those aspects of his writings.

2 Thomas Robert Malthus focused on a problem noticed early on in market capitalism—the increasing economic disparity between the rich and the poor. His analysis led him to conclude that poverty is a moral problem: the poor lack moral restraints in reproduction. Any effort to improve their condition through government relief or higher wages will result in their producing more offspring until they fall back to subsistence levels again. This is the "Iron Law of Wages." Any effort to improve their situation by higher wages, government policy, or charity is doomed to failure. This theory reinforced laissez-faire thinking and justified opposition to any policy proposal on behalf of the lower classes by the more affluent. Conversely, it can be directly linked to arguments that tax rates on the wealthy should be kept as low as possible and that it is immoral and counterproductive to take wealth from productive individuals and transfer it to those who have contributed less to the social good.

3 Karl Marx pointed out failures in the laissez-faire model due to market power and insufficient income for workers to maintain the demand for goods necessary to maintain full employment. Marx saw threats to the continuance of the capitalist system everywhere.

4 John Maynard Keynes revolutionized economic theory with his analysis holding that market economies are inherently unstable, and that they have no self-correcting properties. According to Keynes, government may be the only part of society capable of intervening in the economy to create the demand necessary to maintain full employment. His analysis showed the economy to be much more complex than anything suggested by the classical school. His conclusion was that there are several different areas of monetary and fiscal policy in which the government may successfully intervene. These interventions may also be geared to achieve social goals of the society other than those purely economic in nature.

It may well be that the very survival of a capitalist economy in America is due to the relief from some of its harshest failures (poverty, unemployment, alienation, and income insecurity) by the Keynesian welfare state. The welfare state may result less from the policy choices in search of social justice, than it has become necessary to the survival of a capitalist economy. Government expenditures, both national and state, now account for 30 percent of GDP in the United States.

5 The supply-side approach brought back many of the arguments of the classical school in a slightly different form. The decade of the 1980s saw a concerted effort to return to earlier policy prescriptions of reducing government involvement in social and economic issues. The policies were not successful in achieving the macroeconomic goals claimed. Although the supply-side school as an approach has receded in importance, a conservative perspective with the goal of reducing government influence and its consequent tax burden is still very much alive.

6 Government does have some advantages over private efforts to correct failures in the economy or to influence what, how, or to whom goods will be distributed.

QUESTIONS FOR DISCUSSION

1 Many contemporary followers claim that Adam Smith was above all a supporter of laissez faire. What support is there for this view? On what basis could that view be challenged?

2 Much of the Malthusian analysis has been discredited today, yet he was onto something when focused on the relationship of population and a nation's economic well-being. How would you revise his theory to apply it to developing nations today?

3 The Malthusian analysis had instant appeal to the affluent of his time, while the Marxian analysis had more appeal to the working class. Discuss the psychological appeal of each theory to the self-interest of each group. Is there a way to determine which theory is more in accordance with the facts? How?

4 Contrast the major tenets of the classical school as discussed in this chapter with those of Keynes.

KEY CONCEPTS

fiscal policy	mercantilism
free rider	monetarism
Great Depression	monetary policy
imperfect markets	natural price
Iron Law of Wages	Phillips Curve
John Maynard Keynes	self-adjusting market
laissez faire	Adam Smith
Thomas Robert Malthus	stagflation
market price	supply-side economics
Karl Marx	surplus value

SUGGESTED READINGS

Marc Allan Eisner, *The State in the American Political Economy* (Englewood Cliffs, NJ: Prentice-Hall, 1995).

John Kenneth Galbraith, *The Culture of Contentment* (New York: Houghton Mifflin Company, 1992).

Robert Heilbroner, *The Worldly Philosophers: The Lives, Times, and Ideas of the Great Economic Thinkers,* 4th ed. (New York: Simon and Schuster, 1972).

Robert Heilbroner and Lester Thurow, *Economics Explained* (Englewood Cliffs, NJ: Prentice-Hall, 1994).

John Maynard Keynes, *The General Theory of Employment, Interest, and Money* (New York: Harcourt Brace Jovanovich, 1964; originally published in 1936).

Thomas Robert Malthus, *An Essay on the Principle of Population,* edited by Philip Appleman (New York: W. W. Norton & Company, 1976).

Robert B. Reich, *The Work of Nations* (New York: Vintage Books, 1992).

Adam Smith, *An Inquiry into the Nature and Causes of the Wealth of Nations,* edited by Edwin Cannan (New York: G. P. Putman's Sons, 1877; originally published in 1776). There are many more recent annotated editions available.

Adam Smith, *The Theory of Moral Sentiments,* edited by D. D. Raphael and A. L. Macfie (Oxford, England: Clarendon Press, 1976; originally published in 1759).

6

ECONOMIC POLICY: STRATEGIES FOR TIGHT BUDGETS AND NEW SOCIAL NEEDS

As chapter 5 indicated, prior to the 1930s most policy analysts believed that a market economy would achieve the macroeconomic goals of full employment, price stability, and productivity growth without government intervention. The Great Depression, which was a period of high unemployment, declining incomes, and considerable political unrest, shattered such complacent beliefs. John Maynard Keynes's theories demonstrated how achieving macroeconomic goals required government intervention through monetary and fiscal policies. This was officially endorsed in the United States by the Employment Act of 1946 which committed the federal government to policy goals of achieving maximum employment, production, and purchasing power.

INTRODUCTION

Several economic policy goals are generally accepted by all governments. They include **full employment, price stability** (low levels of inflation), and **economic growth.** The role of the policy analyst is to design policies that will best achieve these goals. In the United States, Congress and the president, along with a host of policy advisers, try to formulate policies to achieve the goals through the political process.

EVOLUTION OF POLITICAL-ECONOMIC THINKING

One of the major effects of the New Deal was that it signified a fundamental change in the role of government in American society. For the first time government tried to change certain market structures to provide more socially acceptable outcomes for an economy in severe distress. The recognition that government may alter market outcomes is a significant change in political philosophy. A laissez-faire view of society no longer described the perfect model of the relationship between government and the economy. It is now widely accepted that there are different kinds of markets in society and that government should intervene in many cases. For example, when an industry produces toxic waste as a negative externality, government should intervene. The government should intervene to provide for public safety in such markets as aviation. Most agree that the government should intervene to require information be provided in food labeling, medicines, and stock offerings, among others. There is no consensus on the question of *how much* and *what kind* of intervention. These are two of the most contentious questions dividing liberals and conservatives on policy issues today.

The market system had so broken down during the Depression that it was unable to put together the factors of production (land, labor, and capital) to produce a satisfactory level of output for the society. The efforts to prime the pump to stimulate economic activity were actually very meager, in the range of a $2 to $3 billion dollar deficit per year. At that time, those deficits seemed rather radical and new government involvement had the unintended effect of further unsettling business confidence. But, as previously noted, John Maynard Keynes's theory suggested that the *total volume of expenditures* that a market spent for goods and services was the critical element leading to prosperity or stagnation. When the volume was high, unemployment was low; when it declined, output and unemployment rose. The volume of expenditure was in turn determined by capital expenditure. Therefore if there was insufficient private business investment, the government could make up the deficiencies by engaging in public capital expenditures such as building roads or schools.

To the New Dealers, this would not be a radical change of capitalism, rather it would amount to government attempting to guide the economy to maintain high levels of employment and nudge the economy toward growth whenever it showed signs of weakening. But to business leaders and ideological conservatives government spending is inherently wasteful. For those who believe in a Social Darwinist, laissez-faire view of society there is always a suspicion that government spending is a thinly disguised entering wedge for socialism. The debate lasted through the 1930s until World War II brought the unprecedented rise in expenditure, and a corresponding decline in unemployment. The federal government mobilized the nation for war and the years of massive output led to a new attitude toward government involvement in the economy.

The changed environment resulted in the passage of the Employment Act of 1946 which signaled a new era. The original version of the bill responsible for creating the conditions that would result in full employment was opposed by the United States Chamber of Commerce, the National Association of Manufacturers, and the American Farm Bureau Federation. Their opposition was such that the original goal of full employment was watered down to providing "maximum employment, production, and purchasing power." But most importantly the law moved the debate from *whether* the government should be involved in directing the economy, to *how* to best achieve a robust economy.

The Employment Act created a Council of Economic Advisers (CEA) which would be confirmed by the Senate and would be responsible for preparing an annual *Economic Report of the President.* Although the Bureau of the Budget was completely under the control of the president, Senate confirmation of the CEA indicated that responsibility for the macroeconomic health of the nation would not be under the exclusive control of the president. The act also created a Joint Economic Committee in Congress to have cognizance in the area of economic affairs which further limited the power of the president.

Problems

Political economic policy is concerned with the interaction of political and economic forces and the way that governmental authority influences economic activity. The policy that results is also, as noted in chapters 3 and 4, the outcome of the competition between coalitions, elite demands as constrained by institutional capacities, and previous policy decisions. Political-economic theories shape the institutional capabilities.

Two models are generally used by officials in contemplating appropriate economic policies. The first is a variation on the classical model referred to as the neoclassical model. The classical model assumed that labor markets performs like other competitive markets. It assumed that there was a wage at which everyone could find employment. As the price of labor fell demand would rise and unemployment would disappear. Ultimately it held that all unemployment was temporary or voluntary. The Great Depression, the continuation of high unemployment despite falling wages, was an undeniable failure of classical theory concerning labor markets finding equilibrium at full employment.

The neoclassical model also assumes that markets generally find their own equilibrium point and are efficient. The state is justified in intervening only in situations of market failure. This model is conservative as the result from market forces is assumed to be efficient and therefore legitimate.

The second model is the Keynesian model. Keynes, as noted in chapter 5, is recognized for providing new insights into the role of the state in the economy and the functioning of markets. Keynes's insight is simplicity itself: Left alone, the economy might not tend toward equilibrium. However policy makers could expand government spending or reduce taxes to stimulate demand. If these policies were pursued correctly and on a large enough scale, these policies could increase economic activity and reduce unemployment. According to his theory, monetary and fiscal policy could be employed throughout the business cycle to maintain low inflation and high employment. One of the fiscal policies that could be used to maintain high employment is the full-employment budget. The full-employment budget is based on the calculations of what government revenues would be at a hypothetical state of full employment. Government expenditures would then be based on that projected level of revenues and expenditures. Keynesianism provided some hope that economic policy could insulate society from the wildly fluctuating business cycles of the past.

It would be difficult to overstate the importance Keynes's economic theory had as a political doctrine. Keynesian theory provided an intellectual framework that justified state activism and social spending for policy makers. Previously policy makers who increased spending during economic downturns were charged with being fiscally irresponsible and threatening to bankrupt the nation. Now the spending could be justified as stabilizing the economy. In fact, programs could be put in place to automatically stabilize the economy by programming spending increases precisely when the economy was contracting. This limited the depth of the business cycle. When the economy begins expanding, social welfare expenditures automatically contract reducing the potential for such rapid growth that excessive inflation results. Ultimately the theory provided the justification for the welfare state. Most advanced industrial democracies have adopted economic policies based on extensions of Keynesian thinking since WW II although they have adopted different means of promoting aggregate demand.

When the economy falters, the deficit increases even if there is no change in tax rates or spending programs. As earnings fall and unemployment rises, government tax revenues, which rely heavily on the personal income, payroll, and corporate taxes, fall. People and corporations pay less tax when their income declines. At the same time some government expenditures for unemployment and welfare benefits will rise. Similarly, when the economy expands, tax revenues rise and unemployment and welfare benefits fall. Changes in tax collections and expenditures are **automatic stabilizing mechanisms** that reduce the impact of economic fluctuations. Automatic stabilizers are important because they adjust immediately to a rising or falling economy and do not require any policy debate to begin working. Therefore the deficit will rise during a recession and shrink during a robust economy, even if there is no change in fiscal policy. So the same fiscal policy could result in a surplus, a balanced budget, or a deficit.

Crude Policy Instruments

Clashes over economic policy emphasized by the major policy makers in the field helped to define the mechanisms government had at its disposal to affect the overall management of the economy. The principal policy tools available to presidential administrations for influencing the economy are monetary policy, regulatory policy, and fiscal policy (including taxing and spending).

There are at least two major problems with using these instruments effectively. The first problem is that even if the goals are accepted, there is considerable debate about the best way to achieve them. **Nowhere is the disagreement regarding how to achieve noncontroversial goals more apparent than the schools of thought regarding market failure.** If unregulated markets generated full employment, price stability, economic growth, and an equitable distribution of income as classical economic theory suggests, there would be no need for government intervention. As has already been pointed out, markets do fail and governments are called upon to intervene. Does government intervention accomplish its goal of economic growth, reduced unemployment, and inflation? If not, government interventions also fail. In the real world, of course, nothing is perfect, so the real choice is between imperfect markets and imperfect policy interventions.

A second major problem for economic policy is that governments may be unable to achieve full employment, prevent inflation, or stimulate economic expansion because those responsible for economic policy are either _unable,_ or _unwilling_ to take the action required. The separation of powers fragments the responsibility for economic policy and weakens the government's ability to control the economy. While the president is by far the single most important player in economic policy, his ability to control events or policy is often overestimated. Since the president submits a proposed budget to Congress annually, and uses all the powers of the office to persuade the rest of the government to accept his approach, he appears to be more of a leader than he actually is. But **fiscal policy** (i.e., taxing and spending), is largely determined by the performance of the economy at the time the budget is introduced to Congress, and the forecast during the period of the budget. Much of the budget includes programs over which a president has little control such as debt refinancing and various entitlement programs.

The President

The executive branch itself contains different departments at the cabinet level such as the Departments of Commerce, Treasury, and Labor each with goals that differ from each other. In addition the Office of Management and Budget (OMB) assists the president in preparing the budget and submitting it to Congress. The OMB tries to submit a budget that reflects the priorities of the president. But federal agencies submitting their budget requests usually believe in the value of their own programs and press for expanded funding. If the OMB lowers an agency's request, the agency may appeal directly to the president, or seek informal support from Congress.

Since Article I of the Constitution provides that Congress alone has the power to "appropriate" money, it assures the budgetary process will involve partisan maneuvering for political advantage. Not surprisingly, politicians often color budget projections to win support for their agendas. The most flagrant examples of predicting unrealistically low projections of inflation and optimistic projections of economic performance occurred during the first two years of the Reagan administration. Ronald Reagan began his presidency promising to eliminate the deficit, increase defense spending, cut taxes, and reduce what he perceived to be the excesses of the welfare state. He held that this agenda would stimulate such economic growth that enough tax revenues would be created to balance the budget by 1984. George Bush, as a presidential candidate called the proposal "voodoo economics." Starting with Reagan's assumption and working backward, former budget director, David Stockman, hastily put together a five-year plan openly referred to as "Rosy Scenario." Stockman and his colleagues' secret calculations showed the deficit rising dramatically. In public he insisted his "Rosy Scenario" projections were valid. In his memoirs, David Stockman stated that he "out-and-out cooked the books . . ." inventing spurious cuts to make the deficit appear smaller.[1] During a presidential election, challengers are anxious to place the blame for any economic failures on the incumbent when offering their own solutions to economic problems.

Monetary policy as a tool to control the money supply is primarily centered on the Federal Reserve banking system. By loosening or tightening the reserve requirements that banks have to maintain on their deposits the Federal Reserve is able to encourage or discourage lending money which is the source of much economic activity. Monetary theory also suggested that it should make more money available to the banking system to lend at low interest rates when they were needed, and reduce funds available when

---

[1]David Stockman, *The Triumph of Politics* (New York: Harper & Row, 1986), p. 383.

money seemed in excess supply by buying or selling bonds. The Federal Reserve did not take this action early in the Depression.

Presidential influence on monetary policy is based upon the power to appoint individuals to the Federal Reserve Board's Board of Governors. The president's subsequent influence after appointment is largely informal, although the relationship is often much closer than press accounts would indicate. The president often works the "good cop/bad cop routine" with the Fed for public consumption when the latter makes a politically difficult decision. The president complains to the press that soft economic conditions are caused by a recalcitrant Fed that refuses to lower interest rates sufficiently. Or, conversely, that inflation could be brought under control if the Fed would only tighten the money supply. Blame is directed toward the Fed since they do not run for election, while the president appears to be a nice guy without sufficient clout to implement his more compassionate goals.

The Policy Makers

Policy makers do not prefer high unemployment to full employment, inflation to price stability, or economic recessions to economic growth. But political entrepreneurs have short time horizons and may not find it in their interest to take the action required to reduce inflation, or get a vigorous economic expansion underway. They may agree with the notion that there is no free lunch, but they are also aware that **the price of lunch may be deferred.** Elected officials prefer policies that provide short-term benefits before Election Day and bills that will not come due until after voters have cast their retrospective votes. Thus, in the American political process, there is a bias in favor of policies with short-term benefits and long-term costs. That fact has profound implications for the conduct of long-term economic growth and stabilization policies as opposed to near-term policies.

In practical terms, suppose that the government increases its expenditures by borrowing rather than raising taxes. The result will be an increase in aggregate demand. **Aggregate demand is the total demand for an economy's goods and services.** The distributional benefits of increased output and employment will be felt almost immediately. The costs of this expansion reflected in higher prices will manifest themselves only months later, hopefully after an election. So from a politician's perspective, the political "goods" arrive first: an increase in employment and a rise in real GDP. The political "bads," higher debt servicing and higher inflation arrive later. Every member of the House of Representatives is never more than two years away from election and averages only a year away from the next election. Every president is never more than four years from an election and averages only two years. Politicians have a very strong incentive to pursue the near-term political "goods" and put off worrying about the "bads" as long as they are in office.

To the extent that presidents do engage in economic tightening, they have a strong incentive to pursue such policies early in their terms and pursue expansionist policies as elections draw near. And to the degree that voters have short memories and limited sophistication of economic policies, they are likely to reward the political entrepreneur who engages in economic expansion just before the election.[2] Survival being a basic instinct among all politicians, these facts of political life also lead to short-term thinking.

Many recent economic problems require the spending of more money by the government, but the string of massive federal deficits in recent years precludes increased spending. A conspicuous solution to increased spending needs and huge deficits is for large tax increases. But such increases would cause pain to taxpayers and threaten a reduction in consumer demand that could lead to greater unemployment long before a reduction in the deficit would reduce inflation or free up new government monies. In this case the political "bads" arrive rather promptly, while the "goods" would likely arrive much later and be felt only gradually. Not surprisingly, the three presidential elections in the 1980s were won by the candidate who took the hardest line against raising taxes. In 1992, presidential candidate Clinton was able to neutralize the appeal of President Bush who had broken his pledge of "no new taxes" by indicating that he himself was a "new kind of Democrat" committed to reducing the deficit by reducing expenditures, and also to cutting taxes for middle-income taxpayers. Once in office though, President Clinton faced pressure to initiate spending cuts but increase taxes, and to do both quickly. If the process was delayed, the fear was that it would be impossible to do either as the 1994 elections approached. Clinton barely achieved the tax increases—receiving not one Republican vote. The increases were limited to wealthier Americans who had received steep tax decreases during the Reagan-Bush years.

Political entrepreneurs thus have a bias toward expansionary fiscal and monetary policies since lower taxes and increased expenditures for special interest groups provide strong support for an incumbent's bid for reelection. Policies to reduce spending and increase taxes cause unrest among voters. Even though the optimal policy often requires long-term strategies, the political incentives for incumbents may not reflect the long-term economic interests of the nation. Political entrepreneurs find it extremely difficult to continue unpleasant policies as the exigencies of elections threaten their futures.

There is considerable irony in the fact that voters deplore the deficits and rail against the inability of governments to control spending, yet threaten to retaliate against candidates who support the painful economic measures needed to end them. The result is a built-in bias favoring lower rather than higher taxes and higher rather than lower expenditures. But cutting government spending inevitably means reducing benefits to someone who is currently receiving them. Voters who are hurt by government policies and lose benefits are thought to have long memories at election time, a notion that definitely has long-term effects on politicians' voting behavior.

MONETARY POLICY AND ECONOMIC HEALTH

John Maynard Keynes, in his theory, believed that the amount of money available in an economy was critical in determining how interest rates would adjust to balance the supply and demand for money. Recall that the money supply in the United States is determined by the Federal Reserve. The Fed has three methods to control the supply of

[2]Thomas D. Willett and King Banaian, "Models of the Political Process and Their Implications for Stagflation: A Public Choice Perspective," in Thomas D. Willett (ed.), *Political Business Cycles: The Political Economy of Money, Inflation, and Unemployment* (Durham, NC: Duke University Press, 1988).

money: (1) it can change the reserve requirements (by raising or lowering the amount of reserves that banks must keep on hand as a percentage of total deposits), (2) it can change the discount rate (the interest rate the Fed charges member banks when they borrow from the Fed), and (3) its most important tool—it can change the amount of reserves in member banks by buying or selling government bonds in open market operations. When the Fed buys bonds, it deposits money in the banks which is added to their reserves. When the Fed sells bonds to the banks, the banks transfer money to the Fed causing their reserves to fall, while the Fed takes the money out of circulation.

Once the Fed has fixed the money supply, the quantity is not affected by other variables such as interest rates. The interest rate really mirrors the opportunity cost of holding noninterest-bearing money rather than putting money in an interest-bearing account. Therefore rising interest rates will result in people putting more of their money into interest-bearing accounts. The interest rate reflects the rate necessary to bring the amount of money demanded and supplied into balance.

The implications of what has been said is that an increased demand for money can be expected to lead to a higher interest rate, and a higher interest rate will reduce the quantity of goods and services demanded. A higher price level for goods will increase the demand for money. Therefore, if the Fed increases the money supply at any given price level, it will lead to a lower interest rate, which will raise the quantity of goods and services demanded. So monetary policy can be described either in terms of the money supply or interest rates.

However, all too often the Fed has been concerned that if "too much money" is available, individuals raise their demand for goods and services. An increase in demand throughout the economy would result in a decrease in unemployment as businesses hire more workers to turn out more goods and services. The end result would be an upward pressure on prices as labor would seek higher wages in a tight labor market. In such a situation the Fed is tempted to reduce inflationary pressures by tightening the money supply and raising interest rates. The end result is that inflation may be reduced at the cost of rising unemployment. One view is that there is a natural rate of unemployment at a little over 6 percent (some think it may have dropped to 5.5 percent because of changes in the labor force). At that level there would be enough slack in the economy to neutralize inflationary pressures.

In the spring of 1998, in a clear political victory for President Clinton, the unemployment level declined to 4.3 percent, its lowest level in thirty years, well below the "natural rate" of unemployment (6 percent). Many had expected that the demand for labor would result in a surge of inflation. There was concern that the Fed's chairman, Alan Greenspan, always on the alert for signs of inflation would raise interest rates to "cool down" the economy from what he characterized as "irrational exuberance." But with inflation stabilized at around 3 percent, the Fed has responded to the Clinton administration officials' frequent comments that they see no signs of inflation by not taking any action.

With both Clinton and the Fed getting high marks for performance and both inflation and unemployment at low levels, some critics suggest that zero inflation should be the primary goal. Proponents of this view argue that the costs of such a policy would be relatively small (an increase in unemployment of about 2–3 percent and a corresponding reduction in the GDP of the same amount) while the gains from zero inflation would be great. Liberals have argued that the price in increased unemployment and decreased production is too great. The goal, they argue, should be to encourage employment not reduce employment through government policy.[3]

Deflation

Ironically, just as many policy makers thought that they had succeeded in taming inflation, even if they were not certain just how, a new threat appeared: deflation. **Deflation is defined as a general decline in the price of goods and services.** The last extreme case of deflation occurred during the Great Depression when prices fell at an average of almost 7 percent a year from 1929 through 1933.

Many policy analysts believe that underlying economic conditions make inflation more likely than deflation, but the financial crisis in Asia is making many very nervous. Political economists do not even agree on exactly what would cause deflation. One view is that global supply is growing faster than demand. As a result, prices are dropping for many raw materials and manufactured goods. Others believe that many governments (like Japan, Canada, and the United States), eager to stop inflation, have kept too tight a control over the money supply which dampens demand.[4]

Since 1997, an increasing number of policy analysts have been concerned about the potential for a deflationary spiral spreading to the U.S. from Asia. A simplified illustration of the gloomy chain of events is worth considering. Japan, Thailand, Indonesia, Malaysia, and South Korea all tried to build a large productive capacity in the same industries at the same time. As a result, there is overcapacity in automobile and high-tech industries. Competition in these industries resulted in declining prices which raised the cost of debt and forced many corporations to reduce costs. Some Asian businesses began going bankrupt. This weakened financial institutions leaving them with little money to lend to credit-worthy borrowers. Reduced prices in Asia made their exports cheaper here, and forced American companies to lower their prices to remain competitive. Anticipating lower prices leads many consumers to put off making purchases, because they expect products to be cheaper if they wait. Reduced profits result, which in turn, causes companies to reduce labor costs by holding the line on wages and even laying off workers. These corporate slowdowns could potentially cause stock market declines that, in turn, would cause stockholders to postpone spending plans. The overall slowdown would reduce government tax revenues from personal and corporate taxes, leading to cuts in government spending. This could cause a decline in the Gross Domestic Product (GDP), as the United States slides into a recession. While this scenario is possible, most policy analysts believe it is unlikely. Prior to Keynes, the classical school would have suggested that governments should not intervene while these cycles played themselves out. Today, policy analysts point out that policy makers can vary interest rates and government spending to stop this downward spiral.

---

[3]George A. Akerlof, William T. Dickens, and George L. Perry, "Low Inflation or No Inflation: Should the Federal Reserve Pursue Complete Price Stability?" *Brookings Policy Brief No. 4* (Washington, DC: The Brookings Institution, 1996).

[4]Christopher Conte, "Deflation Fears," *CQ Researcher* (Washington, DC: Congressional Quarterly Inc., 1998), vol. 8, no. 6, p. 123.

While most policy analysts expect the Asian crisis will have an impact on the U.S. economy, no one is certain how significant the impact will be. Falling prices in Asia will result in reduced exports to those countries from the United States, while simultaneously resulting in an increase in cheaper imports from the area. Alan Greenspan has made clear that the Fed will switch from its anti-inflation stance to an anti-deflation stance if conditions make it necessary.[5] However if the economy slips into deflation the Fed might find it difficult to respond satisfactorily. It cannot reduce interest rates below zero, so it is unclear how far it could go in combating severe deflation. It might also be difficult to maintain the current pleasant blend of the summer of 1998 of low inflation and low unemployment. Workers have accepted very low wage increases in recent years because of job insecurity resulting from competitive global markets. Workers in the United States could not increase their wages in the face of lower wage rates abroad. Therefore tight labor markets in America are not inflationary because global competition is keeping a lid on prices and wages. But as Greenspan noted, "There is a limit to the value of additional job security people are willing to acquire in exchange for lesser increases in living standards."[6] The crux of the problem as some see it is that the traditional concern of the Fed has been to operate on the assumption that inflation is the greatest threat, especially when the U.S. economy is operating at a high level of capacity and low unemployment. The global economy, of which we are now a part, is suffering from deflation. If our policies continue to reflect an excessive concern about inflation, the Fed argues, we will increase the risk of deflation.

The major unknown in this situation is that much of Asia appears to be in a period of plunging asset prices, bankruptcies, moribund consumer demand, and declining economies, and it is not clear how far the economic conditions may slide. President Clinton has asked Congress to appropriate about $18 billion to cover the U.S. share of an international plan to replenish International Monetary Funds (IMF) to deal with the crisis. He made clear how the global economy has changed the landscape of "independent" nation-states in his State of the Union Address in 1998. He said, "If they sink into recession, they won't be able to buy the goods we'd like to sell them. Second, they're also our competitors, so if their currencies lose their value . . . then the price of their goods will drop, flooding our market and others with much cheaper goods, which makes it a lot tougher for our people to compete. And finally, they are our strategic partners. Their stability bolsters our security."

It is clear that monetary policy is much better equipped to deal with inflation than with deflation.

TAXES AS AN INSTRUMENT OF POLICY

The second major economic policy instrument to guide the economy is the ability of the government to *adjust taxes*. Pent-up consumer demand at the end of WW II served as a reminder that the major factor of the nation's total expenditure is always consumption

---

[5]Alan Greenspan, remarks at the annual Conference of the American Economic Association, Chicago, IL, Jan. 3, 1998; available online at http://www.bog.frb.fed.us.
[6]Alan Greenspan, *Monetary Policy Testimony and Report to the Congress,* February 26, 1997; available online at http://www.bog.frb.fed.us.

spending. Therefore through the ability of the government to raise and lower taxes, especially income taxes, the government can quickly raise or lower this broad flow of purchasing power.

The idea of monetary policy was not entirely new in the 1930s, but the idea about the use of taxes and national budgets as management tools of economic policy to counter economic cycles of boom and bust *was* new. Although the government borrows money to finance its operations, taxes collected from a variety of sources are the main reservoir of government expenditures.

But the question of **"who pays?"** is inextricably linked to several other questions regarding tax policy. Tax policy raises the question regarding what is a fair distribution of income? What are the major issues involved in deciding who should bear the burden of taxes? What do political scientists and policy analysts take into consideration when they talk about a fair tax system? Does the American tax system meet the criteria for fairness?

Government intervention is a conscious decision not to leave the provision of certain goods or services to the marketplace. It is a determination that political, not economic considerations will prescribe which services the government will provide. Taxes are required to finance these goods and services. **Therefore, the main purpose of taxation is to move purchasing power from the private to the public sector.** In order to understand and judge these economic policies, their distributional consequences must be understood.

Antitax sentiment has always run high in America. Recall that the American Revolution began as a tax revolt with the dumping of tea into Boston Harbor, because the colonists objected to the taxes levied upon the tea. After the adoption of the Constitution, the government relied primarily upon customs duties to fund the limited national budget. Congress enacted an income tax during the Civil War, but it expired at that war's end. In 1894 Congress passed another income tax bill. That tax was declared unconstitutional in 1895 in *Pollock v. Farmers' Loan and Trust Co.,* 158 U.S. 601 (1895). As a result, the Sixteenth Amendment to the Constitution was passed, which when ratified in 1916 gave Congress the power "to lay and collect taxes on incomes, from whatever source derived."

Although the personal income tax soon became the primary source of revenue for the government, the portion of income paid in taxes in the United States is still well below the percentage of income paid by workers as taxes in other countries. Figure 6-1 illustrates this fact. The bar graph supports the evidence that Americans are not overtaxed. Taxes from all levels of government are expressed as a percent of each country's GDP or output. This is the best measure of relative taxation because it includes not only the tax burden, but an indication of the ability to pay the taxes levied.

The Organization for Economic Cooperation and Development (OECD), one of the most reliable sources of data for international comparisons, found that of twenty-nine countries examined (mostly western, industrialized nations) only three (Korea, Mexico, and Turkey) collect a smaller share of revenues as a percentage of the GDP than the United States.[7]

[7]Organization for Economic Cooperation and Development, *Revenue Statistics 1965–1996,* 1997.

FIGURE 6-1
THE TAX LEVEL AS A % OF GDP IN SELECTED COUNTRIES—1994.
(Includes national and local taxes and social security contributions)

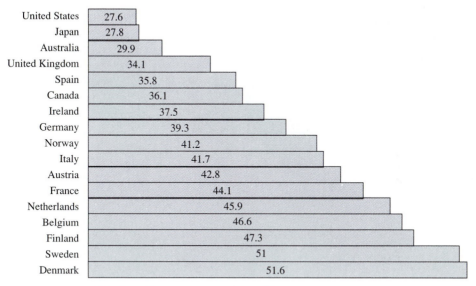

United States — 27.6
Japan — 27.8
Australia — 29.9
United Kingdom — 34.1
Spain — 35.8
Canada — 36.1
Ireland — 37.5
Germany — 39.3
Norway — 41.2
Italy — 41.7
Austria — 42.8
France — 44.1
Netherlands — 45.9
Belgium — 46.6
Finland — 47.3
Sweden — 51
Denmark — 51.6

Source: Statistical Abstract of the United States 1997, p. 844.

Even though Americans are among the least taxed people in the industrialized world, aversion to taxes runs high and politicians are usually rewarded for a vigorous and righteous defense of constituents against rapacious tax collectors. This is often accompanied by an indignant opposition to any increase in social welfare spending, since any reason for increased public expenditures would entail higher taxes. The reality is that when compared to most industrialized nations, the United States is a tax haven.

The OECD reports that if the United States adopted universal health insurance and paid close to the average of all health care expenditures (80 percent) U.S. tax rates would rise to about 35 percent, still well below the OECD average of 39.2 percent.[8] **The American tax burden is very light by any international comparison.**

TAXATION AND INCOME DISTRIBUTION

The government gets its revenue to finance its programs from a variety of tax sources. Figure 6-2 presents a breakdown of the sources of revenue for the national government. The largest single source of revenue is the **personal income tax** followed by **social insurance taxes** and the **corporate income tax.** In addition to income taxes, wages are subject to a **payroll tax** which is levied on a company's payroll (half of which is deducted

[8]*OECD Economic Surveys: United States. 1992, p. 52.*

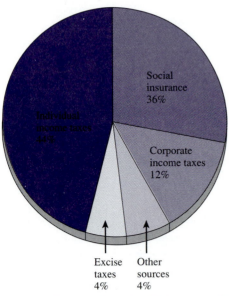

FIGURE 6-2
FEDERAL GOVERNMENT RECEIPTS 1997.

Social insurance 36%

Individual income taxes 44%

Corporate income taxes 12%

Excise taxes 4%

Other sources 4%

Source: Budget for Fiscal Year 1997, Volume 3: Historical Tables, 30 (Washington, DC: U.S. Govt. Printing Office, 1996).

from an employee's paycheck) to finance the Social Security and Medicare programs. The Social Security payroll tax is now the second major source of revenue. Workers transfer part of their earnings to retired workers through mandatory payroll deductions amounting to 7.65 percent of wages on income up to $68,400 in 1998. Employers contributed an equal amount.

Excise taxes, which are taxes on specific products, are a source of revenue for state and local governments, as well as the national government. Politicians find that raising taxes usually costs some voter support. Therefore they prefer that taxes be borne by as small a group as possible, or by such a large group that it is a minimal burden on each payer. Politicians find it easier to impose excise taxes than any other form of tax because they can raise a significant amount of revenue while affecting a relatively small number of voters. Nevertheless, excise taxes have declined in importance as a source of federal revenue. Their share of tax revenues has fallen from 13 percent of federal revenues in 1960 to just over 4 percent in 1992. Taxes levied on the sale of tobacco products or alcohol are often referred to as **sin taxes** based on the idea that use of these products imposes externalities on more sober nonsmokers in the form of air pollution, litter, and health hazards and increases in medical care. Most such taxes are levied on goods with a relatively **inelastic demand.** If the demand were highly elastic, the tax would push sales down significantly resulting in only small government revenues.[9]

Some excise taxes are targeted at purchasers of certain goods who will eventually benefit when the money is spent by the government. Gasoline taxes, for example, are

[9]The decline in sales resulting from the tax that is not offset by the tax revenue generated is referred to as a "deadweight loss" in that no one gets the money. Since a small number of voters buy cigarettes and alcohol, the price increase will not significantly affect sales. A much larger number of voters buy gas, but the political cost to an elected official of a tax on petroleum is acceptable because the deadweight losses are minimal and because the tax burden on each voter is relatively small.

used to finance highway construction. Others such as **luxury taxes** are levied on buyers of expensive nonessential items, such as yachts or expensive jewelry, whose incomes are assumed to be high enough to absorb the costs.

Most states raise most of their revenue from a combination of income taxes and **sales taxes** imposed on the purchase of a wide variety of goods and services (although many states exclude some essential items such as food from their sales taxes). **Property taxes** have traditionally been the main source of revenue for state and local governments, but income and sales taxes are increasingly important.

Principles of Taxation: Fairness and Efficiency

Although no one likes to transfer control over part of their income to the government, most people grudgingly comply. The primary purpose of taxation is to raise revenues to carry out government policy goals, although there are other goals as well such as discouraging the consumption of certain goods. Voluntary compliance is related to the perceived **efficiency** (or neutrality) and **fairness** of the system.

Efficiency Efficiency, or neutrality, suggests that unless there is adequate justification, we should try to interfere as little as possible with the market allocation. The freest movement of goods and services maximizes economic efficiency and therefore overall economic well-being. Unfortunately every tax influences economic activity and the allocation of resources, even in cases where the market process works well and needs no outside regulation. For example, the preferential treatment that allows individuals to deduct the cost of mortgage interest and property taxes on their homes from income taxes distorts the market by increasing the demand for home ownership over that for rental units. Similarly tax laws allow child care payments to be deducted from taxes owed. Unfortunately every tax invites concerted efforts to avoid it. For example the preferential treatment that allows individuals to deduct the cost of mortgage interest and property taxes on their homes distorts the market by increasing the demand for home ownership over rental units. Such preferential treatment, referred to as **tax expenditures,** represents a loss in government revenue just as though the government wrote a check for the amount of the deduction.

Special interest groups receiving preferential treatment are vigorous defenders of their tax subsidy and thus subsidies are very difficult to eliminate.

While there is a bias in favor of allowing the market to resolve many issues, there are many cases where the government must intervene to provide collective goods through the tax system. This immediately brings up the issue of fairness.

Fairness Political scientists, economists, and philosophers have wrestled for hundreds of years with the concept of what constitutes a just and equitable tax system. If the system is perceived as unfair, people are more likely to evade taxes, if possible, or pressure political entrepreneurs more aggressively to reduce their tax burden.

There are two main principles of fairness.

The Benefit Principle **The benefit principle holds that people should pay taxes in proportion to the benefits they receive.** This principle tries to make public goods

THE TWELVE LARGEST TAX EXPENDITURES (LOOPHOLES) IN THE 1997 BUDGET

Tax expenditures are defined as the reduction in tax revenue that results when government programs or benefits are provided through the tax system rather than reported as budgetary expenditures. The reductions are usually made by offering special tax rates, exemptions, or tax credits to programs beneficiaries. Governments introduce tax expenditures primarily to achieve social policy objectives such as transfers to lower income families or to promote economic development and job creation.

The federal government spent $554 billion on tax expenditures in fiscal 1997 according to the Clinton administration's budget request. The largest tax expenditure—the exclusion for employer contributions for health insurance—is also the fastest growing. The main reason the government reports tax expenditures is to improve government accountability by providing a more complete picture of government spending.

Rank	Tax expenditure	Cost to treasury in billions
1	Exclusion for employer contributions for medical insurance	$70.5
2	Exclusion of employer pension plan contributions and earnings	67.0
3	Deduction for mortgage interest on home	53.1
4	Deduction for state and local income taxes	30.6
5	Special treatment of capital gains at death	30.3
6	Accelerated depreciation of machinery	29.5
7	Deduction for charitable donations	26.1
8	Exclusion of Social Security benefits for retired workers	17.3
9	Deduction for state and local property tax payments	16.9
10	Deferral of capital gains on home sales	15.0
11	Exclusion of interest on state and municipal bonds	13.7
12	Exclusion of interest on life insurance savings	11.5

Governments use the tax system to deliver programs to reduce their own administrative costs and reduce compliance costs for recipients. There are several negative aspects to tax expenditures. Their overall cost receives less public scrutiny than is the case for spending programs because it need not be formally approved every year. The benefits of the major tax expenditures tend to go to high-income earners to an even greater degree than do entitlements. This can run counter to the objective of incorporating progressiveness into the tax system. Tax expenditures are big, and automatic, and costs are often hard to control as many the benefits tend to be more open ended and enforcement is often more difficult than for spending programs.

Source: Budget of the U.S. Government, Fiscal Year 1997, Vol. 3: Analytical Perspectives (Washington, DC: U.S. Government Printing Office, 1996), Table 5.1

similar to private goods in that payment for services is commensurate with the amount of goods or services received. If the purpose of taxes is to pay for government services, then those who gain from those services should pay. A toll bridge is justified using the benefit principle. Tolls collected are used to pay the bonds used for bridge construction

FIGURE 6-3
HOW THE FEDERAL BUDGET DOLLAR IS SPENT.

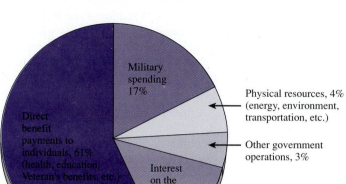

Military spending 17%

Physical resources, 4% (energy, environment, transportation, etc.)

Direct benefit payments to individuals, 61% (health, education, Veteran's benefits, etc.)

Other government operations, 3%

Interest on the national debt 15%

Source: The Budget for Fiscal Year 1997, Volume 3: Historical Tables (Washington, DC: U.S. Government Printing Office, 1996), 49.

and to maintain the bridge. Because those who pay the toll are the same people who use the bridge, the toll is viewed as a fair way to pay for the government service. The more they use the bridge, the more they will pay. Those who do not pay can be excluded. The major disadvantage of this principle is that it will not work for public goods where non-payers cannot be excluded, or where it is difficult to determine who benefits or by what amount. For example, who benefits most from law enforcement and the judicial system, the rich or the poor?

The benefits principle is often used to argue that the more affluent citizens should have a higher tax burden than poorer citizens because they benefit more from public services. For example, the wealthy receive more benefit from a police force than do poor citizens because they have more wealth to protect and their losses would be much greater in the event of theft. Therefore since police protection is more beneficial to the affluent, they should contribute more. The welfare of the wealthy is best served by the Securities and Exchange Commission, the Federal Reserve System, National Security, or by the judicial system. If there were agreement on **who benefits** and **by how much,** taxes could be allocated accordingly. Allocating taxes by this principle provides an incentive to insist that someone else is the main beneficiary. If these taxes could be allocated accurately there would be no income redistribution.

Ability-to-Pay Principle   The ability-to-pay principle claims that fairness requires that taxes be allocated according to the incomes and/or wealth of tax-payers, regardless of whether or not they benefit more. According to this principle, the wealthy may benefit more than the poor from some government expenditures and less than the poor in others. But since they are better able to pay than the poor, they should pay more in taxes. This principle is justified by the argument that all citizens should make an "equal sacrifice." Fairness in this system requires both **horizontal equity** and **vertical equity. Horizontal equity means that individuals who have nearly equal incomes should have nearly equal tax burdens.** This is the concept Plato had in mind when he wrote in Book One of *The Republic,* "When there is an income tax, the just man will pay more and the unjust less **on the same amount of income.**" Horizontal equity is lacking when those with equal abilities to pay are treated differently because of tax deductions, credits, or preferences not available to all taxpayers on equal terms.

Vertical equity states that those with higher ability to pay should pay more taxes than those with less. There is less agreement on *how much more* the rich should pay. In fact, taxes are generally classified according to their **incidence. Tax incidence is the actual distribution of the tax burden on different levels of income.** Tax systems are classified as **progressive, proportional** (sometimes referred to as a **flat tax**), or **regressive** as illustrated in figure 6-4.

A **progressive tax** is one in which the tax rate rises as income rises. Wealthier taxpayers pay a larger percentage of their income in taxes than do low-income taxpayers. A progressive tax redistributes wealth from the more affluent to the less affluent. Most Americans support progressive taxes on the grounds that ability to pay rises more than proportionately with income.

A **proportional tax** is one in which the tax is the same through all income levels. Ordinarily called a **flat tax,** a proportional tax is often praised by its supporters for its efficiency. By assessing a tax as a fixed percentage of income, a wage earner's decisions do not affect the amount of tax owed nor distort incentives. Since theoretically there are no deductions everyone can easily compute the amount of taxes owed, there is little need to hire accountants or tax lawyers. Because the proportional tax is so efficient and imposes only a slight administrative burden on taxpayers, many argue that we should adopt it. But efficiency is only one goal of the tax system. Although some think

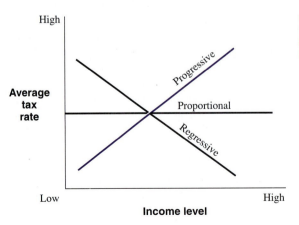

FIGURE 6-4
TAX INCIDENCE: PROGRESSIVE, PROPORTIONAL, AND REGRESSIVE.

that a system in which everyone pays the same percentage of their income is fair, others argue that is not equitable. A proportional tax is **neutral** in regard to income distribution.

Under a **regressive tax** the average rate declines as income rises. It is called regressive because high-income taxpayers pay a smaller percentage of their income than do low-income taxpayers, even though they may still pay a higher amount in absolute dollars. A regressive tax redistributes income from the poor to the wealthy. Regressive tax systems are so manifestly unfair that few *openly* advocate them. A notable exception is George Gilder, a conservative writer with refreshing frankness but doubtful logic who wrote "Regressive taxes help the poor."[10] Gilder's work, which was widely and approvingly read by supply-siders of the early 80s also declared that "To help the poor and middle classes, one must cut the taxes on the rich."[11]

Because state and local governments often rely on sales and property taxes they tend to be regressive. State and local sales taxes increased during the 1980s along with local property taxes. Sales and property taxes are regressive because poorer people must spend a higher percentage of their income for goods and services and housing costs than do the affluent.

In theory, the federal income tax supports the principle of vertical equity by being very mildly progressive. Many critics believe that it **should** be more progressive. There is no agreement on how much more, or even on how the ability to pay should be measured. For example should adjustments be made for catastrophic medical expenses? Or what of families that may have several children in college at once?

Federal tax progressivity has been declining for over two decades. When taxes paid by individuals to federal, state, and local levels of government are combined, the mildly progressive features at the national level are offset by regressive taxes at the local level resulting in a roughly proportional tax system. The trend toward inequality is attributable to the increased influence of those who argue in favor of tax neutrality (proportional). The avowed purpose of the 1986 tax reform was to make the federal tax system more "neutral." By primarily reducing the taxes of those in the highest brackets and cutting government funding for social welfare programs, it intended to reduce the redistributive effect of transferring wealth to the poor.

Many who support the neutrality of the tax system argue that efforts to redistribute wealth through tax transfers are not very effective. They maintain that a progressive income tax reduces the incentives for the more affluent to work and save. They believe in the **trickle-down theory** that holds that allowing the affluent to keep their wealth will result in greater investment and ultimately greater output, improving the welfare of the poor. By encouraging the affluent to invest their wealth, the size of the total economic pie will be increased so that the benefits that trickle down to the poor will exceed any benefits from redistribution through tax transfers. They insist that the fact that some entrepreneurs become extraordinarily wealthy is irrelevant because their actions have improved society.

---

[10]George Gilder, *Wealth and Poverty* (New York: Basic Books, 1981), p. 188.
[11]Ibid., p. 188.

CASE STUDY

LOTTERIES AS A REGRESSIVE TAX

Gambling generates enormous amounts of revenue for governments and the gaming industry. But its enchanting promises of significant benefits for the general welfare frequently do not live up to expectations, because of mismanagement or corruption.

The average voter does not consider the lottery to be a tax. Instead, lotteries are thought to be a form of entertainment that may make the ticket purchaser rich. Political entrepreneurs have discovered that this perspective removes a major barrier to taxation. The transfer of lottery revenues to state treasuries is an implicit tax on lottery bettors. There is a consensus among researchers regarding who bears the burden of state lotteries. It is a decidedly regressive form of taxation in that average lottery sales are highest in low-income areas and are lower in areas of higher economic and educational levels.

This tax is *popular* and avoids the aggressive reaction of the more affluent to any tax increase especially when the benefits accrue to themselves. The result is that states have increasingly resorted to lotteries to increase revenues as a way of sidestepping opposition to tax increases. New Hampshire started the first modern state lottery in 1964. By 1998, 38 states and the District of Columbia sponsored lotteries.

Per capita lottery ticket sales were three times higher in inner-city Detroit than in the suburbs. Of $104 million contributed to Michigan's school aid fund in 1988 by Detroit lottery ticket purchasers they received back only $80 million. The remaining $24 million was transferred to more affluent suburban school districts. Another study of the Florida lottery, which also earmarks profits from sales to go into the general education fund, found that when one includes the tax incidence (who pays) and the benefit incidence (who receives the funds), the tax was regressive for those with incomes below $40,000. The benefits of the net tax are proportionally distributed at incomes between $40,000 and $70,000 and become progressive at incomes above $70,000.

As a result, lotteries violate the tax principles of both neutrality and equity. There is also a question of the ethics of exploiting human desire to extract a regressive tax on the poor.

It is often pointed out that state-sponsored gambling has a negative impact on all Americans by endorsing greed and envy. States spend millions of dollars on lottery advertising annually, implying that possession of money is the most accurate gauge of personal success. Being a "success" means hitting the lottery and becoming rich while being poor designates one as a "failure." Although one's chance of being struck by lightning is greater than winning the lottery, it is the individual's only real hope for success and true happiness. Advertising agencies realize that this appeal will be greater in lower income neighborhoods and concentrate most advertising in those areas.

Sources: Mary Borg, Paul Mason, and Stephen Shapiro, *The Economic Consequences of State Lotteries* (New York: Praeger, 1991); Charles Clotfelter and Philip Cook, *Selling Hope: State Lotteries in America* (Cambridge: Harvard University Press, 1989).

Changes in the tax system in the 1980s are often cited as a major factor in the trend toward greater income inequality. In the early 1940s the federal income tax rate was highly progressive with a top tax rate of 90 percent on high incomes. The top rate declined to 70 percent by 1980. In reality of course because of many loopholes no one paid the top rate. The Reagan reduction in the progressivity of tax rates and the increase in regressive taxes during the 1980s were among the most dramatic changes of the Reagan-Bush administrations. The Reagan administration reduced the rate structure from 70 to 50 percent with a sliding scale, and reduced the lowest rate from 14 to 11 percent. It also lowered the rate on capital gains which also helped the wealthy.

Subsequently, the Tax Reform Act of 1986, raised the bottom tax rate to 15 percent while it further reduced the top rate to 33 percent in return for closing **tax loopholes** (including capital gains). The resulting robust increase in the after-tax income among the more affluent was gratefully accepted. **Tax loopholes consist primarily of tax deductions and exemptions that may be subtracted from personal income to determine the taxable income. This effectively reduces the tax rate if certain conditions are met.** One tax loophole that was left open was the **tax exempt** status of state and municipal bonds. The interest on these bonds is exempt from federal taxes.[12] **Income is tax exempt if income from that source is not subject to taxes.**

Preferential treatment of homeowners compared to renters is the **tax deduction** for the interest on mortgage payments and property taxes. **A tax deduction is money that may be subtracted from total income to determine one's taxable income.** This deduction encourages home ownership. Since homeowners on average have a higher income than renters, this erodes the progressivity of the income tax (see chapter 9). To make matters worse, homeowners are tempted by lenders urging them to consolidate their debts at lower rates of deductible interest through "home-equity" loans. Renters do not have this opportunity and must pay higher, nondeductible interest rates.

All tax loopholes encourage taxpayers to engage in certain types of behavior to avoid taxes. Most loopholes primarily benefit the more affluent and therefore they erode the progressivity of the income tax. The tax reform did not reduce the actual progressivity as drastically as the percentages would indicate because it eliminated many loopholes that allowed the wealthy to legally reduce their **taxable incomes** and pay taxes at the lower rates. **Taxable income is the income that remains after all exemptions and deductions are subtracted from personal income. Taxable income is the income that is subject to taxation.**

Social Security taxes were increased however. This tax is proportional at first, in that it requires individuals and employers to pay the same rate (7.65 percent) on wages up to $68,400 (in 1998). After that the **marginal tax** rate is zero. Rather than exempting low incomes it exempts high incomes. Once the ceiling is reached no more payments are made for the year.[13] Also since only salaries are subject to the payroll tax, while income from interest is untouched, it is ultimately regressive.

Actually an important long-term development occurred in the United States in the first eighty years of the twentieth century. There was a marked movement away from the extreme inequalities that were characteristic of earlier capitalism. There were many

---

[12]Tax-exempt bonds are a curiosity peculiar to the United States. It is a remnant of the doctrine of state sovereignty that originally held that the salaries of state employees must be free from federal tax. States fiercely resist any suggestion of elimination of the tax free status because of the resulting increase in the cost of their borrowing.

[13]Robert Reich pointed out that Michael Milken, who earned $550 million in 1987, fulfilled his 1987 Social Security payment obligations at about 12:42 A.M. on January 1. Social Security exempts investment income, like interest and capital gains. See Robert B. Reich, *The Work of Nations* (New York: Vintage Books, 1992), pp. 198–99.

TABLE 6-1
AVERAGE AFTER-TAX INCOME IN 1994

	Actual	If group's share of the national income remained the same as in 1977	The difference
Lowest fifth	$ 7,175	$ 9,829	$ 2,654
Second fifth	16,540	19,352	2,812
Middle fifth	26,651	27,448	1,797
Fourth fifth	37,226	39,129	1,903
Highest fifth	80,417	71,736	−8,681
Top one percent	374,131	241,176	−132,955

Source: Isaac Shapiro and Robert Greenstein, "Trends in the Distribution of After-Tax Income: An Analysis of Congressional Budget Office Data." *Center on Budget and Policy Priorities* (Washington, DC: August 1997), p. 4.

reasons for the shift, some of which will be developed in chapter 7, and not all of them were due to reasons of public policy. More workers moved out of low-skilled laboring jobs into higher-skilled jobs in factories. Taxes were levied at first only on the wealthy. As recently as the New Deal, it was almost exclusively the wealthy who paid the taxes. The result was that between 1929 and 1981 the share of income going to the top 5 percent of families fell by over fifty percent from 33.5 percent to 14.4 percent. Since the early 1980s, there has been a significant movement against the long tide of greater equalization.

Today just about everyone pays taxes. That means that any shift in tax policies now affects just about everybody. The *Congressional Budget Office* has released tables on after-tax income in 1994. When compared with data the CBO released for 1977, it is clear that the changes in the tax laws have favored those households in the top portion of the income scale even though Presidents Bush and Clinton passed bills to restore some of the taxes for those at the top that had been slashed by the Reagan administration. The *average* after-tax income rose 9.5 percent between 1977 and 1994 after adjusting for inflation. However the bottom two-fifths actually experienced a *decline* during this period. The income of the middle quintile remained relatively unchanged. However the average after-tax incomes of those in the top quintile rose by 25 percent during this period. The top one percent had an average after-tax gain of 72 percent between 1977 and 1994 or almost 8 times the 9.5 percent average gain for everyone.

The bottom 60 percent of the population were all receiving smaller shares by the end of the period. The distribution of after-tax income would be even more uneven if state and local taxes were taken into account since they tend to be regressive. To repeat, these income trends reflect many changes in the economy and not just taxes. The view has been that tax laws could guide the distribution to not exacerbate the disparities.

The tax increases in the 1990 and 1993 budget laws reduced the share of after-tax income received by the top 20 percent from 49.8 to 49.3 in 1994. And the share of after-tax income received by the wealthiest 1 percent of families fell from 12.1 percent in 1992 to 11.4 percent in 1994. Nevertheless, the shares of after-tax income received by the top 20 percent of the population in 1994 were far above their share in the late 1970s.[14]

---

[14]Shapiro and Greenstein, "Trends in the Distribution of After-Tax Income," op. cit., p. 5.

THE CONVENIENT LOGIC OF TARGETING THE RICH FOR INCOME TAX CUTS

In defending the tax bill providing the greatest share of tax relief to high-income taxpayers, many congressional leaders argued that it was because they pay the majority of the federal taxes. But the primary reason that high-income taxpayers pay the majority of federal taxes is that they receive the lion's share of the national before-tax income.

Their logic suggests that as the share of national income received by high-income families grows, and their share of the federal tax payments increases—the need for these affluent families for tax relief grows proportionately. According to this convenient logic, the wealthier those with the highest incomes become relative to the rest of the society, the more they—rather than lower-income families—need tax relief.

The common argument made by conservatives is that tax cuts for the rich actually shift the tax burden upward. So that during the 1980s, the top federal tax rate was cut from 70 to 28 percent. During that time the wealthiest 1 percent increased their share of all income taxes paid from 17 to 28 percent. But in fact **the tax bill of individual millionaires did not rise** during the decade of the 80s—it fell. Over the decade the average tax bill of those who made over $1 million a year fell 35 percent from $980,869 to $634,196. But the rich *as a group* paid a larger percentage of the total federal tax. The top 1 percent increased their share of the national income by about 50 percent. Their share of all federal taxes grew also by about 50 percent (their tax percent would have been higher but tax cuts reduced the amount).

Thus, the rich paid more taxes because they made more; the poor paid less because they made less. No poor person would accept this as a favorable outcome.

Source: Shapiro and Greenstein, op. cit., p. 6. See also, http://www.scruz.net/~kangaroo/L-taxshare.htm.

However the budget agreement of 1997 changed direction from the 1990 and 1993 budget laws that raised taxes on the wealthiest Americans. According to one analysis, estimates are that the richest 1 percent of the population will receive 32 percent of the benefits from the tax cuts when the tax reductions are fully implemented. The top 1 percent will receive more tax cuts than the bottom 80 percent of the population.[15] The top 20 percent of households will receive about 78 percent of the tax cut benefits under the 1997 agreement.

Proposals for Tax Reform

Demand for fundamental tax reform has been fairly high on the political agenda for the last several years. Politicians such as Dick Armey, Bill Archer, Steve Forbes, and Jack Kemp among others have argued that the current tax system needs to be completely replaced with another system that is simpler, fairer, and more growth-friendly. However most of the proposals put forward do more to reduce taxes than reform the system. Reducing tax revenues will make it more difficult to keep the budget balanced especially

[15]Ibid.

after the baby boomers begin collecting Social Security benefits in a few years. Dismantling the tax system is an effective way to take apart collective policies, but it will make meaningful tax reform more difficult. Tax reform will inevitably create new winners and losers.

One policy analyst, William Gale, proposes tax reform that would be revenue-neutral while broadening the tax base, reducing effective tax rates, and simplifying the process.[16] Briefly, he contends that itemized deductions are at the heart of any serious effort at tax reform. Although they are popular and subsidize various activities thought of as "good," they create many problems. He argues that deductions largely subsidize activity that would have occurred anyway. By eroding the tax base they require higher tax rates than would otherwise be necessary. Deductions are also *regressive* in that 90 percent of households with incomes above $75,000 itemize, while less than 10 percent of households below $30,000 itemize.

Deductions under the current system are also unfair, he argues. Why should a high-income household save 40 cents on a dollar of mortgage interest while a low-income household saves 15 cents? Why should homeowners with a large mortgage be able to use a tax-deductible home equity loan to buy a car, when renters with similar incomes cannot? Other deductions for state and local taxes are often justified on ability-to-pay grounds, since the taxes directly reduce household income. However, state and local taxes largely pay for services that households consume, such as schools, roads, and parks. But if taxes buy services they should be part of the taxable income. For instance, a household that paid $30 a month for garbage collection to a private company would not expect a deduction. Why should a household that pays the same amount in local taxes for trash removal get a deduction?[17]

Gale argues for reducing the number of exemptions by one which would raise taxes—but not tax rates. He would also convert the deductions to 15 percent credits. Analysis suggests that this would simplify taxes by reducing the number of itemizers by about 8 million while raising an additional $18–$21 billion per year.

Research on the effects of the progressive income tax on incentives to work and save are inconclusive. The effect of taxes on saving is even more contradictory. Joseph Pechman, a late authority on tax systems has written that "the strongest conclusion one can draw from the available evidence is that the incentive effects of taxation have been relatively small."[18]

In our view, a progressive income tax is perhaps the most effective fiscal tool for reducing extreme inequalities in the distribution of income and wealth inherent in capitalism. The asymmetric income distribution gives rise to great variation of welfare, opportunity, and economic power (see chapter 7). The difficult choice for policy makers is not only how to distribute the tax burden throughout the income levels of the population so that it meets with standards of fairness, but also when to use the taxing power to stimulate economic activity or to restrain the economy from uncontrolled inflation.

---

[16]William G. Gale, "Tax Reform is Dead, Long Live Tax Reform," *Brookings Policy Brief No. 12,* (Washington, DC: The Brookings Institution, 1997).
   [17]Ibid.
   [18]Joseph A. Pechman, "Why We Should Stick with the Income Tax," *The Brookings Review* (Spring 1990), pp. 9–19.

THE PROPOSED CAPITAL GAINS TAX CUT

Proposals to cut the capital gains tax rate would increase income inequality in America since only the affluent receive substantial amounts of their income from this source and would get the preponderance of the benefits. Adoption of a capital gains tax cut would aggravate the trend since the early 1980s of using the tax system to *increase inequality.* Increases in *after-tax* income during the 1980s became more unequally distributed than increases in *before-tax* income.

Tax law prior to 1986 exempted 60 percent of net long-term capital gains income (assets held for 6 months or longer) from tax. The Tax Reform Act of 1986 repealed this preferential treatment. This bill, embraced by then President Reagan and by Congress was an attempt to lower overall tax rates by broadening the base of taxable income. The goal was to provide horizontal equity in each tax bracket. This would improve the efficiency of the tax system by not favoring one form of income over another. The drop in marginal rates at the top bracket went from 50 to 28 percent.

Almost immediately after the bill was passed however, the Republican Party proposed scrapping the capital gains part of the agreement, but keeping the lower overall tax rate on upper-income tax brackets.

As Henry Aaron of the Brookings Institute has pointed out, the question of whether tax rates on income from realized capital gains should be set below rates on other income is an academic question. "More than half of all capital gains are never taxed. Either they are held until the owner dies, after which they are exempt from tax to subsequent owners. Or they accrue to tax-exempt U.S. entities, such as pension funds, or to foreign owners not subject to U.S. tax." Advocates of capital gains cuts claim further cuts might improve investment incentives, but the effect would be small for at least two reasons. The *effective* rate on capital gains is already low (estimated at only 7 percent) because the gains are deferred, or are forgiven for assets held until death and are capped at 28 percent). Also capital gains are only a small part of the overall tax on investments because significant amounts of capital gains go to tax-exempt investors who do not pay the tax anyway. In addition, about one-third of investment is financed with debt rather than equity. Some estimates indicate that if the top capital gains tax rate was cut to 14 percent—as proposed by Bob Dole—it would reduce interest rates by 0.15 percent and raise investment by about 0.2 percent of GDP.

Since capital gains are concentrated in upper-income groups, a cut in capital gains taxes would produce a significant reduction in the tax burden for upper-income families.

Nevertheless, supporters such as George Bush defended the proposal by claiming that it would stimulate growth. He stated, "I am sick and tired of the demagogues who call this a tax cut for the rich. It means jobs, it means savings, and it is good for all Americans." Research indicates that a reduction in the tax on capital gains would result in less government revenues. Supporters insist that a lower tax will create jobs but others insist that that is based upon unrealistic assumptions about the response of investors to increases in the rate of return. Most researchers agree that cutting capital gains would lower investment and the GDP.

Sources: Henry J. Aaron, "The Capital Gains Tax Cut," *The Brookings Review* (Summer 1992), pp. 30–33; *The Washington Post,* Jan. 9, 1990; Kevin Quinn, *False Promises: Why the Bush Capital Gains Tax Cuts Would Not Result in More Saving, Investment, Economic Growth or Jobs* (Washington, DC: Economic Policy Institute, 1990); Gregg Esenwein, "Taxation of Capital Gains," 1990, CRS Issue Brief.

The problem is compounded because control over fiscal power is divided between the president and Congress. Although the Fed has the final authority in determining the money supply, the president and Congress are not without considerable influence in this area as well. Timely coordination of monetary and fiscal policy under such circumstances can become problematic. Since monetary policy is usually positioned to restrain inflationary forces, it would be less effective in combating deflation.

CONCLUSION

1 The theory of John Maynard Keynes provided the intellectual framework of welfare capitalism to justify government's role in guiding the economy when it failed to live up to society's expectations. In the United States the New Deal under Franklin Roosevelt tried to correct the weaknesses in the economy and to strengthen its workings. During the New Deal government stepped in to manage the economy to a greater extent than had ever been done before. By the end of the war, there was an acceptance of the idea that government had a responsibility to manage the economy to create the conditions that would provide for employment opportunities.

2 Monetary policy was developed in a way that had never been done before to encourage or discourage private spending. Fiscal policy especially through government spending to stimulate private investment was developed. In retrospect the amount of spending during the New Deal was insufficient to prime the pump to end the Depression. But a deficit on the scale of World War II would certainly stimulate private investment.

3 The experience of the war showed that economic policy could bring about high levels of employment and resulted in the Employment Act of 1946. These tools of monetary and fiscal policy resulted in a long trend of greater equalization in the American society through the use of monetary and fiscal policy. The trend toward greater inequality can also be encouraged by use of the tax structure. Considerable disagreement has resulted over what the role of government should be in using the taxing power for redistributing income.

4 Government efforts to deal with economic problems ranging from the deficit to entitlements will require a combination of policies. Tax increases, however unpopular are sometimes required. This may be accomplished by a variety of means, including closing loopholes and tax expenditures, as well as by raising marginal tax rates. A reduction in government expenditures and entitlements must be implemented. In some cases this may be accomplished by taxing benefits as well as by reducing payments.

QUESTIONS FOR DISCUSSION

1 Would you consider inflation to be as dangerous to an economy as deflation?
2 In what way has history provided a test for Keynes and his theory of government spending? Was it conclusive?
3 What kinds of problems do large budget deficits pose for the nation's economy? What are the different problems in the short run as opposed to the long run?

4 Budgets are a serious problem. What additional information does a policy analyst need to make a policy assessment of that statement?

5 Why are investments critical in determining the level of prosperity?

6 Is a balanced budget amendment a wise policy? Why or why not?

7 What alternative tax policies are available to the government? What are the positive and negatives associated with each?

8 What are the characteristics of a "good" tax system? Why is vertical and horizontal equity important?

KEY CONCEPTS

automatic stabilizers	proportional tax rate
benefit principle	regressive tax
deflation	tax efficiency
excise taxes	tax exemption
fiscal policy	tax expenditure
horizontal equity	tax fairness
marginal tax rate	tax incidence
monetary policy	tax loophole
progressive tax rate	trickle-down theory
property taxes	vertical equity

SUGGESTED READINGS

Martin Neil Baily, Gary Burtless, and Robert E. Litan, *Growth With Equity: Economic Policymaking for the Next Century* (Washington, DC: The Brookings Institution, 1993).

Congressional Budget Office, *The Economic and Budget Outlook: An Update* (Washington, DC: U.S. Government Printing Office, 1993).

John Cranford, *Budgeting for America,* 2d ed. (Washington, DC: Congressional Quarterly, 1989).

Louis A. Ferleger and Jay Mandle, *No Pain, No Gain: Taxes, Productivity, and Economic Growth* (New York: The Twentieth Century Fund Press, 1992).

Robert Heilbroner and Peter Bernstein, *The Debt and the Deficit: False Alarms/Real Possibilities* (New York: W. W. Norton & Company 1989).

Paul Heyne, *The Economic Way of Thinking* 5th ed. (Chicago: Science Research Associates, Inc., 1987).

Kevin Phillips, *The Politics of Rich and Poor* (New York: Random House, 1990).

James M. Rock, *Debt and the Twin Deficits Debate* (Mountain View, CA: Mayfield, 1991).

7

THE POLITICS AND ECONOMICS OF INEQUALITY

The phrase "the American dream" refers to the widespread belief in an open, vigorous, and progressive community committed to equal opportunities for all in which life would improve for each generation. It includes the belief that the condition of the American society and life opportunities would improve with each generation. As the nation approaches a new millennium the American dream is in trouble. The gap between the incomes of poor and affluent citizens is larger in the United States than in any other industrialized country. Many Americans now complain that hard work and playing by the rules no longer ensure upward mobility or even maintain one's position on the economic ladder. Many find economic security more elusive than ever and fear that their children's generation will not fare as well financially or socially as they have done. These concerns are being expressed while the economy is experiencing a long expansion since the last recession in 1991 and with unemployment in the spring of 1998 at its lowest level (4.4 percent) in thirty years. Inflation stands at a mere 1.6 percent. What has caused these anxieties? Those who are already the most prosperous are benefiting the most from this long period of prosperity while the least well-off are falling behind. The income gap between the richest and the poorest Americans is widening, while the number of people in the middle class is actually declining.

INTRODUCTION

There is increasing interest in equality and the distribution of national income. It has long been known that extreme inequality is a major cause of political instability in many developing countries. Even in a wealthy country like the United States, economic inequality is associated with poverty, crime, political alienation, and social unrest.[1] Since great inequality in income and wealth is a social problem it is a problem for the policy agenda. Whether the government should reduce the great inequalities between the rich and poor is vigorously debated. Part of the uncertainty arises from the imperfect knowledge about the relationship between inequality and economic growth. It is often held that there is a trade-off between equality and efficiency suggesting that policies aimed at reducing inequality reduce economic growth. Because the trade-offs are not known precisely there are sharp disagreements in evaluating policy choices. For example, the data clearly show that an expanding economy has benefitted the rich much more than the poor as the rich have become significantly richer in both absolute and relative terms, while the poor are only now recovering their income levels achieved prior to the recession in 1991 and have lost ground relative to the wealthy. Some have argued that public policy could have prevented this development. Others claim that while inequality increased, that is the price that must be paid to achieve economic growth.

The framers of the Constitution wrote that one of the ends of government was to "promote the general welfare." In today's terminology, **if "human development" is the end, then economic growth is the means.** In this scenario the quality of growth is as important as its quantity. Otherwise, economic growth might be inequitable and futureless rather than providing hope and participation in economic society. Economic growth and equitable human development must go hand in hand if they are to succeed in the long term.

The concept of egalitarianism has been a cornerstone of American social and political culture. This view is embedded in the preamble to the Constitution when it states: "We hold these truths to be self evident, that all men are created equal, that they are endowed by their Creator with certain inalienable rights, among them are life, liberty, and the pursuit of happiness." This liberty, to be protected by government, would permit each person to acquire material goods according to his or her abilities. But the result has been an inequality of outcomes.

During the 1930s, President Franklin D. Roosevelt inaugurated the New Deal. The depression caused a crisis in the country which resulted in "one-third of the nation ill-fed, ill-housed, and ill-clothed." Government responsibility to narrow the gap between rich and poor was largely accepted by liberals and conservatives alike after the New Deal. That responsibility was seriously challenged in the 1980s by a resurgence of conservatism under Ronald Reagan. Supply-side economic thinking defended economic inequality as a source of productivity and economic growth.

We hear a great deal about political equality, which typically means that individuals are equal before the law, and that regardless of ability or income, each has the right to vote. There appears to be an assumption that this narrow technical political equality is **the** significant equality in the United States and we disregard or minimize the fact of economic inequality. Most countries of the western world have policies designed to **reduce** the differences between rich and poor. In those countries most concede that the role of government should not be to widen the gap between rich and poor but rather, to reduce it.

---

[1]See the *Economic Report of the President, 1997,* chapter 5, which discusses the gap in economic rewards as a policy issue.

This chapter examines the major changes in wealth and income distribution beginning in the late 1970s. In the first two decades after World War II the United States, as well as most other industrialized economies, experienced decreasing income inequality which was associated with the post-war boom. During this period real family incomes doubled and poverty rates declined dramatically. Starting about 1973 there was a decade of economic stagnation coupled with two recessions, which resulted in falling average incomes, slightly increasing levels of inequality, and higher levels of poverty. But from the early 1980s to the present, the economy has experienced sustained economic growth, with the exception of a recession at the end of the Bush administration in 1991. During this period there has been some growth in average incomes (mostly through working more hours) and continuing higher rates of poverty than expected in a growing economy. The poverty trend has not kept pace with improvements in income, in part because income is becoming more unequal. There has been a considerable divergence with the rate of growth in income and wealth highest for those at the top and dropping at increasing rates throughout the lower levels. Other industrialized states have experienced similar patterns. The policy analysts must ask: What has caused these trends? In this process the policies of different countries have had a significant impact on the trends toward greater economic inequality.

It is largely a matter of public choice as to how much inequality the society will permit. Growing inequality has become a politically charged topic in recent years, which raises the question, **why should society care about the degree of income inequality?** Is there something public policy can or should do to reduce growing inequalities? Some conservatives have argued that significant differences in economic inequalities do not necessarily have policy implications. They argue that the wealthy are inclined to invest their money creating jobs and contributing to faster economic growth. Others have denounced raising such issues in a policy context as engaging in the divisive politics of envy and "class warfare" and threatening the American consensus that we are a "middle class" nation with only a few poor and a few rich at the extremes. Others see the growing inequality as a serious threat to society's political, social, and economic well-being. They argue that income inequality causes "spillover" effects on the quality of life, even for those not necessarily in poverty. Wide economic disparities result in frustration, stress, and family discord, which increases the rates of crime, violence, and homicide.[2] Those possessing the economic means to move into protected communities do so. Increasingly Americans move into gated communities with round-the-clock security. The middle-class flight from the poorer neighborhoods results in the progressive deterioration of the housing and public education system (see chapters 9 and 10). Support for public schools declines. Wide disparities in income tend to coexist with an underinvestment in human capital as measured by reduced spending on education, lower literacy rates, and increased high school drop out rates. A lower skilled workforce means that society ultimately pays the price through lower levels of productivity and economic growth. Robert Putnam has suggested that the breakdown of social cohesion brought about by income inequality threatens the functioning of democracy. He found that low levels of civic trust spill over into a lack of

---

[2]See R. G. Wilkinson, *Unhealthy Societies: The Afflictions of Inequality* (London: Routledge, 1996).

confidence in government and low voter turnout at elections. It is well known that the poor are less likely to vote. Political representation is further distorted by inequalities in political campaign contributions. It is estimated that the richest 3 percent of the voting population accounts for 35 percent of all private campaign contributions during presidential elections.[3] There is a serious concern that too much inequality could lead to a situation in which the society could enter into a cycle in which lack of trust and civic engagement reinforces a public policy which does not result from the collective deliberation about the public interest, but merely reflects the success of campaign strategies.[4]

EQUITY AND EQUALITY

To many of the leaders of the American Revolution democracy was looked upon as the completion of the human struggle for freedom. The framers of the Constitution were well aware of the difficulty of reconciling individuality and liberty with democratic equality. James Madison expressed his concern over the inherent conflicts a democratic society would have to address when he wrote that the "most common and durable source of factions" in society is "the various and unequal distribution of property."

Thomas Jefferson's bias in favor of equality is well known. He believed that the innate differences between men were small.[5] He wrote:

> I am conscious that an equal division of property is impracticable. But the consequences of this enormous inequality producing so much misery to the bulk of mankind, legislators cannot invent too many devices for subdividing property. . . . Another means of silently lessening the inequality of property is to exempt all from taxation below a certain point, and to tax the higher portions of property in geometrical progression as they rise.[6]

He went on to say that the government should provide "that as few as possible shall be without a little portion of land" as the "small landholders are the most precious part of a state."[7]

Americans have often boastfully quoted Alexis de Tocqueville's observation of "the equality of conditions" in the United States in the 1830s. Indeed Tocqueville perceived that the Americanization of the world in terms of the ever increasing equality of conditions was inevitable. He realized that the creation of democratic forms of government was not the end of the struggle, but that it was a continuous process. And he believed that inevitably the rest of humanity would finally arrive at an almost complete equality of conditions. His central concern was over the difficulty of reconciling individuality

---

[3]Robert Putnam, "The Strange Disappearance of Civic America," *The American Prospect* (Winter 1996), pp. 34–48. See also Sidney Verba, Kay Schlozman, and Henry Brady, *Voice and Equality: Participation in American Politics* (Cambridge: Harvard University Press, 1996).

[4]Robert Putnam, "Bowling Alone: America's Declining Social Capital," *Journal of Democracy* (January 1995), pp. 34–35.

[5]Garry Wills develops the thesis that the idea of "all men being created equal" was more than just rhetoric. See Garry Wills, *Inventing America: Jefferson's Declaration of Independence* (New York: Doubleday, 1978).

[6]Thomas Jefferson, *The Papers of Thomas Jefferson*, vol. 8, Julian P. Boyd, (ed.), (Princeton: Princeton University Press, 1953), p. 682.

[7]Ibid.

and liberty with democratic equality. He sensed a growing "Aristocracy of Manufacturers" who had no sense of public responsibility and whose aim was to use the workers then abandon them to public charity. He believed that the manufacturing aristocracy:

> is one of the harshest which ever existed in the world. . . . the friends of democracy should keep their eyes anxiously fixed in this direction; for if ever a permanent inequality of conditions and aristocracy again penetrate into the world, it may be predicted that this is the channel by which they will enter.[8]

Writing a century later, Keynes pointed out that we could hardly expect business to act on behalf of the well-being of the workers let alone the entire society. He noted that in democracies the government has the responsibility to protect the economic well-being of the nation. The main failure of capitalism according to Keynes is its "failure to provide for full employment and its arbitrary and inequitable distribution of wealth and incomes."[9] Keynes was not opposed to economic inequality. However, he expressed his concern over the degree of inequality when he wrote "I believe that there is social and psychological justification for significant inequalities of incomes and wealth, *but not for such large disparities as exist today.*[10] What was required he said was a collective management of the system which would be as efficient as possible without offending our notions of a satisfactory way of life. The problem then becomes, what is a socially optimal amount of economic inequality?

Although the current intellectual climate is less supportive of an egalitarian position than a decade or two ago, it is still true that in most western countries significant majorities believe that a bias in favor of equality to reduce a large income gap accords with a democratic approach.[11] (see Table 7-1)

While we may declare our sympathy for policies favoring equality, most of us would support inequality if it resulted from certain conditions:

1 People would agree that inequality is justified if everyone had a fair (not necessarily equal) chance to get ahead.[12] Not only would most people not object to inequality in the distribution of wealth or income if the race was run under fair conditions with no one handicapped at the start, they would actively support it.

However, the situation becomes murky quickly. Many people do try to compete for scarce highly paid jobs by attending college so their future incomes will be higher. Some may **choose** not to attend college, while others may have grown up in families that could not afford to send them or to provide a background conducive to preparation for college. For those people, the resulting lower income is not voluntary.

---

[8]Alexis de Tocqueville, *Democracy in America,* as in William Ebenstein and Alan Ebenstein, *Great Political Thinkers* (New York: Harcourt Brace Publishers, 1991), p. 641.

[9]John Maynard Keynes, *The General Theory of Employment, Interest and Money* (London: Macmillan Publishers, 1936), p. 372.

[10]Ibid., p. 374.

[11]No poll has asked if it is the responsibility of the government to increase the gap between rich and poor, presumably few would support such an idea. Yet many proposed policies do just that.

[12]See especially in this regard, Robert Heilbroner and Lester Thurow, *Economics Explained,* revised, (Englewood Cliffs: Prentice-Hall, 1994), pp. 216–218. This discussion on the bias in favor of equality relies heavily on this source.

TABLE 7-1
ATTITUDES TOWARD GOVERNMENT RESPONSIBILITY
TO REDUCE INCOME INEQUALITY BETWEEN PEOPLE

Country	% agree government responsible
Italy	81
Hungary	77
Netherlands	64
Britain	62.9
Germany (All)	58.6
United States	27.9

Source: U.S. News & World Report (August 7, 1989), p. 29.
From Gallup International Research Institute.

What parameters make conditions fair? Of particular concern is the fairness of inheritances. What of the genetic inheritance of talent? Much of our most important human capital is carried in our genes, with the ownership of productive resources just an accident of birth. Is it fair that some individuals through their genetic endowment, a factor beyond the control of the person so equipped, have high innate intelligence, the ability to become professional athletes, or highly paid model because of their appearance; while the genetic inheritance of others determines that they will be both mentally and physically limited or even both? We usually do not worry too much over this kind of inheritance but its effects are very real.

What of the inheritance of gender? Studies make it plain that females born in the United States doing the same job as men receive approximately 70 percent of the pay received by a male. Is that fair? What about the inheritance of those who did not pick their parents wisely and grew up as an ethnic minority in a culturally deprived family in a ghetto neighborhood as opposed to a child born to a white privileged family who can afford the richest environment and best schools available for their children?

Then there is the income differential resulting from inherited wealth. Many of the super-rich in America got that way through merely inheriting large sums of money. That it should be possible to pass some wealth on from one generation to another is generally conceded, but whether large fortunes should be able to be passed on virtually intact is frequently challenged.[13]

Any discussion of inheritances suggests the **role of chance** in income distribution. Chance operates not only in inheritances, but also in the wider region of income differentials. One individual hits a lottery jackpot, another finds a superhighway built adjacent to her farm increasing its value several times, another unexpectedly finds oil on his land. On the other hand, a worker may find himself out of work for a prolonged period

---

[13]Conservatives are often the most supportive of the theory of Social Darwinism, which suggests that society is a place of competition based upon the principle of "survival of the fittest" in which those most fit win in the competition for material goods. Supporters of Social Darwinism tend to be most opposed to the passing on of large inheritances from one generation to the next, because it nullifies the fairness of the competition. Someone who inherits $10 million does not have to "compete" and prove their ability through competition.

due to a recession beyond his control, or the victim of an expensive debilitating illness, or that highly paid position she trained for disappeared.

2 No one objects to inequalities if it reflects individual choice. If an individual decides to turn his back on the secular world, become a Franciscan, and take a vow of poverty, no one would object. If someone decides to take a job that offers financial incentives because of unpleasant or inconvenient working conditions, or because it is more dangerous we will not object to her higher wages. The problem is that frequently these decisions do not result from free choices but are brought about by circumstances. A person raised in a ghetto with no opportunity to sacrifice **current** income to improve skills through education so that a **future** income will be higher, may not have the option of choosing to work in a highly paid profession.

3 People accept inequality when it reflects merit. Nearly everyone believes in the correctness of higher pay when it can be shown that it is justified by a different contribution to output.[14] Some people work longer hours than others, or work harder when on the job. This may result in income differences that are largely voluntary. Other workers acquire experience over time which may result in their earning a higher wage. This is part of the justification for a wage differential based on seniority.

4 People accept, and even support inequality, when they are persuaded that the inequality will benefit everyone. Often the common good is thought to include an increase in the Gross Domestic Product (GDP), since greater productivity typically means a brisk demand for labor, higher wages, and greater economic activity. Therefore, the argument is often made by some politicians and some economists that policies encouraging inequalities that benefit those with higher incomes are justified because they will lead to higher savings for the wealthy that will ultimately be translated into investments, which will create the jobs enriching the prospects of everyone else. The proposal for a lower capital gains tax made by conservatives is just such a suggestion. This is the trickle-down theory which suggests that if the well-to-do only had more money, they would be more highly motivated to invest more of it in the hope of making a profit,[15] and these investments would create more jobs, thus helping society in general.

These four general principles describe how the unequal distribution of income and wealth *is* defended. There is no suggestion that this is the way we *should* think about inequality.

---

[14]**Economic discrimination** occurs when duplicate factors of production receive different payments for equivalent contributions to output. This definition is difficult to test because of the difficulty of measuring all the relevant market characteristics. For example, the average black person earns less than the average white person, and the average woman earns less than the average man. Some of the differentials are easily accounted for. The average black is about six and one-half years younger than the average white. Younger workers earn less than older workers based upon work experience. Proportionately more black workers live in the South, where wages still lag behind wage scales in other areas. Women are less likely to have majored in a technical subject than men. It might not be discrimination if a woman with a high school diploma receives a lower salary than a man with a college degree (although discrimination might help in explaining their educational achievements). It is clearly too simplistic to try to measure discrimination by merely comparing the typical incomes of different groups. The question is not, "do blacks, earn less than whites do?" but: "Do blacks earn less than whites do *with like market characteristics* (work experience, age, education, etc.)?"

[15]We could achieve the same goal without yielding to inequality by financing the investment through taxation and government purchases (public investment) rather than through private investment through savings.

THE FUNCTIONAL THEORY OF INEQUALITY

There is a theory that maintains that inequality is **functionally imperative** because no stable system can long survive without it.[16] According to the **functional theory of inequality,** society must first distribute its members into the various jobs or roles defined by the society and then motivate them to perform their tasks efficiently. Some jobs are more important than others in the sense that the successful performance of them is crucial to the welfare of the whole society.[17] Additionally, some tasks require skills that are either difficult or scarce because they require special training. To ensure that the most important jobs are performed competently, every society provides a system of unequal rewards to produce incentives to channel the most competent people into the most important and difficult jobs. This ensures the greatest efficiency in the performance of these jobs.

It should be emphasized that according to this theory, "a position does not bring power and prestige because it draws a high income. Rather it draws a high income because it is functionally important and the available personnel is for one reason or another scarce."[18] **The population comes to understand that inequality is functional.** The system of unequal rewards works to the advantage of the whole system by guaranteeing that jobs essential to society's welfare are performed efficiently and competently.[19]

Milton Friedman believes that the market is the most efficient way of filling the most important positions with the most capable people. Equality of opportunity is the principle that allows the market to select the most competent individuals:

> No society can be stable unless there is a basic core of value judgments that are unthinkingly accepted by the great bulk of its members. I believe that payment in accordance with product has been, and in large measure still is, one of these accepted value judgments or institutions.[20]

The functional theory of inequality is intuitively appealing. But it immediately raises several problems.

Trade-Offs Between Equality, Equity, and Efficiency

Equality and **equity** of income are not the same. Equality deals with income in terms of "the same amount," while equity refers to "fairness." Equality deals with what

---

[16]The functional theory of inequality is a variation on The Marginal Productivity Theory of distribution (MPT) which holds that the income of any factor will be determined by the contribution that each factor makes to the revenue of the endeavor. Its income will be higher or lower depending on the ability and willingness of the suppliers of the factors of land, labor, and capital to enter the market at different prices. But at each price, factors will earn amounts equal to the marginal revenue they produce. The result, in theory, is that there cannot be exploitation of any factor in a perfect market.

The functional theory challenges the assumption of the Marginal Productivity Theory that a perfect market exists. If it does not, then the earnings of each factor may not reflect their contribution to output. The MPT cannot explain the variation of incomes due to nonmarket factors such as discrimination, imperfect markets, and other factors.

[17]Kingsley Davis and Wilbert Moore, *Some Principles of Stratification* (Reprint Series in Social Science) (New York: Columbia University Press, 1993).

[18]Ibid.

[19]James Madison, in *The Federalist #10,* clearly states that it is a primary function of governments to protect individual freedom which will lead to inequalities in income based upon differing abilities and interests. He notes that this is the basis for factions, which he laments. The most common and enduring source of factions is the unequal distribution of property. This poses a major dilemma for governmental administration.

[20]Milton Friedman, *Capitalism and Freedom* (Chicago: University of Chicago Press, 1962), p. 167.

incomes **are** and variance from a standard, while equity is the normative question of what incomes **should be.**

The main argument against an equal distribution of income is based upon **efficiency.** An unequal distribution does provide incentives. To illustrate the point, imagine the consequences if the society decided to achieve equality by taxing away all individual income and then dividing the taxes collected equally among the entire population. Realizing that harder work would no longer lead to a higher income would eliminate an important incentive. Any incentive to forego current consumption to purchase capital goods would also be abolished since there would be no chance of additional income. Since all rewards for harder work, investing, taking risks by developing capital, land, and entrepreneurship would disappear, the gross national product would decline dramatically. This suggests that policies that increase the amount of economic equality (or reduce inequality) may reduce economic efficiency—that is, lower the incentive to produce (thus lowering the GDP).

A second argument against an equal distribution of income or wealth is based on the concept of equity. As noted earlier, people with different natural abilities and who make unequal contributions to output should not receive the same income. An equal distribution is not equitable if individual contributions are unequal. The American society has been based on the idea of equality of opportunity rather than equality of results.

The case in favor of an equal distribution of income must include the argument that an unequal distribution leads to unequal opportunities. Some income differences arise because of differences in **wealth.** Many with income-producing assets such as stocks and bonds may receive sizeable incomes from them. Not only are these individuals able to acquire additional income-producing assets such as land or capital investments (i.e., more stocks and bonds), but they are also more able to invest in human capital through training and education to increase even further the amount of income they can earn in the future. A person with less wealth is, by contrast, less able to invest in other productive factors such as land and capital, or in education. Therefore an unequal distribution tends to be perpetuated and even increased because of the unequal market power of those who already have wealth, unless the government intervenes through taxes and transfers of income.

A second argument made by those in favor of a more equal income distribution is that a highly unequal distribution providing a great deal for the few and little or nothing for the many creates political unrest and threatens the stability of the society. When 25 percent of the population lives at the subsistence level and the top 10 percent which receives most of the income also dominates the political and economic levers of power, the poor may be driven to rebel against the economic and political elites.

Third, it may be argued that a highly unequal distribution of income can, contrary to the conservative view, inhibit investment in capital which is crucial to economic growth. While it is true that investment usually comes from people with higher incomes, if relatively few members of a society have most of its income, the rest of the population cannot put significant demand into the economy to stimulate growth. With a lack of investment incentives, the wealthy may opt to use their incomes for personal consumption instead.

Liberals sometimes undermine their case for more equality by denying that their proposals will have any harmful effects on incentives. Conservatives, on the other hand, undermine their case against greater equality by making greatly exaggerated claims about the loss of efficiency that would arise.

Qualifications to the Theory

The functional theory of inequality of income distribution is open to some criticisms which do not demolish it, but which significantly narrow the range of inequalities that can be justified as functionally imperative.

To begin with, it is relatively easy to determine which skills are in scarce supply, but difficult to tell which jobs are the most important to the welfare of a particular society. Questions of comparable worth, for example, are notoriously complex problems. After agreement is reached regarding the extremes—for example the importance of the cardiovascular surgeon compared with the street-sweeper—it becomes very difficult to determine the relative importance of jobs more at the "center"—managing a corporation versus teaching young children, for instance, or working as an accountant versus being a dentist. How does one decide?

Those supporting the functionalist approach usually shift from an assessment of the **relative importance** of any particular position to assessing its **relative skill** level and the **scarcity** of that skill in the society.

Scarcity of needed skills becomes the primary test, then. But this runs into another set of problems: Some professions, like physicians, can affect the supply of skilled personnel in that occupation. The profession tries to promote the economic interest of its members by increasing their income. Competitive conditions would attract more members potentially developing a surplus and driving incomes down. So the profession will typically try to limit its membership through occupational licensing creating a contrived scarcity. Many occupations require a state license. Frequently the licensing process is very strongly influenced by the profession that claims that it alone is competent to judge the criteria necessary for training and certification. The members of the profession justify their control by citing the need to exclude "quacks." But the certification, whether for architects, accountants, lawyers, or physicians, has substantial economic value. Frequently the license is fundamentally a way to raise wages in a particular profession by limiting competition. Typically licenses are granted by a panel of practitioners in the field who determine how many are to be granted and to whom. The potential for conflicts of interest is apparent.[21]

The point is that once the first criterion of the functionalists—the importance of a particular kind of job—recedes into the background, the functionalist interpretation of the second criterion—the scarcity of needed skills—becomes doubtful.

Functionalists emphasize the positive side of their theory and ignore its negative aspects. The theory does identify the value of talent and shows how rewarding various talents motivates those who possess them to work efficiently. However, it ignores the demotivating effects for those with fewer talents. Those at the higher end of the income stream can be motivated with the aspiration to bonuses, higher wages, life and health insurance benefits, promotions, and pension programs. But workers at the lower end of the income stream cannot be motivated by higher pay, for at least two main reasons: (1) Low income at this end of the pay scale must provide the differential to fill the higher positions with competent and conscientious workers. (2) The money needed to pay some

---

[21]See in this regard, Doug Bandow, "Doctors Operate to Cut Out Competition, *Business and Society Review* (Summer 1986). Bandow illustrates that entry into the medical profession is essentially controlled through the use of licensing arrangements, which increase health care costs and decrease the options available to patients.

people more, must be taken from those who will be paid less. Thus, in functionalist theory, the workers on garbage trucks who are quick and efficient cannot be rewarded by higher pay or bonuses, although they may be valued employees. As these individuals get older, and slower, they must continue to work because of the need to provide for their families even under the most adverse conditions. Consequently low income, unemployment, and the threat of unemployment are concentrated among those jobs where the skill levels are the lowest and the supply of people having the skills is the greatest. In sum, the carrot motivating those at the upper-income levels requires the stick to motivate those at the lower levels of income. Functionalist theory rarely mentions this.

Finally for the functionalist system of inequality to operate smoothly, the society as a whole must see it as working to benefit the entire population. Most of the population must also believe that their tasks and their income levels reflect their skills and their relative contributions to the society. The stratified system will then rest upon a consensus in which even those at the lower end of the income stream understand that their low wages and the threat of unemployment are necessary motivators to keep them working. Not surprisingly, those who wholeheartedly believe in the system tend to be found at the upper end of the income stream. Those at the lower levels cannot both believe in the system *and* have a sense of self esteem.

TRENDS IN INEQUALITIES IN INCOME AND WEALTH

There is no established theory of inequality to guide us to an optimal amount of inequality. Anyone interested in studying the social structure of America must begin by examining the disparities of income and wealth. **Income is defined as the total monetary return to a household over a set period, usually a year, from all sources consisting of wages, rent, interest, and gifts.** Income refers to the flow of dollars within a year. Labor earnings (wages) are an ever larger component of total income as one moves down the income ladder. Income tends not to be as unequally distributed as wealth. **Wealth refers to the monetary value of the assets of a household minus its liabilities (or debt), which is its net worth.** Wealth includes the accumulation of unspent past income and is a source from which capital income is realized.

Income

The issue of income and wealth inequality is slowly forcing its way onto the public agenda. It has been slowed by economic growth during the Clinton administration which has pushed the unemployment rate to its lowest level in twenty-five years. Nevertheless growing inequalities are of such magnitude that it has gained momentum. The inequities in the class structure of our society are deeply rooted. The standard policy solution to unemployment and its consequent effect of increasing inequality was to engage in expansive monetary and fiscal policy to stimulate economic activity. John F. Kennedy explained that "a rising tide lifts all boats." During the past quarter century it has become clear however that the rising tide of economic growth was not lifting all boats equally. The yachts of the wealthy were indeed raised by a full tide, while the canoes of the poor were swamped and covered with flotsam and jetsam on the bottom. For most of this century the income distribution had remained relatively stable, but since the 1970s there

EEK & MEEK reprinted by permission of Newspaper Enterprise Association, Inc.

has been a pronounced increase in the gap between the incomes of the well-to-do and those of middle- and lower-income families.

An analysis of income trends in each of the fifty states reveals that inequalities in income between the top fifth of the families and the bottom and middle of the income distribution have grown significantly over the past twenty years.

How Much Income Inequality?   In 1996, the real median income was $35,492 which means that half of the households received more and half less. The upper income limit of the lowest percentile was $14,768 while it took $119,540 to get into the top 5 percent in household income. Table 7-2 illustrates that the bottom two quintiles were still below their 1990 pre-recessionary level at the end of the Bush administration. Between 1975 and 1996, the most recent year for which data are available, income inequality grew.

Another way to look at the growth in inequality is to look at the change in real income in each quintile. The average income of households in the top quintile grew 38.8 percent, from $83,221 (in 1996 dollars) to $115,514 in 1996. During the same period, the average income in the bottom quintile grew by only 1 percent from $8,470 to $8,596 in 1996 dollars. Consequently, the ratio of the average income of the top 20 percent of households to the average income of the bottom 20 percent increased from 9.8 to 13.4. The income gap continued to widen for the first two years of the Clinton administration. Finally, the Council of Economic Advisers' *The 1998 Economic Report of the President*,

TABLE 7-2

MEAN HOUSEHOLD INCOME OF QUINTILES: 1975 TO 1996
(Income in 1996 Dollars)

Income dispersion	1975	1985	1990	1996
Lowest Quintile	8,470	8,453	8,637	8,596
Second Quintile	20,112	20,896	21,644	21,097
Third Quintile	32,907	34,610	35,751	35,486
Fourth Quintile	47,787	52,048	53,902	54,922
Fifth Quintile	83,221	96,008	112,642	115,514

Source: U.S. Department of Commerce, Bureau of the Census, *Money Income in the United States: 1996,* Pub. P-60-197, p. xii.

TABLE 7-3
SHARE OF AGGREGATE INCOME RECEIVED BY EACH FIFTH AND TOP 5 PERCENT OF
HOUSEHOLDS—IN FIVE-YEAR INTERVALS: 1976–1996
(Income in 1996 CPI-U adjusted dollars)

Year	Lowest	Second	Third	Fourth	Highest	Top 5 percent	Gini ratio
1996	3.7	9.0	15.1	23.3	49.0	21.4	0.455
1991	3.8	9.6	15.9	24.2	46.5	18.1	0.428
1986	3.9	9.7	16.2	24.5	45.7	17.5	0.425
1981	4.2	10.2	16.8	25.0	43.8	15.6	0.406
1976	4.4	10.5	17.1	24.8	43.2	15.9	0.397

Source: U.S. Census Bureau: The Official Statistics.
http://www.census.gov/hhes/income/income96/in96agg2.html

reported that, "Since 1993, household income has grown in each quintile of the income distribution, with the largest percentage increase going to the poorest members of our society. Maintaining a full-employment economy is essential if this progress is to continue."[22] However, over the long term, the slight improvement in income inequality pales in comparison to the damaging trends of the last two decades.

This unequal distribution is portrayed in table 7-3 which reports the Gini indexes of the shares of aggregate income by each quintile and the top 5 percent. The Gini index measures the increasing inequality at each five-year measurement. The Gini index provides a measure of income concentration by ranking households from the lowest to the highest based on income divided into groups of equal population size (20 percent each, or quintiles). The aggregate income of each group is then divided by the overall aggregate income to determine shares. The Gini index ranges from 0—indicating perfect equality where everyone has an equal share—to a 1 or perfect inequality where all the income is received by one recipient or group of recipients. The data reveal that each of the quintiles from the lowest through the fourth declined in its share of aggregate income over the twenty-year period with the lowest losing the most ground followed by each other fifth declining by lesser percentages. The bottom 20 percent saw its share of aggregate income decline by 18 percent, while the second 20 percent declined by 16 percent, the third by 13 percent, and the fourth lost 6 percent. Only the top fifth steadily increased its share of aggregate income over this period (by 13 percent), while the top 5 percent increased its share of aggregate income by a whopping 34.5 percent. Since the census data do not include capital gains, the actual total-income figures for those at the top are actually significantly higher.

Wealth

An examination of wealth provides a more complete picture of family economic well-being than does income. The richest man in America is Bill Gates, who in his early forties, is worth an estimated $40 billion, which is equal to the combined net worth of

[22]*The 1998 Economic Report of the President,* Council of Economic Advisers, Feb. 10, 1998.

the bottom 40 percent of U.S. households.[23] Power also flows from wealth. Fortunes can be a source of political and social influence that goes beyond having a high income. Large holdings of wealth can also be transferred to succeeding generations which includes the transmission of power and influence associated with it. There is a correlation, although not a strong one, between wealth and age, since older individuals typically have worked more years and have accumulated more assets. There is also a correlation between income and wealth in that those with high income generally have more wealth.[24]

Through the first three-quarters of this century, distinctions based upon class became progressively less important, and opportunities for upward mobility expanded. That stopped during the 1970s, and since then American society has been moving in two directions. Wealth and income in the United States have become much more concentrated since 1980. Both poverty and wealth are increasing together, indicating that the distance between the rich and poor is widening.

The most recent study completed by the Federal Reserve based on data compiled over the last ten years found that as expected from their earlier work, wealth is highly concentrated, with the top ½ percent of the wealthiest households owning more than a quarter of household net worth in 1995. This latest study which applied consistent weights with their earlier studies "show[s] a statistically significant increase in the share of household net worth held by the wealthiest ½ percent of households from 1992 to 1995, driven in large part by a rise in their share of personal businesses."[25]

The most recent data found that the top ½ percent of the population held 23 percent of the total net worth in 1989 which grew to 27.5 percent of net worth in 1995 (see table 7-4). The net worth of the wealthiest 1 percent of the households increased from 30.3 percent in 1989 to 35.1 percent of the net wealth in 1995. In 1989 the top 1 percent had 30.3 percent of the nation's wealth compared to 32.5 percent of the bottom 90 percent of the households. By 1995, the top 1 percent had more wealth (35.1 percent) than the bottom 90 percent of the population which had just 31.5 percent of the nation's wealth to share between them. The increased share of wealth held by the rich was offset by a decline in the share of net worth held by the bottom 90 percent, and a decline in the share of net worth held by those in the 90th through 99th percentile from 37.1 percent to 33.2 percent of the nation's wealth. Only the top 1 percent increased their share of the nation's wealth in this period with the largest gains going to those in the top ½ percent.

An increase in the percentage of business assets held by the top ½ percent was of major importance in increasing their share of total wealth. In 1995 that group held about 60 percent of all business assets. This group's share of all bonds also increased by about 10 percent of those held to almost 47 percent. The increased share of overall net worth of the top ½ percent of households in 1995 resulted from their increase in the share of business and bonds which came mostly at the expense of the group between the 90th and 99th percentiles. The top ½ percent's share of the total value of trusts also increased to

[23]Mary H. Cooper, "Income Inequality," *CQ Researcher* (April 17, 1998), p. 341.

[24]Edward N. Wolff, *Top Heavy: A Study of the Increasing Inequality of Wealth in America* (New York: The Twentieth Century Fund, 1995), p. 6.

[25]Arthur B. Kennickell, Board of Governors of the Federal Reserve System and R. Louise Woodburn, Ernst and Young, "Consistent Weight Design for the 1989, 1992 and 1995 SCFs, and the Distribution of Wealth" (August 1997), Board of Governors of the Federal Reserve System, p. 32.

TABLE 7-4
CHANGES IN CONCENTRATION OF WEALTH BETWEEN 1989 AND 1995.
(in percent)

Item	All households 1995 (billions)	Top 0.5% 1989	Top 0.5% 1995	Next 0.5% 1989	Next 0.5% 1995	Next 9% 1989	Next 9% 1995	Remaining 90% 1989	Remaining 90% 1995
Assets	$24,461.0	21.4	24.2	6.5	6.9	35.0	31.0	37.1	37.9
Principle residence	7,613.2	4.2	5.2	2.8	2.7	29.6	25.7	63.4	66.4
Other real estate	2,690.2	35.3	27.1	7.3	8.8	38.5	45.9	18.9	20.2
Stocks	2,747.2	29.5	31.5	8.8	10.7	43.2	42.2	18.4	15.6
Bonds	1,142.3	36.8	46.5	8.8	9.3	41.9	34.5	12.5	9.7
Trusts	529.7	28.1	33.8	17.4	10.5	40.8	42.5	13.7	13.1
Life insurance	651.1	9.4	11.0	6.5	6.2	32.6	27.8	51.4	55.0
Checking accounts	265.9	4.5	11.6	6.9	4.6	39.8	26.0	48.8	57.7
Thrift accounts	893.5	6.8	7.8	4.7	8.2	38.7	40.9	49.8	43.1
Other accounts	2,035.0	11.8	19.8	8.5	7.0	38.8	35.2	40.9	37.9
Businesses	4,018.2	46.2	59.9	9.6	11.5	35.3	20.8	8.9	7.7
Automobiles	1,108.2	3.9	2.6	1.9	1.9	19.8	17.8	74.4	77.6
Other assets	766.7	24.1	26.6	8.9	4.8	42.8	39.2	24.2	29.3
Liabilities	3,941.2	12.5	6.8	2.2	3.0	23.1	19.3	62.1	70.9
Principle residence debt	2,650.7	1.9	2.7	1.1	1.8	18.6	17.2	78.4	78.4
Other real estate debt	582.3	37.7	23.5	5.4	10.2	39.9	41.0	17.0	25.2
Other debt	708.1	8.4	8.3	1.2	1.5	13.7	9.6	76.6	80.6
Net Worth	20,519.8	**23.0**	**27.5**	**7.3**	**7.6**	**37.1**	**33.2**	**32.5**	**31.5**
Total Income	4,300.7	9.7	8.1	4.0	3.4	21.3	19.6	65.0	68.9

Source: Arthur B. Kennickell and R. Louise Woodburn, *Consistent Weight Design for the 1989, 1992 and 1995 SCFs, and the Distribution of Wealth*, Board of Governors of the Federal Reserve, August 1997.

almost 34 percent. Stocks also constitute a major portion of the assets of the wealthy as they possess over 31 percent of the value of all stock held. In the category of liabilities, it is noteworthy that the wealthiest group significantly reduced its debt during this period. In 1996 about 2.7 million households in the United States had a net worth that exceeded $1 million.

The bottom 90 percent of the households by contrast, holds most of its wealth in their homes, which is their largest investment, and their automobiles. Money held in checking accounts and the cash value of life insurance policies are a significant form of savings for this group. With the significant increase in the stock market over the last several years it is noteworthy that the share of stock and mutual funds owned by the bottom 90 percent fell between 1989 and 1995. While the money share of this group rose by over a third, the holdings of the other groups rose even more rapidly. The figures on income and wealth show a skewed distribution with a fat lower tail and a thin and long upper tail.

Lorenz Curve and the Inequality of Income and Wealth, 1995

The Lorenz Curve (figure 7-1) illustrates the variance of the percentage of the population that has a net worth from a given value. If every household had the same income and wealth, the distribution would follow the 45 degree complete equality line. Any variance from equality will result in the graph falling below the line of equality. The shaded area shows the amount of income inequality. The larger this area, the more unequal is the distribution of income. If there were no government policies to transfer income from the rich to the poor, the income inequality would be even greater.

The country is moving in the direction of greater inequality as indicated by both tables 7-3 and 7-4. What is of particular concern is that the next downturn in the economic cycle could bring higher unemployment and result in the poor falling further behind. Reductions in the social safety net will result in greater hardship for many. The United States, once more egalitarian than many European nations, now has one of the most unequal distributions of wealth and income in the industrialized world.

We might speculate that the institutional framework is critical in explaining trends in inequality in different countries.[26] There are many factors that may have an impact on the level of inequality such as: demographic changes, the entry of women into the labor market in ever greater numbers, changes of family structure such as the delay of marriage, an increase in single-parent households, the levels of unemployment tolerated, the increase in the temporary labor force, industrial relocation to cheaper labor countries, and tax and transfer programs.

Simon Kuznets's law holds that the transition from a rural economy to an industrialized economy results in an initial rise in economic inequality followed by more equality only after reaching some threshold level of development.[27] Thus Kuznets argued that income distribution follows a U-curve in which economic expansion makes poor people

---

[26]See for example, A. Henley and E. Tsakalotos, "Corporatism and the European Labour Market after 1992," *British Journal of Industrial Relations* (1992), vol. 30, no. 4, pp. 567–86. See also S. Marglin and J. Schor (eds.), *The Golden Age of Capitalism: Lessons for the 1990s* (Oxford: Clarendon Press, 1990).

[27]Simon Kuznets, "Economic Growth and Income Inequality," *American Economic Review* (1955), vol. 45, pp. 1–28.

FIGURE 7-1
LORENZ CURVE SHOWING CUMULATIVE PERCENTAGE OF WEALTH AND INCOME IN 1995.

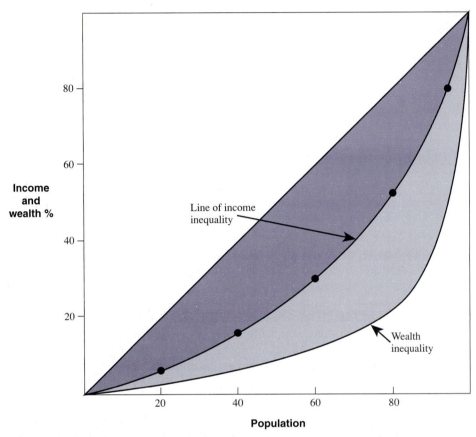

If everyone had the same income and wealth, the distribution would follow the 45° complete equality line. The darker shaded area shows the amount of income inequality in 1995. The lighter shaded area shows the inequality in the distribution of wealth. The larger the shaded area the greater the inequality.

relatively poorer during the initial stage of a country's development and relatively richer at more advanced stages. Kuznets presented historical data to show the swing in inequality that took place in various countries in the course of their development. He showed, for example that income inequality in the United States peaked in the 1890s, and did not begin to decline until after World War I. Later research by Lampman on the distribution of wealth, as opposed to income, found a similar pattern of increasing inequality of wealth, with a decline in the gap occurring between the late 1920s and continuing through the next several decades.[28]

[28]Robert J. Lampman. *The Share of Top Wealth-Holders in National Wealth, 1922–1956* (Princeton, NJ: Princeton University Press, 1962). Other research confirmed the Kuznets-Lampman research in various countries. See Peter Lindert and Jeffrey Williamson, *Explorations in Economic History* (1985), vol. 22, pp. 341–77.

Between 1935 and 1945 there was a clear trend toward a more equal distribution of income in the United States, primarily because: (1) The end of the Depression and a wartime economy provided full employment, significantly raising the wages of labor. (2) During the war, a more progressive income tax and excess-profits taxes reduced the after-tax income of the rich more than that of the poor. (3) Labor scarcity during the war reduced discrimination against minorities and increased economic opportunities for them. (4) Union membership quadrupled and increased the relative income of labor.[29]

In the decade between 1945 and 1955, the trend toward greater equality continued but at a much slower pace as unions began meeting more resistance after the war, and continued prosperity meant continued employment and educational opportunities for minorities. From 1955 through about 1980 the distribution of income remained relatively constant, largely because governments at all levels imposed taxes that were less progressive than in former years. Since 1980 inequality in income has increased. The increase results from a scaling back of progressivity in the federal income tax, and a reduction in federal funding of a variety of social welfare programs resulting in increased regressive taxes at the state and local level. It also results from the decline in the number of middle-class jobs and the accompanying rise in the proportion of jobs in the service sector that pay lower wages.[30]

Theories Regarding Long-Term Growth and Income Inequality

An important contribution to the discussion is a study by Torsten Persson and Guido Tabellini who found that long-run growth rates of income are positively associated with measures of income equality in a study of forty-eight countries.[31] Their examination found a negative relation between the inequality of wealth and economic growth. Other studies have found a link between inequality which causes "political instability" which in turn depresses investment and reduces economic growth.[32]

Other theorists have developed models that illustrate how financial imperfections create inequalities that perpetuate and increase inequalities in the future. For example, Galor and Zeira developed a model in which children receive bequests from their parents, who in turn leave bequests to their children.[33] This process is continued for each succeeding

---

[29]See James Willis, Martin Primack, and Richard Baltz, *Explorations in Economics* (Redding, CA: CAT Publishing Co., 1990), 3d ed. p. 43.

[30]For a time, there was debate among scholars over whether wage inequality was increasing, and whether real wages have declined in absolute terms. The trends and data are now clear, and there is general agreement that both trends are occurring. See especially, Bennett Harrison, Barry Bluestone, and Chris Tilly, "Wage Inequality Takes a Great U-Turn," *Challenge,* vol. 29 (March–April 1986), pp. 26–32. Also, Bennett Harrison and Barry Bluestone, *The Great U-Turn: Corporate Restructuring and the Polarizing of America* (New York: Basic Books, 1988).

[31]Torsten Persson and Guido Tabellini, "Growth, Distribution, and Politics," in Alex Cukierman, Zvi Hercowitz, and Leonardo Leiderman (eds.), *Political Economy, Growth, and Business Cycles* (Cambridge, MA: MIT Press, 1993), pp. 3–22.

[32]Alberto Alesina and Roberto Perotti, "Income Distribution, Political Instability, and Investment," National Bureau of Economic Research Working Paper 4486, 1993. See also, Roberto Chang, "Income Inequality and Economic Growth: Evidence and Recent Theories," *Economic Review,* Federal Reserve Bank of Atlanta, (July/August 1994).

[33]Oded Galor and Joseph Zeira, "Income Distribution and Macroeconomics," *Review of Economic Studies* (1993), 60, pp. 35–52.

generation. Going to school, especially college and beyond is a good investment because an educated person can be a highly skilled and more productive worker and receive a higher income than a more poorly educated and lower skilled worker. The income of the educated and presumably more productive worker will grow faster than the less educated worker. Presumably everyone would like to get an education and receive higher wages. But only those with large enough bequests can afford to pay for their education. This leads to a population split between wealthy families earning high incomes and poor families whose members are more poorly educated, receiving low wages, and caught in a poverty trap. In this model the families that become wealthy or poor, and consequently the economy's growth rate and income distribution, is largely dependent on the initial distribution of wealth, which determines which families can pay for education. As the rich outdistance the poor, they balk at suggested high taxes needed to improve the education of the poor.

This model is in many ways supportive of a less traditional view of education. Why is it that jobs with greater educational requirements usually offer higher wages? The conviction that educated people are more productive is not accepted by everyone. Some claim that the educational system primarily **sorts** individuals by ability. Skills like self-discipline and intelligence that lead to success in college are the same abilities that lead to success in the job market. Therefore individuals with these skills stay in school longer and achieve academic success. Employers try to hire those whom the educational system has suggested will be the most productive workers. Education is partly an investment in human capital and partly consumption. Education is one way to acquire human capital, and while it may also signal innate abilities, it is usually some combination of the two. Highly educated people do earn higher wages than do less highly educated people. Education may indeed be a cause of the higher wages, but the higher wages may also be a cause of education. Many people enjoy going to college and view it as a consumption good (and not only an investment good). We would expect people with greater wealth to consume more of the education good. Just as wealthier people buy more luxurious mansions, so richer people buy more education. Yet it would not be suggested that because rich people live in posh mansions, buying a mansion will make you rich.

A more radical view holds that the wealthy are better positioned to buy the best education available and keep their children in school regardless of ability. In this view education sorts people according to their social class, not according to their ability. The more privileged members of society consequently pass their economic position on to their children while making it appear that there is a legitimate reason for businesses to give them higher earnings. See chapter 8 for a fuller discussion.

Inequality in OECD Countries

One study of income distribution in OECD countries found trends toward greater equality from the 1950s through the early 1970s. Since then there has been a distinctive pattern of an increase in inequality in those countries that emphasize a *laissez-faire* approach to capitalism, such as the United States, Canada, and England. Other countries with more corporatist institutions, such as Germany, Sweden, and Denmark, have a greater tendency to intervene with social welfare programs and have adjusted with much smaller increases in inequality.[34]

However, there has been a resurgence of income inequality in American society that is abrupt enough to be called the "Great U-Turn" by Harrison and Bluestone who place the beginning of the increased inequality in the early 1970s.[35] Similar increases in inequality of earnings for men have been documented in Canada, Sweden, and Australia.[36]

The most comprehensive analysis of income inequality has been developed by the Luxembourg Income Study (LIS) project, which uses sources in eighteen industrialized nations and applies the same definitions to each. The Luxembourg Study, based on census survey data from each country, found that the most corporatist countries had a less unequal distribution of income. The Luxembourg Study confirmed that inequality generally declined throughout all the OECD countries until about 1974 after which inequality began to rise. Since that time "the living standards of the least well-off families tended to decline as overall inequality rose."[37] They also found evidence that the income shares of the middle classes also have declined.

As figure 7-2 shows, children living in the richest American households are by a large margin the most affluent of any industrialized country. Those children living in poor American households are poorer than the children of any other country except Ireland and Israel, the two poorest countries in the study. The gap between rich and poor children is the greatest in the United States and the smallest in Ireland. The gap is greater in the United States largely because welfare programs are less generous here than in other OECD countries.

The Luxembourg Income Study concluded that while the United States has a high real level of income, it is the middle- and high-income children who reap the benefits. "The average low-income child in the other seventeen countries is at least one-third better off than the average low-income American child."[38] In 1996, the number of persons living in poverty was 36.5 million or 13.7 percent of the population. In 1996, 20.5 percent of children under age 18 were poor, a larger percentage than any other age group. Children under the age of 18 represent 40 percent of the poverty population even though they are only 27 percent of the total population.[39]

[34]See M. Sawyer, "Income Distribution in OECD Countries," OECD, *Economic Outlook, Occasional Studies* (July 1976), pp. 3–36.

[35]Bennett Harrison and Barry Bluestone, *The Great U-Turn: Corporate Restructuring and the Polarizing of America* (New York: Basic Books, 1988). Bennett and Bluestone's research has been confirmed by other scholars. See Lester Thurow, "A Surge in Inequality," *Scientific American* (1987), vol. 256 (5) pp. 30–37. Also, Frank Levy and Richard C. Michel, "The Economic Future of American Families: Income and Wealth Trends," (Washington, DC: Urban Institute, 1991).

[36]Gordon Green, John Coder, and Paul Ryscavage, "International Comparisons of Earnings Inequality for Men in the 1980s," *Review of Income and Wealth* (1992), vol. 38 (1), pp. 1–15.

[37]Francis Green, Andrew Henley, and Euclid Tsakalotos, *Income Inequality in Corporatist and Liberal Economies: A Comparison of Trends Within OECD Countries,* Studies in Economics, University of Kent, (November 1992), p. 13.

[38]Luxembourg Income Study.

[39]Leatha Lamison-White, U.S. Bureau of the Census, Current Population Reports, Series P60-198, *Poverty in the United States, 1996,* (Washington, DC: U.S. Government Printing Office, 1997).

FIGURE 7-2

THE GAP BETWEEN RICH AND POOR CHILDREN IN 18 OECD COUNTRIES.

Gap Between Rich and Poor (Thousands of Dollars)

	Poor Households* With Children	Gap (poor–affluent)	Affluent Households # With Children
Ireland	$ 6,692	$20,493	$27,185
Israel	7,781	$25,611	33,392
United States	10,920	$54,620	65,540
Australia	11,512	$38,351	49,863
Britain	11,580	$32,353	43,933
Italy	12,552	$31,728	44,280
France	13,000	$38,835	44,835
Canada	13,662	$42,512	56,174
Austria	14,321	$25,590	39,911
Netherlands	14,529	$28,087	42,616
Germany	15,257	$36,617	51,874
Luxembourg	15,396	$34,675	50,071
Norway	16,575	$27,254	43,829
Belgium	16,679	$30,583	47,262
Denmark	17,268	$29,058	46,326
Finland	17,303	$24,687	41,990
Switzerland	18,829	$40,673	59,502
Sweden	18,829	$27,323	46,152

*POOR includes after-tax income, including government benefits like food stamps and an Earned Income Tax Credit, for a family of four that is poorer than 90 percent and richer than 10 percent of the households.

#AFFLUENT means richer than 90 percent of the households in the nation and poorer than 10 percent of the households.

All figures are in 1991 dollars, with foreign currencies converted using adjustments for national differences in purchasing power.

(Source: Luxembourg Income Study.)

GLOBAL INEQUALITIES

Not only are the gaps between rich and poor in the United States wider than in the past, there is evidence that similar pressures that increase inequality are being felt worldwide. There is also a widespread myth that the developing nations are closing the gap between themselves and the developed nations. The belief is that we are witnessing a leveling of the differences between the rich and poor nations.

A United Nations survey has concluded that the wealthiest and the poorest people—both within and among countries—are living in increasingly separate worlds. The UN survey entitled *Human Development Report 1996,* compiled by the United Nations Development Program found that the United States is moving into a category of countries, including Brazil, Guatemala, and the United Kingdom, where economic inequality is most pronounced. The report found many of the most equitable societies are in Asia, where economic growth has been the fastest while the division of national wealth has been the most equitable. In Japan and Indonesia, for example, the average income of the poorest quintile as a percentage of the average per capita income was 43.5 percent (in the United States the poorest quintile average was only 24 percent of the average per capita income). Several other economies in Asia including Hong Kong, Malaysia, the Republic of Korea, and Singapore have maintained rapid economic growth and have maintained relatively low inequality.

The report found that since 1960, no country was able to follow a course of lopsided development—where economic growth was not matched by human development for more than a decade without falling into crisis. During the past three decades, "every country that was able to combine and sustain rapid growth did so by investing first in schools, skills, and health while keeping the income gap from growing too wide.

A central theme of the Human Development Report is that, contrary to the conventional wisdom, *income and wealth inequality is harmful to economic growth.* "The new insight is that an equitable distribution of public and private resources can enhance the prospects for further growth."

The report concluded that we live on a planet which increasingly represents "two worlds." Far from narrowing, the per capita income gap between the industrial and developing worlds tripled between 1960 and 1993, from $5,700 to $15,400.

The Human Development Report's other findings included:

- The net worth of the world's richest 358 billionaires is equal to the combined annual incomes of the poorest 45 percent of the world's population (2.3 billion people).
- Eighty-nine countries are worse off economically than they were a decade ago. Seventy developing countries have lower incomes than they did twenty-five years ago. In nineteen countries, per capita income is below the 1960 level.

Source: Human Development Report 1996, published for the UN Development Program by Oxford University Press, 1996.

Policies to Reduce Poverty and Inequality

Concerns about inequality are inseparable from concerns about the well-being of the poor. The success or failure of some aspects of economic policy are relatively easy to measure. Does the system, along with public policy, reduce levels of poverty? If this measure is applied to the American economy, there is a mixed record. Poverty declined throughout the post-war years until 1978 when it leveled off at 11 percent of the population. Since then it has drifted up to between 13 and 15 percent (see figure 7-3). (See also Appendix A.)

POVERTY DEFINED

A goal of organized society is to eliminate poverty. In many societies the larger part of the population is equally poor, while in others income is distributed unequally between middle- and upper-income groups. Equality and inequality are relative concepts, while poverty is an absolute. **Poverty exists when people lack an income sufficient to provide the necessities of life.** The American economy has performed rather well in producing and distributing goods and services, nonetheless, **in 1996, 57.5 million people—21.6 percent of all Americans—would have been poor if government benefits were not counted as part of their income.**

Poverty results for the same reasons as inequality in the distribution of income: discrimination, inadequate human capital, and chance. Any theory of inequality should be able to account for the differences in income and wealth detailed here. The interdependence among the variables make a complete accounting for the differences difficult.

Age   Some differences in income and wealth are clearly related to the differences in people's ages. One way to measure income and wealth is to compare an individual's lifetime statistics with the information in any given year of his/her life. Generally income increases with age until age 55 when earnings begin to decline, and then drops significantly with retirement. Wealth typically increases until about age 60. We would also expect to find that the income of different age cohorts would display a similar pattern.

In 1996 the poverty rate for individuals under 18 was 20.5 percent, while the poverty rate for people 18 to 64 declined to 11.4 percent (figures include government benefits). The poverty rate for those 65 and over (10.8 percent) was even less than for the population as a whole. However, they were more likely than the non-elderly to have incomes just above the poverty level. In 1996, people aged 65 and older were 12 percent of the population but only 9 percent of the poor. Since retirees hold a large share of wealth even though their income from wages is often zero, any theory of inequality must take into consideration the life cycle aspect of income and wealth.

Those under 18 are about 25 percent of the population but constitute 40 percent of the poor. Of those under 6 years of age living in families with a female householder, no spouse present, 58.8 percent were poor, compared with 11.5 percent of those children in married-couple families.[40]

---

[40]Leatha Lamison-White, op. cit. p. 6.

FIGURE 7-3
NUMBER OF POOR AND POVERTY RATE: 1959 TO 1996.

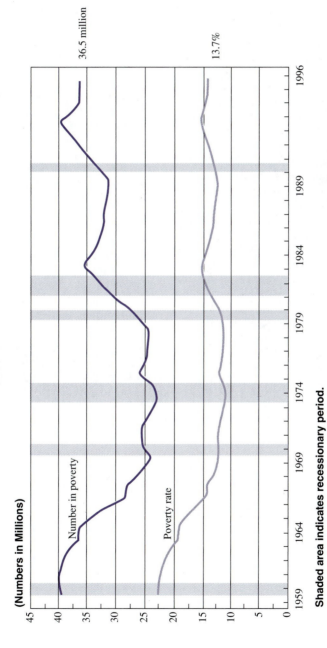

(Numbers in Millions)

Number in poverty — 36.5 million

Poverty rate — 13.7%

Shaded area indicates recessionary period.

(Source: Leatha Lamison-White, Bureau of the Census, Current Population Reports, Series P60-198, Poverty in the United States: 1996, U.S. Government Printing Office, Washington, DC, 1997.)

THE INCOME PARADE

We might dramatize the problem of inequality and poverty by lining up our roughly 65 million families according to size of income, starting with the smallest, along an imaginary road around the world at the equator, 25,000 miles long. That would mean that a family averaging 3.8 people would be found every 2 feet. Assume that the height of the middle family is 5'10" (70") representing the median household income of $35,082 in 1996. Let us assume that our height is also 5'10" so we can look the middle family directly in the eye. What would this parade look like?

For over the first 1,000 miles we will see families of tiny dwarfs beginning from a few inches high to just under one foot tall as we approach 1,100 miles. For the next 2,000 miles or so these grotesque creatures grow from about one foot tall to just over 23 inches in height representing all those families whose income is less than $10,000. They are generally poorly educated. We notice that they are about three times as likely to be black, twice as likely to be Hispanic, and three times as likely to be female heads of households and sickly children.

For the next 2,250 miles, or more than one fifth of the parade, we see these dwarfs increase in size to almost 3 feet tall. They are still more likely to be young, poorly educated, minority, and female. During the next 5,000 miles their height grows from 3 feet to about 4'10".

At the half-way point in the parade we see people whose faces are at our level. When the parade is about three-fifths over we begin to appreciate what it is like to have others tower over us as we towered over the dwarfs. Here people go from 6'8" to almost 10 feet tall. Now the individuals begin to get gigantic. During the next 5,000 miles the height in the parade reaches 15 feet. Then as we reach the last 2,000 miles we find those with incomes over $75,000 and whose height goes from 15 feet and up. These people have the dimensions of King Kong. At $150,000 a year, family members tower 30 feet in the air. Those with incomes of $1 million per year and above are taller than skyscrapers beginning at 200 feet high. The super wealthy, those with incomes over $10 million annually, are half a mile tall.

Employment Status   In 1996, for all people 16 years of age and older, over 70 percent worked and 44 percent worked full time. Of all poor people 16 years old and over, 41 percent worked, but only 10 percent worked year-round, full time. Households with a head who is unemployed are both income and wealth poor. The main exception is among retirees who tend not to be poor. For both groups, transfers are an important source of income.

Education   There is a strong correlation between the education level and the economic performance of households. College households receive more income from business and capital sources than other groups; households that have completed high school are mostly laborers, and households with less than a high school education receive the largest share of income from transfers and the lowest share from labor, capital, and

TABLE 7-5
POVERTY IN THE UNITED STATES: 1996

Characteristic	% Below Poverty 1996
Total	13.7
Related children in families under 18	19.8
Related children in families under 6	22.7
Unrelated subfamilies	45.6
Female head of household	24.2
Black	26.1
Hispanic	26.4
Foreign born	21.0
Not a citizen	26.8
Under 18	20.5
65 and older	10.8

Source: Leatha Lamison-White., "Poverty in the United States: 1996," *Current Population Reports*, p. vii.

business sources.[41] The **transfers** consist of cash or in-kind benefits given to individuals as outright grants from the government. Understanding the factors that determine how much education an individual receives is a critical factor in understanding inequality.

Marital Status   Compared to single households with or without dependents, married households have significantly higher incomes and own a substantially higher amount of wealth. This tends to be the case even if the income and wealth of married households is divided by two to account for double-income households. The poverty rate for families was 11 percent, while married couples had a poverty rate of 5.6 percent. However, families with a female householder, with no spouse present stood at 32.6 percent. And 54 percent of all poor families had a female head.

Race and Hispanic Origin   The poverty rate was lower for whites than for other racial and ethnic groups, most poor people in America (67.5 percent) were white and 45.1 percent were non-Hispanic white. The poverty rate was 11.2 percent for all whites, 28.4 percent for blacks and 29.4 percent for persons of Hispanic origin.

Absolute and Relative Poverty

The definition used by the government is the absolute poverty standard developed for official government use by the Office of Management and Budget in 1969. The U.S. government attempts to define a **poverty line** below which the annual income level is not adequate to provide basic necessities. The poverty line in use today was devised in

---

[41]"Dimensions of Inequality: Facts on the U.S. Distributions of Earnings, Incomes, and Wealth," *Quarterly Review—Federal Reserve Bank of Minneapolis* (Minneapolis, Spring 1997), p. 3.

the 1960s based on the minimum cost of a nutritionally balanced and adequate diet. The amount needed for this diet was multiplied by three because data available at the time suggested that the typical family spent about one-third of its income on food. The figure is then adjusted for different consumption requirements of differing sizes of households. Using this **absolute poverty level** definition, families or individuals with income below their "Poverty Income Threshold" are classified as poor. If your income passes above that criterion you are, by definition, not poor. Since then the poverty thresholds are adjusted annually for inflation using the consumer price index (CPI). The **poverty rate** is the percentage of families whose incomes fall below the poverty line. In 1998 the poverty guidelines defined a single individual to be in poverty if his or her income did not exceed $8,050, $10,850 for a two-member household, $13,650 for a family of three, and $16,450 for a family of four.

The official poverty definition is based on pre-tax money income only, excluding capital gains, and excluding the value of *noncash* benefits such as employer-provided health insurance, food stamps, Medicaid, or public housing (but including all cash benefits).

Interestingly, although definitions of what constitutes "middle class" are less precise, by one definition, a household income between two and five times the poverty level is defined as "middle class."[42] Individuals or families above the poverty threshold but with less than twice the poverty income are classified as "poor" or "working class" but not in "poverty."

In 1996, the number of people below the official poverty level was 36.5 million, which equals 13.7 percent of the population. Without government intervention, inequality and poverty would be even greater. The federal income tax which is mildly progressive and different federal and state transfer programs have worked to reduce inequality. In addition, several policies have been added over the years to reduce inequality by improving the conditions of those at the bottom of the income distribution.

Another way to measure poverty is to include government cash and non-cash benefits as income while subtracting federal income and payroll taxes from income. We can then compare the number of people who would be poor if government benefits were not counted as part of their income to the number who are poor after including government benefits. The difference between the levels of those two measures would indicate the number of people lifted out of poverty by government safety net programs while providing a measure of the impact of those programs.

In 1996, the most recent year for which data are available, 57.5 million people, or 21.6 percent of the population would have been poor if government benefits were not counted as part of their incomes. When government benefits are counted, the number of poor declined to 30.5 million, 11.5 percent of the population.[43] Thus government benefits lifted almost half (46.9 percent) above the poverty line. Those remaining had incomes so low that they were still in poverty after counting government benefits. Those receiving benefits were "less deeply poverty stricken" than they would have been without those benefits. A measure called the **poverty gap** refers to the depth of poverty. The poverty gap

---

[42]*Economic Report of the President,* to the Congress, February 1998, (Washington, DC: Government Printing Office, 1998), p. 125.

[43]*Strengths of the Safety Net: How the EITC, Social Security, and Other Government Programs Affect Poverty* (Washington, DC: Center on Budget and Policy Priorities, 1998), p. 7.

RELATIVE POVERTY AND DEPRIVATION

The use of an absolute level to measure poverty in the United States is criticized by some who argue the standard is arbitrary. People living in countries such as Haiti or Ethiopia might feel elated to live at the poverty line in America, and even consider themselves fortunate. Still members of a poor family in the United States would find little comfort in knowing their income was greater than the average income of Ethiopia. Any measure of poverty must be gauged by income levels within that country.

Today many poor people have a standard of living including modern utilities such as central heat, electricity, refrigeration, radios, and televisions unattainable by the wealthiest individual in 1800. The refrigerator was once a convenience for the middle and upper classes. However, it revolutionized the food distribution system in the United States so that even a poor person now finds it a necessity. But the cost of the refrigerator is a significant burden on a poor family. In some other countries where most of the population lives on farms, and the technology is structured differently, a refrigerator may still be considered a luxury. In one sense it takes more money to even be poor in America today.

Clearly the concept of poverty will vary with time and place and will depend on where it is being examined. Therefore, there is an approach to measuring poverty that applies a relative standard. A **relative poverty level** designates the poor as those who fall too far below the average income. This definition makes it more difficult to reduce poverty, since the poverty line will ratchet upward as the nation's economy grows. If the income of the poor grows, allowing a greater control over economic goods, they are better off. But what if everyone else's income has grown by the same percentage? The poor will not have improved their relative position. Although they have more income, they may not feel more content.

The relative standard erodes the distinction between the poor and the non-poor. Rather than a sharp line dividing the poor and the non-poor, we begin to think of a line of people from the most impoverished to the most fabulously wealthy. This illuminates the problem of poverty as one of the magnitude of the disparities of income. As Alan Blinder writes, "The poor are so poor because the rich are so rich."[*] According to this standard, poverty can be eliminated by moving toward an equal distribution of income.

[*]William J. Baumol and Alan S. Blinder, *Microeconomics: Principles and Policy,* 4th ed. (New York: Harcourt Brace Jovanovich, 1988), pp. 441.

is the total amount of money needed to lift all those below the poverty threshold exactly to the poverty line. In 1996, the poverty gap, before counting government benefits, was $200 billion. Government benefits reduced the poverty gap to $61 billion. Thus government programs reduced the depth of poverty by about two-thirds ($139 billion).

Poverty Reduction and the Earned Income Tax Credit (EITC)

The bill creating the first EITC was signed into law in 1975. The law basically assists low-income workers by refunding some or all of their taxes, or, if they have very low wages, by writing them a small check at tax time. The EITC was seen as a device to get people off welfare by making eligibility contingent upon having a job. It also helps lift many workers above the poverty line. The EITC was designed to avoid a work disincentive by adding to the wages of low-income workers. This results in benefits that go to those in poverty who have a parent who works at least half time. The largest EITC benefits go to families with earnings equal to what a full-time worker earning the minimum wage throughout the year would earn. The EITC is seen as encouraging work and family responsibility.

There has been a concern over cash assistance programs that provide a maximum benefit to those who receive no income, but then reduce the benefit as the recipient's income from work rises. This disincentive to work has been *the* major trepidation of policy makers regarding welfare policy. Since the EITC appears to address this problem it has received broad support.

The EITC is the most effective safety net program for children in working poor families, lifting 4.6 million people, including 2.4 million children, out of poverty in 1996.[44] The EITC was especially effective in moving Hispanic children out of poverty (over 30 percent) because the proportion of poor children living in families with a full-time worker is larger for Hispanics than for either whites or blacks. Its impact on poverty rates is greater among children than among adults because it is targeted to families with children. The EITC also lifted more poor children in the South out of poverty than in any other region in the country because the South has more working families with wages below the poverty level than any other region.

In an effort to reduce the deficit and the size of government, Republicans in Congress proposed a reduction of the EITC benefits. Its supporters argued that a reduction would reduce the work incentives which are a central feature of the bill. The expansion of the benefit in 1993 is associated with increases in the employment rate of single mothers with children.[45] Providing a wage subsidy also avoids the criticism leveled by some critics of minimum wage laws, that a higher minimum wage results in some workers being laid off.

Social Security and Reducing Poverty Among the Elderly

Since the administration of Franklin Roosevelt, Social Security has provided elderly Americans with a basic safety net in their retirement. Of all the groups within the population, the elderly are most dependent on government programs. Currently about 90 percent of married couples one of whom is 65 or older receives Social Security benefits. Social Security is the only form of pension income for about half of these households. In fact Social Security accounts for over three-quarters of the money income (which includes money from work, interest, and other pension sources) for the elderly in the bottom two quintiles. Social Security accounts for about 25 percent of the income for those in the highest quintile and about half the income for those in the next highest quintile. In fact, Social Security lifts close to 15 million people above the poverty line

---

[44]The analysis of the Center on Budget and Policy Priorities compares the number of people who are poor after all government programs and federal income and payroll taxes are counted, but before the EITC is counted, with the number of people who are poor after counting government programs and taxes, plus the EITC. The difference is the number of people lifted out of poverty by the EITC. See CBPP, *Strengths of the Safety Net,* p. 42, fn. 7.

[45]*The Economic Report of the President,* February 1998, p. 99.

EITC

The EITC was enacted in 1975 to offset the adverse effects of Social Security and Medicare payroll taxes on working poor families and strengthen work incentives. The EITC is a refundable tax credit administered through the income tax system. If a family's credit exceeds its tax liability, the family receives a refund check for the difference from the IRS. If a working family earns too little to owe federal income tax but qualifies for the EITC, the IRS sends the family a check. Since enactment in 1975 it has been expanded several times.

This program pays no benefits to those who do not work. Benefits rise as earnings increase. The maximum benefits are $2,210 for families with one child and $3,656 for families with two or more children for tax year 1997. Working families with one child receive the maximum benefit if they have earnings of at least $6,500 and an adjusted gross income of no more than $11,930. Working families with two or more children get the maximum benefit if they have earnings of at least $9,140 and an adjusted gross income of no more than $11,930. Benefits phase down as income rises above $11,930 and are completely phased out for families with two or more children at $29,290. Today approximately 20 million workers get tax credits averaging about $25 per week. The credit ranges from 7 cents to 40 cents per dollar earned. It phases down as a worker approaches the top limit and ends when a family's earning reach between $400 and $500 per week. Only low-income families that live with and care for children may receive benefits under the EITC. Amendments added by President Clinton in 1993 expanded the program and also provided a small credit for childless workers.

Source: Center on Budget and Policy Priorities, *Strengths of the Safety Net,* p. 18.

and millions more from near poverty. In 1960, the poverty rate for the elderly was twice that of the rest of the population. Since then the poverty rate for this group has declined and, as noted previously, is slightly less than for other adults. Social Security has been a key factor in this decline. The Social Security benefit schedule is progressive, and although some benefits are subject to partial taxation, the benefits are not means tested. This allows many people to add other sources of income such as pension benefits to the Social Security benefits to achieve a level of income in retirement close to the level of their working years. A high proportion of the elderly of all races receive Social Security. The program lifts 77.7 percent of the white, 51.5 percent of the black and 46.1 percent of the Hispanic elderly who would otherwise be poor out of poverty.[46]

Social Security is responsible for lifting more elderly people out of poverty than all other transfer programs combined. Nine out of ten elderly people who are lifted out of poverty by government programs are lifted out by Social Security. It also eliminated 83.2 percent of the poverty gap among the elderly before the receipt of other government transfers.

Often overlooked is the fact that Social Security also provides payments to roughly 5 million disabled adults and 3 million children every month. About half the children who receive benefits have lost one or both parents. In short, Social Security is a most

[46]Center on Budget and Policy Priorities, *Strengths of the Safety Net,* op. cit., p. 24.

A TOP HEAVY WINNER-TAKE-ALL SOCIETY

Politicians frequently applaud the "globalization" of the American economy as promising new products and prosperity for the American consumer. Some fear that globalization has imported third-world inequalities to the United States rather than promoting equality abroad. Edward N. Wolff, in his work, *Top Heavy*, carefully documents how the U.S. economy has moved from one of the most egalitarian nations to one with the most unequal distribution of income and wealth among industrialized nations. Wolff is most disturbed about the fact that during most of the last fifteen years virtually all of the growth in marketable wealth accrued to the top 20 percent of households, while the bottom 40 percent of all households saw their wealth decline in absolute terms. This period was also accompanied by a growing proportion of households with zero or negative net worth.

If the policy goal is to moderate rising inequality, then direct taxation of wealth is one proposed remedy. He would provide for estate taxes and a more effective capital gains tax rate among other policy proposals.

Robert Frank and Philip Cook's work *The Winner-Take-All Society*, put forward a provocative and compelling hypothesis to explain part of the increase of within-group inequality. Their thesis is that a new trend, aided by technology, has expanded winner-take-all markets, where more and more people compete for ever fewer but bigger prizes. In such markets small differences in performance translate into rewards far out of line with marginal differences in performance. Winners or top performers in such markets collect far greater rewards than do those whose performance is only slightly inferior. Winner-take-all markets have spread from the performing arts and sports to virtually every part of economic life so that huge wage differences for minor differences in performance may now be observed in investment banking, medicine, academia, and management. Improvements in computing and telecommunications technology facilitate the flow of information, while transportation costs have declined. These factors increase the competition to hire the best performers, dramatically increasing their wages. While there are some benefits for consumers, this market concentrates rewards among a small handful of winners and dramatically widens the gap between rich and poor.

Frank and Cook assemble compelling evidence for their hypothesis, but what is unknown is how much of the observed increase in inequality may be assigned to the expansion of winner-take-all markets.

Source: Edward N. Wolff, *Top Heavy: A Study of the Increasing Inequality of Wealth in America* (New York: The Twentieth Century Fund, 1995); Robert Frank and Philip Cook, *The Winner-Take-All Society* (New York: Free Press, 1995).

valuable program that replaces income in the event of retirement, disability, or death. By this means it serves to reduce the inequality in income between certain groups.

The Minimum Wage as a Policy to Reduce Poverty and Inequality

The wage gap between those who receive high returns for their labor and those at the bottom reflects the high rewards going to those at the top in a winner-take-all society being matched at the lower end of the distribution by an erosion of the value of wages at the bottom. In fact, the low wages paid to many workers and whether the minimum wages that employers can pay should be raised, is an issue that often divides liberals and conservatives. Supporters of a minimum wage view it as a way to assist the working poor without any government outlay.

The minimum wage is a reference point for many employers and employees in many job markets. Typically about 10 percent of the labor force earns the minimum wage. The erosion of the after-inflation value of the minimum wage was cited as being responsible for between one-quarter and one-third of the increase in wage inequality between 1979 and 1989 and continued to increase inequality through 1996.[47] The Clinton administration pushed strongly for federal minimum wage increases in two stages from $4.25 to $4.75 an hour in 1996 and again, to $5.15 per hour effective on September 1, 1997. This was still significantly below the $5.74 average minimum wage rate (in 1995 dollars) in the 1970s. That is an erosion of 35 percent which is significant for the working poor. In 1979, a minimum wage earner working full time could support a family of three above the poverty level. By 1995, he or she would be $3,318 below the poverty level (of $12,158). In fact with the new minimum wage of $5.15 an hour, a full-time minimum wage worker would earn $10,712 but in 1998 a two person family falls below the poverty line at $10,850 and a three person family would need $13,650.

Clinton supported a further increase in the minimum wage which was introduced in Congress as The Fair Minimum Wage Act which would raise the minimum wage to $5.65 an hour in 1999, and then to $6.15 in 2000. The real increase, after taking inflation into account, in the year 2000 would be about $0.60 higher or the equivalent of $5.72 in 1997 dollars, still well below the poverty level for a family of three. It should also be noted that a higher minimum wage would reduce government credits and payouts for EITC.

Conservatives oppose the legislation as a threat to current economic growth. The basic argument in favor of the minimum wage, and of raising it, is that it raises poor people's income. Poor people often have little power to bargain for higher wages. Employers, even with highly profitable workers, have little incentive to pay more than the minimum necessary to supply the needed labor. The minimum wage is a way to help those on the bottom to get a better share of growing prosperity. Those opposed argue against raising the minimum wage, or even having a minimum wage at all, because they argue that it raises the cost of labor and creates unemployment. They also argue that the wage increase is poorly targeted, in that the gains would go mostly to teenagers in high-income families. The theory suggests that although some workers who will remain employed may benefit by an increase in wages, this is offset by other workers losing their jobs altogether, thereby causing an increase in inequality, the opposite of its intended effect. In fact, the expanding economy absorbed both wage increases with a declining unemployment rate so that by February of 1998 there were indications of continued upward pressure on wages.

Families in the lowest quintile received 39.5 percent of the gains. Nationally about 10 million workers (9 percent of the labor force) received a pay increase due to the increase in the minimum wage. The average increase was $0.42 per hour (in the range

[47]Lawrence Mishel, Jared Bernstein, and Edith Rasell, *Who Wins With a Higher Minimum Wage?* Briefing Paper (Washington, DC: Economic Policy Institute, 1995).

A MAXIMUM WAGE LAW?

The discussion of ways to reduce inequality focuses almost exclusively on ways to supplement income upon a Malthusian subsistence level of wages. Another way to reduce inequality would be to set a maximum wage.

Actually the idea is not a new one as Aristotle suggested that a citizen should not be allowed accumulation "more than five times the minimum qualification." He believed that legislators should aim at the equalization of property and that it be in moderate amounts to discourage luxuriousness. Thomas Jefferson, as already noted, indicated a desire to relieve the poor of all taxation and increase taxes geometrically on the wealthy as income increased. As recently as World War II, President Roosevelt suggested taxing all income over $25,000 per year at 100 percent to prevent war profiteering.

While workers' wages rose 16 percent from 1989 to 1995, corporate profits rose 23.3 percent and CEO salaries jumped 54 percent in 1996 alone.

Unlike low-salaried employees, who have no power to increase wages even with improving productivity, CEOs with their stock-option grants, cushy retirement deals, sign-on bonuses, and iron-clad severance packages, have made a farce of any effort to link executive pay to performance. In 1997, average compensation of the top executives at the largest U.S. companies was $8.7 million, an increase of 37.8 percent over 1996, with the bulk coming from stock options. For most CEOs their compensation gains bore little relation to how well their companies—or their stockholders—did. The up-front aspects of pay are in fact shrinking in importance in relation to options, long-term incentive plans, and perks. The 37 percent increase in 1997 was 14 times the 2.6 percent raise earned by blue-collar workers and over 9 times the 3.8 percent for white-collar workers, according to the Bureau of Labor Statistics. **In 1997 the average boss earned 326 times what a factory worker did**. As recently as 1970 the average ratio of CEO

between $4.25 and $5.14). The minimum wage benefitted primarily low-income families with 57 percent of the increase going to working families in the bottom 40 percent of the income scale.[48] Females account for 58 percent of the minimum wage workforce and were also especially benefitted by the increase.

Several factors account for the growing inequality in the United States relative to many other economies. There has been a reduction in government transfers to the poor in the United States along with an increase of single-parent families, a decline in manufacturing industries, and a relocation of industry in the southern states and abroad. There has been an increasing number of women, part-time, and temporary employees in the labor market with labor now receiving a smaller share of the national income. A reduction in the progressivity of the income tax also contributes to the well-being of those at higher income levels. It is difficult to avoid the conclusion that the commitment to a welfare state during the Roosevelt administration and lasting through the early 1970s

[48]Jared Bernstein, *America's Well-Targeted Raise,* Economic Policy Institute Briefing Paper (Washington, DC: Economic Policy Institute, 1997).

income to factory worker income was 40 to 1, approximately the same ratio as in Japan today.

In view of the huge pay increases executives have received, recent attempts by corporations to gain special exemptions from immigration rules to permit the hiring of foreign skilled workers for jobs they claim Americans are unqualified to perform is ironic. "There's no scarcity of skilled American workers, they just don't want to give skilled workers wage increases. What if we turned that around and said that because top executives are pulling in these huge pay increases we should declare an executive shortage? I don't hear anyone saying we should be importing business leaders. It's just incredible chutzpah on the part of executives."*

Some suggestion has been given to linking the income of the rich to that of poorer workers to ensure that the rising tide of a growing economy really would lift all boats and not just the yachts. At the current min-

imum wage of $5.15 per hour a minimum wage worker would earn $10,712 per year. If a CEO were limited to 50 times the lowest paid worker his/her wage would be $535,600. A CEO desiring a raise would have a vested interest in raising the pay of the lowest paid workers who are without bargaining power. It would be a statement of values that there should be a relationship between the top and bottom in the economy. It would also make a statement about how much inequality the society was willing to tolerate.

Another way of approaching the problem would be to prevent a company from deducting that part of an executive's compensation that exceeded 50 times that of the lowest paid worker. Or a company might receive a tax incentive if the highest paid worker received less than 40 times what the lowest paid worker received. Shareholders would become more active in forcing executive compensation to be measured against a standard of performance.

Source: This section is indebted in part to "Executive Pay," *Business Week,* April 20, 1998.
*Mary Cooper, "Income Inequality," *The CQ Researcher,* (April 17, 1998), p. 354.

---

was always a tenuous consensus at best which began to seriously unravel in the early 1980s. The American economy is still undergoing a restructuring through the creation of many millions of low-skill and low-technology jobs. In fact the combination of low wages and low or increasingly nonexistent transfer programs to help the poor has in fact served to concentrate increases in poverty in families with children. Some European countries, such as Great Britain under Margaret Thatcher, have dismantled parts of their social welfare structure with an inevitable increase in inequality as well.[49]

Welfare as We Knew It

The same market forces that carry winners on a surging tide also swamp individuals in smaller boats who need assistance. One way to assist those individuals is for the government to provide a lifeline through the welfare system. **Welfare refers to various**

[49]K. McFate, *Poverty, Inequality and the Crisis of Social Policy* (Washington, DC: The Joint Center for Political and Economic Studies, 1991).

government programs that provide assistance to the poor. Most of these programs are "means tested" in that the recipient must be sufficiently impoverished to qualify for the assistance. There is tension concerning the view that society has a moral obligation through public policy where necessary to meet basic human needs. Such programs are always controversial because they cost taxpayers money and many fear they reduce the commitment to individualism and self reliance. Critics committed to the Social Darwinist principles of rugged individualism and survival of the fittest believe such benefits are **unearned** and therefore go to the **undeserving poor.** The result of this is that the generosity of such programs varies with each liberal or conservative tide.

President Lyndon Johnson declared a "War on Poverty" in 1964. Several antipoverty programs were created or expanded during his administration. The most contentious program was **Aid to Families with Dependent Children (AFDC)** which began in 1935 under the provisions of the Social Security Act. It was originally devised to assist widows not covered by Social Security. It was expanded during the "war on poverty" to provide help to female heads of households below the poverty line. Families with an unemployed male in the house were disqualified. This proviso was meant to make it difficult for men to receive any benefits. It targeted aid to assist the children of the poor on the premise that they were not responsible for their poverty.

A major criticism of AFDC is that, as originally set up, a family with a father who could work but was unemployed was not eligible for AFDC benefits. As a consequence an unemployed father or one with a low-paying job made his family ineligible by his presence. The children would get more money if the father left. Many fathers did leave, and others felt forced to ostensibly leave to obtain assistance, and then return surreptitiously. In 1988, the Family Support Act, acknowledged the weaknesses in the bill that encouraged the breakup of families and made eligibility standards slightly more generous. It tied benefits to work, permitting two parents in the home as long as one of them worked. If employment could not be found, then community service or other unpaid work was acceptable. Programs that require welfare recipients to accept public service jobs or participate in job training is called **workfare.** Through the Family Support Act, states can make participation in a training or employment program mandatory and enact penalties on any recipient who refuses to accept a job that is offered them.

Finally, the federal funding portion varies between states, based upon the per capita income of the particular state. Federal funding as a percent of the total is highest in states with the lowest per capita income. Federal funding averages approximately one-third of the total throughout the United States. Consequently, benefit levels and eligibility requirements show a wide variation, as each state determines its own definition of requirements for food, clothing, and shelter. It then determines the AFDC payments that are calculated according to their own definition of need requirements. Ironically the federal funding matching formula reimbursed states at a declining rate. The federal government would reimburse a state at a higher rate for the first $50 than for the second $50 paid to a family. Several states, especially in the South, such as Alabama and Mississippi which have some of the nation's poorest families set very low levels of funding, which had the effect of encouraging needy families to migrate to higher-paying states. Other states, particularly in the North, enforced residency requirements more strictly to discourage individuals from migrating to their state. Residency requirements were declared unconstitutional in 1969,[50] and since that time no state can bar a citizen from another state from moving in and receiving the public services made available to other citizens within its jurisdiction. Without those restrictions the mobility of those receiving welfare increased markedly, so that by the mid-1970s their long distance mobility was greater than that of nonrecipients.[51] A state with more generous welfare benefits provides incentives for their resident poor to continue on in the state and for the poor from other states to move there. The net in-migration results in an increased poverty level in some states that causes policy makers to be concerned that their progressive policies attract and retain the poor from other areas and overburden their capabilities.

A second program associated with the War on Poverty is the **Food Stamp** program. Actually a food stamp program existed between 1939 and 1943. However the current program was established in 1961. Under this program families with incomes below the poverty level and with less than $2,000 in disposable assets, can purchase food stamps to buy food. The dollar amount a family is eligible to receive, and the amount they are required to pay for them is based on family income. The higher the family income, the more they must pay for the stamps. Spending for this program increased rapidly until 1981 when President Reagan eliminated 1 million recipients by tightening eligibility requirements through an administrative limit on the allowable income of recipients and cutting funding for the program. Unlike AFDC, the Food Stamp program is fully financed by the federal government. In 1996, over 20 million Americans received food stamps.

Criticisms of the War on Poverty

AFDC and food stamps are two programs that have been most apparent in the effort to fight poverty. There has been widespread criticism of various aspects of these programs by both liberals and conservatives. But conservatives have been more critical of the fundamental nature of the programs. They often argue that these programs attack the **symptoms** of poverty in the short-run, while leaving the **causes** of poverty undisturbed. Providing families with food stamps or AFDC improves their financial situation and makes the poverty more bearable, but does nothing to end their dependence on such handouts. And the poor are given incentives **not** to increase their work effort. A frequently heard criticism is that such welfare programs provide an incentive for low wage earners to become "needy," by establishing a disability, or another child to qualify for

---

[50]*Shapiro v. Thompson,* 394 U.S. 618, 1969. The case involved a Massachusetts resident who moved to Connecticut and applied for AFDC after two months of residency. She was turned down based on a one-year residency requirement in the state. The lower court noted the "chilling effect on the right to travel" caused by the requirement and held that it denied Thompson the equal protection of the law as guaranteed by the Fourteenth Amendment. The Supreme Court noted that it created two classes of residents, based upon those who lived in the state one year or more and those for less than a year. The Court held that it was a "device well suited to discourage the influx of poor families in need of assistance."

[51]See Paul E. Peterson and Mark C. Rom, *Welfare Magnets: A New Case for a National Standard* (Washington: The Brookings Institution, 1990), p. 17. Between 1976 and 1980, 13 percent of the poor moved across state lines versus 11 percent of the nonpoor. Between 1981 and 1985, 15 percent of the poor moved across state lines versus 10 percent of the nonpoor. Between 1986 and 1987, 5 percent of the poor and 3 percent of the nonpoor households moved to another state, ibid., p. 16.

assistance. In this way, critics claim, such welfare policies provide incentives to create the conditions they are supposed to alleviate.

Clinton and Ending Welfare as We Knew It

President Clinton campaigned with a promise to "end welfare as we know it," which placed welfare reform at the center of the political debate. Clinton's proposal had three parts. First, he pushed through an increase in the earned income tax credit. Second, he proposed that Congress require that all employers offer their workers a minimal health insurance package. Third, Clinton proposed that government should serve as an employer of last resort for those unable to find work after two years on welfare. Congress adopted the first proposal while rejecting the requirement for employer-based insurance and the proposal for the government to be an employer of last resort. The Welfare Reform Bill signed into law in 1996 was extraordinary in that it broke with a principle that extended back to the Great Depression that individuals and families who are poor are entitled to government assistance. Most people use welfare benefits to tide them over relatively brief periods of unemployment or other difficulties, however there is evidence that the longer one is on welfare, the more difficult it is to get off. The bill limits the time families can be on welfare by ending cash assistance unless the head of the household begins to work within two years. Families now have a lifetime benefit limit of five years, although states may waive that requirement for up to 20 percent of their families. This was justified by many who felt that allowing people to not work for long periods encourages dependence on handouts while destroying initiative, self-confidence, and earning power.

Critics argue that the bill is based upon popular myths that most people on welfare are not truly needy, and proffering welfare seduces able-bodied people away from available productive employment. A second myth, critics charge is that subsidies for children is the cause of the increase of out-of-wedlock births.

The welfare reform legislation signed by Clinton significantly alters the safety net. The welfare reform bill replaces AFDC with a block grant program called Temporary Assistance to Needy Families (TANF) and the Personal Responsibility and Work Opportunity Reconciliation Act (PRWORA). Although the time limits received most media attention, **its most important feature is the transfer of power from Washington to the states.** Under AFDC, each dollar a state appropriated for welfare was matched by federal money from $1 to $4 under a formula providing greater largesse to the poorer states. Under TANF, states receive a fixed block grant determined by the size of their AFDC grants in the previous few years. If a state wants to spend more it has to raise the entire amount from its citizens. States must submit plans indicating how they will use the federal monies but they have a wide latitude to determine eligibility requirements and benefit levels for their particular state. Previously, if a state raised 25 to 50 cents for the poor it would be matched by a dollar from the federal government under AFDC. Now each dollar beyond the block grant must be paid for in its entirety by the state. The block grant will not rise due to inflation, so its real size will quickly begin to shrink. State legislators have quickly caught on that reducing TANF outlays by a dollar adds a full dollar to money that can be spent for sports arenas, convention centers, or schools, therefore the share of state budgets going to the poor will decline. Close to half the states have limited eligibility and adopted time limits more restrictive than those suggested by Congress.

States are not required to provide detailed reports of child welfare related to the Social Services Block Grant (SSBG) expenditures to the federal government. PRWORA reduced funding for the SSBG by 15 percent and abolished the Emergency Assistance program that provided funds for children under the Social Security Act. The Social Security Administration estimates that by 2002, at least 180,000 children who would have qualified under the prior law will be denied SSI.[52] PRWORA changes may affect the incidence of abuse and neglect of poor children in that research consistently reports that the best predictor of child abuse and neglect is income.[53] Thus if families face reduced economic circumstances, child abuse and neglect will likely increase.

The welfare bill mandates $54 billion in welfare programs over a five-year period. Most cuts will come in the Food Stamp Program and in reducing benefits to legal immigrants. States may deny benefits to individuals convicted of a felony involving the possession, use, or distribution of a controlled substance. Since a higher percentage of families served by child welfare agencies have drug abuse problems than in the general population, this will make it more difficult for some to obtain the economic resources necessary to take care of their children. Close to half the state plans submitted indicate that welfare recipients who have additional children will not receive an increase in benefits. States also have the freedom to deny benefits to children born to those on welfare. Governor Tommy Thompson (R-WI) vetoed a bill to provide health care for the poor once welfare was ended.

The main effects of the 1996 welfare reform law will be felt more fully beginning in early 1999 as families begin to become ineligible for assistance due to the time limits taking effect. The ratio of the number of children who receive cash assistance and food stamps to the number of children who are poor before receipt of government benefit will continue to decline. The data for 1997 show sharper declines in the number of children receiving cash assistance and food stamps between 1996 and 1997 than occurred between 1995 and 1996. Between the summer of 1996 and the summer of 1997, the average number of recipients of means-tested assistance programs dropped by 16 percent (from 12.2 million to 10.2 million recipients) more than any single-year drop in recent years. Also, between 1996 and 1997, average monthly participation in the Food Stamp Program fell by more than 3 million people (a decline of 12.6 percent). Of that number close to 1.5 million were children.[54] Such large declines in the number of children who are poor before government benefits are counted indicates a weakening of the safety net for the poor and a reduced commitment for government action to alleviate the conditions of the poor.

[52]Rob Geen and Shelley Waters, "The Impact of Welfare Reform on Child Welfare Financing" (Washington, DC: The Urban Institute, Nov. 1997), Series A, No. A-16.

[53]Ibid.

[54]Center on Budget and Policy Priorities, *Strengths of the Safety Net* (Washington, DC: Center on Budget and Policy Priorities, March 9, 1998), p. 3.

CORPORATE WELFARE REMAINS ACCEPTED

The Republican takeover of Congress in 1994 resulted in promises to cut wasteful spending, shrink government, and overthrow the welfare state. The new Republicans were all too happy to expand federal welfare for business. It should be clear that the increase has been a bipartisan effort with the Clinton administration also anxious to increase business subsidies.

For example, the Agriculture Department's Market Access Program (MAP) has actually *increased* subsidy outlays by $14.5 million to promote the export of goods produced by agribusiness. Enterprises like McDonalds, Ernest and Julio Gallo, Tyson Foods, Pillsbury Company, Campbell Soup Co., Pepperidge Farms, Jim Beam, Ralston Purina, Welch's Food, Inc., and the Wine Institute have all received government subsidies. The question is whether it is right to take money from average taxpayers for the benefit of business interests. Put bluntly: McDonalds, Tyson Foods, and Gallo Wine should pay to promote their own products. The fundamental principle is that the policy role of government is to fulfill critical common goals that cannot be achieved privately, not to redistribute wealth toward private parties based on the size of campaign contributions. When major corporations coopt legislators to transfer tax dollars from ordinary citizens and small businesses with more modest political connections, it warps the entire political system. The availability of hundreds of billions of dollars in taxpayer money has encouraged the creation of Political Action Committees (PACs) and the consequent diversion of special interest money into politics. Companies such as Archer Daniels Midland simply buy access to politicians in both parties. Such access is not available to most of those who pay the bill.

Of course the recipients of corporate welfare insist that they are not the true beneficiaries, but those who might be employed by a more prosperous corporation are the true beneficiaries. Much corporate welfare is delivered indirectly. For example the $1.4 billion sugar price support program is backed by quotas on imported sugar, which cost consumers several billion dollars a year. About 40 percent of the benefits of the program go to the largest 1 percent of sugar farms. Estimates of the cost of protectionism through quotas and tariffs on over 8,000 products which primarily enrich domestic producers run as high as $80 billion. Ethanol, a corn-based substitute for gasoline is expensive but receives tax credits for firms that produce ethanol and exemption from federal excise taxes worth over $500 million a year. Companies like Archer Daniels Midland, which dominates the ethanol market, contribute heavily to Democrats and Republicans alike. They are the primary beneficiaries.

Spending money on corporate interests increases the inequality in the distribution of wealth and income and leaves less money available to assist the less well-off and thereby reduce inequality.

Source: This section relies heavily on Doug Bandow, "Corporate Welfare Remains Unchecked" *Business and Society Review,* no. 97, 1996, pp. 10–13.

New Policy Initiatives   The most obvious difficulties for young mothers in joining the labor force is the high cost of child care and the loss of medicaid that accompanies low-paid employment. The most cost effective scenario for many poor young mothers is stay home and care for her children—not work at a minimum wage job while someone else cares for them. Increasing child care subsidies may be the most politically acceptable way of supporting unskilled mothers in their effort to work.

Secondly, losing access to Medicaid is a serious obstacle for many unskilled mothers. This makes low-wage work not economically viable. A minimal approach would allow all low-income families to buy into Medicaid for some percentage of their earnings through a payroll tax for, say something roughly equivalent to Social Security deductions.

ETHICS AND DISTRIBUTIVE JUSTICE

Philosophers of various types—moral, political, economic—and practical politicians have debated the distribution of income and justice throughout history. Thomas Hobbes, a conservative political philosopher in the seventeenth century wrote:

> And whereas many men, by accident become unable to maintain themselves by their labour; they ought not to be left to the charity of private persons; but to be provided for, as far forth as the necessities of nature require, by the laws of the Commonwealth.[55]

More recently, Thomas Carlyle, a nineteenth century economist and philosopher wrote:

> It is not to die, or even to die of hunger, that makes a man wretched . . . all men must die. . . . But it is to live miserable we know not why; to work sore and yet gain nothing; to be heart-worn, weary yet isolated, unrelated, girt in with a cold, universal Laissez Faire.[56]

John F. Kennedy lamented the practical problem for public policy when he said, "If a free society cannot help the many who are poor, it cannot save the few who are rich."[57] **Distributive justice** is basically an ethical problem. The National Conference of Catholic Bishops issued a call for its members to work for greater "economic justice in the face of persistent poverty [and] growing income gaps." It held that all people have a right "to just wages and benefits" in a society in which the moral measure of the economy is "how the poor and vulnerable are faring."[58] Political scientists and economists may discuss the political and economic difficulties and consequences of certain policy choices, but have no special claim to moral insights. The dominant philosophies of distributive justice vary significantly in their views on equity in the distribution of income.

Natural Law

Natural law theorists generally held that each person has the right to the product of his or her own labor. This view conceded that there would be an inequality of income since each factor of production should receive a return proportional to its contribution to output. Those who owned factors of production or who were more productive because of special skills or intense effort would receive a return that would equal that factor's

---

[55]Thomas Hobbes, *Leviathan,* Meridian Books (New York: World Publishing Company, 1963), p. 304.
[56]*International Encyclopedia of the Social Sciences,* quotations volume, #19, from *Past and Present,* (London: Chapman and Hall, 1845, 2d ed. 1903), pp. 210–211.
[57]Inaugural Address, Jan. 20, 1961.
[58]National Conference of Catholic Bishops, *A Catholic Framework for Economic Life* (November, 1996).

portion, or the marginal revenue product in economic terms. Many of these philosophers suggested that an unequal power relationship frequently resulted in labor not receiving its fair share. The "just wage" theory was developed which reinforced the contention that employers had an obligation to not use their greater market power to enrich themselves unjustly at labor's expense.

This philosophy recognized that the major advantage of distribution according to marginal productivity was that everyone had a vested interest in raising the marginal productivity of their factors which would result in increased productivity and greater total income. These writers also recognized the difficulty of measuring the contribution of each factor precisely, and generally accepted the validity of the "trickle-down" theory of prosperity.

The late Arthur Okun, an economist who favored a more equal distribution of income for ethical considerations, described the equity versus efficiency argument in terms of a "leaky bucket" analogy. Redistributing income from the successful to the unsuccessful is like using a leaky bucket to transfer water from one barrel to another. In the process of making the transfer, some water will leak away and is lost for good. The point is not to stop the redistribution, but to recognize that there are substantial costs, including administrative costs, as well as reduced incentives to work for the recipient.

The goal should be to reduce the leaks as much as possible. It does not mean that welfare expenditures should be cut back. For example, no one would object to providing a starving child with a nutritious meal even though it may cost $4.00 to provide the child with a $2.00 meal. But it does suggest that solving the problem of poverty may be more costly than often presumed.

Utilitarianism

The utilitarian theory as espoused by Jeremy Bentham (1748–1832) and John Stuart Mill (1806–1873) challenged the justification for inequality. Bentham saw all humankind as seeking to avoid pain and to increase happiness. In a political society all pain and pleasures are comparable which provides a legislator with a calculus for determining policy. Policies should be calculated to bring about the greatest good for the greatest number. **Utilitarianism is a political philosophy which holds that governments should select policies to maximize the total benefit of everyone in society.** Therefore, since people are fundamentally alike, then the total **utility** of society will be greatest when income is distributed equally.

The utilitarian approach has provided an approach to determine the "correct" distribution of income.[59] An additive social welfare function may be defined as the total of all individuals' utilities living in the society. The basic rationale for the utilitarian views of income distribution rests upon the law of diminishing marginal utility. It assumes that:

1 Individuals have identical utility functions. Two individuals would therefore receive the same number of **utils** from a given amount (say $1,000) worth of consumption.

---

[59]See Michael Katz and Harvey Rosen, *Microeconomics* (Boston: Richard D. Irwin, Inc., 1991), pp. 670–72, for a more complete treatment of this model.

2 Everyone is subject to the law of decreasing marginal utility of consumption.
The marginal utility for an extra dollar is less for someone who is rich than for someone
who is poor. Increasing an individual's level of consumption will make that person better off, but at an ever decreasing rate. Consequently, the loss in utility in a dollar taken
from a rich person is less than the gain in utils by the poorer recipient. Accordingly, the
reduction in inequality will increase the total utility for society. The total utility of society would be greatest when income is distributed equally.

**3 The total amount of consumption available is fixed and unaffected by policies
that redistribute wealth.** Consider a United States with only two people, Jim and
Christy, and suppose we wanted to divide $1,000 between them in a way that would yield
the most Total Utility. If we assume that Jim and Christy enjoy money equally, that is,
their **marginal utility** schedules are the same as shown in figure 7-4, we can prove the
following conclusion: the optimal distribution of income is to give $500 to Jim and $500
to Christy, which is point E. If the income distribution is unequal, we can improve things
by moving closer to equality.

Although the law of diminishing marginal utility makes certain assumptions, a utilitarian would reject a completely equal distribution because it is clear that people do
respond to incentives. If money is redistributed from Christy to Jim, both will modify
their behavior based upon the incentives they receive from such action. Secondly, the
amount of money in society is not fixed. The utilitarian conclusions would suggest a
policy of complete equality. One criticism of this approach is, as has already been suggested, that people may have different marginal utility schedules. Some may be more
concerned with material goods than others. Nor is it proven that a person with high
income gets less utility from their last dollar than does a poor person. It is not possible
to objectively measure satisfaction. Nonetheless, it is reasonable for a government to
assume the validity of the first two assumptions since different intensities of the psychological satisfaction for consumption by various individuals cannot be known. Nor
can they be proven. The government should act, when designing policy, as if everyone
does have an identical marginal utility function.

FIGURE 7-4 OPTIMAL DISTRIBUTION OF INCOME.

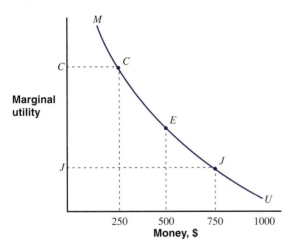

If Christy and Jim have identical
marginal utility schedules (MU), the
optimal way to distribute $1,000 is to
give $500 to each. A redistribution
toward equality will maximize
society's total utility.

If income is not distributed equally
their MU will be unequal, so a
redistribution can make society
better off. Points C and J represent
an income distribution in which
Christy gets $250 (and has marginal
utility C) while Jim gets $750 (and
therefore has marginal utility J).

The main weakness appears to be in the third assumption. In order to improve every-ones' utils the benevolent dictator must want economic growth allowing for increased consumption by all. The dilemma is that the total amount of money is *not* independent of distribution since complete equality destroys incentives to produce more. Equal dis-tribution would clearly provide a disincentive for individual work decisions thereby reducing total income.

Liberal Theory

John Rawls, a contemporary philosopher, has proposed a modern variant on the theory of the social contract that he advances as an appealing alternative to utilitarianism. See chapter 4 for a fuller treatment of liberal theory. Rawls maintains that rational self-interested people would choose principals of justice to govern society in which they were going to live, **if** they did not know, when they chose the standards, what their own place in society would be.[60] He believes that inequality and injustice result from the reality that people know too much about their endowments of assets and skills when they enter into bargaining concerning their political, social, and economic rewards. Those who are already better endowed with political, social, and economic resources refuse to agree to any arrangement (such as a seriously redistributive tax system) that would give away these benefits. The rational self-interest of those so privileged will not only not allow a social consensus for a more equal distribution to emerge, they will favor a system sup-porting inequality to allow them to keep their higher income.

In fact, everyone has a vested interest in a particular position. Those with high incomes favor a system of inequality, and those with low incomes advocate equality since it will improve their position.

Rawls's argument is based upon the notion that an objective view would emerge if everyone operated behind a "veil of ignorance" in which they have no knowledge of whether their place in society will be rich or poor. In this "original position" people would be motivated to choose principles that are impartial and fair to everyone because if you chose principles that favor some people over others, you might find that you placed yourself in a disadvantaged position when the "veil of ignorance" was lifted.

Government should adopt the **maximin criterion** which maximizes the utility of the worst-off person in society. Rawls argues that rational self-interested individuals would act as risk avoiders since they realize that they could end up at the bottom of the income distribution, and therefore they want the minimum income to be as high as possible. They would generally agree that social, economic, and political opportunities must be distributed equally. Since everyone would be equally situated in the original position, and not know how they would fare in advance, they would opt for risk aversion. They would be concerned for the welfare of the poor, since they would not be sure they would not end up being poor themselves. Consequently a consensus would develop in favor of equalizing the distribution of income, unless some other distribution could leave every-one better off. By transferring income from the wealthy to the poor, policy improves the well-being of those less well-off.

---

[60]John Rawls, *A Theory of Justice* (Cambridge, MA: Harvard University Press, 1971). Also John Rawls, "Some Reasons for the Maximin Criterion," *American Economic Review* (May 1974), pp. 141–46.

The implication of this theory for public policy is clear. Government should champion policies that move society in the direction that would be supported by everyone in the "original position," that is toward more equality. This would not lead to a completely equal society, however, since if incomes were completely equal the incentives to produce would be destroyed leaving everyone worse off. The maximin criterion allows for income and wealth disparities because the disparities will raise income and increase society's ability to help the poor. By stressing society's poor, it would favor greater redistribution than does utilitarianism.

A criticism of this theory is that in the original position, some would be less risk averse than others. Some might be willing to risk benefitting at the expense of others. Or depending upon the odds, it might be rational to risk being $100 poorer, but if you win, you might be $500 richer. A second criticism is once again the trade-off between equality and efficiency. Equality will be gained at the expense of efficiency in that there is no incentive to produce more if it will be taken away.

Conservative/Libertarian Position

A final view of inequality is the conservative position which in this case is very similar to the libertarian view. The earlier views see the aggregate income of society as a quasi-collective good that permits some redistribution to achieve social objectives. By contrast, conservatives and **libertarians** argue that society has no legitimate claim on anyone's income. Society's appropriate function is to enforce contracts willingly entered into, provide a system of justice, and provide national defense.

This position places an emphasis on establishing a fair *process* for the initial competition rather than the final *distribution* of rewards. Government's efforts should be directed toward creating a level playing field with equal opportunities to seek economic rewards regardless of sex, race, religion, or national origin. They would generally agree that the struggle for equal opportunity is not over but progress has been impressive. Legal barriers have largely been eliminated and attitudes have become much more enlightened.

It would be unreasonable to expect progress in eliminating discrimination to change the structure of the market economy and the attendant inequality. Once equal rights are provided to individuals so everyone has the same opportunity to use their talents to achieve economic success, the economy merely picks new winners and losers. The elimination of constraints on women and the rise in their educational level and income potential has undercut the economic support for marriage. With less dependence on a husband's earnings, divorces have increased and more children are being born outside the traditional marriage relationship. The resulting increase in childhood poverty and poverty in female-headed households, especially for those of lower educational achievement, should not be surprising. The market still works impersonally in distributing smaller rewards to those who are less productive because of chosen lifestyles, not based on racial or gender discrimination. There is now less of an external rationale for failure. Charles Murray and Richard Herrnstein argue that the differences in cognitive ability are significant and largely inherited.[61] With the elimination of barriers to success, cognitive

---

[61]Richard Herrnstein and Charles Murray, *The Bell Curve: Intelligence and Class Structure in American Life* (New York: The Free Press, 1994).

abilities become more important in a modern economy and one's economic position will increasingly depend on the inherited differences of ability. Affirmative action policies to change the outcome of rewards is not justifiable. Government has no ethical justification to alter the distribution of income.

CONCLUSION

1 In the United States there has always been tension between a commitment to egalitarian principles and a commitment to meritocracy. The Functional Theory of Inequality contends that inequality is necessary to motivate people to work hard and produce economic goods as efficiently as possible. The Functional Theory has certain weakness and must be qualified. If the amount of inequality permitted is basically a social question, then the question to be addressed is how much inequality to allow.

2 Data on the distribution of income reveals a growing disparity in the income of those in the top and bottom quintiles. In 1975 the top quintile earned about 9.8 times the income of the poorest quintile. By 1996 the richest fifth of the families had about 13.8 times the wealth of the poorest fifth. The disparity between the richest and the poorest children in the United States is greater than that in all but two countries. The trend toward greater inequality is increasing in the United States, but other OECD nations also feel the pressure.

3 Government programs of in-kind transfers and other programs are designed to alleviate some aspects of poverty and to reduce the numbers of people in poverty. Poverty is more likely to afflict the young than the old. Female heads of households are represented out of proportion to their numbers along with the more poorly educated and minorities. It is important to understand the life cycle of poverty to design policies targeted to reduce poverty while trying to avoid reducing the incentives to work. The Earned Income Tax Credit and the Minimum Wage law have been two very effective programs in reducing poverty levels of children and low-income wage earners. Social Security has been the most effective transfer program to reduce poverty among the elderly.

4 Tax policy is perhaps the most obvious policy tool that could be used to reduce income inequalities. Tax proposals currently advanced, such as a national sales tax or a flat tax, would fall more heavily on the poor and increase the difficulties. A more progressive tax would reduce inequalities. An annual wealth tax of 3 percent on the top 1 percent would provide about $250 billion annually to the treasury that could be used to reduce taxes on the poorest Americans, or provide education or health care benefits.

5 The Welfare Reform Act of 1996 has ended the entitlement of the poor to welfare. It reduces the amount of federal funding for welfare and turns much of it over to the states to administer in the form of block grants. The bill was motivated by a view that welfare had an unintended side effect of discouraging welfare recipients from taking the initiative to get out of poverty on their own.

6 Political philosophers, like policy analysts and political economists, have differing views about the appropriate role of government in changing the distribution of wealth and income in our society. Most philosophical schools, including the natural law, utilitarian, and liberal social contract theories, suggest government responsibility to reduce inequality. The utilitarian views of Jeremy Bentham and John Stuart Mill would approve of policies that improve the total utility to all of society. Liberals like John Rawls would approve of those measures if they would help the poor at least as much as those who are well off. Conservatives and libertarians would approve only of a minimalist state that enforces laws that encourage a level playing field but does not interfere with the inequality that results.

QUESTIONS FOR DISCUSSION

1 What is the Functional Theory of Inequality? Is it in need of qualification?
2 Is public policy to blame for the growing income inequality in the United States?
3 What can public policy do to correct the tendency toward greater inequality?
4 In thinking about distributive justice, is it possible to develop a model to tell us what is the right amount of inequality?
5 What groups are most likely to live in poverty?

KEY CONCEPTS

absolute poverty	maximin criterion
AFDC	natural law
efficiency	poverty gap
equality	poverty rate
equity	relative poverty
functional theory of inequality	transfers
income	utilitarianism
libertarianism	utility
Lorenz Curve	wealth
marginal utility	workfare

SUGGESTED READINGS

Barry Bluestone, "The Inequality Express," *The American Prospect* (Winter 1995).
Gary Burtless and Kent Weaver, "Reinventing Welfare . . . Again: The Latest Version of Reform Needs a Tune-Up," *The Brookings Review* (Winter 1997).
Robert H. Frank and Philip J. Cook, *The Winner-Take-All Society* (New York: The Free Press, Martin Kessler Books, 1995).
Andrew Hacker, *Money: Who Has How Much and Why* (New York: Scribner, 1997).
Bennett Harrison and Barry Bluestone, *The Great U-Turn: Corporate Restructuring and the Polarizing of America* (New York: Basic Books, 1988).
Robert Putnam, "The Strange Disappearance of Civic America," *The American Prospect* (Winter 1996), pp. 34–48.
Garry Wills, *Inventing America: Jefferson's Declaration of Independence* (New York: Doubleday, 1978).
Edward N. Wolf, *Top Heavy: A Study of the Increasing Inequality of Wealth in America* (New York: The Twentieth Century Fund Press, 1995).

APPENDIX A–INCOME STATISTICS BY STATE

State	Average poverty % 1995–1996	% Affected by minimum wage increase	Median household income 1995–1996 average	Wealth>$600,000 <$10 million Net Worth number*	amount#
United States	13.8	8.9	$35,287	3,654.9	4,037,539
Alabama	17.1	14.0	28,530	39.4	44,305
Alaska	7.7	3.6	51,074	4.2	4,227
Arizona	18.3	9.9	31,706	44.6	49,913
Arkansas	16.1	14.8	26,850	20.1	20,383
California	16.8	10.0	38,457	638.2	734,921
Colorado	9.7	6.1	41,429	52.8	56,406
Connecticut	10.7	4.6	41,775	69.7	76,009
Delaware	9.5	6.2	37,634	8.1	7,552
D.C.	23.2	5.5	31,811	24.0	21,608
Florida	15.2	10.1	30,632	249.5	299,367
Georgia	13.5	9.4	33,801	77.4	83,035
Hawaii	11.2	3.0	42,944	32.3	35,655
Idaho	13.2	10.7	34,175	9.2	10,701
Illinois	12.3	6.8	39,375	183.3	220,761
Indiana	12.3	9.3	34,759	48.4	55,484
Iowa	10.9	9.0	34,888	35.4	30,772
Kansas	11.0	11.8	31,911	30.8	32,209
Kentucky	15.9	10.4	31,552	34.2	39,302
Louisiana	20.1	15.3	29,518	32.5	36,086
Maine	11.2	7.9	34,777	17.6	14,380
Maryland	10.2	5.7	43,123	69.5	78,338
Massachusetts	10.6	5.0	39,604	113.5	107,777
Michigan	11.7	7.2	38,364	89.5	92,013
Minnesota	9.5	6.0	40,022	57.7	57,846
Mississippi	22.1	16.5	27,000	15.1	16,870
Missouri	9.5	8.1	35,059	52.9	59,642
Montana	16.2	11.9	28,631	15.0	12,868
Nebraska	9.9	8.8	33,958	23.2	23,798
Nevada	9.6	6.2	37,845	16.5	21,423
New Hampshire	5.9	5.1	39,868	14.8	17,780
New Jersey	8.5	4.6	46,345	164.0	180,251
New Mexico	25.4	12.3	25,922	13.8	14,927
New York	16.6	7.6	34,707	375.8	412,705
North Carolina	12.4	9.2	34,262	88.2	96,943
North Dakota	11.5	13.6	30,709	14.4	11,847
Ohio	12.1	8.7	35,022	123.3	130,219
Oklahoma	16.9	14.6	27,263	34.8	34,434
Oregon	11.5	7.3	36,470	28.1	37,447
Pennsylvania	11.9	8.9	35,221	143.0	159,134
Rhode Island	10.8	7.3	36,695	15.9	13,975
South Carolina	16.5	11.3	32,297	45.7	43,146
South Dakota	13.2	10.2	29,989	12.1	10,804
Tennessee	15.7	8.7	30,331	55.9	52,641
Texas	17.0	12.0	33,029	192.7	226,567
Utah	8.1	8.6	37,298	12.3	12,021

| State | Average poverty % 1995–1996 | % Affected by minimum wage increase | Median household income 1995–1996 average | Wealth>$600,000 <$10 million Net Worth | |
				number*	amount#
Vermont	11.5	7.0	33,591	7.0	5,453
Virginia	11.3	8.4	38,252	73.6	79,647
Washington	12.2	5.4	36,647	60.9	73,961
West Virginia	17.6	14.8	25,431	16.1	14,550
Wisconsin	8.7	6.6	41,082	42.1	49,114
Wyoming	12.1	12.5	31,707	5.4	5,824

*numbers are in thousands
#money amount is in millions of dollars
Sources: Bureau of the Census, The Official Statistics; Barry Johnson, *Personal Wealth,* 1992–1995; Statistics on Income Bulletin, Winter 1996–97, vol. 16, no. 3, Internal Revenue Service.

8

CRIME: THE POLICY QUAGMIRE

In 1996, the FBI reported nearly 13.5 million criminal offenses. This represents the lowest annual crime count in ten years. According to FBI data, during the first six months of 1997 violent crimes decreased by 5 percent and property crimes by 4 percent. Yet most Americans are unimpressed by this decline. Public opinion polls in the mid-1990s showed crime overtaking the economy as the biggest perceived problem facing the nation. U.S. citizens read daily newspaper accounts of car theft, mugging, child abuse, robberies, murders, drug sales, and vandalism. This, along with sensational stories of bombings and shooting sprees makes Americans clamor for public policies to thwart the "crime wave." Ironically, while everyone agrees that crime is a serious problem, few have much perspective on it. Most public reaction to crime reflects anecdotal experience springing from fear, not reasoned thinking. In this chapter we explore the crime problem by asking **how much crime is out there, what are its causes, and how can policies be created that prevent crime, punish criminals, and protect the innocent from becoming victims.**

HOW MUCH CRIME?

FBI director J. Edgar Hoover conceived of the "Ten Most Wanted" list of criminals in the 1950s as a way to build public awareness about the extent of crime. Now nearly fifty years later, this list of ten is a "quaint" public relations device in a world of mass media and instant communication. False perceptions and fear about crime result in part from the constant media attention given to various vicious, licentious, or mindlessly violent acts committed in the United States. U.S. society, for example, is frequently characterized as the most crime ridden in the world. Yet, when careful comparisons of cross national data are made, this conventional wisdom falls short. Research shows that while the United States has higher levels of lethal crime than comparable nations, it has lower levels of minor violence and property crime.[1]

One less emotional approach to evaluating America's crime problem begins with a look at crime statistics. The FBI publishes an annual report on crime entitled *The Uniform Crime Report* (UCR).[2] This statistical summary, compiled from data supplied by state and local agencies, presents a detailed breakdown of criminal activity in the United States. The most commonly cited UCR statistic is the **crime index,** a highly aggregated measure of the volume and rate of reported crime.[3] Table 8-1 shows a data trend which demonstrates a rise in the crime index over the twenty years from 1973 to 1992 and a more recent decline during the mid-1990s back to the levels of the mid-1980s. Other UCR data give a yearly snapshot of the level of criminal activity. UCR data for 1996 (the latest available) tell us that geographically the largest volume of crime occurred in the South (40% of the total) followed by the West (24%), the Midwest (21%), and Northeast (15%).[4] Table 8-2 shows this regional distribution more accurately by breaking out the incidence of crime according to population distribution. Except for the South, all regions of the country have experienced declining crime rates. According to the UCR, crime is highest in the metropolitan areas and lowest in rural counties. Not surprisingly most offenses occur during the heat of August while the least occur in February.

Thirteen percent of reported crime is violent in nature. Violent crime includes murder, nonnegligent manslaughter, forcible rape, robbery, and aggravated assault. All violent crimes involve force or the threat of force. Firearms were used in 29 percent of assaults, robberies, and murders, knives in 15 percent. The UCR reports that ". . . the proportion of violent crimes committed with firearms has remained relatively constant in recent years."[5]

Murder nationwide reached a high in 1991, with 24,703 murders reported.[6] The volume was down by 4 percent in 1992, and by 17 percent in 1996 when the murder count totaled 19,645 or a rate of 7.4 murders for every 100,000 people.[7] Most murder victims, like offenders, were male (77%) between 20 and 34 years old (43%). Seven out of ten murders involved the use of firearms. Most murder victims knew or were related to their assailants. Nearly one-third of the murders resulted from arguments. Most murders occurred in large cities, though murder rates in 1996 declined in all four geographic areas.

Over one-third of violent crimes were robberies. The 1996 UCR reported that $500 million were lost to robberies, again the lowest since 1987. According to UCR data, all

[1]James Lynch, "Crime in International Perspective," in James Q. Wilson and Joan Petersilia (eds.), *Crime* (San Francisco: ICS Press, 1995).

[2]Federal Bureau of Investigation, *Crime in the United States 1996* (Washington, DC: U.S. Government Printing Office, 1996).

[3]The crime index includes murder, nonnegligent manslaughter, forcible rape, robbery, aggravated assault, burglary, larceny-theft, motor vehicle theft, and arson.

[4]It is important to note that the South consists of the largest number of states and includes populous ones like Maryland, Virginia, Florida, and Texas, along with the District of Columbia. This may explain why the crime index there is higher than in other regions.

[5]*UCR, 1996,* p. 6.

[6]*UCR, 1992,* p. 11.

[7]U.S. Department of Justice, Federal Bureau of Investigation, *Proportions of Crime in the United States 1996* (http://www.fbi.gov/pressrel/ucr/ucr.htm) 4/28-98, p. 2.

TABLE 8-1
INDEX OF CRIME, UNITED STATES 1977–1996, PER 100,000 INHABITANTS

Year	Crime index total*	Violent crime**	Property crime**	Murder and non-negligent manslaughter	Forcible rape	Robbery	Aggravated assault	Burglary	Larceny-theft	Motor vehicle theft
1977	5077.6	475.9	4601.7	8.8	29.4	190.7	247.0	1419.8	2729.9	451.9
1978	5140.3	497.8	4642.5	9.0	31.0	195.8	262.1	1434.6	2747.4	460.5
1979	5565.5	548.9	5016.6	9.7	34.7	218.4	286.0	1511.9	2999.1	505.6
1980	5950.0	596.6	5353.3	10.2	36.8	251.1	298.5	1684.1	3167.0	502.2
1981	5858.2	594.3	5263.9	9.8	36.0	258.7	289.7	1649.5	3139.7	474.7
1982	5603.6	571.1	5032.5	9.1	34.0	238.9	289.2	1488.8	3084.8	458.8
1983	5175.0	537.7	4637.4	8.3	33.7	216.5	279.2	1337.7	2868.9	430.8
1984	5031.3	539.2	4492.1	7.9	35.7	205.4	290.2	1263.7	2791.3	437.1
1985	5207.1	556.6	4650.5	7.9	37.1	208.5	302.9	1287.3	2901.2	462.0
1986	5480.4	617.7	4862.6	8.6	37.9	225.1	346.1	1344.6	3010.3	507.8
1987	5550.0	609.7	4940.3	8.3	37.4	212.7	351.3	1329.6	3081.3	529.4
1988	5664.2	637.2	5027.1	8.4	37.6	220.9	370.2	1309.2	3134.9	582.9
1989	5741.0	663.1	5077.9	8.7	38.1	233.0	383.4	1276.3	3171.3	630.4
1990	5820.3	731.8	5088.5	9.4	41.2	257.0	424.1	1235.9	3194.8	657.8
1991	5897.8	758.1	5139.7	9.8	42.3	272.7	433.3	1252.0	3228.8	659.0
1992	5660.2	757.5	4902.7	9.3	42.8	263.6	441.8	1168.2	3103.0	631.5
1993	5484.4	746.8	4737.6	9.5	41.1	255.9	440.3	1099.2	3032.4	606.1
1994	5373.5	713.6	4660.0	9.0	39.3	237.7	427.6	1042.0	3026.7	591.3
1995	5275.9	684.6	4591.3	8.2	37.1	220.9	418.3	987.1	3043.8	560.4
1996	5078.9	634.1	4444.8	7.4	36.1	202.4	388.2	943.0	2975.9	525.9
% Change rate/100,000										
1996/1995	−3.7	−7.4	−3.2	−9.8	−2.7	−8.4	−7.2	−4.5	−2.2	−6.2
1996/1992	−10.3	−16.3	−9.3	−20.4	−15.7	−23.2	−12.1	−19.3	−4.1	−16.7
1996/1987	−8.5	+4.0	−10.0	−10.8	−3.5	−4.8	+10.5	−29.1	−3.4	−.7

*Because of rounding, the offenses may not add up to totals.
**Violent crimes are offenses of murder, forcible rape, robbery, and aggravated assault. Property crimes are offenses of burglary, larceny-theft, and motor vehicle theft. Data are not included for the property crime of arson. All rates were calculated on the offenses before rounding.
Source: UCR, 1996, p. 62.

TABLE 8-2
INDEX OF CRIME, REGIONAL OFFENSE, AND POPULATION DISTRIBUTION, 1996

Region	Population	Crime index total	Violent crime*	Property crime*	Murder and nonnegligent manslaughter	Forcible rape	Robbery	Aggravated assault	Burglary	Larceny-theft	Motor vehicle theft
United States total**	100.0	100.0	100.0	100.0	100.0	100.0	100.0	100.0	100.0	100.0	100.0
Northeastern states	19.4	14.9	17.9	14.6	14.1	13.4	22.3	14.7	14.3	14.2	17.4
Midwestern states	23.4	21.5	19.8	21.7	20.1	24.7	18.6	19.9	20.3	22.5	19.7
Southern states	35.1	39.6	39.1	39.6	42.8	39.3	35.2	41.0	42.0	39.7	34.9
Western states	22.1	24.0	24.1	24.0	23.0	22.6	23.8	24.3	23.5	23.5	27.9

*Violent crimes are offenses of murder, forcible rape, robbery, and aggravated assault. Property crimes are offenses of burglary, larceny-theft, and motor vehicle theft. Data are not included for the property crime of arson.

**Because of rounding data may not add to totals.

Source: UCR, 1996, p. 63.

235

TABLE 8-3
ROBBERY, PERCENT DISTRIBUTION, 1996

	United States total	Northeastern states total	Midwestern states total	Southern states total	Western states total
Total*	100.0	100.0	100.0	100.0	100.0
Street/highway	51.2	65.6	60.3	44.7	47.0
Commercial house	13.5	8.3	11.1	14.2	16.3
Gas or service station	2.4	2.5	3.0	2.2	2.5
Convenience store	5.9	4.5	4.1	7.6	5.5
Residence	10.6	7.7	9.8	14.1	8.8
Bank	2.0	1.3	1.7	1.6	3.0
Miscellaneous	14.4	10.3	10.1	15.6	17.0

*Because of rounding, percentages may not add to totals.
Source: UCR, 1996, p. 63.

types of robberies declined except for bank robberies. Table 8-3 gives a percentage breakdown of data on robbery for 1996.

Nonviolent, property crime, which includes larceny-theft, burglary, and motor vehicle theft, equaled nearly 12 million reported offenses in 1996. The total dollar loss of property was estimated at about $15 billion, with the average loss per offense being about $1,274.00. Twelve percent was motor vehicle theft; the FBI estimates an average 1 out of every 147 registered motor vehicles were stolen nationwide during 1996.

As part of these UCR summary statistics, the FBI also reports **"clearance rates."** These are offenses cleared by arrest or "other exceptional means."[8] The 1996 clearance rate was 22 percent or about 3 million arrests. Clearance rates have remained stable over the past ten years, with more than 700,000 persons arrested for violent crimes. Typically, property crime represents the lowest clearance rate. The violent crime clearance rate was 47 percent in 1996.

Juvenile arrests (under the age of 18) rose 21 percent over the five-year period 1992 to 1996. Six percent of all persons arrested nationally were under the age of 15. Most juvenile arrests resulted from larceny and theft.[9]

In 1994, the FBI began collecting hate crime statistics. Hate crimes are not distinct crimes but are motivated by prejudice based on race, religion, ethnicity, sexual orientation, or disabilities—both mental and physical. These crimes are committed against persons, property, and society. **The UCR reported in 1996 that racial bias represented the largest proportion of bias-motivated offenses.** Most hate crimes against persons took the form of intimidation; vandalism was the most common hate crime against property.

[8]Examples of "exceptional means" include death of the offender or denial of extradition.
[9]A recent *Knight-Ridder News* article (1 June 1998) reported that arrests of girls have "skyrocketed." Between 1992 and 1996, violent crime arrests for girls increased 25 percent while boys' rates remained steady. The number of girls committing violent crime is still relatively small (15 percent of all minors).

It is tempting to conclude that the drop in overall crime statistics indicates "progress" in the "war on crime." Data alone fail to give the full picture. Much data underreport the extent of particular crimes, for example rape. The UCR reported rape dropped to the lowest level since 1989. In 1996, 71 out of every 100,000 women were raped. Yet, two studies conducted in the 1990s found a significantly higher incidence of rape victimization than UCR data reflected.[10] Looking at existing data, criminologist Elliott Currie comments, "While guarded optimism may be in order, complacency is not. And there is no guarantee that the respite that we are now enjoying will last."[11] To fully understand what has been accomplished in fighting crime, we need to take a more careful look at the causes of crime and the criminal justice system.

CRIME: A DEFINITION

When we speak of the crime problem, what do we mean? How is crime defined? In their book *Crime and Human Nature,* Harvard University scholars James Q. Wilson and Richard J. Herrnstein explore the meaning of crime.[12] Wilson and Herrnstein tell us that crime is not easily defined or measured. Yet it is very common. In fact, the authors explain, "Using interviews and questionnaires, scholars have discovered that the majority of all young males have broken the law at least once by a relatively early age."[13]

As a concept, crime is vague and hard to categorize. Categories of crime like property crime and crimes against persons, white-collar crime, victimless crime, or public corruption fall short because they are not mutually exclusive. Moreover, crimes have different social costs. For example, most people fear property loss from street crime yet the financial loss from white-collar crime is far greater. For example, an article in the *St. Petersburg Times* in the early 1990s described the widespread consumer fraud caused by watering down fruit juice. The newspaper article estimated a $1.2 billion per year loss to consumers.[14]

Obviously, some crimes are more abhorrent and more destructive of the social fabric than others. Wilson and Herrnstein argue, then, that **"a crime is any act committed in violation of the law that prohibits it and authorizes punishment for its commission."**[15] A serious crime is aggressive, violent behavior categorized as murder, rape, assault, and theft.

One way to gain an understanding about crime is to look at the **causes of criminal behavior.** This approach focuses attention on the criminal and his or her relationship to the rest of society. A second approach explores the processes and characteristics of the

[10]A study conducted by The National Crime Victim Center and the Crime Victims Research and Treatment Center at the Medical University of South Carolina entitled *Rape in America* (1992) found that every year in America 683,000 women are forcibly raped. Partly in response to this finding, the Bureau of Justice Statistics completed a redesign of its National Crime Victimization Survey and reported in *Violence Against Women: Estimates from the Redesigned Survey (NCJ-154348)* that women reported about 500,000 rapes and sexual assaults to interviewers.

[11]Elliott Currie, *Crime and Punishment in America* (New York: Henry Holt & Co., 1998), p. 4.

[12]James Q. Wilson and Richard J. Herrnstein, *Crime and Human Nature* (New York: Simon and Schuster, 1986).

[13]Wilson and Herrnstein, *Crime and Human Nature,* p. 21.

[14]"Not All Fruit Juice is Pure as Label Says," *St. Petersburg Times* (November 1, 1993), p. 1A.

[15]Wilson and Herrnstein, *Crime and Human Nature,* p. 22.

HOW ACCURATE ARE THE NUMBERS?

Conventional wisdom says, "No data are better than bad data." How accurate are crime statistics? The most commonly reported numbers are those collected by the FBI in its *Uniform Crime Report* (UCR) and the Census Bureau in its *National Crime Victimization Survey* (NCV). Both data collections are made annually; both report on similar crimes, though the NCV surveys do not include arson and homicide. Both collections also suffer from errors of measurement and bias, and both under-report crime.

The UCR data are based on police reports. Underreporting is largely due to unwillingness on the part of citizens to call the police. Not surprisingly, much petty theft (like someone stealing your wallet) goes unreported. Most people wager the police cannot do much about the loss, so why bother. A second source of inaccuracy comes from the reporting methods used. Some police departments do a better job reporting crime than others. Perhaps their collection techniques are better. Sometimes it is in a department's best interest to report crime; it reflects a job well done, It might even help the department's budget alloca-tion. On the other hand, sometimes a police department would rather not report as much crime. It raises questions about the compe-tence of the police force. If the FBI dis-covers intentional underreporting, it refuses to publish the statistics of the offending agency until the discrepancies are cor-rected. Further, when the UCR data are collected the police report all crimes com-mitted in a given locality. Consequently, big cities, like New York, which experience lots of commuters and visitors report high crime rates.

Police reports also emphasize certain types of crimes and not others. Selling drugs for example, is not included. And if several crimes are committed by a criminal at once, only the most serious is counted.

Victimization studies are equally flawed. The Bureau of the Census ran-domly selects households for inclusion in the study. In 1991, about 83,000 people age 12 or older participated in the NCV survey. NCV, too, underreports crime, but for dif-ferent reasons. NCV studies only count personal and household crimes, not crimes against business. Consequently, they are not as sensitive to crime rates overall, nor are the rates they report as volatile as UCR statistics. On the other hand, NCV studies report up to three times the number of

---

criminal justice system established to deal with crime. Here one asks how effectively the system protects the innocent and punishes offenders. This perspective concentrates largely on the legal system. When looking at the criminal justice system, one also asks how well it operates in reducing the level of crime. Specifically, one wonders if our cur-rent decentralized (even if highly federalized) system of criminal justice can work con-structively to lower the level of crime.

CAUSES OF CRIME: WHAT DO WE KNOW?

Judging from the amount of crime reported, many observers feel very little is known about causes of criminal behavior. Wilson and Herrnstein argue overall that "crime is as broad a category as disease, and perhaps as useless. To explain why one person has ever committed a crime and another has not may be as pointless as explaining why one

crime victims that police reports do. It makes sense that if five people are robbed at gunpoint, the victim study presents a different tally than the police report.

Other factors also skew the data collected in each report. Victims are likely to report some kinds of crime to the police and others, like rape, to interviewers. Women are more likely to report to interviewers that they have been robbed than that they have been assaulted (possibly by a relative). Over time people also forget or grow confused about when a crime occurred, so human error tends to creep into NCV data since the information is collected longer after the crime than most police reports. Further NCV interviews include data from the previous year. All this makes data from the two sources difficult to compare. **Moreover, any comparisons should keep in mind that UCR data reports perpetrators while NCV data reports victims.**

So, are no data better than bad data? It depends. Certainly if crime statistics are used for political convenience, the public is not well served. But if policy makers use the data with an awareness of their inaccuracies and a sense of appropriateness to the crime issue, then they serve a valuable purpose.

Generally, it is wise to consider these aggregated data as providing a good sense of **long-term trends.** The data from year to year probably do not indicate much. Large differences probably do indicate something. These widely cited studies give researchers some sense of the amount of crime occurring throughout the country. As noted by James Q. Wilson, they do not specify the **prevalence** of crime or the **incidence** of crime. In other words, they do not indicate what proportion of a given population consists of criminals or the number of crimes committed per year by the average criminal, indicators that would give a more valid measure of crime in the United States. Wilson warns that the best statements about crime are those supported by as many different measures as possible.

Sources: James Q. Wilson (ed.), *Crime and Public Policy* (San Francisco: ICS Press, 1983); U.S. Department of Justice, *Criminal Victimization in the United States, 1992* (Rockville, MD: Bureau of Justice Statistics, March 1994), p. 9.

---

person has ever gotten sick and another has not."[16] But, in fact, scholars who study the determinants of criminal behavior know quite a bit about its etiology or origin. This scholarly endeavor forms the field of **criminology.**

Criminologists have proposed many scientific, empirically testable theories of criminal behavior. George B. Vold and Thomas B. Bernard in their book *Theoretical Criminology* assign criminologists as social scientists to one of three essentially different ways of thinking about crime.[17] They describe these three frames of reference as follows:

Two frames of reference focus on the behavior of criminals. The first argues that behavior is freely chosen, while the second argues that it is caused by forces beyond the control

[16]Wilson and Herrnstein, *Crime and Human Nature,* p. 21.
[17]George B. Vold and Thomas J. Bernard, *Theoretical Criminology* (New York: Oxford University Press, 1986).

of the individual. The third frame of reference views crime primarily as a function of the way criminal law is written and enforced.[18]

Given these different points of departure, it is no wonder there is a great deal of scholarly disagreement among criminologists over the causes of crime. Those who see a life of **crime as one freely chosen** describe people as rational. A criminal act is considered like any other act—as a rational purposeful choice whose aim is to promote one's best self-interest, much as a choice is described by public choice theory. This "classical" view is highly legalistic and emphasizes ways society can maximize the cost and minimize the benefits of criminal behavior.

The second perspective, **criminal behavior as caused,** is deterministic. In other words, it proposes that people behave as they have been determined to behave. This perspective has dominated the field of criminology. The "positivist" school of criminal behavior looks for causes in biology, psychology, and social settings. Positivists argue that social scientists will **never be able to say what causes a person to commit a crime, but research can determine what factors predispose or increase the risk of a life of crime.** Some of the criminologists holding this view even question the efficacy of punishment in dealing with criminal behavior.

The last perspective, **the behavior of criminal law,** emerged in the 1960s when, as Vold and Bernard explain, ". . . some criminologists [began] to address a very different question: why some individuals and behaviors are officially defined as criminal and others not."[19] These scholars ask why, given a place and time, certain people and behaviors are defined as criminal.

Thus, the field of criminology offers compelling theoretical arguments and divergent explanations. Some criminologists argue crime relates to intelligence, hyperactivity, or chromosomal characteristics. Others assert that poverty and economic inequality lead people to criminal behavior.

A traditional view associated with sociologist Emile Durkheim (1858–1917) argued that in the process of social change and modernization societies became highly differentiated. A consequence of differentiation was "anomie" or a breakdown in social norms and rules. Crime is one normal consequence of anomic society. It is a price society pays for progress. Many criminologists and sociologists in the tradition of Durkheim look to society as a whole to explain criminal behavior.

More recent explanations, like strain theory, offer the intuitive appeal of a causal relationship between social inequality, lack of economic opportunity, and crime.[20] Some see crime as learned behavior. Others offer a Marxist interpretation. All theories of criminal behavior have been extensively criticized. They are afflicted with a large number of theoretical and empirical problems and offer limited guidance to the policy making community.

In the introductory chapter to their book on crime, Wilson and Herrnstein summarize the facts we do know. They write:

---

[18]Vold and Bernard, *Theoretical Criminology,* p. 9.
[19]Vold and Bernard, *Theoretical Criminology,* p. 13.
[20]For an excellent discussion of strain theories see Vold and Bernard, *Theoretical Criminology,* pp. 185–204.

Predatory street crimes are most commonly committed by young males. Violent crimes are more common in big cities than in small ones. High rates of criminality tend to run in families. The persons who frequently commit the most serious crimes typically begin their criminal careers at a quite young age. Persons who turn out to be criminals usually do not do very well in school. Young men who drive recklessly and have many accidents tend to be similar to those who commit crimes. Programs designed to rehabilitate high rate offenders have not been shown to have much success, and those programs that do manage to reduce criminality among certain kinds of offenders often increase it among others.[21]

For the policy maker, individual indicators of crime like age, gender, personality, or intelligence do not translate easily into practical policy. Even policies emphasizing the deterrence of **criminogenic factors** like drugs, alcohol, and guns are hotly debated (see later sections of this chapter).[22] As a result, policy attention shifts to an area more easily identified and controlled, the criminal justice system. Here, consideration is given to the relative costs of legal protection and punishment and the efficient delivery of criminal justice services.

CHARACTERISTICS OF THE CRIMINAL JUSTICE SYSTEM

There is no single criminal justice system. What exists is a jumble of legal avenues. Mapped out, these legal avenues look more like a very poorly designed interstate road system and far less like a carefully constructed legal structure.

The American criminal justice system is **decentralized.** It consists of local, state, and federal jurisdictions. Again, this reflects the American historical experience. When drafting the Constitution, the Founding Fathers left most criminal law to the states. They wanted criminal law to reflect community standards and enforcement to be localized.

The Courts

Different state and local criminal jurisdictions follow somewhat similar organizational patterns, although they often use different names to describe similar functions. The design and size of jurisdictions vary. To fully understand all the systems of each jurisdiction would need a separate look. Nevertheless, they all share **basic similarities in organization and process.** Generally, at the bottom of each state system are courts of **limited** or special jurisdiction. They hear civil cases and criminal misdemeanors.[23] The next level of courts has **general jurisdiction.** Here **the state prosecutes individuals accused of serious crimes**—felonies and certain types of important civil cases. **The appeals courts** review and rule on the legality of decisions made by the lower courts. State supreme courts are the top appellate courts within this judicial system.

---

[21]Wilson and Herrnstein, *Crime and Human Nature,* p. 19.

[22]Mark H. Moore, "Controlling Criminogenic Commodities: Drugs, Guns and Alcohol," in James Q. Wilson (ed.), *Crime and Public Policy* (San Francisco: Institute for Contemporary Problems, 1983), pp. 125–43.

[23]In a civil case individuals bring action against one another hoping to recover financial damages. A misdemeanor is a crime less serious than a felony punishable by less than a year in jail.

Organizationally the federal court system is divided into ninety-seven district courts and ten courts of appeal. Again, cases originate in federal district court and move upward in the appeals process to the U.S. Supreme Court. The Supreme Court hears only those cases with far-reaching policy implications.

Many people take part in the administration of justice. Key participants include police officers, prosecutors, public defenders, judges, wardens, psychiatrists, and parole officers. Often, they have competing goals. Some seek to protect citizens' rights under the law, others see that punishment is effectively carried out. **Ultimately there is a struggle between speed and due process of law, between protection and punishment.**

Our criminal justice system seeks to **investigate and arrest, prosecute, determine guilt or innocence, and punish and/or rehabilitate.** The process from arrest to sentencing has changed little from colonial times. A crime is investigated and an arrest is made by the police. The prosecutor seeks an indictment and an arraignment follows. A trial consists of the admission of evidence and questioning of witnesses until a verdict is reached. If guilt is determined, a judge or jury establishes the appropriate sentencing. From there the penal system takes over.

Understand, too, that most criminal cases never follow this process; rather a **plea bargain** is forged. Here a defendant pleads guilty to a certain charge in exchange for the court dropping more serious charges or the promise of a lighter sentence. In the United States, if a defendant pleads guilty, there is no trial. By reducing court loads and avoiding long and costly trials, plea bargaining expedites the judicial process. Critics argue that the plea bargain works against those who insist on the Constitutional right to trial by jury. But trials too can work against defendants. As noted by one author, "If defendants exercise this right, they risk a harsher sentence."[24]

The Role of the Police

Because the police are the most visible part of the criminal justice system, much attention focuses on their effectiveness. Writes one author: The police represent ". . . that 'thin blue line' between order and anarchy."[25]

The United States has no national police force, and state and local police agencies operate autonomously. Local autonomy has its roots in America's historic opposition to any type of standing army. Today the FBI catalogs 13,032 police agencies or 2.3 law enforcement officers per 1,000 inhabitants.[26]

The chief function of the police is keeping the peace, not enforcing the law. Police officers share a subculture not unlike the military subculture. Police departments are organized to follow a chain of command, and regulations and discipline govern police behavior. As peacekeepers, the police use patrolling techniques to protect public safety and enforce the law.

Many argue that the police have been restricted in their ability to exercise their **investigative and arrest powers.** These powers to stop, question, detain, use force, and to

---

[24]Marianne LeVert, *Crime in America* (New York: Facts on File, 1991), p. 116.
[25]James A. Inciardi, *Criminal Justice,* 3d ed. (New York: Harcourt Brace Jovanovich, 1990), p. 168.
[26]*UCR, 1992,* p. 289.

search have been constrained by Supreme Court decisions. Much public policy debate about the criminal justice system centers on legal decisions critics claim have tied the hands of law enforcement agencies.

During the tenure of Supreme Court Justice Earl Warren (1953–1969), a revolution in **procedural rights** occurred. Because the rights of the accused are the same as the rights of the innocent, Constitutional protections against unjustified searches, admission of hearsay as evidence, and inadequate legal defense apply. Since the 1960s, the rights of the accused have been expanded. This expansion may have been stopped by the appointment of more conservative justices to the Supreme Court during the Reagan-Bush years.

The Exclusionary Rule   One such expansion involved the exclusionary rule, which prohibits illegally obtained evidence from being introduced in a court of law. Despite the arguments by critics that the rule protects only the guilty, the Supreme Court fully extended the principle to the state justice systems in *Mapp v. Ohio* (1961).[27] *Mapp* produced immediate reactions from enraged police departments throughout the country, which felt it seriously diminished their legal investigative powers. Conservatives feared that criminals would now be able to walk away due to mere legal technicalities.

The exclusionary rule was eventually set back by the **"good faith" exception** enunciated in *U.S. v. Leon* (1984). Here the Supreme Court ruled that, though a search was determined to be technically illegal, if the police acted in good faith, the evidence obtained could be introduced in court.

Custodial Interrogation   The Supreme Court extended the right to counsel at state expense to all felony cases with *Gideon v. Wainwright* (1963). Shortly afterward the Court moved even further to protect defendants by addressing police conduct during arrest and interrogation in *Escobedo v. Illinois* (1964), when it decided suspects have the right to counsel back to the point of arrest. And two years later, in *Miranda v. Arizona* (1966), it required police to inform every suspect of his or her Constitutional rights upon arrest. These cases and others represented the belief that convictions often resulted from confessions obtained through inappropriate interrogations by the police—in other words, from defendants who were unaware of their Constitutional rights in regard to criminal matters. Since most convictions result from confessions, once again bitter reactions followed. New York City's police commissioner argued that "if suspects are told of their rights they will not confess."[28]

Many argue the Miranda decision has reduced the effectiveness of confessions as a crime-fighting tool and symbolizes an obsessive concern for the rights of the accused. However, the original strength of the Miranda rule has been diluted through decisions

---

[27]In 1957, Cleveland police officers sought entrance to the home of Mrs. Dollree Mapp, in search of a man suspected of an earlier bombing and of gambling paraphernalia. The police forced their way into Mrs. Mapp's home, forcibly arresting her, and conducted what was later established to be an illegal search. The Supreme Court ruled that evidence seized from Mrs. Mapp's home was illegally obtained and therefore not admissible in any courtroom in the country.

[28]Robert F. Cushman, *Cases in Constitutional Law* (Englewood Cliffs, NJ: Prentice-Hall, 1979), p. 400.

reached in cases beginning with the 1970 Burger Court.[29] Chief Justice Warren Burger, a Nixon appointee espoused a "law and order" position. More recently, concern with custodial rights has centered on the use of plea bargaining, as discussed earlier. Today the number of defendants deciding to "cop a plea" far exceeds those opting for jury trials. Some critics maintain the practice subverts justice by violating Constitutional protection against self-incrimination and the guarantee of a fair jury trial. But its widespread use also lessens pressure on the criminal justice system.

Often manipulated, blamed, or even hated, police departments are caught in the cross fire of criminal justice policy debates. The police find it difficult to balance the demands for more aggressive anticrime measures, which require more expenditures and greater intrusiveness on people's lives, with demands that they adhere to Constitutional protections ensuring proper investigative and arrest procedures. Increasingly the police are forced to use discretion, or selective enforcement of the law, in doing their job.

Police Theory

In September 1994, President Clinton signed a $30 million dollar crime bill into law. Critics of the law denounced its lack of coherence and proposed benefits, while its proponents argued that the law represented a fundamental change in the role the federal government played in crime fighting. The centerpiece of the law is the **Community Oriented Policing Services (COPS)** program which proposed hiring 100,000 new police officers. Community-oriented policing represents a change in police strategy. The first large, organized police force was set up in London in 1830; New York and other large cities followed.[30] Before that, policing was a voluntary, citizen-based effort. To these early police departments, a policy of high visibility and low response time was very effective. According to criminologist Lawrence W. Sherman, "There is substantial evidence that serious violent crime and public disorder declined in response to the 'invention' of visible police patrol."[31]

Over the past twenty-five years, **research has shown that police visibility really does not matter anymore.** An influential experiment was done by the Kansas City, Missouri police which compared crime rates in three groups of patrol beats. One group was given two to three times as much coverage as the others, another group no coverage, and a third group normal police coverage. Results showed no difference in crime across the groups.[32] Researchers speculate that changes in population density resulting from the growth of suburbs in the 1950s and 1960s have reduced the effectiveness and practicality of police visibility and quick response time. As Carl Klockers explains,

---

[29]For example, in 1975 the Supreme Court ruled that, even if a suspect asserts the right to remain silent during interrogation, the police can commence questioning him or her about another crime *(Michigan v. Mosley)*. Beginning in the 1980s, a series of cases were heard which dealt with issues of public safety. In *Berkemer v. McCarthy* (1984) the Court held that roadside questioning of suspected drunken drivers does not require Miranda warnings.

[30]Lawrence Sherman, "The Police," in Wilson and Petersilia, *Crime* (ICS Press: San Francisco, 1995), p. 330.

[31]Sherman, p. 330.

[32]George L. Kelling, Tony Pate, Duane Dieckman, and Charles Brown, *The Kansas City Preventive Patrol Experiment* (Washington, D.C.: The Police Foundation, 1974).

". . . it makes about as much sense to have police patrol routinely in cars to fight crime as it does to have firemen patrol routinely in fire trucks to fight fire."[33]

Yet police visibility does make a difference if it is concentrated and directed at **"hot spots"** or high crime times and places. For example, a police "crack down" or ". . . sudden, massive increases in police presence or enforcement activity" are very effective especially if they are short in duration and unpredictable.[34]

Today, the police are adopting strategies which emphasize "security guard" activity and "public health" prevention. Community-based policing treats a neighborhood the same way a security guard treats a client's property, by looking for risk factors for crime. Security guards, however, protect private property while the police protect public space. The police cannot use trespassing laws to protect public space. They rely on risk factors like traffic stops to control handguns, Repeat Offender Programs (ROP) to track parolees, and curfews and truancy regulations to monitor juveniles. Using public health strategies, police departments consider long term trends and "situational factors" that contribute to crime. They use this analysis for example, to make recommendations to communities for siting automatic teller machines or procedures at business closing hours. Both of these approaches represent a new "philosophy" of policing, one which emphasizes prevention, problem solving, and peacekeeping alongside traditional law enforcement. Gradually police strategy is moving toward a balance between the taxpayer demand for "fair share" approaches to policing and focused, risk reduction strategies.

Prisons: Perspectives on Punishment and Correction

By the 1960s not only had the orientation of the courts changed, but so had public attitudes toward crime. The decade was in many ways a turning point in criminal justice policy. Citizens had come to fear crime as never before, in part due to increasing street crime, drug use, and civil rights protests. Consequently President Lyndon Johnson declared a "war on crime" and established a presidential commission to study the psychology, sociology, and appropriate policy response to crime in America. Commission recommendations led to passage of the Omnibus Crime Control and Safe Streets Act in 1968. This act was viewed by some as a way to offset criticism that the country had "gone soft" on crime.

The emphasis on "law and order" continued through the 1970s. President Richard Nixon supported increased funding to local governments via the Law Enforcement Assistance Administration to conduct research into and carry on programs directed at crime abatement.[35] By the 1980s, both President Reagan and President Bush fought hard for strict law enforcement policies along with protection for victims' rights and stricter drug laws. And the emphasis has not been just at the federal level. A recent study reports:

---

[33]Carl Klockers (ed.), *Thinking About Police* (New York: McGraw-Hill, 1983).

[34]Sherman, p. 332.

[35]The Law Enforcement Assistance Administration (LEAA), now defunct, grew out of the earlier Office of Law Enforcement Assistance set up within the Department of Justice. The LEAA was set up to financially assist local governments efforts to fight crime.

TABLE 8-4
PRISON POPULATIONS 1995: INTERNATIONAL COMPARISON

Selected countries	Prisoners per 100,000 population
Russia	690
United States	600
Ukraine	350
Singapore	287
Canada	115
China	103
England/Wales	100
Germany	85
France	81
Ireland	55
Japan	37

Source: Marc Mauer, *Americans Behind Bars: U.S. and International Rates of Incarceration* (Washington, DC: The Sentencing Project, 1995).

Criminal justice is the fasting growing area of state and local spending, expenditures grew 232% between 1970 and 1990. In comparison, public expenditures on hospitals and health care increased 71%; public welfare, 79%; and education, 32%.[36]

The Clinton administration continues this emphasis. President Clinton launched his second term with passage of the 1994 Crime Bill. This law represented a shift in philosophy for the Clinton administration. Frustrating his Republican counterparts, Bill Clinton swiped the crime issue and campaigned on crime as a central pillar of his presidency. Among the "new Clinton" proposals, a "one strike, you're out" rule for violent criminals and drug offenders living in public housing, school uniforms, curfews, statements inveighing the entertainment industry for showcasing drugs and violence, and nearly $8.7 billion spread over six years to help states build more prisons.[37]

According to Marc Mauer, Assistant Director of "The Sentencing Project," criminal justice policies in the United States continue to become more punitive. Mauer explains, "Russia and the United States remain far ahead of other nations in the degree to which they use incarceration, with the rate of incarceration of 690 per 100,000 for Russia and 600 per 100,000 for the United States in 1995. The U.S. rate is higher than at any previous time and is 6–10 times the rate of Western European nations."[38]

Despite recent trends, no explicit philosophy serves as an underlying rationale for American criminal justice policy. Traditionally such policy has been based on one of four competing philosophical attitudes about punishment—**retribution, deterrence, incapacitation, or rehabilitation**—emphasis on which particular attitude reigns at any

---

[36]U.S. Advisory Commission on Intergovernmental Relations, *Guide to the Criminal Justice System for General Government Elected Officials* (Washington, DC: U.S. Government Printing Office, 1993), p. 11.

[37]David Johnston with Steven Holmes, "Experts Doubt Effectiveness of Crime Bill," *The New York Times* (Sept. 14, 1994), p. 16.

[38]Marc Mauer, *Americans Behind Bars: U.S. and International Rates of Incarceration, 1995* (Washington, DC: The Sentencing Project, 1995), p. 1.

given time depends on shifting national values, as described previously, and growing or waning fears about crime.

Retribution is the age-old philosophy of "an eye for an eye." Now often referred to as a policy of "just deserts," it emphasizes punitive sanctions: Criminals must pay their debts to society through punishment that "fits the crime."

Somewhat related is the philosophy of incapacitation. This postulates that, through restraint or incapacitation, criminals are **removed from society so that they can no longer endanger others.** Incapacitation emphasizes citizen protection and crime prevention.

Rehabilitation seeks to reintegrate criminals into society through corrections programs and services. More humanitarian in its outlook, this philosophy looks to social causes to explain crime. As noted earlier, humanistic philosophy has dominated twentieth-century thinking and policy making about crime.

In recent years deterrence philosophy has come to the fore. Here, some argue **that the effective use of sentencing will function as an example to deter would-be offenders (general deterrence) or to convince criminals not to commit another crime (specific deterrence).**

Often the appeal of a particular philosophy is tied to our assumptions about human nature. In an effort to sort through competing policy approaches, David Gordon has laid out the logical flow of conventional criminal justice policy.[39] He notes that liberal and conservative philosophies about crime correspond to liberal and conservative positions on other social issues. Both liberals and conservatives share the assumption that criminal behavior is irrational. To a conservative, the problem and the solution are for the most part straightforward. Social order, as reflected in the law is rational. Because criminal behavior is irrational, it must be met with a response that protects public safety. Policies to combat crime must emphasize forces which deter crime. This translates into more police, more equipment, and more prisons.

On the other hand, liberals, although they agree that criminal behavior is irrational, also see imperfections in the social order. And because the system is imperfect, they note, some people are more likely to be driven toward a life of crime. As Gordon states, "Criminality should be regarded as irrationality, but we should nonetheless avoid blaming criminals for irrational acts."[40] Liberals postulate relationships between poverty and racism and crime. Consequently, their answer to crime is found in more research, more technology, more professional help for criminals. Liberals argue that societies will never rid themselves of crime till the root causes are discovered and eliminated.

The conservative emphasis on law and order and protection leads to policies promoting incapacitation and deterrence. The liberal emphasis on justice and equality has a stronger connection to rehabilitative techniques.

Sometimes laws contradict ideological integrity. For example, all but three states—Kentucky, Nebraska, and New Mexico—have enacted a version of **"Megan's Law"** that requires convicted sex offenders to register with their local police after their release from

---

[39]David M. Gordon, "Capitalism, Class and Crime in America," in Ralph Andreano and John J. Siegfried, *The Economics of Crime* (New York: John Wiley and Sons, 1980).

[40]Gordon, "Capitalism, Class and Crime in America," p. 98.

prison and allows officials to publicize names of some offenders. Despite a string of court challenges which argued that the registration represented an additional punishment, appeals courts have determined that "Megan's Law" is an administrative action and not a criminal penalty. Some, including members of the various state civil liberties unions, oppose the registration arguing that the decision about how to characterize an offender (one of three groups ranging from low to high risk; all information including name, address, physical description, and detailed criminal history are published on high risk offenders) can lead to prejudice and mistakes. Liberals and conservatives alike are torn between offender and victim rights.

More recent economic analysis of crime began to question traditional liberal and conservative assumptions in another way.[41] These scholars challenge the assumption that criminal behavior is irrational. Building upon nineteenth-century utilitarian thinking, they argue that criminal behavior is a rational choice, as follows:

> A person commits an offense if the expected utility to him exceeds the utility he could not get by using his time and other resources at other activities. Some persons become "criminals," therefore, not because their basic motivation differs from that of other persons, but because their benefits and costs differ.[42]

The rational choice model of crime claims that criminals rationally calculate the cost/benefit ratio of an act. In doing this, they consider the likelihood of being caught, the probability of punishment, and the length and nature of their possible punishment. Solutions to crime from this perspective can be found in an analysis of why criminals make the choice they do and in the development of cost- or punishment-optimizing policies to deter people from making that choice. Public policy should thus aim at raising the cost of crime disproportionately to its potential benefits.

Notions of deterrence pervade current policy for combating crime. One example of this is the renewed practice and enthusiasm for **definite and determinate sentencing policies.** A definite sentence sets a fixed period of confinement that allows no reduction by parole. A determinate sentence is a fixed confinement, set by the legislature, with parole eligibility. These contrast with the more customary indeterminate sentence, which offers more court discretion and is based on a correctional (not deterrent) model of punishment.

The Implications of Punishment and Reform

Although crime-fighting policies have moved increasingly toward deterrence, many find fault with this logic. They question the assumption of criminal rationality, arguing that **even if individuals knew that the risk** of being caught for committing a crime was low, **most people would not commit that crime.** This is particularly true of violent crime. Further, critics point out that the assumption that criminals understand and weigh the

---

[41]See in particular the work of, Gary S. Becker, "Crime and Punishment: An Economic Approach," *Journal of Political Economy,* vol. 76, no. 2 (April 1968), and Gordon Tullock, "An Economic Approach to Crime," in Andreano and Siegfried, *The Economics of Crime.*

[42]Quoted from Gordon, "Capitalism, Class and Crime in America," in Andreano and Siegfried, *Economics of Crime,* p. 100.

possible costs/punishments for their criminal acts lacks empirical support. Many analysts argue that it takes more than the threat of punishment to keep people in line.[43]

Those who defend deterrence argue that, while **particular deterrence,** or the effect of deterrence on criminals, may be hard to prove, it is likely to have a great **general** effect. They claim the average citizen is less likely to commit a criminal act because of the "demonstration effect" of punishment. However, critics argue that such an effect is nearly impossible to prove or disprove.

Some refine deterrence policy by asserting a relationship between **the certainty and severity of punishment and the level of crime.**[44] In other words, they claim criminal behavior is deterred if the punishment is swift, certain, and severe. This proposition reinforces arguments used against the more traditional rehabilitative policies. Research has found that traditional rehabilitation has achieved only limited success. Alfred Blumstein explains that by the mid-1970s studies showed that "rehab" programs had a "null effect."[45] In other words, corrections programs broke even on reducing recidivism.[46] Recidivism seems more closely associated with personal characteristics of the criminal and to the outside environment to which the prisoner returns upon release. As Robert Blecker explains, this led policy makers to pass laws like the Sentencing Reform Act of 1984, in which Congress[47]

> . . . rejected rehabilitation as an outmoded philosophy, abolished parole, and established the United States Sentencing Commission to fix sentences for a vast range of federal crimes based largely on a philosophy of giving each criminal his just deserts.[48]

The resulting "get tough" policies on crime led to longer sentencing. A recent National Research Council study states that **average prison time served per violent crime approximately tripled between 1975 and 1989, returning to the levels of the 1950s.** But this does not seem to have had the desired deterrent effect either. Crime data since 1975 show longer sentences have not reduced the level of crime. As noted in the National Research Council study,

> . . . if tripling the average length of incarceration per crime had a strong deterrent effect, then violent crime rates should have declined in the absence of other relevant changes. While rates declined during the early 1980s, they generally rose after 1985, suggesting that changes in other factors . . . may have been causing an increase in potential crimes.[49]

Some even argue that longer sentences may have aggravated the crime problem. Certainly longer sentences put more pressure on prison resources (see fig. 8-1 for growth

[43]See the recent work of James Q. Wilson, *The Moral Sense* (New York: Free Press, 1993), which argues that to combat crime, societies need to nurture more private virtue.

[44]See studies noted in Albert J. Reiss, Jr. and Jeffrey A. Roth (eds.), *Understanding and Preventing Violence* (Washington, DC: National Academy Press, 1993), pp. 291–94.

[45]Alfred Blumstein, "Prisons, Populations, Capacity and Alternatives," *Crime and Public Policy* (San Francisco: ICS Press, 1983), p. 232.

[46]Recidivism is recurring criminal behavior.

[47]Sentencing Reform Act of 1984, Pub. L. 98-473, 98 Stat. 1987 (1984).

[48]Robert Blecker, *Haven or Hell? Inside Lorton Central Prison: Experiences of Punishment Justified* (unpublished internal study of Lorton Prison conducted in 1990 by Robert Blecker, Professor of Law, New York University Law School).

[49]National Research Council, *Understanding and Preventing Violence* (Washington, DC: National Academy Press, 1993), p. 292.

FIGURE 8-1
SENTENCED PRISONERS IN STATE AND U.S. FEDERAL INSTITUTIONS, 1925 to 1990.

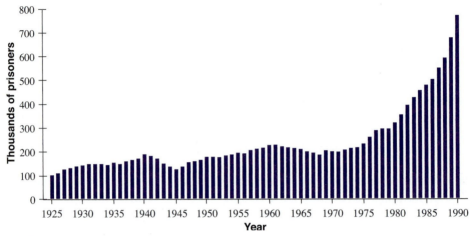

(*Source of data:* Sourcebook of Criminal Justice Statistics, *1989, U.S. Department of Justice, Bureau of Justice Statistics, Washington, DC, 1991.*)

in prison population) and raise costs. A recent study reports that "the United States has more of its population behind bars than any other country in the world."[50] The annual operating expenditure per inmate is estimated today at about $15,000. But a number of experts fear that jailhouses and prisons have become "schools for crime." Blumstein points out how some critics argue ". . . prison is harmful because it socializes prisoners, especially younger ones, into a hardened criminal culture."[51] The box entitled "Who Is in Prison?" describes the current prison population.[52]

How society finds a suitable mix of retribution, deterrence, incapacitation, and rehabilitation to fight crime is a practical issue, but it also has important moral dimensions. Robert Blecker makes the following trenchant critique: "What actually happens to prisoners—their daily pain and suffering inside prison—is the only true measure of whether the traditional concepts have meaning, the traditional goals are fulfilled, the traditional definitions apply."[53]

INGREDIENTS OF VIOLENCE: DRUGS, GUNS AND POVERTY

Crime abatement has been linked with policies aimed at low levels of drug and gun use, along with policies designed to lift people out of poverty. The relationship between these factors and crime is controversial. Politicians often proclaim such policies because they

[50]U.S. Advisory Commission on Intergovernmental Relations, *Guide to the Criminal Justice System for General Government Elected Officials* (Washington, DC: U.S. Government Printing Office, 1993), p. 11.

[51]Alfred Blumstein, "Prisons: Populations, Capacity and Alternatives," *Crime and Public Policy* (San Francisco: ICS, 1983), p. 232.

[52]U.S. Advisory Commission, *Guide to the Criminal Justice System,* p. 30.

[53]Blecker, *Haven or Hell?* p. 1152.

WHO IS IN PRISON?

Age—half are over 28

Race—47 percent are black, 38 percent white, 12 percent Hispanic, and 3 percent other

Education—only 38 percent have completed high school

Marital status—20 percent are married and 54 percent were never married; 80 percent of the females have at least one child, and over 40 percent of them had their first child before the age of 18

Drug and alcohol use—54 percent admitted to being under the influence of drugs and/or alcohol at the time of the crime; drug testing surveys show a higher percentage

Family crime—about 40 percent had an immediate family member with a prior incarceration record

Prior criminal record—82 percent had a prior felony conviction. Almost half of inmates with nonviolent records were in prison for at least the third time. Only 7 percent were nonviolent first offenders, and over 25 percent of these were convicted of drug trafficking.

Source: U.S. Advisory Commission, *Guide to Criminal Justice System,* p. 30.

appeal to voters. But prudent analysis shows that the connection between drugs, guns, poverty, and crime is not obviously direct or causal.

The War on Drugs

The shattering effects of drug dependency lead citizens to endorse just about any program directed at eliminating illegal drug use. Public drug policies are based on medical, commercial, and moral concerns, and increasingly they are connected with crime policy. Most Americans support a "war on drugs" and believe any efforts to decriminalize drug use are morally bankrupt. But the links between drugs and crime are unclear, and the empirical evidence demonstrating their relationship is weak.

Supply and demand considerations govern current drug policies. Reducing drug supplies through interdiction and the punishment of drug traffickers and reducing demand through the education, incarceration, and rehabilitation of drug users form the basis of the government's antidrug strategy. This strategy relies heavily on the criminal justice system for its effective implementation. Most Americans buy into the argument that drugs and crime are closely related. Consequently, they support employing the resources of the criminal justice system to fight the war on drugs. But is doing so justified?

Illegal drugs today include a wide range of psychoactive products such as opiates, cocaine (and its derivative crack), amphetamines, PCP, and hallucinogens. Medical research reveals that the behavioral response to these various drugs differ significantly from one person to the next and one drug to another. But setting up good scientific research on drug use and behavior to learn more is difficult. Reactions to drugs are highly individualistic and depend on factors like how much and how often a drug is taken.

THE ENDURING DEBATE: CAPITAL PUNISHMENT

In October 1993, the state of Maryland began preparing for its first criminal execution in more than twenty-five years. Despite the legal and moral debate that has threatened the use of capital punishment, most Americans still support it. But the death penalty raises a number of problems, including proportionality of punishment, consistency of state statutes, and the vagaries of sentencing.

When the Bill of Rights was added to the Constitution, few intended the Eighth Amendment's "cruel and unusual punishment" to preclude capital punishment. The concern was to assure that punishment was proportional to the offense. Flagrant acts of punishment like burning at the stake were outlawed. The use of capital punishment continued historically. It peaked in the 1930s and began to decline precipitously in the 1960s. Critics denounced the variability in state statutes and pointed out that the poor, blacks, and underrepresented groups were more likely to be executed. By the 1960s, the NAACP and the ACLU had mounted a campaign against the use of capital punishment, making the issue one of public policy debate.

Beyond the question of arbitrary use, others raised the larger question of "evolv-ing standards of decency." They argued that, though our colonial ancestors found no moral distaste in imposing the death penalty, perhaps contemporary standards of decency had changed. These two concerns, combined with growing worry that juries lacked sufficient directions in imposing the death penalty, led to a virtual moratorium on its use by the late 1960s.

Perhaps inevitably the question came before the Supreme Court. The first challenge to the death penalty addressed questions like the legality of "death qualified juries," that is, jurists selected for their willingness to impose the death penalty. The Court ruled such juries unconstitutional. The Court also invalidated the death penalty mandated under the Federal Kidnapping Act.

The major challenge to the death penalty occurred in the 1972 case *Furman v. Georgia*. The Supreme Court in its decision temporarily struck down the death penalty because of the "arbitrary, capricious and racist manner" in which it had been applied. Essentially the Court reacted to how the death penalty had been used, not to the death penalty per se. Though the decision was complex, it did leave two legal avenues open to the states. States could pass laws which established a bifurcated procedure for the death penalty. Here defendants would face a trial to establish

Scientists do know that different drugs elicit different reactions.[54] For example, heroine and opiates tend to inhibit behavior, though it is not at all clear what happens during periods of withdrawal. The chronic use of these drugs may affect the central nervous system and lead to aberrant social behavior. Drugs like cocaine, LSD, and PCP, and amphetamines produce effects not unlike alcohol. In small doses, individuals tend to act out in a disruptive fashion, while higher doses lead to more disorganized, clumsy behavior that may have an inhibiting effect on social interaction. Crack cocaine may lead to a psychotic state, though no direct relationship has been established. **Essentially, the analysis of individual drug use and crime levels show no consistent relationship.**

[54]For a detailed summary of the leading scientific research on drugs and their effects, see the study prepared by the National Research Council already cited, Reiss and Roth (eds.), *Understanding and Preventing Violence.*

culpability. If found guilty then a second proceeding would follow to establish grounds for the death penalty. The other legal avenue available to states was to make the death penalty mandatory for certain crimes.

The Supreme Court ruled on the legality of the two-step procedure in *Gregg v. Georgia* (1976). In this case, the Court ruled that the death penalty for murder did not necessarily constitute cruel and unusual punishment. Further it declared the bifurcated system Constitutional. However, the Court ruled in *Woodson v. North Carolina* (1976) that the death penalty may not be made mandatory.

Despite the fact that the Gregg case upheld the Constitutionality of the death penalty, a series of rulings has eroded the jury discretion in applying the statutory guidelines. In addition to these fundamental legal questions, other objections have been voiced regarding the cost and effectiveness of the death penalty. While some are persuaded that it is a cost-effective form

of punishment, others point out that given the need to guarantee procedural safeguards its costs are much higher than other forms of punishment. In other words, the studies show that the deterrent effect of the death penalty is far from proven. Comparisons show few differences in crime rates for those states with the death penalty and those without it. And in states with the death penalty, comparisons of the crime rate before and after an execution show no differences. Many conclude that the death penalty is popularly supported by Americans and politically useful. Some elected officials, however—among them the former Governor of New York, Mario M. Cuomo—have argued forcefully for life in prison without parole as a preferable sentence. As noted by Cuomo in a *New York Times* editorial, "That alternative is just as permanent, at least as great a deterrent and—for those who are so inclined—far less expensive than the exhaustive legal appeals required in capital cases."*

*Mario M. Cuomo, "New York State Shouldn't Kill People," *The New York Times,* June 17, 1989, p. 23.
Sources: Donald D. Hook and Lothar Kahn, *Death in the Balance: The Debate Over Capital Punishment* (Lexington, MA: D. C. Heath, 1989); Bonnie Szumski, Lynn Hall, and Susan Bursell (eds.), *The Death Penalty: Opposing Viewpoints* (St. Paul, MN: Greenhaven Press, 1986); *Gregg v. Georgia,* 428 U.S. 153 (1976); *Woodson v. North Carolina,* 428, U.S. 280 (1976).

Data in figure 8-2 illustrate this comparison for cocaine use in five major American cities. As explained by researcher James Inciardi:

New York, with the highest cocaine prevalence of the five cities, and Los Angeles, with the second lowest, have the lowest homicide rates. The New York, Miami, and D.C. data resemble, if anything, an inverse relationship between homicide rates and arrestees' cocaine use.[55]

While the physiological connection between drugs and crime is not verifiable, **economic arguments** are persuasive. Do drug addicts steal or kill to feed a drug habit? Again, good data to confirm this proposition are hard to come by. One study found the

[55]Reiss and Roth (eds.), *Understanding and Preventing Violence,* p. 188.

FIGURE 8-2
HOMICIDE RATES, 1985–1989 AND COCAINE USERS IN SELECTED CITIES.

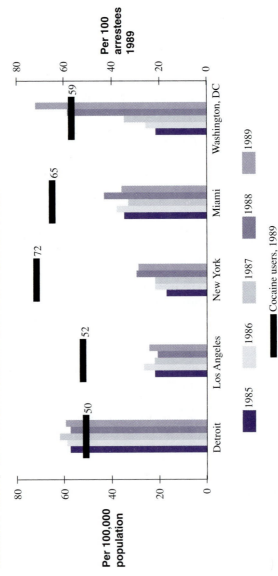

Per 100,000 population

Per 100 arrestees 1989

Detroit   Los Angeles   New York   Miami   Washington, DC

50   52   72   65   59

■ 1985 ■ 1986 ■ 1987 ■ 1988 ■ 1989 ■ Cocaine users, 1989

(*Sources: National Research Council, Understanding and Preventing Violence, p. 188; J. A. Inciardi,* The Crack/Violence Connection within a Population of Hard-Core Adolescent Offenders, *paper presented at the National Institute on Drug Abuse, Technical Review on Drugs and Violence, September 26, 1989, Rockville, MD.*)

empirical support for economic violence to be very inconclusive. But the report's first author, P. J. Goldstein further concludes from a study done on the New York City Police Department that drug-related violence can be categorized as "systemic" rather than just "economic."[56] That is, it can be understood as the result of factors having to do with the overall drug "marketplace," in line with the following analysis: Current public policy aims at **minimizing the supply of drugs.** An artificial drug scarcity results, which drives up the price of drugs. Dealers capture these **excess profits,** and drug users are forced to find ways to pay the contrived high prices. Among the reactions to this "systemic" condition is violence resulting from territorial disputes, gang warfare, battles with police and informers, the creation of black markets, and the lure of corruption. Prostitution increases, and drug dealers enter the school yards. A logical extension of this argument is the "iron law of prohibition." If all drugs are prohibited, dealers have a greater incentive to traffic in the more profitable and more dangerous drugs. In other words, if the punishment for dealing marijuana is the same as that for dealing cocaine, then logically it is preferable to deal cocaine, which is more profitable.[57] Analysts point to the rising use of expensive "designer drugs" as an indication of this trend.

One public policy direction consistent with this reasoning is **decriminalization** of drugs. Not surprisingly, some elected officials have concluded that, given the costs of combating drug use, decriminalizing them makes the most sense. Proponents of this position argue that studies fail to confirm drug use causes crime, and that maybe coincidentally criminals just use drugs. In addition, some worry that effective drug programs will infringe on civil liberties.

Decriminalization has only a small following. Most Americans simply will not accept the risk. It is estimated that as many as 6 million people already use drugs, and legalizing them could lead to even greater numbers. Yet the costs of treating drug use as a crime are also great. Prison overcrowding, caseload pressure, and ballooning police and military budgets raise practical questions about the policy (see fig. 8-3). Some argue that deemphasizing the crime connection and reemphasizing the public health aspects of drug use is a more viable and appropriate course.[58] This approach would target education and rehabilitation rather than interdiction and prosecution as its main goals.

Gun Control

Like drugs, guns represent something tangible policy makers can control in the fight against crime. Policy makers point to the experience of other countries, like England, which have far lower crime rates and tough gun control policies. But the relationship

---

[56]P. J. Goldstein et al., "Drug Related Involvement in Violent Episodes, Final Report" (National Institute on Drug Abuse) (New York: Narcotic and Drug Research, Inc., 1987). See also P. J. Goldstein, "Drugs and Violent Crime," in N. A. Weiner and M. E. Wolfgangs (eds.), *Pathways to Violent Crime* (Newbury Park, CA: Sage, 1989).

[57]This argument is presented by David Boaz, "The Case of Legalizing Drugs," in Herbert Levine (ed.), *Point Counter Point Readings in American Government,* 4th ed. (New York: St. Martin's Press, 1992).

[58]In October 1993, Attorney General Janet Reno agreed to a new approach to fighting the war on drugs. Drug offenders arrested in Washington D.C., would come before a "drug court" rather than the D.C. Supreme Court. The drug court would supervise intensive treatment for nonviolent drug offenders. The goal, as expressed by Attorney General Reno, is to deal with the underlying problems of drugs rather than adjudicate for criminal charges. Other drug court experiments have been set up in Florida's Dade and Broward counties.

FIGURE 8-3
STATE PRISON POPULATIONS.
The category "other" includes gambling, weapons offenses, driving under the influence of alcohol, nonviolent sex crimes, commercial vice, etc.

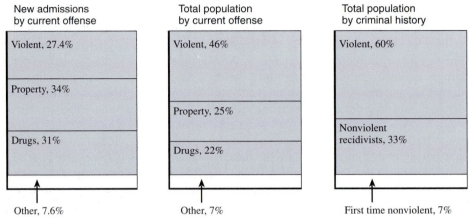

(*Source of data:* Prisons and Prisoners in the United States, *U.S. Department of Justice, Bureau of Justice Statistics, Washington, DC, 1992.*)

between guns and crime is very complex. While analysts concede that tough gun laws could mitigate crime, they argue that those laws would not work unless all states agreed to the same standards.

Gun control policies affecting the **availability, use, distribution, and deadliness** of guns are already in place in the United States. Congress passed the Federal Gun Control Act in 1968 in reaction to public outcries over the assassinations of Senator Robert Kennedy and Reverend Martin Luther King, Jr. The act emphasized restrictions on the availability and distribution of guns. It **banned** mail order sales of guns and outlawed sales to convicted felons, fugitives, and individuals with certain mental illnesses. It restricted private ownership of automatic and military weapons. The law required that gun dealers be **licensed** by the Bureau of Alcohol, Tobacco and Firearms (ATF) and that the serial numbers on all guns sold by licensed dealers be recorded. It also required that individuals buying guns from licensed dealers must show proof of identification and residency and certify their eligibility to own guns.

Despite this effort to control the distribution and availability of guns, gun ownership today is widespread. The ATF estimates 150 to 200 million firearms are privately owned. Most are used for hunting, sport, or self-protection. Twenty-four percent of privately owned guns are easily concealed handguns, which are used disproportionately in homicides. Estimates provided by the FBI indicate that in 1989 about 60 percent of all homicides resulted from gun attacks and that the cost of gun injuries was about $14 billion.[59]

These frightening statistics have led to a groundswell of support for more effective gun control. Many states have tightened their gun ordinances by insisting on waiting periods before purchase, licensing of purchasers, and laws against carrying concealed

[59]Dorothy P. Rice et al., *Cost of Injury in the United States: A Report to Congress 1989* (San Francisco and Baltimore: Institute for Health and Aging, University of California, and Injury Prevention Center, The Johns Hopkins University, 1989).

weapons. But these stricter requirements are often undercut by the less demanding regulations of neighboring states. Frustration has mounted sufficiently that Congress finally passed the popular **"Brady Bill."** The bill, named after presidential press secretary James Brady, who was seriously wounded in the 1981 assassination attempt on President Ronald Reagan, requires a background check and a five-day "cooling off" period prior to purchasing a gun. Despite widespread popular support, the Brady Bill met with ongoing congressional opposition. Its passage came only after a threatened filibuster attempt by Senate members and an aggressive advertising campaign mounted by the National Rifle Association (NRA). Both failed to sway public sentiment. In an emotional ceremony, President Clinton signed the Brady Bill shortly after Thanksgiving 1993.

However, many gun enthusiasts complain that legislation like the Brady Bill misses the point. Their common refrain, "Guns don't kill people, people kill people," reflects their belief that gun control will not solve the crime problem. Further, they argue that gun control violates individual rights. Supported by the aggressive lobbying of the National Rifle Association (NRA), gun control opponents challenge any attempts to curtail their right to own and use weapons. They base their opposition on the right to bear arms protected by the Constitution's Second Amendment and on what they perceive as a common sense judgment that ownership of guns is uncontrollable. They find efforts to control certain types of guns—for example, the ban on imported assault rifles imposed by President Bush—to be illogical, particularly when no such ban was placed on similar domestic-made weapons. Opponents also point to studies that show no difference in crime patterns between jurisdictions with strict gun laws and those without.[60]

Despite this opposition, though, increasingly the public opinion has coalesced around the demand to do something to counteract gun availability.[61] Recent school violence— the most horrifying—two boys, 11 and 13, killing four schoolmates and a teacher, and injuring ten others—has led to renewed demand for gun control.[62] Children with access to firepower, perhaps spurred by the indiscriminate violence absorbed from TV, movies, and video games, alarm even die-hard opponents of gun control. Scholars point out that gun use tends to be an **instrumental act much more than an intentional act.** They point to the fact that firearms are rarely used by serial killers. Tragically gun availability has changed victimization patterns. Empirical evidence supports the conclusion that, **while guns do not increase the overall levels of crime, they seem to increase the seriousness of criminal attacks.**[63] One study concludes:

> Where guns are available, commercial targets are robbed more than individual citizens, and young men more frequently than elderly women. Similarly, in domestic assaults husbands are more frequently the victims. Thus the most important effects of guns on crime

---

[60]The National Research Council reports estimates showing that only one out of six firearms used in crimes was illegally obtained.

[61]A study of children's hospitals reported in *The Washington Post* (November 26, 1993) estimated the average cost of treating a child for a gunshot wound at more than $14,000. One study reports that gunshot wounds are the fifth leading cause of death for children under 14.

[62]On March 24, 1998, in Jonesboro, Arkansas, two boys opened fire on classmates. In April 1998, a 14-year-old boy killed a teacher and wounded two students and another teacher when he opened fire at an eighth grade graduation dance in Edinboro, Pennsylvania. And on May 22, 1998, a 15-year-old Oregon high school student killed three of his classmates in a high school cafeteria and wounded twenty-six others.

[63]Mark H. Moore, "Controlling Criminogenic Commodities: Drugs, Guns and Alcohol," in *Crime and Public Policy* (San Francisco, ICS Press, 1983), p. 130.

are that they increase the seriousness of criminal attacks and effect the distribution of vic-timization; they do not seem to markedly increase the overall levels of criminal attack.[64]

Poverty and Crime

Does poverty cause crime? The connection between these two societal illnesses is far from simple. Yet many propose that the antidote to crime is the elimination of poverty. Unfortunately, what research tells us about the relationship between poverty and crime is inconclusive and sometimes misleading.

Much of the research about crime and poverty takes as its starting point assumptions about criminal behavior. In this model, individuals choose crime over employment when crime seems a more expedient course of action. They do this particularly **if the risk of being caught is low and the utility (money) to be gained is high. It follows, then, that the appropriate reaction to this rational choice is to increase the deterrent (pun-ishment) for prospective criminals.** A further implication is that poor people are more likely to make this rational calculus then members of other segments of society. They have less to lose than those who have sufficient income sources.

Empirical research advanced to confirm this rationale is common but methodologi-cally weak. Many studies use unemployment statistics to measure poverty, but these have proven to be very unrefined measures, neither reliable nor valid. Time series studies comparing crime rates and unemployment statistics fail to explain mounting crime rates, nor do they show that unemployment causes crime. Cross-sectional studies comparing crime rates and unemployment trends across different geographic areas are even more difficult to interpret. States and cities differ widely in the nature and extent of the crimes committed within their jurisdictions. Fluctuations in differing labor markets make unem-ployment figures difficult to compare. Nonetheless, the intuitive sense that if individu-als have jobs they are less likely to commit crimes has resulted in the government promoting jobs programs. Yet the effects of this approach have been unclear, leading some to wonder if the causes of unemployment and crime are the same, if some people simply cannot succeed economically no matter what help they receive, or if the problem is simply that criminals choose a life of crime (a return to rational choice notions). Analysts continue to struggle with these questions. Though unable to explain how crime factors relate, **researchers continue to point to correlations between delinquency, homicides, and the socioeconomic characteristics of communities.**

Indicators like population density of households, residential mobility, family disrup-tion, the presence of gangs, gun density, and drug distribution typically characterize low-income communities. All correlate with high crime rates. Studies point out that the three factors of population density of households, residential mobility, and disrupted family structures are particularly significant indicators of crime.[65] They are typical of commu-nities with high numbers of teenagers and single-parent households.

Research concludes that poverty today goes hand in hand with significant social dis-organization. In his study, *The Truly Disadvantaged: The Inner City, The Underclass*

---

[64]As noted in Moore, "Controlling Criminogenic Commodities," p. 130.
[65]National Research Council, Reiss & Roth (eds.), *Understanding and Preventing Violence*, p. 133.

and Public Policy, William Julius Wilson writes of the social isolation of the inner city.[66] Beyond the extreme racial segregation of inner cities in relation to other parts of the social fabric, there is a further breakdown within these communities themselves. People live side by side but do not know one another. Great mistrust exists among neighbors. In these communities, unlike poor communities of the past, parenting becomes highly individualistic. Everyone is a stranger. Intergenerational relationships fall apart. There are no positive identifications with a neighborhood, no explicit community norms, and no sanctions against delinquent behavior. A street culture develops with its own set of norms and symbols. Embedded in this is a deep distrust for established institutions such as the police, schools, and businesses. Furthermore, given the current ongoing structural economic change toward service production and away from traditional industrial production, little opportunity exists in these communities to find good jobs and move out of the inner city culture. Crime is convenient, pervasive, and attractive.

The crisis for public policy makers is where and how to break into this cycle. In the 1970s, theories took hold proposing the concept of "defensible space."[67] Here the objective was to create a more livable and more easily protected environment. City planners took hold of these ideas and experimented with better architectural design, improved lighting, and more green space. Twenty years later, these experiments have met with mixed success. While still aware of the need to make communities more hospitable, studies now recommend the use of more informal social controls. Community watch programs, beat police patrols, and exact change requirements for public transportation are all examples of the changing emphasis. Increasingly policy makers have come to consider crime and poverty as social illnesses that need not just deterrence, but improvements in areas such as public health. The complex relationship between crime and poverty defies any simple solution. Better studies, improved social and anticrime programs, and better economic opportunities may help shed light on the issue.

WHITE-COLLAR CRIME

White-collar crime is defined as illegal activity conducted in the course of one's occupation. This differs from **organized crime,** which is economic gain through illegal business practices like gambling, loan sharking, prostitution, and narcotics. Organized crime *is* one's occupation; white-collar crime is perhaps more insidious. The activities of white-collar criminals cut across business and politics, the professions, and labor organizations.

Too often white-collar offenders hide behind corporate or professional sanctuaries. This leads to claims that white-collar criminals experience more lenient penalties. Critics say white-collar crime is just a "better racket." Unfortunately the criminal justice system reacts differently to white-collar crime than street crime. Some criminologists theorize that judges and criminal justice personnel are often reluctant to view white-collar crime as seriously because they identify with the socioeconomic standing of these offenders. To illustrate this, consider the S&L crisis of the 1980s. After the Reagan

---

[66]William Julius Wilson, *The Truly Disadvantaged: The Inner City, The Underclass and Public Policy* (Chicago: University of Chicago Press, 1987).

[67]Oscar Newman, *Defensible Space: Crime Prevention through Urban Design* (New York: Macmillan, 1973).

TABLE 8-5
PRISON SENTENCES FOR S&L OFFENDERS AND
SELECTED FEDERAL OFFENDERS

	Mean prison sentence (mos.)
S&L offenders	36.4
All federal offenders, convicted of	
Burglary	55.6
Larceny	27.5
Motor vehicle theft	38.0
Counterfeiting	29.1
Federal offenders, with no prior convictions, convicted of	
Property offenses (non fraudulent)	25.5
Public order offenses (regulatory)	32.3
Drug offenses	64.9

Sources: Data from *Federal Criminal Case Processing 1980–90* (Washington DC: U.S. Department of Justice, Bureau of Justice Statistics, 1992), 17; *Compendium of Federal Justice Statistics, 1988* (Washington DC: U.S. Department of Justice, Bureau of Justice Statistics, 1991), 43.

administration deregulated the S& L industry, some S&L owners and executives violated laws and regulations by engaging in fraudulent, unsafe business practices. This resulted in billions of dollars of losses.[68] Table 8-5 compares prison sentences for savings and loan offenders with selected federal offenders. The authors of this study concluded that the latter offenders often received longer sentences, ". . . despite the fact that these crimes almost never approached $500,000 the average S&L offense."[69] White-collar offenders typically have resources to use to mount a good defense and as argued by Richard Posner, ". . . efficient legal institutions will seek to minimize costs and maximize gains by penalizing white-collar offenders with monetary sanctions obtained through less costly civil or administrative procedures rather than seeking imprisonment through the cumbersome criminal justice system."[70]

Classifications of white-collar crime include "theft after trust" such as financial manipulations, fraud, and acceptance of bribes, or "restraint of trade" like phony limited partnerships and pyramid schemes. Embezzlement, or crime by an individual in a subordinate position against a strong corporation contrasts with corporate crime which includes, price fixing, and "collective embezzlement," or crime *by* a corporation *against* a corporation. In their study of the savings and loan crisis of the 1980s, *Big Money Crime*, researchers Kitty Calavita, Henry N. Pontell, and Robert H. Tillman explain that, " 'collective embezzlers' were not lone, lower-level employees," but thrift owners and

[68]Charles Keating, Don Dixon, and Erwin Hansen were the three best known of the thrift defendants.
[69]Kitty Calavita, Henry N. Pontell, and Robert H. Tillman, *Big Money Crime* (Berkeley: University of California Press, 1997), p. 164.
[70]Richard Posner, "Optimal Sentences for White-Collar Criminals," *American Criminal Law Review* 17 (Winter 1980): 409–18.

managers, acting within networks of coconspirators inside and outside the institution. Indeed, this embezzlement was company policy."[71]   Corporate crime is distinctive because its primary objective is to advance corporate interests, thus Calavita et al., find many similar characteristics between corporate and organized crime. Both are premeditated, organized, continuous, and develop connections to public officials to avoid prosecution. These types of crimes reflect the dark side of the business subculture of competition and profit maximization. Crimes like false advertising, misuse of campaign funds, and occupational and environmental violations are further examples of betrayals of the public trust by business and political leaders. Ironically, most citizens worry little about or are unaware of the effects of this activity. In fact, the systematic study of white-collar crime did not take hold until recently.[72] Yet while the average bank heist nets a robber $10,000, the average computer crime has reached a figure of $430,000.[73] Another study reports that ". . . about 30 percent of business failures were the result of employee dishonesty . . . about 15 percent of the price paid for goods and services goes to cover the costs of dishonesty."[74]

The general lack of documentation and prosecutorial activity regarding this kind of activity is not surprising. The nearly invisible and very diffuse nature of white-collar crime makes it hard to investigate and often complicated. One investigator complained that it was like "doing someone else's checkbook."[75] Paper trails are papered over, increasingly with the help of computers and other sophisticated forms of technology. Nevertheless the FBI has established a special branch of forensic accountants and lawyers to investigate and prosecute white-collar criminals. In 1987, the U.S. Congress enacted the "Computer Fraud and Abuse Act," which has been supplemented by various state laws to counteract computer fraud and abuse. Computer specialists are now routinely members of law enforcement agency staffs. This, combined with new tougher sentencing guidelines, means the criminal justice system is starting to focus on these illegal operations.

With the white-collar crime price tag estimated at approximately $200 billion per year, society can no longer afford to allow professional and business standards alone to regulate the workplace.[76] In the aftermath of the savings-and-loan crisis, which cost the American taxpayers about $180 billion, the heavy artillery of criminal law is increasingly being used.[77] Many Americans have yet to learn that there is a much greater

---

[71]Calavita, et al., p. 63.

[72]"White-collar crime" as a term was first used by Edward Sutherland in an address to the American Sociological Society in 1939.

[73]Paul W. Keve, *Crime Control and Justice in America* (Chicago: American Library Association, 1995), p. 33.

[74]Charles R. Wagner, *The CPA and Computer Fraud* (Lexington, MA: Lexington Books, 1979).

[75]Comment quoted by reporter for "Sheriff's Investigation Follows More Paper Trails," *St. Petersburg Times,* August 30, 1993, p. 1.

[76]See Chantico Publ. Co., *Combating Computer Crime: Prevention, Detection, Investigation* (New York: McGraw-Hill, 1992). Also see Francis T. Cullen, William J. Maakestad, and Gray Cavender, "The Ford Pinto Case and Beyond: Assessing Blame," in *Justice, Crime and Ethics* (Cincinnati: Anderson Publishing, 1991).

[77]See Congressional Budget Office, *Resolving the Thrift Crisis* (Washington, DC: U.S. Government Printing Office, April 1993). See also F. Stevens Redburn, "The Deeper Structure of the Savings and Loan Crisis," *PS: Political Science and Politics,* vol. 24, no. 3 (September 1991), p. 436.

property loss associated with white-collar criminal activities than with street crime. Paradoxically, crime prevention funds are allocated in just the opposite way.

CONCLUSION

1 While Americans are united, often passionately, over the need to fight crime, no public policy problem is more elusive. Science offers advances in medical treatment and environmental protection, but tells us little about how to keep peace in our streets.

2 How much crime is there? Newspaper accounts give the impression that crime-free, safe neighborhoods no longer exist. The days of unlocked cars and houses are of another era. Systematic studies of crime like FBI and police reports along with academic studies confirm this impression and tell us that violent crime in particular has reached record levels. The associated physical, emotional, and financial costs have forced policy makers at all levels to put crime at the top of their agendas.

3 What are the causes of crime? Efforts to answer this question have so far offered minimal direction to policy makers. Diverse theories point to a range of possible origins, but none explain conclusively why some individuals commit criminal acts and others do not. More is known about specific conditions associated with crime, like the use of drugs, the availability of guns, and poverty. Unfortunately, policy recommendations based on this knowledge are controversial and too often aimed at achieving political aims rather than true solutions.

4 How can the American criminal justice system create effective policies to control crime, punish offenders, and protect the innocent? The criminal justice system is the crossroads for testing our resolve to protect the rights of the victims and of the accused before conviction yet to punish offenders. Often bogged down by its own size and complexity, the system is characterized by the right to legal appeals, pervasive plea bargaining, and complex sentencing requirements. The police, the front line in fighting crime, typically suffer "whiplash" from the need to observe procedural safeguards, protect victims, and respond to society's demand that they catch the criminals.

5 Consequently, crime abatement creates a policy quagmire. There is no consensus and there are no viable remedies. A rough starting point is the healthy uneasiness about current crime control practices voiced by individuals like Attorney General Janet Reno. Reno calls for redirection in fighting crime to emphasize prevention and the welfare of children, rather than tougher punishment. Despite this, President Clinton's $30.2 billion crime bill passed after an aggressive partisan battle over what some representatives saw as "social pork." The resulting biggest crime bill in history suggests few of the links between public health and education. It called for $13.4 billion in grants to localities to hire more police, $9.9 billion to build more prisons, and just $5.5 billion for crime prevention programs—the pork. The bill also banned nineteen more assault weapons, increased to sixty the number of federal crimes punishable by death, and introduced the so-called three strikes penalty for repeat offenders. It appears that the future portends stronger gun control laws, more prisons, new antidrug campaigns, and increased police visibility as the plan of action.

6 This chapter's discussion calls for a warning: Finding the answer to crime has proven as intractable as eradicating any of humanity's most deadly diseases. Like disease, crime rots the social system. Analysts know that until the true root causes of this social illness are determined, money spent and prisons built will only treat the symptoms.

QUESTIONS FOR DISCUSSION

1 Is there a relationship between public expenditure and crime abatement?
2 How accurate are crime statistics? Why is crime underreported?
3 Compare and contrast leading theories of criminal behavior. What policy guidance have they offered?
4 Describe the competing philosophies of criminal justice. How does deterrence differ from other philosophies?
5 Discuss contemporary police theory. What policies reflect these new approaches?
6 What are the implications of a decentralized criminal justice system?
7 Is the "war on drugs" winnable? What is the theory underlying decriminalization?
8 Do "guns kill people" or do "people kill people?" Discuss.
9 Why are Americans less concerned about white-collar crime? How important is the "fear factor" in our criminal justice policy?

KEY CONCEPTS

Brady Bill	deterrence
clearance rates	due process
Community Oriented Policing Service (COPS)	incapacitation
crime index	plea bargain
criminal justice system	procedural rights
criminogenic factors	rehabilitation
criminology	retribution
decriminalization	white-collar crime

SUGGESTED READINGS

Ralph Andreano and John J. Siegfried (eds.), *The Economics of Crime* (New York: John Wiley & Sons, 1980).

Hugh Adam Bedau, *The Death Penalty in America*, 3d ed. (New York: Oxford University Press, 1982).

Elliott Currie, *Crime and Punishment in America* (New York: Henry Holt and Company, Inc. 1998).

James A. Inciardi, *Criminal Justice*, 3d ed. (New York; Harcourt Brace Jovanovich, 1990).

Joseph E. Jacoby (ed.), *Classic of Criminology* (Prospect Heights, IL: Waveland Press, 1988).

Marianne LeVert, *Crime in America* (New York: Facts on File, 1991).

Jeffrey Reiman, . . . *And the Poor Get Prison* (Needham MA: Allyn & Bacon, 1996).

Albert J. Reiss, Jr., and Jeffrey A. Roth (eds.), *Understanding and Preventing Violence* (Washington DC: National Academy Press, 1993).

Tom R. Tyler, *Why People Obey the Law* (New Haven: Yale University Press, 1990).

George B. Vold and Thomas J. Bernard, *Theoretical Criminology*, 3d ed. (New York: Oxford University Press, 1986).

James Q. Wilson (ed.), *Crime and Public Policy* (San Francisco: ICS Press, 1983).

James Q. Wilson and Richard J. Herrnstein, *Crime and Human Nature* (New York: Simon and Schuster, 1985).

James Q. Wilson and Joan Petersilia (eds.), *Crime* (San Francisco: ICS Press, 1995).

9

EDUCATION POLICY: LOW GRADES FOR NATIONAL EFFORT

In this chapter we focus on the widespread societal concern referred to as the "crisis" in education. Perceived need to improve education, particularly at the primary and secondary levels is now a major public agenda issue. When it comes to public policy toward schools, almost everyone has ideas about how to improve them. Everyone can claim a certain amount of expertise regarding school, because everyone attended school at one time, and their children or the children of friends and relatives are in or have attended school. Apathy and complacency among the public have been replaced with increasing interest as education has become a policy issue of national importance. Alarm over the problem in education has many different, and sometimes contradictory, sides. Many express fears about the decline in the quality of education. They believe this is the reason that America is losing its competitive edge in international trade. Others are concerned about the lack of equal treatment in the school system especially for the disadvantaged. This chapter will examine the validity of these criticisms and suggest policy solutions for the problems identified.

INTRODUCTION

Education is a distinct departure from other services provided by the government. Unlike social welfare or health care, which are concerned with the maintenance of human capital, education seeks to **develop** it. Yet widespread dissatisfaction with the American educational system makes it clear that it is one area of public policy where many feel the current system deserves a failing grade. Unfortunately little consensus exists about **what** should be done to resolve the problems or **who** has the primary responsibility for taking corrective action.

Education policy provokes debate because no policy issue is more important to the nation's future. Most of the demands to improve the quality of education are prompted by economic anxiety: There are concerns that the economy will not prosper or be competitive against technically advanced nations without an improvement in the educational level of the labor force.[1] Ironically, the education and skills of labor also affect the income of management. If lower-level employees cannot do their jobs properly, American companies cannot be competitive in a world market.[2] This means the disappearance of jobs at the management level also. The United States simply cannot afford to have an uneducated and unskilled labor force.

While school systems must prepare students with more advanced and complex skills than ever before, they must also cope with new kinds of demands. Schools today must assimilate a population less competent in English than twenty years ago. In addition, a larger percentage of students come from families receiving welfare than was the case previously, and more students come from single-parent households. Economic disadvantage often translates into problems at school.

Indicators of poor scholastic performance are everywhere. The schools must cope with low academic achievement, criminal and antisocial behaviors, alcohol abuse, adolescent pregnancy, and high drop out rates. These failures were documented in a series of critical reports in the 1980s that urged immediate remedial steps be taken.[3]

The study by the National Commission on Excellence in Education linked the decline in the quality of education in the American school system to the deterioration in American international economic competitiveness. The report, *A Nation at Risk*[4] stated that:

> Our Nation is at risk. Our once unchallenged preeminence in commerce, industry, science, and technological innovation is being overtaken by competitors throughout the world. . . .
>
> [T]he educational foundations of our society are presently being eroded by a rising tide of mediocrity that threatens our very future as a Nation and a people. What was unimaginable a generation ago has begun to occur—others are matching and surpassing our educational attainments.
>
> If an unfriendly foreign power had attempted to impose on America the mediocre educational performance that exists today, we might well have viewed it as an act of war.

The report went on to state that our society and its educational institutions appear to have lost sight of the basic purposes of education and the disciplined effort needed to achieve them.[5]

The reaction to the commission's study was to spur a reform movement in education. Many states reacted by increasing their graduation requirements and raising academic

---

[1] Pearl M. Kamer, *The U.S. Economy in Crisis* (New York: Praeger, 1988), p. 108.

[2] Lester Thurow, *Head to Head: The Coming Economic Battle Among Japan, Europe, and America* (New York: William Morrow, 1992), p. 55.

[3] The National Commission on Excellence in Education, *A Nation At Risk: The Imperative for Educational Reform,* April 1983.

[4] Ibid.

[5] The National Commission on Excellence in Education proposed several traditional proposals for reform including strengthening graduation requirements, higher pay and qualifications for teachers, and a longer school year or longer school days. President Reagan responded to the commission by presenting his own proposals including abolishing the Department of Education and permitting prayer in the schools. See Edward Fiske, "All at Once Everyone Is Worried About Schools," *New York Times,* 8, May 1983.

TABLE 9-1
AVERAGE SCHOLASTIC ASSESSMENT TEST (SAT) SCORES*

	1967	1970	1975	1980	1985	1990	1995	1996	1997
Verbal	543	537	512	502	509	500	504	505	505
Math	516	512	498	492	500	501	506	508	512

*Scores for 1995 and prior years have been recentered by the College Entrance Examination Board.
Source: Statistical Abstract, 1997, p. 177 and Educational Testing Service.

standards. Enrollments have gone up in mathematics and science. But on the whole, academic performance has not shown significant improvement over the past twenty years and performance gaps between racial groups has improved only slightly. The efforts to reform American education that came after the commission's report are still in progress and therefore receive a grade of incomplete.

On the positive side, the report of the National Commission on Excellence in Education can claim some success. The report *A Nation At Risk* recommended that states raise graduation requirements and that schools require a core academic curriculum. A consensus formed among parents, teachers, and students that schools need more academic rigor to combat the academic decline resulting from a combination of grade inflation, the increase of nonacademic courses, and reduced homework requirements. Many states have raised graduation requirements and added the recommended curriculum called the "New Basics" which includes four years of English, three years each of math, science, and social studies, and two years of a foreign language for those intending to go on to college. The number of high school students who studied the New Basics—including two years of a foreign language—increased from less than 15 percent in 1982 to 39 percent in 1994.

The Scholastic Assessment Test (SAT)

Less than half of all high school graduates take the **Scholastic Assessment Test (SATs).**[6] SAT scores began to decline in the late 1960s and reached a low point in the early 1990s. Average math scores dropped from 516 in 1967 to a low of 492 in 1980, but bounced back to 508 in 1996. Average verbal scores fell from 543 in 1967 to 500 in the early 1990s and have only begun a modest rebound in the late 1990s. In 1994 the College Board recentered the SAT scores at 500 based on the levels established in 1990. By accepting the new standard, critics point out that it validates the mediocre performance of 1990.

Why SAT scores have declined is a matter of debate. Some dismiss the decline as a shift in the pool of students taking the SAT. They contend that a smaller and more elite percentage of high school students were college bound in the 1960s. As college admission opened up to a larger percentage of high school graduates, a growing number of less-well-prepared students have been included in the pool. But declines also occurred at the top end of the distribution. In 1972, for example, 116,585 students (11.4 percent

---

[6]The American College Testing (ACT) program is also widely used to assess the achievement level of high school students along with other characteristics.

NATIONAL CURRICULUM CONTENT STANDARDS

The **Goals 2000** (*Educate America Act:* Public Law 103-227) legislation included provisions for the codification of National Education Goals; the establishment of national education standards; and assistance in financing state education standards. It was held that goal setting would be meaningless unless progress toward the goals could be measured and reported to the nation. To that end it was concluded that there should be standards defining what students needed to know in each subject and assessments to measure student performance.

Goals 2000 enacted into law the six goals originally adopted by President Bush and the nation's governors in 1990 and added two new goals (4 and 8). These goals provide that by the year 2000:

1 all children will start school ready to learn;
2 the high school graduation rate will be at least 90 percent;
3 students will master a challenging curriculum at grades 4, 8, and 12;
4 teachers will have access to professional development opportunities;
5 U.S. students will be first in the world in science and math achievement;
6 all adults will be literate;
7 schools will be free of drugs, violence, and firearms; and
8 every school will promote parental involvement in education.

What Are These Standards?
The national curriculum content standards provide a general description of the broad knowledge and skills students should master in different subjects at different grade levels (e.g., goal #3), but do **not** constitute the curriculum for any subject. They offer benchmarks against which state and local curricula can be judged, as well as guidance for assessments of teacher development. Supporters argue that achievement of the third goal requires national standards for the curricula that must be mastered, and direction should be provided for needed educational improvements. It would also provide public measures for judging curriculum and school quality, particularly in comparison to other states and nations. In 1992 the National Council on Education called for high national curriculum standards because expectations for student per-

of those taking the SAT) scored above 600 on the verbal test. By 1983 only 66,292 (6.9 percent of the total) scored above 600. Since that time the percent scoring above 600 has languished at around 7 percent.[7]

There is no relationship between the diversity of test takers and the decline in test scores. In 1980 math scores reached their lowest level when less than 20 percent of those taking the test were from minority backgrounds. In the late 1990s almost a third of the test takers were from minority backgrounds, yet math scores increased significantly. One reason for the improvement in the math scores may be attributed to the New Basics math requirements. Because of these requirements in the past fifteen years, the number of high school graduates who have taken geometry increased from 45 to 70 percent. However, they have also resulted in students taking a wider variety of courses in "language arts" rather than courses that emphasize grammar, syntax, and spelling.

[7]Diane Ravitch, *Student Performance Today,* Brookings Policy Brief, no. 23, (Washington, DC: The Brookings Institution, 1997).

formance in many states and school districts were too low. Therefore assessments should measure student performance against standards rather than against other students' performance.

Opposition to the standards is based on the argument that such standards will lead to a national curriculum under federal direction. Others argue that standards could create standardization, driving out local innovation. They also argue that national standards could result in insurmountable hurdles for disadvantaged students. Finally, some argue that many states are already developing standards making federal ones unnecessary.

It should be noted that the *Goals 2000* law does not require states and localities to adopt any national curriculum content standards or adopt curricula aligned with the standards. And the 103rd Congress included language in *Goals 2000* reiterating prohibitions against federal influence over the curriculum of any state and explicitly prohibiting any requirement that state curriculum standards be nationally certified.

The decline in SAT scores would seem to provide a logical argument for national standards in math and English. **National standards** could offer rigor and substance in material to be mastered. Unfortunately governors and politicians from both political parties oppose national standards as "federal standards" in which the federal government could pressure or punish states who failed to meet "national standards." Most politicians have responded by supporting "local standards." This is most unfortunate if we want to develop a world-class educational system. There may be different ways to teach science or mathematics, but the fundamental principles do not vary between Maryland, California, or Japan. Students in Atlanta need to understand the same principles as those in Montreal. National standards would provide a rational basis for defining excellence and preparing students to compete internationally.

Source: This section relies heavily upon James B. Stedman's "National Curriculum Content Standards," Congressional Research Service Report for Congress, May 16, 1995. And also James B. Stedman and Wayne C. Riddle, "Goals 2000: Educate America Act: Implementation Status and Issues." *CRS* July 18, 1995.

A recent study suggests that the drop in SAT scores may explain the decline in productivity rate in the labor force over the last two decades.[8] To the extent that test scores do measure intellectual achievement, even imperfectly, the decline in test scores slows the growth of American productivity. The American educational system imparts knowledge and skills less well than the school systems of other countries in math and science so that by the end of high school American students were four grade equivalents behind Japanese students with the same number of years in school. There is a cost to the nation, in forgone productivity and earnings, that can be associated with the low academic achievement of the average American worker who joins the workforce after high school.[9]

[8]John Bishop, "Is the Test Score Decline Responsible for the Productivity Growth Decline?" *American Economic Review,* vol. 79 (March 1989), pp. 178–97.
[9]Charles Schultze, *Education: A Memo to the President* (Washington, DC: The Brookings Institution, 1992).

International Comparisons

American students usually lag behind their contemporaries in other countries overall and among the most advanced students. The most recent and largest international comparison of student achievement ever administered is the Third International Math and Science Study (TIMSS). This study conducted in 1996 included forty-one countries. Comparing fourth graders, American children were behind Austria, the Czech Republic, Hong Kong, Japan, the Netherlands, and South Korea but were still well above the international average in math and science. However, American eighth graders scored well below the international average in mathematics and only slightly above the mean in science. Just 5 percent of American eighth graders scored in the top 10 percent in math compared to 34 percent of South Koreans, and 32 percent of Japanese students. In science, 13 percent of the American students and 18 percent of both South Korean and Japanese students placed in the top 10 percent. These are disappointing scores, especially when one considers that America spends more money per capita on education than any other country except Finland. Only in the United States, however, are a majority of the education workers nonteachers (55 percent).[10] A survey in 1991 by the Organization of Economic Cooperation and Development found, for example, that in Australia, Belgium, Japan, and France teachers made up 80 percent of all education workers.[11]

Traditionally, American education has been a local issue and only since World War II have states increased their influence over education through increased funding. The federal government's role in education was limited typically to financial assistance until the passage of the Elementary and Secondary Education Act in 1965 (ESEA). To understand the constraints on education policy, one must be aware of how public education evolved in the United States.

THE STRUCTURE OF AMERICAN PUBLIC EDUCATION: AN OVERVIEW

In the past, much of education was the responsibility of the family. This **informal education** took place primarily in the home, with relatives and friends serving as teachers. Learning in this context took place largely through the socialization process and imitating the behavior of elders. This was because in an economy based on tradition, production techniques changed at a glacial pace, and the needed knowledge and skills were passed from one generation to the next through apprenticeships and work experience.

In more advanced market economies, however, production techniques change more rapidly, requiring greater adaptability to the new skills needed by workers. Productivity growth is fostered by workers with more education who can more easily adapt to new work requirements than workers with less education. Modern societies have developed **formal education** systems in which professional teachers guide the learning process. The state has become largely responsible for transmitting culture, literacy, and technical knowledge.

Most modern societies, spell out the right to education in their Constitutions. However, education is not mentioned in the U.S. Constitution, which was drafted in 1787, when formal education was a rarity and not perceived as critical to society or its citizens.

---

[10]*Statistical Abstract of the United States: 1997,* p. 168.
[11]Diane Ravitch, *Student Performance Today.*

In the early years of the nation, education was the responsibility of the ministry of the various congregations. As a result public elementary and secondary education, funded by tuition payments from parents, was not begun by states until the early 1800s. Traditionally, once having developed education systems funded by tax revenues, states have jealously defended their authority and control over public education. Private schools educated the children of the affluent.

Most businessmen of the early nineteenth century opposed efforts to require compulsory school attendance or taxation to support public education. The struggle to create publicly funded school systems in the various states was taken up as a crusade by educational reformers in the 1830s. Paradoxically, the drive to provide public schools, financed by property taxes, was given a boost by immigration. Successive waves of immigration generated the fear that unless the new arrivals were "Anglicized" the "American character" would be destroyed. The arrival of Catholics and Jews in increasing numbers caused growing concern among the established elites. In fact, the "Know-Nothing" party of the 1840s developed from fear of a Catholic takeover. Catholic and other religiously affiliated schools were founded not only to reinforce religious values, but also to escape societal religious discrimination.

Providing schools where foreigners learned American customs, morals, and language, meant the system had to be tuition free for all newly arrived poor immigrants as well as for second and third generation Americans. The public school system reflected American nativism and was designed to anglicize recent arrivals. Public school education was justified as a public good that reduced distinctions between people and created a unified citizenry.

There is still uneasiness in the United States regarding parochial schools. Critics see these institutions as maintaining religious and cultural identities different from mass culture. Still the United States has the largest number of religious and private elementary, secondary schools, and universities in the world. Private and parochial schools enroll 14 percent of all elementary school children, 9 percent of all secondary school students, and 28 percent of all college students.[12] Many are hardly distinguishable from public schools. Others are known as elite academic institutions. Many elite prep schools which began with a religious purpose, have dropped any formal religious affiliation. These boarding schools (such as Phillips Exeter, Groton, Choate) provide the children of families of established wealth and distinction with advantaged access to the most prestigious universities and from there to corporate and political leadership.

In the United States, unlike most other industrialized societies, **education is a state and local responsibility rather than a national one.** The Supreme Court rejected the idea that education is a federal responsibility in a 1973 Texas case in which it ruled that education was not a fundamental right guaranteed by the Constitution.[13] The public educational system historically provided one school per community for children from all social levels (segregation by race was a glaring anomaly). Limitations in transportation kept residents, their workplace, and schools in close proximity. Since World War II, the automobile has fostered the separation of workplace from residence, and the development of large socially homogeneous school districts. This coincided with the

---

[12]Figures are projected for 1998. *Statistical Abstract, 1997*, no. 233, p. 153.
[13]*San Antonio Independent School District v. Rodriguez*, 411 U.S. 1, 93 S. Ct. 1278 (1973).

erosion of the egalitarian principle that underlay the notion of public education. It also led to an erosion in the traditional local control of education. As school districts became larger and state and even federal governments increased their financial contributions, they began to exercise more control over school policy while the influence of parents and sometimes local school boards declined.

Local property taxes within the district, which often are identical with local political boundaries, typically provide close to half of school finances. But dependence on local property taxes resulted in highly unequal funding available per student between property-rich and property-poor districts. Lawsuits challenging the fairness of relying on local property taxes for funding has resulted in states steadily increasing their contribution to local school districts.[14] Today states overall provide more funding than do local districts. In 1994, states contributed 34.3 percent of the money needed for public elementary and secondary education while local districts contributed 27 percent. The federal government contributed 8 percent while businesses contributed the remainder.[15] States now establish standards for education within their boundaries, while local control is exercised within the constraints permitted by state governments.

EDUCATION: A QUASI-PUBLIC GOOD

Recall that in chapter 1 we pointed out how competitive markets are very efficient mechanisms for meeting consumer demand. Why, then, should government be involved in providing education when a competitive market is such an efficient mechanism? The answer lies in the idea that education is a good for which private decisions about how much to buy do not lead to a socially optimal level of output. In other words, private "interests" lack incentives to provide education for everyone. This is an instance we referred to earlier as **market failure.** Defenders of public education point to the important external effects on the welfare of others associated with having an education. Such goods are termed **quasi-public goods.**[16]

Education has attributes of both a private and a quasi-public good. The individual receives the primary benefits of that education through higher income, satisfying work, and pleasant working conditions. But positive externalities result from improving the educational level of a society. When individuals demand education based upon their private expectations without regard to these positive external benefits, the result is education will be under-produced. These external benefits justify government subsidizing the production of education.

---

[14]See John Augenblick, "The Current Status of School Financing Reform," in Van Mueller and Mary McKeown (eds.), *The Fiscal, Legal, and Political Aspects of State Reform of Elementary and Secondary Education* (Cambridge, MA: Ballinger, 1986).

[15]Statistical Abstract, 1997, p. 156.

[16]Recall that our earlier definition of a **pure private** good is characterized by excludability and depletability. A **pure public good,** in contrast, is **not depleted (nonrivalness)** by an additional user. Secondly, it is extremely difficult **to exclude (nonexcludability)** people from the benefits if they do not pay for them. If the community buys national security, a newborn child in the community is also protected at no additional cost. The marginal cost approaches zero. And the new child does not interfere with the protection afforded the rest of the community.

Functionalism

Public support of education has long been touted because of its positive impact on society. **Functionalism** is the view that society can exist in harmony because its institutions spring from a shared culture. Consequently, the family, the educational system, and the economy, among other institutions, perform specific "functions" necessary for the survival of society. The function of education is to (a) transfer societal values, (b) produce a more informed citizenry, (c) produce workers with more productive skills, and (d) provide for "equal opportunity" by providing everyone, regardless of circumstance, with basic education skills. School serves as a "halfway house" to assist a child's passage between the familiar world of the family and the impersonal world of adult careers and community life.[17] Considerable research supports the contention that the more education one has, the more likely one is to be knowledgeable and active in the democratic process and familiar with its current events.[18]

Functionalism supports the notion that all members of society should have an equal chance for educational and economic success. This meritocratic ideal strongly supports equality of **opportunity,** but not equality of **outcomes.**

A public education system fosters greater equality because it provides the knowledge and skills necessary to perform those jobs that society rewards highly. Thus, wealthier members of society are not able to monopolize access to highly paid jobs. By broadening the equality of opportunity, education encourages social mobility.

Critics of functionalism accuse it of disregarding the social class divisions in society perpetuated by the educational system. They charge that students are separated into vocational, general education, and college prep programs along the general class lines of their families. One researcher suggested a similar sorting mechanism takes place in the way curriculums are presented in different communities.[19] Many hoped that as education became more available and equally distributed, children from disadvantaged families would get as much education as those from advantaged families. That has not happened.

---

[17]Kevin J. Dougherty and Floyd M. Hammack, *Education & Society* (New York: Harcourt Brace Jovanovich, 1990), pp. 13–14.

[18]See for example, William H. Flanigan and Nancy H. Zingale, *Political Behavior of the American Electorate,* 6th ed. (Boston: Allyn and Bacon, 1987), p. 18. They state that one of the factors in voting is a sense of civic duty reflected in the attitude that a good citizen has an obligation to vote. "Since such feelings are usually a prime focus of the political socialization carried on in the American educational system, turnout is highest among those with the longest exposure to this system: Length of education is one of the best predictors of an individual's likelihood of voting" (p. 18). They go on to state that because education is associated with relative affluence, people who vote are usually somewhat better off in socioeconomic terms than the aggregate population. "This bias is likely to increase in low-stimulus elections, as greater numbers of occasional voters drop out of the electorate, leaving the field to the better educated and more affluent who rarely miss an election" (p. 18).

[19]For example, one study of three communities—(a) an affluent community with politically active adults; (b) a lower-middle-class community—with reduced levels of involvement; and (c) a working class neighborhood with primarily apolitical adults—concluded that the students in each community were being taught to play "different" political roles. Only in the affluent community were students taught the subtleties and nuances of decision-making and given the expectation that they should be a part of the process. The lower-middle-class group were taught the "responsibilities" of citizens in a democracy. The school curriculum in the working-class neighborhood covered mechanics and procedures without stressing the utility of participation. See Edgar Litt, "Civic Education, Community Norms, and Political Indoctrination," *American Sociological Review,* 28 (February 1963). Also reprinted in Richard Flacks, (ed.), Conformity, Resistance, and Self-Determination (Boston: Little Brown, 1973), pp. 136–41.

Therefore, the critics claim, while education can provide social mobility, it tends to "transmit inequality from one generation to another."[20] One study shows that high school graduates who are in the top quartile in socioeconomic status are almost twice as likely to go on to college as those in the bottom quartile.[21] The gaps in educational achievement are a major factor in the transmission of inequality. Another study by Christopher Jencks and his colleagues found that about 40 percent of the association between male childhood family background and adult occupational status was due to the student's educational attainments, after controlling for the effects of IQ test scores. In other words, upper-class graduates received higher-status jobs than working-class graduates because they got more education.[22]

Pierre Bourdieu, a French sociologist and leading critic of higher education, has focused on the glaring inequalities in the distribution of wealth and status that persist despite the expansion of educational opportunities for everyone.[23] He is concerned with how inequalities of position endure over generations. Bourdieu argues that individuals use education to maintain their positions of privilege. The educational system has displaced the family, church, or workplace as the determinant variable for the transmission of **social stratification.** Since democratic societies originated in a rebellion against privilege and therefore affirm a belief in the essential equality of individuals, privileged groups cannot openly claim a right to dominating positions. Modern democracies rely on indirect and symbolic forms of power rather than physical coercion to maintain authority. Dominant groups have found that higher education can transmit social inequalities by converting them into academic hierarchies.[24] Several points are stressed in Bourdieu's research. His investigation supports other findings that academic performance of students is highly correlated with parents' cultural background. This further relates to degree of success in the labor market which hinges on both the **amount** of education received and the academic **prestige** of the institution attended. Ultimately, educational institutions frequently develop their own academic interests and agendas. These may differ significantly from those proclaimed by the existing social order.

---

[20]Dougherty and Hammack, *Education & Society,* p. 248. It should be noted that there is evidence of social mobility in America. One survey taken among American men in 1973 found that 51 percent were in a higher job status than their fathers, while only 17 percent were lower. See David L. Featherman and Robert M. Hauser, *Opportunity and Change* (New York: Academic Press, 1978), p. 93.

Education does have a powerful impact on income and occupational prestige, with about two-thirds of this effect being unconnected to family background. See Christopher S. Jencks, et al., *Who Gets Ahead?* (New York: Basic Books, 1979), pp. 224–27.

[21]Dougherty and Hammack, *Education & Society,* p. 248. If the comparison is restricted to high school graduates who score in the top quarter in academic ability, the gap widens. Socioeconomic status was measured by a composite of parents' education, the father's occupation, and family income.

[22]Jencks et al., *Who Gets Ahead?,* pp. 214–18. Also reported in Dougherty and Hammack.

[23]See Pierre Bourdieu, "The School as a Conservative Force: Scholastic and Cultural Inequalities," in John Eggleston (ed.), *Contemporary Research in the Sociology of Education* (London: Methuen, 1974), pp. 32–46. Also, Pierre Bourdieu, "Cultural Reproduction and Social Reproduction," in Jerome Karabel and A. H. Halsey (eds.), *Power and Ideology in Education* (New York: Oxford University Press, 1977), pp. 487–511 and Pierre Bourdieu and Jean-Claude Passeron, *The Inheritors: French Students and Their Relation to Culture* (Chicago: University of Chicago Press, 1979).

[24]Bourdieu and Passeron, *The Inheritors,* p. 153.

Class Conflict Model

Another explanation for the expansion of education in the United States argues that education grows to meet the rising technical skill requirements of jobs. Given this premise, the **class conflict model** claims that employers use education to screen workers although no demonstrable connection exists in most cases between education and job performance. According to this model formal education developed to meet the growing problems created by industrialization and urbanization in the United States. Rather than meeting objectives like supplying workers with more complex technical skills or reducing social inequality, public education has provided social control by instilling behavior attributes like obedience, discipline, and respect for and compliance with authority.[25] In this view, educational credentials rank workers rather than measure skills.[26] Thus, employers are willing to give a preference to more educated workers in hiring and salary because those workers are more willing to accept traditional corporate values.[27] Thus, education serves to legitimize inequalities rooted in the economic structure of society.

Research by Gregory Squires concluded that the upgrading of the educational requirements related to work cannot be explained in terms of the increasing technical skill requirements of jobs.[28] He points to the growing **underemployment** particularly among college graduates. Employers frequently raise the educational specifications of jobs in reaction to an increase in the supply of better educated workers. And better educated workers receive the preferred positions within the job structure. With the expansion of schooling, both employers and occupational groups increasingly require formal education as an entry requirement.[29] One result is that individuals have responded by acquiring higher levels of

[25]Gregory D. Squires, "Education, Jobs, and Inequality: Functional and Conflict Models of Social Stratification in the United States," *Social Problems,* vol. 24, no. 4 (April 1977) pp. 436–37. Also reprinted in Dougherty and Hammack, p. 549.

[26]Lester C Thurow, *Generating Inequality* (New York: Basic Books, 1975).

[27]Squires, "Education, Jobs, and Inequality," pp. 436–50. Reproduced in Dougherty and Hammack, pp. 548–60.

[28]Squires, *Education, Jobs, and Inequality,* p. 445. The Department of Labor estimates increases in the amount of formal education required as a result of the increased technical skill requirements of jobs, and the Census Bureau reports on the increasing educational achievement of workers, show that educational accomplishment has risen faster than technical skill requirements (Squires, p. 550). In fact, when technological change affects skill requirements, workers typically learn the additional skills on the job. The effect of applying principles of Adam Smith's division of labor with Frederick Taylor's principles of scientific management has, in fact, resulted in fragmenting many skilled occupations into several unskilled jobs, thereby reducing the skill requirements for many clerical, service, craft, and even some professional and technical careers (Squires, p. 551).

There is a misconception that a change from farm laborer to assembly line worker or from blue-collar to white-collar jobs represents an increase in skill requirements. However, while an assembly line worker may use more sophisticated machinery than the farmer, the assembly line worker is not necessarily a more highly skilled worker (Squires, p. 551).

[29]Floyd M. Hammack, "The Changing Relationship Between Education and Occupation: The Case of Nursing," in Dougherty and Hammack, *Education and Society,* p. 561. Hammack points out that requiring greater educational achievement and "credentials" increases the prestige of a profession while encouraging higher pay and control over access to the profession. Thus efforts to abolish the apprenticeship system of "reading the law" and requiring the attendance of law school after obtaining a bachelor's degree and then passage of the bar exam has reduced the access of lower-class individuals to the profession.

He also notes efforts by leaders of the nursing profession to improve the prestige and power of their occupation by increasing the educational requirements. They propose that all registered nurses hold at least a bachelor's degree, thereby abolishing entrance into the profession through three-year hospital "diploma" programs,

EDUCATION AS MARKET SIGNALING

The concept that education is an investment in *human capital* is widely known. Your decision to go to college rather than enter the labor force is costing you significant amounts of money in foregone current job opportunities as well as tuition payments and other costs associated with a college education. Although there are many reasons to attend college, including the joy of learning, social development, and other benefits, human capital theory analyzes the education decision as if it were purely a business decision. From this perspective the optimal investment in education is to stay in school until the marginal revenue (expected in higher future income) equals the marginal cost of additional schooling.

Human capital theory suggests that college graduates should receive an increased income that at least compensates them for their extra investment in education. Can you reasonably expect your investment to pay off? The theory implies that those with a college education can demand higher pay as a return on their investment. It assumes that students acquire skills as they successfully complete high school, and gain even

more skills improving their productivity as they invest in a college education.

Other social scientists challenge this view of how education raises income. One view claims that the educational process teaches students little in the way of relevant knowledge or skills for subsequent job performance. Rather the educational system *sorts* people according to ability. Supporters of this view claim that competencies like perseverance, intelligence, and self-discipline are needed to succeed in college and also correlate with success in the labor force. A college degree indicates to employers that the individual is a high-quality worker who can be trained easily thus lowering productivity costs. Employers are therefore willing to pay a differential to more highly educated workers because they will be more productive on average.

Academic credentials thus provide a mechanism by which better educated workers may separate themselves from those with less education. Suppose the labor force is divided equally between low- and high-skilled workers: A low-skilled worker has a marginal revenue product MRP (the additional revenue when the firm uses an additional unit of input) of $300 per week.

educational achievement to improve their competitive position within the job market, thereby continuing the ever higher spiral of educational credentials and requirements.

Several studies have noted that the problem of underemployment is increasing.[30] As the gap between the supply and the demand for college graduates continues to increase, competition between them extends further down in the labor market, leaving those with less education with even fewer job opportunities. Thus, the wage gap between those with high school degrees or less and those with college degrees increases, while both groups experience underemployment. More highly educated workers receive higher pay,

---

or two-year associate degree programs. Hammack concludes that this effort is not required by the technical skill requirements of the health care they provide, but by the desire to counter the greater authority and prestige of the doctors with whom they work (pp. 561–73).

[30]See for example, Denis F. Johnston, "Education of Workers: Projections to 1990," *Monthly Labor Review,* 96 (November 1973), pp. 22–31. Also see James O'Toole, "The Reserve Army of the Underemployed," *Change,* 7 (May 1975), pp. 26–33.

And the other half of the work force, high-skilled workers, have a marginal revenue product of $500 per week.

If an employer cannot be sure whether a new worker has the qualities of a high- or low-quality worker when first hired, the wage will be based upon the *anticipated* MRP. Thus the firm will calculate that a new hire has a 50 percent chance of being a high-quality worker and a 50 percent chance of being a low-quality worker, and pay a wage based upon the expected MRP of $400 (.50 × $300 + .50 × $500 = $400).

Since firms pay the average MRP, low-quality workers are better off—since they receive $400 rather than $300, while high-quality workers are worse off since they receive $400 rather than $500. High-quality workers would like to signal the firm that they possess the characteristics associated with high productivity in the labor force. The educational system provides the means for them to signal the firm in a way that low-quality workers would be *unable* to do. Employers are aware of the correlation and screen workers based on

their education. Although education by itself does not increase a worker's productivity, it signals to the employer the probable possession of other qualities that improve productivity.

Signaling does not change the *average* wage, only its distribution. It has a positive effect on the income of the more highly educated workers, and a negative effect on the incomes of those less educated.

A more radical view holds that the wealthy are able to buy the best education regardless of ability. Education thus sorts people according to social class, not ability. In this way, education is a device by which the privileged members of society are able to pass on their favored position to their already privileged successors while providing the appearance of legitimacy for higher wages. In this model, education does not enhance ability, but does cultivate noncognitive traits like discipline, respect, obedience, and acceptance of the values of the business culture.

Source: A. Michael Spence, "Market Signaling: Informational Transfer in Hiring and Related Screening Processes," *Harvard Economic Studies* (Cambridge: Harvard University Press, 1974), vol. 143.

but it is based upon the amount of education rather than the content of learning or the skills required for the job.

This important point suggests implications for the popular belief that the primary reason the United States has lost ground to Germany and Japan in economic competition is that the American labor force is not highly skilled. According to the Department of Labor, salespersons, cashiers, clerical help, janitors, waiters and waitresses, receptionists, cashiers, and truck drivers are among the fastest growing occupations in the American economy.[31] Most jobs created in the last decade of this century will be in low-skilled occupations, and only about one-fourth of the jobs will require a college education.[32] The high-wage jobs in manufacturing that used to give high school graduates, especially males, a relatively high-paying job have been replaced by low-paying jobs in

[31] *Statistical Abstract, 1991,* p. 398.
[32] See Henry M. Levin, "Jobs: A Changing Workforce, a Changing Education?" Reprinted in Dougherty and Hammack, *Education & Society,* pp. 574–82.

the service sector. These low-wage jobs not only make it difficult for workers to purchase more education for their children, but they provide few benefits like health insurance or a pension program. This raises the following questions: Should access to a college education be a right rather than a privilege? Should government policy concentrate on policies to produce better jobs, rather than low-wage jobs?[33]

Human Capital Theory

Closely related to the functionalist view of education in sociology is the **human capital theory** in economics. Human capital theory argues that education makes individuals inherently more productive and therefore more highly valued workers. Adam Smith included education with national defense and justice as essential policies of the government. He said that the capital stock of a nation includes the:

> useful abilities of all the inhabitants or members of the society. The acquisition of such talents, by the maintenance of the acquirer during his education, study, or apprenticeship, always costing a real expense, which is a capital fixed and realized, as it were, in his person. Those talents, as they make a part of his fortune, so do they likewise of that of the society to which he belongs. The improved dexterity of a workman may be considered in the same light as a machine or instrument of trade which facilitates and abridges labour, and which, though it costs a certain expense, repays that expense with a profit.[34]

Interestingly, Adam Smith also supported free public education financed by taxes to counter the reduced mental stimulation of those individuals who perform repetitious jobs in modern industry that require little mental exertion. He wrote:

> The man whose whole life is spent in performing a few simple operations, of which the effects too are, perhaps, always the same, or very nearly the same, has no occasion to exert his understanding, or to exercise his invention in finding out expedients for removing difficulties which never occur. He naturally loses, therefore, the habit of such exertion, and generally becomes as stupid and ignorant as it is possible to become. . . . His dexterity at his own particular trade seems, in this manner, to be acquired at the expence of his intellectual, social, and martial virtues. But in every improved and civilized society this is the state into which the labouring poor, that is, the great body of the people, must necessarily fall, unless government takes some pains to prevent it.[35]

During preindustrial periods the value of individuals to society was measured primarily in physical productivity rather than mental ability. The size of a nation's population was a strong indicator of the nation's power. With the advent of the industrial and commercial revolutions, it became apparent that a nation's power was less depen-

---

[33]See for example, Gary Burtless, (ed.) *A Future of Lousy Jobs? The Changing Structure of U.S. Wages* (Washington, D.C.: The Brookings Institution, 1990).

[34]Adam Smith, *The Wealth of Nations,* edited by Edwin Cannon (New York: G. P. Putnam's Sons, 1877), Book 2, Chapter 1. Smith did not develop this idea beyond the statement quoted. Theodore Schultz and Gary Becker are usually given credit for developing human capital theory. See Theodore W. Schultz "Investment in Human Capital." *American Economic Review,* 51 (March 1961), pp. 1–17. See also, Gary Becker, *Human Capital* (New York: National Bureau of Economic Research, 1964).

[35]Ibid., pp. 616–17.

dent on physical labor and more dependent on brain power. A country with the largest population was not necessarily the most productive or powerful. The ability of colonial England and France to control far more populous territories illustrated this.[36]

Education can be thought of as an **investment in human capital** much like a firm invests in physical capital. Just as a corporation commits some of its profits to buying new equipment to generate more profits at a later date, the individual may reduce current income (and consumption) by investing in education in the hope of increasing future income. By obtaining a college degree, you anticipate that your diploma will help you earn more money or result in a more pleasant job than a high school friend who did not continue on.

Those with more human capital should be more productive than those with less. The productivity and quality of labor will be largely determined by the education and skill of the workforce. The educational process replicates many of the skills the job market rewards generously. The return for those skills may be paid in the form of wages. This may also include a return on the human capital acquired through education.

Measuring the Returns to Human Capital: What is Education Worth?

Ordinarily, there is a positive relationship between education and lifetime earnings. High school graduates ordinarily have higher lifetime earnings than those without a high school degree, and college graduates will earn more during their lifetime than high school graduates.[37] This leads to the conclusion that one is better off with more rather than less education. Because more education **correlates** with higher lifetime earnings, does not prove that higher education **causes** the higher earnings.

Further, estimates of educational benefits may be too low because of the difficulty of distinguishing between consumption and investment benefits.[38] Education is not only an investment, but also a consumption good. Many enjoy learning while the process is going on.

---

[36]Roe J. Johns, Edgar L. Morphet, and Kern Alexander, "Human Capital and the Economic Benefits of Education," in Dougherty and Hammack, Education & Society, pp. 534–35.

[37]Theodore Schultz in an address to the American Economic Association in 1960 first recognized education as an investment in human capital. He suggested that education should be examined the same way that investment in machinery and equipment is examined. When the addition of ever greater amounts of reproducible capital was added to a fixed supply of land and labor, it would result in diminishing returns. However when returns did not diminish, it seemed possible that improvement in the quality of human resouces might be the answer. See Theordore W. Schultz, "Investment in Human Capital," *American Economic Review* (March 1961), pp. 1–17.

[38]Many look upon their school days, especially their college years, as the most rewarding years of their lives. Therefore if half the cost of education is assigned to consumption, then the benefits derived, compared to investment, would be doubled. The share assigned to consumption and investment might vary with the focus of the education. Vocational training, on-the-job apprenticeships, work-study programs or other study, or training designed for a particular job may have less consumption and more investment aspects. On the other hand the study of art, drama, music, and the humanities may have a higher consumption portion than the study of some of the sciences. In any case, the difficulty of assigning portions of educational cost to consumption and investment has resulted in most studies attributing all cost to investment, thus underestimating the rate of return to education.

TABLE 9-2
AVERAGE INCOME BY HIGHEST DEGREE EARNED: 1996

Charac- teristic	Not a high school graduate	High school graduate	Associate's	Bachelor's	Master's	Profes- sional	Doctorate
All persons	$14,013	$21,431	$27,780	$36,980	$47,609	$ 85,322	$64,550
Age: 18–24	6,837	11,376	13,774	16,145	22,770	20,262	19,583
25–34 yrs	13,742	20,243	24,288	31,658	37,033	50,019	40,366
35–44 yrs	17,313	23,926	31,230	42,056	51,184	111,026	62,808
45–54 yrs	17,197	25,661	32,238	44,115	54,508	93,517	75,070
55–64 yrs	18,692	24,766	33,474	45,055	44,443	89,158	68,293
65 yrs or more	10,803	16,443	16,004	26,442	31,258	58,844	60,885

Source: Statistical Abstract, 1997, p. 160. From U.S. Bureau of the Census, unpublished data.

Costs and Benefits of Human Capital Investment

Who pays for the costs of education? In regard to the public school system, governments at the federal, state, and local level underwrite the cost of education. Those costs are **subsidized** through taxes, especially at the elementary and high school levels where compulsory attendance is required at least through age 16. Individuals during the years of their elementary and high school education forgo minimal income since the law precludes significant employment below the age of 16. Parents and other adults pay through their taxes, but not usually exorbitant amounts since the costs are absorbed by many people.

A college education is far more expensive since the government does not fully subsidize its costs. The student, or their parents, must pay directly for room, board, tuition, books, and other assorted fees. In addition, the individual receiving the education can forgo significant income during the typical 4½–5 year period it increasingly takes to complete a college degree. After the college education is completed, it may take time before college graduates surpass high school graduates in income levels since the latter have already acquired four years of seniority and experience on the job. The return on human capital investment is illustrated in Table 9-2.

Education and Productivity

Government subsidies of college-level education are often justified because of the expansion of national output arising from the college-educated worker's increased productivity. For example, a highly educated researcher may invent new processes to save the ozone layer. This research rewards the inventor, but also brings benefits to society. Increasing the number of trained scientists promotes increased research and development (R&D), a major factor in stimulating productivity. Ultimately highly educated and skilled managers add to the output of any firm by creating an environment conducive to improved efficiency and productivity.

Improved productivity is necessary to maintain and improve living standards in the United States, and is particularly important when one considers the increasing economic

TABLE 9-3

EARNINGS BY HIGHEST DEGREE AND FACTORS OF GENDER AND RACIAL/ETHNIC BACKGROUND (1996)

Charac-teristic	Not a high school graduate	High school graduate only	Associate	Bachelor's	Master's	Profes-sional	Doctorate
Sex:							
Male	$16,748	$26,333	$33,881	$46,111	$58,302	$101,730	$71,016
Female	9,790	15, 970	22,429	26,841	34,911	47,959	47,733
White	14,234	22,154	28,137	37,711	48,029	85,229	64,608
Male	17,032	27,467	34,286	47,016	58,817	100,856	72,542
Female	9,582	16,196	22,547	26,916	35,125	48,562	45,202
Black	12,956	17,072	26,818	29,666	38,294	(B)	(B)
Male	14,877	19,514	33,674	36,026	41,777	(B)	(B)
Female	10,739	14,473	22,113	25,577	35,222	(B)	(B)
Hispanic*	13,068	18,333	23,406	30,602	36,633	(B)	(B)
Male	14,774	20,882	24,021	35,109	38,539	(B)	(B)
Female	9,809	14,989	22,883	25,338	33,390	(B)	(B)

*Persons of Hispanic origin may be of any race. (B) indicates base figure too small to meet statistical standards for reliability of a derived figure.
Source: Statistical Abstract, 1997, p. 160.

competition from abroad. It is of fundamental importance, then to determine what types of educational skills have the greatest impact on worker productivity. There is considerable evidence that literacy and problem-solving skills in specific contexts are of primary importance.[39] A key to worker productivity is the ability to identify problems that occur in a work-related context and to synthesize new information and develop problem-solving strategies. This includes the ability to understand directions and to formulate appropriate questions. Other studies have found that worker's scores on tests of mathematical skills are significantly correlated with their supervisor's evaluations of their productivity. Mathematical ability may be particularly related to worker productivity because it typically requires a step-by-step approach to problem solving.

Some argue education policy should emphasize instruction in the skills of practical problem solving as opposed to instruction by means of lower-order skills such as recall and drill often used to teach arithmetic computation. There is concern that schools provide the former primarily to college-bound students.[40]

[39] See Richard L. Venezky, Carl F. Kaestle, and Andrew M. Sum, *The Subtle Danger: Reflections on the Literacy Abilities of America's Young Adults* (Princeton, NJ: Educational Testing Service, 1987).

[40] For example, Venezky, Kaestle, and Sum (*The Subtle Danger,* p. 22) found that over 90 percent of young adults could follow simple directions and make inferences when all the necessary information was in one sentence. However 30 percent of the same group encountered difficulties in problem solving when they had to gather data from several sentences to solve multistep problems. The expanded use of computers as instructional aids in the classroom is often advocated as one way to improve student learning.

UNEQUAL PAYOFFS FOR CAPITAL INVESTMENT

Investing in education has been considered a guarantee of a good job and upward mobility. Increasingly, however, relatively high-paying manufacturing jobs for high school graduates have been replaced with low-paying jobs in the service sector. The shrinking job market for well-paying, male-dominated jobs in the manufacturing sector for high school graduates resulted in a decline in median male earnings of 9 percent in real terms in the decade from 1988 to 1998. White male high school graduates were the biggest losers. It was in large measure due to this decline in male wages that women's wages appear to have increased from 46 percent to 54 percent of the average male wage. Wages for high school graduates have declined since the mid-1970s.

Investing in a high school education provides less return than in the past. Investing in a college education may provide greater job security although it may not result in an increase over a college income in the 1960s and 1970s.

Moreover, gender, racial, and ethnic discrimination still play a significant role in determining the jobs and wages available to different individuals, often overriding the investment in education. Table 9-3 shows the average return on investment in education for women in 1996. A comparison shows that males get a greater return on their investment in education than do females at every level. While a comparison of age and education may not include other factors, such as continuous years in the labor force, the implications are too apparent to be ignored. These results challenge the theory of human capital investment that claims wages are based upon productivity which is in turn dependent upon an investment in education that improves the quality of labor. According to the theory, the wage gap should disappear as women and minorities invest more in education. This clearly has not happened.

Human capital theorists contend that people choose between investing in education or entering the job market after calculating the costs of an education and the income that will be lost during the period of education, as well as whether their lifetime earnings will exceed lifetime earnings (and working conditions) of those with less education. According to the theory, women and especially minorities choose to invest in less education because they place a greater value in current earnings rather than future earnings. This of course ignores other factors such as their current economic status which may not permit a greater investment in education, or growing up in a neighborhood with poor schools and a poorer preparation for college. It also ignores the fact that investment in a college education for minorities is not as sound an investment as for white males in terms of the expected long-term expected payoff. Human capital theory holds that wages received are determined by the amount of education and skills invested in by the individual, but it overlooks the factors of cost, access, and discrimination in public education and in the job market. Thus it is a view supportive of conservative policy positions that see low educational achievement as a purely personal problem (or decision) and not a political problem.

TRENDS IN AMERICAN EDUCATION

The success of American education, especially when compared to European nations, reflects the nation's revolutionary origins. The Founding Fathers rejected the idea of a hereditary aristocracy and emphasized the equality of all citizens. Alexis de Tocqueville, in the early nineteenth century, noted that equality was the dominant value in American society, along with a culture of individualism that supported personal freedom to pursue interests without hindrance by the government. In this view, social conditions should enable individuals, whatever their pedigrees, to compete for positions on the basis of merit alone (though in the nineteenth century gender and race were sufficient grounds for exclusion from consideration for all higher-level positions).

One **goal** of the educational system in the United States **is to equalize differences in wealth and circumstances so that individuals can progress according to their abilities.** Unfortunately, according to critics, the results of American public education in the past reflected differences in the wealth of students' parents, and often do so today also:

> For despite the promise of American education, it was organized in such a way that it acted as an overwhelmingly powerful mechanism for preserving and promoting racial and social class segregation. Today its effects are so pervasive that probably no other public policies or government actions are as important in preserving inequality from one generation to the next.[41]

The mechanism for perpetuating inequality was and is the American method of financing public schools primarily through property taxes. Since property taxes reflect the value of the property within local school districts, the amount of money raised to support education on a per capita basis varies immensely from district to district.

School district boundaries reflect societal divisions between affluent and poor, white and black and Hispanic students. Central city school systems tend to receive fewer funds and have disproportionate numbers of poor and minority students. Children attending these schools typically exhibit poorer academic performance than students attending suburban schools. "White flight" to suburban school districts, the result in part of efforts to escape mandated desegregation of inner-city schools, has introduced a racial and ethnic factor into these educational problems. Concern over the strong association between the family background and success in scholastic performance has led to much research and a number of theories.

Despite the promise in the landmark decision by the Supreme Court in *Brown v. the Board of Education (1954),* the condition of public education in the United States still tends to be separate and unequal. Despite the virtual elimination of de jure segregation, most minority children today still attend de facto racially segregated schools. Litigation in over thirty state courts reveals continuing widespread disparities in per pupil spending between poor and middle-class school districts. Both problems appear intractable. Public schools, for all their virtues, have not been very helpful to those children who need it most. The system that helped assimilate generations of disadvantaged European immigrants is not working very well for the most disadvantaged members of society.[42] The same educational system that once was seen as a poor child's ticket out of the slums is seen by many as part of the system that today traps the poor in the slums.

---

[41]David B. Robertson and Dennis R. Judd, *The Development of American Public Policy: The Structure of Policy Restraint* (Boston: Scott, Foresman, 1989), p. 246.

[42]Joseph P. Viteritti, "Stacking the Deck for the Poor: The New Politics of School Choice," *The Brookings Review* (Summer 1996), vol. 14, no. 3.

ASSESSING FACTORS IN LEARNING

Researchers have developed two general approaches for analyzing educational achievement: student-centered and school-centered explanations.

Student-Centered Focus

Ordinarily, **student-centered theories** are put forward by functionalists. These "elitist" interpretations emphasize the qualities the student brings into a learning environment. They view these qualities as the primary reasons for success or failure in the school.

Many of these arguments suggest a **cultural deficit** works to provide poor and working-class students with behavior patterns and attitudes different from the white middle- or upper-class culture reflected in the public educational curricula.[43] The **cultural deprivation theory** holds that working-class and nonwhite students perform poorly because they are not raised in a manner to develop the skills that encourage school success. Such children come to school without adequate language and auditory discrimination skills. This view holds that the effectiveness of the elementary and secondary educational systems depends on the quality of the home environment, which becomes increasingly important in secondary school. The lack of learning resources attending impoverishment has the effect of reducing the cognitive skills of poor children.

The student-centered theory has been attacked for letting schools escape criticism by focusing blame on the deprived children. Critics argue that "blaming the victim" allows policy makers to avoid facing the need for fundamental changes in the educational system.[44] They contend that, if society is sincerely interested in improving the work-related skills of the labor force of the future, it must improve the quality of the lives children lead outside of school. This is of particular concern since one child in five in the United States lives in poverty.

Cultural difference theory rejects the cultural deprivation theory. It claims that the lack of educationally important skills is not due to any inadequacy in working-class or minority households, but results from children being raised in oppressed subcultures. It sees the low educational aspirations and achievements of working-class and minority students as reflecting the inequalities inherent in the class structure.[45]

Some student-centered critics see school failure as a long-term effect of elitist and meritocratic school procedures which lead to different educational conditions for the advantaged and the disadvantaged. This view accounts for low student achievement by attributing it to individual inadequacies, rather than to schools that do not serve their students well. Whatever their weaknesses, student-centered interpretations do delineate the

---

[43]Dougherty and Hammack, "Factors Influencing Academic Learning," *Education & Society*, ch. 6, p. 340.

Arthur Jensen, an educational psychologist, argued the student-centered view that, since remedial education frequently failed, scholars must take seriously the argument that working-class and minority students do less well educationally because they have less intelligence due to an inferior genetic makeup. The geneticist argument has been attacked primarily on the basis of cultural biases of the test and social factors including family upbringing and schooling (pp. 340–41).

[44]Ibid., p. 341.

[45]Ibid., p. 342.

differences between the skills and characteristics that students bring to school and those that lead to success in classroom settings.

School-Centered Explanations

School-centered theories shift the focus from students to the educational process. Until the mid-1960s, this approach started from the premise that a major reason disadvantaged students get less education is because they go to inferior schools, while, in contrast, middle- and upper-income students attend schools having substantially more resources and more experienced teachers. This explanation has an appealing inherent logic.

Researchers began to investigate schools commonly considered effective and compared them, where possible, with schools commonly regarded as ineffective. This approach provided insight into the critical performance factors within the larger population of schools. By the late 1970s and early 1980s, a number of studies reached the inescapable conclusion that **school organization does have an important impact on learning.**

Interestingly, one of the more weighty arguments in favor of the significance of school organization on the learning process came from the late James Coleman.[46] In a study, whose results were published in 1982, Coleman and his colleagues at the University of Chicago used the *High School and Beyond* (HSB) data set to conduct a comparative study of public, parochial, and private schools. They concluded that parochial school students generally received the highest scores on achievement tests, followed by private school students, and finally public school students. This finding remained constant even when background characteristics of students, such as family income or parental education, were controlled. The study also found that parochial schools, primarily those serving inner-city racial minorities, were more integrated than public schools.[47] Parochial and private schools consistently did a better job of educating the typical student than public schools, and much of the superior performance originated in important organizational differences.

Coleman's study created political controversy. The controversy was stimulated by its finding that parochial and private schools are more effective than public schools. Many in the public educational community rejected the study out of hand. But Coleman and his colleagues established an important theoretical point that **schools matter.** "Effective schools research," as studies of school organization came to be called, suggest that it should be possible to identify how structural features of schools can condition teacher behavior and expectations and influence student success. Using this approach, schools

[46]James S. Coleman, Thomas Hoffer, and Sally Kilgore, *High School Achievement: Public, Catholic, and Private Schools Compared* (New York: Basic Books, 1982).

[47]A Rand Corporation study in 1990 concluded that parochial schools had particular success with disadvantaged and minority students. Although minority students score lower than their white classmates in both Catholic and public schools, the gap decreases significantly by the eleventh grade. Children from single-parent families drop out at twice the rate of those with both parents in the home. Children in single-parent homes drop out only at the same rate as those with both parents in Catholic schools however.

Although the educational level of parents of parochial school students exceeds that of public school parents, Catholic schools' achievement advantage over public schools is the greatest for children whose parents have the least education. Reported in *The Baltimore Sun,* Tim Baker, "Successful Schools are Right Under Our Noses," June 3, 1991.

JUSTICE AND EDUCATIONAL EQUALITY

John Rawls and Robert Nozick offer two conflicting philosophical approaches for considering the problem of inequality in education. Rawls holds that only those inequalities are justified which are to the benefit of the least advantaged. Only inequalities of position or resources that result in greater productivity and thereby provide greater benefits to all, may be justified. The implication is that Rawls would attempt to delete the "accidents of birth" wherever possible, thus creating a full equalization of opportunity for each child. By moving toward equality, individual liberty is lost to the central authority that imposes that equality.

Robert Nozick's position is based upon the entitlement of the individual to whatever property he or she has legitimately acquired. Accordingly, for him the imposition of equality in benefits signifies a loss of rights for the affluent as well as the poor. The extreme position of Nozick would suggest no public education. Public education is by definition redistributive. But according to Nozick, in regard to education, each child is entitled to the untaxed benefits of his or her family's resources to the extent that the family chooses to apply those resources to the child's education. This would make all education private and paid for by each family according to its ability and desires. By moving in the direction of individual liberty, equality is lost to the variations in market power enjoyed by different individuals.

Because of the issue of school financing, parental choice of schools based upon residence conflicts with the attempts by states and federal agencies to reduce inequality. This problem arose as schools were no longer primarily financed from independent towns and cities. The schools reflected the social diversity within their communities so the poor and affluent had access to the same program of studies, which encouraged Rawlsian equality. But each school district was thought to be entitled to its own resources even if there was inequality between districts, which accorded with Nozick's position. Note that the policy decision to levy taxes for public schools so long ago resulted in surrendering control over resources for schooling to government authority.

With the shift in recent decades of the responsibility for financing public educa-

are identified whose students perform much better than typical for comparable students elsewhere. Researchers have then tried to isolate those factors that differentiate such atypically effective schools. Comparing "effective schools" with those commonly regarded as "ineffective" also provides insight into the general elements of effectiveness within the educational system.

No single factor makes a school exceptional. **Effective schools,** these studies have concluded, are charaterized by several ingredients that conventional wisdom has suggested all along were important:

- **Clear school goals,** and strong principal, or school-based leadership. (Schools should have a mission rather than operate from force of habit.)
- **School autonomy.** Effective schools are free from extensive outside bureaucratic controls.
- **High expectations on the part of teachers** and principals for student performance.
- **Vigorous leadership and involvement by the principal** in the instructional program.

tion away from local government to the state and federal levels, the issue of liberty versus equality has become more prominent. But now it involves the liberty of the local school district (not the individual) to freely allocate its own resources, versus equity among school districts (not individuals) restricting district liberty. The basic conflict is between those who appeal for financing by the state based on principles of equity, versus those who protest that resources should not be redistributed to other districts. In this issue there are policy alternatives that tend toward the positions of Rawls or Nozick, and a third that is somewhat of a compromise. The first would emphasize equality by providing full funding by the states. The extreme position precludes the liberty of individual districts to spend more on education by taxing themselves more heavily, insisting complete equality of funding for all children. A second option, more closely in tune with Nozick's views, would maintain local funding and local decisions regarding the level of expenditure. State and national funds would supplement local financing but without regard to the level of the local tax burden for education.

A third alternative would encourage some aspects of both Rawls's and Nozick's principles. Rather than taking away rights from those who feel entitled by their economic power to opt for the school of their choice through residence, those rights might be expanded to include others who do not have that choice. Permitting choice would increase equality rather than inequality by allowing individuals otherwise effectively excluded by economics from the residential area of the school to choose a school other than that of closest residence. By exercising that right inequality is reduced. Full equality is not realized, however. The liberty of the affluent to maintain socially homogeneous schools is restricted. Importantly, however, a new liberty (option) is provided for the less privileged who previously were without it.

Source: This section draws heavily upon James Coleman, "Rawls, Nozick, and Educational Equality," *The Public Interest,* vol. 43 (1976), pp. 121–28.

- **Rigorous academic standards** with high teacher expectations regarding students graduating from high school, going to college, becoming good readers, and being good citizens.
- **Professionalism among the teachers.** Teachers spend their time actually teaching and monitoring their students, and providing feedback to them. Teachers rely on tests they have developed in judging student achievement.
- **Principals and teachers are able to experiment and adapt techniques and procedures in response to circumstances encountered.**[48]

The research on effective schools comes at a time when dissatisfaction with the educational system has reached a critical level. It is consistent with the views of those who suggest a "back-to-basics" approach that accentuates order and discipline, emphasizes basic skills, includes more tests to measure progress, and promotes higher educational

[48]See Stewart C. Purkey and Marshall S. Smith, "Effective Schools: A Review," *Elementary School Journal,* vol. 83 (March 1983), pp. 427–52, for a good review of the characteristics of effective schools research.

standards. Coleman and others found in their research that Catholic parochial schools tend to be more effective and provide a significantly better education than public schools, due to their focus on just such aspects of education.[49]

In the private education sector the formal right to control a school is vested with a church, a corporation, or a nonprofit agency that has the legal right to make all the educational decisions. In the public education sector, different interests struggle over educational decisions. Ironically, though, a basic market or "choice" principle gives parents and students a more influential role in private-sector schools than in the public educational system. Those who run private or parochial schools have a strong motivation to please their clientele because they know that if people do not like the educational services they receive, they can switch. This is invariably a strong possibility since the low-cost public school system is always an alternative. Moreover, private sector schools that cannot attract a clientele of sufficient size must be able to pass along the higher per pupil charges to the families of the students they are able to attract or to their sponsoring organizations. Otherwise they will go out of business.[50] This is a strong financial motivator to be responsive to parents and provide a good education.

Coleman's conclusions have been supported and reinforced by the more recent research findings of Anthony Bryk and his colleagues reported in their work, *Catholic Schools for the Common Good*.[51] Their most significant finding is that Catholic schools have been particularly effective in educating inner-city minority students. Many inner-city parochial schools have been very successful although their student profiles are very similar to those associated with failing public schools. These parochial schools are typically more racially integrated and operate at a per capita cost of between 50 and 60 percent of public schools. Most would agree that racial equality can be achieved only by eliminating the differences in the average academic performance of blacks and whites. However, half of all African Americans, but only 20 percent of whites, in public school attend inner-city schools. In the largest American cities, the racial differences between inner-city and suburban schools are even greater. In Chicago, Dallas, Detroit, Houston, Los Angeles, and Washington, over 85 percent of the public school students are minorities.[52] In fact, today's private school students are more integrated than those attending public school. According to 1992 Department of Education data, 37 percent of private school students are in classrooms whose share of minority students is close to the national average, compared to only 18 percent of public school students.[53]

[49]See for example, James S. Coleman, "Families and Schools," *Educational Researcher* 16 (August–September 1987), pp. 32–38. Particularly for research comparing public and private schools, see James S. Coleman, Thomas Hoffer, and Sally Kilgore, *High School Achievement: Public, Catholic, and Private Schools Compared* (New York: Basic Books, 1982); also Coleman and Hoffer, *Public and Private High Schools,* 1987.

The findings of effective schools research have been challenged along with the policy implications by several scholars. A full issue of *Sociology of Education,* 55 (April–July 1982) and the *Harvard Educational Review,* 51 (November 1981), pp. 481–545 were devoted to a critique of the Coleman, Hoffer, and Kilgore study.

[50]John E. Chubb and Terry M. Moe, *Politics, Markets, and American Schools* (Washington, DC: The Brookings Institution, 1990), pp. 32–33.

[51]Anthony Bryk, Valerie Lee, and Peter Holland, *Catholic Schools for the Common Good* (Cambridge, MA: Harvard University Press, 1993).

[52]Paul E. Peterson and Jay P. Greene, "Race Relations & Central City Schools: It's Time for an Experiment with Vouchers," *The Brookings Review* (Spring, 1998).

[53]Ibid., p. 36.

Research findings suggest that factors are at work in the public educational system that directly conflict with several of the indicators which make for effective schools. For example, John Chubb and Terry Moe have concluded that a public educational system with low or declining quality may not keep parents from moving into a school district, and it is even less likely to cause existing residents to leave. Rather it might prod them to consider a private school. If they choose that option, it reduces the number of disgruntled parents in the public school system and reduces the average dissatisfaction of those left in the public sector.[54] The major disincentive to leaving is that **public education has a very low cost.** Therefore the worth of private or parochial schools must be far superior to public schools to attract students. Or, stated differently, the low cost of public schools permits them to attract students without being particularly good at teaching them.

Once **parents make a choice** in favor of a public school despite their apprehensions, they may try to correct perceived problems in methods or performance through the democratic process. The political struggle for control over the public schools involves parents, student advocacy groups, teachers, teachers' unions, administrators, business groups, local school boards, state governments, and the federal government. Victory comes in the form of tenuous compromises regarding goals that could vanish with a shift in political power. Thus schools will be directed to:

> . . . pursue academic excellence, but without making courses too difficult; they will be directed to teach history, but without making any value judgments; they will be directed to teach sex education, but without taking a stand on contraception or abortion. They must make everyone happy by being all things to all people—just as politicians try to do.[55]

The winning coalition inevitably sets up a bureaucratic arrangement to force compliance upon the losers and to insure against the risks of future defeat by opponents who would like to impose their own rules. Bureaucratic control means that teacher behavior will be regulated in minute detail and through enforcement procedures set up by the winners that permits verifying teacher compliance with rules and standards.

Thus, the tendency to blame the public education bureaucracy for the educational problems is to misunderstand the nature of the problem. It is true that bureaucrats are rewarded for devising rules and regulations and for setting standards of policies and programs defined in the past. But the bureaucrats are put into place by the victors of the political struggle to enforce compliance with their vision of what education should be.[56] Not to put bureaucrats in place would result in an uncertain political victory and an inability by the victors to enforce their terms.

[54]Chubb and Moe, *Politics, Markets & America's Schools,* p. 33. This is the best analysis to date of the problems of public education in America and alternative approaches to resolving them.

[55]Ibid., p. 54.

[56]*The Baltimore Sun* (June 3, 1991) reported that the parochial school system in Baltimore costs about $2,000 per student or less than half the cost of the Baltimore public schools. Bureaucracy accounts for a major portion of the difference. Parochial schools educate 31,002 students in 101 schools in Baltimore and the surrounding counties with a central staff of 16 people. By comparison the Baltimore public school system employs 570 people in its headquarters to run a system of 108,000 students in 180 schools. Comparable per-student staff levels would drop the public school bureaucracy from 570 to 56 people.

Parochial schools have some advantages in that they do not try to educate children with severe learning disabilities, handicaps, or discipline problems. Those advantages do not entirely account for the superior results.

Nor are teachers necessarily to blame for problems in public education. Good teaching consists of skilled operations that are extremely difficult to measure in formal bureaucratic assessments. Educational output results from the interaction between a teacher and a student. That is the primary relationship in education. Professionalism requires that teachers have the freedom to exercise their judgment in applying their knowledge and teaching skills to the specific students and circumstances they encounter. When the system is bureaucratized, the most important relationship for the teacher is with the supervisor, not the students. Increasing bureaucratic regulations and reporting standards guarantee that teacher discretion will be reduced and initiative stifled.[57]

Market-Oriented Reforms and "Effective Schools"

The obvious implication of the "Effective Schools" type of research is that policy alternatives need to be implemented that will move the educational system in the direction of decentralized educational "markets." Advocates argue this would give parents more choice in selecting a school for their children. It would also force schools to compete for the financial support that would come through parental choice of schools. As a necessary component of choice, proponents point out, schools must be given greater autonomy in deciding their academic programs, principal, and staff, and how to compete for students. Thus they would resemble private and parochial schools more closely. The projected benefits would be a public education guided more by markets and less by politics, and therefore it would be less prone to the debilitating effects of excessive bureaucratic controls. Subjecting schools to fewer bureaucratic requirements, but to more competition, the market mechanism would reward clear goals and efficiency. Finally, proponents argue, the choice exercised by the consumers of education—parents and students—should foster more positive and cooperative affiliations between parents, students, and the school.[58]

The Debate Over Market Mechanisms

The firestorm of controversy generated by the Coleman study on education in America demonstrates that education is not an issue that neatly divides liberals and conservatives. Typically conservatives have supported the student-centered analysis of educational problems. They have stressed the abilities and attitudes students bring to school, not what schools do to educate students. Student-centered arguments range from "geneticist" views at one end of the spectrum ascribing the lower educational attainment of

---

[57]The problem of increased bureaucratic control has increased as responsibility for funding has moved from localities to the states and with the growth of federal regulation. Court decisions on funding equity and racial integration have also contributed to the trend. Increased regulation has also contributed to instruction taking a smaller portion of educational expenditures, declining from 68 percent in 1960 to 61 percent in 1980. Also between 1960 and 1984 the number of nonclassroom personnel grew 400 percent, approximately 7 times the growth rate of classroom teachers. See John E. Chubb and Eric A. Hanushek, "Reforming Educational Reform," in Henry J. Aaron (ed.), *Setting National Priorities: Policy for the Nineties* (Washington, DC: The Brookings Institution, 1990), pp. 223–24.

Teachers' unions, in supporting greater autonomy for teachers, promote a formalization of teacher authority by imposing strict procedural rules for decision-making between a principal and the teaching staff. This also has the consequence of reducing the principal's ability to take effective action to obtain teachers with the greatest teaching skills. The result is that the principal and the staff are both stuck with each other.

[58]Ibid., p. 230.

disadvantaged students largely to an inferior gene pool, to "cultural difference" views that impute working-class or minority students' educational distress to their rebellion against school discipline or the intolerance of middle- and upper-class school culture regarding disadvantaged subcultures. In between is the "cultural deprivation" view attributing academic inadequacies to a deficient home life that fails to develop the skills and attitudes necessary for academic success. Conservatives tend to see these problems as being outside the purview of educational policy.

Liberals, on the other hand, have usually focused on school-centered explanations. Many liberals are very troubled by the impossible conditions teachers frequently confront when trying to carry out their educational tasks in public schools—the lack of a clear sense by many school systems of their education purpose, and their refusal to involve teachers in the process of curriculum design. Liberals tend to favor smaller and more focused schools that are permitted the freedom to adapt to local conditions.

The implications of the Coleman study and the subsequent research regarding what constitutes effective schools are threatening to many of the groups who helped install the bureaucracies which implement and defend educational policies opposed to "effective schools" research conclusions, whether those groups are in other respects conservative or liberal in their views. For example, both the National Educational Association and the American Federation of Teachers, disagree with the notion of school choice.

School Choice and Vouchers

The proposal for a free market model of education as an alternative to a government monopoly became a significant policy issue in 1990 when John Chubb and Terry Moe published their important work, *Politics, Markets, and America's Schools.*[59] Their study gave support for student choices regarding schools. In their view consumer choice drives competition for establishing school systems where schools determine their own policies, curriculum, hire their own teachers, and compete for students like private schools now do. They argue it would be a better system, especially for poor children most in need of choice.[60] As they see it this would give the disadvantaged more of the same choices that the affluent already have. Affluence gives the ability to buy homes in the preferred public school district or to opt for private school alternatives. The affluent have also been able to press for the best principals, teachers, and facilities. It is only equitable to provide an open enrollment plan (market oriented) to give the disadvantaged families the same market power to choose that the affluent have always had. Currently, the poor have no choice. The idea of giving the poor the same options as those exercised by the more affluent members of society appears inherently democratic.

Policy Action

One concern frequently expressed is that "choice" would be rigged against the poor. A major concern of many liberals has been that school choice programs would provide

---

[59]Chubb and Moe, *Politics, Markets, and America's Schools.*
[60]As quoted in Linda Chion-Kenney, "The Choice Debate," *The Washington Post,* 10 February 1992, B5. Also Chubb and Moe, *Politics, Markets, and America's Schools.*

CHOICE AND MARKET OPTIONS

A range of plans exist that allow parents some choice and introduce elements of market competition into the public education system.

Magnet Schools

Magnet schools usually build an advanced academic curricula around interested faculty, parents, and students. This concept permits students to attend the magnet school from anywhere in the district (intra-district choice). Students usually choose between the magnet school and the normal high school. A frequently voiced criticism is that magnet schools tend to attract the best teachers and students from the district, resulting in a net loss in quality to the other schools in the district. The benefits to the magnet school may be offset by the losses suffered by the traditional schools in the district. Typically the organizational constraints of the large school system remain in force.

School Choice Plans (Open-Enrollment)

Intra-district open enrollment allows students to choose any public school within their school district. *Inter-district* choice plans permit families to send their children to public schools in other districts. The overall results have been favorable. Parents have expressed satisfaction. In East Harlem, a school district in New York, test scores in reading and math went from the bottom of thirty-two school districts to sixteenth.[61] The greatest drawback is that public authorities allow students who cross district lines to transfer only the share of educational costs contributed by the state. When costs exceed the amount guaranteed by the state, the district they left actually receives the local contribution as a benefit, while the district they enter must make up the difference. This inflicts a penalty on the host school that attracts pupils which is the very opposite of what free-flowing market forces would do.[62]

Teachers' unions are supportive of choice in public schools as an alternative to reduce the argument for giving assistance to parents to send their children to private schools.

Tuition Tax Credits

These move beyond magnet schools and open-enrollment plans and toward market forces by abolishing the monopoly that

---

[61]See Edward B. Fiske, "Letting Parents Choose a Public School: The Idea Now Has Champions in the White House," *The New York Times* (11 January 1989). See also Raymond Ja Domanico, "A Model for Choice: A Report on Manhattan's District 4," Education Policy Paper 1, Center for Education Innovation, Manhattan Institute for Policy Research, June 1989.

[62]See Chubb and Hanushek, "Reforming Educational Reform," pp. 237–38.

---

an additional advantage for the affluent who would leave public schools for more exclusive private academies at the expense of public schools. It would contravene the policy goals if vouchers would permit parents to select the public or private school of their choice and give it their share of the tax revenue spent on schools. The objection is basically, "Why should the taxpayer subsidize the parents who want to use their taxes to pay a significant portion of the $18,000 to $28,000 that elite schools charge?" Low income families would not be able to pay the difference between the value of their voucher and the tuition costs of elite academies. Legislators in Wisconsin provided one solution to the problem by limiting eligibility for state vouchers to families whose income did not exceed 175 percent of the federal poverty level. The bill provided state vouchers in the amount of $2,987 (in 1990) for students in Milwaukee to attend nonsectarian private schools of choice. The bill was the result of effort by the poor and minority parents and

public school districts exercise over the supply of publicly supported education. Giving parents a credit against their federal or state taxes for some portion of private or parochial school payments makes such schools more affordable and increases the pressure on all schools, whether public or private to become more competitive. The Supreme Court's decision in *Mueller v. Allen,* 463 U.S. 388 (1983) established the legality of a Minnesota law allowing parents of children in elementary and secondary schools to deduct tuition from their income taxes.

A limitation on tax credits, some argue, is that it would provide only a small portion of the typical private school tuition. And it would provide less of a tax benefit to parents with low incomes than those with high incomes.

Voucher Plans
These move beyond the confines of tuition tax credits by providing parents of school-age children with a certificate or voucher that could be used only to pay for school. The goal of vouchers would be to provide full payment for the student's education at any public or publicly approved private school. The school receiving a voucher would turn the certificate in to the issuing government for reimbursement. Such vouchers would provide all families with the market power now exercised only by the affluent. One variation on the proposal would provide the educationally disadvantaged with a voucher of greater value, which would make those students more attractive to schools that otherwise might not want them. Government would retain the right to set requirements regarding eligibility, admission, graduation, teacher certification, and any other societal goals it found warranted for participating public and private schools. Providing such broad educational choice would encourage all schools to improve their educational output to stay ahead of the competition.

Voucher plan support has been overwhelmingly Republican and suburban. More recently with many inner city schools having failed, inner-city residents and African Americans have become much more supportive than suburbanites who generally support the suburban public schools their children attend. Public sentiment is shifting toward vouchers. In 1997, 44 percent of the public favored vouchers, up from only 24 percent in 1993.

Source: This section is broadly adapted from Chubb and Hanushek, "Reforming Educational Reform," pp. 235–40. See also Rochelle L. Stanfield, "A Turning Tide on Vouchers," *National Journal,* Sept. 27, 1997.

---

political leaders who were frustrated with the ineffective educational system. The bill was amended in 1995 which increased the value of the voucher to $3,200 and permitted the vouchers to be used at parochial schools.[63] The Ohio legislature passed a similar measure for low-income students in Cleveland.

Researchers from Harvard and the University of Houston found that students who attended private schools on the voucher program scored higher on math and reading tests

---

[63]The vouchers have been increased in value annually to keep pace with inflation. In 1996 their value was raised to $3,600.

Another proposal to prevent vouchers becoming a subsidy for the affluent to attend expensive private schools if they were to be issued to all students, was to limit their use to schools that would accept the voucher as full payment.

after four years than did youngsters who stayed in the public school.[64] As a result of this experience a new model of school choice designed to give children the chance to attend a high quality public, private, or parochial school has evolved. As a result means-based proposals have been introduced or are being seriously considered in Connecticut, Maryland, Massachusetts, Minnesota, California, Texas, Pennsylvania, and New Mexico. By focusing assistance to students on the basis of economic need it targets those who are most poorly served by the educational system.

Certainly means testing the program does eliminate concern over the elites taking advantage of the system by leaving the public educational system.

Legal Obstacles

Proposals to provide federal aid to states to allow middle- and low-income children to attend public, private, or parochial schools of choice were stymied by broad opposition. The teachers' unions believe that choice undermines their interests and warned that the proposal, if widely enacted, would destroy public education because most parents would not choose to send their child to a public school if given an alternative. Others expressed fears that the proposal would result in many middle-class students leaving the public school system while the poor would be left behind in underfunded government-run schools. Others raised Constitutional arguments that the plan would provide government funds to religious schools and thereby violate the First Amendment requirement to maintain a separation of church and state.

Strict separationists including the American Civil Liberties Union, teachers' unions, and others argue that school choice or voucher programs that would include parochial schools would have the "primary effect" of advancing religion and would therefore be unconstitutional. The Supreme Court has continued a prohibition against direct public assistance to religious institutions, but in recent years has provided standards that would permit parents to receive aid to send their children to religious schools. Three basic requirements for aid to be permissible are: that the assistance must be provided to the parent or child rather than to a religious institution, secondly, any benefit that accumulates to a religious institution must result from the parental decisions, and third, funds must be appropriated on a neutral basis as regards religion and made available to everyone regardless of whether they attend a public, private, or parochial school.[65] The Rehnquist court has stressed that parents who wish to have their children attend sectarian schools are entitled to the same rights and privileges as those who desire a public education for their children. The Supreme Court held that a Minnesota tax deduction for educational purposes, whether for secular or parochial schools, did not "establish a religion." Nor do state-provided scholarships "establish a religion" as long as they can be used at any school whether Catholic, Protestant, Jewish, Muslim, or secular.[66]

---

[64]*New York Times,* "Study Shows Voucher Pupils Thriving in Private Schools," 13 August 1996, p. A8.
[65]Viteritti, *Stacking the Deck for the Poor,* p. 12.
[66]*Mueller v. Allen,* 463 U.S.388 (1983).

Opponents of the inclusion of sectarian schools in a voucher system have increasingly attempted to make their case on provisions found within state constitutions.[67] Both the Wisconsin and Ohio programs are being challenged in state courts.

In the United States, the Democratic Party, which has long felt that education is its issue, finds itself torn between its desire to defend the educational establishment or support the desires of their working-class members who want choice. Republicans have eroded the Democrats' advantages by appealing to traditional Democratic party constituents, especially ethnic minorities and Catholics, and supporting choice.

DROPOUTS

Policy concern over high school dropouts stems from the importance of having an educated workforce. Technological advances have increased the demand for skilled labor to the point that a high school education is increasingly a minimum requirement to enter the labor force.

Students who drop out of school before completing their high school education exact a high cost on themselves and American society. On average, dropouts have higher rates of unemployment and earn lower wages than those who graduate. The average annual income of dropouts is approximately two-thirds of the income of high school graduates ($14,013 versus $21,431 see table 9-2). Women who drop out of high school are more likely to become pregnant at an early age, and are more likely to be single parents.[68] They are also more likely to receive public assistance. Half of all families on welfare are headed by high school dropouts.[69] The stress and frustration associated with dropping out means an increased risk to turn to crime for financial support; dropouts account for about half the prison population and a disproportionate share of death row inmates.[70]

The *Goals 2000: Educate America Act* signed into law by President Clinton in 1993 calls for a high school graduation rate of 90 percent for the nation's schools by the year 2000. The *School-to-Work Opportunities Act,* signed in 1994 is intended to provide new initiatives to build systems that will prepare young people for jobs requiring higher skills and paying higher wages.

Despite a steady reduction in high school dropout rates throughout this century, it remains a very serious problem in many cities. Students from lower socioeconomic status (SES) groups in large cities are overrepresented in the dropout population where dropout rates of 30 percent and higher are not uncommon.[71]

[67]David M. Ackerman, *Choice Programs and State Constitutions: The Inclusion of Sectarian Schools,* Congressional Research Service, Report for Congress, March 2, 1992.

[68]Marilyn McMillen, *Dropout Rates in the United States: 1995,* U.S. Department of Education, National Center for Education Statistics, NCES 97-473.

[69]Karl L. Alexander, Doris R. Entwisle, and Carrie S. Horsey, "From First Grade Forward: Early Foundations of High School Dropout," *Sociology of Education,* vol. 70 no. 2, p. 87.

[70]About one- quarter of federal inmates are dropouts and about half of all state prisons inmates are dropouts. See C. W. Harlow, *Comparing Federal and State Prison Inmates, 1991,* U.S. Department of Justice, Office of Justice Programs, Bureau of Justice Statistics, September 1994, NCJ-145864.

[71]Deborah B. Strother, *Phi Delta Kappan,* 68 (December, 1986), pp. 325–28. Reprinted in Dougherty and Hammack, *Education & Society,* p. 256. The dropout rate from high school which was 90 percent in 1900, dropped to 80 percent by the 1920s, to 50 percent by the early 1950s, and to the low 20s by the mid 1970s. See *Dropouts in America* (Washington: The Institute for Educational Leadership, 1987), pp. 11–12.

Defining the Dropout Problem

To provide a detailed picture of dropouts in the United States, the National Center for Education Statistics (NCES) defines and calculates three different types of dropout rates. Each defined type examines a different aspect of dropouts. The types of dropout rates are:

Event dropout rates which describe the proportion of students who leave high school each year without receiving a diploma. This measure is useful in providing information about how effective the school system is in keeping students enrolled.

Status dropout rates provide cumulative data on dropouts within a specified age range. Status rates are higher than event rates as they include, for example, dropouts from last years tenth and eleventh grades as well as this year's dropouts. The status rate is valuable in revealing the *extent* of the dropout rate in the population. This data is helpful in estimating what resources should be dedicated to education and training to help dropouts develop the necessary job training skills.

Cohort dropout rates provide a measure of what happens to a cohort of students over a period of time. Repeated measures of a cohort reveal how many students starting in a specific grade drop out over time. Such studies provide more background and contextual data on those who drop out than are available in other sources.

Indicators for Dropping Out

Nationally about 14 percent of potential high school graduates quit before graduation.[72] In considering the NCES report on status dropout rates for 1995, the most recent year for which figures are available, it confirms the findings of earlier studies that found that race and ethnicity are strongly associated with dropping out of school. The data shows that the status dropout level for Hispanics is definitely higher than for blacks or whites between the ages of 16 and 24, the gap between the rate for blacks and whites is closing. Twenty years ago black dropout rates were over 10 percent higher than for whites. Over the last twenty years the rates fell for both groups, but the smaller gap is the result of a more rapid rate of improvement for blacks than for whites.

During this same period the dropout rates for Hispanic youths has remained far above that of either whites or blacks at around 30 percent. In 1995 over half the Hispanic dropouts had not completed the tenth grade compared to 31 percent of white dropouts and 27 percent of black dropouts.[73] Why is the rate so high for Hispanics? Some Hispanics immigrate to the United States, enter the labor force, and never enter the school system. Among those who do enter the school system, dropout rates are often the result of language difficulties (32 percent for those speaking Spanish in the home versus 14 percent for those who speak English).[74]

Table 9-4 also highlights the significance of family income in explaining dropout rates. Young adult members of families in the lowest quintile are eight times more likely to be without a high school diploma than those from families with high incomes. Table

[72]*School Dropouts: Everybody's Problem* (Washington: The Institute for Educational Leadership, Inc., 1986), p. 1.
[73]U.S. Department of Education, NCES, 97-473, p. vi.
[74]Ibid., p. 15.

TABLE 9-4
STATUS DROPOUT RATES, AGES 16–24 BY SEX, RACE-ETHNICITY, INCOME, AND REGION: OCTOBER 1995

Characteristics	Status dropout rate	Percent of all dropouts	Percent of population
Sex			
Male	12.2	51.0	50.1
Female	11.7	49.0	49.9
Race-Ethnicity*			
White, non-Hispanic	8.6	48.7	67.9
Black, non-Hispanic	12.1	14.7	14.6
Hispanic	30.0	34.7	13.9
Family income**			
Bottom quintile	23.2	40.2	20.8
Middle income	11.5	54.4	56.7
Top quintile	2.9	5.4	22.5
Region			
Northeast	8.4	12.9	18.3
Midwest	8.9	17.6	23.7
South	14.2	42.8	35.9
West	14.6	26.8	22.0

*Due to relatively small sample sizes, American Indian/Alaskan Natives and Asian/Pacific Islanders are included in the total but are not shown separately.
**Low income is defined as the bottom 20 percent of all family incomes for 1994; middle income is between 20 and 80 percent of all family incomes; and high income is the top 20 percent of all family incomes.
Source: U.S. Department of Education, NCES, *Dropout Rates,* p. 14.

TABLE 9-5
STATUS DROPOUT RATE, AGES 16–24, BY INCOME AND RACE-ETHNICITY: OCTOBER 1995

Family income	Total	White non-Hispanic	Black non-Hispanic	Hispanic
Total	12.0	8.6	12.1	30.0
Family Income				
Bottom quintile	23.2	18.6	20.1	38.9
Middle income	11.5	8.8	8.7	28.2
Top quintile	2.9	2.6	3.2	8.7

Source: U.S. Dept. of Education, NCES, 97-473, p. 16.

9-5 compares racial group, income, and dropout rate and demonstrates that the higher the income status the lower the dropout rate. At each income level there is no significant difference between white and black dropout rates. About 97 percent of children from families in the top quintile complete high school, compared with about 73 percent from those in the bottom quintile.

The dropout pattern for Hispanics is consistent with the dropout pattern for blacks and whites throughout the income scales. But since it remains at a higher level at each point, the higher dropout rate appears to be caused, at least in part, by other factors than income. Since 1981–82, dropout rates declined by over 40 percent overall, but the dropout rate for those in the bottom quintile remained virtually unchanged.

Growing up in poverty does not determine school failure. But when the difficulties of deprivation are not alleviated by the dedication of substantial resources and the commitment of concerned adults, it is extremely difficult to succeed. There is little help in many poor rural communities or in many inner-city schools. As Theodore Sizer, a former Dean of the Harvard School of Education, wrote:

> The hard fact is that if you are the child of low-income parents the chances are good that you will receive limited and often careless attention from adults in your high school. Most of this is realism that many Americans prefer to keep under the rug, of course; it is no easy task for the poor in America to break out . . . of their economic condition. But a change of status that is a matter of moderately poor odds becomes impossible when there is little encouragement to try.[75]

Because the dropout problem is concentrated in certain urban centers and rural pockets, it is practically invisible to most of society and therefore ignored. In fact there is a real reason for concern that while upgrading standards may encourage many students to work harder, the higher standards will contribute to higher dropout rates for minority and disadvantaged students.[76]

Higher standards usually do not come with funding for remedial programs. Increasing the number of required courses and upgrading course content may result in teachers adding units to a course but allowing less time to aid students who are falling behind.[77] There are many programs with substantial funding to promote "excellence" in education, but few that take "equity" into account which may be essential in helping potential dropouts to remain in school.

Who Drops Out and Why

Students drop out of school for reasons that are largely unchanged over several decades. In a study entitled *High School and Beyond* conducted by the National Center for Education Statistics, researchers found that the most often cited reason for leaving school was poor academic performance. High-risk students frequently find school to be a hostile environment where they are confirmed as failures daily. School agendas prize uniformity, harmony, regulation, and intellectual competition. These behaviors are often especially difficult for high-risk students. Their rebellion against those behaviors leads to truancy, suspension, or other forms of misconduct within school. They were more

---

[75]Theodore B. Sizer, *Horace's Compromise: The Dilemma of the American High School* (Boston: Houghton Mifflin, 1984), pp. 36–37. Quoted in *Dropouts in America*, p. 3.

[76]A study completed in 1985 examined thirty-two state initiatives in education and found just ten programs focusing on disadvantaged or underachieving students. See MDC, Inc., *The States' Excellence in Education Commissions: Who's Looking Out for At-Risk Youth* (Chapel Hill, NC: 1985). Since that time, at least fifteen other states have initiated programs although new funding for such programs has been difficult.

[77]There is some concern that raising requirements to be eligible to participate in extracurricular activities, such as sports, drama, or band, to a "C" may take away an important incentive for some to stay in school. Most agree that no one benefits from watered down courses or an emphasis on extracurricular activities. Yet it must be recognized that at-risk students may need additional assistance to be encouraged to stay in school and meet the higher requirements.

likely to report that they were not popular with their classmates, were less likely to take part in extracurricular activities, and felt estranged from school life. Males who were older than average for their grade (they tend to have been retained in grade at least once) and racial and ethnic minorities (other than Asian Americans) were more likely to experience "disciplinary" problems and become dropouts. Dropouts by and large are capable of doing the academic work however. They are inclined to be underachievers as indicated in the *High School and Beyond* survey which found that their tested achievement was 7 to 12 percentiles higher than their grades.

A variety of programs have been developed to increase pupil retention. First, programs should address those school practices that discourage high-risk students and substitute practices and arrangements that encourage them to remain in school until graduation. Recommendations of several studies include the following.

1 Higher requirements should be accompanied with support for low-achieving students. Higher standards without additional assistance for those with lower aptitudes and achievement will reinforce their sense of failure and negative view of school.

2 Promotion policies. The dropout rate among students who have repeated a grade is more than double those who have not been held back. This connection begins as early as the first grade. Research shows that holding a child back a grade in elementary school is less cost effective than providing the special services the student needs to perform at the grade level. Several states are instituting standardized tests to determine competence for promotion and graduation. If such programs are implemented without remedial programs, they may simply divide "winners" and "losers" without identifying where help is needed. Retaining a student without remedial help is a form of punishment.

3 School and class size. The larger the school and classes, the more problems reported by both teachers and students with the quality of teaching. Teacher workloads are increased with overcrowded classrooms making it difficult to provide individual attention or provide remedial help in learning difficulties. Students experiencing problems in overcrowded classrooms find teachers less accessible, increasing the student's feeling of frustration and alienation with the activities of school. The greatest overcrowding occurs in poorer school districts where there is insufficient funding to provide extra classroom space or hire the additional teachers needed.

4 Lack of support for minorities. Many ethnic minority students, primarily Hispanic, suffer from attending schools that do not provide sufficient bilingual education. Few Hispanic children with limited English proficiency, even in areas where they make up the majority of the class, are placed in a bilingual program.

5 Work-study programs. Schools should develop programs to provide relevant work experiences for students who are faced with the necessity of helping to provide a family income.

The dropout phenomena is not new. However the predicament of those who drop out of school is exacerbated by an increasingly technological society. Policies to reduce the dropout rate must deal with several interrelated components of the problem. They include: (a) low academic achievement, (b) high truancy rates, (c) alienation from teachers and classmates, and (d) home factors that include economic pressures to work and low parental support for the student's academic success. Programs to deal with the problem will require the financial support necessary to provide for teachers and counselors to work with high-risk students and those needing remedial help to stay in or who return.[78]

FEDERAL POLICY IN ELEMENTARY AND SECONDARY EDUCATION

Unlike many other countries, the national government in the United States does not operate a school system, and therefore does not employ teachers or principals. Since the federal government's role in education is secondary to state and local governments' function, its ability to initiate policy is also necessarily constrained. State and local governments alone have the constitutional authority to decide whether teachers will receive merit pay or authorize choice plans.

The policy making problem is not insurmountable. However, policy cannot be directly mandated. By offering grants to states or school districts that adopt certain reforms, the national government can encourage progressive policies. For example, the government could make money available to states that adopt choice plans.

The federal government could also provide national standards and goals for achievement and provide assistance for innovative plans to meet those goals on an experimental basis. By requiring an acceptable means of measuring changes and effectiveness, and making the results public, it would encourage the adoption of effective programs. This task is made more difficult by the opposition of conservatives to anything except block grants.

POST-SECONDARY EDUCATION

The United States differs from most industrial nations in that it lacks an organized post-secondary education system for the student not intending to go to college. As Lester Thurow points out, other nations invest much more heavily in the postsecondary skills of the noncollege-bound. Britain, France, and Spain spend more than twice as much as the United States in this area, Germany spends over three times as much, and Sweden almost six times as much.[79]

In the United States, firms do not want to spend significant sums to educate their workers. They fear that employees will take their skills to other employers without training programs who could pay higher wages since they have avoided the cost of those programs. Local governments avoid postsecondary vocational training for the same reason. Students may take their skills to a different region of the country. Moreover, the higher taxes necessary to pay for such educational programs might encourage industry to relocate beyond the tax region and become a free rider on the better-trained work force. Community colleges come closest to providing the technical intermediate level training for high-level technicians and semi-professionals needed by a complex industrial society.[80]

---

[78]Strother, "Dropping Out," pp. 325–28. Also reproduced in Dougherty and Hammack, *Education & Society,* p. 256–63.

[79]Lester Thurow, *Head to Head,* 1992, p. 275.

[80]See Arthur M. Cohen and Florence B. Brawer, *The American Community College* (San Francisco: Jossey-Bass, 1982).

According to Thurow, the problem in the United States is that there are too many people in college and not enough qualified workers. With high school graduation rates (approximately 86 percent in the United States versus 94 percent in Japan and 91 percent in Germany), the United States' labor force is undereducated and less competent than the labor forces in Japan and Germany.[81]

Those who graduate from American colleges make up the gap in education. However, first-rate economies require not only first-rate college graduates, but also very competent and skilled technical workers. The skills of the workers in the bottom half of the population affect the wages of the top half. If workers cannot staff the production and service processes competently to operate an efficiently producing society, the management and professional jobs that go with those processes also disappear.[82]

CONCLUSION

1 There is widespread evidence that the quality of elementary and secondary education in the United States is lagging behind that of many other countries. The system is not performing adequately in terms of educational output as measured through standardized international achievement tests.

2 The United States is atypical in that education is primarily a state and local policy issue. Constitutionally, states are responsible for educational systems. The federal government's ability to influence policy is primarily through the carrot of financial assistance. The result is that education policy has never been a major aspect of national policy. It is frequently a matter of symbolic politics. As recently as 1980, Ronald Reagan campaigned on the platform of abolishing the Department of Education since education was not a question for national policy.

3 In 1993 Congress passed and President Clinton signed into law the *Goals 2000: Educate America Act* which provides for national Education Policy Goals of raising educational standards in mathematics, science, and reading. It also set a requirement of being able to measure whether or not the policy was achieving those goals through the creation of national standards. Conservative opposition quickly forced a reconsideration of national standards. The act also set a goal of increasing the secondary school completion rate to 90 percent.

4 There are several theories regarding the benefits of education. Functionalism stresses that education prepares individuals for various positions in the job market. Other theories contend that education should promote equality, but the system in fact reinforces social stratification. Human capital theory is one of the major justifications for government intervention and for treating education as a quasi-public good.

5 Recent studies to improve the quality of education have focused on the factors that affect learning. Student-centered and school-centered factors are both involved in the learning process. School-centered approaches are the primary interest of "effective-schools" research. This research suggests that decentralized systems that encourage market competition are strongly correlated with effectiveness in educational achievement.

---

[81]Thurow, *Head to Head,* p. 159.
[82]Thurow, *Head to Head,* p. 55.

6 No one proposal can be expected to resolve all the problems connected with American education. The evolution of the educational system in the United States occurred long after the drafting of the Constitution. As a result, education has been primarily a state and local responsibility. This is decidedly unlike many other countries where education is a function of the national government based upon their more recently drafted constitutions. Countries noted for educational excellence, such as Japan, have strongly centralized ministries of education that set national standards. West Germany and Britain are exceptions. West Germany vests its Lander (or states) with educational authority in a manner similar to the arrangement in the United States, while Britain gives its Local Educational Authorities considerable autonomy. A strongly centralized system will not work in the United States since state and local governments are jealous of their authority over education.

7 There are almost 16,000 school districts in the United States, none of which uniformly turns out students that outperform foreign students in their educational systems. The system of school choice might introduce an element of market competition among American schools that would make them more effective. But choice should be accompanied by the national standards to be met on achievement tests. Since national standards are opposed by conservatives who fear "federal" influence, the alternative may have to be standards determined by disciplines. One example is the history standards developed by the National Center for History in the Schools.

8 High school dropout rates are reflective of serious social stratification problems in the society and a need for remedial assistance to encourage greater equality of educational opportunity. Meaningful vocational programs should also be added to many school programs.

QUESTIONS FOR DISCUSSION

1 Do you think the economy grows because of its investment in human resources, or does it invest in education because it is growing and can afford it?

2 Explain the concept of "human capital investment." In what ways can education and training be considered investment? In what ways can they be considered consumption?

3 How can we measure the return on human capital investment?

4 Is there any reason to believe that Americans are becoming overeducated? What criteria would you use to decide?

5 What aspects of education seem to be more consistent with the market-signaling view of education than with the human capital view?

6 What are the considerations regarding parental choice and equal opportunity? Should the use of vouchers extend to permit parents to choose the type of education for their children?

7 What steps would be necessary to improve the performance of U.S. elementary and secondary students to the level of their counterparts in other countries?

KEY CONCEPTS

choice	*Goals 2000*
class conflict model	human capital theory
Coleman report	magnet schools
effective schools	market signaling
functionalism	meritocracy

national standards
pure public good
quasi-public goods
Scholastic Assessment Test
school-centered theories

student-centered theories
tuition tax credits
underemployment
voucher plans

SUGGESTED READINGS

Clifford Adelman, (ed.), *Assessment in American Higher Education: Issues and Contexts* (Washington, D.C.: Government Printing Office, 1986).

K. L. Alexander and A. M. Pallas, "Curriculum Reform and School Performance: An Evaluation of the 'New Basics.'" *American Journal of Education,* 92 (1984), 391–420.

Arthur N. Applebee, Judith A. Langer, and Ina V. Mullis, *Crossroads in American Education: A Summary of Findings* (Princeton, NJ: Educational Testing Service, 1989).

S. Bowles and H. Gintis, *Schooling in Capitalist America* (New York: Basic Books, 1976).

Ernest L. Boyer, *High School: A Report on Secondary Education in America* (Washington, DC: Carnegie Foundation, 1983).

John E. Chubb, "Why the Current Wave of School Reform Will Fail," *The Public Interest,* 90 (Winter 1988), 28–49.

John E. Chubb and Terry M. Moe, *Politics, Markets & America's Schools* (Washington, DC: The Brookings Institution, 1990).

John E. Chubb and Terry M. Moe, "Politics, Markets, and the Organization of Schools," *The American Political Science Review,* 82 (December 1988), 1065–87.

David K. Cohen and Eleanor Farrar, "Power to the Parents?—The Story of Education Vouchers," in Nathan Glazer (ed.), *The Public Interest on Education* (Cambridge, MA: Abt Associates, 1984).

James S. Coleman, Ernest Campbell, Carol J. Hobson, James McPartland, Frederic D. Weinfeld, and Robert L. York, *Equality of Educational Opportunity* (Washington, DC: Government Printing Office, 1966).

James S. Coleman, Thomas Hoffer, and Sally Kilgore, *High School Achievement: Public, Catholic, and Private Schools Compared* (New York: Basic Books, 1982).

James S. Coleman, Thomas Hoffer, and Sally Kilgore, *Public and Private Schools* (Washington DC: National Center for Education Statistics, 1981).

Randall Collins, "Some Comparative Principles of Educational Stratification," 47 *Harvard Educational Review,* vol. 47 (1977), pp. 1–27.

Richard Freeman, *The Overeducated American* (New York: Academic Press, 1976).

Eileen Gardner, (ed.), *A New Agenda for Education* (Washington, DC: Heritage Foundation, 1985).

Arthur R. Jensen, "How Much Can We Boost I.Q. and Scholastic Achievement?" 39 *Harvard Educational Review,* vol. 39 (1969), pp. 1–123.

Stephanie Kasen, Patricia Cohen, and Judith S. Brook, "Adolescent School Experiences and Dropout, Adolescent Pregnancy, and Young Adult Deviant Behavior," *Journal of Adolescent Research,* vol. 13, no. 1, pp. 49–72.

Caroline H. Persell, *Education and Inequality* (New York: Free Press, 1977).

Theodore W. Schultz, "Investment in Human Capital," *American Economic Review* (March 1961), 1–17.

Lester Thurow, *Investment in Human Capital* (Belmont, CA: Wadsworth 1970).

U.S. Department of Education, National Center for Education Statistics, *Dropout Rates in the United States,* NCES 97-473, by Marilyn McMillen, project officer. Washington DC: 1997.

Paul Willis, *Learning to Labour* (New York: Schocken, 1977).

10

HEALTH CARE: DIAGNOSING A CHRONIC PROBLEM

Health expenditures in the United States continue to outpace inflation. Rising from less than 6 percent of GDP in 1960 to more than 14 percent today, they continue to grow faster than the Consumer Price Index (CPI). Many policy analysts believe that these expenditures are rising at a rate that is unsustainable. Health care in the United States has been absorbing an ever larger share of the Gross Domestic Product. However, while many Americans have comprehensive health insurance coverage ensuring access to the best medical care in the world, over 44 million, about 17 percent, have no health insurance coverage. Millions more have such limited coverage that a serious illness would leave them economically impoverished. Many are afraid to seek proper health care for fear of losing their coverage. The rising cost of health care has made affordability, once a concern primarily of lower-income households, an increasing middle-class worry. The rising cost of medical care has been cited by various pollsters as of greater concern to the public than any other issue. Two major problems in health care confronting policy makers are: the excessive **increase in costs** and the growing gap in **access** to health care. Not surprisingly a very high percentage of the population believes the American health care system is in need of fundamental reform.

This chapter provides an overview of the ideological debate that has taken place over the last four decades concerning health care. It begins with a history of health care in the United States and how it has fallen short of public expectations. This is followed by some comparative data with health care delivery in other countries. We then discuss some broadly defined choices facing the American society and Congress regarding health care, and what policy analysis has to say about the economic effects of these choices and the implications for American public philosophy.

INTRODUCTION: THE GROWING CONSENSUS ON THE NEED FOR CHANGE

As we approach the turn of the century, escalating health care costs are forcing every industrialized nation to consider reforms of their health care system. The foundation for the first national health care program was put in place in 1883 by Bismarck, the first chancellor of the modern German state. However, as recently as a little more than 100 years ago in America, health care was a relatively minor concern in most people's lives. When people became ill, they hoped that their body's natural defenses along with bed rest and home remedies would improve their condition. Usually the individual would get better without a physician's intervention. But not always! In either case, medical care was not usually much help. There were few standards regarding medical education in America. The early 1900s saw a medical revolution driven by the widespread application of scientific theory and principles in medical care. The **Flexner Report** of 1910 was very critical of the quality of medical education at the time and encouraged strict standards of education as a requirement to become a certified practitioner of medicine. The American Medical Association (AMA) effectively closed down inferior medical schools while improving the economic status of physicians by limiting the number of physicians produced. Many practitioners in the early part of this century still saw themselves as professionals who provided care to everyone without regard to ability to pay. Hospitals were often run by religious or charitable organizations and charged fees to those who could pay, but provided care to everyone despite financial ability.

Proposals for a publicly financed universal health care system in America were made before World War I but garnered little support. Although private health insurance was introduced in the early part of the twentieth century, it was not until the emergence of Blue Cross in the 1930s, that health care began to change. Before then very few Americans had prepaid health insurance that covered hospital or doctors' bills. In the 1930s and 1940s, labor unions, strengthened by New Deal legislation, pressed for higher wages *and* fringe benefits. President Franklin D. Roosevelt considered adding medical care to the Social Security legislation in 1935 because so many poor and unemployed during the Great Depression had no secure access to health care. Blue Cross developed a vigorous campaign to persuade the middle class that the availability of private insurance made national health insurance unnecessary and even illegitimate in that private, not public programs, were the American way. Roosevelt decided that adding health care to legislation already deemed radical by opponents would destroy his chances for passage of Social Security by Congress.

The situation changed rapidly during World War II when unemployment virtually disappeared. Companies were not allowed to raid rival corporations' workers by offering higher pay because strict wage controls to fight inflation were in effect. However the tax code, after energetic lobbying efforts by a growing insurance industry and labor unions, allowed employers to claim the cost of health insurance as a tax-deductible business expense. Insurance premiums were not counted as wages or taxable income to workers. This approach allowed companies to increase workers' incomes without raising wages per se.

After the war, the lack of medical insurance coverage was seen as a problem primarily of the poor and the elderly. President Truman made coverage of those groups and workers without employment-related health insurance, a National Health Insurance (NHI) goal of his administration. His program was defeated, largely because of opposition by the American Medical Association (AMA). However, Truman's efforts did get health care on the public policy agenda.

Employer-based health insurance grew rapidly in the decade after World War II and provided a ready supply of cash to finance developments in medical care. Union contracts negotiated with large corporations included health benefits; nonunion employers soon followed suit as workers increasingly came to expect such benefits subsidized by their employers. Almost every major company provided health benefits to their employees as a standard fringe benefit by the end of the 1950s. Initially the expense was not a major cost item for employers so the bill for health benefits was largely invisible.

The trend toward increasing health care coverage through work-related insurance continued until the 1980s. This arrangement resulted in health insurance companies becoming a **third-party payer** for the insured workers. **The recipient of the health care services usually had only a minor deductible or co-payment to pay, and the insurance company became the major payer for the health care.**

Insurance companies as third-party payers became the dominant form of reimbursement for health services and had a profound effect on health care delivery in the United States. The practice of medicine became a business and priorities were adapted to the new approach. Instead of treating health problems first and thinking of payment second, the filling out of insurance forms came first and providing care came second. The family doctor in solo practice who provided health care became part of a health care professional group with a receptionist, nurse, and various technicians and administrative personnel.

HEALTH CARE AND THE DEVELOPMENT OF IMPERFECT MARKETS

Separating the health care consumer from the payer may lead to an increased demand for health care services. A physician's willingness to supply those services and then bill the insurance company leads to the problem shown in a simple supply/demand curve (fig. 10-1).

In this **imperfect market,** health care costs are rising more rapidly than the cost of other goods and services. Since insured patients often do not experience out-of-pocket expenses at the time of care, they tend to request any medical service that provides any benefit at all. Physicians and hospitals typically receive payment retrospectively after submitting bills based upon the treatment provided to an insurer known as a third-party payer. These "fee-for-service" charges are usually paid as long as they are considered "customary, prevailing, and reasonable" by the insurance company. Insurers now complain that physicians are rewarded in a **fee-for-service** system for providing more medical care than is optimal from a cost-benefit perspective. The more treatment that uses sophisticated diagnostic techniques—magnetic resonance imaging (MRI), for example—or new methods of treatment, the higher the payments tend to be to the providers. In this system, patients and physicians both have incentives to demand health care that provides any aid at all without regard to the cost to any third-party payer. Many studies

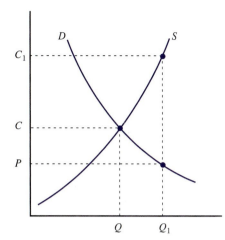

FIGURE 10-1
IMPLICATIONS OF THIRD-PARTY PAYER ON DEMAND FOR HEALTH CARE.
In a user-pay approach, the consumer would choose the quantity (Q) of health care at cost (C). In a third-party payer system the user can buy more health care (Q_1) at a lower price (P) because of his low deductible or co-payment, while the third party's payment provides the necessary reimbursement to supply the higher quantity of health care (Q_1) at a higher cost (C_1) than in a user-pay system.

have supported the conclusion that many procedures prescribed by physicians are unnecessary.[1] Without spending limits, patients do not face budget constraints when consuming health care, as they do when purchasing other goods.[2] Physicians in turn do not worry about the costs because insurance companies, not the patient, are paying. This leads to resources being diverted from developing new drugs, diagnostic equipment, and other means of increasing patient services. Under this system the pay of health care providers, especially physicians' incomes, increased in both relative and absolute terms when compared with the population as a whole.

Health care does not meet the requirements of free market competition since restrictions have been placed on entry into the medical field. The need for medical resources is potentially unlimited, but the supply of those resources is not. In a market-driven system there are not enough providers or money to give care to everyone. The American Medical Association, backed by state regulation, allocates the right to perform health care services among a variety of medical professionals, reserving the most important and well-paying responsibilities for physicians. In the name of protecting the public, but also protecting the privileged position of its own members, the AMA has restricted access to medical accreditation through the regulation of the medical education process, testing and licensing procedures, and other requirements. Graduates of medical school have to complete longer residency requirements ranging from three to seven years depending on the specialty the resident wishes to enter. These longer residency programs lead many to feel that after such a significant financial investment and the monumental time commitment to enter their field, they deserve to be handsomely rewarded.

Health care is increasingly seen by practitioners as similar to any other business activity. Those with adequate insurance receive whatever care they need and are not significantly affected by rising costs. To keep costs low, insurance companies make it

[1]See John Wennberg, "Outcomes Research, Cost Containment, and the Fear of Health Care Rationing," *New England Journal of Medicine,* vol. 323 (October 25, 1990), pp. 1202–4.

[2]Henry J. Aaron, "Health Care Financing," in Henry J. Aaron and Charles L. Schultze (eds.), *Setting Domestic Priorities* (Washington, DC: The Brookings Institution, 1992), p. 25.

HEALTH CARE AND MORAL HAZARDS

A **moral hazard** refers to the reduced incentive of policyholders to protect themselves from what they are insured against. It is yet another example of a *market imperfection*.

A moral hazard is the increased probability for an insured party to change his/her behavior after a contract is made at the expense of the insuring party because that behavior is now protected.

For example, an individual *un*insured against the hazard of theft would personally sustain any financial loss resulting from burglary. Since the individual bears the entire financial risk, she has a significant incentive to take precautions against theft by installing and using window and door locks or installing burglar alarms. However, when an individual buys an insurance policy that protects against theft, the incentive to take precautions is significantly reduced. The fewer precautions the homeowner takes to prevent theft, the greater the chance of theft, and ultimately the liability of the insurance company.

Insurance companies try to reduce the problem of moral hazard by requiring a policyholder to share some costs of any claim. Cost sharing generally takes two forms. **Deductibles** in health insurance generally require the purchaser to pay the initial medical charges up to some predetermined limit. So a health policy might not cover the first $250 of health care in a year. Many health insurance policies also require **co-payments** (or *coinsurance*). Under a co-payment arrangement, the insurance company pays for 75 or 80 percent of a physician's bills, and the policyholder pays the remaining 20 or 25 percent.

Moral hazards encourage higher health care expenditures than is medically warranted. Individuals have incentives to seek more care, including high-cost low-benefit care, when there is a third-party payer. Retrospective billing that cannot be determined until after a hospital and physician have provided the services and have reported the costs to the patient, the insurance company or Medicare, encourages the use of more services than medically indicated.

Part of what is claimed to be a moral-hazard contribution to rising health care costs is a subjective judgment, however. A jogger, with insurance, who falls and twists an ankle while running may have X rays taken to determine if there is a fracture. Without insurance, the person may hope it is just a sprain that will heal in a few days by giving the ankle rest. Whether seeking medical attention in such a situation is excessive or not is unclear. It is also unlikely that possessing health insurance would increase one's incentive to take risks that might lead to cancer. Also, a cancer patient who receives large insurance payments is still less fortunate than healthy people who do not. Consider an individual spending a week at a resort hotel, and another spending a week in a hospital recovering from major surgery. The patient will have more resources devoted to his or her well-being; however, we would all prefer to spend a week at the resort hotel and forgo the need to have the same medical services devoted to our welfare.

Finally, the concern with the insured patient as the focal point of a moral hazard is misplaced. The major choice made by the patient is typically that of the physician. After that choice, the physician acts as the patient's agent and decides what diagnostic tests to run, which medical procedures are appropriate, which hospital to use, and what the follow-up procedures will be.

expensive and difficult for those most needy of health care services to get insurance. The health needs of the uninsured promptly exceed the ability of humanitarian caregivers to supply them. And rising health care costs mean that almost any health care is prohibitively expensive for the uninsured. Some in the health care industry are still committed to the notion of providing health care to all who need it despite their ability to pay. The system tries to meet the need by **cost shifting,** or spreading out the cost for caring for the poor and uninsured by increasing the charges to those with insurance. The result drives up health care costs for providers, employers, and insurance companies, and creates a larger division between the haves and the have nots in health care coverage. This commitment creates tremendous strains in the health care system in America.

THE INTRODUCTION OF MEDICARE AND MEDICAID

Progressives and labor unions had proposed compulsory national health insurance since shortly after the turn of the century, but were always overwhelmed by the combined opposition of business and the medical profession. The Johnson administration placed the policy goal of getting the federal government to accept responsibility for paying the health care costs of the "have nots"—the poor and the elderly through Medicaid and Medicare at the top of the "Great Society" agenda. The poor could not afford health insurance and not infrequently their physical condition would have precluded their coverage in any event. Since most insurance was employment based, retirees found that advancing age made them ineligible for private insurance coverage or it was prohibitively expensive. This at a time when they were most in need of health insurance. The legislation was passed by an overwhelmingly Democratic Congress in 1965 over the opposition of the medical profession.

Medicare

Medicare, in contrast to Medicaid, is strictly a federal program, not related to income level. It is the largest federal health program, serving more than 30 million elderly and 3 million disabled Americans. The major requirement for access to Medicare is to have reached the age of 65, and to have worked in employment covered by Social Security or railroad retirement. It was designed to relieve the threat of financial ruin due to medical expenses among the elderly, although there are significant gaps in its coverage.

Congressional Budget Office (CBO) projections are that Medicare spending, including offsetting premiums, will increase from $187 billion in 1997 to $246 billion in 2002. The Balanced Budget Act of 1997 will slow the growth of Medicare spending, especially between 1997 and 2002. Nevertheless, Medicare's share of the federal budget is expected to increase from less than 12 percent in 1997 to 16 percent by 2008.[3] The law restrains the rate of increase in payments to fee-for-service providers and expands coverage of preventive services in the fee-for-service sector.

---

[3]Congressional Budget Office, *The Economic and Budget Outlook: Fiscal Years 1999–2008.* (Washington, DC: Government Printing Office, 1998), p. 123.

MEDICARE BENEFITS

Medicare consists of two separate programs, Parts A and B. It has three separate funding sources: general revenues, premiums paid by beneficiaries, and a payroll tax paid by workers and their employers. Part A, officially known as the Hospital Insurance (HI) program, pays all covered costs of hospital care, except a $736 deductible in 1996, for up to 60 days per illness. Medicare will pay for an additional 30 days, less a coinsurance payment ($184 per day in 1996). Part A helps pay for a semi-private room, meals, regular nursing services, rehabilitation services, drugs, medical supplies, laboratory tests and X rays, and most other medically necessary services and supplies. Medicare does not pay for personal convenience items such as a telephone or television, private duty nurses, or extra charges for a private room unless it is medically necessary.

Part A is financed by the HI portion of the Social Security payroll tax that is 1.45 percent of an employee's wage paid by both the employer and employee (2.90 total). When people speak of Medicare "going broke" they are usually referring to the status of the Part A Hospital Insurance Trust fund that the 1997 Trustees Report projects will go broke in 2001.

Everyone eligible for Part A and all Americans 65 or older can enroll in Part B, technically known as the Supplemental Medical Insurance (SMI). This coverage is available to individuals at a monthly premium ($46.20 in 1995). Beneficiaries' premiums originally covered about 50 percent of the program costs, but by 1995 premiums covered about 31 percent of costs— budget appropriations from general revenues pay for the remainder. Part B provides a great return for recipients, so about 98 percent of those eligible for Part A elect coverage under Part B. Between 1992 and 1997, Medicare Part B grew 14 percent faster than the economy. "Bankruptcy" is not an issue with Medicare Part B because any gap between expenditures and the income from beneficiary premiums is paid out of general revenues. The annual subsidy in Medicare Part B in 1997 was about $1,620 per beneficiary. The annual taxpayer subsidy was $52 billion in 1996 and is expected to grow to $89 billion by 2001. The projected depletion of the trust fund for Part A and the increasing cost to taxpayers of Part B led the Public Trustees to warn in their 1997 report that Medicare cannot stay exactly as it is and it is misleading to think that any part of the program—beneficiary premiums, provider payments, controls on use, covered services or revenues—can be exempt from change.

Medicare Part B picks up where Part A leaves off. It pays for a wide range of medical services and supplies, but perhaps most important for recipients, it helps pay doctor bills. It covers 80 percent of allowed physician's fees after an annual $100 deductible has been met. This coinsurance share of the bill may be more than the 20 percent of the Medicare-approved amount. For example, a patient is responsible for paying 20 percent of whatever a hospital charges, not 20 percent of a Medicare-approved amount. It also helps pay for: outpatient hospital services, physical and occupational therapy, home health care, durable medical equipment such as wheelchairs, hospital beds, and oxygen equipment prescribed by a doctor for home use.

Changes made by the Balanced Budget Act have blurred the distinction between Part A and Part B. A more useful distinction today is that between payments for Medicare enrollees in group plans and payments for enrollees in the fee-for-service sector. The

Balanced Budget Act expands the number of risk-based plans (essentially Health Maintenance Organizations). More health service options for medicare recipients became available in late 1998. CBO projections are that risk-based plans will grow from 14 percent of Medicare enrollees in 1998 to 38 percent in 2008.

Medicaid

Medicaid was designed, when enacted in 1965, to be a health insurance program financed jointly by the federal government and the states providing basic medical care for the poor. In fact, though it is the dominant public program financing health care service for the poor, it covered only 45 percent of the poor and near-poor in 1996. To qualify for Medicaid assistance, one must first become eligible for welfare support in the **state of residence.** It does not cover all of the poor because in addition to being poor one has to meet other criteria such as receipt of Supplemental Security Income (SSI) benefits, eligibility for public assistance, or membership in particular demographic groups (such as low-income children or pregnant women). Since **states** administer the Medicaid, they determine who is eligible to participate in this program created by the **national** government.

Participating states in the program are obligated to provide a certain federally mandated minimum package of services to recipients. Other options are provided only at state discretion. Within the federal government mandates, states have a good deal of flexibility to establish their own income levels for eligibility and benefit packages. And within states, Medicaid spending can vary significantly by the beneficiary group. States that meet federal eligibility requirements receive matching payments from the federal government based upon the state's per capita income. The federal government's contribution to the states' programs ranges from an 80 percent subsidy for the poorest states to only 50 percent for the most affluent states. Accordingly there are large variations in coverage and expenditures between states. In 1994 for example, the total per capita Medicaid expenditures varied from a high of more than $4,800 per low-income person in the most generous state to a low of less than $1,000. The states with the highest per capita expenditures tend to have the lowest federal match of Medicaid funds because they tend to be the richest states.[4]

In recent years, many states have expanded Medicaid coverage to groups like poor children and pregnant women who do not otherwise qualify for cash assistance though they have low incomes. The recently enacted **Temporary Assistance to Needy Families** (TANF) program which replaces AFDC, keeps the eligibility rules for Medicaid essentially unchanged. TANF work requirements and the limited duration to receive those funds may reduce Medicaid participation rates.

Children account for half of all individuals covered by Medicaid. Adults in families with children covered by Medicaid account for another 23 percent of Medicaid enrollment. Nevertheless, among poor children, 3.4 million (23.3 percent) were uninsured in 1996, almost twice the 12.7 percent of children above the poverty line. Health insurance

---

[4]David Liska, *Medicaid: Overview of a Complex Program,* The Urban Institute, Series A, No. A-8, May 1997.

coverage for persons under 18 differs sharply from the other most vulnerable group, the elderly. Largely because of Medicare, only 1.1 percent of the elderly are without health insurance, compared with 14.8 of Americans under 18 years of age.[5]

The Impact of Medicare and Medicaid   Although some doctors spoke of boycotting Medicare, they quickly realized that it was a windfall that guaranteed payment that many physicians had provided earlier by cost-shifting for reduced fees. Medicare and Medicaid greatly increased access to health care for the elderly and the poor. Medicare was the first occasion in which the government underwrote health care for a significant segment of the American population. However, by defining health care as a right due only to the elderly, and not all citizens, it has set back the movement for national health insurance.[6] Literally, the most explosive problem in Medicare is the "time bomb" that will begin to go off after about 2005 as baby boomers reach age 65. The ranks of Medicare beneficiaries will increase rapidly adding pressure to the federal budget, though at first, baby boomers will add relatively young and healthy recruits to Medicare. The relative low cost of the new enrollees will offset some of the financial impact of their numbers for several years.

Medicare HMOs are a major growth sector in the health care industry. Medicare enrollees who join, turn their Medicare eligibility over to an **HMO,** which covers the out-of-pocket expenses that Medicare does not cover. These programs have led to even more cost-shifting and dividing of the health care market. The increase in the demand for medical care by the disabled and the elderly under Medicare and the poor under Medicaid, has helped drive up the price of health insurance. Companies increasingly resist higher insurance premiums for their workers. And more and more corporations have reduced or dropped their insurance coverage altogether.

The government has tried to limit the cost of the care it supplied through Medicare and Medicaid, by limiting the quantity of care it will supply while making enrollee's liable for a higher percentage of the cost. A three-tier system of health care coverage has evolved that is rather unique to the United States, in which those who are fully insured have excellent medical care available to them, those under Medicare and Medicaid have more limited health care available to them, and increasing numbers of the uninsured receive the most limited health care.

RECENT STEPS TOWARD COST CONTROL

The health care system in America really consists of separate markets. The system has responded to the "haves" whose well-funded insurance plans encouraged demand for new and expensive technological developments in health care. Critics of the current system claim that exempting health insurance premiums paid by employers from taxable income creates an incentive for many individuals to be **over-insured.** If employer-paid health insurance premiums were taxed like regular income, their argument goes, the

---

[5]Robert Bennefield, *Children Without Health Insurance,* Census Brief, CENBR/98-1, Issued March 1998.
[6]See David Rothman, *Beginnings Count: The Technological Imperative in American Health Care* (New York: Oxford University Press, 1998).

government would take in about $45 billion in additional taxes each year. In the view of these critics, since insurance pays most medical bills, many individuals have no incentive to ask questions about the cost of their health care or to compare the costs of different alternatives. Insured patients rarely pressure doctors to consider costs when ordering tests or providing treatments.

During the 1960s, health care expenditures grew at twice the rate of inflation. This, coupled with increased competition from abroad in the 1970s, began to squeeze corporate profits. Thus, in the 1980s, continuing health care inflation and a weakening economy resulted in increased pressure to contain medical costs. The first reaction of employers was to shift health care costs to employees by increasing the worker's share of health insurance premiums, deductibles, and co-payments.[7] A number of employers, particularly smaller ones, have also reduced coverage or elected not to insure employees at all.[8] Increasingly, employers are reducing their health care cost burden by subsidizing only their employees' insurance and requiring the workers to pay the entire premiums for dependents if they want insurance for them. This **cost sharing** is often justified as a **cost containment** effort by companies on the theory that, by making employees bear a larger portion of medical costs, they will demand less low-benefit health care. This reduction in demand in turn is supposed to put a downward pressure on health care prices. In reality such **cost shifting** has reduced access to health care for **underinsured** employees.

The average amount of time workers must wait before qualifying for health benefits at a new employer has increased to fifty-seven days.[9] Until recently, new employees were usually not covered for **preexisting medical conditions** such as cardiovascular diseases, cancer, diabetes, asthma, or any condition requiring ongoing treatment. Many individuals were forced to stay in a job rather than take another position that was more desirable because of "preexisting medical conditions" that would not be covered in a new insurance plan. President Clinton sponsored the **Health Insurance Portability and Accountability Act** passed by Congress in 1996 that prohibited employers from refusing to cover preexisting conditions for new employees who had been covered elsewhere within sixty-three days of starting the new job. Many workers who have insurance are in fact "uninsured" for conditions known to require health care expenditures. And many insured workers face the problem of employers and insurers altering the type or amount of coverage under policies already in force.

There are more than 1,500 health insurance companies in the United States, each of which offers several distinct plans. Many companies offer their employees several

---

[7]Thomas Bodenheimer and Kip Sullivan, "How Large Employers Are Shaping the Health Care Marketplace," *The New England Journal of Medicine,* Health Policy Report, vol. 338, no. 14, April 2, 1998, p. 1003.

[8]One study found that the number of employers who paid the full premiums for their workers dropped from 61 percent in 1985 to 45 percent in 1991. For family coverage, the number dropped from 36 percent in 1985 to 23 percent in 1991. See *Hay/Huggins Benefit Report: Annual Survey of 1000 or More Employers* (Philadelphia: Hay Huggins, 1985, 1991). Cited in Aaron, "Health Care Financing," p. 29. See also Bodenheimer and Sullivan, "How Large Employers," p. 1003.

[9]David Hilzenrath, "Employee Health Benefit Costs Rising Modestly, Survey Shows," *The Washington Post,* 16 June 1998, p. C3.

insurance plans and require them to choose among those offered. In addition to all the health insurance companies, each of the fifty states and several federal agencies also pay health care bills. The costs of conforming to the different reimbursement procedures and filling out the diversity of forms involved contributes significantly to the growing administrative portion of total health care expenditures. Physicians and hospitals must hire workers to respond to each insurer's unique set of claims forms, procedures, and billing codes. One reform that would reduce administrative costs would be to require all insurance firms and corporate payers to agree on a standardized set of claims forms and billing codes. Although estimates vary regarding precisely how much could be saved, there is general agreement that billions of dollars could be saved from the well over $100 billion now spent on administrative costs.

Community and Experience Rating

Blue Cross and Blue Shield plans, reflecting their origins as nonprofit entities, originally offered insurance based upon **"community rating."** This meant that different employee groups were charged the same rates, based on the average cost of health care for broad groups of people, despite the age or the health experience of a particular firm's work force. Profit-oriented insurance firms, confronting intense competitive pressure to lower costs and boost profits, began to offer policies at lower costs than Blue Cross and Blue Shield based upon **experience rating. Experience rating provides for different insurance rates based upon the predicted average health care costs of a particular company's labor force.** This saves money for employers with younger workers and for workers in certain occupations and industries. However it raises premiums and cost sharing for workers in higher-risk occupations and for companies with older workers and more retirees.

The market implications are clear. Every insurance company feels pressure to offer insurance based upon experience rating or be driven out of business. The impact on those who seek insurance is equally unavoidable. Workers in certain high-risk industries or occupations can obtain insurance, if at all, only by paying rates several times higher than those paid by workers in low-risk industries or jobs.

Competitive health insurance markets inevitably lead to efforts to shift costs to consumers. The result may be positive when, for example, private insurers use the incentive of experience rating to reward positive behavior such as offering nonsmokers lower insurance rates. But incentives for reducing costs overall may reduce the ability of insurance to provide as broad a coverage in the future as it has in the past.

The problem of uncertainty in health insurance coverage produced by competition is affecting large groups of insured people. One strategy used by insurance companies is to significantly raise their rates each year for current subscribers. At the same time, the companies invite all their policyholders to reapply for a low rate offered to new subscribers. Those discovered during the previous period of coverage to have significant illnesses or preexisting conditions are turned down for the new insurance when they apply. They are forced to stay with their old policies and their rapidly escalating rates. This allows insurers to escalate premiums for those who have illnesses to unaffordable levels within a few years. Such underwriting procedures sort out the healthier clients from those with health problems.[10] People fear that if they disclose every little medical occurrence, they will be refused coverage. However, they also fear that if they do not disclose a medical problem and subsequently make a substantial claim, they may be denied coverage for failing to provide a full disclosure of their medical history.

If there is evidence that a medical condition is going to cost an insurance company money, it does not have to provide coverage for it. The insurance industry defends high premiums, waiting periods, condition-specific payment denials, and denial of coverage to people with preexisting conditions as necessary to protect companies from the moral hazard of people who only want to pay for insurance when they need it. The practices are actuarially sound and permit more affordable rates for other employers and employees. Many workers agree, and contend that they cannot afford to subsidize others. This approach by definition, however, is at variance with the idea of insurance as a way to spread risk. Competition in the insurance market now means insurance companies search for ways to avoid risks rather than for ways to share them. Employer-based coverage has become insecure and insured workers face the threat that their coverage will dissolve when they need it most.

Insurance companies prefer to insure those who are the least likely to have health care claims. Many insurance companies have resorted to occupational blacklisting to avoid high-risk employees. Among blacklisted occupations, for example, are gas station attendants, taxi drivers, security guards, and those working for liquor and grocery stores because of the increased likelihood of injuries due to robberies. Florists and hairdressers are often blacklisted because insurers insist the higher proportion of gays working in these job categories means an increased likelihood of AIDS. Health care workers including doctors, dentists, and nurses are sometimes blacklisted because it is claimed that they have a high rate of health care use because of their special medical knowledge.[11] Other occupations such as logging, commercial fishing, and construction are sometimes excluded because of the high risk of injury associated with them.

Experience rating is now moving from the work group to the individual level. Especially for small companies, insurers may exclude certain categories of individuals from coverage—for example, newborns with medical problems such as heart murmurs. Some states have begun to respond with laws to prevent certain types of exclusions.

In response to the rising costs of health insurance or its unavailability, many companies have become **self-insured,** which also relieves them of state insurance regulations. Under the federal **Employee Retirement Income Security Act (ERISA)** of 1974, passed to encourage the development of employer pension programs, companies may structure their own health plans if they act as their own insurers rather than using an insurance company. The law permits companies to hold funds needed for medical claims in company accounts, thereby permitting them to realize investment income from those

---

[10]Paul Cotton, "Preexisting Conditions 'Hold Americans Hostage' to Employers and Insurance," *JAMA,* vol. 265 (1991), p. 2451. The article pointed out that a survey of 2,000 employers who offered insurance in 1987 found 57 percent had preexisting condition clauses in the health policies they offered to workers. Although such clauses were more common with small employers (64 percent of firms with less than 500 employees), they were also common in large firms (45 percent of companies with more than 10,000 employees).

[11]Michael D. Reagan, *Curing the Crisis: Options for America's Health Care* (San Francisco: Westview Press, 1992), p. 49.

INSURANCE AND ADVERSE SELECTION

Recall that the moral-hazard problem occurs when one party to a contract engages in opportunistic behavior *after* a contract is made. In contrast, the adverse-selection problem arises *prior* to entering the contract. The adverse-selection problem occurs when a party enters a disadvantageous contract on the basis of incomplete or inaccurate information. This happens generally because the cost of obtaining the information makes it difficult to determine if the agreement is truly mutually beneficial. For example, an insurance company may not know the real intention or risk involved in the contract. In that case, the party with superior information may entice the other party into an inequitable contract. A contract is inequitable if either one of the contracting parties would not have entered into it if it had the same information as the other party.

One market response by insurers is to devise contracts to reveal the true risks of the parties involved. Insurers, especially of small companies, may refuse to insure a company until it supplies a health status profile of all its employees. If any of the employees or their dependents have a potentially costly illness, such as severe arthritis, those employees or their dependents may be excluded from the plan if state law permits. Or the insurer may raise rates to take any such conditions into account. The insurer may even deny a company insurance. Insurance companies include clauses that permit them to raise rates or cancel a company's insurance as experience indicates, usually on an annual basis. Deductibles, caps, and co-payments are efforts by insurance companies to prevent "excessive" demand for health care.

Sources: Mark J. Brown, "Evidence of Adverse Selection in the Individual Health Insurance Market," *The Journal of Risk & Insurance,* vol. 59, no. 1 (March 1992), p. 13; M. S. Marquis, "Adverse Selection with a Multiple Choice Among Health Insurance Plans: A Simulation Analysis," *Journal of Health Economics,* vol. 11, no. 2 (August 1992), p. 129.

funds and pay out benefits themselves rather than using an insurance company—they are exempt from all state taxes and regulations governing health insurance. The original purpose of the health section exemption was to allow companies with employees in several states to offer uniform health care coverage throughout those states. But companies soon discovered self-insuring was a way to avoid state laws mandating certain minimal coverage and to allow them to restructure health plans to reduce costs.[12] ERISA preempts the authority of the states to regulate self-insured employer health plans. Its impact has grown as more firms have self-insured for health benefits.

None of these measures slowed the inflation in health care. Employers' health care costs rose 18.6 percent in 1988, 16.7 percent in 1989, and 17.1 percent in 1990.[13] By 1989, employees' health insurance premiums represented 8.9 percent of wages, up from

[12]In the early 1970s, prior to ERISA, only 5 percent of American workers were covered by self-insured plans. That number grew to 66 percent by 1988. See General Accounting Office, *Health Insurance: Cost Increases Lead to Coverage Limitations and Cost Shifting* (GAO/HRD 90-68) (Washington, DC: Government Printing Office, May 1990), p. 21.

[13]Bodenheimer and Sullivan, "How Large Employers," p. 1004.

CASE STUDY

SELF-INSURANCE AND EMPLOYEE
VULNERABILITY

A case that made the national news concerned Joe McGann, an employee of the H & H Music Company of Houston for five years. In 1987 Joe developed AIDS. As the first of his medical bills began to trickle in, his employer decided to take advantage of ERISA and drop its commercial medical coverage and become self-insured. The company's self-insurance plan limited its coverage for AIDS—and only for AIDS—to a lifetime limit for each employee of $5,000. Joe McGann reached that limit in a few months. McGann died in 1991 at the age of 47. He was dependent for the last three years of his life on Medicaid and the charity of physicians. A lawsuit was filed to prohibit employers from singling out one disease or individual employees in cost-reduction moves. The broader concern was that any disease such as cancer could be singled out if an employee were stricken. H & H argued that it had the right to structure its benefits any way it chose in its self-interest.

Legal arguments on behalf of McGann did not challenge the right of a company to change its benefits in response to workforce conditions or economic circumstances, but claimed that, by focusing its cost-saving efforts on one individual, it had violated the anti-discrimination clause in the ERISA legislation. Neither the district court nor a federal appeals court found any violation by H & H. On appeal to the Supreme Court, the Bush administration instructed the Solicitor General to urge the Court not to hear the case, arguing that H & H was acting within its rights. In the end the lower court ruling was allowed to stand.

Another case illustrates the difficulty the courts have in reviewing ERISA cases. Florence Corcoran was in an employer-sponsored health plan using Blue Cross as administrator and United Health Care as the utilization reviewing agency. Mrs. Corcoran, who had a history of pregnancy-related problems became pregnant with what was viewed as a high-risk pregnancy. Although her obstetrician recommended (and another obstetrician concurred with a second opinion) hospitalization as the due date approached so that the fetus could be monitored, United Health Care overruled stating that hospitalization was not medically necessary. Instead limited in-home nursing care was authorized. When the nurse was not available, the fetus developed problems and died. The Court found that, under the ERISA law, the Corcorans had no remedy for damages. The Court expressed its frustration with cost containment features of the law and expressed a desire that Congress amend the law so that it would truly safeguard the interests of employees.

Sources: Corcoran v. United Health Care, Inc., 965 F.2d 1321 (5th Cir. 1992). Also testimony of Families USA Executive Director Ron Pollack before the Labor, Health and Human Services, Education and Related Agencies Subcommittee of the Senate Appropriations Committee re Current Problems with the Federal Employee Retirement Income Security Act of 1974 (ERISA), May 14, 1998.
Malcolm Gladwell, *The Washington Post,* 20 August 1992.

just 2.2 percent in 1965. This accelerated inflation from 1988 through 1990 dealt a severe blow to fee-for-service health insurance. Auto companies pointed out that health insurance accounted for about $700 of the average-priced American-made car compared to only $200 of the cost of a car made in Japan.

The Managed Care Revolution

A revolution has occurred in the U.S. health care system with breathtaking speed. In 1985 just 15 million Americans were enrolled in employer-sponsored HMOs. By 1996, 50 million Americans received their care through this system. And another 50 million were enrolled in **preferred provider organizations (PPOs).**[14] Authority was seized from physicians and hospitals by entrepreneurs hoping to maximize profits. When prepaid group health plans first began they were vigorously opposed by organized medicine that succeeded in getting laws passed in several states barring such consumer-controlled cooperatives.[15] Richard Nixon saw HMOs as an appealing alternative to liberal backed national health insurance plans. The Nixon administration repackaged prepaid group health care plans as HMOs, with federal legislation providing for endorsement, certification, and assistance.[16] More importantly the administration pushed a law through Congress—the Health Maintenance Organization Act of 1973—that provided $375 million over five years for grants and loans to help start HMOs, and required businesses with more than twenty-five employees to offer at least one HMO as an alternative to conventional insurance if one was available in the area. Today, organized medicine opposes the heavy-handedness of meddling by those outside the medical profession in pursuit of cost cutting.

The term **"managed care"** became the term of common currency in the late 1980s to refer to clinical practices in prepaid plans. It was meant to convey the idea that concern for patient welfare would be best served by professional management to ensure efficient, quality health care in the best interest of the patient in the competitive environment of corporate medicine. Now, only a decade later, many critics believe that managed care means "managed costs" to minimize health care resources spent on the patient and maximize profits for the employer and the insurer.

The dominant players have become those who pay the premiums (corporate management and government administrators). Organized medicine, usually vigilant to any threat to independence, did not realize the implications of managed care until too late. They are now caught between the pressure for cost control by HMOs which often put financial pressure on physicians to ration health care in a miserly fashion, and patients anxious about the quality of care.[17]

Large employers developed three strategies to control the cost of health care.

1 Channeling employees into managed care. Many large corporations in the early 1990s simply contracted with an HMO or a PPO and required all employees who wanted to be insured to join. Their employees were given no choice. In many large companies employees may be given a choice of health plans in which the employer pays a fixed amount per employee for health insurance. Employees typically receive a booklet during

---

[14]Ibid., p. 1004.

[15]W. Crowley, *To Serve the Greatest Number* (University of Washington Press, 1996).

[16]Robert Kuttner, "Must Good HMOs Go Bad? The Commercialization of Prepaid Group Health Care," *The New England Journal of Medicine,* Health Policy Report, vol. 338, no. 21 (May 21, 1998), p. 1558.

    Actually Paul Ellwood, a Minneapolis physician, met with officials from the Nixon administration to make his case for prepaid insurance and coined the phrase "health maintenance organizations" while making his case that a fee-for-service system penalized health providers who returned patients to health.

[17]Kuttner, "Must Good HMOs Go Bad?" p. 1558.

an open-enrollment period in which the health plan choices are listed. If an employee selects a higher cost plan, the company makes the same premium payment as for a lower cost plan, the employee must pay the difference through higher payroll deductions to receive the high-cost plan. Corporations are aware that employees are very sensitive to small differences in the cost of premiums.[18] Twenty-six percent of health plan enrollees switched to a cheaper plan when monthly premiums for their plan rose by only $10.[19] A recent survey found that 44 percent of all companies offered their workers only one health plan.[20] Approximately half of all large companies provide some choice for their employees while less than 10 percent of employees in small companies have choice.

2 Negotiating Strength Through Corporate Health Coalitions. A second strategy of employers to control health costs was to form coalitions with other corporations in a region to purchase health insurance. Some large employers in California discovered, when comparing premium costs with HMOs, that the same HMO charged different rates to different companies. The differentials could not be completely explained by age or gender differences or variances in the benefit package. They concluded that the different rates were primarily related to what the HMOs could negotiate with each corporation. In reaction to these findings, a joint purchasing alliance was formed in California between thirty-three companies representing over 3 million employees. This enhanced negotiating authority resulted in an unprecedented decline in health care costs for three years in a row.[21]

3 Direct Contracting. The third corporate strategy involves directly contracting between a coalition of corporations and systems of health care providers. Some companies seeking low-cost health care came to believe that physician group HMOs and hospitals had formed alliances that amounted to regional oligopolies making it difficult for corporations to negotiate lower fees. In this system employers bypass the managed-care plans and contract directly with organized groups of providers called "care systems." This method typically requires primary care physicians to be affiliated with only one care system and not serve as a "gatekeeper" for different managed-care systems. This system challenges the model of the HMO insurer because the premiums go directly to the care system rather than to an insurer, which causes the insurer to lose control over those health care dollars.[22] Many physicians find that to win contracts the care system bids low. They feel they are working even longer hours with no increase in salary. Actually doctors' salaries have rebounded from the initial decline brought on by managed care. *The New York Times* reports that, "A survey of 1996 incomes . . . showed physicians' average earnings rising to the threshold of $200,000 for the first time."[23]

[18]D. Scanlon, M. Chernew, and J. Lave, "Consumer Health Plan Choice: Current Knowledge and Future Directions," *Annual Review of Public Health,* 1997, vol. 18, pp. 507–28.

[19]Bodenheimer and Sullivan, "How Large Employers," p. 1004.

[20]Hilzenrath, "Employee Health Benefit Costs."

[21]Ibid.

[22]Thomas Bodenheimer and Kip Sullivan, "How Large Employers are Shaping the Health Care Market-place," Second of Two Parts, Health Policy Report, *The New England Journal of Medicine* (April 9, 1998), p. 1084.

[23]Peter T. Kilborn, "Doctors Pay Regains Ground Despite the Effects of H.M.O.'s." *The New York Times* (22 April 1998), p. 1.

CASE STUDY

CLASHING CULTURES:
PROFESSIONALISM AND THE
COMMERCIALIZATION OF HEALTH CARE

A generation ago professional medical care presumed that a patient's welfare was the paramount consideration. Hospitals and health insurance plans were mostly non-profit, community institutions. There were no third parties with invested capital seeking to maximize returns from the physician's care or hospital services.

Some socially oriented (or nonprofit) managed care systems, in addition to treating the ill, emphasize prevention and patient education. By putting physicians on salary there is no incentive to overtreat a patient as in a fee-for-service system. Money saved by reducing unnecessary surgery or other care can be directed toward preventive care. These plans also monitor what their physicians do to educate them about the "best practice" and reduce unjustified variations from it.

Market-oriented HMOs have additional features. Corporations employing physicians seek profits by selling services. The physician-employee ceases to be a free agent. Commitment to patient care is subordinated to the need to assure corporate profitability. These managed care plans almost always require that physicians' incomes be tied to meeting profitability requirements. Physicians who provide "too

much" care may be "deselected" from the HMO. Most plans require that physicians get authorization for various treatments and tests usually thought of as routine such as X rays. Failure to get authorization may result in a denial of payment. It is not unusual for physicians to subsequently be told that their care was excessive and have deductions made from their salary.

Almost 90 percent of HMOs require that primary care physicians serve as gatekeepers. As gatekeepers, they often have a financial incentive not to refer patients to appropriate specialists. A pool of money is set aside for the gatekeeper. Whenever a patient is referred to a specialist, the cost of the care is subtracted from the pool of money. At the end of the year, the gatekeeper is allowed to keep any money remaining in the pool. Such financial incentives create stark ethical dilemmas. The financial incentive to withhold or limit care is pervasive throughout the managed care industry.

Many of these programs try to exclude patients from coverage who are high risk. The traditional group plans accepted all who applied to spread the risks. For-profit HMOs practice risk avoidance in the interest of profits. In so doing they deny care to those most in need. This shifts the cost of caring for the sickest patients to other plans that are then viewed as (incorrectly) high cost and therefore less efficient.

Source: Robert Kuttner, "Must Good HMOs Go Bad?" Part One. "The Commercialization of Prepaid Group Health Care," *The New England Journal of Medicine,* vol. 338, no. 21, May 21, 1998.

Backlash Against Managed Care

Employers, who willingly included health insurance as a fringe benefit to attract workers in the 1940s watched their health care expenditures soar over the next decades. Large employers began taking an active part in trying to hold costs down only in the last fifteen years and are reshaping the health care marketplace. By the late 1990s, over 150 million people were covered by some form of managed care through an HMO, a preferred

FIGURE 10-2
PERCENT OF AMERICANS WHO SAY
HMOs AND OTHER MANAGED CARE
PLANS HAVE:
Percentages do not add up to 100 because
"No effect" and "Don't know" responses are
omitted.

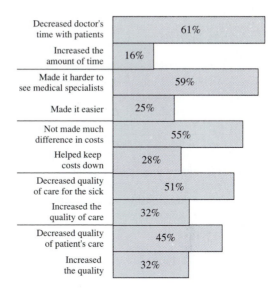

Decreased doctor's time with patients	61%
Increased the amount of time	16%
Made it harder to see medical specialists	59%
Made it easier	25%
Not made much difference in costs	55%
Helped keep costs down	28%
Decreased quality of care for the sick	51%
Increased the quality of care	32%
Decreased quality of patient's care	45%
Increased the quality	32%

(*Source: Adapted from Kaiser/Harvard/
Princeton Survey Research Associates,*
National Survey of Americans' Views on
Managed Care, *November 1997.*)

provider plan (PPO) that provides care through a wider network of doctors and hospitals who will accept a lower negotiated fee, or a point-of-service (POS) plan that will allow members to choose providers outside the HMO for a higher cost to the employee. The managed-care industry gained 86 percent of the insured health care market largely by holding down premium increases.

Cost has become such a dominant consideration for employers that in a 1998 survey of 1,583 companies with 200 or more employees, 73 percent of the employers said "costs" were "very important" when choosing a health plan. Whether a health plan had received accreditation was "very important" to 27 percent and how well it had fared on standardized performance measures was "very important" to only 8 percent.[24] Quality is important however, because employees who are unhappy with their health care are often unhappy employees. Employees who are ill and miss work reduce productivity and are costly to employers.

Large employers who switch from one HMO to another seeking the lowest cost plan force families to leave their family physician for one in the new plan. In managed care programs individuals have very little or no choice about who their primary care physician is going to be. Many changes in health care delivery occur not to improve health care but to reduce the cost of doing business for the employer.

Most health care consumers are concerned that managed care plans do not provide them with the care they need when they are sick. A 1997 survey makes clear that a majority of Americans believe that HMOs have had an adverse effect on the quality of health care.

[24]Hilzenrath, "Employee Health Benefit Costs." This survey is consistent with an earlier survey by M. Freudenheim, "Assessing HMOs by a New Standard: A Patient's Progress." *The New York Times,* 16 July 1996, p. A1.

PATIENTS' RIGHTS

In the United States the right to health care was overtaken by a movement to establish rights in health care. The right to health care required legislation and financing, while rights in health care needed only judicial decisions. It was not until the early 1970s that the courts established all patients' rights to informed consent. The courts made clear that they would treat the doctor-patient relationship not as an arm's-length business relationship, but as a fiduciary relationship (based upon trust). Before obtaining a patient's consent to treatment, the physician must give the patient basic information so that the patient (not the physician) can make an informed decision about whether to proceed. This information includes a description of the proposed treatment, expected risks and benefits, alternative treatments (including no treatment) and their risks and benefits, the probability of success and the main anticipated problems of recovery. This may seem rather commonplace today, but it was unconventional at the time and disapproved of by physicians and had to be imposed on them by the courts.

In *Roe v. Wade* (1973) the Supreme Court ruled that pregnant women have a constitutional right of privacy that includes their right to end a pregnancy in the absence of a state's ability to demonstrate a countervailing and compelling state interest. The case suggests that the Constitution limits interference by the state in the doctor-patient relationship. Also, in 1973, the American Hospital Association issued a patients' bill of rights. Although it was vague, it did include many basic concepts of patients' rights such as the right to complete information about diagnosis, to refuse treatment, and to have confidentiality maintained. In the 1977 case of Karen Ann Quinlan the courts affirmed that competent patients have the right to refuse any medical treatment including life-sustaining treatment. More recently patients, while competent, can designate another person to

About three out of five say that managed care plans made it harder to see medical specialists and that it reduces the time that doctors spend with patients. Fifty-five percent of those surveyed also said they were "somewhat worried" that if they were sick their "health plan would be more concerned about saving money than about what is the best medical treatment."[25] More HMO than fee-for-service subscribers complained about their health care program. An escalation of complaints and a number of highly publicized lawsuits over wrongfully denied health care encouraged both state and federal lawmakers to consider legislative responses.

RECENT REFORM EFFORTS

In 1993 President Clinton, hoping to provide health insurance for all Americans, proposed a National Health Security Act. The president's plan was defeated. In response, the president has proposed a series of incremental health care reform bills. Employment-based insurance may discourage some workers from changing jobs because of "pre-existing conditions" and may create difficulties in obtaining insurance in a new job. Also,

[25]Ibid.

make treatment decisions for the patient, if he or she becomes incompetent. Patients were also granted access to their medical records and to basic emergency treatment.

Patients' Rights in Managed Care

The doctor-patient relationship in more traditional health care systems becomes more problematic under managed care. Managed care systems try to transform the patient into a consumer. Typically patients (not consumers) seek medical attention when they are sick. Sick people are not on an equal footing to bargain, and must be able to trust their physicians to be on their side in dealing with pain, suffering, or disability. The choice of the health care plan and that of the physician is severely constrained in managed care. Managed care systems threaten the independence of physicians as professionals, while treating the patient as a consumer of health care limited to a particular provider of services. That is why the new patients'-rights movement tries to preserve the traditional doctor-patient relationship, and to eliminate the financial conflicts of interests that threaten that relationship. There is a real effort to shift power from managed care companies, insurance companies, and health care facilities to patients and their physicians.

The federal government responded with legislation in areas that received significant attention such as "drive-through-deliveries." Several states also responded with statutes to limit "drive-through-mastectomies." There is interest in limiting cases in which medical decisions are made by nonphysicians and to remove "gag rules" restricting physicians' conversations with their patients about treatment options.

Source: George J. Annas, "A National Bill of Patients' Rights," Legal Issues in Medicine, *N Engl J Med* (1998), 338, 695–99.

losing a job becomes even more catastrophic when a family loses health care in addition to wage income. As mentioned earlier, in 1996 Clinton successfully pushed for a law (The Health Insurance Portability and Accountability Act) making it easier for people to keep their health insurance when they lose or change jobs, or start their own business. The president, in response to criticism of "drive-by deliveries," supported a congressional bill to require health insurance plans to provide coverage for at least forty-eight hours of hospital care for new mothers.

In his State of the Union address in 1998, President Clinton urged Congress to pass a Patient's Bill of Rights. Addressing the concerns of many Americans, he said, "You have the right to know all your medical options, not just the cheapest. You have the right to choose the doctor you want for the care you need. You have the right to emergency room care, wherever and whenever you need it. You have the right to keep your medical records confidential."[26] The president continued to press the issue when he released an Executive Memorandum a month later directing all federal health plans, which serve over 85 million Americans, to comply with the President's Quality Commission's Consumer Bill of Rights. He reissued his challenge to Congress to pass legislation so

[26]Text of President Clinton's State of the Union message, *New York Times,* January 28, 1998, A19.

THE UNINSURED

In 1978, about 12.3 percent of the population below the age of 65 did not have health insurance. The rate increased to 14.8 percent in 1986. In 1996 approximately 41.7 million people in the United States (15.6 percent of the population) had no health insurance coverage during the entire calendar year. This figure was up 1.1 million from the previous year. This number is more than at any time since the passage of Medicaid and Medicare in 1965. Not surprisingly, low-income families are more likely to be uninsured than middle- or high-income households. In fact, 30.8 percent of the poor (11.8 million people) had no health insurance of any kind in 1996, which was double the rate for the entire population. The poor comprised 27 percent of all uninsured people although they make up 13.7 percent of the total population. The poor were more likely to be covered by Medicaid than any other type of insurance.

Young adults between the ages of 18 and 24 are more likely than any other age group to be uninsured (28.9 percent). In contrast, because of Medicare, the elderly were the most likely to be insured with only 1.1 percent without any coverage. Among ethnic and racial groups, Hispanics had the highest probability of lacking coverage, while African Americans had the lowest uninsured rate among the poor. Education and lack of insurance were inversely related. Among all adults as the level of education rose, the likelihood of being uninsured declined. Among those employed who are uninsured, there is a correlation between those who work part-time and lack of insurance (22.4 percent). Many firms classify workers as part-time if they work less than 35 hours per week in the majority of weeks they work in a year. By classifying workers as part-time they are typically not eligible for benefits such as health insurance. Workers, whether full- or part-time, were more likely to be insured than nonworkers. However, among the poor, workers actually had a higher uninsured rate than nonworkers. Over one-half of the poor full-time workers were uninsured in 1996 (52.2 percent).

Those born outside the United States were more likely to be without health insur-

that a patients' bill of rights will become the law of the land. The directive provided: "Guaranteed access to needed health care providers to ensure that patients are provided appropriate high quality care; access to emergency services when and where the need arises; confidentiality of medical records to ensure that individually identifiable medical information is not disseminated and to provide consumers the right to access and amend their own medical records; grievance and appeals processes for consumers to resolve their differences with their health plans and health care providers."[27]

By requiring all federal health plans to support a "Patient's Bill of Rights" (including Medicare, Medicaid, the Federal Employee Health Benefits Program, the Department of Defense Military Health Program) the government placed great pressure on many health care providers to announce their own "voluntary" patient's rights plans. Several of these proposals are put forward primarily as a marketing strategy to help health plans compete on an equal basis.

While the president's national bill of rights for patients provides a basic outline, many believe that it is incomplete. They are pressing for legislation that permits members to

[27]http://www.whitehouse.gov/WH/Work/022098.html

ance (33.6 percent) than were natives (13.7 percent). Poor immigrants fared the worst with over half lacking health insurance (54 percent). Seventeen percent of those who are naturalized citizens had no coverage compared to foreign-born noncitizens who were uninsured (42.4 percent).

Health insurance coverage rates increase as income rises. The average percent of persons without health insurance ranged from 7.6 percent among those in households with incomes of $75,000 or more to 24.3 percent in households with incomes less than $25,000. Of 143 million workers, 53.1 percent had employment-based health insurance policies. The proportion varied by size of employer, with firms employing less than twenty-five people being least likely to have insurance policies, while 92 percent of the firms with 1,000 or more employees offered health insurance plans in 1993. Some workers without policies may be covered by employment-based coverage through another family member.

Number of Uninsured Children is Increasing

In 1996, 1 in 7 children (10.6 million) had no health insurance. Of those, most uninsured children are not poor (about 7.2 million were above the poverty level). Poor children were much more likely to lack health coverage with almost one-fourth (23.3 percent) or almost twice the 12.7 percent of the children above the poverty line. The increase in the number of children lacking health insurance is largely attributable to the falloff in Medicaid coverage. Children between 12 and 17 years of age were less likely to have health care coverage than younger children.

Source: Robert Bennefield, *Health Insurance Coverage: 1996,* Current Population Reports, Census Bureau, P60-199, Issued September 1997. "Natives" are persons born in the United States, Puerto Rico, or an outlying area of the United States, such as Guam or the U.S. Virgin Islands, and persons who were born in a foreign country but who had at least one parent who was a U.S. citizen. All other persons born outside the United States are "foreign-born."

---

sue their health plans directly for harm caused by wrongful acts on the part of health care plans. Other recommendations include an independent third-party review process for resolving HMO members' complaints; the collection and publication of detailed information of complaints; and standard descriptions of HMO services and limitations to ease comparison shopping among plans. There is wide support for reform of managed care, and several bills have been introduced into both houses of Congress. Republican leadership is divided over the wisdom of government regulations however, so passage is uncertain. Conservatives are gratified that the health insurance industry is gearing up for a major advertising campaign to convince the public that government regulation will drive up the cost of health care and lead still more companies to not offer health care to their employees. The Congressional Budget Office estimates that the Consumer Bill of Rights would add 0.3 percent to existing premiums.[28]

The managed care industry is undertaking an expensive campaign to defeat consumer protection legislation based upon the argument that it would drive up costs to consumers.

[28]"Consumer Bill of Rights Would Raise Costs by 0.3 Percent for Employers, CBO Projects," *BNA's Health Care Policy Report* (Washington, DC: Bureau of National Affairs, March 16, 1998).

THE DEFEAT OF THE CLINTON HEALTH CARE PLAN

President Clinton's electoral victory was based upon a call for change in several public policy areas, including the American health care system. A variety of forces, including the health insurance industry, voters fearing a reduction in health coverage, corporations fearing tax increases, and conservative members of Congress opposed to any increase in government involvement were able to defeat Clinton's comprehensive proposal. There was, it seems, a consensus that *something* should be done about health care, but not *what* should be done.

Many believe that affordable health care for all is the final missing piece of the social safety net first woven by Franklin Roosevelt. For those people the political system failed when it rejected Clinton's initiative. But for those who believe that the Clinton plan would have mutilated a flawed but workable health care system, the political system appeared to have worked exactly as the founding fathers had designed, in other words a system that would make change difficult.

Bill Clinton came to the White House with an exuberance believing that "the system" could work. He hoped to convince the nation that government could be a positive force in the lives of Americans. If the nation could be mobilized to address its social problems, history could be changed through wide support for public policy. Haynes Johnson and David Broder describe how the system frustrated Clinton in their work "The System." Theirs is the best account by far of the struggle within "the system" over Clinton's health care bill.

They point out that the press largely ignored the substance of the bill "such as portability of coverage, long-term care, mental health services, and rural health facilities." Instead the press focused on who was winning and who was losing. They also blame Ira Magaziner, a brilliant but arrogant consultant, who was enlisted to work with Mrs. Clinton in developing the plan for not showing sufficient respect for Congress. They also fault the president for not becoming more involved when Mrs. Clinton was attacked and his leadership was needed.

Johnson and Broder argue that one of the main reasons for the bill's defeat was the role of special interest groups. They detail how very early in the process over thirty organizations met in secret as the "No Name Coalition" to plan a strategy to destroy the proposal. Some were insurers who were concerned about restrictions on their freedom in the market, others were small employers who were concerned about increased costs, while others were ideolog-

This has brought attention to the costs associated with compensation for high-level HMO executives. A recent report by the Families USA foundation found that the twenty-five highest paid executives in the twenty companies studied made $153.8 million in annual compensation, excluding unexercised stock options in 1996. The average compensation was over $6.2 million per year (the median was over $4.8 million).[29] These same executives had stock options valued at $337.4 million.

[29]Families USA Foundation, *Premium Pay: Corporate Compensation in America's HMOs,* April 1998.

ical conservatives who oppose any deviation from laissez faire free market forces. Millions were spent by interest groups on persuasive advertisements. Since polls showed women were more in favor of health care than men, a particularly effective commercial showed an average American couple "Harry and Louise" discussing the merits of the plan in which Louise forcefully explains to a confused husband why it is a bad plan.

The time taken to construct the plan permitted opposition to peel off some potential supporters like the rings of an onion. Big business stood to gain from expanded coverage, but its instinctively conservative leaders were persuaded that the plan would lead to large bureaucracies and excessive red tape. Hospitals and physicians stood to benefit significantly from the prospect of more patients who would be covered and less worry about reimbursement. But they were persuaded that government might prove to exert a greater downward pressure on prices for their services than HMOs.

The second major reason for the defeat of the health care plan was the aggressive opposition by the Republican Party. Newt Gingrich designed a plan of "coagulation" that exhorted Republicans to "clot every-

body away from Clinton." He saw that the defeat of the health care plan was essential to stopping the Clinton momentum and gaining control of the House. Many Republicans who had been willing to compromise with the Democrats saw the advantage of killing any plan for which Democrats could take credit. "Playing on mistrust and fears of government enabled Gingrich to use the health care battle as a powerful symbol of the failings of the liberal welfare state."

This legislative effort to provide for universal health insurance failed, but it did succeed as never before in focusing attention on problems within the system. The bill's rejection was a statement in favor of the imperfect market for health care. Many would argue that the market is bringing about those restrictions that its adversaries predicted the Clinton plan would dictate: less choice, higher patient costs through increased deductibles and higher co-payments, and increased threats to the quality of care. At the same time, more companies stopped offering job-related insurance altogether, and the number of uninsured Americans continues to climb. The debate over health care continues.

Source: Haynes Johnson and David S. Broder, *The System: The American Way of Politics at the Breaking Point* (Boston: Little, Brown, 1996).

Public Dissatisfaction

Because of these factors many believe that the current managed care system has serious problems and critics have started to question the whole health care arrangement in the United States. The question is raised: **Should health insurance be employment based?** The United States has a system based primarily on **voluntary private insurance.** Premiums are collected by competing private insurance companies from participating employers, which then reimburse health care providers for services rendered. Increasingly, the insurer may own the HMO provider. Most people who were insured (about 70.2 percent) were covered by private insurance through a plan offered by an employer (their own or through a relative such as a parent or spouse) in 1996.[30] The remaining number of insured people were covered through Medicare (13 percent), Medicaid (11 percent), or military health care systems. Competing health insurers set their premiums according to the risk characteristics of individuals or the community of individuals. Consequently, poor people are less likely to be offered group insurance in their low-skill job and are unable to afford insurance (about 42 million people were uninsured in the United States in 1998).

From an economic perspective, tying health insurance to employment costs lower-paid employees more. That is, it is a regressive method of providing health care. The employee indirectly pays the entire cost of the health care insurance premium. One recent study showed that employment-based insurance cost workers in the lowest 10 percent of households 5.7 percent of their wages, but only 1.8 percent of the income of the highest 10 percent.[31]

Employers are less interested in the health care services for their employees than in reducing the costs of doing business. Because of this the percentage of the working-age population in the United States with employment-based health insurance fell from 69 percent to 64 percent between 1987 and 1996.[32] Increasingly employers are simply not offering insurance to their workers. There is a trend away from higher-paid union jobs with fringe benefits like health insurance to nonunion service jobs with fewer benefits; more employees are classified as part-time and are not eligible for fringe benefits; and increasingly lower-wage and part-time employees forego employment-based insurance that includes higher employee costs along with higher deductibles. Due to the ongoing erosion of employment-based coverage for workers and jobs that are no longer as long-lasting or stable as they once were, linking health insurance to employment will be even more untrustworthy in the future.

Some problems of American health care are clear. Medical costs are soaring. It is not a matter of too little spending. The United States spends more on health care than any other industrialized nation, and costs are still rising faster than the general rate of inflation. In 1995, the United States spent 14.2 percent of its GDP on health care and had 42 million citizens with no health care coverage. The average of twenty-seven OECD countries, all with universal health care coverage, was 7.6 percent of GDP. Germany, the next highest spending country for health care, spent 10.4 percent of its GDP, but had virtually 100 percent of its population covered. Despite spending almost two times the OECD average, the United States was behind these countries in some critical measures of health care.

Life expectancy has generally increased around the world in recent years, but the low ranking of American life expectancy has persisted. The United States ranks 17th in life expectancy and 14th in infant mortality.

A number of studies have concluded that the high U.S. mortality rate in comparison to other economically developed countries is a consequence of its relatively unequal

[30]Robert Bennefield, "Health Insurance Coverage: 1996," *Current Population Reports,* Census Bureau, pp. 60–199, September 1997.

[31]Thomas Bodenheimer and Kip Sullivan, "The Logic of Tax-Based Financing for Health Care," *International Journal of Health Services,* 1997, vol. 27, pp. 409–25. See also *N Engl J Med* 1998, 338, p. 1087.

[32]Ibid., p. 1086.

TABLE 10-1
COMPARISON OF INFANT MORTALITY AND EXPECTATION OF LIFE AT BIRTH

Country	Expectation of life at birth: 1997	Infant mortality rate: 1997*	Percent of 1995 GDP expenditures
UNITED STATES	76.0 (years)	6.2	14.2
Australia	79.6	5.0	8.6
Austria	76.7	5.8	7.9
Belgium	77.2	6.1	8.0
Canada	79.3	5.5	9.6
France	78.6	6.0	9.8
Germany	76.1	5.9	10.4
Greece	78.3	7.2	5.8
Hong Kong	82.4	5.0	n.a.
Italy	78.2	6.8	7.7
Japan	79.7	4.4	7.2
Netherlands	77.9	4.8	8.8
Spain	78.5	6.1	7.6
Sweden	78.2	4.5	7.2
Switzerland	77.8	5.4	9.8
Taiwan	76.3	6.9	n.a.
United Kingdom	76.6	6.3	6.9

*Number of deaths per children under 1 year of age per 1,000 live births in a calendar year.
Source: Statistical Abstract, 1997, pp. 832–833, 835.

income distribution and more limited health care access for the poor.[33] A number of studies have noted that income and education are inversely associated with death from all causes. It has also been documented that people in a lower socioeconomic level are more likely to smoke cigarettes, be overweight, and lead a sedentary lifestyle. Therefore a leading hypothesis is that "the elevated mortality risk associated with low levels of income and education is primarily due to the higher prevalence of health risk behaviors among people who are poor and/or have low educational attainment."[34] The study found that those in the lowest income category were more than three times as likely to die during the follow-up period of the study than those in the highest income group when age and other socio-demographic variables were controlled. They also found that while education was related to health behaviors, income was the strongest predictor of longevity. Education was related to mortality through its association with income. The study showed quite convincingly that the risky behaviors associated with lower socioeconomic lifestyles explain no more than about 12 percent of the observed higher mortality rate. The authors conclude that other factors such as depression, hopelessness, low self-esteem, reduced social support, and heightened levels of anger that make up the harsh and adverse environment in which poorer people live are likely to account for most of the causes of premature death (heart attack, strokes, etc.).

[33]Harriet Orcutt Duleep, *Social Security Bulletin,* Summer 1995 (Washington, DC: Publications Office, 1995).
[34]Paula M. Lantz, et al., "Socioeconomic Factors, Health Behaviors, and Mortality: Results from a Nationally Representative Prospective Study of U.S. Adults," *JAMA,* June 3, 1998; 279, 1703–8.

THE RIGHT TO HEALTH CARE

At the present time there is no general constitutional right to medical care. Throughout the past four decades, Americans have been involved in an ideological debate about whether the poor should have the same chance at avoiding a preventable illness or of being cured from a given illness as the affluent have. What makes this question ever more pressing is that all other industrialized nations have answered that question in the affirmative. The debate raises many questions concerning the parameters of such a "right." For example, do federal or state governments have a duty to the medically uninsured? Would such an obligation extend to all the uninsured, or only to the poor who are uninsured? If there is a right to health care how much care does a person have a right to?

The Constitution is silent on the issue of health care and so far the Supreme Court has not spelled out a federal right to health care. The Constitution was framed before health care was considered to be a right of a country's citizens or a way a government could enhance individual freedom. The framers were more concerned with protecting citizens *from* heavy-handed interferences in personal freedoms. Nonetheless,

arguments have been made that a denial by the state or federal government of a minimal level of health care for the poor violates the equal protection guarantees under the Fourteenth Amendment. The Court has not found health care to be a fundamental right. However, where a person is confined to a prison, there exists a right to adequate medical care (see *Estelle v. Gamble,* 429 U.S. 97, 103–105, 1976). The court held that "deliberate indifference to serious medical needs of prisoners" violates the specific constitutional prohibition against cruel and unusual punishment.

The court has used the "rational basis" standard of review to assess the constitutionality of distinctions in providing health care. For example, the court held that a state could refuse public assistance for abortions that were not medically necessary under a program that subsidized medical expenses otherwise associated with pregnancy and childbirth. It held that poor pregnant women were not denied equal protection of the laws because the abortion provisions were rationally related to a government "interest in protecting the potential life of the fetus" (*Maher v. Roe* 432 U.S. 464, 1977).

Even though there is no constitutional right to health care services, Congress has

Another study of the relationship of the gap between the rich and poor on health found that for treatable conditions like tuberculosis, pneumonia, and high blood pressure, mortality rates were higher in states where the income gap was wider. The study found that "the size of the gap between the wealthy and less well-off, as distinct from the absolute standard of living enjoyed by the poor, appears to be related to mortality."[35] Income distribution may be a proxy for other social indicators, such as the degree of investment in human capital. The lack of a universal health care in the United States is an indication of a lack of investment in human capital.

[35]Bruce P. Kennedy, Ichiro Kawachi, and Deborah Prothrow-Stith, "Income Distribution and Mortality: Cross Sectional Ecological Study of the Robin Hood Index in the United States," *BMJ* (1996); 312, 1004-7, p. 1006.

enacted statutes which establish and define the legal rights of individuals to receive medical care from the government. Pursuant to Congress' authority in the Constitution to "make all Laws which shall be necessary and proper" and to "provide for the general Welfare," as well as its power "to regulate Commerce . . . among the several States," it has enacted Medicare and Medicaid statutes. Congress is free to expand or circumscribe those rights with additional legislation.

Congress has also provided a statutory right to health care in legislation like the Hill-Burton Act which provides funding for hospital construction with the proviso that hospitals accepting federal funds must provide a reasonable amount of medical care for those unable to pay. Under the law, ironically, an individual indigent patient is eligible for free care, but not necessarily entitled to free care. The hospital's obligation is to provide uncompensated care for the poor as a group, and no rights are created for particular patients to receive such care (See *Newsom v. Vanderbilt,* 653 F.2d 1100, 1121 [6th Cir. 1981]).

Governmental obligations to provide medical care for the poor may be found in some state constitutions, and more frequently in state statutes. Fifteen states have constitutional provisions that either authorize or require medical care for the poor. States are always free to provide greater protections than those provided at the national level (federal rights generally set minimum standards for the states). Some statutes such as this California state statute are mandatory and broad:

> Every county and every city and county shall relieve and support all incompetent, poor, indigent persons and those incapacitated by age, disease, or accident, lawfully resident therein, when such persons are not supported and relieved by their relatives or friends, or by their own means, or by state hospitals or state or private institutions. (Cal. Welf. & Inst. Code section 17000)

Statutes in some other states also provide specific rights for medical care for the poor under limited circumstances.

Source: Kathleen S. Swendiman, "Constitutional and Statutory Rights to Health Care," *CRS Report for Congressional Research Service,* The Library of Congress 94-64A, 1994.

THE OPTIONS

Everyone agrees that the current U.S. system of providing health care is in need of reform. There is little agreement however about what the reform should be. Proposals range from minor and very incremental tinkering with the current system to a fundamental restructuring of health care that would involve a universal single-payer system like Canada's. These proposals should be judged by their potential for being adopted as well as by their likelihood of providing health care coverage for everyone while containing prices and maintaining quality.

Option 1: Incremental Health Reform

The proposals that represent the smallest departure from the current system are those that suggest that the status quo has much to commend it. They point out that most Americans do have health coverage, and most are satisfied with the care they receive even while they acknowledge fear concerning the continued availability and quality of health care. The status quo has a certain legitimacy because the free market has provided those with sufficient coverage (though not all to be sure) with access to some of the highest quality health care in the world. That such medical care is expensive is not surprising. Those who support this position claim that the current system's shortcomings can be resolved by extending coverage to the uninsured.

Building on existing programs and administrative structures already in place offers a ready-made foundation for incremental expansions. There are proposals for expanding health insurance coverage for those people most at risk: permitting Medicare buy-ins by older adults, Medicaid or other health expansions for poor children, and financing care for the unemployed.

Medicare Extension   The president's budget includes two proposals that would increase health insurance by expanding the federal Medicare program. The administration proposes to allow people 62 to 64 years of age to enroll voluntarily in Medicare if they do not have employment-based health insurance or Medicaid. The eligibility requirements would limit the potential enrollment to about 75 percent of those between the ages of 62 and 64. Those enrolling would have to pay high monthly premiums ($316) to reflect the average expected costs of benefits ($389 a month) if everyone in that age group participated. Those who enrolled in this program would continue to pay higher premiums after age 65 (an additional $14 per month until age 85) to pay for additional benefits received. The Congressional Budget Office (CBO) estimates that the higher premiums before and after age 65 would increase spending by less than $1.4 billion over five years.

Medicare Buy-In for Displaced Workers Ages 55 to 61   The Clinton administration also proposes to extend Medicare to allow a limited number of workers from age 55 to 61 (and their spouses) who lose health insurance because of a job loss to buy into the Medicare program. This program would be available only to individuals who meet several eligibility requirements related to their job loss. They must have had employment-based health insurance for the 12 months before losing their job and have exhausted the 18 months of unemployment benefits available under the Consolidated Omnibus Budget Reconciliation Act of 1985 **(COBRA).** Premiums for the buy-in for displaced workers would initially be set at $400 *per person* and would be updated annually. Less than 190,000 workers annually would meet the requirements to be eligible for this insurance. As the baby boom population hits the 55- to 64-year-old age bracket at the turn of the century, the number of uninsured older adults is expected to become an increasingly serious problem.[36]

Clinton's proposal is seen as astute by many. People aged 55–65 tend to be healthier than older retirees. Their premiums will infuse the actuarial pool with many healthier subscribers. At the same time people in this age group are often medically insecure.

---

[36]Karen Davis, "Incremental Coverage of the Uninsured," *JAMA* (September 11, 1996), 276, pp. 831–32.

When people in this age group are laid off due to corporate downsizing and lose their job-related coverage, they find private health insurance prohibitively expensive. There are many people in this age group who are forced to wait until they become eligible for Medicare to obtain a needed operation. Extending Medicare to the next most vulnerable segment of the population in terms of those likely to lose their health insurance gets high ratings in public opinion polls. The proposal would expand a known quantity gradually to a healthier population. Not surprisingly, the private health insurance industry dislikes the proposal. Republicans are also distrustful of the idea because it is a program like Social Security or the original Medicare which bonds voters to big government.

Health Insurance for Children   Being uninsured is a powerful predictor of reduced access to health care, and the primary reason families have no coverage is their inability to pay for it. Children in families without health insurance are obviously far less likely to get medical care than those in families with insurance.[37] There are some 10.6 million uninsured children nationally. The Balanced Budget Act of 1997 created a new State Children's Health Insurance Program (S-CHIP), as Title XXI of the Social Security Act to provide funds to states to enable them to expand the provision of child health assistance to uninsured, low-income children.[38] But the CBO estimates that Title XXI and other enhancements to the Medicaid program will cover only about 2 million out of the 10.6 million currently uninsured children.[39] Title XXI was a hesitating small step forward because Congress did not want to create a new individual entitlement.

Such small measures resulted in well-known writer Uwe Reinhardt to comment forcefully in the *Journal of the American Medical Association,* that we seem to be interminably involved in debating the question: *As a matter of national policy, and to the extent that a nation's health system can make it possible, should the child of a poor American family have the same chance of avoiding preventable illness or of being cured from a given illness as does the child of a rich American family?*[40] Reinhardt points out that the "yeas" in all other industrialized nations have won that debate decades ago and those nations have worked to put health insurance and health care systems in place to carry out that decision. He deplores that only in the United States have the "nays" so far won. He states:

> As a matter of conscious national policy, the United States always has and still does openly countenance the practice of rationing health care for millions of American children by their parents' ability to procure health insurance for the family or, if the family is uninsured, by their parents' willingness and ability to pay for health care out of their own pocket or, if the family is unable to pay, by the parents' willingness and ability to procure charity care in their role as health care beggars.[41]

---

[37]P. Newacheck, J. Stoddard, D. Hughes, and M. Pearl, "Health Insurance and Access to Primary Care for Children," *N Engl J Med* (1998), 338, pp. 513–19.

[38]See "State Children's Health Insurance Program: Title XXI, Social Security Act," 1997, Section 2101(a).

[39]Congressional Budget Office, "Budgetary Implications of the Balanced Budget Act of 1997" (Washington, DC: Government Printing Office, December 1997), table 11.

[40]Uwe E. Reinhardt, "Wanted: A Clearly Articulated Social Ethic for American Health Care," *JAMA* (1997), 278, 1446–7.

[41]Ibid.

As already noted, every indication is that the number of the uninsured will grow. When other socioeconomic factors such as income or family status are controlled, uninsured Americans receive about 60 percent of the health services as insured Americans. When they are hospitalized, uninsured Americans (adults as well as children) die from the same illness at almost three times the rate observed for equally situated insured patients.[42] Over the long run, uninsured Americans die at an earlier age than similarly situated insured Americans.

Still, as Reinhardt observes, many of the elite in America believe that rationing by price and ability to pay serves a high national purpose. Although he points out that virtually everyone who shares that view:

> [T]ends to be rather comfortably ensconced in the upper tiers of the nation's income distribution. Their prescriptions do not emanate from behind a Rawlsian veil of ignorance concerning their own families' station in life. Furthermore, most . . . who see the need for rationing health care by price and ability to pay enjoy the full protection of government-subsidized, employer-provided, private health insurance that affords their families comprehensive coverage with out-of-pocket payments that are trivial relative to their own incomes and therefore spare their own families the pain of rationing altogether.[43]

It is surprising to observe such unwavering support for subsidized insurance for the middle class and above in the Congress that claims to lack the resources to afford every parent and child the security and health benefits that come with universal health insurance, a privilege that parents and children in other countries have long taken for granted as a right.

Financing Health Insurance for the Unemployed   Most workers are insured through job-related insurance. Loss of a job typically triggers a loss of health insurance coverage. Even though the Consolidated Omnibus Budget Reconciliation Act (COBRA) provisions allow workers to continue coverage for a time, most find that it is not feasible at a time when families are under the financial strain of job loss. As a result, only about 20 percent of those eligible participate. One proposal is to use unemployment funds to pay COBRA premiums or partially subsidize health care premiums for unemployed workers to help maintain equilibrium when money is scarce. Such a method which would subsidize the costs of coverage for the uninsured would broaden access to care at a time when market forces are closing doors to the unemployed.

For both unemployed and uninsured workers, and uninsured children, the simplest way for a state to extend coverage is to raise the state's current Medicaid eligibility limits. A Medicaid expansion would avoid the need to create new programs to cover those whose incomes are just above the current Medicaid limits. No new bureaucracy is needed and funds would not be spent on duplicating administrative structures or costs. The larger populations would offer states an advantage when negotiating with health providers and help states get the most for their health dollars.

---

[42]J. Hadley, E. Steinberg, and J. Feder, "Comparison of Uninsured and Privately Insured Hospital Patients," *JAMA* (1991), 270, pp. 374–79.
[43]Reinhardt, "Wanted," p. 1447.

Option 2: Universal Health Care

A second option is to replace the current system which is based upon private insurance with a system based on a government-sponsored health care plan in which the entire system is controlled by the government. Since all other industrialized countries have national health care systems, there are several different models one might use for comparison purposes. Government pays the providers of health care in all other systems. Two aspects of the **single-payer plans** are of interest: first, it makes health care a right, and removes the insecurity regarding its availability and cost; second, single-payer plans have been much more successful in containing the proportion of its GDP devoted to health care than has the United States. These plans replace the myriad health insurance companies and the literally thousands of different plans that currently exist in the United States. The obvious advantage of a centralized system is that it provides universal coverage as a right, while making a single payer a powerful negotiator in holding down costs.

By eliminating duplication and standardizing forms and benefits, administrative costs are also reduced. Since there is universal coverage, doctors are confident of reimbursement without wrestling with eligibility criteria, a bewildering variety of forms, and different rules for different situations or locations. Since coverage is not linked to employment, it is portable within a nation, which enhances job mobility. Employers also benefit since they can hire employees who best fit their needs without regard to whether someone is a high-health-risk hire or has a preexisting medical condition that might affect the company's insurance costs. A single-payer system also eliminates the costs of marketing competitive health insurance policies, evaluating and pricing insurance risks, and billing and collecting premiums. This has kept down the administrative costs which range from about 2 to 4 percent in countries with national health, compared to over 7 percent of U.S. health expenditures. The General Accounting Office (GAO) concluded after studying the Canadian health care system:

> If the universal coverage and single-payer features of the Canadian system were applied in the United States, the savings in administrative costs alone would be more than enough to finance insurance coverage for the millions of Americans who are currently uninsured. There would be enough left over to permit a reduction, or possibly even the elimination, of copayments and deductibles, if that were deemed appropriate.[44]

Since everyone is guaranteed access to medical care on the same terms and conditions, they are treated much more equitably than in the United States where ability to pay is a major factor in determining treatment. There is no means testing for eligibility as there is for Medicaid in the United States.

The single-payer plan changes the nature of medical care from a market good available to those with sufficient resources to a right which, ironically is closer to what the United States had when medical care was largely regulated by social forces, with nonprofit hospitals and physicians who felt more of an obligation to care for a patient regardless of ability to pay (although with cost shifting wherever possible).

---

[44]General Accounting Office, *Canadian Health Insurance: Lessons for the United States* (Report to the Chairman, Committee on Government Operations, House of Representatives) (Washington, DC: U.S. Government Printing Office, June 1991), p. 3.

The single-payer plan replaces rationing by market forces with rationing by the government. The winners under the job-related health insurance program, those with jobs that bring health insurance benefits, are apprehensive about change, while the losers are poorly organized to press for inclusion especially when the prevailing public philosophy tends to be tilted against government inclusion. Politically, any move toward a single-payer system would have to overcome very long odds. Any attempt to introduce it would be met by gargantuan lobbying efforts on the part of current health insurance carriers whose function would be eliminated and by health care providers who would oppose the market power of government in maintaining cost control. They would unite, as they did in 1994 in opposition to Clinton's Health Security Plan, to enlist consumers to oppose such a plan for reducing consumer choice and control. Politically, a single-payer plan is not likely to be adopted in the current political climate.

There is significant confusion and mistaken notions about foreign national health care systems within the United States. During the debate on health care reform in 1994 and its aftermath, advocates of various policies, partisan politicians, and the popular press recounted horror stories emanating from foreign universal health care systems such as those in Canada and Germany. These countries were particularly significant because both the Canadian and German systems contain several features that many policy analysts thought might be attractive to many Americans. Recent cross-national public opinion studies on the performance of the health care systems in Germany, Canada, and the United States for the Harvard School of Public Health and reported in *Health Affairs* provide new insight about how these individuals view their health care system.[45]

The survey found Canadians to be the most satisfied and Americans the least satisfied with their health care system, with Germany in the middle. The authors did not examine whether the higher level of dissatisfaction expressed by Americans was because they had unpleasant experiences with the health care system or perhaps to a broader tendency to be more critical of their institutions. In an earlier survey (1990) of ten nations, in only four (Canada, the Netherlands, West Germany, and France) did more than 40 percent of the population report satisfaction with their health care arrangement, with the United States having the lowest satisfaction rate.[46] Among physician health care providers, only 23 percent of American physicians, 33 percent of the Canadian physicians, and 48 percent of the West German physicians said their respective health care systems were working well.[47] It is ironic that many policy analysts found the German and Canadian models valuable because of the financing arrangements that provide universal coverage and control costs. Both countries maintain health care spending at less than 10 percent of GDP with universal coverage while the United States spends over 14 percent of GDP and has 42 million Americans without coverage. The survey found however that a plurality of Americans believe that we spend too little on health care. But

[45]Robert J. Blendon, John Benson, Karen Donelan, and Robert Leitman, "Who Has the Best Health Care System? A Second Look," *Health Affairs,* Winter 1995.

[46]Robert J. Blendon, Robert Leitman, I. Morrison, and Karen Donelan. "Satisfaction with Health Systems in Ten Nations," *Health Affairs* (Summer 1990), pp. 185–92.

[47]Dietlind Wahner-Roedler, Peter Knuth, and Rudolf Juchems, "The German Health-Care System," *Mayo Clinic Proceedings* (1997), 72, pp. 1061–68.

as previously noted, support for increased spending would probably be lower in all countries if individuals thought they would have to pay more in taxes or premiums.

Americans are clearly aware of the concerns about equity in the health care system. A clear majority of Americans, 55 percent, believe that wealthy or influential people always get better medical care than those who are less well off, compared to 39 percent of Germans and 29 percent of Canadians. Americans were more inclined to think that their health care system does not treat them fairly (28 percent), compared to 22 percent of Germans and 11 percent of the Canadians.

Finally, 20 percent of Americans reported having problems paying medical bills during the previous year, while only 6 percent of Canadians and 3 percent of Germans had problems. In a survey of physicians, patients' inability to afford necessary treatment was considered a serious problem by 73 percent of the American physicians, 25 percent of the Canadian and 15 percent of the West German physicians.[48] More Americans reported difficulty in obtaining health care they thought they needed.

The survey was taken just after strong national efforts to contain costs in the national health care systems in Canada and Germany took place. The survey reflected a rising unhappiness with the Canadian and German health care systems. However, the Canadian public is not disenchanted with its health care system, but rather with the reduction in government funding. Clearly Americans do not rate their system as highly as Canadians and Germans rate their systems. Americans appear to want universal coverage and security found in the other programs but a smaller role for the federal government in its operation.

Universal Health Care: Case Studies of the German and Canadian Health Care Systems

The German health care system is of interest because it was the first national health insurance system (established by Bismarck in 1883) and is a benchmark against which all other national health programs are measured. In Germany, as in Japan, France, and the Netherlands, participants pay into nonprofit compulsory insurance funds which are used to reimburse health care providers through negotiated contracts. In Germany the law requires individuals (up to a certain income) to have health insurance. Premiums are a percentage of one's income, independent of the number of family dependents or health risks, and are deducted from each worker's paycheck. All are entitled to the same services, including preventive care as well as treatment of illness. The German system is highly decentralized and consists of over 1,000 autonomous sickness funds that are either regional or employment-based. These sickness funds provide coverage for about 90 percent of the population, an additional 8 percent covered by the sickness fund choose additional private insurance primarily for in-hospital care, and about 2 percent are covered by special arrangements. Less than 0.5 percent of those in the very highest income level have opted out of the system and have no coverage.[49] All workers with incomes below

---

[48]Ibid.
[49]Ibid., p. 1062.

about $45,000 (U.S.) must by law contribute to the sickness fund. The average premium rate is about12.85 percent of earnings up to a fixed maximum with the employer and employee each paying 50 percent of the premium. Workers earning above this threshold can continue to pay into the fund or opt for private insurance and not contribute to the fund. However, most workers continue to pay into the fund. If a worker becomes unemployed there are provisions to assure that the premiums are paid out of other funds (such as the unemployment fund, the old-age fund, or disability insurance).

Patients are free to choose their primary care physician. Since physicians are reimbursed by the fund, no money passes between a physician and the patient. The physician submits a bill with a list of all reimbursable treatments rendered during the quarter to the regional association. The reimbursable health care is translated into points on a fee schedule for the different services provided. All physicians in a region submit their bills quarterly. The point value of a given physician's bill is added to all other physicians' submissions and divided by the budget available. This method has led to a reduction in physicians' relative income, which has been exacerbated by a steady increase in the number of physicians in Germany. Hospital-based physicians are paid a fixed salary by the hospital based on specialty and seniority.

There is a steadily increasing number of physicians in Germany due partly to the constitutional right of all qualified students to a state-subsidized medical education. Since the sickness funds must be split among the physicians in a region, it has the effect of depressing physician incomes. In 1990, there was one physician for every 323 people in Germany and one per 435 in the United States.[50]

Any assessment of German health care would have to conclude that the system has achieved its goal of (1) universal coverage and access, (2) high-quality care, (3) the ability of patients to choose their physicians, and (4) relative success at controlling costs. Germany's health care expenditure as a percentage of the GDP is 10.8 percent (or 73 percent of the U.S. share of health care spending), but it provides access to health care to virtually all of its citizens, compared to the United States which spends 14.2 percent of its GDP on health care but still has almost 16 percent of its population without any coverage. Germany also has lower infant mortality rates and longer life expectancy of its population than does the United States.

Several factors have conspired to put enormous pressure on the German government to cut spending. Since reunification, unemployment has risen to about 10 percent, the costs of rebuilding the former East Germany are higher than expected, and the shift of business operations to lower-cost labor in eastern Europe have all contributed to the need to cut spending. Budget cutters are looking to health care as a place to cut funds. Health benefits are generous. Germans can consult as many doctors as they want, as frequently as they want, with no co-payment. Full-time workers can get three weeks of spa treatment every four years, fully paid by insurance, if prescribed by their doctor. Sickness funds, in an effort to attract new subscribers, offer exercise classes and yoga.[51]

There is a lack of financial reserves in the sickness fund that is putting stress on the system. If the rules for providing health benefits do not change, future health payroll tax

[50]Ibid., p. 1065.
[51]Dale Rublee, "Uneasy Marks," *Hospitals & Health Networks,* May 5, 1998.

rates must rise. In Germany, as in Canada, the health insurance system deals a better hand to low-wage workers who receive the same health benefits as high-wage earners who pay more in taxes. But the society accepts the arrangement as basically fair and something everyone has a stake in. Whatever accommodations the government makes, it is very unlikely that they will tamper with the basic universal and equal access provisions of the health care system.

Key Aspects of the Canadian Health Care System

The Canadian model has also been of special interest to the United States because of the similarities between the two nations. Two aspects of the Canadian system especially are of interest: first, it makes health care a right, and removes the insecurity regarding its availability and cost; second, Canada has been much more successful in containing the proportion of its GDP devoted to health care than the United States. The **Canada Health Act of 1984** (CHA) affirms the commitment of Canadian health care policy to protect, promote, and restore the physical and mental well-being of residents of Canada, and to provide reasonable access to health services without financial barriers. Because constitutional authority for health care delivery rests with the provinces, the federal government achieves its goal by establishing the criteria and conditions for the provinces and territories to satisfy in order to qualify for their full share of the federal transfers for health care services.

The CHA sets out five criteria that the provinces must meet. **Universality** requires that all residents of the province be entitled to public health insurance coverage. **Accessability** requires reasonable access unimpeded by financial or other barriers to medically necessary hospital and physician services for residents, and reasonable compensation for physicians and hospitals. **Comprehensiveness** requires that all medically necessary services provided by hospitals and doctors be insured. The federal law also requires that the coverage be **portable** which means that coverage moves with a resident throughout Canada or outside the country (outside the country coverage is limited to the coverage the individual has in his or her own province). Finally, the law requires that health care have **public administration** which requires that the administration of the insurance plan of a province be carried out on a not-for-profit basis by a public authority.

Canadian health care has preserved two features in particular that surveys consistently show are highly regarded in the United States; first, Canadians choose their own physician, and secondly, physicians receive their incomes based on fee-for-service. Canadian physicians are also free to not accept patients.

A general misperception of Canadian health care concerns the view that shortages of health care personnel and equipment in the Canadian system result in excessive waiting periods for health care services and a consequent significant usage of U.S. health care facilities by Canadians who do not want to wait. Interestingly, there was no significant difference between Canadians (16 percent) and Americans (15 percent) who had to wait more than a week to schedule a doctor's appointment. Only 6 percent of Germans waited that long. However, 6 percent of Germans reported going to another country to seek medical treatment in the previous year, compared to 1 percent of the Canadians and ½ percent of Americans.

It is true that Canadians must wait for some elective hospital services longer than Americans. But provincial governments have been successful in shortening the waiting periods significantly in the last several years. So although emergency cases are treated immediately, there are queues for some nonemergency and elective services. Waiting lists are necessary because some forms of medical technology are less available in Canada (especially magnetic resonance imaging). One study comparing seven hospital services in the United States and Canada found average waiting times significantly shorter in American hospitals for four of the services, but significantly more expensive in American hospitals for six of the seven services.[52] The study concluded that U.S. hospitals provided higher prices and faster care for those patients who were adequately insured than did Canadian hospitals with all patients having complete coverage.

Some American observers suggest that such waiting would not be acceptable in the United States. But Canadians defend this egalitarian aspect by pointing out that you have to wait your turn for nonemergency procedures even if there are two poor people ahead of you. In the United States, they point out, if you are affluent or have comprehensive insurance you can get immediate treatment, but if you are poor or uninsured you may not get any treatment. Americans dependent on Medicaid must wait for many types of health care if they receive it at all.

One measure of satisfaction with health care is the number of people who go abroad to seek medical attention. About one percent of all Canadians have gone abroad to seek health care. The major portion of Canadian expenditures on health care in the United States are incurred by retired Canadian "snowbirds" who spend their winters in Florida and not those who cross the border to avoid delays in Canada. By contrast, just under ½ percent of Americans seek medical attention outside the United States, and most of these expenditures are incurred by uninsured Americans who go into Canada (and seek health care with two Canadian photo I.D.s). Canada has tried to reduce this drain by American "free-riders" by requiring additional proof of qualification procedures. By contrast, 6 percent of Germans reported going to another country to seek medical treatment in the previous year.

Canada has publicly funded its universal health insurance since 1972 through shared financing by the federal government and the ten provincial and two territorial governments. Each province and territorial authority administers its own program through a public agency according to federal standards. In 1971, Canada and the United States were spending about the same percentage of their GDP on health care, 7.5 and 7.6 percent, respectively. By 1995 the share of Canada's GDP spent on health care had risen to 9.6 percent, while U.S. spending reached 14.2 percent. Canada has achieved universal health care coverage while spending over 40 percent less of its GDP on health care. This Canadian performance is attributed, in part, to an efficient public administration in the health services sector. The Canadian infant mortality rate is lower than that of the United States (5.5 versus 6.2 per 1,000 live births, respectively) and life expectancy is longer

---

[52]Chaim Bell, Matthew Crystal, Allan Detsky, and Donald Redelmeier, "Shopping Around for Hospital Services," *JAMA* (1998), 279, 1015–17. The seven services were: magnetic resonance imaging of the head without gadolinium; a screening mammogram; a 12-lead electrocardiogram; a prothrombin time measurement; a session of hemodialysis; a screening colonoscopy; and a total knee replacement. Waiting times were measured in days until earliest appointment and charges were converted to American currency.

(79.3 years versus 76 years). The World Competitiveness Report of 1991 ranked Canada first in the world for the "quality and availability of health care to employees and their families."[53]

Canada, like Germany and the United States (and all industrialized countries) is under the pressure of escalating costs to reform their health care system. Massive cuts in federal transfers to Canada's provinces has kindled a debate about "social justice." When the Canadian health care program came into being almost thirty years ago, the federal government provided about half the funds for health care within the provinces. Since 1995 the federal portion has been reduced to about 20 percent. This has resulted in significant cost cutting and elimination of service, a beleaguered core of health care providers and a very unhappy public. As this book goes to press, the Canadian Medical Organization is siding with an unhappy public demanding that the existing mechanism be kept, but demanding major increases in federal government funding. Canadians are not unhappy with their system, only the reduced funding.

CONCLUSION

1 Health care is an imperfect market. The result is a series of perverse incentives. Until approximately 1985, fee-for-service health care combined with third-party payer insurance reimbursement to stimulate excessive treatment and drive up costs. Today managed care health delivery often reverses the process and creates incentives to deny crucial care.

2 The current debate over health care is about basic values and priorities in America. A primary question is whether we as a nation should recognize health care as a **right** and not a **privilege** for those who can afford it. Almost all other industrialized nations recognize health care as a right. If there is a consensus that health care should be a **right,** then society has a collective **obligation** to provide some agreed-upon standard level of care. The market forces in health care are unable to provide the access that a **right** demands. Nor do market forces provide the cost control that the economic well-being of society requires.

3 There are many who doubt the government can run a more efficient system and maintain control over costs. Others point out the success of the public sector in running programs ranging from defense to police protection. Seeking government action to implement the collective will in health care is no different. They think the remedy is for government to shoulder its responsibility, not shirk it.

4 The market structure in health care resulted in rapidly rising costs. Health insurance relieved many of significant out-of-pocket expenses when they were sick. There is an inclination to overutilize health services. Health care providers also have an incentive to provide every service available. The use of low-benefit high-cost services encouraged the development of increasingly costly high-tech medicine that drove up health care costs.

5 Large employers, with the assistance of legislation pushed by Richard Nixon, brought about a revolution in health care delivery through the development of HMOs.

[53]http://strategis.ic.gc.ca/SSG/hs01267e.html

The development of managed care systems were a direct response to escalating health care costs. The changing health care structure has frequently placed physicians in impossible ethical dilemmas by providing economic incentives to reduce medical treatment. This strained the trust that patients have in their physician to be their advocate in health care. The result has been a decline in confidence in the health care system by many Americans, while health care costs continue to exceed inflation rates.

6 As a nation, the United States spends a larger percentage of its GDP on health care than any other country in the world, but still does not provide guaranteed access to about 16 percent of the population (42 million Americans). The uninsured have a higher death rate than can be explained by their lower socioeconomic standing. As a result of Medicare and Medicaid passage in 1965, coverage has been extended to the elderly and to the very poor. But for many of the working poor insurance is not affordable.

7 President Clinton tried to promote a bill to provide universal coverage by making it affordable. If successful, the United States as the richest nation in the world would have joined other industrialized states in providing health care to those less well off. The bill's fate was sealed when interest groups argued their self-interested positions rather than the "general welfare." After the defeat of the proposed legislation, the administration has gone back to the effort of incrementally expanding health care.

8 Germany and Canada offer two models of universal health care that are feeling cost containment pressures but are determined to maintain the basic principal of universal access based upon equality of care for all.

QUESTIONS FOR DISCUSSION

1 Should health care be a right or a privilege? Why?

2 Why are health care costs rising faster than the rate of growth in the GDP despite various attempts to contain costs?

3 Why have insurance companies shifted from risk sharing to risk avoidance? What, if anything, can be done about this phenomenon?

4 Explain how health care is rationed in the American system of health care delivery. How does this differ from the rationing system in a system of universal health care? Which is fairer? Why?

5 How is it possible for the United States to spend almost twice as much as many countries that provide their citizens with universal health care (and have better health indicators than the United States) while we still have so many without regular access to health care? Is this a demonstrated case of market failure? How could this be tied in to the inequality in the distribution of income noted earlier?

KEY CONCEPTS

adverse selection
COBRA
community rating
co-payment
cost shifting
deductible
ERISA

experience rating
Flexner Report
Health Insurance Portability and
 Accountability Act
HMOs
imperfect markets
managed care

Medicaid	self-insured
Medicare	single payer
moral hazard	third-party payer
preferred provider organization (PPO)	TANF
patients' rights	

SUGGESTED READINGS

Thomas Bodenheimer and Kip Sullivan, "How Large Employers Are Shaping the Health Care Marketplace," in two parts *The New England Journal of Medicine* (1998), 14, pp. 1003–7 and 15, pp. 1084–87.

Haynes Johnson and David S. Broder, *The System: The American Way of Politics at the Breaking Point* (Boston: Little, Brown, 1996).

George Kaplan, Elsie Pamuk, John Lynch, Richard Cohen, and Jennifer Balfour, "Inequality in Income and Mortality in the United States: Analysis of Mortality and Potential Pathways." *British Medical Journal* (1996), vol. 312, pp. 999–1003.

Robert Kuttner, "Must Good HMOs Go Bad?" in two parts, *The New England Journal of Medicine* (1998), vol. 338, no. 21, pp. 1558–63, and vol. 338, no. 22, pp. 1635–39.

Paula M. Lantz, James House, James Lepkowski, David Williams, Richard Mero, and Jieming Chen, "Socioeconomic Factors, Health Behaviors, and Mortality," *JAMA* (1998), vol. 279, no. 21, pp. 1703–8.

John E. Ware, Martha Bayliss, William Rogers, Mark Kosinski, and Alvin Tarlov, "Differences in 4-Year Health Outcomes for Elderly and Poor, Chronically Ill Patients Treated in HMO and Fee-for-Service Systems," *JAMA,* vol. 276, no. 13, pp. 1039–47.

11

CRISIS IN URBAN AND HOUSING ISSUES

The study of housing, in the context of public policy is an interdisciplinary undertaking. It is concerned with the politics and economics of housing costs and housing policy processes and strategies. Sociology provides analysis of neighborhood interactions and the impact of homelessness. Geography and land use planning provide studies on the spatial aspects of social, political, and economic forces.

Housing is central to the study of urban affairs because shelter is one of every person's most basic needs. The availability and quality of housing available in a metropolitan area reflects that community's ability to provide its citizens with a fundamental need. As a commodity in the market system, the ability of the market to match supply to the demand for housing shows the successes and failures of the market. When market outcomes result in negative outcomes for too many citizens, there are calls for the government to intervene and change them.

This chapter examines housing, the land use that very directly affects the welfare of families. During the Great Depression, millions of Americans lost their homes to bank foreclosures. Housing starts came to a virtual halt. A majority of those in the home building industry were unemployed due to lack of demand. Builders, banks, and those needing shelter looked to the national government for help. The response of the Roosevelt administration was the National Housing Act of 1934 that declared: "The general welfare and security of the Nation and the health and living standards of its people require . . . the realization . . . of the goal of a decent home and suitable living environment for every American family." This chapter examines the difficulty in reaching that goal.

HOUSING POLICY AND THE "AMERICAN DREAM"

Housing is of special importance in the U.S. economy and public policy. A house is the largest single consumer purchase for the majority of Americans. Owning a home has become part of the "American Dream." Thus, there is a belief that a strong relationship exists between the quality of housing and the quality of life.

Housing is a **merit good. A merit good is a good or service that the government considers desirable and therefore encourages by subsidies or regulation.** Some argue that an unsubsidized market can do a sufficient job of allocating housing resources in the quantities desired for those with money. In their view, there is little need for government financial support in the housing market except for low-income housing assistance. Housing is important because it has the ability to satisfy two of Abraham Maslow's most basic physiological (food and shelter) and safety (security) needs. Also, according to Maslow's hierarchy, being able to control where we live and to determine the setting and appearance of a dwelling can enhance self-esteem and self-actualization. Lack of control over these factors can increase alienation and reduce one's sense of self-worth.

Housing can also influence how we relate to other household members affecting what Maslow referred to as our need for belongingness and love. We might expect those with no fixed address to exhibit higher levels of anxiety and depression. The anguish of those with no fixed abode has a special place in Judeo-Christian thought. The Old Testament admonishes the faithful to be kind to the stranger and to remember that they were once "strangers" wandering in the land of Egypt. And the New Testament recounts that Christ was born in a cave as there was "no room in the inn." Christ spoke of his own sense of homelessness when he said, "the foxes have their lairs and the birds in the sky have their nests, but the Son of Man has nowhere to lay his head."

Economic and Political Aspects of Home Ownership

Substandard housing has been held responsible for disease and crime. Physically unsuitable housing has an impact on the safety and well-being of its occupants. If it is unclean, poorly or unsafely heated or ventilated, or has unsanitary plumbing it may have negative effects on the occupants. If left alone, it causes the deterioration of nearby housing. Homebuilding creates jobs and provides housing stock in communities, which in turn attracts other kinds of employment. The foregoing factors provide the ingredients for powerful bipartisan, political constituencies in housing, especially in regard to home ownership. Indeed, encouragement for the idea of home ownership has come from the leadership of both political parties. In 1968, President Lyndon Johnson said that "owning a home can increase responsibility and stake out a man's place in his community. . . . The man who owns a home has something to be proud of and reason to protect and preserve it."[1] President Ronald Reagan said that home ownership "supplies stability and rootedness."[2] Both political parties have pledged to work for a decent home for every citizen.

---

[1]Lyndon B. Johnson, "The Crisis of the Cities," the President's Message to the Congress on Urban Problems, February 12, 1968.

[2]Ann Mariano, "Action Urged to Keep Public Housing Units Available to Poor," *The Washington Post,* 13 July 1985.

It has long been held that home ownership promotes social stability because the individuals owning homes have a stake in the system. Recall that voting was originally limited to male property holders on the theory that they would vote more responsibly than those without property. Consequently, government at all levels has provided housing assistance for households at all income levels.[3]

For most individuals home ownership provides a psychological and financial confidence not typically identified with rental occupancy. Purchase of a home severs the dependency relationship between tenant and landlord. It also allows families to accumulate wealth through the equity they have in their homes. **Equity in homes is the main source of wealth for most families.**

In April 1994, survey research firms conducted the Fannie Mae National Housing Survey to determine American attitudes toward home ownership. Just over 86 percent of those surveyed believed that people are "better off owning," while 74 percent said the best time to buy a home is "as soon as you can afford it." By an overwhelming majority, both owners (86 percent) and renters (84 percent) agreed that a home is a good investment. As shown in table 11-1, the survey found that Americans do associate home ownership with a host of positive effects on the economy and their neighborhoods.

In addition to these personal gains, some analysts argue, there are broader societal gains related to home ownership. In their view, homeowners are able to save at a higher rate than renters. This occurs through the portion of their mortgage payments paid directly on the principal that builds up home equity, the appreciation of the worth of their homes over the years, and the tax advantages homeowners enjoy. These savings make funds available for national investment, which stimulates greater economic growth. Also, homeowners are more likely to maintain and improve their property than renters, and maintenance and renovation extend the life of the housing stock. Moreover, studies confirm that homeowners are more likely to vote in local and federal elections than are renters.[4]

A major problem in our market economy is that labor markets drive the wages of many wage earners below the level where they can buy minimum quality housing without sacrificing other basic needs. That is, their income is so low that homebuilders cannot produce decent housing at the price level many low income wage earners can afford. This is particularly true in an emerging global economy in which low-skilled American workers must compete directly with workers in even lower wage countries. Housing is a problem in every country of the world in that there is a gap between the cost of building and maintaining housing at a profit and the level of housing expenditures that are affordable by the less affluent in the society.[5] Under central planning, the economies of Eastern Europe, until the last decade, directed state investments in industry rather than housing. The result was a shortage in the housing stock that

---

[3]The government has, in fact, supported home ownership beginning with the Homestead Act in 1860, and extending through the federal income tax in 1913 right up to the tax policies in effect currently. However, it is debatable that homeowners are more responsible than renters in all respects: There is some evidence that free-rider behavior leaving neighborhood improvements to others extends across both groups.

[4]Raymond J. Struyk, *Should Government Encourage Home Ownership?* (Washington, DC: The Urban Institute, 1977). Homeowners' greater propensity to vote at present may well reflect their economic status relative to the average renter, rather than being related to home ownership per se.

[5]R. Allen Hays, "Housing," in *Handbook of Research on Urban Politics and Policy in the United States,* Ronald K. Vogel (ed.), (Westport, CT: Greenwood Press, 1997), p. 294.

TABLE 11-1
POSITIVE EFFECTS OF HOME OWNERSHIP

Positive effects	% Americans agreeing
Economy in area	57
Young people obtaining college degrees	54
Families getting ahead financially	54
Neighborhood safety	49
People voting in elections	49
Positive overall effects on community	49

Source: Fannie Mae, *Fannie Mae National Housing Survey 1994*
(Washington, DC: U.S. Government Printing Office, 1994), pp. 3–4.

crowded families into cramped apartments. Underinvestment resulted in poorly constructed housing as well.

Still others criticize the American fixation with the higher level of investment in housing as having largely occurred through governmental taxing and spending policies that have directed investment funds into real estate at the expense of new plants and equipment. In this view, overinvestment in facilities that provide instant gratification for some, such as new houses, is encouraged, while the necessary investment in factories that provides long-term benefits for everyone is discouraged.[6] Critics also contend that home equity loans give undue advantage to homeowners—who tend to be more affluent than renters—because they are cheaper than other consumer loans. The critics contend, in other words, that these loans help "the rich get richer."

Other critics have argued that the market responds very efficiently to consumer demand for expensive housing that includes an implicit preference for segregation by class. For the affluent, the purchase of a home is seen as an investment. Along with the structure, the homeowner's purchase includes the purchase of social status and social homogeneity that is included in the purchase price. Since these factors become a part of the cost of home ownership, each buyer has a financial interest in maintaining the status and social integrity of the community.[7]

HOUSING AND POLITICAL TRENDS

From Farms, to Cities, to Suburbs

Throughout much of Europe's history, cities were densely populated areas where everyone could live within city walls that protected the population from attack. The poor and outcasts were excluded from the town as were certain operations like farming that required more land, or tanning operations that gave off noxious fumes. Those living or working outside the urban area were in the **suburbs**—a term that suggested something less than urban areas. Cities tended to expand roughly in concentric circles as wider

[6]Alfred L. Malabre, Jr., *Beyond Our Means* (New York: Vintage Books, 1987), pp. 42–43. Malabre also claims that housing policy has encouraged excessive indebtedness and overspending as more and more Americans have been going into deeper debt by borrowing against equity in their homes (p. 44).
[7]Hays, "Housing," p. 294.

circles were built to protect an ever expanding population. In North America there was less concern about foreign attack than about opportunities in the expansive bounty of nature. Many sought agrarian living away from the crowded and unhealthy conditions of city dwellers. Rivers became important energy sources during the industrial revolution. Mills and factories attracted a laboring population that lived close to the industrial engines.

Thomas Jefferson believed that the ideal society would be composed of farmers with enough property to provide support for the social order. He believed that an equitable distribution of property would help prevent excessive concentrations of wealth and power. Therefore, he thought property ownership was useful in deterring civil disorder and revolution. Nineteenth-century America was primarily agrarian, and reflected the Jeffersonian ideal of the yeoman farmer. However, social patterns in much of twentieth-century America have reflected an excitement for cities as the centers of culture and the very heart of industrial production and national prosperity. Throughout the nineteenth and well into the twentieth century, most American cities were manufacturing centers.

In the 1880s railroads and streetcars enabled middle-class residents to move further away from the center of the city while the poorest workers continued to live within walking distance of the industrial nerve center. The pattern of urban development was one of a commercial district with adjacent industrial areas and residential neighborhoods in town extending out along streetcar and rail lines.

Although housing is one of everyone's most basic needs, until the experience in this century of two world wars and the Great Depression few thought that government had any direct responsibility to provide housing. Although the U.S. government began experimenting with housing programs during the Depression, most believed that, once the economy was stabilized after World War II, the government's role would recede in the face of advances in the housing industry. Nevertheless, several factors conspired to increase the role of government in housing, not decrease it.

The post–World War II economic boom, assisted by federal housing mortgage subsidies and the purchase of newly affordable cars, enabled more people than ever to consider moving to the suburbs to escape the unpleasantness of crowded city life.[8] The absence of buildable land for new homes in cities and an increase in real incomes from the 1950s and continuing to the present also exacerbated the decline of central cities by expediting the exodus to the suburbs. Suburban development patterns promoted greater segregation by income. The realities of the housing market ultimately determined that the "less affluent" would live in the older, deteriorated housing inventory in the central cities.

Local governments outside the city began adopting zoning ordinances separating different types of developments into different areas. As suburban sprawl moved further from the center of cities, businesses followed the shifting population channeled by zoning laws into areas separated from housing. Business parks and shopping malls

[8]The movement to the suburbs is not a recent phenomenon in reaction to the decay and deterioration of inner cities. The movement toward less densely populated areas began by the turn of the century and actually preceded the automobile. It was not apparent at first because growth at the fringes was still largely inside city limits. See William G. Grisby and Thomas C. Corl, "Declining Neighborhoods: Problem or Opportunity," *Annals of the American Academy of Political and Social Science,* vol. 465 (January 1983), p. 90.

were interspersed throughout suburbia. Suburban development is extremely expensive because of the need to build roads, streets, sewers, and water lines to support the suburban spread. The need to keep up with the demand for new services was a major contributor to the anti-tax revolt of the 1980s to limit property taxes (California's Proposition 13 is the best-known example). These restrictions deprived many jurisdictions of needed revenue to provide the infrastructure and services for suburban development. Suburban jurisdictions came to depend more heavily on sales taxes to finance required services. Jurisdictions in need of revenue now find that zoning for malls and shopping centers will provide higher revenue than residential zoning which requires more expensive infrastructure.

There is such fragmentation of government responsibility in the many small municipalities surrounding cities that meaningful land-use planning becomes difficult. Suburban development often led to an exodus of residents and jobs from the central city leaving only those too poor to leave behind. The result is a decentralization of jobs and people and concentrated poverty. This process has racial overtones. Those who are white and poor often live in pockets in a metropolitan area. Those who are African American and poor tend to be concentrated in neighborhoods in the central city. As the donut expands into the suburbs, the barren hole in the center grows as well.

Central cities retain many facilities that cannot be easily reproduced in the suburbs, such as large hospitals and medical facilities, museums, and art galleries. Moreover, the "central" locations of cities sustain central business districts (CBDs) that employ suburbanites. Jobs utilizing primarily communication skills rather than manual labor thrive in cities, so that suburbs become "bedroom" communities with many of their residents commuting daily to work in nearby big cities. Ironically, many of the urban dwellers living closest to the CBDs offering highly paid jobs find themselves excluded from such employment.

The Undesirable Consequences of Concentrated Urban Poverty

The exodus of nonpoor residents and many businesses reduces the ability of the cities to provide adequate services to their residents. First, the flight of these tax sources reduces the per capita fiscal resources left in the cities putting pressure on those governments to raise taxes or cut services or both. Since suburban residents live in a community with fewer poor residents, they can avoid their fair share of public costs of dealing with poverty. This further encourages people to move to the suburbs from central cities and entices even more residents to the community who wish to avoid the full costs of paying the nation's fiscal burden for the poor.

The housing market reflects these preferences through demand but may heighten the impact. For example, when a bank redlines a neighborhood, it reflects the declining demand for houses in the community by those who could keep up the market value of housing, while it also cuts off credit from those investors who still find the area desirable, that is, those who might rescue it from the spiral of decline.[9] Thus large cities that have a disproportionate share of the nation's poor must bear the "excess social burden."

[9]Hays, "Housing," p. 299.

Those living in the suburbs often also benefit from the amenities cities have to offer while largely avoiding their costs. Urban facilities such as roads, public sanitation, and mass transportation are used by everyone, but paid for out of the declining tax bases of lower-income city residents. On the other hand, suburban communities benefit from their more affluent property tax bases, which assure them of superior public schools, parks, and other amenities that are nominally public, but are in fact inaccessible to all but the local community dwellers.[10]

Cities with higher than normal poverty rates are high-cost places to live and work and are afflicted with crippling social problems despite the means-tested transfers flowing to many of the urban poor. One strategy that would make cities more attractive to the non-poor would be to relieve big cities of the excess financial burdens that separate them from the suburbs. The redistributive responsibilities of poverty should reside with all citizens and the federal government. Federal block grants could be targeted to recognize the disproportionate impact of poverty concentrated in large cities. At the state level, regional taxation and service delivery between cities and the suburbs can help spread the costs of poverty.

Another strategy is to provide incentives to break up the pockets of concentration of the poor in major cities by providing housing vouchers. By breaking up the concentration of poverty, inner city fiscal burdens can be reduced while attracting middle-income households and businesses to the city.[11]

By the end of the 1950s, as a result of the movement toward the suburbs, the American population was almost equally divided between urban areas (one-third), suburbs (one-third), and rural areas (one-third).[12] **In 1990, the United States became the first country ever to have more people living in the suburbs than urban and rural residents combined.**[13]

The trend toward a suburban society cannot be overestimated in terms of its impact on American politics. Topography initially shapes the desirability of land for various uses. The structures that are built on the land and their function affect the desirability of the land for subsequent purposes. Much of urban politics is shaped by this basic struggle over physical space. Neighborhoods are designed for housing within a certain range of economic value. Residents fight to prevent any activity or use that might negatively affect their property values. Investors are seeking a maximum return on their investment.

---

[10]Wallace Smith, "Housing America," *The Annals of the American Academy of Political and Social Science* (Beverly Hills, CA: Sage, 1983), pp. 10–11.

[11]Joseph Gyourko and Anita A. Summers, "A New Strategy for Helping Cities Pay for the Poor," *Brookings Policy Brief No. 18* (Washington, DC: The Brookings Institution, 1998).

[12]The definition of what constitutes a city, or what is a rural area, is a subjective judgment complicated by the growth of suburban areas (neither rural or urban). In 1910 the Census Bureau defined any incorporated town with 2,500 residents as urban. The definition slowly shifted so that by 1980 an area had to have a minimum population of 50,000 and have "built-up" characteristics to be classified as urban.

The U.S. Census and American Housing Survey (AHS) now uses what are termed metropolitan statistical areas (MSAs) in an effort to create more useful boundaries for urban areas. MSAs typically include cities **and** close-by suburban areas. However, they are rather imprecise and also present research problems. For example, some MSAs include entire counties that have close economic relationships with central urban areas. In the West, some counties are so large that an MSA may extend from coastal Seattle inland fifty miles to the Cascade mountains.

[13]Kenneth Jackson, "America's Rush to Suburbia," *The New York Times,* 9 June 1996.

HOUSING LOCATION AND
NEIGHBORHOOD CHANGE

What factors shape a family's choice of
where to live? Families in similar situations
often engage in parallel decision-making
processes that have the cumulative effect of
forming identifiable neighborhoods. Several
models have been developed to explain
neighborhood change. The filtering-down
theory is one such model.

The Filtering-Down Theory
This model holds that as the incomes of
families rise, the families will be able to satisfy their increased demand for housing by
buying newly built housing. Newly constructed housing will usually be built away
from the central city because urban lots are
too small to satisfy the preference of upper-
income families, and the cost of buying sufficient land and demolishing existing
construction is prohibitive. Suitable vacant
land at lower opportunity cost is usually
available outside the city.

This means an empty house, and there
are two likely scenarios for the home that
has been vacated. First, it may be purchased by a family having socioeconomic
characteristics similar to the previous owners. In this case, the neighborhood remains
unchanged, and no filtering occurs.

A second possibility is that families of
similar economic backgrounds are not
interested in buying the property at the
price paid by the original owners, even

though the quality of the housing has not
declined. The equilibrium price of housing
in the neighborhood thus falls and becomes
affordable to households with incomes
lower than those who moved away.
Families with incomes below those of the
families that have moved will clearly benefit from this filtering operation.

As lower-income groups filter into
such homes, a variety of changes are
likely. The less affluent will be less able
to afford the same levels of maintenance
as the previous more affluent owners.
Studies suggest that the level of maintenance can affect the rate of neighborhood
change. Those in a neighborhood going
through this filtering toward lower-income
families anticipate lowered property values, or if they plan to move themselves,
they expect that maintenance and upkeep
will not result in an appreciation of property values and they invest less in that
maintenance.

What Starts the Process
There is reason to believe that the filtering-
down process is the result of negative externalities of pollution, congestion, noise, or
fear of crime that increase as one moves
toward the central city. Once a neighborhood is identified as blue collar or working
class, as opposed to white collar or middle
class, in the minds of those in the housing
market, the shift to the next lower income
group may accelerate.

Source: John P. Blair, *Urban & Regional Economics* (Homewood, IL: Richard D. Irwin, 1991),
pp. 415–19.

The socioeconomic sorting of neighborhoods whose residents have similar incomes,
as explained by the filtering-down and tradeoff models, is especially encouraged in a
culture in which material status is highly regarded. One of the strongest forces affecting the use of housing space is the tendency for people to group themselves according
to economic, cultural, or social stratification. By attracting people of like income levels, suburban communities become economic enclaves. Robert Reich has pointed out

that similar incomes, and the similarity in tastes that go with them, increasingly define communities.[14] People hope that by living near people like themselves they will find agreeable neighbors or friends for their children. The price of housing in a neighborhood is often taken as a strong indicator of the social characteristics of its residents. As Allen Hays states it:

> There are three basic motivations for this sociospacial structuring: (1) to structure social relations by limiting interactions to neighbors who share "desirable" traits according to the individual's value structure; (2) to create a neighborhood that, by its location and aesthetics, is a visible symbol of one's social standing; and (3) to preserve the investment value of one's property, which is viewed as a direct result of (1) and (2).[15]

This structuring that attracts people to affluent neighborhoods has a negative impact on those on the bottom rungs of the socioeconomic ladder. Those with the most economic power choose the most attractive spaces, while those on the bottom rungs must settle for what is left over. Those at the bottom of this stratified system are physically isolated from opportunities that might enhance their upward mobility and thereby the isolation contributes to the self-perpetuation of their poverty.[16] All federal housing programs that try to improve the lives of the poor by providing low-income housing in housing areas of high incomes have had to contend with the "NIMBY" (not in my back yard) reaction.

People in the same community usually have neighborhood associations that serve to protect and defend the integrity of the area against any threat to property values or the construction of low-income housing or a factory nearby. The result is to reduce the community's sense of a common purpose with the larger society. Gated communities— enclaves with security guards posted at the community entrance and surrounded by walls are becoming increasingly popular. Many choose to reside in gated communities because they believe that such housing reduces the risk of unwanted daily intrusions while providing improved personal security. Gated communities usually deliver the security against intrusion and falling home prices they promise. Such suburban community dwellers frequently substitute their involvement in and sense of belonging to their community for involvement in the larger society. Defending the local community's property values can provide a self-image of performing a civic duty. But it implies a separation from communities beyond the confines of one's own neighborhood. Gated communities reinforce an exclusive community culture, where the tension between the individual and society tilts toward the individual's self-interest.[17]

Political parties have sought to exploit suburban America's uneasiness. Prior to the 1960s, the Republican Party had a tradition of being at least as committed to racial liberalism as the Democratic Party. But as legislation with real substantive content began to be seriously pressed, Republican support began to decline. Bills establishing rent

---

[14] Robert B. Reich, *The Work of Nations* (New York: Vintage Books, 1992), p. 278.

[15] Hays, "Housing," p. 293.

[16] Ann C. Case and Lawrence Katz, *The Company You Keep: The Effects of Family and Neighborhood on Disadvantaged Youths* (Cambridge, MA: National Bureau of Economic Research, 1991). See also Hays, op. cit.

[17] Robert E. Lang and Karen A. Danielsen, "Gated Communities in America: Walling Out the World?" *Housing Policy Debate,* vol. 8, issue 4, *Fannie Mae Foundation,* http://www.fanniemaefoundation.org/Housing Research/Abstracts/HPDebate.

supplements for the poor, open-housing policies, the model cities program, a rat erad-ication program, and a new federal cabinet-level Department of Housing and Urban Development were passed over the opposition of most Republicans in the House and Senate.[18] The Republican Party has increasingly adopted an adversarial stance toward government-sponsored urban programs, claiming they are examples of flawed gov-ernment intervention into areas best left to the free market.

European urban dwellers have not shown the same inclination to move to the suburbs as their incomes rise. In Europe, cities are thought of as centers of civilization. The cen-tral city represents a vital asset for society. Therefore, those who live in suburban and rural areas are more willing to pay taxes to beautify and maintain urban centers. As a result, the political cleavage between cities and suburbs evident in the United States has not occurred in Europe.

A clear example of this difference can be seen in the handling of transportation issues. Most Americans live outside cities in suburban areas and their concerns focus on free-ways as the solution to urban transportation problems. By contrast, in Europe, interest in the quality of the environment takes priority over accessibility. Investment in public transportation within cities is emphasized as a strategy to ease congestion. The use of automobiles is discouraged, and in some cases, banned altogether. Also in Europe, highly developed intercity rail systems deliver travelers from one city center to another. Train depots located in central urban areas encourage business locations nearby and attract highly paid professionals to live in areas easily accessible to railway terminals. The United States lacks a well-developed high-speed rail system and relies instead on air travel. Airports are mainly located outside cities. This often results in their becoming significant areas for business location.

Political Implications

Housing patterns have profoundly influenced American political issues. Unlike cities of an earlier era that housed rich and poor alike and had to provide services for them all, today most middle- and upper-income families have moved to the suburbs. American cities are left with a population of minorities largely poor and less well educated than suburbanites, living in older deteriorated housing. The suburbs, by contrast, contain middle- and upper- income families who are better educated, live in newer housing, and identify only with their local suburban interests. William Schneider argues that America unfortunately prefers the private over the public. Upwardly mobile suburban dwellers are highly tax-sensitive when governments use their money to solve what are perceived to be other people's problems.

The "elitist" suburban view tends to believe that government has too much power, that taxes should be kept low, and that people should solve their own problems.[19] There is another more cynical view that government **cannot** solve most problems because offi-cials are incompetent, or controlled by special interests, and cannot be trusted to do what

---

[18]Thomas Ones Agnus and Mary D. Agnus, *Chain Reaction: The Impact of Race, Rights, and Taxes on American Politics* (New York: W. W. Annoys & Company, 1991), p. 62.

[19]William Schneider, "The Dawn of the Suburban Era in American Politics," *The Atlantic,* vol. 270, no. 1 (July 1992), p. 37.

THE TRADEOFF MODEL: SPACE VERSUS ACCESS

This model (fig. 11-1) aims at explaining housing location and starts with the proposal that rents are higher the closer one is to the center of a city and decline as one moves further away. The higher rent close to the center results from access to urban goods that make the land more valuable. Offsetting the desirability of access, and a factor in the choice of housing location, is the fact that, all things being equal, families prefer more space to less space. If one lives in the suburbs but commutes to the city for work, travel costs (including time) must be considered in the calculation of which is the more desirable residential area. The outward movement effect caused by the wish for space is stronger than the travel cost effect, resulting in neighborhoods of higher-income families in a metropolitan area's outer ring. In addition, although the central city is still the site of a plurality of jobs, jobs have increasingly shifted to suburban locations, easing transportation costs.

FIGURE 11-1
THE TRADEOFF MODEL: SPACE VERSUS ACCESS.
Space versus access with increasing income. (*Note:* As income increases, the original equilibrium is disturbed, resulting in a relocation because the desire for more space and cheaper land in outlying regions is stronger than the desire for better access to the central city.)

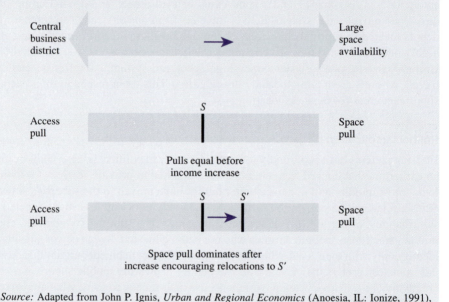

Source: Adapted from John P. Ignis, *Urban and Regional Economics* (Anoesia, IL: Ionize, 1991), pp. 419–20; John P. Blair, *Urban & Regional Economics* (Homewood, IL: Richard D. Irwin, 1991), p. 419.

is right. Together these views make up a powerful antitax, antigovernment coalition.[20] Many people want to live in the suburbs so they can control government, including taxes, education, and other services. Nationwide, suburban voters tend to be the most

[20]Ibid., p. 37.

Republican in presidential elections, although they are more likely to vote for Democratic candidates in congressional and state elections.

City governments lack adequate tax bases. They need redistributive tax programs that would transfer financial resources from the suburbs to the cities. However, suburban voters recoil from the prospect of their tax dollars going to the cities. Recent Republican presidential candidates have appealed to suburban voters by campaigning against Great Society programs that primarily helped the cities. Similarly, Democratic presidential candidates have increasingly taken up the cause of the "forgotten middle class" while downplaying urban programs. Cities tend to vote for Democratic presidential candidates, but are often outvoted by an overwhelming concentration of voters in the suburbs. This has not gone unnoticed by the leadership of both parties. Mayors of many cities feel frustrated when their agenda items are given low priority by both parties.

Nevertheless, government must be involved in housing, because private housing markets cannot provide sufficient quantities of affordable housing for a significant portion of the population. This appears to be true in all advanced countries. The rationale for federal intervention in the U.S. housing market has focused on the policy goal of providing every American with "a decent house in a suitable living environment." The government's role has emphasized **improving the quality of the housing inventory** by stimulating new construction and reducing the number of substandard housing units.[21]

Physical Condition of Housing Units

Housing conditions have improved significantly since the end of World War II due primarily to the brisk growth in per capita and household incomes. Problems with physical deficiencies in housing units are less common than problems in affordability for both home buyers and renters. The physical deficiencies where they do exist are higher in rental units than owner-occupied housing.

Some seize upon the improvements in housing during the last decades as an indication that the United States has dealt with housing problems more successfully than most critics are aware. As would be expected, lower-income renters were more likely than high-income renters to live in physically deficient dwellings: 18 percent of all very-low-income renters and 14 percent of all low-income renters lived in units judged physically deficient, while only 8 percent of higher-income renters were so housed.[22]

---

[21]Lawrence B. Smith, Kenneth T. Rosen, and George Fallis, "Recent Developments in Economic Models of Housing," *The Journal of Economic Literature,* vol. 26 (March 1988), p. 41.

[22]An index developed by the Congressional Budget Office (CBO) defines units needing rehabilitation as those lacking complete plumbing or kitchen facilities, or having two or more of eleven different structural defects. The defects include (1) three or more breakdowns of six or more hours each time of the heating system during the previous winter; (2) three or more times completely without water for six or more hours each time during the preceding ninety days; (3) three or more times completely without a flush toilet for six or more hours each time during the preceding ninety days; (4) a leaking roof; (5) holes in interior floors; (6) open cracks or holes in interior walls or ceilings; (7) broken plaster or peeling paint over more than one square foot of interior walls or ceilings; (8) unconcealed wiring; (9) the absence of a working light in public hallways for multiunit structures; (10) loose or no handrails in public hallways for multiunit structures; and (11) loose, broken, or missing steps in public hallways for multiunit structures. See Congressional Budget Office, *Current Housing Problems and Possible Federal Responses* (Washington, DC: Government Printing Office, 1988), p. 8.

THE TIEBOUT MODEL AND GOVERNMENT

Charles Tiebout, in 1956, developed a model of local government financing that considered a house purchased in an area as including a bundle of goods and services which vary depending upon what is offered by the local government. In the twentieth century, government bestows value on private property by providing police protection, roads and streets, sewage, power and water systems, public transportation, schools, and other services. The different levels of services provided will result in different tax burdens in different communities. More and better community services with lower taxes will increase demand for housing within a community. If differing communities have equal housing services, the one with the lowest tax rate will be the most attractive. By "voting with their feet," households choose jurisdictions on the basis of the fiscal package of the services offered and the cost mechanism to pay for them. Property tax increases that result in a more attractive mix of services provided will be capitalized into property values.

Other nongovernmental amenities such as community prestige, friendly neighbors, and pleasant surroundings add to the community's attractiveness. On the other hand, negative features such as pollution and unsafe streets may not only be negative externalities in themselves, but have the effect of increasing taxes on property values.

Individual preferences for an area include the actual housing as well as the public services and other aspects of the community's external environment. People's choices will be based not only on their preferences but their willingness and ability to buy different bundles of public services.

Source: Charles M. Tiebout, "A Pure Theory of Local Expenditures," *Journal of Political Economy,* vol. 64, no. 3 (October 1956), pp. 416–24.

Those opposed to government rehab programs complain supporters have changed their definition of deficient housing. They claim that, if higher standards are constantly applied, the housing problem will never be resolved since units acceptable under older standards, even if they do not deteriorate, will be considered unacceptable under new standards.

Table 11-2 shows the types of improvements that have occurred in owner-occupied housing between 1970 and 1996. The trends indicate increases in square footage, the number of bathrooms, the percentage of new units with central air conditioning, and the number of units having parking facilities. Every category of amenity grew except for number of bedrooms. This may reflect smaller family sizes and the growth in vacation and retirement communities.

THE HOMELESS

One of the more troubling developments in recent years for those concerned with housing policy issues has been the increasing numbers of the severely disadvantaged in our society. It is at this level that the policy goal of "a decent house in a suitable living environment" for every American has clearly not been achieved. And future trends are ominous. Not only are the numbers of the homeless increasing, but the numbers of precariously

TABLE 11-2
CHARACTERISTICS OF NEW PRIVATELY OWNED SINGLE-FAMILY
HOUSES COMPLETED, 1970–1996

Characteristic	Percent of units		
	1970	1980	1996
Floor area, ft²			
Under 1200	36	21	9
1200–1599	28	29	21
1600–1999	16	22	23
2000–2399	21	13	18
2400+		15	30
Bedrooms			
2 or fewer	13	17	13
3	63	63	56
4 or more	24	20	31
Bathrooms			
1½ or fewer	20	10	9
2	32	48	41
2½ or more	16	25	49
Central air conditioning	34	63	81
Fireplaces			
1 or more	35	56	62
Parking facilities			
Garage	58	69	86
Carport	17	7	1
No garage or carport	25	24	13

*Median size was 1385 ft² in 1970, 1595 ft² in 1980, and 1905 ft² in 1990.
Source: Statistical Abstract, 1993, 1997.

housed families forced to double up in their living accommodations, the numbers of low-income families paying more rent than they can afford, and the numbers of homeowners delinquent in mortgage payments indicate that housing problems are getting worse.

Homelessness is not a new phenomenon, but has always been a part of the American socioeconomic landscape and history. In the nineteenth and early twentieth centuries, transient homelessness, consisting of poor workingmen without families living in skid row sections of major cities, was established. Cheap hotels and restaurants thrived in such neighborhoods. Prior to the 1930s, private charities and local governments provided almost all of the aid to the poor and homeless. The Great Depression overwhelmed the charitable institutions of the time. During the Great Depression in the 1930s, the transient homeless consisted primarily of young men who left home in search of work so as not to be burdens on their parents. World War II marked a change, and the demand for labor remained high enough after the war to ensure that homeless rates stayed low throughout the 1950s and 1960s compared to the 1930s. By the mid-1970s, urban renewal projects had demolished many of the cheap flop-house hotels. By the late 1970s, the homeless were seen with increasing frequency sleeping on steam grates, doorways, park benches, and other highly visible places in American cities. Women began to appear among the homeless with increasing frequency as well.

Throughout much of American history, the reaction of society to homelessness has ranged from indifference to fear and contempt. But recently public concern with homelessness appears to have increased with the growing awareness of the problem. In New York state, public interest lawyers sued New York City claiming that the state constitution and the city's charter made "shelter" an entitlement. The case was settled in 1981 by a consent decree in which New York City agreed to provide shelter on demand.[23]

Defining Homelessness

To be homeless is to be at the very bottom of the socioeconomic ladder in America. The spreading epidemic of homelessness is only the most obvious indication of the growing problem of poverty in America, and the homeless are only the most visible of those inadequately housed, whose numbers are growing even faster and reaching into the American mainstream. A Department of Housing and Urban Development report in 1984 defined a person as homeless if his or her customary nighttime residence met any of the following criteria:

> a) in public or private emergency shelters which take a variety of forms—armories, schools, church basements, government buildings, former firehouses and where temporary vouchers are provided by private and public agencies, even hotels, apartments, or boarding homes; or b) in the streets, parks, subways, bus terminals, railroad stations, airports, under bridges or aqueducts, abandoned buildings without utilities, cars, trucks, or any of the public or private space that is not designed for shelter.[24]

These poor clearly do not have access to traditional standard dwellings such as homes, apartments, rented rooms, or mobile homes. Peter Rossi, a professor of sociology, in his work *Down and Out in America,* defines **literal homelessness as not having customary and regular access to a conventional dwelling.**[25]

How Many Homeless Are There?

The homeless, in the definition above, are a subset of the very poor in our society. Policy makers need a reasonable estimate of the extent of the problem of homelessness in order to effectively deal with it. Unfortunately there are no firm statistics on the number of homeless people in America. The National Alliance to End Homelessness, a Washington-based advocacy group for the homeless acknowledged the difficulty in obtaining an accurate census of the homeless in its 1995 annual report. The Alliance estimated that on any given night, about 750,000 Americans are homeless. It also estimated that between 1.3 and 2 million people would experience a period of homelessness during the course of a year.[26]

---

[23]See Peter H. Rossi, *Down and Out in America: The Origins of Homelessness* (Chicago: The University of Chicago Press, 1989) for an excellent description of the evolution of the characteristics of the homeless.

[24]United States Department of Housing and Urban Development (HUD), *A Report to the Secretary on the Homeless and Emergency Shelters* (Washington, DC: Office of Policy Development and Research, 1984).

[25]Rossi, *Down and Out in America,* p. 11. Professor Rossi points out that homelessness is not an absolute condition but actually a matter of degree.

[26]National Alliance to End Homelessness, *Annual Report 1995,* p. 4.

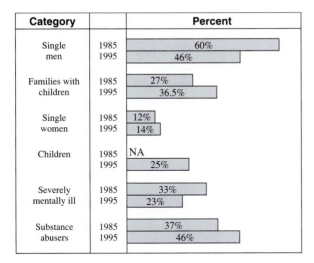

Category		Percent
Single men	1985	60%
	1995	46%
Families with children	1985	27%
	1995	36.5%
Single women	1985	12%
	1995	14%
Children	1985	NA
	1995	25%
Severely mentally ill	1985	33%
	1995	23%
Substance abusers	1985	37%
	1995	46%

FIGURE 11-2
THE CHANGING HOMELESS POPULATION. (*Source:* U.S. Conference of Mayors, *A Status Report on Hunger and Homelessness in America's Cities: 1995, December 1995.*)

Many more people are "precariously housed." That is, they live in conventional dwellings but their hold on their lodgings is precarious. The precariously housed are chronically poor people who live in constant risk of becoming homeless. They must rely on inadequate incomes, and lacking the security of enough food, are completely dependent upon the good will of friends or relatives. Professor Rossi estimates that approximately 7 million people may fall into this category. These precariously housed individuals make up the pool from which people cycle in and out of homelessness.

It is not surprising, then, that efforts to profile the composition of the homeless population result in varying figures. For example, the 1995 report of the *U.S. Conference of Mayors* reported on a survey of twenty-nine major cities (fig. 11-2).

The number of adult males declined by 14 percent over the decade while the number of families with children grew by almost 10 percent to 36.5 percent. Over half the single males had never married, while more than a third lived alone before becoming homeless. Peter Rossi found that a major contrast between the homeless population in recent years and that in the 1960s is the increase in the number of women. Women with children make up about 34 percent of the homeless population.[27]

Another contrast between the homeless in the 1960s and currently is that the new homeless are younger. The average age in earlier studies was around 50. Recent studies show the median age to be around 36, with the range extending primarily from age 28 to 46.[28] The homeless are also increasingly African American. Earlier studies suggested that about 75 percent of the homeless were white. The percentage of the homeless drawn from minority populations varies from city to city based upon the minority composition of the area, but a clear majority nationally are now African American.

The increasing number of families with children is another foreboding indicator of future challenges to society. Twenty-five percent of the 750,000 homeless are children

[27]Rossi, *Down and Out in America,* p. 39. The number of homeless women varies widely between cities (from about 7 percent in Austin, to over 20 percent in New York). By all accounts, however, the percentage of homeless women prior to the 1970s was relatively insignificant.

[28]Rossi, *Down and Out in America,* p. 40.

which is more than all the children in a major city like Pittsburgh. The infant mortality rate among the homeless is roughly 30 percent higher than that for babies born into families living in homes. Oftentimes, homeless families are separated because some shelters will accept only women and young children, while others will accept only men and older boys. Young children who are homeless often show signs of emotional distress. Unstable housing can put them far behind their peers in physical and cognitive development. Homeless children find getting to school difficult, and academic achievement even more difficult. Many worry that their parents will be gone (to look for a job, or to another shelter) when they leave school.[29]

The Causes of Homelessness

Any effort to develop an effective policy to deal with homelessness must not only identify who the homeless are but must determine what has caused these people to become homeless. The theories that have been advanced to explain homelessness fall into four general categories.[30]

1 Falling incomes. One theory holds that rising homelessness has been caused by declining incomes of low-income workers. It suggests that the homeless are the victims of the impersonal forces of the economy.

2 Reductions in safety net programs. A second theory maintains that the upsurge in homelessness is related to government cutbacks, particularly at the federal level, in welfare benefits such as Aid to Families with Dependent Children (AFDC), food stamps, unemployment assistance, and housing assistance. Moreover, states have reacted to recent economic downturns and federal cutbacks by reducing their own programs. In all areas of assistance other than Social Security, which is indexed to inflation, there has been a significant erosion of government payments.[31] Reducing social program spending or new restrictions on program eligibility may have erased the only margin of protection that kept some from becoming homeless.

3 Affordability of housing and the homeless. Another theory focuses on affordability, stressing the reduced availability of housing for low-income families. According to this theory, the major factor in contributing to homelessness today is the fact that the gap between the number of low-income renters and the number of affordable units has been growing since the early 1970s. So real incomes were falling while real housing costs were rising. The result for many is homelessness. For those who manage to avoid homelessness, the result is higher-cost-housing and the increased risk of homelessness.

4 Individual pathologies. Still another theory stresses the personal pathologies of individual homeless people. It centers on the lack of personal abilities or skills of

[29]Children's Defense Fund, *The State of America's Children,* 1991, p. 108.

[30]See William Tucker, *The Excluded Americans: Homelessness and Housing Policies* (Washington, DC: Regnery Gateway, 1990), pp. 4–10. These theories also apply, although perhaps not as critically, to those who are precariously housed and to those who are low-income renters and homeowners.

[31]For example, AFDC was created for families where unemployment was due to an absent, disabled, or dead parent. In 1992 the median benefit was $380 for a family of three. But in thirty-nine states, the maximum AFDC grant for a three-person family was less than the federally set fair market rent for a modest two-bedroom apartment in the states' lowest-cost areas. See Children's Defense Fund, *The State of America's Children, 1991,* p. 113. (See also chap. 7.)

the homeless, which may be compounded by psychological disabilities and substance abuse. In the early 1970s, federal legislation shifted mental health care to the "least restrictive" community-based setting, meaning deinstitutionalization. This shift was seen as humane, since numerous abuses of patients at state mental institutions had come to light. But almost immediately it was clear that many deinstitutionalized patients were not receiving the necessary care to function in a noninstitutional setting. However, deinstitutionalization was completed by the mid-1970s, so the increase in homelessness in the 1980s cannot be explained by this earlier process. Between 1985 and 1995 the percentage of the homeless who were mentally ill actually declined from 33 percent to 23 percent.

Each of the theories has some validity, but none provides a completely satisfactory answer to what causes homelessness. According to one study, there is a correlation between cities with high rates of poverty and high per capita incomes and cities with high rates of homelessness. The study found that income inequality directly affects the housing market. The affluence of people with good jobs or skills elevates the cost of most housing beyond what poor or nonworking households can afford.[32] Finally, it found that cities with high costs of living tend to pay higher disability benefits than cities with lower costs of living—but not enough to compensate for the extra expenses for the poor. So high-cost cities with higher disability payments were actually associated with higher rates of homelessness.

Policy Action for the Homeless

The term "homeless" suggests that the policy issue would be solved if those without a fixed abode could be provided affordable housing. Some homeless-care providers suggest that the problem is more complex than just providing housing. Providing housing for a significant number would solve the problem. But for many others the issue involves personal responsibility and accountability. As Christopher Jencks wrote:

> If no one drank, took drugs, lost touch with reality, or had trouble holding a job, home-lessness would be rare. But if America had a system of social welfare comparable to that of Sweden or Germany, homelessness would also be rare. In those countries job training is far better, unskilled jobs pay better, benefits for the unemployed are almost universally available and the mental health system does much more to provide housing for the mentally ill. It is the combination of widespread individual vulnerability and collective indifference that leaves so many Americans in the streets.[33]

Several policy options might alleviate some of the problems of the homeless. In 1994 President Clinton issued a plan to reduce the homeless population by one-third by spending $2.15 billion in 1995. His plan recommended a "continuum of care" which combined shelter, education, substance-abuse counseling, job training and medical treatment.[34] Many of the homeless are discarded workers with little education and few working skills,

---

[32]Martha Burt, *Over the Edge: The Growth of Homelessness in the 1980s* (Washington, DC: Urban Institute Press, 1991), p. 45.

[33]Christopher Jencks, "The Homeless," *The New York Review of Books,* April 21, 1994, p. 22.

[34]Richard L. Worsnop, "Helping the Homeless," *CQ Researcher* (Washington, DC: Congressional Quarterly Inc.), vol. 6, no. 4 (January 1996), pp. 73–96.

and a robust economy increases job availability for low-skilled labor. Job-training programs that develop interpersonal skills and job responsibility attitudes would offer significant hope for reducing homelessness. A liberalization of welfare benefits, which have not kept pace with inflation, and a relaxation of eligibility rules for those benefits would make housing more affordable for many. New housing programs would help others: Many states provide almost no housing assistance to single people, especially single males, who make up the greatest portion of the homeless population.

There is some evidence that American sympathy for the homeless is receding. Recent surveys by the National Law Center on Homelessness and Poverty found that many cities have enacted or enforced restrictions on occupying public spaces, or otherwise selectively enforced laws rarely applied to the non-homeless. The center conceded that some concerns about the use of public space are legitimate in that city residents do not want people living or begging in the streets. But instead of criminalizing these activities and attacking the homeless, they argue cities should attack homelessness.[35]

The homeless are merely the most visible portion of the population experiencing housing deficiencies. Many of the homeless eventually do obtain housing, either on their own or by being taken in by friends or relatives for varying lengths of time. A much larger portion of the poor population does not move into the streets, but "doubles up" with relatives or friends. Such displaced people have to be considered in the overall determination of housing needs. There is a growing gap between what individuals can afford to pay for shelter and what it costs to build and maintain housing. This is no longer a problem affecting only those in poverty, but also middle-income wage earners.

HOUSING AFFORDABILITY

Homelessness is the most compelling and obvious evidence of the failure to achieve the nation's housing policy goals. However, there are millions of Americans who manage to maintain roofs over their heads only by giving up other necessities of life or by living in badly deteriorated housing. The source of most housing problems is the widening gap between the cost of housing provided by the private sector, and the income available to pay for it.

There is a widespread misconception that housing subsidies are aimed primarily at the poor and the homeless, when in fact the middle- and upper-classes have been the beneficiaries of the most generous government assistance. Middle- and upper-income groups have been the primary *target population* of government subsidies. Most government policies encourage a higher level of ownership than the market would produce.

The concept of "affordability" has changed over time. At one time many researchers suggested that housing was affordable if it cost no more than 25 percent of pretax income for households at the poverty level. By the 1980s that had risen to 30 percent. The Congressional Budget Office considers households to have **affordability problems when they pay out of pocket more than 30 percent of their**

[35]National Law Center on Homelessness and Poverty, *No Homeless People Allowed* (December 1994), pp. ii, vi. Also quoted in Wornsop, "Helping the Homeless," p. 87.

HOUSING: HOW MUCH CAN HOUSEHOLDS AFFORD?

One method of determining how much a family can afford for housing is based upon *percentage of income*. This is the most widely used standard for housing affordability. In the 1950s, 20 percent of income was the standard rule of affordability. In the 1960s it rose to 25 percent, and in the 1970s to 30 percent. Since 1981, 30 percent of income has been the amount that families receiving government subsidies have been required to contribute toward their housing costs.

The major criticism of this approach is obviously that fixed percentages are arbitrary—affordability may more accurately be viewed on a sliding scale, with the maximum affordable percentage varying with income and household size and type. This is based on the fact that housing costs constitute a fixed basic claim on a household's disposable income. Subsequent expenditures must adjust to what is left after housing expenses have been met. On a sliding scale, some low-income households might be able to afford less than 30 percent of their income for housing. At upper income levels over 50 percent of net income could be spent on housing, and the remainder would more than adequately cover other expenses.

A second method approaches the problem in reverse and determines the *market basket costs of basic necessities* such as food, clothing, and health care first. These are viewed as making the fixed claim on the disposable income of a household, with the remainder being taken as what the household can "afford" for housing. This is usually considerably less than 30 percent. However, note that most of the poor do not receive housing subsidies and must pay more than 30 percent of their income for housing. Renters usually have higher cost burdens than owners.

Sources: James Poterba, *Housing Price Dynamics: The Role of Tax Policy and Demography* (Brookings Papers on Economic Activity) (Washington, DC: The Brookings Institution, 1991), vol. 2, no. 2, pp. 184–203; Steve Max, "Bring Down the High Cost of Home Ownership," *Social Policy,* vol. 17 (Spring 1987), pp. 54–55.

income for housing—roughly the tenant contribution toward rent in assisted housing set by statute.[36] But in fact households with very low incomes find it difficult to pay even 30 percent of their income for housing since housing costs constitute a fixed basic claim on disposable income each month, and all other expenses—even those for other necessities—must be adjusted to fit what is left over. This contrasts with the situation for those with high incomes who also own homes: The higher the incomes of homeowners, the larger the mortgages they are likely to have since they can deduct their mortgage interest against the taxes they owe on those high incomes.

[36]In the CBO's explanation, housing costs for renters include tenant payments due to the landlord, utility costs not included in the rent payment, and renters' insurance. Housing costs for homeowners include mortgage payments, real estate taxes, property insurance, and utilities. Both measures exclude federal subsidies. Housing costs for homeowners are computed by the CBO without taking tax benefits and equity gains into account, both of which reduce the real cost of home ownership. Conversely, opportunity costs of capital tied up in the home are also not included, which increases the real cost of home ownership. Nor do CBO housing costs include expenditures for maintenance and repairs, which also increase the cost of owning a home. See Congressional Budget Office, *Current Housing Problems and Possible Federal Responses* (Washington, DC: U.S. Government Printing Office, 1988), p. 8.

Most low-income households are renters, while most middle- and upper-income households are homeowners. Since Franklin Roosevelt recognized that "one-third" of the nation was ill-housed, and initiated public policies to increase home ownership, the rate of ownership has risen from 44 percent in the 1940s, to an all-time high of 66 percent in 1998.

CAUSES OF THE LOW-INCOME HOUSING CRISIS

Fading Numbers of Homeowners and Rising Numbers of Renters

The basic problem is very straightforward: **Shifts in the economy have produced a growing number of workers whose average wages are insufficient to pay enough in**

SEGREGATION IN HOUSING

Segregation in residential housing in the United States is plain. In one sense cities have become more integrated. In recent years, large cities have more diverse populations living within their metropolitan areas. Segregation persists, however, in that different racial groups still live in clearly identifiable neighborhoods. Despite many predictions that segregation would decline because of less prejudicial attitudes by whites, the increasing market power of a growing African-American middle class, and fair housing legislation, most African Americans continue to reside in predominantly African-American neighborhoods. Race is still a central cleavage in American society.[37]

Housing segregation may be based primarily on economics rather than on racial discrimination. Nevertheless, the result is de facto racial segregation. The comparatively low incomes of African Americans and other minority families could be based upon the fact that lower-income workers must locate in areas of low-quality housing based upon simple market forces. However, low-income African Americans are segregated from whites of the same income level.

Discrimination Can Raise the Price of Housing for Minorities
In most metropolitan areas, there is a concentration of minority housing in the central city surrounded by primarily white housing in the suburbs. An increase in the white population can be accommodated by an expansion of the suburban area around the city. Within the city, there are boundaries of racial transition between minority and white populations, and an increase in the African-American population will not be easily accommodated by an expansion of the housing supply, especially if the whites resist. Whites may resist selling or renting to minorities by being less flexible regarding the terms of leases than when dealing with whites. The result is to raise the rent for minorities to a level where whites near the frontier are willing to rent to minorities. Real estate agents may also **steer** prospective minority buyers into housing areas dominated by their minority group and not inform minority clients about housing availability in white neighbor-

[37]See Douglas S. Massey and Nancy Denton, "Trends in the Residential Segregation of Blacks, Hispanics and Asians: 1970–1980," *American Sociological Review,* vol. 52 (December 1987), p. 823.

rents or mortgages to make the building of low-income housing profitable. In the 1990s, home prices in many markets rose less rapidly than in the 1980s and even declined in several areas. And mortgage rates were lower than they had been throughout much of the 1980s, but lower interest rates, which translate into lower monthly mortgage payments, have done little to improve many renters' prospects of buying a home.

U.S. HOUSING POLICY

The outcome of the housing market in the United States leaves much of the public dissatisfied. But since in a mixed economy, people are opposed to total government control, the policy outcomes tend to be a series of narrow interventions designed to deal with individual aspects of the problem. Therefore, the greatest challenge for policy analysts

hoods. Sellers also typically put their houses on the market for more than they expect to be offered. This allows them negotiating room to accept lower bids if made by whites, but to resist lower offers made by non-whites.

On other occasions, African Americans may not necessarily pay more for housing. **Blockbusting occurs when real estate brokers or agents encourage whites to sell quickly at low prices "before it is too late" and minorities take over the neighborhood.** The intention is to buy properties at low prices and quickly resell them to African Americans to earn commissions from the fast turnover. The quick turnover of houses with whites moving out and African Americans moving in encourages other whites to sell quickly at low prices. If possible, realtors sell to African Americans at higher prices. In either case, neighborhoods that might have become desegregated are quickly resegregated from all white to all African American.

Not infrequently, banks have been reluctant to lend money to African Americans who want to buy homes in white neighborhoods, fearing that if the borrowers defaulted, the financial institution would be left with properties whose value had declined. Some banks engaged in what is termed **redlining—refusing to lend money to certain buyers applying for mortgages in particular neighborhoods.**

The Civil Rights Act of 1968 prohibited steering, blockbusting, redlining, and other forms of discrimination in the sale or rental of housing. The act has not resulted in significant changes in housing patterns, however. The reasons are rather clear. Discrimination has become more subtle. Income inequalities make it very difficult for many African Americans to buy in more expensive white neighborhoods. Housing segregation perpetuates school segregation as well.

Sources: Dan Gilmor and Stephen Doig, "Segregation Forever?" *American Demographics,* vol. 14 (January 1992), pp. 48–52; Douglas Massey, Andrew Gross, and Mitchell Eggers, "Segregation, the Concentration of Poverty and the Life Chances of Individuals," *Social Science Research,* vol. 20 (December 1991), pp. 397–420; Veronica M. Reed, "Civil Rights Legislation and the Housing Status of Black Americans: Evidence from Fair Housing Audits and Segregation Indices," *The Review of Black Political Economy,* vol. 19 (Winter/Spring 1991), pp. 29–42.

FIGURE 11-3
ESTIMATED FEDERAL HOUSING SUBSIDIES AND TAX
BREAKS BY INCOME QUINTILE (1992 FIGURES).

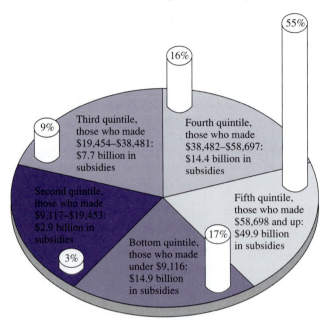

is to develop an analytical framework to indicate which alternatives best address specific issues and to evaluate those policies implemented.

Policies may be classified according to the critical choices implicit in their purpose. As already indicated one classification is the *population targeted.* We often think of housing assistance as aimed primarily at the poor, because housing projects are more visible, while in fact those in the middle class and the affluent are the beneficiaries of the most generous programs encouraging home ownership. Government policies in America support a much higher level of ownership than the housing market with no government intervention would produce.

The second major choice regarding housing relates to the *process* of intervention. In the United States the tax system has been the most powerful form of intervention.

Although both political parties support the availability of decent housing, moving beyond the rhetoric reveals great differences in view regarding **how** this should be done, **who should benefit,** and **who should pay.** Public policies favoring housing have taken several forms in the United States, including (1) tax deductions, (2) mortgage assistance, and (3) low-income assistance.[38] These are in addition to other government economic actions such as interest-rate policies to encourage the purchase of housing and zoning laws to provide a stable environment for a high-cost long-term investment.

---

[38]In this section we are heavily indebted to a clear exposition of these housing policies presented by John P. Ignis, *Urban and Regional Economics* (Anoesia, IL: Ionize, 1991).

Tax Benefits

Government assistance to middle- and upper-income families in housing takes the form of a distributive policy. **Tax deductions on the interest paid on home mortgages are available to all who can afford to buy a home. The recipients do not have to compete for the benefit as if there were limited funds available.** The amount of the subsidy is related to the amount of interest paid. **Those who can afford to carry larger mortgages or pay higher local property taxes receive larger subsidies.**

Easily the largest housing subsidy program is the ability of homeowners to take a deduction on mortgage interest and local property taxes from their federal income taxes. **A tax deduction is an amount of money that may be subtracted from income before a taxpayer computes his or her taxable income.** The ability to avoid paying taxes on income spent on mortgage interest and property taxes may substantially reduce taxes and give homeowners preferential treatment when compared to renters. Since homeowners are, on average, more affluent than renters, this special treatment reduces the progressivity of the income tax. The tax deduction often more than compensates for the **real interest paid on mortgages.**[39] Therefore, upper-income households have a particularly strong incentive to buy homes. For them, a home is viewed "primarily as an investment rather than as necessary shelter."[40] The combination of tax deductions and inflation can result in a distortion of the housing market in which builders provide too many large houses to produce tax shelters for the affluent, and too few low-priced houses for the poor. Housing subsidies in the form of tax deductions that reduce the cost of owning a house for middle- and upper-income families amounted to $72.5 *billion* in 1995.[41] The income tax deduction for mortgage interest totaled $58.3 billion and homeowner deductions for local property taxes totaled $14.2 billion. In fact the mortgage interest deduction alone was almost three times the size of the entire budget for the Department of Housing and Urban Development in 1995.[42] This tax expenditure would be more acceptable if most of the money went to help a majority of the people. But it does not. Those with the highest incomes and the most expensive houses get the largest tax breaks. Recent data from the Joint Taxation committee shows that 1.2 percent of taxpayers with incomes over $200,000 received $12.6 billion in mortgage interest deduction (21.6 percent of the entire amount) in 1995. The top 5.6 percent of all taxpayers, those with incomes over $100,000, received half (49.7 percent) of the total tax deduction.[43]

Although only 21.3 percent of all taxpayers actually take advantage of the mortgage interest deduction, the proportion of those that do are overwhelmingly in the highest tax brackets. For instance in 1995, 82.5 percent of taxpayers with incomes over $200,000 took the deduction worth an average of $9,763. But of those with incomes just between $40,000 and $50,000 only 28 percent took the deduction saving only $952 on their taxes. While only 6.6 percent of those earning between $20,000 and $30,000 took the

---

[39]The **real rate of interest** is defined as the nominal rate of interest minus the rate of inflation. The **nominal rate of interest** is defined as the interest rate actually paid in current prices.

[40]Anthony Downs, *Rental Housing in the 1980s* (Washington, DC: Brookings Institution, 1983), p. 33.

[41]Peter Dreier and John Atlas, "Why Should Our Tax Code Underwrite the Lifestyles of the Rich and Famous?" From *The New Democrat,* Jan/Feb 1997.

[42]Ibid., p. 1.

[43]Ibid., p. 2.

deduction which saved them on average only $502. The mortgage interest deduction is of no use to those lower income families that cannot afford to buy homes, and is of little value to those that can.

Although the home mortgage deduction is usually defended as a major tax break for the middle-class, the statistics clearly indicate that it mainly benefits those upper income homeowners. Nor, it turns out, is this the only path to widespread home ownership, as neither Canada nor Australia have a mortgage interest deduction but their home ownership rates of about 65 percent of all households are roughly the same as ours.[44]

It is clear to all who are familiar with the home mortgage deduction that it is inequitable, however the real estate industry lobby, known for their generous campaign contributions, resist any challenge to the tax break. In 1986, Congress limited the mortgage deduction to the interest paid on no more than two homes. In 1987, Congress limited the amount of the principal eligible for the interest deduction to $1 million. Relatively few affluent taxpayers were seriously constrained by that provision. It is worth noting that flat tax proposals put forward by the Republican Majority Leader Dick Armey would eliminate all deductions for mortgage interest.

Over the past several years, the Congressional Budget Office (CBO) has recommended options to reduce the federal deficit. One recommendation it has consistently made is to eliminate the mortgage deduction entirely for second homes. On its face it appears eminently fair to eliminate tax breaks for vacation and investment homes when many cannot afford a first home. It would save the government about $400 million annually. However it would run into the determined opposition from the vacation industry in many states, and in particular such states as Maine, Florida, Colorado, and Arizona.

The CBO has also suggested limiting mortgage interest deductions to $12,000 for an individual return or $20,000 for a joint return which would affect roughly the top 5 percent of taxpayers allowing a family to finance a fixed rate mortgage of about $225,000. This provision would generate an additional $6.1 billion annual tax savings for the government. Finally, the CBO has proposed lowering the limit on the amount of principal eligible for the interest deduction from the current $1 million to $300,000. This would affect only a few homeowners and generate an additional $3.8 billion in tax savings. A *Time*/CNN poll in May 1995 asked: "As you know, the tax code subsidizes mortgage loans, even for the most expensive homes. One proposal would limit the tax deduction to $300,000 in mortgage principal, and would save the treasury $35 billion over 5 years, while affecting only 1.2 million of the wealthiest taxpayers. Would you favor or oppose such a limit?" Interestingly 68 percent of the respondents would favor the limit with almost no difference in opinion between Democrats and Republicans.[45]

Homeowners are favored in additional ways. Under previous legislation, a couple age 55 or over would not be taxed on capital gains up to $125,000. Conditions of this legislation include selling a primary residence on a one-time basis, as long as they lived in the house for the previous three years. Revisions to the federal tax code in 1997 expanded the benefits accruing to homeowners upon the sale of their home. Individuals

[44]Ibid.
[45]Ibid., p. 3.

HOME MORTGAGE TAX DEDUCTIONS
AND HORIZONTAL EQUITY

Mortgage and property tax deductions by homeowners are tax expenditures from the perspective of the government. A **tax expenditure is a provision of the tax code that reduces an individual's tax bill, and hence revenue collections by the government.**

The tax deductions associated with **home ownership are also held to violate a tax principle that those who are equals in all pertinent tax respects should be treated equally.** For example, suppose than Jim and Katherine are neighbors, each earning $50,000 per year. The only difference is that Jim owns his home while Katherine is renting her house. Since they have equal incomes, most observers would say that they **should** pay the same income tax. Because of the favorable tax treatment of homeowners, however, they probably will not. Suppose Jim pays $3,000 in property taxes and has a $100,000 mortgage at 10 percent interest, which costs him about $10,000 a year in interest costs. Since the property taxes and mortgage interest are tax deductible, he is able to deduct $13,000 per year in housing costs. Katherine pays $13,000 per year in rent, which is not tax-deductible. Her tax burden is significantly higher than Jim's.

The inequity could be remedied in several ways. One would be to allow renters to deduct their rent from their income tax, or the mortgage and property tax deductions could be disallowed. A third alternative would be to require the homeowner to add the value of housing (or imputed rent) which is calculated by adding their mortgage and property tax payments to their income.

now may realize capital gains of up to $250,000 (or $500,000 per couple) in a sale of a primary residence occupied for at least two years and without any age requirement. There is no limitation on the number of times this may be done, nor is there any requirement that the profit money must be rolled over into the purchase of another home to realize the tax savings.

Also, since about 65 percent of households own their own home, homeowners form a very powerful interest group. Many nonowners also aspire to home ownership. These groups successfully argued the convenient logic that Congress should continue to encourage home ownership as a support for responsible citizenship. They also argued that tax deductions raise home values higher than would be the case without the deductions and repealing them would reduce those values and thus ultimately the demand for home ownership. The tax advantages of homeowners remain untouchable to politicians. However, reductions in the marginal tax rates have resulted in reductions in the size of this type of tax expenditure.

Mortgage Assistance

Most home buyers make down payments on their houses and borrow the remaining money needed to purchase their homes. In 1996, the average homeowner had a mortgage with an average ratio of loan to purchase price of 80.5 percent on mortgages

TABLE 11-3
RECENT HOME BUYERS—GENERAL CHARACTERISTICS

Item	Unit	1976	1990	1996
Median purchase price	Dollars	43,340	131,200	153,200
First-time buyers	Dollars	37,670	106,000	130,100
Repeat buyers	Dollars	50,090	149,400	170,700
Average monthly mortgage payment	Dollars	329	1,127	1,087
Percent of income	Percent	24.0	33.8	32.6
Percent buying—				
New houses	Percent	15.1	21.2	22.7
Existing houses	Percent	84.9	78.8	77.3
Single-family houses	Percent	88.8	83.8	82.6
Condominiums	Percent	11.2	13.1	14.2
For the first time	Percent	44.8	41.9	44.7
Average Age:				
First-time buyers	Years	28.1	30.5	32.4
Repeat buyers	Years	35.9	39.1	41.1
Downpayment/Sales price	Percent	25.2	23.3	19.5
First-time buyers	Percent	18.0	15.7	12.4
Repeat buyers	Percent	30.8	28.9	25.3

Source: Statistical Abstract, 1997, p. 730.

averaging over $123,000.[46] The national government has expanded the supply of funds available to home buyers by making mortgage loans more secure for lenders. This has the effect of reducing interest rates and making homes more affordable.

The best known government mortgage-assistance program is the Federal Housing Administration's (FHA) program, which began in 1934 to insure lending institutions against defaults by borrowers. **Insuring home mortgages is a subsidy to the middle class and has been the major way the federal government has intervened in the housing market.** Under the FHA program, a buyer can get up to 97 percent of the value of the property insured. That means the borrower need only make a 3 percent down payment to obtain a loan for the 97 percent balance that is fully insured for the lender upon payment of a small fee paid to the FHA. The Veterans Administration has a similar loan guarantee program. In 1995, 22 percent of all mortgages were FHA- or VA-insured.[47]

These programs contributed greatly toward the move to the suburbs after World War II. They were so successful in a period of generally rising prices that even when defaults occurred the outstanding balances were usually recouped. They actually made money for the government. In fact, they were so successful they spawned a whole private mortgage insurance industry.

[46]*Statistical Abstract, 1997,* p. 730.
[47]*Statistical Abstract, 1997,* p. 727.

Low-Income Housing Assistance

The U.S. Department of Housing and Urban Development (HUD) operates three major federally-funded programs that provide housing assistance to low-income families: public housing, Section 8 certificates and vouchers, and Section 8 project-based programs. It is important to keep in mind that **housing assistance is not an entitlement.** There are many more eligible families than there are families who receive assistance. Each year, Congress appropriates funds for a number of new commitments. The number of commitments funded annually has been cut back in recent years. Since housing assistance for low-income families is not an entitlement program, and since it is provided through several different approaches, a number of recurring questions are raised each year concerning its funding. They include the following: What types of households should have priority for receiving assistance? How large a subsidy should households receive? How many households should receive housing assistance?

The result is that there are long waiting lists for housing assistance in many areas of the country.[48] Census data indicate that there are 5.3 million families without any housing assistance living in "worst case housing needs" which means these families live in substandard housing or pay over half their income in rent.

Housing assistance can become available to families through turnover or increased federal funding. However, since 1995 there has been no net increase in the supply of federally subsidized housing for poor families. In fact, as older public housing units are demolished and some Section 8 contracts are not renewed the number of households receiving federal housing subsidies has begun to decline for the first time in the history of the programs. However the Clinton administration has proposed an increase of 103,000 Section 8 vouchers (50,000 welfare-to-work and 34,000 for homeless) as part of its FY1999 budget, targeted to the homeless and those moving from welfare to work.

Eligibility   To be eligible for federal housing assistance a family's income must be at or below 80 percent of the median income of an area (which averaged $34,920 for a family of three in the nation's metropolitan areas in the winter of 1998). Federal law specifies that a majority of the subsidies must be targeted to families at or below 50 percent of the median metropolitan area income (which averaged $21,825 for a family of three). Families who receive housing assistance must pay 30 percent of their income in rent. Thus their rent rises and falls with family income fluctuations.

Public Housing   Public housing consists of rental units owned and operated by public housing authorities (PHAs). There are approximately 1.2 million public housing units, of which about 550,000 are occupied by families with children. Families and elderly households living in public housing pay subsidized rents which go directly to the PHA and are used to help meet the operating and maintenance costs of public housing. Tenants' required rent payments are adjusted to any changes in their income. Changes

---

[48]Barbara Sard and Jennifer Daskal, "Housing and Welfare Reform: Some Background Information," *Center on Budget & Policy Priorities,* Hn0026@handsnet. Unless otherwise noted, this section relies heavily on their study.

in rent payments directly affect the amount of funds available to the PHA for operations and maintenance. The assistance provided was originally project-based in that a household had to live in a designated low-income housing development in order to receive the subsidy. Denying choice proved to be stigmatizing for low-income tenants, in that their place of residence identified them as disadvantaged. Furthermore, by concentrating large numbers of low-income persons in one place, the policy unintentionally intensified the social pathologies associated with poverty. It tended to create negative, destructive social environments in many public and private housing projects.[49]

This system often resulted in an adversarial relationship between the tenants and the managing entity. Since the tenants had little individual or collective stake in the project, individual or collective destructive behavior often resulted. Additionally, PHAs often neglected the physical and social environment because they had insufficient funds. Private developments often neglected repairs since short-term fees or tax incentives were the main motivation for investors.

Section 8 Tenant-Based Vouchers and Certificates **Rental vouchers** are viewed as the preferred method for the restoration of household choice, as well as a more efficient form of subsidy. Recipients of vouchers and certificates can use these subsidies to rent housing among ordinary housing developments in the private market, as long as it is approved by the local PHA. This avoids the isolation and stigma attached to a "housing project." Nevertheless, even with vouchers, low-income households' choices are limited by the supply and cost of housing and continued discrimination. Many suburban jurisdictions have erected their own barriers to mobility by favoring very low density settlements with little affordable rental housing.[50] Racial hostility and discrimination, overt and covert, are unfortunately still with us, so despite housing vouchers' mobility potential, in many jurisdictions recipients are still heavily concentrated in areas of high poverty. The private market solution to communities, as noted earlier, works to intensify social homogeneity in the more exclusive neighborhoods combined with a disinvestment or exploitative investment in lower-income neighborhoods.[51]

Even so, vouchers help families move to apartments closer to where jobs are which helps to decrease the concentration of poverty in a housing project, or even in a given neighborhood. Tenants pay 30 percent of their income in rent, and the PHA pays the landlord the difference between the tenant contribution and the full rental cost. If a tenant with a voucher rents housing that costs more than the PHAs designed co-payment standard for the apartment, the tenant must pay all of the additional cost. The number of vouchers and certificates available for low-income workers has been constrained by a congressional requirement that vouchers that are returned must not be reissued for a period of three months. That reduces the number of vouchers in circulation by about 25 percent (or 40,000 vouchers). As tenants use vouchers to rent private housing and move out of troubled public housing projects, HUD has begun demolishing public housing projects.

[49]Hays, "Housing," p. 298.
[50]John J. DiIulio, Jr., "In America's Cities," *The Brookings Review* (Fall 1997), vol. 15, no. 4, p. 8.
[51]Ibid., p. 299.

President Clinton has launched the most ambitious reform of public housing since the programs begun under Franklin Roosevelt in the 1930s. In an effort to change the physical face of public housing, the administration plans to demolish 100,000 public housing units (approximately one-twelfth of the total public housing stock) by the year 2000. They will be replaced with smaller-scale, economically integrated, affordable housing developments. At the administration's request, Congress has temporarily repealed the rules favoring the poorest households. PHAs are encouraged to create more "mixed income" developments through admission policies that include working families and to emphasize programs to help existing residents increase their own incomes.[52]

Project-Based Section 8 Assistance   Project-based Section 8 assistance refers to rental units in privately owned buildings. The owners receive a subsidy from the federal government. These units are similar to public housing in that the subsidies are valid for specific housing units and cannot be used to rent housing of a low-income recipient's choice. Tenants pay their share of the rent directly to the unit's owner. The subsidy amount is paid by the federal government. PHAs do not have any administrative responsibility for the project-based Section 8 program, with the exception of requiring the owner to maintain a moderate level of upkeep and rehabilitation.

How Welfare Policy Can Impact Housing Policy

The 1996 welfare law, as indicated earlier, replaced the Aid to Families with Dependent Children (AFDC) program with the Temporary Assistance to Needy Families (TANF) block grant. In 1996, about one-quarter of the families receiving AFDC/TANF benefits lived in assisted housing. This ratio varied significantly from state to state because the supply of housing assistance is more limited in some states than in others. So that in Massachusetts, for example, over 40 percent of AFDC families received housing assistance, while only 12 percent of AFDC families received housing assistance in California.[53]

Welfare policy can affect housing policy, for example, as families hit TANF time limits, or are penalized for failure to comply with TANF work requirements, housing authorities will be faced with losses in revenue. This will in turn reduce rental payments and require an increased subsidy reducing the amount of total money available unless Congress makes more money available for housing.

Data from the 1995 American Housing Survey indicate that about half of working poor families with children that receive no housing subsidy pay at least half of their income for rent. High housing costs leave many low-income families trying to move into the workforce with insufficient money for the increased costs that often accompany employment, such as additional clothing and food costs, child care, and transportation to and from work. Reducing a low-income worker's housing cost burden can provide some families with the stability they need to get and retain a job. Reciprocally, housing assistance permits a worker to move closer to a location where employment opportunities are and receive work opportunities reducing the need for TANF.

[52]Ibid., p. 9.
[53]Ibid., p. 2.

HOUSING POLICY AND LIBERAL-CONSERVATIVE PERSPECTIVES

Since the 1930s, housing and urban policy have undergone considerable growth and realism in addressing these very difficult and complex problems. Since about 1980 there has been an increasing attack on the legitimacy and the efficacy of collective public action. The unrelenting attack holds that government action is almost certainly inept. And although the stated claim of the criticism is to "improve" or "streamline" public policies, its underlying goal is the disengagement of the public sector from such efforts. If this occurs, resources would not have to be redistributed from the more affluent elements in society to pay for them.

Central to this position is a denial of society's moral obligation to assist the poor in any but the most limited and punitive ways. The poor are viewed from a Malthusian perspective as totally responsible for their own fate through their moral inferiority. Government programs are seen as rewarding the immorality of their recipients and thereby exacerbating, rather than ameliorating, their problems. Accompanying this rejection of the poor is an unquestioning devotion to and faith in the "free market" or market-like solutions for the problems of the poor. And these "free marketers'" faith is undisturbed by the vast subsidies provided to the nonpoor by the tax system and other subsidized goods and services. Meanwhile privatization of public housing is touted as a radically new concept in (as if public housing were ever anything more than a marginal solution for the disadvantaged) a housing system that is overwhelmingly private.

Conservative critics attacked liberals in the 1980s for their "naive faith" in the ability of "quick-fix" federal programs. Conservative critics correctly pointed out the potential of unjustified optimism for unkept promises in this approach. And it was conservatives who suggested housing vouchers, that ultimately proved more efficient and less stigmatizing than some other approaches. However the mode of attack could be best described as not conservative but reactionary since it tends to indiscriminately dismantle previous collective efforts with no viable alternatives remaining.

The highest priority for those involved in housing policy must be given to the need to restore the fundamental legitimacy of the policy process in the eyes of the public. A progressive position must be developed that is realistic about the difficulty and the cost of solving housing and other problems and yet clear in its conviction that collective solutions are absolutely essential if real progress is to be made. The current conservative critique of public policy is popular because it resonates with a suspicion of government and the poor.

However public opinion surveys repeatedly show strong elements of compassion for the less fortunate and a belief in the value and necessity of public efforts to help them. Therefore appeals for collective action must genuinely support and foster those values. Housing and other social programs must actively encourage individual responsibility and independence on the part of their beneficiaries. However, until the underlying social and economic structural factors that create poverty are addressed, other programs cannot succeed.

Source: R. Allen Hays, "Housing," in Ronald K. Vogel (ed.), *Handbook of Research on Urban Politics and Policy in the United States* (Westport, CT: Greenwood Press, 1997).

The exponential growth of suburban and exurban areas has major implications for housing and urban development concerns. Today, the suburbs are the major job generators in the new economy. The suburbs, in the 1990s, are responsible for over 85 percent of the jobs in the lower paying and lower skilled service and retail trade sectors. Not surprisingly, unemployment rates in central cities are frequently one-third to one-half higher than in the surrounding suburbs. Secondly, cities today continue to lose middle-class families which destabilizes the neighborhood and increases the concentration of the poor in urban ghettoes. This is perhaps the most disturbing trend which is largely ignored in the welfare and housing debate—the explosive growth in concentrated, and especially minority poverty, in urban America. The Clinton administration's 1997 "State of the Cities" report found that the poverty rate in cities rose almost 50 percent between 1970 and 1995, from 14.2 percent to 20.6 percent. The residential concentration of poverty separates the poor from the location of jobs as well as middle-class role models, while it reinforces social isolation. The poor who live in concentrated poverty are more likely to drop out of high school, become pregnant as teenagers, and to remain unemployed than their counterparts in socioeconomically mixed neighborhoods. Housing and urban policy must consider the entire dynamic in trying to deal with this problem.

CONCLUSION

1 Political rhetoric in the United States from Thomas Jefferson to the present has been very supportive of home ownership as an important way to give families a stake in society. Besides providing for a basic necessity of life, it is seen as producing political and social stability. Plentiful housing encourages other forms of employment and job creation within a community, and home ownership allows individuals and families to save at a higher rate than renters, thus contributing to the pool of capital available for further economic expansion. However, questions have been raised as to whether the overall emphasis on investment in home ownership in this country causes underinvestment in capital plants and equipment that would be more beneficial to the economy in the long run.

2 The movement from city to suburbs by the more affluent has had a profound impact on American politics. It has left urban areas with a falling tax base of lower-income workers to pay for the many public services required by both the remaining urban residents and suburban commuters. In addition, many move to suburban communities for the express purpose of avoiding the problems of cities; they form an antitax and antigovernment voting coalition that has exacerbated the problems of cities in terms of the federal and state aid available to local communities.

3 The homeless are not new on the American scene, but their numerical increase in recent decades is indicative of an upsurge in poverty that is also reflected in the increase in housing problems. The homeless are the most visible evidence of the failure of American national housing policy. Urban renewal programs in inner-city districts have dramatically reduced the number of single-room occupancy hotels that used to serve as low-income housing for the very poor. That cheap housing has not been replaced with acceptable new low-income housing. Shelters at best provide only short-term housing and are not a permanent solution to the problem of homelessness.

Any serious public policy effort to deal with homelessness must first identify the homeless population and determine their needs. A profile of today's homeless shows that they differ from those in the past, tending to be younger and including more women and families. Serious policies must include job training and opportunities for employment in occupations that pay enough to make housing affordable. In addition, they must include counseling, education, and health care programs. The very poor in the United States are victims of falling incomes and reductions in the government safety net programs that used to place a floor under those in poverty; when they are homeless, they are also a reflection of the increased cost of suitable housing.

4 More Americans are spending an ever increasing percentage of their incomes on housing, leaving them with insufficient means to purchase other necessities such as food, clothing, and health care. The number of renter households has increased dramatically since 1970. But their average income, after adjusting for inflation, has declined significantly. During this same period the amount of low-cost unsubsidized housing also dropped by 50 percent.

5 The greatest housing subsidies go to those whose incomes place them among the wealthiest 20 percent of the population. Those subsidies take the form of the mortgage interest tax deduction and property tax deduction allowed on federal income tax forms and ironically are the only housing subsidies that can be considered entitlements. Currently there are waiting lists for individuals trying to get into subsidized housing. The number of low-cost, unsubsidized rental units has declined, and government assistance programs have not been increased to help those in poverty afford more expensive housing. The rising cost of unsubsidized housing is the main reason for the increasing housing problems experienced by several segments of the population, including the homeless, the precariously housed, and those paying an excessive amount of their income for rent who are also unable to afford to purchase a home.

6 In the last fifteen years the viability of collective effort in the area of housing has been challenged as unworkable and unjustified. Without the political mobilization of individuals, community action and other committed groups the flow of assistance to those at the bottom of the income distribution at adequate levels would be choked off.

QUESTIONS FOR DISCUSSION

1 Is homelessness primarily a problem of unemployment? If so, why did it worsen even as the unemployment rate was declining in the 1960s?
2 Is rent control responsible for the decline in available housing stock for the poor? Do moderate rent control regulations solve the problems raised by critics of such policies? Why or why not?
3 Why are so many people homeless in the United States compared to most European nations? What is the difficulty such individuals have in getting their lives back on track?
4 What is the significance of the movement to the suburbs for U.S. housing policy?
5 What is the responsibility of the public sector (federal, state, and local), in addressing the problem of housing and urban policy?
6 How do ideological views shape housing policy?

KEY CONCEPTS

affordability

blockbusting

filter-down theory

merit good

rental voucher

suburb

tax deduction

tax expenditure

The Tiebout Model

The Tradeoff Model

SUGGESTED READINGS

John P. Blair, *Urban & Regional Economics* (Homewood, IL: Richard D. Irwin, 1991).

Martha R. Burt and Barbara E. Cohen, *America's Homeless: Numbers, Characteristics, and Programs That Serve Them* (Washington, DC: The Urban Institute Press, 1989).

Jacqueline Jones, *The Dispossessed: America's Underclasses from the Civil War to the Present* (New York: Basic Books, 1992).

Jonathan Kozol, *Rachel and Her Children: Homeless Families in America* (New York: Crown Publishers, 1988).

Alfred L. Malabre, Jr., *Beyond Our Means* (New York: Vintage Books, 1987).

Henrey Miller, *On the Fringe: The Dispossessed in America* (New York: Lexington Books, 1991).

Jamshid A. Momeni (ed.), *Homelessness in the United States* (New York: Greenwood Press, 1989). (2 vols.)

Jamshid A. Momeni (ed.), *Homelessness in the United States—Data and Issues* (New York: Praeger, 1990).

Peter Rossi, *Down and Out in America: The Origins of Homelessness* (Chicago: University of Chicago Press, 1989).

Raymond J. Struyk, Margery A. Turner, and Makiko Ueno, *Future U.S. Housing Policy: Meeting the Demographic Challenge* (Report 88-2). (Washington, DC: Urban Institute Press, 1988).

William Tucker, *The Excluded Americans* (Washington, DC: Regnery Press, 1990).

Ronald K. Vogel, *Handbook of Research on Urban Politics and Policy in the United States* (Westport, CT: Greenwood Press, 1997).

12

ENVIRONMENTAL POLICY: DOMESTIC AND INTERNATIONAL ISSUES

Until recently, many environmentalists have directed their efforts toward persuading the public that there is in fact an environmental crisis. The increase in public concern about environmental issues is nothing less than a major change in attitudes. Measurable degradation of air and water quality, oil and sewage spills, and contaminated beaches and drinking water have served to dramatically focus our attention on growing stresses on the environment. Public opinion polls now regularly reveal that overwhelming majorities of Americans think more should be done to protect the environment.

Global warming is now accepted by the overwhelming majority of the scientific community as a genuine and severe threat. In a 1995 report to the United Nations, 2,500 of the world's leading climate scientists, declared that the recent heating of the atmosphere is caused by carbon emissions from oil and coal combustion, not by the natural variability of the climate. The ten hottest years on record have all occurred since 1980. The depletion of ozone from the atmosphere, the destruction of the rain forests, world population growth, and the emission of excessive amounts of "greenhouse gases" all contribute to the fragility of the earth's environment.

Environmental policy is distinctive because of the scientific nature of the fundamental questions raised. Environmental issues are complicated and multifaceted. Environmental choices are often intertwined with consequences for energy policy. The technical nature of scientific debates may discourage some from trying to inform themselves on the issues. Nevertheless, energy and environmental issues have a very real impact on the average person's daily life. Those who support major initiatives typically want assured energy resources at reasonable prices with acceptable environmental consequences. This is very difficult to accomplish in fact.

INTRODUCTION

During the last two decades, the deterioration of the environment has moved from an issue of personal inconvenience to a major issue on the public policy agenda. People have become aware that population growth and the accompanying growth of industry and traffic congestion contribute to environmental damage. Air quality has deteriorated because of auto and industrial emissions. Smog has become a major problem for most major cities of the nation.

Despite increased awareness and scattered efforts since the 1960s to pass legislation to protect the environment, environmental disruptions have surfaced with increasing frequency and urgency. Environmental issues have emerged in different forms, including projected scarcities of energy resources, damage from acid rain, deforestation and soil erosion, water shortages, depletion of the ozone layer which protects life from harmful ultraviolet radiation, and the "greenhouse effect" which has started a long-term global warming trend.

EMERGING ENVIRONMENTALISM

The present-day concern with environmental issues has its roots in the conservation movement that began in the 1880s. The conservation movement was led by President Theodore Roosevelt and a few scientists and politicians who were largely motivated by a concern for resource conservation and management. It was driven by a fear of resource exhaustion and a need to manage natural resources before they were destroyed. This approach tried to make rational choices based upon utilitarian principles of "the greatest good for the greatest number," from an economic perspective. This movement did not have significant public support, and was largely viewed as elitist and anti-populist.

The Sierra Club and the Audubon Society were organized at that time to call attention to the environmental destruction caused by the unrestricted and destructive exploitation of the nation's resources. The preservationist movement had an interest in preserving the natural state of wilderness and scenic areas by creating national parks in resource-rich areas. Few political elites got involved, but neither did most Americans seem to take seriously the damage that unregulated growth and development was inflicting on the environment.

The publication of Rachel Carson's *Silent Spring* in 1962, warned of the effects of the concentration of toxins as they move up the food chain, and argued that a fragile balance in nature was being upset by the excessive use of pesticides like DDT—for example, on bird reproduction. She articulated the concerns of many who were troubled by environmental degradation and were struggling to comprehend its implication for our future.

Then in 1962 President Kennedy convened a White House Conference on Conservation. Kennedy and a Democratic Congress passed the **Clean Air Act** of 1963 despite fierce opposition led by the business community. The act had a complicated enforcement procedure that relied upon state action to initiate lawsuits against polluters. The Johnson administration passed The Water Quality Act of 1965, which established national standards for water quality. Federal grants were made available to states for sewage treatment plants to improve water quality. But again conservatives wrote provisions into the law allowing states to formulate plans to meet the federal standards. Prior to 1970, the federal government provided technical advice and assistance and funding for specific environmental projects, while deferring to state governments as possessing the primary enforcement responsibility. The increased public concern about the environment resulted in the passage of several pieces of legislation in the early 1970s. Both Republicans and Democrats vied with each other to prove themselves as the real champions of the environment.

Congress passed the National Environmental Policy Act of 1969 (signed by President Nixon on January 1, 1970), which required and Environmental Impact Statement (EIS) for any major federal construction. The EIS must show that government projects either will not significantly impact the environment or that satisfactory steps can be taken to mitigate damage. The Environmental Protection Agency (EPA) was created in 1970; prior to that, many different agencies in several federal departments, such as Interior and Agriculture, had responsibility for monitoring and regulating air and water pollution. The EPA was given the responsibility to enforce environmental laws ranging from toxic waste and air and water pollution to regulation of solid waste and pesticide use.

In 1970, Congress renewed the Clean Air Act and set national standards for ambient air quality. Congress also set a timetable for the reduction of auto hydrocarbon, carbon monoxide, and nitrogen oxide emissions. The 1970 act was intended "to protect and enhance the quality of the Nation's air resources so as to promote the public health and welfare."[1] The EPA was directed to promulgate National Ambient Air Quality Standards (NAAQS), in an effort to limit the amount of certain pollutants in the atmosphere that adversely affect public health. The pollutants cited were sulfur oxides, particulates, carbon monoxide, hydrocarbons, nitrogen oxides, and photochemical oxidants. The act required states to adopt plans to meet NAAQS requirements. After approval by the EPA, each state was required to enforce its plan. The EPA was given the authority to prepare and enforce a state plan if it did not meet federal requirements. The EPA was also to set exhaust emission standards for the auto industry and require the use of catalytic converters and the use of fuels with reduced lead.

The Water Pollution Control Act Amendments of 1972, passed over President Nixon's veto, attempted to limit the discharge of pollutants into navigable waters by 1985. It provided $25 billion in grants for local governments to build waster treatment plants and to install the best available technologies by 1983. The Clean Water Act of 1977 allowed for more flexibility in meeting compliance deadlines and effluent limitation requirements.

Industrial expansion after World War II resulted in the disposal of enormous amounts of solid and hazardous wastes into the atmosphere and water and on land. The potentially dangerous impact on the atmosphere and groundwater of hazardous waste dumping was apparent. Since the states controlled waste disposal, some industries were encouraged to shop for states with the weakest regulatory controls. Congress finally responded with the Resource Conservation and Recovery Act of 1976, which required that hazardous waste storage and disposal be regulated so as to minimize the threat to public health and the environment. The EPA was authorized to establish standards for the disposal of hazardous waste.

---

[1]Pub. L. 91-604, 84 Stat. 1713 (1970).

The spate of environmental legislation in the 1970s was impressive in its magnitude and scope. One serious drawback in several pieces of legislation was that the EPA had to negotiate with state and local governments to obtain compliance. The agency did not have the personnel or the budget to force compliance in an efficient manner.

Nonetheless, many states began to complain that they were overburdened by these environmental laws. By the late 1970s, critics began complaining that environmental legislation was causing inflation and slowing down economic growth. Business and conservation groups began mounting a counterattack against environmentalists. They ultimately argued that, while the excesses of the past could not continue, "reasonable" future controls would allow the environment to purify itself. They pointed out how a certain amount of pollution is inevitable in a growing economy. Therefore, they claimed, the benefits of any environmental regulation must be balanced against the economic costs to business. There was general acceptance of the view that little additional legislation to protect the environment was necessary. Ronald Reagan wove these views into his campaign for president in 1980; he was not opposed to "reasonable" environmentalism, he said, but the government had gone too far. Government bureaucrats, especially at the EPA and the Department of the Interior, were out of control on environmental issues, he claimed.

Ronald Reagan's campaign theme to get government regulators off the backs of business was a significant factor in his victory in 1980. He interpreted his victory as clear support for a reversal of the federal government's role in environmental protection. His administration moved immediately to repeal several regulations approved by the Carter administration. He appointed individuals, such as Ann Gorsuch Burford to the EPA and James Watt as Secretary of the Interior, who were openly hostile to the federal government's role in environmental policy.[2] Several thousand employees of the EPA were fired, including many attorneys experienced in environmental law. The entire staff of the President's Council on Environmental Quality, whose views were unapologetically pro-environment, was fired.

The Reagan administration required any new EPA regulation clear a **cost-benefit analysis** hurdle that had a built-in bias against regulation. The administration claimed that it was using cost-benefit analysis as a neutral tool to make sure that the dollar benefits of any proposed regulation exceeded the dollar costs. The problem is that no uncontested dollar value could be assigned to the value of a human life, let alone on an

---

[2]Ann Burford had been a vocal critic of all environmental regulation from Colorado before going to EPA. Under her leadership, the EPA routinely approved states' requests for more autonomy from federal regulation in managing environmental programs. She was forced to resign in 1983 after evidence was made public that strongly suggested clandestine collusion between the EPA and the industry it was to regulate. For example, the amendments to the Clean Air Act of 1977 regulating lead content in gasoline were based on public health concerns. Agency records showed that there had been thirty meetings between officials at the highest levels of EPA and the petroleum industry before setting leaded gasoline standards required by the 1977 amendments. However, EPA officials did not meet with public health officials or even request data on the effect of lead levels on health.

James Watt was a leader of the "Sagebrush Rebellion," which was an effort by businessmen, lobbyists, and state officials to pressure the federal government to ease federal regulation, and thereby the costs, of public land used by cattle, mining, and real estate interests. As Secretary of the Interior, he antagonized environmentalists by selling and leasing federal lands at a fraction of the commercial market value to mining and timber interests.

endangered species like a spotted owl or the beauty of a natural setting, while the costs incurred by industry were more precisely quantifiable. As a result most new regulations were predestined to fail the test of cost-benefit analysis. The Reagan administration was less interested in protecting the environment than in encouraging industrial growth through reduced regulation.

In 1988, George Bush campaigned for vigorous action to improve the environment. He indicated that he wanted to be known as "the environmental President." Indeed, one of his more famous charges against his opponent, Michael Dukakis, was that he had not done enough to clean up the pollution of Boston Harbor. During the first two years of his term, President Bush supported amendments to the Clean Air Act, put areas of the U.S. coastline off limits for oil exploration, approved an increase in the EPA budget, and was generally supportive of other environmental issues.

Bush introduced a clean air proposal in 1989 which helped members of Congress whose clean air proposals had been beaten back by the previous administration. Ultimately Congress approved the Clean Air Act Amendments of 1990, which provided far stricter and more costly regulations for industry than those proposed by Bush. The legislation was signed into law by Bush and was designed to ensure that air quality throughout the United States would meet certain standards by reducing emissions from industry and motor vehicles, including pollutants that cause acid rain. It also set standards for phasing out chemicals that reduce ozone in the stratosphere.

Environmentalists became disenchanted during the last two years of George Bush's term, however. They charged that his administration undermined the most dynamic provisions of the Clean Air Act. A coalition of cities and business interests claimed that the costs of compliance with environmental regulations were too high. Vice President Quayle's Council on Competitiveness allowed businesses to appeal for a relaxation of environmental regulations if they were shown to raise costs. Based upon the council's recommendations, the government waived rules that would have restricted pollutants from the automobile, chemical, and pharmaceutical industries.

In addition, Bush refused to support an environmental treaty at the "Earth Summit" held in Rio de Janeiro in June 1992 until its provisions designed to slow global warming were watered down. He also refused to sign a second treaty at the same meeting designed to protect endangered species.

In the 1992 presidential campaign, Bush dismissed his Democratic opponents, Bill Clinton and Al Gore, as dangerous "environmental crazies." Then candidate Clinton campaigned on a pledge to be an activist on the environment and if elected to reverse his Republican predecessors' weak record on environmental protection. Environmentalists took heart in 1993 when Bill Clinton became the first Democratic president to occupy the White House since 1981. Gore was the author of *Earth in the Balance,* which supported tougher environmental laws. His basic premise was that the choice presented between saving jobs or the environment is false.

In response to complaints from states and localities that the Environmental Protection Agency (EPA) habitually wrote environmental regulations requiring compliance without providing money to achieve the conformity amounting to an "unfunded mandate," Clinton tried to introduce greater flexibility into the system. EPA administrator Carol Browner tried to allow states and businesses greater leeway as to how they could come into compliance. President Clinton's effort to compromise and entice greater support from industry for environmental regulation was evident in his handling of the dispute between the Endangered Species Act and environmental activists trying to protect the spotted owl on one side and the logging industry on the other. He promised to provide $1.2 billion to develop alternative industries to logging in the Northwest, while saving thousands of acres of old growth forests needed by the owls to survive. In 1994 Clinton proposed lifting the logging restrictions on private lands within the spotted owl's habitat.

The administration was forced to back down or was defeated by Congress in several of its environmental goals. For example, when Interior Secretary Babbitt proposed raising the below-market fees that over 27,000 ranchers pay to graze cattle and sheep on public lands and reduce taxpayer subsidies to the livestock industry, industry opposition forced him to abandon the effort. Other administration proposals to elevate the EPA administrator to the Cabinet and to overhaul the clean water act and the Safe Drinking Water Act, and to strengthen the superfund they were all defeated by Congress.

After the Republicans took over both houses of Congress in 1994, they set out to implement the "Contract With America" which included legislation to reduce the federal government's ability to enact regulations. The first legislation passed to this end was a law to limit unfunded mandates. It requires the federal government to pay for most regulations it imposes on states and localities.

A second bill called the Risk Assessment and Cost-Benefit Act was a revival of Reagan's attack on environmental protection. It would have required the EPA and other agencies to perform cost-benefit analysis and risk assessment analysis involving extensive scientific and economic tests. Opponents charged that the goal of the measure was a thinly disguised plan to wreck regulatory agencies by tying them up with costly paperwork requirements. A filibuster by Senate Democrats eventually blocked the Republican "regulatory reform." But the bill was symbolic of the opposition of the Republican-controlled Congress to further environmental regulation. President Clinton was thrown on the defensive and took a policy stance designed to neutralize the Republican momentum of environmental deregulation. The administration has taken the position that some reform is needed but we should look for cost-effective solutions.

MARKET FAILURE AND THE ENVIRONMENT

Government has a function of providing the legal framework within which economic activity takes place. **Governments also have a role to play when markets fail to produce efficient outcomes.** Here we focus primarily on negative externalities and their relation to energy resource consumption and the closely related concern of environmental protection. One of government's primary policy roles is to provide remedies for the inefficiencies resulting from externalities. In an earlier chapter we noted that **externalities exist when a producer or a consumer does not bear the full cost (negative externality) or receive the full benefit (positive externality) of economic activity.** Externalities result in costs or benefits for third parties.

Keep in mind that externalities do not pass through the market system. Thus, the market cannot allocate them. The fact that externalities, whether positive or negative, do not pass through the market system, results in some of our most intractable problems. This point is worth emphasizing since the American preference for markets is based upon the principle of consumer sovereignty. But the production of certain goods and services has significant effects on people other than those directly involved in buying or selling the goods, since certain of their costs are being transferred to unwilling consumers.

Pollution is the classic example of an externality problem. Pollution is the production of wastes that we do not want, such as industrial wastes, smoke, congestion, or noise. These externalities exist for two reasons. The first is technical: We do not know how to produce some goods without waste products. Second, even if we do know how to produce goods without waste, their production or consumption may be very expensive without those externalities. For example, an automobile manufacturer may find it cheaper to drain industrial waste into a nearby river than to ship it to a waste dump. Neither the factory owners nor the customers pay for this use of the river. The river is a scarce resource, however, and degrading it does not take into account the rights of those downstream to use it to fish, swim, or enjoy it for other forms of recreation or natural beauty. Consequently, the cost of the pollution is borne by the public at large.

This is an **external cost**—a cost not reflected in market prices. **That cost, moreover, is imposed on the public without its consent.** In this example, since the cost of such pollution is not reflected in the price of the automobile, the factory will tend to produce more cars (and pollution) than is socially desirable.

The inefficient allocation of resources caused in this way is shown in figure 12-1. A market with external costs (negative externalities) allocates resources inefficiently. P_1, the **private marginal cost** of producing cars, the cost borne only by the producer, does not include all opportunity costs of production. The **social marginal costs**—the marginal costs of pollution—exceed the **private marginal costs.** Although the market price is at E, the efficient allocation of resources is found at Q_2 and the price at E'.

Thus there arise demands for the government to intervene and change the market outcome through laws and regulations. Those who argue against government intervention to control externalities emphasize that business is, or can be, socialized to be responsible through voluntarism. But there are many instances where feelings of social responsibility and voluntarism are not sufficient. In the early 1960s, despite mounting public pressure to reduce auto pollution, car manufacturers lobbied against legislation to mandate pollution control devices. The auto makers in a public relations campaign gave assurances that they were conducting research, but solving the problem was extremely difficult. In 1963, California passed a law requiring pollution control devices on all new cars sold in California one year after a state board certified that at least two systems were available at reasonable cost. California certified four devices, made by independent parts manufacturers, and mandated their requirement on 1966 model cars. Although automobile manufacturers had insisted that they would not be able to produce such devices before 1967 at the earliest, they announced that they would be able to install emission control devices on their 1966 model cars.[3]

We have already seen how positive externalities, such as those resulting from education, will tend to be undersupplied in the market. In such cases, government may respond to raise output to a socially optimal level by subsidizing students' costs through loans or

---

[3]Lawrence White, *The Regulation of Air Pollutant Emissions from Motor Vehicles* (Washington, DC: American Enterprise Institute, 1982), p. 14.

FIGURE 12-1
EQUILIBRIUM OF A MARKET WITH NEGATIVE EXTERNALITIES
(POLLUTION).

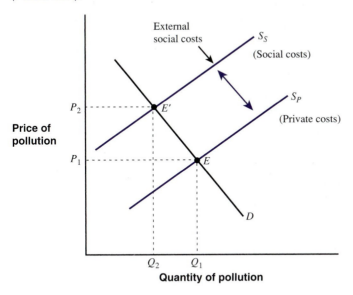

FIGURE 12-2
A MARKET WITH POSITIVE EXTERNALITIES WILL BE
UNDERSUPPLIED.

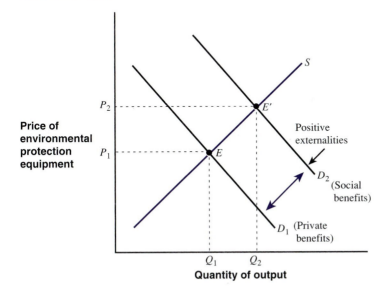

research programs. Likewise, government must oversee solutions to negative externalities. As figure 12-2 suggests, economic efficiency requires greater expenditures on environmental protection than would occur in a free market. The equilibrium price (E) does

not include the positive benefits received by others. If a firm installs pollution control equipment in its smokestacks, it will have a social marginal benefit higher (E') than its private marginal benefit. A firm that takes only its private interests into account will operate at point E, and not voluntarily install equipment to provide a situation where marginal social benefits equal the marginal costs for society (E'). A major public policy role for the government, then, is to correct for market inefficiencies that result from externalities.

ENVIRONMENTAL PROTECTION AND RATIONAL CHOICE

Policy Debates on Environmental Issues

As with other public policy issues examined in this book, there is spirited debate regarding what role, if any, the government should play in environmental policy. Most people admit to being concerned about environmental degradation at some threat level. But individual views differ markedly about the perceived level of threat to the environment from different sources (such as global warming, ozone depletion, or deforestation). Experts often differ regarding the nature of the threats as well as the most effective responses to the threats. Frequently, there is sufficient scientific uncertainty to allow people to reach different conclusions based upon the same evidence.

Global Warming: Clear Facts and Hazy Conclusions

Over a century ago a Swedish chemist Svante Arrhenius theorized that all the carbon dioxide and other gases being released from burning vast amounts of coal were trapping solar heat in the earth's atmosphere similar to the way the glass roof and walls of a greenhouse trap solar energy. He predicted that industrialization would release more gases into the atmosphere trapping increasing amounts of solar heat, causing global temperatures to rise several degrees. Only in recent years however has scientific study proven that the Earth is getting warmer due to the environmental effects of greenhouse gas (GHG) concentrations. **Greenhouse gases refer to atmospheric gases that are almost transparent to incoming solar energy, but trap infrared energy reflected from the earth's surface.** There are about twenty such gases, but scientists primarily focus on carbon dioxide (CO_2), the predominant greenhouse gas which occurs naturally, as do other GHGs such as methane, nitrous oxide, and water vapor. Carbon dioxide has an atmospheric lifetime of between 100 and 200 years.[4] So even if the world stopped burning all coal and oil tomorrow, climatic instability would continue for many years.

As solar radiation, or heat from the sun, approaches the earth, a fraction is absorbed by the atmosphere and by the earth's surface; the rest is reflected back into space. GHGs permit solar radiation to pass relatively freely to the earth's surface, but then trap significant amounts of solar energy in the atmosphere that would otherwise be reflected back into space and reflect the heat back to the earth's surface at different rates. About 30 percent of the solar radiation that reaches the earth is absorbed and the rest is reflected

---

[4]Ross Gelbspan, "A Global Warning," *The American Prospect* (March–April 1997), p. 37.

FIGURE 12-3
THE GREENHOUSE EFFECT.

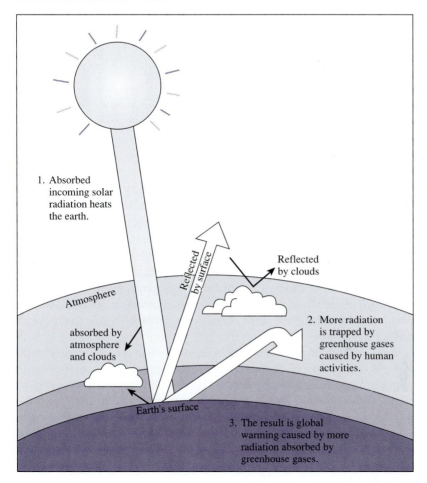

1. Absorbed incoming solar radiation heats the earth.

Reflected by surface

Reflected by clouds

Atmosphere

absorbed by atmosphere and clouds

2. More radiation is trapped by greenhouse gases caused by human activities.

Earth's surface

3. The result is global warming caused by more radiation absorbed by greenhouse gases.

back into space. Without the **"greenhouse effect"** to prevent some radiation from escaping, life on earth would be impossible. The earth would be about 0 degrees Fahrenheit. The GHGs produce the greenhouse effect, without which the earth's temperature would be about 60 degrees Fahrenheit colder. At the other extreme, a runaway greenhouse effect, extremely unlikely, could change the long term weather patterns and make the earth unbearably hot.

In 1995 the United Nations' Intergovernmental Panel on Climate Change (IPCC), a worldwide network of 2,500 of the world's leading scientists studying the problem announced that the evidence of global warming was "undeniable." Research confirms the **global warming theory,** which holds **that the earth is being warmed because of an increase in carbon dioxide and other trace gases in the atmosphere.** This increase is caused by the burning of fossil fuels in automobiles, aircraft, home heating fuel, and factories. **Chlorofluorocarbons (CFCs),** a man-made chemical, make up a much smaller portion of GHGs and have radiative properties giving them a warming potential several thousand times greater than carbon dioxide. Global warming is not only a theory, it is a fact. Average global temperatures have risen about one degree Fahrenheit in the last century. Research has shown a strong connection between average temperatures and GHGs in the atmosphere. Over the next century, the level of GHGs, especially carbon dioxide in the atmosphere is expected to double resulting in global warming of between three and seven degrees. The consequences of an increase of that magnitude could cause severe problems and disruptions for human society. The heating of the atmosphere is projected to cause sea levels to rise by about three feet in the next century, causing disastrous flooding. In parts of the United States for example a three-foot rise would extensively flood areas like New York City, Houston, Charleston, South Florida, and many coastal towns along the East coast. Many other countries such as the Netherlands, Egypt, Bangladesh, and China would face even more extreme problems.

Some scientists, although a minority, criticized the IPCC for putting forth a global warming **worst-case scenario.** They argue that there was a confusion between acknowledging that global warming exists and the magnitude of that warming and warned against taking premature actions to reduce emissions that would slow the economy.

Now that there is a recognition of the reality of global warming the policy debate shaping up is what to do about it. How accurate are the computer generated models of global warming? Do we need to act? Can we determine the cost of reducing GHGs? Who will pay for it? Would global warming irreparably damage the environment or create public health problems?

Most political leaders around the world have been reluctant to act on the early warnings for fear that reducing emissions of carbon dioxide would require actions that would undercut economic growth. International pressure to take action has begun to build however. For example, deforestation in Brazil increases the amount of carbon dioxide in the atmosphere by destroying the trees necessary to absorb it. When the trees are burned even more carbon dioxide is added to the atmosphere. Recently a Dutch official warned the president of Brazil that if his government failed to curb deforestation of the Amazon basin, the Netherlands would cease to exist, as rising temperatures would melt polar ice caps and raise the sea level.[5]

Climate Treaty

The United States and about 130 other countries signed the United Nations Framework Convention on Climate Change, the first binding agreement dealing with climate change. Signatories agreed to reduce their greenhouse gas emissions to 1990 levels by the year 2000. At the Earth Summit in Rio de Janeiro more countries signed the climate change convention, bringing the total to 165. Developing countries were given extra time to meet the targets and were promised financing and technology to help them meet their targets. It soon became clear however that few countries would meet their targets.

[5]Mary H. Cooper, "Global Warming Update," *CQ Researcher,* Nov. 1, 1996.

ACID RAIN

Acid rain refers to the process by which sulfur dioxide and nitrogen oxides are pumped into the atmosphere by coal-fired electric utilities, industrial furnaces, and motor vehicles, where they combine with water vapor and return to earth either as acidic rain or in a dry form. While electric utilities are responsible for over two-thirds of all sulfur oxides, motor vehicles are responsible for over 40 percent of all nitrogen oxide emissions in the United States. Sulfur dioxide is about twice as acidic as nitrogen oxides. Predictably, NO_x emissions are more evenly dispersed around the nation than sulfur oxides, which are concentrated in the Ohio Valley. However, by building high smokestacks, electric utilities and industries in the Ohio Valley have reduced local sulfur dioxide concentrations. These oxides are then usually carried by the prevailing winds for hundreds of miles in a northeasterly direction before returning to earth in precipitation.

Acid rain contributes to the deterioration of metal and stone in buildings and statues. It has also been linked to health problems like asthma, emphysema, and chronic bronchitis. The New England states and Canada have linked the acidity of rivers and lakes with the destruction of aquatic life and the killing of many forest trees to emissions originating in the Ohio Valley. Canada has expressed its exasperation with what it considers to be American insensitivity over the need to reduce sulfur oxide emissions.

The amendments to the Clean Air Act of 1990 did establish goals and deadlines for a two-phase reduction in sulfur dioxide emissions, reduced NO_x emissions, and "caps" on future sulfur dioxide emissions; they also created a system of marketable "allowances" for allocating reductions from different emissions sources.

Since 1995, electrical utilities have a permit for each ton of sulfur dioxide they emit. These permits are distributed in limited supply to firms each year by the government. The permits can be bought and sold between the utilities. The permits roughly reflect the per ton pollution control costs. It was expected in the early 1990s when the permits were being designed that they would cost about $1,100 per ton. By 1997, they were selling for around $100. Compliance costs have been less expensive than either industry or the EPA had predicted.

Source: This account relies heavily on Thomas H. Moore, "Acid Rain: New Approach to Old Problem," *Editorial Research Reports,* no. 9 (March 9, 1991). *Note:* Acidity is measured by a pH scale which ranges from 0 to 14. A reading of 0 is most acidic, while 7 is neutral. A pH reading above 7 indicates alkalinity. Unpolluted rainfall is slightly acidic and has a pH level of about 5.6. "Acid rain" is considered to be precipitation with a pH reading below 5.6. Some acid rain falling in the eastern United States has a pH in the range of 3.5.

On Earth Day in 1993, President Clinton announced his Climate Change Action Plan which included a series of voluntary programs to persuade companies to cooperate with federal agencies to improve energy efficiency and reduce GHGs. The goal was to have the United States meet its goal of reducing its carbon emissions to 1990 levels by the year 2000 through voluntary actions rather than mandatory regulations. There have been some very positive actions taken, particularly by the electric utility industry to reduce greenhouse emission, but on the whole it quickly became apparent that voluntary actions would not enable the United States to meet its emissions goal. In July of 1996, the United

States announced that it had abandoned its call for voluntary steps to reduce greenhouse gas emissions and would press instead for legally binding targets and timetables in the treaty negotiations in Kyoto, Japan, where negotiators were to try to produce a climate change treaty. But many industries within the United States were adamantly opposed to binding targets and timetables and vigorously sought help in Congress to defeat any agreement that required mandatory cuts. There were also great divisions between the wealthy world and the poor countries in which the OPEC countries warned that many of the scenarios of global warming was based on flawed models and was a plot by the wealthy to maintain their status relative to the poor. Not surprisingly the Kyoto summit failed to produce a meaningful agreement.

Failing binding agreements, rising sea levels present grim choices for policy makers. They are very stark and clear: retreat from the sea's encroachment, or try to fend it off. Over the years, homes and businesses have been built closer to the ocean. Estimates of the cost to protect the current U.S. coastline against a 1-meter rise in the sea level are about $300 billion. Even then there are no guarantees the protective measures would work. Measures designed to be permanent frequently turn out to be only temporary. Efforts to protect one beach often displace the ocean's energies to a different coastal area. The alternative is to limit coastal development, and require property owners to bear the cost for property damage due to storms and flooding.

Many scientists believe that the stakes are so high that a worst-case scenario is the only prudent policy perspective. They argue that policy makers typically design programs based upon a worst-case analysis when evaluating military threats because if they do not and the worst case happens the results could be disastrous. They feel the same perspective should be adopted to reduce global warming so that situations do not arise which are irreversible. However, best-case scenario advocates point out that since scientific efforts to measure global warming have yielded ambiguous results, demand for government to "do something" are largely based on emotional arguments.

Ozone Depletion

Ozone is a pale blue gas made up of oxygen. Ninety percent of all atmospheric ozone is found in the stratosphere from approximately 12 to 35 miles above the earth. Most of the upper level ozone is concentrated about 25 km from the Earth's surface in the "ozone layer." **Ozone occupies only a small fraction of the earth's atmosphere but its existence is extremely important to all forms of life on Earth since it is the only gas that absorbs lethal ultraviolet radiation (UV-B) from the sun and reduces it to reasonably safe levels.** While ultraviolet radiation is necessary to synthesize vitamin D, it also damages DNA, which is the protein code necessary for cell reproduction. Animal and plant life on earth have adapted to "natural" levels of UVB. Without such UV protection most life forms, including plants and animals, experience cell damage with major consequences including a decrease in photosynthesis activity in plants and cancer in humans. Without the ozone layer, much higher levels of UVB would reach the earth's surface, wiping out most life on the planet.

Ozone is not discharged into the air by any source. **It is produced when ultraviolet (UV) sunlight splits an oxygen molecule and the resulting single oxygen atom combines with two-atom oxygen molecules forming a molecule with three-oxygen**

atoms (O_3). Ozone, an unstable atom, is primarily **produced** over the tropics, where solar radiation is strongest, and then **diffused** through air circulation toward the polar regions. Therefore, ozone tends to be spread thinner at the poles. The only reason it exists in the upper stratosphere (12 to 35 miles above the earth's surface) is because, until the last several decades, generally it did not come into contact with other highly reactive elements. Although we often refer to an "ozone layer," what actually exists is a diffu- sion of O_3 throughout the upper reaches of the stratosphere, not a "layer" of pure ozone. If the ozone in the stratosphere were compressed to surface pressures, the ozone layer would be less than ½-inch thick.

In 1985, a team of British and American scientists confirmed the existence of a "hole" in the ozone layer over the Antarctic which lasted for several weeks of the Antarctic spring. Subsequent discoveries of ozone depletion over other areas of the earth, espe- cially over the Arctic, led to considerable research to determine the specific forces behind ozone destruction.

Studies by the National Aeronautics and Space Administration (NASA) found by 1988 that the ozone layer around the entire globe was decreasing by 8 percent, a rate much faster than had been previously suspected.

The evidence now makes clear that ozone depletion is primarily caused by man-made chlorofluorocarbons (CFCs) which contain the ozone-destroying catalyst chlorine. CFCs have been used worldwide for over sixty years. CFCs enter the atmosphere from man- made products like refrigerants in refrigerators, aerosol sprays, solvents like carbon tetra- chloride and methyl chloroform used primarily as cleaning agents in the electronics industry, and the materials used to make insulating plastic foam expand in products like Styrofoam, food packaging, and foam cushions. Chemicals like Halon, used primarily in fire extinguishers, have a much greater ozone depleting potential than other CFCs.

CFCs have a particularly stable chemical structure, unlike ozone, and have expected lifetimes of twenty-five to thirty years per molecule before they disintegrate. They are insoluble and therefore unaffected by rainfall. Scientists estimate that it takes between six to ten years for the average CFC molecule to reach the stratosphere by convection and diffusion. Once there, **UV radiation decomposes the CFCs, producing chlorine which acts as a catalyst in breaking down ozone.** The resulting chlorine atom is not used up in the process. Regenerated, it can break down well over 100,000 molecules of ozone before it is destroyed by the intense radiation of the upper atmosphere. The level of chlorine in the atmosphere is estimated to be about six times higher now than at the turn of the century.

Because of the long life cycle of CFCs and the time lag before they get to the strato- sphere, the full effects of ozone depletion will not be felt for decades. Even if the pro- duction of CFCs were to end by the year 2000, the level of chlorofluorocarbons in the stratosphere would continue to increase until about the year 2015 when peak levels of UVB radiation would strike the earth. The persistence of CFCs in the atmosphere will prevent the "hole" in the ozone layer from filling in for at least forty-five years. Ozone levels will not be restored before about 2075.

The discovery of ozone depletion led to predictions of sharply increased incidents of skin cancer and resulting deaths worldwide. Skin cancer is manifested in basal and squamous cell carcinomas. These nonmelanoma skin cancers are linked to the ultraviolet rays absorbed throughout a lifetime. They are usually disfiguring rather than fatal.

Melanoma is less common, but is often fatal. The skin, the largest human organ, defends itself by producing melanin when exposed to the sun's rays, which acts to filter out UV. Data indicate that an increase in UVB will reduce plant yields—especially of soybeans, the world's leading protein crop. Other studies have concluded that phytoplankton at the bottom of the food chain is susceptible to destruction by increased UVB exposure. Reduction of phytoplankton will reduce the food available to other fish and sea mammals.

In 1991, satellite data indicated that ozone was being depleted from the stratosphere at twice the rate reported only three years earlier. And in 1992, NASA released a study indicating that a "hole" in the ozone, comparable to that which has already appeared over the Antarctic, could appear over the northern hemisphere.

Policy Choices

Ozone depletion, like global warming, is a problem of global proportions. As such, it requires a response that includes not only a national commitment, but international efforts. CFCs come primarily from the wealthier nations of the northern hemisphere. Poorer nations produce only a small portion of the CFCs but they share the social costs. Thus the wealthy nations are imposing a negative externality on the rest of the world.

In recent years, substitute products like hydrofluorocarbons (HFCs) have been used which have performance characteristics similar to CFCs in refrigerators, but since they have no chlorine, they will not deplete the ozone layer. Nitrous oxide is another ozone-destroying chemical carried to the upper atmosphere. This compound results from fossil fuel combustion in automobilies among other things. This helps drive the search for "cleaner" automobile engines.

In 1978, CFCs aerosol spray cans were banned by the Environmental Protection Agency. Intense lobbying by industry and a reluctant Reagan administration precluded any further regulatory activity. The 1985 discovery of the ozone "hole" over Antarctica alarmed scientists and aroused environmentalists around the world. Overwhelming pressure to take action resulted. The Montreal Protocol of 1987 represented an agreement by thirty-four countries to reduce the production of CFCs by 50 percent by the year 2000. In 1988, NASA announced that research indicated the ozone layer was being depleted at a faster rate than previously thought. The Montreal Protocol was amended **to completely phase out the production of most CFCs by the year 2000.** The protocol provided funding of $250 million, provided by the developed countries to assist the developing nations in their switch to non-CFC-producing products. This protocol has now been signed by over 100 countries.

The Clean Air Act Amendments passed by Congress in 1990 represented a major break with the "benign neglect" attitude that previously characterized the policy toward ozone depletion. The bill required the EPA administrator to identify and, within two years of enactment, bar the sale or distribution through interstate commerce of nonessential products that release Class I substances into the environment.[6] It also barred any

---

[6]Class I substances were defined in the Clean Air Act Amendments as all fully halogenated chlorofluorocarbons (CFCs), halons, carbon tetrachloride, and methyl chloroform.

Class II substances include those having a reduced ozone depletion potential, which means they can be used during a transitional phaseout period of all CFCs.

person (effective January 1, 1994) from distributing or selling any aerosol product that contains any Class II substance or plastic foam product. It established a national policy of ending the production and use of CFCs and carbon tetrachloride by the year 2000. Methyl chloroform must be phased out by 2002. The EPA also issued a rule requiring car repair shops to use equipment that captures and recycles CFCs. Technicians servicing auto air conditioners must use EPA-certified equipment and be trained in the proper procedures for its use.

Supporters of the legislation argued that there was enough convincing evidence to take action. In this case, they pointed out, absolute proof was not necessary when the worst-case consequences could be catastrophic.

HAZARDOUS WASTES

The awareness of the dangers from toxic-waste dumps was symbolized by the public reaction to the discovery that a subdivision of Niagara Falls, New York, known as Love Canal had been built directly over a 20,000-ton highly toxic chemical waste dump. Many of the residents of Love Canal suffered a wide range of serious illnesses from birth defects to cancers as a result of the toxic contamination of the area. The approximately 900 families living in the neighborhood eventually received relocation benefits from the government. The company responsible for dumping most of the waste was no longer in business. Their struggle made national news and helped raise public consciousness and galvanize public opinion in favor of legislation. Love Canal motivated Congress to pass a law to clean up hazardous waste in 1980. It was known as "Superfund" and dramatized the debate between environmentalists and businesses. The law was based on the "Polluter Pays Principle" which states that polluters are responsible for cleaning up the hazards to the environment that they create. The Polluter Pays Principle started out as an economic principle but became a legal one.

Because of the high costs involved, the debate over who should pay has been contentious from the start. Many in industry claim that since all Americans have profited from cheaper consumer goods that resulted from the improper disposal, taxpayers should pay for the clean up. Environmentalists argue that since polluters have profited most directly from imposing negative externalities on the general public they should be liable for the cleanup. The Comprehensive Environmental Response, Compensation and Liability Act (CERCLA) of 1980 is based, however, on the polluter pays principle by holding anyone who produces or handles hazardous wastes "strictly, jointly and severally" liable for cleanup and damages caused. Some in the industry argue that this provision can unfairly penalize firms in the chain who act responsibly and force them to pay for the improper acts of other firms. They argue for example that they should not be held responsible for the negligence of waste haulers or the improper actions of the operators of a waste dump. The law as amended to allow the EPA to release from liability polluters that contributed only a small amount of toxic wastes to a site.

Until the law was passed there was no effort to define, measure, or take a census of hazardous waste sites. In 1994 President Clinton proposed overhauling the superfund law. He requested a $300 million appropriation to pay for cleaning up "orphan" sites polluted by companies that were no longer in existence was insufficient. He was criticized by environmentalists for proposing different remediation standards for superfund sites according to their anticipated future use. A site for industrial development or a high-way would not have to meet the same standards as an area targeted as a site for future housing. When the measure was taken up in 1995 the "proposals more closely reflected the business interests represented by the new congressional majority," and there was a stalemate.[7] The superfund's taxing power was not renewed at the end of 1995 and the Congressional Budget Office estimates that the $3 billion the fund has received in envi-ronmental tax revenues will sustain the program through fiscal 2000. Congress will take up the superfund's reauthorization again by the year 2000.

POPULATION

The sheer numbers of the world's **population** growth raises the specter of a collision between the expanding needs of human beings and the limits on the human ability to increase production. Understanding the relationship between population, pollution, and poverty is necessary before one can consider policies to deal with these issues.

Throughout most of human history, the population has grown very slowly with the net death rate nearly equal to the birth rate, both of which were high. *The crude birth rate minus the crude death rate equals the increase in population for that year.* Mortality declined just as life expectancy increased beginning in the late seventeenth century in Europe. Improving infant survival rates led to potentially much larger populations to produce the next generation of children.

The world's population reached 1 billion around 1830. By 1900 the Earth had a pop-ulation of about 1.6 billion people. In the span of only fifty years, by the middle of the century, another billion had been added to the world's population. Significantly, 80 per-cent of the growth had taken place in the world's developing nations. In 1995, just forty-five years later, the world population grew by another 3 billion people, with over 90 percent of the increase occurring in developing countries. It took several million years of human history to reach the first billion, about 130 years to reach the second, and today a new billion is added in about eleven years.[8] It now stands at 5.9 billion, and is grow-ing by about three people every second, or more than **a quarter of a million people every day.** As an illustration, the world is adding a city the size of New York every month. Between 90 and 100 million people—roughly equivalent to the population of Mexico—will be added each year of this decade. A billion people, almost the popula-tion of China, will be added over the decade. About 97 percent of the world's popula-tion growth takes place in poorer and developing countries. In some countries, the rate of increase is over 3 percent per year, which means the population will double within twenty years. The result is that social dislocations caused by population growth are more severe in the poorer countries, which also tend to have the fewest natural resources. Several million will migrate to more industrialized countries, but most will remain in the country of their birth, taxing the natural resources and adding to the burden of the local society.

---

[7]Mary Cooper, "Cleaning Up Hazardous Wastes," *CQ Researcher,* vol. 6, no. 32 (Washington, DC: Congressional Quarterly Inc., August 1996), p. 759.

[8]Carl Haub, "Global and U.S. National Population Trends," http://www.gerio.org/CONSEQUENCES/summer95/population.html

Global Projections

The recent population growth all over the world resulted not from increased birth rates but from worldwide decreases in the death rate. Death rates had already been lowered in the industrialized states by the beginning of the twentieth century. While death rates continued to decline more gradually in developed states, they plummeted in developing countries when advances in public health and medicine were introduced.

Poor countries have traditionally sustained high levels of population growth to support agricultural production. But the modernization of agricultural production in those countries has displaced labor-intensive sharecropping systems in favor of mechanized farms using seasonal wage labor. As a result, urban areas have grown rapidly as unemployed farm workers search for jobs in cities. Continued population growth in many poorer countries has led to overcultivation and the destruction of rain forests in a search for new arable land. Desperately poor people are often driven to further ravage the environment in their struggle to survive. In many cases, the consequence is an actual decline in per capita agricultural production and a further increase in poverty. The gap between rich and poor widens. Hence, all to often, agricultural development has not only failed to eliminate poverty but has increased it, with unfortunate consequences for population growth and the environment.

A key measure of a country's population growth is the *total fertility rate* (TFR), defined as the average number of children women will bear in their lifetime, based upon the age and the specific rates for a specific region.[9] Women in developing countries today bear an average of about 3.4 children, or 4.1 when numbers for the much-lower fertility of giant China with over 21 percent of the world's population are removed. Either figure is down considerably from 6.1 TFR in the early 1960s. Only in sub-Saharan Africa do women still average 6.1 children each. But if the TFR remains constant, the world population would rise from 5.9 billion today to 22 billion by 2050 and still be growing at over 4 percent per year.[10]

Almost one-third of the world's 5.9 billion people are age 14 or less. These potential parents are already alive and reaching their reproductive years. An international environmental disaster characterized by starvation, unemployment, poverty, and civil unrest is not idle speculation. The basic concern regarding population growth has been put forward by the U.S. National Academy of Sciences and the U.K. Royal Society as follows:

> If current predictions of population growth prove accurate and patterns of human activity on the planet remain unchanged, science and technology may not be able to prevent either irreversible degradation of the environment or continued poverty for much of the world.[11]

Because population growth rates are not evenly distributed around the world, there will be significantly altered population densities. For example, Europe and North America made up about 22 percent of the world population in 1950, but by 2025 they will make up less than 9 percent. By contrast, Africa, which made up 9 percent of the

---

[9]Haub, "Global Trends," p. 2.
[10]Haub, "Global Trends," p. 3.
[11]U.S. National Academy of Sciences and the Royal Society of London, "Population Growth, Resource Consumption, and a Sustainable World" (Joint Statement, February 27, 1992).

world's population in 1950, will make up approximately 20 percent in 2025. Over 90 percent of the global population growth over the next thirty-five years will occur in the developing countries of Africa, Asia, and Latin America.[12] The sheer numbers indicate that there will be an increasing impact on the environment.

Migration from one country to another is also at an all-time high. In the mid-1990s about 125 million people, mostly in developing countries, lived outside the country in which they were born. At the same time there is a systematic shift from rural to urban living. Problems arise when cities grow so rapidly that governments cannot provide the necessary public services, such as adequate housing and sanitation, and when the job market is unable to absorb all those who move to the cities.

Gender Equality

Studies increasingly focus on the different economic and social conditions faced by the world's women and men. Women around the world bear a greater burden of poverty and ill-health, and have more limited access to education, jobs, and political power. Women are less educated than men throughout the world. Two-thirds of the world's illiterate adults are women, and 70 percent of the children not enrolled in primary school are girls.[13] Women with more education tend to have fewer children because of delayed marriage and improved opportunities for employment. Any number of studies support the conclusion that an improvement in the status of women pays other dividends as well through productivity increases.

Population Models

There are two views of the ability of developing countries to adjust to changes in the environment and population growth to avoid economic decline. One is the **"Cornucopian"** position of Julian Simon, who opposes all attempts to restrain population growth. He believes that **people are the highest resource,** so it is unbelievable that a society can have too many people. According to Simon, people will use their creativity to develop technologies to provide for an ever growing population. Cornucopians historically have been right in that technological progress has allowed most Western economies to avoid the dire warnings of Malthus because output grew faster than population. In developed societies, food production has increased faster than expected because of technological improvements, and populations have grown more slowly than anticipated. Higher standards of living and improved health care have increased life expectancy and reduced infant mortality. These factors have contributed to population growth. They have been offset, however, by the fact that children become an economic liability in developed societies. This has encouraged family planning and has contributed to the stabilization of populations in developed countries.

---

[12]Nafis Sadik, "World Population Continues to Rise," *The Futurist* (March/April 1991).
[13]Lori S. Ashford and Jeanne A. Noble, "Population Policy: Consensus and Challenges," *Consequences,* vol. 2, no. 2, p. 4.

U.S. POPULATION TRENDS

The United States is the most populous of the developed countries and also has one of the highest population growth rates of the industrialized nations: about one percent annually. By the end of 1998 the U.S. population reached 270 million. This adds 2.5 million people to the population each year. The annual growth is equal to a city about the size of San Diego. This is in sharp contrast to Europe which adds less than a million people per year to a population of about 728 million.

Immigration contributes roughly a third of the annual U.S. increase, although the natural increase of births minus deaths is substantial at about 1.7 million per year. The TFR rate has receded slightly to about 2.0. If it remains at its present rate it will maintain its replacement rate.

The United States is undergoing a significant change in its geographic distribution. The stream of immigrants into the United States is highly directed toward six states (California, New York, Texas, Florida, New Jersey, and Illinois). And within these states the flow is primarily to a few metropolitan areas. The population within the United States is also shifting to the South and West.

The nation is also undergoing significant changes in ethnic composition. One-fourth of the present population of the United States is now composed of racial minorities, which are defined as anyone who is not white and non-Hispanic. The Hispanic population is projected by the Census Bureau to rise from 27.7 million in 1996 to 90 million by 2050 due to a combination of immigration and higher fertility (from 10 percent to 22 percent of the population).

Source: Carl Haub, "Global and U.S. National Population Trends."

Developing countries have also benefitted from improved health care. There are fewer incentives for family planning in developing agrarian societies. In agrarian societies children are an economic asset as a source of labor. In countries without pension programs or social security, children may also be a source of support for parents in old age. As a result, family planning is not as popular in developing countries, and their populations are growing much faster than those in developed countries. Unfortunately, many less-developed agrarian countries have not been able to avoid Malthusian predictions because of diminishing marginal productivity. As more people live on a fixed amount of land, the output per worker declines. Even though the economies are growing, per capita growth is negligible or even declining.

The other view is known as **"neo-Malthusian,"** and as its name implies, its proponents believe that in the long run population will exceed the means of subsistence. Populations will increase to the limit that natural resources can support.

Paul Ehrlich is a leading exponent of the neo-Malthusian view. He developed an "Impact Equation" to explain the relationship between human beings and their environment: $I = P \times F(P)$, in which I is the total impact, P is the population, and F is a *function which measures the per capita impact.*[14] The larger the population, the greater the impact on the environment. A world population of less than 1 billion people in the 1600s had less of an environmental impact than a population of 6 billion people at the end of this century. A larger population puts more stress on clean water and air than a smaller population.

In addition to the size of the population, lifestyles have an impact on the environment. The lifestyle of an individual in an affluent country like the United States creates more of an environmental burden than the lifestyle of the typical Ethiopian. Americans make up about 5 percent of the world's population but are responsible for producing over two-thirds of the world's atmospheric carbon monoxide and almost one-half of its nitrogen oxide emissions.

Many charge that there are ethical implications for such affluence. They argue that if Americans ate less meat, more land could be used to raise grain to feed hungry people abroad. Currently, about one-quarter of the world's cropland is devoted to producing grains and other feed for livestock. About 38 percent of the world's grain production is now fed to livestock. In the United States this amounts to about 135 million tons of grain annually of a total production of 312 million ton per year, sufficient to feed a population of 400 million people on a vegetarian diet.[15] A move away from diets high in animal protein foods toward a diet higher in vegetable protein would result in more grain being available for populations in poorer countries.

During the 1970s, the United States encouraged developing countries to voluntarily limit population growth before it began to seriously erode living standards. In 1974, the United Nations held an intergovernmental conference on population. The United States lent its strong endorsement to the program and actively encouraged nations to adopt education programs for family planning and was a major donor to the United Nations Population Fund (UNFPA) and the International Planned Parenthood Federation and other family planning programs in developing countries. At the conference, many developing countries criticized the U.S. position arguing that poorer countries needed more economic assistance, not contraceptives. At a similar conference a decade later in Mexico City the positions were reversed. Most developing countries were now in favor of family planning programs and actively sought assistance for that purpose. However, in the 1980s, Reagan-style conservatism opposed national family planning programs.[16] The Reagan and Bush administrations stopped all financial assistance for family planning and refused to cooperate with multilateral efforts to reduce population growth. Some nations that are usually closely allied with the United States, such as Canada, the United Kingdom, Japan, and Germany, actually increased their donations to UNFPA to try to fill the void. In the last three decades the percentage of couples using contraceptives worldwide has increased fivefold, from less than 10 percent in the 1960s to over 50 percent in the 1990s. One recent study indicated that family planning programs were

[14]Paul R. Ehrlich and John P. Holdren, "Impact of Population Growth, vol. 171 (March 26, 1971), pp. 1212–17.

[15]Henry W. Kindall and David Pimentel, "Constraints on the Expansion of the Global Food Supply," in *Ambio,* vol. 23, no. 3, May 1994. The Royal Swedish Academy of Sciences.

[16]See Garrett Hardin, "Sheer Numbers: Can Environmentalists Grasp the Nettle of Population?" in *E, The Environment Magazine,* vol. 1, no. 6 (November/December 1990), pp. 40–47.

responsible for averting over 400 million births.[17] It varies considerably from country to country however. In developed countries it exceeds 70 percent, while in some developing regions it remains below 15 percent.

There are several reasons why the threat of population growth fails to attract our attention as a critical problem. The world's population grows by over *250,000 people a day, every day.* What networks report as **news** usually involves climactic occurrences rather than daily happenings. Nevertheless, many of the consequences of overpopulation such as deforestation, malnutrition and starvation, and toxic waste do make the news on a daily basis.

Another reason overpopulation does not seem a serious threat is that Thomas Malthus' dire warnings of economic collapse resulting from growing populations have so far failed to materialize. While many aspects of the Malthusian analysis have proved wrong, Malthus did focus on at least two important points: that growing populations could be a problem, and that there is a relationship between the numbers of people and poverty. A growing population within a nation means that the national economy must grow by at least the same rate just to maintain the same standard of living. A country with a population growth rate of 2.7 percent a year must maintain economic growth of 2.7 percent just to maintain the status quo. Continual economic growth rates above that level are very difficult to maintain. It is rather like running up a down escalator. Since much of the population growth rate is occurring in underdeveloped countries, it means that their industrial revolutions can be undone by a Malthusian revolution. Another factor that militates against the perception that population growth is a problem is that many individuals and businesses benefit from population increases. Landlords, banks, manufacturers, and merchants all stand to benefit by providing a growing population with goods and services.[18]

Policy Choices

Population, poverty, and pollution are related in complicated ways. World population has grown beyond an optimal level of "carrying capacity" at the present stage of technological development. At least 1.5 billion people today, over 1 in 5, live in absolute poverty. Population growth rates tend to be much greater in poorer countries than in the developed countries.

People do create wealth and earn incomes. Without people there would be no wealth or income, but the more people there are, the greater the impact on the environment. Larger populations often reduce the income per person and the output of economic goods produced per worker. A country can reduce poverty (increase per capita income) by

---

[17]Ashford and Noble, "Population Policy," p. 5.

[18]Hardin, "Sheer Numbers," p. 43. Lester Milbrath took a survey in which respondents were asked if they would prefer a society that emphasized environmental protection **over** economic growth or a society that emphasized economic **growth** over environmental protection. Business leaders were more likely to choose economic growth over environmental protection. In contrast, the U.S. public chose environmental protection over economic growth by a ratio of 3 to 1 in 1982. When people were asked if they would prefer to live in a society that emphasized economic growth versus one that **limited** economic growth, they overwhelmingly chose economic growth. See Lester Milbrath, "The World Learns about the Environment," *International Studies Notes,* vol. 16, no. 1 (Winter 1991), p. 15.

increasing income while holding its population constant, or by holding income steady while decreasing its population.

The commitment to work to reduce poverty is seen by many policy makers as a moral obligation. It is also necessary for the preservation of the environment and the health of the world economy. A healthy environment can more easily support the present or growing population than a devastated one. Policies to protect the environment are necessary to reduce poverty. Pollution and poverty are twin problems. **Economic development programs to reduce poverty must take into account the necessity of environmental protection. But it is not easy to work toward the seeming antithetical goals of reducing pollution while promoting economic development.** Poorer countries have few incentives to limit greenhouse gases. They do have an incentive to transfer the added costs of pollution to the global environment as an externality, giving themselves a cost advantage in the process.

Threats to the environment are global and thus require international cooperation. However, political power often lies with the wealthier members of society who have much at stake in accommodating the current economic interests of business leaders. Political leaders in most countries tend to remain fixated with narrow aspects of sovereignty and feel they are accountable solely to their domestic constituents. Moreover, nations differ in their contributions to environmental degradation. The wealthier nations of the north make a greater per capita contribution to environmental degradation by emissions of GHGs through the burning of fossil fuels. In poorer countries, overpopulation contributes to environmentally unsound deforestation. The destruction of watersheds by bringing less arable land under cultivation threatens many ecologically fragile areas, along with the economic viability of the countries in question.

The Clinton administration holds that population stabilization policies must have a high priority to stop environmental degradation. Improving the status of women is a part of this strategy. Women who are given a choice will have fewer children. The recent tribal violence in Rwanda occurred in a country with one of the highest fertility rates in the world. Its population grew at the rate of 3.6 percent per year between 1980 and 1990. There are more than eight children for every adult female in Rwanda. The arable land has been so depleted that between 1980 and 1990 food production fell by 20 percent. Tribal and religious conflict is aggravated by a rapidly growing population in poverty. The poor have little to lose by violence.

To reduce world poverty, per capita income in poor countries must be raised. However, there is no realistic way poor countries can achieve the economic development needed for them to significantly raise their standards of living unless their population growth rates are decreased. During the Reagan-Bush years, the United States rejected the policy solution of encouraging birth control efforts in poor nations through the UN. The Clinton administration has since reversed that position and encouraged UN efforts to reduce high population growth rates.

Population control is an important first step in reducing poverty levels, but others are needed also. One possibility would be to encourage technology transfers of low-population, energy-efficient production procedures to poorer countries. In addition, subsidizing the investment costs of installing the equipment needed to implement those procedures would be beneficial.

POLICY RESPONSES

Politics is said to be the art of the possible. The task of the political scientist engaged in policy analysis, then, is to devise solutions derived from principles that different interests share. Policy responses that result in non-zero-sum solutions are generally to be preferred. For example, many businesses view environmentalists' concerns with alarm, fearing that any regulatory measures will drive costs up to intolerable levels. Business leaders tend to dismiss negative externalities as inevitable by-products of market forces. Environmentalists, for their part, tend to view businesses as callous for pursuing profits without sufficiently considering the needs of the environment. The ideal solution would accommodate the needs of both sides, not sacrifice one set of needs to the other.

Command and Control

Diametrically opposed views such as those just described lead to bitter struggles and political polarization. Simply put, government finds itself pressured to outlaw a negative externality, even though many oppose any regulation. Thus the government may adopt **direct regulation in which it determines permissible levels of pollution, and may fine or shut down firms that exceed them** while allowing pollution by other firms that remains within the defined limit.

This regulatory technique is usually referred to as the **command and control** approach because it requires such heavy government involvement. It requires the government to determine the maximum safe level of emissions and then set uniform standards for every smokestack or waste pipe. Policy analysts are uncomfortable with it because the standards promulgated are usually "all or nothing" in nature and do not necessarily reach their stated goals as efficiently or as fairly as possible. The standards require every company to meet the same target regardless of differing costs. This is inefficient because some businesses may have to use more expensive technologies to control pollution than others. Perhaps more importantly, businesses have no incentives to reduce pollution below the standards set by the government. They have no incentives to develop or utilize technologies to exceed the regulated targets. Money that might be used to develop technologies to further reduce pollution is often diverted to fighting the standards or getting an exemption based on the threat of eliminating jobs if the standard is imposed.

Market Incentive Programs

Years of huge budget deficits, anemic economic growth, and sharp foreign competition have inspired searches for policies that reduce bureaucratic intrusion into business decisions. At the same time, policy makers wish to be sensitive to the need for cost-effective solutions to get a high rate of return for the regulatory effort.

Political scientists recognize that pollution externalities represent a failure of the market in which the production of a good exceeds the optimal level. Business and consumers tacitly agree to pass some costs on to the public. Since firms can pass the costs of pollution on society, they have little incentive to consider them in business decisions. To the contrary, any firm that unilaterally tried to reduce external costs would be less competitive in the market. However, rather than rejecting market mechanisms as a source of help in favor of direct regulation, or forsaking pollution control by returning to laissez-faire economic policies, policy analysts recognize that market incentives might suggest creative solutions. **Market incentive programs try to make the market price of a good include the cost of any negative externality.**

There are several ways to ensure that environmental costs are included in choices made by firms and individuals.

Tax Incentives   **A tax incentive program uses taxes to provide incentives for individuals to pattern their behavior in a way that achieves the desired goals.** This tactic charges a fee (tax) on the amount of good consumed that generates pollution, or imposes effluent charges. The threat of taxes are a stick to encourage the desired behavior to protect the environment.

For example, suppose that 100 gallons of gasoline are consumed each month in a society consisting of just three people. And suppose they mutually agree that total gas consumption should be reduced by 15 percent. Let us assume Mrs. A uses 50 gallons per month, Mr. B uses 35 gallons, and Ms. C uses 15. **Direct regulation** would require that each decrease their consumption by an equal percentage (15 percent each) to achieve the reduction. The difficulty with this approach is that it does not reward anyone for saving more than he or she is required to save. It may be that Mrs. A could easily reduce her consumption by 10 gallons with little inconvenience, and Mr. B can easily reduce his by 15 gallons, while Ms. C has always been frugal and would find it difficult to reduce her consumption by more that 1½ gallons (10 percent) per month.

On the other hand, if they agree to levy a tax of 25 cents per gallon on the gasoline they consume, each will have an incentive to reduce consumption. Mrs. A will likely reduce her consumption by 10 gallons (20 percent) and pay $10 in taxes, Mr. B will reduce his by 15 gallons (42 percent) and pay $5 in taxes, while Ms. C will reduce her consumption by 1½ gallons (10 percent) and pay $3.38 in gas taxes each month.

In this illustration, the tax achieves the goal more efficiently than direct regulation. Since the incentive to conserve is included in the price, each person has to choose how much to reduce their consumption. Each is influenced by the marginal utility of consuming an additional gallon. Those who consume less pay less in taxes. The tax gives individuals an incentive to reduce their consumption as much as possible, and to find new ways of reducing consumption. For example, they may buy more fuel-efficient cars, use carpools, consider public transportation alternatives, or consider walking short distances instead of driving.

A variation on this market-based incentive is to provide a subsidy (a carrot rather than the stick). For example, a business could receive a tax credit for installing pollution abatement equipment, such as a scrubber, in a smokestack. Society is still better off with less pollution, since the gap between the market price and the social costs is reduced. Businesses almost invariably will prefer subsidies to taxes. Policy analysts typically prefer tax incentives because they encourage companies to seek greater efficiency in reducing consumption or reducing pollution rather than just achieving a defined standard.

Marketable Permits   **In the marketable permit approach, the government establishes an upper limit of allowable pollution and gives permits to businesses to emit some fraction of that total.   If companies reduce their pollution (or consumption) below the level allocated to them, they receive a permit they can then sell to another firm that has chosen not to reduce its emissions to less than its allowable amount.** For example, a utilities firm may want to expand production but under an emissions cap may be unable to do so unless it can purchase permits to increase its emission of pollutants.

This method is aimed at encouraging firms to significantly reduce their pollution in order to generate marketable permits for other firms that for one reason or another do not find such a reduction worthwhile.   The 1990 Clean Air Act explicitly uses this market incentive to deal with pollution.   The act provides for a 10-million-ton reduction in sulfur dioxide emissions from the 1980 level by the year 2000.   Nitrogen oxide emissions must be reduced by 2 million tons under the 1980 level by the year 2000.   The law also provides a cap limiting emissions to about 50 percent of 1990 levels by 2000.   To meet these goals by the year 2000, the permits issued by the EPA are designed to reduce the amount of pollution allowed each year.   Utilities will be forced to take a number of actions to reduce the levels of emissions: install scrubbers, switch to low-sulfur coal, implement conservation measures, close down obsolete plants, use renewable energy sources such as hydroelectric power where feasible, build new more efficient utilities and transfer the emission allowances to the new plant.   The act also contains a system of pollution "allowances" that encourages utilities to exceed their required reduction of pollutants and recover their costs by selling their marketable certificates to other companies.

Assessing Policy Approaches

Market incentive policies like taxes, subsidies, and marketable permits are attractive to policy analysts for many reasons.   They reduce the market inefficiency of pollution by discouraging undesirable activities that produce externalities.   Pollution charges require businesses to share the burden of the costs of externalities, and therefore to include them in their daily business decisions.   Firms for which pollution reduction is cheapest will reduce pollution more, while those for whom reduction is expensive will have to reduce it less.   Such policies also make the price consumers pay for an externality more closely reflect its cost.

Since pollution cannot be reduced to zero, many see market-based incentives as a pragmatic approach to achieve the **optimal level of pollution.   The optimal level of anything produced from a purely economic perspective is the point at which its price reflects the marginal costs of its production.**   The difficulty is in accurately determining the marginal social cost of pollution and setting the incentives appropriately.   If properly set, firms will pursue pollution abatement to the point that the marginal cost of pollution abatement equals the marginal social benefit control.   If the tax is too low, firms will commit to insufficient environmental protection, while if it is too high, production of the good will be cut back too much.

Market approaches to controlling pollution are rapidly gaining acceptance among many involved in policy making. For example, many states have instituted market-based incentives known as "bottle-bills": A deposit must be made on the purchase of beverages in aluminum or plastic bottles, which is refunded when empty containers are returned. The effect has been to reduce litter and promote recycling.

Nevertheless, there is still significant skepticism regarding market-based incentives, for several reasons. Many environmentalists oppose them because it seems that selling permits to pollute legitimizes pollution. Many business firms oppose market approaches because they involve taxes which are associated negatively with government interference. Also businesses and their lobbyists often prefer direct-market regulation because they have become very effective at countering this approach. For example, they can appeal for a delay in the implementation of regulatory rules citing economic hardship and the possibility of layoffs due to increased costs, and often get what they want.

ETHICS AND ENVIRONMENTALISM

The appeal of market approaches to encourage environmentally sound policies is their efficiency. The market provides a framework in which trade takes place based upon the choices of individuals between a given supply and demand for goods. Through cost-benefit analysis the government can try to set policy while relying upon the *efficiency* of the market to be reproduced even as centralized government decisions aimed at protecting the environment are incorporated into the market process. This is built on the assumption that the policy goals embody an ethical *consensus* that can be promoted better by market mechanisms than by any other means.

There are problems with this utilitarian approach. Cost-benefit analyses are carried out by individuals, and individual preferences may provide a weak foundation for policy making. Individual preferences are the result of personal experiences, which are necessarily limited and based on incomplete information. Even if we were willing to accept individual preferences, we may have a problem in translating the aggregate conflicting preferences into a single policy decision. Another major objection to this form of utilitarianism is that it may result in decisions that are an affront to our sense of justice. Cost-benefit analysis would permit the loss of income of thirty families at $30,000 per year each rather than the loss of one person's income at $1 million. That is, cost-benefit analysis does not require (or preclude) us from taxing distribution. Cost-benefit analysis then cannot be the sole guide to decision making on environmental matters.

Environmental Justice

The poor have always suffered more than the affluent because of the deleterious effects of inferior living conditions. Industrialization had added to the environmental threats to health that more heavily burden the poor than the wealthy. We have noted how housing policy generally stratifies society with the poor living in deteriorating urban areas close to factories and pollution, while the wealthy move to the suburbs. Discrimination against minorities can compound the problem, making them even more likely to live in areas where hazardous waste and other toxins make for unhealthy living conditions. The

POLLUTION AND PUBLIC HEALTH

Many pollutants are a serious threat to health. Over 2,000 deaths per year from cancer are attributed to air pollution. The Harvard School of Public Health calculates that over 50,000 deaths a year are caused by particle pollution (particles of soot 10 microns or less in diameter that are inhaled). These particles are so small that they fall within legal limits of particle pollution. The deaths occur mostly among asthmatics, children with respiratory problems, and the elderly with bronchitis, emphysema, and pneumonia.

Ozone pollution has reached levels dangerous to health in many cities in the last several summers. Ozone is produced at ground level when volatile organic compounds (VOCs), primarily from auto emissions, solvents, and industrial facilities, react with NO_x and sunlight. Since ground-level ozone is created by a chemical reaction in the atmosphere, the amount of it created is closely related to the weather. Ideal weather conditions for the formation of ozone include dry, stagnant, and hot conditions with intense solar radiation.[20] Ground-level ozone is acrid-smelling and toxic when it is part of the smog around us.

Love Canal has come to symbolize the dangers associated with toxic waste, when chemicals including benzene, dioxin, and trichlorethylene contaminated the soil of school and housing areas along the canal in Niagara Falls.

Despite the dangers of pesticides highlighted by Rachel Carson and others, their use continues to grow. About 1 pound of pesticide for every person on the earth (5.6 billion people) is applied on farm crops every year. According to the UN World Health Organization (WHO), over 1 million people per year suffer health problems such as dermatitis, nervous disorders, and cancers. The U.S. National Cancer Institute has established a link between farmers who use a herbicide, 2,4-D and lymphatic cancer. The use of insecticides is often lethal to various animal species as well. For example, carbofuran, a toxic granular insecticide used on crops in the United States, kills well over a million birds that ingest the granules. Pesticide runoff kills well over 2 million fish in waterways.

The greatest health danger may come from nuclear waste. The civilian nuclear power industry has been unable to find a safe way to dispose of such waste. The problem is that it remains dangerous for hundreds of thousands of years. No permanent storage system has yet been devised that can isolate radioactive waste from the rest of the environment and that is satisfactory to those who support or oppose nuclear power.

[20]Susan L. Mayer, *Air Quality Trends: Effects of New Data on Compliance with Standards* (CRS Report for Congress, 92-783 ENR) (Washington, DC: Congressional Research Service, October 30, 1992), p. 8.

Sources: Shirley A. Briggs, "Silent Spring: The View from 1990," *The Ecologist,* vol. 20, no. 2 (March/April 1990); Jack Lewis, "Superfund, RCRA, and UST: The Clean-Up Threesome," *EPA Journal* (July/August 1991).

Council on Environmental Quality's 1971 annual report acknowledged that poor non-white Americans were disproportionately impacted by environmental degradation.[21] And the General Accounting Office found in a 1983 study that three of four hazardous-waste facilities in the Southeast were in African-American communities.

[21]Mary H. Cooper, "Environmental Justice," vol. 8, no. 23, *CQ Researcher* (June 1998), p. 537.

When the environmental movement began in the 1970s, it largely reflected the views of some of the more prosperous upper-income people in the United States. However, since the mid-1980s minorities and the poor have increasingly assumed a leadership role.[22] President Clinton assumed office in 1993 promising to restore the role of the government in environmental protection. Carol M. Browner, appointed by Clinton as EPA administrator, pledged that the EPA would be committed to a leadership role in environmental justice. In 1994 President Clinton issued Executive Order 12898 requiring all federal agencies to include the achievement of "environmental justice part of its mission."

In 1996 in Chester, Pennsylvania, residents brought suit against the Pennsylvania Department of Environmental Protection which had issued a permit to Soil Remediation Services to build a waste facility in Chester. A citizens group in Chester, which is mostly minority, charged that they had become the main waste dump site for mostly white Delaware county. Their suit was filed under Title VI of the 1964 Civil Rights Act, which prohibits agencies that receive federal funds from practicing racial discrimination by effecting "policies or practices [that] cause a discriminatory effect."[23]

There are several ethical principles that should be included in any evaluation of costs versus benefits in policy making. The residents of Chester won their case in the 3rd District Court setting a precedent allowing a poor minority community to pursue a charge of environmental racism even if the discrimination was not deliberate. The state appealed and in June of 1998 the Supreme Court agreed to decide whether lawsuits alleging environmental racism can be brought in federal court.

General Philosophical Principles

There should be a preference for policies that are not irreversible. Many policy choices will make it very difficult to go back and choose an alternative that was rejected. But policy choices should not be of the sort that irrevocably close out other options. For example, many conservationists feel that policies aimed at preserving endangered species from extinction should rank above those aimed at maintaining jobs since new jobs can be created but once a species is extinct its loss is irreversible.

Policies should give special consideration to those most vulnerable to the consequences of policy choices. For example, the poor may find themselves at the mercy of decisions made by the more economically powerful members of society. Dolphins, whales, or spotted owls are affected by human choices. Later generations will have to live with results of decisions made today regarding the use of fossil fuels versus nuclear energy.

Policies should give a preference to strategies that provide the maximum sustainable yield of benefits. The most obvious application of this principle is setting maximum levels of fish catches. While no one owns the ocean, the fish, or the mammals such as whales that live within it, everyone has an incentive to exploit those resources but no

[22]Ibid.
[23]Ibid., p. 542.

incentive to manage or conserve them. The problem of the commons may be dealt with by setting up regulations and incentives to encourage the management of the common stock in question to its maximum sustainable yield. This principle is consistent with the goal of protecting those most vulnerable to the spillover effects of policy choices as well. Since later generations are vulnerable to present-day choices, setting maximum sustainable yields would guarantee that succeeding generations would be provided with benefits roughly equal to those enjoyed by those making the decisions today.

This principle would also encourage renewable energy sources such as solar, wind, and wave energy over the use of scarce nonrenewable forms of energy.

CONCLUSION

1 Environmental issues have taken center stage in public policy debates just in the last three or four decades. Almost every environmental issue is related to the impact of man on the environment. Nature everywhere tends to be treated as a mine or a dump. As mankind makes more and more demands on the environment we use up natural resources, destroy habitats for wildlife, increase biological extinction, and increase environmental pollution. The earth's natural systems such as climate and temperature, the ozone layer, and water supply have all been affected by human demands that outrun the earth's capacity.

2 Although many other countries initially lagged behind the United States in environmental regulation, many have now overtaken us. The emergence of "green parties" have emerged in Europe that have pushed some European standards beyond that of the United States.

3 Environment is a policy issue in which local standards are not enough. It is increasingly recognized that global environmental degradation requires global solutions. Meaningful actions are difficult to achieve however when populations resist any increase in cost as a threat to material affluence. Markets do not provide an efficient outcome when negative externalities exist because business firms have a market incentive to not take the marginal social costs into account in their business decisions. To do so would put them at a competitive disadvantage.

4 Business interests usually react negatively to any government regulation that they fear will drive up costs. The Republican Party has emerged as the standard bearer of those who believe environmental regulation in America increases the costs of production, and damages the nation's competitiveness. They generally oppose new environmental measures and would prefer less regulation.

5 Environmentally the world faces tradeoffs regarding the environment. Eliminating all pollution would be impossible. However the earth does appear to be nearing a real environmental crisis. When private people cannot solve the problem of externalities, such as pollution, the government has a responsibility to step in. The problem is that the special interest groups resist any regulation that would limit their negative externalities. The crucial problem in devising market-based programs is to determine the level of incentives needed to achieve the optimal policy outcome, which is where the marginal cost of the program equals its marginal benefit.

QUESTIONS FOR DISCUSSION

1 Why do the negative externalities of pollution occur?
2 What are the possible solutions for the market failure represented by pollution?
3 How can a business enterprise achieve both its own goals of greater productivity and resulting higher profits and society's goal of protecting the earth against the negative consequences of individual and business activity?
4 How would a political scientist respond to the following suggestion: "Pollution is unacceptable and must be eliminated"?
5 Should government try to reduce their nations' population growth rates? If so, what policies would you recommend?

KEY CONCEPTS

acid rain
chlorofluorocarbons (CFCs)
Clean Air Act
Cornucopian
direct regulation
environmentalism
externalities
global warming

greenhouse effect
marketable permits
market failure
market incentive programs
merit goods
neo-Malthusian
population

SUGGESTED READINGS

Wilfred Beckerman and Jesse Malkin, "How Much Does Global Warming Matter?" *Public Interest* (Winter 1994).

R. J. Berry (ed.), *Environmental Dilemmas: Ethics and Decisions* (New York: Chapman & Hall, Inc., 1993).

E. Bromley and M. Cernea, "The Management of Common Property Natural Resources: Some Conceptual and Operational Fallacies" (World Bank Discussion Paper No. 57) (Washington, DC: World Bank, 1989).

Lester Brown, *The Twenty-Ninth Day* (New York: W. W. Norton, 1978).

John Byrne and Daniel Rich, *Energy and Environment: The Policy Challenge* (Energy Policy Studies, vol. 6) (New Brunswick, NJ: Transaction Publishers, 1992).

Paul R. Ehrlich, *The Population Bomb* (New York: Ballantine Books, 1968).

Paul R. Ehrlich and Anne E. Ehrlich, *Healing the Planet: Strategies for Resolving the Environmental Crisis* (Redding, MA: Addison-Wesley, 1991).

Albert Gore, *Earth in Balance: Healing the Global Environment* (Boston: Houghton Mifflin, 1992).

Garrett Hardin, *New Ethics for Survival* (New York: Viking Press, 1972).

Michael W. Hoffman, Robert Frederick, and Edward S. Petry, *Business, Ethics, and the Environment: The Public Policy Debate* (New York: Quorum Books, 1990).

Michael J. Lacey, *Government and Environmental Politics* (Baltimore: The Johns Hopkins University Press, 1991).

Francesca Lyman, "As the Ozone Thins, the Plot Thickens," *The Amicus Journal,* no. 13 (Summer 1991).

Patrick Michaels, *Global Warming: Failed Forecasts and Politicized Science* (St. Louis, MO: Center for the Study of American Business, July 1993).

Linda Starke (ed.), *State of the World, 1994: A Worldwatch Institute Report on Progress Toward a Sustainable Society* (New York: W. W. Norton, 1994).

13

AMERICAN FOREIGN POLICY

U.S. foreign policy making has usually been studied as a field of specialization separate from the making of domestic public policy. The distinction builds on the idea that foreign policy concerns higher "national" rather than lower "special" interests. It further rests upon the notion that foreign policy questions frequently involve governmental organizations that focus primarily on foreign issues which elicit different political reactions. Indeed a primacy for foreign policy as the most important area of public policy has been claimed.

Economic issues today are increasingly replacing international political and military strategies as dominant issues on the foreign policy agenda. With the collapse of the Soviet Union, economic development and international trade questions have replaced the concern with possible nuclear military conflict. The clear distinction between foreign and domestic policy is less apparent. This shift has been accompanied by an increased participation by Congress in the debate and more involvement by the general public.

INTRODUCTION

This chapter examines the characteristic traditions of American foreign policy. Why did the United States pursue a policy of containment from 1947 through the early 1990s? How will the end of the Cold War impact the future of U.S. foreign policy? What is the effect on foreign policy of the increasing interdependence in the world community? This chapter also takes a look at the tools of foreign policy, a short history of foreign policy since World War II, and some major challenges to American foreign policy in the future.

THE SETTING OF AMERICAN FOREIGN POLICY

As the last years of the twentieth century approach, the United States now must re-examine its foreign policy. To confront the challenge of communist expansion, Harry Truman reorganized the national security structure in 1947 and developed the "containment policy" which endured for over forty years. Now that the communist threat has been removed, many of the basic premises that guided foreign policy since World War II must be reexamined.

At the conclusion of World War II, the U.S. economy was largely immune to the effects of economic conditions around the world. This is no longer the case in the late-1990s. At the end of World War II, the United States was committed to the reconstruction of the economies of war-ravaged Europe and Japan. But today Americans feel the stress of economic challenge from the European Community and Japan. The United States is thrust into a dominating role by virtue of its being the sole remaining superpower, while its military and economic ability to influence world politics has declined. The recent U.S. frustration with Japanese Prime Minister Ryutaro Hashimoto's reluctance to cut taxes to propel Japan and the rest of Asia out of its economic slump is a good example of this.

Continued leadership by the United States will depend on its ability to deal with issues concerning free trade, protection of the global environment, support for democracies, promotion of worldwide economic development, and prevention of weapons proliferation.

Foreign policy may be defined as actions the government takes or attempts to achieve its goals in its relationships with other nations. Foreign policy, then, is the product of how government officials, who represent the state, act. The **foreign policy process** refers to how the decision makers identify, choose, and implement external policy.

Most Americans pay attention to foreign policy only when it fails, although expectations about what foreign policy can achieve are often unrealistically high. Many specific issues of foreign policy are less predictable than domestic policy problems. Much of foreign policy is made in **reaction** to what happens in other parts of the world. Over 180 nations are simultaneously pursuing their own foreign policies, which impacts U.S. decisions. As a result, policy issues may suddenly make a public appearance without long gestation periods, appearing like thunderclaps as lead stories on the evening news. As this book goes to press, Nigeria's failure with democracy tops the news as rioters in Lagos accuse their military government of killing popular political leader Moshood Abiola. U.S. policy makers struggle to find "a valid transition process" to usher in civilian rule.[1]

Considerable attention is focused on high policy issues like **crisis management,** or dealing with surprise situations that appear to threaten the **national security.** Economic policy and foreign policy are increasingly intertwined, as are the links between domestic and international economic issues. Such policy issues are often called **"intermestic" policies because they involve a mixture of international and domestic policies.**

---

[1]"Abiola Backers Riot in Nigeria," *The Washington Post,* 9 July 1998, p. A21.

CHARACTERISTICS OF AMERICAN FOREIGN POLICY

The American approach to foreign policy reflects the nation's unique historical experience as a country geographically isolated from Europe, its views of foreign affairs formed primarily by its domestic experiences.

AN AMERICAN SENSE OF DESTINY AND MORAL SUPERIORITY

The United States has traditionally perceived itself as the world's first modern democracy espousing the principles of egalitarianism. European concepts of nobility and heredity titles had no place in this new nation. Americans believed that individual freedom and social justice would lead immigrants to improve their stations in life. The lack of hereditary status or rank placed responsibility for one's station in life squarely upon the individual. Status and prestige would be measured by one's financial success. Power, in this new society, was the natural consequence of the possession of money. In the old world status, money, and prestige were the consequence of one's inherited position, not of intelligence or merit. Thomas Paine pointed out in *Common Sense* that the natural result of such a system was that ignorance and stupidity prevailed in affairs of state of Europe.

The United States was the first "new" nation born in a revolution championing democracy. Americans, from the earliest days of the Republic, have believed that they have a special destiny to be a beacon of hope to the rest of the world. A system based upon freedom, opportunity, social justice, and faith in the goodness and rationality of all human beings was thought to be obviously morally superior to European concepts based upon hierarchy, exploitation, and war. John Quincy Adams depicted it most vividly:

> Wherever the standard of freedom and independence has been on shall be unfurled, there will be America's heart, her benedictions and her prayers. But she goes not abroad in search of monsters to destroy. She is the well-wisher to the freedom and independence of all. She is the champion and vindicator only of her own.[2]

Americans have believed it their obligation to encourage the spread of freedom and social justice throughout the world. **The challenge for the United States has been to find a way to serve as an example of freedom and justice in an environment in which problems are resolved through power.**

PRAGMATISM

An additional consequence of being a "new nation" with an emphasis on **"individualism"** was that there was not a set pattern or traditional way of doing things. Americans quickly established a penchant for inventiveness and creativeness in solving problems. This utilitarian approach led to the conclusion that whatever works is good. Americans were admired for their "Yankee ingenuity" and their ability to get things done.

---

[2]Quote from George Kennan, Testimony before the Senate Foreign Relations Committee, February 10, 1966, in *Supplemental Foreign Assistance Fiscal Year 1966—Vietnam: Hearing before the Senate Foreign Relations Committee, 89th Cong., 2nd Session* (Washington, DC: Government Printing Office, 1966), p. 336.

Historically, foreign policy has been seen as distinct from domestic policy and generally secondary to individual concerns regarding domestic policy such as jobs, inflation, or taxes. Foreign policy did not seem very important to most Americans until after World War II. Presidents have therefore had considerable discretion in formulating their foreign policies.

What has resulted is a foreign policy that is reactive to external pressures and characterized by discontinuity. These ad hoc policies emphasize short-term rather than long-term goals. This approach was reinforced by the fact that U.S. foreign policy had never suffered a serious reversal until the late 1960s.

Isolationism and Moral Interventions

During most of the nineteenth and early twentieth centuries, the United States was protected from external threats by two oceans and weaker neighbors to the north and south. This long isolation allowed the nation to concentrate on the domestic aspects of nation building: exploring and settling its expansive territory, developing its national identity, strengthening its governmental institutions, and encouraging participation by its population in the industrial revolution.

During this period America felt secure in the Western Hemisphere and largely maintained its isolation from involvement in the intrigues of European politics. Forays into the international arena were typically justified as being necessary deviations from isolationism to defend the national security.

The United States was decidedly more involved in the politics of the Western Hemisphere however. President James Monroe warned European nations, in the Monroe Doctrine enunciated in 1823, that further colonization of the hemisphere would not be tolerated, and declared a special right of the United States to exercise hegemony in North and South America.

Geographic isolation allowed American democracy to develop without the threat of invasions. By contrast, nations like Germany, France, and Russia were repeatedly both aggressors and victims of aggression. Highly centralized governments, in contrast to the decentralization of American politics, became the norm in Europe. Not surprisingly, Europeans frequently emphasized the subordination of the rights of the individual, such as free speech and other individual liberties, to those of the state in the interests of national security. Rather than the American notion of the state being the servant of the people, European thinking often stressed individual responsibility to the state.

One result of the American experience has been to define foreign policy and goals in broader terms than just physical security. They include a preference for democratic over nondemocratic states and a belief that freedom should follow the American flag. The Mexican-American War of 1848 was justified as necessary to fulfill America's "Manifest Destiny" of building a democratic state from the Atlantic to the Pacific and therefore seen as part of America's domestic policy. American involvement in international politics was typically seen as a response to an outside provocation against the American will. When the German government decided to wage unrestricted submarine warfare in 1917, the United States was forced to enter World War I. That involvement then became a crusade to "make the world safe for democracy." But after the war, the United States rejected membership in the League of Nations and pursued a self-conscious "return to normalcy" in the form of renewed isolationism.

Franklin Roosevelt justified his foreign policy in the late 1930s as a need to "quarantine" the disease of totalitarian Nazism. Aid to England was justified as necessary after the defeat of France in 1940 because the United States could not survive alone in a totalitarian sea. However, it was the catastrophic blunder of the Japanese attack on Pearl Harbor followed within hours by Hitler's declaration of war against the United States that **forced** a declaration of war by the U.S. Congress. American involvement in both world wars occurred as a result of decisions made abroad.

AMERICAN FOREIGN POLICY MAKING

Who has responsibility for the conduct of foreign policy? And how is foreign policy made in America? This chapter can only briefly consider the primary policy makers and some of the more important instruments they have to implement their policies.

The President and Congress

The Founding Fathers were fearful of the accumulation of too much power in any one branch of government. They were especially careful to circumscribe the powers given to the president to ensure against the acquisition of dictatorial powers. Article II of the Constitution gives the president the right, with the advice and consent of the Senate, to make treaties and to appoint ambassadors. The Founding Fathers also designated the president as the Commander in Chief of the military and indicated that the executive could receive foreign ambassadors. These powers do not justify the conclusion that those at the Constitutional Convention thought the president should dominate in making foreign policy. In fact, foreign policy was viewed as a minor matter to the framers. The new nation was thousands of miles from the European cauldron. George Washington's well-known warning in his farewell address to **avoid entangling alliances** is indicative of the framer's attitudes.

The president was designated the Commander in Chief of America's armed forces, but only Congress was allowed to declare war. The drafters of the Constitution specifically gave Congress the responsibility to "provide for the common defence." They further gave Congress a role to play in the confirmation of all high-level diplomatic and military officials. Finally, they gave Congress the authority "To make all Laws which shall be necessary and proper for carrying into Execution the foregoing Powers, and all other Powers vested by this Constitution in the Government of the United States. . . ."

The Constitution's grant of authority to the president had the potential for an expansive interpretation by Chief Executives as opportunities presented themselves. The Constitution is silent on many aspects of foreign policy. For example, if Congress has the authority to declare war, should it also be responsible for negotiating peace? Various presidents have taken the position that the specific Constitutional grants of authority to the office, although meager, include "implied powers" to take whatever actions holders of the office think necessary in new circumstances; this has established precedents for future Chief Executives. The result has been the accumulation of far more power in the hands of the president in the area of foreign affairs than the Founding Fathers contemplated. Yet a president's authority is very sensitive to the individual's ability to persuade the public and Congress to support presidential positions.

There is a distinctly different perception regarding how **domestic and foreign policy should be made.** The Founding Fathers carefully separated governmental authority among the three branches and placed checks on the exercise of power, and particularly on the president's power, on the theory that too much power is likely to be abused. However, some critics argue that in foreign policy **executive power should be concentrated.** A weak Chief Executive is unable to act with dispatch to protect the nation's vital interests. These critics believe that foreign policy should be made differently than domestic policy, especially in crisis situations like war. During World War II, Congress ceded to the president emergency powers for the duration of the war. Almost immediately after the war ended, the United States found itself involved in the Cold War. Some believed that this situation required the president to continue to exercise emergency powers as long as required by these new circumstances.

However, if a president acquires sufficient power to act almost unilaterally in foreign affairs, there is the danger that restraints on domestic presidential authority will wear away. Congress, particularly through various of its committees, has exercised considerable influence on foreign policy. Unfortunately, when Congress asserted a greater role in foreign policy making because of the collapse of a consensus on foreign policy goals during the Vietnam War, many complained of "congressional interference."

What is the proper congressional role in foreign policy making? Should public opinion play a significant role, or is the public too uninformed?

In the past, the foreign policy process involved only a small elite group that provided input based upon its members' supposed expertise. This is in contrast to the formulation of most domestic policy issues, where the emphasis is on a broad democratic participation in the process. Most problems involving "crisis management" issues require the formation of quick responses and are dealt with by experts at the top of the executive branch's foreign policy bureaucracy. Presumably they formulate the "best" strategy to deal with each such problem.

Longer-term security strategies frequently involve the need for congressional approval and funding. They require an expanded number of players in the planning and negotiation stages of their adoption.

When a policy question involves **intermestic** issues, it is more likely to resemble domestic policy formulation. That is, it involves a wide spectrum of interest groups claiming a right to be heard. The congressional debate involving NAFTA and the involvement of interest groups with the issue greatly expanded the scope of the conflict and encouraged negotiations and compromises.

The president has foreign policy institutions to advise him on foreign and military issues. The Department of State is the oldest of all the cabinet departments, which makes the secretary of state (Thomas Jefferson being the first) the ranking cabinet member. Its primary objective is to carry out foreign policy to promote the long-range security goals of the country. American ambassadors, along with over 8,000 foreign service officers who work for the State Department, represent the United States at foreign embassies and international organizations around the world.

The secretary of state is the president's primary foreign policy adviser. Secretaries of state have only as much policy making authority as the president chooses to delegate. Presidents like Eisenhower and Reagan gave their secretaries of state broad discretion to make foreign policy decisions. Others, like Kennedy, Carter, and Bush, took a more active part in foreign policy decision making. Some contend that this has resulted in reducing the State Department to managing routine affairs, with important foreign policy matters being run out of the White House. President Clinton set domestic issues as the centerpiece of his first term in office, leading many experts to complain that his foreign policy lacked coherence, direction, and determination. As his second term winds down, Clinton seems to have found a path even though critics still describe its substance as "social work" and lacking in geopolitical instinct.

Some recent administrations have appointed National Security Advisers with offices in the White House to provide advice on foreign policy matters. Such an arrangement bypasses the formal institutional provisions of government. National Security Advisers have access to military, intelligence, and diplomatic sources of information and have become very influential in establishing foreign policy. For instance, Richard Nixon and Jimmy Carter relied primarily on Henry Kissinger and Zbigniew Brzezinski rather than their secretaries of state for advice. Communications technology now permits presidents to have direct access with foreign heads of state or to speak directly to their own military commanders in the policy making process.

The National Security Organizations

National Security Council (NSC)   Created in 1947 to help presidents integrate the "domestic, foreign, and military policies" that affect national security, the NSC's statutory membership includes the president, vice president, secretary of state, and secretary of defense. The director of the Central Intelligence Agency (CIA) and the chairman of the Joint Chiefs of Staff (JCS) serve as advisory members. The president's assistant for national security affairs serves as the day-to-day director of the NSC. Technically the agency does not make decisions since that is the responsibility of the president, but it does offer policy guidance and advice. Its statutory authority indicates that it has **advisory** authority only. It does not have any **operational authority.**

Department of Defense (DOD)   The secretary of defense officially presides over the Department of Defense and is the president's main military adviser. The Defense Department comprises all the military services and is responsible for about 70 percent of the government's equipment purchases. The commanding officers of each of the services and a chairman comprise the **Joint Chiefs of Staff (JCS),** who advise the secretary of defense as well as the president. Friction frequently develops between the members of the JCS as they try to strengthen the roles of their respective services in military planning.

The Intelligence Community   **Intelligence refers to the process of collecting, analyzing, protecting and using information to further the national interests.** Prior to the surprise attack on Pearl Harbor, the United States had no centralized agency for

IRAN-CONTRA: A FAILED ATTEMPT AT FOREIGN POLICY MAKING

In an effort to obtain the release of American hostages held in Lebanon and to provide aid to the Contras in Nicaragua, the Reagan administration decided upon a plan that used the NSC. Despite being limited legally to an advisory role, the NSC staff became involved in covert operations. The plan was to secretly sell arms to the Iranians in exchange for their assistance in gaining the release of six American hostages being held by terrorists in Lebanon. There were different shipments of arms to Iran, and one American hostage was released after each delivery. The terrorists maintained their supply of hostages to trade for arms by capturing three more Americans.

Lt. Col. Oliver North diverted funds from the sale of U.S. property, which should have gone to the U.S. treasury, to Swiss bank accounts where some of the money was used to support the Contras in Nicaragua. This was done without the knowledge of Congress. Congress had passed the Boland Amendment to prevent the sale of weapons to terrorist organizations and to prohibit any U.S. government aid from going to the Contras. The administration solicited confidential donations from wealthy American citizens and from foreign governments so that the president could continue to aid the Contras despite the congressional ban. These funds were to be under the control of "The Enterprise" to avoid the Constitutional check of congressional control of funding. The Constitution provides that foreign policy is to be made by the president and the Congress working together. But the Reagan administration was attempting to privatize foreign policy since Congress was not acceding to the president's will.

In November 1986 the Lebanese newspaper *Al-Shiraa* reported that the U.S. government had been selling HAWK missiles to Iran. An executive order by Reagan had officially listed Iran as a government which sponsored terrorism and the Arms Export Control Act prohibited arms shipments to states so identified. President Reagan had publicly stated his opposition to negotiating with terrorists and discouraged other nations from selling arms to Iran. Reagan claimed that he had not been informed of the diversion of funds. The action was also alleged to be in violation of the requirement of the president to provide notification to the appropriate intelligence oversight committee in Congress before implementing covert operations.

intelligence gathering. Then during World War II President Roosevelt created the Office of Strategic Services (OSS) to gather and analyze intelligence to aid in military planning. The OSS also conducted covert operations against enemy forces and their war-making capabilities.

After World War II, the OSS was disbanded and a small Central Intelligence Group provided information to the government. Soviet control of Eastern Europe and concern over communist expansion suggested a need for accurate up-to-date information about the capabilities and the intentions of other national leaders. The CIA was created by the National Security Act of 1947 to advise and make recommendations to the departments of the government about issues and situations related to national security.

The new CIA was to collect and analyze intelligence about foreign countries and disseminate the resulting intelligence reports to those in the American government who needed the information in their decision making. The intelligence community makes use

Lt. Col. North readily admitted his involvement in the affair, and that he had lied to Congress concerning these activities. National Security Adviser Robert McFarlane and Oliver North accompanied the first shipment of arms to Iran, bringing additional gifts of a cake baked in the shape of a key (to symbolize the key to friendship between the two nations) and a Bible signed by President Reagan. North also admitted to efforts to deceive Congress and to destroy incriminating evidence. He defended his actions by saying that he was given to understand his superiors were aware of the full range of his activities and approved of them. He contended that he believed President Reagan was also aware of what he was doing. He indicated that he would do whatever asked by the president.

Admiral John Poindexter claimed full responsibility for the decisions to siphon the money to the Contras. He said that he thought the president would have approved, but that he had not informed him, so Reagan had no knowledge of the operation. Poindexter claimed that the "buck stops here with me."

The experts on Iran and foreign policy planners from the Departments of State and Defense and the CIA were never included in the policy process. Their involvement in such activities was very explicitly prohibited by the Boland Amendment. The Secretary of State, George Schultz, implied that the State Department would not involve itself in such amateurish schemes. Then Vice President George Bush explained that he "was out of the loop" despite his position on the NSC.

The policy was a failure on every score. Constitutional procedures and laws were violated. There were as many hostages at the end of the debacle as at its beginning. Those involved showed contempt for democratic principles and procedures. The result was bad policy administered incompetently. Publically proclaiming an uncompromising policy of not giving in to terrorist blackmail exposed some hypocrisy in the administration and yet secretly doing so damaged the authority and credibility of the President.

Source: Report of the Congressional Committees Investigating the Iran-Contra Affair, with Supplemental Minority and Additional Views, S. Report No. 100-216 (Washington DC: U.S. Government Printing Office, November 1987).

of classified sources of information, but most information is collected from open sources such as news stories, public documents, and diplomatic reporting. Intelligence is distinguished however, by its sources and methods, which are not available to everyone.

The most controversial aspect of intelligence has to do with **covert action, which involves the secret operations designed to influence events in other countries while attempting to conceal the sponsoring government's involvement.** Covert actions may include propaganda, political, economic, or paramilitary operations.

Many scholars argue that covert action is not intelligence per se. However, it is a function that most governments assign to their intelligence branches because their organizations for clandestine information collection makes them well suited to many forms of covert action. CIA covert action has ranged from funneling money to finance anticommunist political parties in Italy's national election in 1948, to helping overthrow foreign governments, such as the one in Iran in 1953 or the government in Guatemala in

1954. CIA covert action launched U-2 flights over the Soviet Union in the 1950s, and the invasion of Cuba at the Bay of Pigs in 1961. The CIA was involved in the destabilization of governments in Indonesia, Chile, and Vietnam. It was also involved, in violation of its charter, in efforts to infiltrate and disrupt the student protest movement against the U.S. involvement in Vietnam.

Congress was concerned about problems created by intelligence organizations within the U.S. democratic structure. Democracies are based upon openness and a free flow of information, while intelligence organizations are relatively closed and place restrictions on access to information. Therefore, Congress provided that the agency would have no police, law enforcement powers, or internal security functions. The CIA was prohibited by law from collecting information about U.S. citizens.[3] The statute creating the CIA provided that nothing in the law was to be construed as authority to withhold information from the intelligence committees on the grounds that providing the information would constitute unauthorized disclosure.[4]

During the early years of the Cold War, Congress did not appear to want to be fully informed about what the intelligence community was doing. But when the national and government consensus on foreign policy began to erode during the Vietnam conflict and rumors began to surface about CIA violations of its charter, Congress began to assert its authority over intelligence operations. Since the 1970s, the role of Congress in intelligence matters has increased dramatically. The intelligence community has become like the rest of government. And the House and Senate permanent Select Committees on Intelligence have become, like other committees, the patrons as well as the overseer of "their" government agencies.[5] The Reagan and Bush administrations and conservatives, not used to Congress vigorously exercising its prerogative in this area, claimed that intelligence gathering is an executive function and that congressional meddling in the area weakened national security. It was this misguided sense of executive prerogatives that led ultimately to Iran Contra.

Although the precise figure is classified, the intelligence community's budget for fiscal 1994 was about 27.7 billion.[6] Estimates today indicate that intelligence avoided drastic cutbacks and has maintained a flat budget.

With the end of the Cold War, the CIA is having to shift its focus to global problems of nations trying to buy or build nuclear weapons, international terrorism, and international economic trends. The products of American intelligence gathering have been increasingly made available upon request to the United Nations to support peacekeeping operations in areas like Somalia, Croatia, and Rwanda.

---

[3]Counterintelligence activity within the United States is carried out by the Federal Bureau of Investigation.

[4]National Security Act of 1947, Title V—Accountability for Intelligence Activities.

[5]Thomas E. Mann (ed.), *A Question of Balance: The President, the Congress, and Foreign Policy* (Washington, DC: The Brookings Institution, 1990), p. 70.

[6]Tim Weiner, "C.I.A. Is Rebuffed on Spying Budget," *The New York Times,* 17 July 1993, p. 7. The CIA receives about $3 billion. About $23 billion goes to various military intelligence agencies, including the National Reconnaissance Office, which is responsible for the design and procurement of all reconnaissance satellites and for their management once in orbit; the National Security Agency, which conducts electronic eavesdropping, decryption, and encryption of U.S. codes; the Defense Intelligence Agency, which analyzes military intelligence; and the intelligence branches of the military service. The remainder goes to the intelligence bureaus of the Departments of State, Justice, Energy, and the Treasury.

CIA AT THE CROSSROADS

Intelligence is basically a dedicated support service for government policy makers. In theory, intelligence should gather and process information from a variety of sources and present it in an objective fashion. However, intelligence is irrelevant without policy. Its purpose is to provide foreign policy makers with accurate information upon which to base their decisions. A major difficulty is that policy makers prefer that intelligence findings support their goals. Conversely policy makers are unhappy with intelligence that undermines a preconceived policy. In such cases the information is often discounted or ignored by policy makers. But if the intelligence community shades its analysis to please a policy maker, it risks policy and intelligence failures.

Unfortunately the CIA has been drawn into partisan politics more frequently in recent years, which undermines its credibility. The agency rebuffed Richard Nixon when he tried to use it in his efforts to cover up the Watergate scandal. A few years later, Gerald Ford appointed George Bush as Director of Central Intelligence (DCI); Bush was a former Chair of the Republican National Committee—an inherently partisan position—and had no experience in intelligence. When Ronald Reagan appointed William Casey, who had managed his campaign, as the new Director of Central Intelligence, any semblance of nonpartisanship was removed. Casey cooperated with the turning over of covert operations to "The Enterprise" to avoid congressional control. In 1991, President George Bush nominated Robert Gates, who had worked closely with William Casey during Iran-Contra to the post. His nomination was also controversial because analysts in the CIA charged that he presented the White House only with intelligence supportive of administrative policy. President Clinton appointed George Tenet as DCI.

Much of the criticism of the intelligence community centers around covert action. Is covert action an appropriate policy tool to be used by democratic governments? How can its drawbacks be minimized so that it is worth continuing? What controls should be placed on covert action? Should the CIA's covert action be limited to political, propaganda, and economic operations? Should paramilitary covert operations be separated from the CIA and placed with some other group like the military?

Economic intelligence is an increasingly important aspect of information collection. In addition to studying economic trends or trade policies, some governments see nothing amiss in using intelligence organizations to steal U.S. corporations' proprietary secrets. A serious debate is taking place about whether the CIA should provide proprietary help to American corporations since many foreign companies receive assistance from their governments. There are great risks involved. Business relationships with companies in other countries might be soured by suspicions that American firms have an unfair advantage. There is also the increasing problem of defining an American company, as many companies have overseas subsidiaries, or are international holding companies.

THE GLOBAL ACTORS

Nation-States

A nation consists of individuals usually bound together by shared history, culture, and language, and who live in a geographic area that provides them with a uniqueness that distinguishes them from others. When people organize into a political group as a means of defense of their identity or other interests, they may claim to be a nation-state. Not surprisingly, nation-states, like individuals, see the world from their own perspectives.

The number of nation-states has expanded more in the last half of the twentieth century than in any comparable time in world history. In 1945, there were 67 nations. The end of colonialism saw the emergence of new nation-states. And more recently the disintegration of the Soviet Union saw the reemergence of the Baltic states as well as other former Soviet republics which proclaimed their independence. By the mid-1990s there were 187 sovereign states.[7] The number has increased recently as the result of the recent phenomenon of failed states like the Soviet Union or Yugoslavia. Other states like Somalia are collapsing and Canada is threatened with disintegration.

The nation-state, or simply state, exists in a world populated by other states each pursuing its own "national interests." The sovereign state is the main political actor in the international system. Each state lays claim to sovereignty. **Sovereignty** means that a state's government has supreme control over the body politic and that it is free from any external control. The highest purpose of the state is to defend itself against external challenges to its sovereignty. Every state claims the right to pursue its own interests at the expense of others, limited only by the constraints of international law.

Sovereignty means that the government has the legal right, and presumably the power to require citizens to comply with its policies. From an international perspective, sovereign equality means that states are equal in their legal status despite differences in size or economic power. Therefore, no government can require other states to agree to a policy. As in other areas of foreign policy, the ideal is for international problems—say of an economic nature—to be resolved through negotiation.

In practice, governments may find themselves challenged for control of the state by internal as well as external forces. No state's sovereignty has ever been absolute. Today, states cannot control information or capital flows across their borders, and international economic integration nibbles away at what once were their sovereign prerogatives. Even advanced powerful nations like the United States find aspects of their sovereignty evaporating. Meanwhile, new nations insistent on sovereignty discover that it does not give them the independence for which they struggled.

The environment of the state system in which nations still must coexist as the primary actors constrains states to be vigilant to any threat to their political, military, and economic security. Survival in a world where states still claim the rights of independence and self-defense among other attributes of sovereignty means that states must still ultimately rely upon "self-help." Many policies stem from the nature of the current international system in which there is, as yet, no international organization that can protect states from hostile acts of other nations. States must ultimately try to advance their interests as a way to increase their security against the possibility of attack. Thus many claim that foreign policy is a product of the state system and not of the existence of states themselves.

---

[7]*Statistical Abstract, 1992*, pp. 820–22. In addition, there are 37 "Areas of Special Sovereignty and Dependencies."

Nonstate Actors

States were perceived to be the sole actors in the international system until well after World War II. Although other organizations and groups, such as the International Telegraphic Union [now the International Telecommunications Union (ITU)], had been around for well over a century, they were not thought of as having any independent power. Such organizations known as **intergovernmental organizations (IGOs),** are voluntary associations of states in which there is a perceived mutual advantage to be gained by cooperation. IGOs may be regional, such as the Organization of American States (OAS) or the European Economic Community (EEC), or global, such as the United Nations (UN). They can in turn be classified according to their goals, which may be narrow, such as the North American Free Trade Association (NAFTA), or all-encompassing, such as the United Nations.

These organizations, of which the best known is the United Nations, may have political, military, economic, or humanitarian purposes. The United Nations was founded in 1945 as the successor to the League of Nations, which was the first attempt at a permanent international organization designed to maintain the peace, created after World War I. Founders of the UN hoped to provide for world order based upon the rule of law and cooperation rather than conflict and the law of the jungle. It embodies the determination "to save succeeding generations from the scourge of war which . . . has brought untold sorrow to mankind." These words in the preamble to the Charter are based on the conclusion that warfare has long since outlived its usefulness as a tool of diplomacy. The UN Charter is a treaty to which the U.S. Senate has given its advice and consent, and as such its provisions are presumably binding on the United States, as well as on all its members. All members of the UN agree under Article 2 "to fulfill in good faith the obligations assumed by them in accordance with the present Charter." In particular, Article 2, paragraph 4, provides the following:

> All Members shall refrain in their international relations from the threat or use of force against the territorial integrity or political independence of any state, or in any other manner inconsistent with the Purposes of the United Nations.[8]

The Charter gives the Security Council the primary responsibility for the maintenance of international peace and security.[9] Article 42 provides that the Security Council may take "such action by air, sea, or land forces as may be necessary to maintain or restore international peace and security" by using the military forces of UN members.

---

[8]The purpose of the Article is to outlaw the aggressive use of force by states, which was acceptable in the classical period of international law that did not recognize any authority above the individual nation-state. The Charter does allow the use of force by states in their self-defense, as Article 51 provides: "Nothing in the present Charter shall impair the **inherent** right of individual or collective **self defense** if an armed attack occurs. . . ." (emphasis added)

Article 2 obviously has not prevented the threat or use of force by states against other states. The major difference since the startup of the UN has been that countries try to defend their use of force either as self-defense or as being otherwise consistent with the purposes and principles of the UN.

[9]Article 24.

THE EUROPEAN ECONOMIC COMMUNITY

Some parts of the world are experiencing the reemergence of nationalism. This is especially true where nationalism had been suppressed by the division of the world into bipolar camps during the Cold War. While ethnic and minority groups demand the right to self determination in many of these cases, there are other examples of states moving in the direction of giving up their independence to form larger economic and political unions.

This can be seen most clearly in Europe with the establishment of the European Economic Community (EEC; usually referred to as the Common Market). The EEC is a customs union, with free trade between the members. This stimulus provides a larger marketplace and greater competition for companies within the bloc. Originally consisting of six member states, it has grown to twelve members—in 1993 members included Ireland, the United Kingdom, Belgium, Netherlands, Luxembourg, Denmark, Germany, France, Spain, Portugal, Italy, and Greece. In 1967 the European Atomic Energy Community (EURATOM), the ECSC, and the EEC joined together to form the **European Community (EC).**

In 1985, the member states committed themselves to work toward a more integrated Europe by 1992, at which time they would undertake to eliminate all barriers to internal European trade. In December 1991 at the EC meeting in Maastricht, Netherlands, the members agreed, among other things, to a goal of monetary union by the end of the 1990s. The treaty proposed a common foreign and defense policy as well. A common currency (the European Currency Union, ECU) was to be in place by 1999 if political problems could be overcome.

Economic integration induces pressure for political integration. The Maastricht Treaty proposed significant political and economic integration. The treaty included a "European citizenship," which would guarantee rights to Europeans in any other European country including voting rights and the right to seek office. But financial strains caused by German deficits incurred to reunify the country give evidence that the nations still have political obstacles to overcome to bring the final monetary union about.

Nongovernmental Actors

While nongovernmental actors are not new in the international system, the surge in their numbers and their development as major players in the international community since World War II is remarkable. Unlike IGOs, which are creatures of the states they represent, nongovernmental or **transnational organizations (NGOs)** are private groups that have programs in more than one country. Such organizations usually downplay nationality. NGOs have their own interests that they pursue in different states' territories.

The International Committee of the Red Cross (ICRC) is an example of an NGO that supports humanitarian projects in many countries. Its success has been based on its strict impartiality in pursuing its goals of humanitarian relief, which allowed it to operate in all the belligerent nations during World War II. The ICRC has been a major player in drafting treaties on the laws of war.

A nongovernmental organization that predates the modern nation-state and wields global influence is the Catholic Church. It is involved in social issues around the world.

A continuing sense of national and cultural identity and language differences retard the movement toward larger political union. Another major obstacle to the appeal of union with a larger community is the reality that the individual nation-state is still responsible for education, housing, health care, and maintaining employment in its labor force through economic policies. These policies differ between nations and in their comprehensiveness, level of funding, and tax rates. Without greater parity between these national policies, a common currency will be extremely difficult to achieve. The movement toward a larger association is clear, but overcoming these last impediments will not happen quickly.

As it is, the European Community poses an impressive economic challenge to the United States. The nations of the EC have a combined total production slightly larger than the U.S. GDP and a larger population. There is concern that the effort to develop European economic unity will lead to additional growth of about 5 percent in the next ten years. Policy makers in the United States are concerned that a single market within the EC could become a tool to increase trade within Europe while reducing trade with the world beyond the EC's boundaries. The United States has argued against high EC protective tariffs. This is an important concern for trade policy since approximately 25 percent of all U.S. exports and imports go to or arrive from EC countries.

The move toward market economies in Eastern Europe and the former Soviet Union has also opened up potential markets for which the United States and the EC will compete. The European Community has not only the obvious geographic advantage over the United States in this competition, but its members also have cultural ties as well. Because of the economic challenge of the EC, the United States negotiated the North American Free Trade Agreement with Canada and Mexico.

Sources: Walter Goldstein, "Europe After Maastricht," *Foreign Affairs,* vol. 71, no. 5 (Winter 1992); Peter Ludlow, "The Maastricht Treaty and the Future of Europe," *The Washington Quarterly,* vol. 15, no. 4 (Fall 1992); Jorge G. Castaneda, "Can NAFTA Change Mexico?" *Foreign Affairs,* vol. 72, no. 4 (September/October 1993).

In developed Western countries, the Church hierarchy has taken positions on the need for governmental action to reduce social and economic inequalities through programs to help those in poverty. In the United States, the National Conference of Catholic Bishops (NCCB) opposed the 1991 Gulf War, and opposed aid to the Contras in Nicaragua in the 1980s. The NCCB has supported an increase in foreign aid to less developed countries, while at the same time it has opposed the sale of military weapons abroad. The Bishops have also expressed their opposition to the view that the use of nuclear weapons could be an ethical defense strategy. Domestically, they have supported a redistribution of wealth toward the poor, supported gun control and opposed abortion. Catholic Relief Services, an overseas aid program, sponsored by American Catholic Bishops, is one of the largest NGOs that distributes food provided by U.S.A.I.D. (U.S. Agency for International Development). In the developing world, many of the Catholic clergy have been actively involved in social justice issues. Governments must use a great deal of circumspection in dealing with such a large organization having worldwide membership.

Multinational corporations (MNCs) are the most noteworthy flood of new NGOs in the post–World War II period. Increasingly, corporations transcend national boundaries. Many of them have branches involved in production and sales located throughout the world. Such corporations develop a multinational rather than a national orientation.

MNCs offer tremendous benefits by creating jobs, helping to train labor forces, bringing new technologies to countries, and providing competition. MNCs also work to reduce international tension. A company with operations in different countries wants friendly relations between them. However, multinational corporations cause problems for national governments. Unlike a domestic corporation that can be dealt with through domestic policies, if an MNC does not like the policies of a particular government, such as taxes or environmental regulations, it can move its operations to a country it finds more hospitable. Nations often compete with each other to influence multinationals to locate within their countries by offering very attractive economic conditions. For example, American investors might form a holding company with a subsidiary for cargo ships incorporated in Honduras to avoid U.S. maritime laws and high wages. Their financial transactions and profits might be handled by Bahamian banks to circumvent American financial disclosure laws.

Many MNCs have greater sales and profits than the gross domestic products of many states. Large corporations have a profound impact on politics in America. It is not surprising, then, that MNCs can threaten the stability of governments in some countries where they operate. In many instances the multinationals can use their leverage to control governments rather than the governments controlling the multinationals. American multinational corporations are spread out across the world, so that, when an American buys a Pontiac from General Motors, over half the money paid goes to Germany, South Korea, Japan, Taiwan, the United Kingdom, and Singapore. In the process, the world is becoming more cosmopolitan, and somewhat Americanized.

In a defensive reaction against MNC penetration, many nations have created their own "corporate champions." Some countries proceeded to develop an industrial policy in which they consolidated whole industries. For example, Britain consolidated its automobile manufacturers into British Leyland and its steelmakers into British Steel. France supported Renault as its automobile manufacturer and Unisor and Sacilor as its steel manufacturers.[10] In some cases these corporations were owned outright by their governments.

Foreign corporations, usually aided by their home government's policies toward business, began to challenge the United States in high-quality, high volume production of standard goods. As patents expired, less-developed countries insisted on coproduction agreements, and as foreign nations improved their educational systems, U.S. technological advantages began to shrink. By the beginning of the 1990s, the United States, which has about 22 percent of the world's GDP, imported over 45 percent of the manufactured exports from all of the developing countries.

Many foreign MNCs, to reduce transportation costs and to avoid any effort to keep cheaper foreign products out of the American market, began buying and building plants in America. Not surprisingly, Honda, Toyota, and Mercedes were aggressively courted

---

[10]Robert Reich, *The Work of Nations* (New York: Vintage Books, 1992), pp. 66–67.

by the U.S. state governors who hoped new plants would be located within their borders. MNCs also contribute heavily to political candidates through political action committees (PACs). Increasingly MNCs operate in disregard of international boundaries. Consequently, business decisions made in one nation will affect employment in other countries.

The Global Village

The rapid pace of political and economic change taking place throughout the world is rearranging the international landscape. American foreign and military policy is being deeply affected by the shift from the old divisions between developed industrialized societies and developing, primarily agrarian, Third-World states to the new situation of industrialization cropping up all over the world. During the last quarter of the twentieth century, some advanced nations have been driven toward high-skill, information-intensive jobs, with lower-skill agrarian and manufacturing jobs being exported to Third-World nations. But the shift taking place is uneven and has many observable overlaps. Even the most technically advanced nations, like the United States, have manufacturing sectors where low-skill labor predominates. Opposition to the North American Free Trade Agreement was a futile effort to prevent more of these jobs from slipping away to Mexico. And there are countries like China and Brazil that are primarily agrarian with some smokestack manufacturing centers that have enclaves of high technology.

Technical societies need many dependable connections with other nations. The change from agrarian to industrialized in high tech economies around the world has been accompanied by a rapid growth of IGOs from about 200 on the eve of World War I to over 4,000 by the early 1980s. Over 30,000 treaties have been registered with the United Nations since 1945. In 1991 the United States was party to over 1,000 treaties and over 12,000 international agreements.[11] The irony is that the most powerful and advanced state in the world is the most constrained by treaties an other agreements, and the least able to act recklessly. By contrast, the least developed are the least connected. Weak economies, often with only natural products or resources to sell, do not need many external links.

COMING IN OUT OF THE COLD WAR

The Cold War has ended, but a brief summary of the major events of that period is in order to clarify the new challenges the new era presents.

American-Soviet Competition

The wartime alliance between the United States and the Soviet Union began to show severe strains by the end of the war in 1945. From 1945 until the collapse of the Soviet

---

[11]According to the *Yearbook of International Organizations* (Munich: K. G. Sauer Verlag, 1993), vol. 1, p. 1667, the total number of international organizations grew from 10,437 to 14,147 between 1981 and 1992.

T.I.A.S. *(Treaties and International Agreements Series)* published by the State Department, which contains all treaties and agreements in force to which the United States is a party, contained over 283 pages listing bilateral treaties and over 138 pages listing multinational treaties in its 1993 edition.

NAFTA: WINNERS AND LOSERS

The North American Free Trade Agreement (NAFTA) ratified by Congress in November 1993 marked a singular victory for free trade proponents. Over a fifteen year period, NAFTA eliminates barriers to trade among the United States, Canada and Mexico. Free trade agreements (FTAs), differ from economic unions, like the European Union, in that **they lack a common external tariff** and have **no institutional infrastructure beyond dispute settlement agencies.** Despite this, the NAFTA debate provoked heated protest from organized labor and environmental groups, especially in the United States. Ross Perot turned NAFTA into a campaign issue during the 1992 presidential elections, when he warned Americans against the "giant sucking sound" NAFTA would create as it took jobs away from American workers.

To date, much of the economic calamity forecasted has not occurred. A Department of Commerce report on NAFTA issued in 1997 found: (1) two-way trade with Mexico and Canada grew 44 percent since the agreement was signed; (2) between 1993 and 1996 U.S. exports to Canada (United States' largest trading partner) rose 33.6 percent and exports to Mexico rose 36.5 percent; and (3) exports to Canada and Mexico supported about 2.3 million jobs since 1993. Other findings summarized from various analyses of NAFTA's economic implications show that Mexico has reduced tariff barriers to the United States from an average of 10 percent to approximately 2.07 percent. Mexico has also dismantled various protectionist rules and regulations representing a shift from almost "police state characteristics" toward a liberalization of its trading practices. Most businesses give a "thumbs up" on NAFTA too. An American Chamber of Commerce/Mexico report entitled "NAFTA's Success: A Three Year View from Mexico," found the NAFTA experience "overwhelmingly positive." This despite Mexico's economic crisis which resulted in a devaluation of the peso. The devaluation translated into lowered purchasing power for Mexican middle-class consumers. Analysts caution that the precariousness of Mexico's economic climate makes a sound evaluation of NAFTA's consequences difficult to conduct.

President Clinton hoped to ride in on NAFTA's success and expand his trade liberalization agenda. As a June 1998 *Business Week* article argued "If the President can pull off even half of his new agenda, he might be remembered as the strongest Democratic advocate of free trade since John F. Kennedy." Clinton urged European nations to join the United States in new rounds of global talks to reduce trade barriers and offer more accommodating labor and environmental standards. But, unlike earlier administrations, Congress stood in the way of Clinton's crusade

Union in 1991, American foreign policy was dominated by two fundamental principles: The first was the primacy of national security. The threat of an expansionist Soviet communism forced all other issues into a subordinate position relative to national security. Thus U.S. initiatives such as the Marshall Plan, which had humanitarian and economic stabilization aspects, were mainly driven by enlightened self-interest to increase Western security. The roughly equal bipolar distribution of military power between the United States and the Soviet Union became the single most defining aspect of international politics after World War II.

by failing to give him **"fast track"** trade negotiating authority. Fast track authority would give the executive branch exclusive control over negotiation of trade agreements. Congressional approval would still be necessary but Congress could not amend an agreement.

NAFTA is not without its critics. **Initial public outcry about NAFTA centered on job loss.** Organized labor's vehement opposition created a deep rift with the Clinton administration as labor leaders fueled fear that NAFTA would benefit the "elite" leaving the average American worker behind. Some of labor's outcry is well founded. American factories, *maquiladoras,* located just over the border of the Rio Grande have sprung up in large numbers in Mexico, contributing to a population surge and environmental degradation. These highly labor intensive factories have attracted large numbers of Mexican workers. Some argue this creates a "win-win" situation. Business takes advantage of labor surplus (and its lower wages), while employment in Mexico grows. Recently, *maquiladoras,* laborers have begun to react. Recognizing their lowered wage status, welders at the Han Young factory—a tractor chassis assembly plant—went on strike after failing to win union recognition. Mexican President Ernesto Zedillo Ponce de Leon joined forces with Congressman David Bonior (D-Michigan) to pressure President Clinton to intercede on behalf of labor. This incident illustrates for many one of the major weaknesses of the NAFTA accord, its inability to enforce labor law.

Another criticism of NAFTA targets its environmental mandate. From the onset **critics argued that "greening" trade agreements was a bad idea.** Consumer advocate Ralph Nader has been particularly outspoken in his criticism of NAFTA's failure to adequately enforce environmental regulations. In a 110-page report entitled "NAFTA's Broken Promises: The Border Betrayed," Nader's Public Citizen group decries the air pollution and waste dumping, it argues, results from NAFTA related industry. Nader's group criticizes NAFTA's environmental enforcement arm (North American Agreement on Environmental Cooperation, NAAEC) for broken promises and inadequate inspections. In an ironic twist to the NAFTA uproar, Nader joined forces with arch-conservative Pat Buchanan to protest the NAFTA agreement.

Florida citrus and tomato farmers and North Dakota wheat farmers complain bitterly about export surges from Mexico and Canada. Canadian citizens fret over the cultural hegemony of the United States, while Mexican officials worry over their flagging economy's ability to live up to the agreement. Ultimately the much heralded "Yukon to Yucatan" agreement has yet to fully live up to expectations. Yet it is far from the disaster predicted by many.

The clear division between East and West led each superpower to construct alliances to better defend itself against threats from the other bloc. The United States ringed Russian with the North Atlantic Treaty Organization (NATO), the Australia, New Zealand, and the United States Treaty (ANZUS), and the U.S.-Japan Security Treaty. The Soviet Union created the Warsaw Pact to counter NATO. Each side tried to convince other states to join their bloc. The bloc antagonisms convulsed universal international organizations to which both belonged such as the United Nations, as each superpower tried to get those organizations to support its own goals.

NATO: EXPANSION OR DISASTER?

The U.S. Senate by a vote of 80–19 approved the expansion of NATO to include Poland, Hungary, and the Czech Republic. Efforts to build bipartisan support for enlargement began during President Clinton's first administration. By 1994, Clinton was on board despite strong opposition in the Pentagon and the State Department. How and why the U.S. Senate gave its blessing to what critics perceive as a provocative move has as much to do with American voter indifference as anything else. For example, most Americans, when asked, were unable to name the three new NATO members. Pundits argue that foreign policy lost its panache when the Cold War ended. Those, like President Clinton, who argued that enlarging **NATO will "erase Europe's dividing lines,"** expressed various reasons for their support. Conservatives, with the backing of the U.S. arms industry eyeing a lucrative market, viewed building a larger NATO coalition as a sound military instrument for redividing Europe and keeping the Russians out permanently. Liberals argue the opposite claiming NATO as an effective political tool for building a united Europe.

But the naysayers, including such prominent foreign policy experts as the "author of containment" George F. Kennan are deeply critical of the Senate vote. Kennan called enlargement **"the most fateful error of U.S. policy in the entire post–Cold War era."** What motivates this fear includes both strategic and economic issues. To many, NATO enlargement **jeopardizes Russia's rapprochement with the West.** Initiatives like the "Partnership for Peace" do little to calm the Russian government's antagonism. Critics argue that history demonstrates the futility of excluding former adversaries. At present, Russian President Boris N. Yeltsin has had little choice but to indicate that he will live with enlargement especially now that five of the sixteen NATO members have ratified enlargement. He must accede to the likelihood that by NATO's 50th anniversary in 1999, there will be three new members.

Beyond strategic concerns, economic questions remain. While the Clinton administration estimated the cost of enlargement at $1.5 billion over the next ten years, the Congressional Budget Office put the cost of enlargement at $61 billion to $125 billion over fifteen years for American and European taxpayers. It is not clear how this cost will be apportioned among members. Most European governments hope that **the U.S. will foot most of the bill.** Faced with serious economic problems, the three proposed members will be forced to spend scarce resources on weapons some claim they do not need. Finally, now that the door has opened, many wonder **which countries come next.** The Baltics, Bulgaria, Romania, and Slovenia hope to be in the next wave of enlargement. Russia, critics claim, will not stand idly by while every country on its western flank joins a military bloc.

So **while many expound on the principled basis for enlargement as a signal of cooperation and trust, skeptics respond that the U.S. backing reflected short-sided politics.** Americans from Central Europe (especially in key states like New York, Michigan, and Ohio) pushed for the inclusion of their motherlands. Time will tell if enlargement succeeds in creating a more democratic, stable and secure Europe. Or, in the words of former State Department Soviet affairs analyst Helmut Sonnefeldt, it forces Russia to define itself increasingly in opposition to all things American.

The second major American foreign policy principle, supportive of the first, consisted of the development of an ideological commitment to market capitalism and opposition to any deviation as socialistic and evil. Repressive dictatorships fending off democratic demands to hold elections quickly learned to denounce their domestic opponents as communist-inspired. They were oftentimes hailed as courageous leaders who had to take repressive measures against ruthless communist opponents. They might receive aid and support from the United States to train their police against opposition forces, as the Shah of Iran did for many years.

As World War II ground to an end, the United States anticipated a new era of cooperation with the Soviet Union that would provide for a stable peace in Europe. Territory of the Soviet Union had suffered catastrophic invasions over the last couple of centuries by Napoleon, by Germany in World War I, by Western powers during Russia's civil war after World War I, and again by Germany in World War II. Although the Soviet Union narrowly escaped defeat at the hand of Germany in the war, it emerged as the major European power by the end of the war. But Western hope that the several years of wartime cooperation would convince Stalin of the peaceful intentions of Britain and the United States was short-lived. To increase Soviet security, the Soviet army imposed control over the nations of Eastern Europe. After World War II elections were never held in those countries or their democratically elected leaders were overthrown; Eastern European nations were reduced to satellites of the Soviet Union.

The United States and the Soviet Union emerged from World War II as the two dominant powers in the world. This bipolar division in which the two superpowers confronted each other extended the competition even to Third-World countries. Each side perceived themselves to be in a zero-sum game in which the slightest gain in power for one was seen as a loss of power and reduced security for the other.

The Soviet army's seizure of authority over Eastern Europe led President Truman to initiate a **policy of containment** in 1947.[12] Under this policy, which was followed on a bipartisan basis until the disintegration of the Soviet Union in 1991, the U.S. goal was to block and contain any expansionist effort of the Soviet Union. In its application, it assumed that communism was a unified subversive force directed and controlled from the Kremlin. Truman felt that the realities of the distribution of international power left the United States no choice but to act to counter communist initiatives anywhere in the world.

Peaceful Coexistence

After the death of Josef Stalin in 1953, Nikita Khrushchev eventually succeeded the Soviet leadership. Khrushchev said nuclear war would leave no winners and that the

---

[12]Actually George Kennan is given credit as the architect of the containment policy. The proposed policy appeared in an article entitled "The Sources of Soviet Conduct," in the journal *Foreign Affairs*. Writing under the pseudonym "Mr. X," Kennan stated that the Soviet strategy was based upon convenient ideology and the conditions inside Russia. Its goal was not world domination, but rather that all governments bordering Russia should be favorably disposed to itself. Kennan proposed a long-term policy of containment of Russia expansionism to buy time for internal changes to occur within that country. He favored a political strategy of containment. He was opposed to the militarization of the concept and therefore opposed to our involvement in Vietnam.

Soviet-American military rivalry was too dangerous. He proposed that both sides agree to peaceful coexistence in which both major powers would compete by economic rather than military means. Nevertheless, Khrushchev viewed assistance to struggles against colonialism as a central element of Marxist principles which he could not renounce.

President John F. Kennedy accepted the concept of peaceful coexistence, and offered as a peaceful challenge to the Soviet Union a race to put a man on the moon within the decade of the 1960s. But this did not mean that Kennedy intended to compromise the policy of containment. In his 1961 inaugural address, he promised that America would "pay any price, bear any burden, meet any hardship, support any friend, oppose any foe to assure the survival and success of liberty."

All too frequently during the Cold War, the United States came to the aid of authoritarian regimes claiming that their democratic opponents were communist sympathizers. In other instances, the United States helped overthrow democratically elected governments such as Guatemala in 1954, if it was thought that they were less anticommunist or pro-American than their opponents.

The Cold War modified the traditional mistrust of foreign intervention. Victory in World War II led to an overconfidence in the ability of the United States to intervene in any foreign dispute and achieve whatever goal it desired. Many Americans abandoned their preference for isolationism in favor of the "higher goal" of containing communism. Even so, significant interventions against communism—such as Korea and Vietnam—produced widespread domestic opposition. This also resulted in the United States deviating from its historic principle of siding with democratic regimes against undemocratic regimes. The imperative of containing communism was the justification for raiding unsavory governments while failing to aid democratic forces.

Cuba

Fidel Castro came to power in Cuba in January 1959 when he overthrew the dictator Fulgencio Batista. Castro immediately began to consolidate close relations with the Soviet bloc. In 1961 the new Kennedy administration was presented with a plan put together under the Eisenhower administration by the Central Intelligence Agency to overthrow Castro. The CIA plan assumed that a small group of Cuban exiles would be able to establish a beachhead in Cuba, which would lead to large defections from Castro's army and a popular uprising. It was implemented, and the exiles landed at Cuba's Bay of Pigs. But the invasion was an unmitigated disaster.

The failure of the United States to overtly intervene with its own force when the covert intervention failed led Khrushchev to miscalculate Kennedy's determination to fight communism. Khrushchev began building launching sites in Cuba for medium- and intermediate-range Soviet ballistic missiles. If Kennedy failed to respond, it would indicate to our NATO allies what some were beginning to fear, that once the United State was vulnerable to attack, it would not risk nuclear war to protect Europe from the Soviets. Failure to respond once the missiles were in place would reinforce Khrushchev's boast that world power was shifting toward the Soviet Union.

The Soviet move in Cuba was predicated on the belief that the United States did not possess the will to use force in the defense of its interests. Kennedy knew that allowing such a misperception to stand was dangerous because it would lead the Soviets to carry out additional challenges to Western security such as Khrushchev threatened over Berlin. So Kennedy stood firm during the Cuban missile crisis: He placed a "quarantine" around Cuba against the shipment of additional missiles there, and demanded the removal of all missiles already in Cuba before they became operational. The overwhelming conventional military superiority of the United States in the Caribbean and its nuclear superiority, along with Kennedy's determined stance, left Moscow little choice but to back down.

Shortly after the Cuban missile crisis, both the Soviet Union and the United States were distracted from their aggressive direct rivalry with each other. The embarrassing blunder in Cuba was a major factor in Khrushchev's ouster by Leonid Brezhnev in 1964, and Brezhnev himself felt forced to concentrate on a massive buildup of conventional and nuclear forces. At the same time, the United States became preoccupied with domestic issues and the war in Vietnam.

Vietnam

After the Cuban missile crisis, the United States two years later faced the shock of Kennedy's assassination in November 1963. Kennedy's successor, Lyndon Johnson, whose main interest was domestic policy, wanted to undertake progressive social reforms, many of which had been proposed by Kennedy, that he termed the Great Society. But even as he worked toward that end, and started pushing civil rights bills through Congress, he became increasingly involved in the unraveling of the situation in Vietnam.

The logic that ensnared the United States in Vietnam was the dubious domino theory: If South Vietnam fell to communist forces, it would be like a falling domino that would cause other dominoes in Southeast Asia, such as Laos and Cambodia, to fall in succession. During World War II, Franklin Roosevelt adamantly opposed any suggestion that France should be allowed to reclaim its colony in Indochina after Japan was defeated. But when communists seized power in the northern part of Vietnam after the war, every President from Truman to Nixon felt compelled to incrementally increase American aid first to the French and then to successive noncommunist regimes in the south of the country in an effort to prevent a communist victory there also. The strategy never worked, however. The autocratic rule of several leaders in South Vietnam provided fertile ground for the recruitment of South Vietnamese into guerrilla activity against the American effort—guerrilla activity directed by Ho Chih Minh's communist forces from the north.

The Vietnam War resulted in the deaths of over 55,000 American troops and about 600,000 North Vietnamese. As the conflict dragged on, many Americans began to question the morality of their country's use of force in Vietnam. The traditional American view that democratic principles were incompatible with power politics began to reassert itself. Vietnam challenged the notion that the policy of containment could be used to justify military intervention regardless of cost in lives and material. The consensus in support of containment policy remained but for the first time serious questions were raised concerning how to most effectively pursue the policy.

The intervention in Vietnam subordinated domestic politics to foreign policy issues. The decision to invest resources in fighting the war diverted their being used to deal with the nation's domestic problems in the areas of health, education, pollution, and crime in the streets.

Supporters of the war argued that those who complained that military expenditures shifted resources away from more pressing social issues were prolonging the war by encouraging the enemy while discouraging the American soldier in the field. In fact as H. R. Haldeman's diaries make clear, President Nixon concluded by late 1970 that the war was unwinnable. He was concerned that a pullout in 1971 would result in an adverse reaction in the 1972 elections. Haldeman noted in his diary that he planned "a continued winding down and then a pullout right at the fall of '72 so that if any bad results follow they will be too late to affect the election."[13] The United States withdrew the last of its ground troops in 1973. The end of the South Vietnam government was by that time inevitable although its final collapse occurred in 1975.

Detente

By the end of the Vietnam War, the illusion of omnipotence possessed by the United States in 1962 was gone. The optimism of the early 1960s that U.S. power and moral righteousness could encourage democracies and justice throughout the world collapsed with the fall of South Vietnam to the communists in 1975. It was replaced by a new awareness of the difficulties involved in democratic nation-building abroad and a fear that the wielding of international power could corrupt the nation using it. Americans became disillusioned and weary with their nation's Cold War role and the rationale that justified intervention based merely on anticommunism. The strains resulting from the war showed that the nation was not invincible militarily nor invulnerable economically.

By the early 1970s, the failure of U.S. policy in Vietnam led the United States to pursue a policy of detente. Detente refers to a relaxation of tension between the United States and the Soviet Union during the Nixon, Ford, and Carter administrations. Detente was begun during the Nixon administration with an attempt to use trade to encourage friendlier relations with the Soviet Union. It was not a rejection of the Cold War or the policy of containment so much as a tactical shift in the pursuit of American interest when the strategic superiority of the United States was gone and many American were demanding that more attention be paid to domestic issues.

Detente was also useful to the Soviet Union. During the first twenty years of the Cold War, the United States embargoed the shipment of products that might have any military application or promote the economic strength of the Soviet Union. The effect was to encourage the Soviet economy to remain self-sufficient and independent. The Soviet economy was stagnating by the early 1970s due to the diversion of so many resources to its military needs. The communist government was unable to delivery on its promise of more consumer goods, including food. Since Brezhnev considered the structural reforms later undertaken by Gorbachev as too radical, he needed detente to import Western consumer goods technology, and food. Henry Kissinger and subsequently President Jimmy Carter used trade to reward or punish Soviet foreign policy. The hope was the Soviet

---

[13]H. R. Haldeman, *The Haldeman Diaries: Inside the Nixon White House* (New York: G. P. Putnam's Sons, 1994), p. 221.

need for American wheat and computers would result in the Soviets exercising self-restraint in foreign policy to avoid a cutoff in American trade. Events revealed the limitations of using trade as a foreign policy tool. But the use of economic carrots and sticks under detente did encourage the Soviet economy to become more dependent upon the American economy.[14]

During the 1970s several agreements between the United States and the Soviet Union on arms control, trade, and technology transfer issues were concluded. Detente continued despite strains created over issues like Angola and Ethiopia until late in 1979. In November of that year, militant elements in Iran seized fifty-two Americans at the U.S. embassy in Teheran, and a month later the Soviet Union invaded Afghanistan. President Carter began taking a tougher stand toward the Soviets. He embargoed shipments of grain to the Soviet Union, and began giving military aid to forces in Afghanistan fighting the Soviet occupation.

All this caused difficulties for detente and shifts in American attitudes. The situation of the hostages in Iran prevented a retaliatory strike against the Iranian militants and seemed to symbolize the impotence of a policy that emphasized accommodation when dealing with revolutionary fundamentalists. Nor was the wheat embargo popular. Sanctions against the Soviets hit American business with the prospect of lost sales and workers with lost jobs. Also trade embargoes can be effective only if an adversary cannot obtain the commodities elsewhere. The Soviet Union learned very quickly how to encourage competition between nations seeking markets for their products. Upset over the hostages and over lost trade because of Carter's embargo encouraged a major shift in public attitudes away from detente and toward a more assertive international role for the United States occurred.

Ronald Reagan, who had long espoused a firm stance on foreign policy issues, benefited from the mood swing. Many believed that detente enabled the Russians to advance their interests at the expense of the United States. In the 1980 Presidential campaign, Reagan supported significantly increased defense spending and indicated a greater willingness to use military force in pursuit of containment. He also promised American farmers that if elected he would end President Carter's embargo on wheat to the Soviet Union.

Gorbachev and the Disintegration of Soviet Communism

Leonid Brezhnev's foreign policy, which sought nuclear parity with the United States, had been achieved at the cost of a stagnant Soviet economy. When Mikhail S. Gorbachev came to power in the mid-1980s, he was unlike any other Soviet leader since the communists came to power in Russia in 1971. He was far more sophisticated and less ideological than his predecessors. He, like Reagan, benefited from a changing mood among the Russian people, who were beginning to press for improved living standards. Several years of bad harvests had resulted in the rationing of some basic foods like meat and sugar. Food had been imported from the United States since the 1970s. By the end of that decade, the Soviet economy had literally come to a standstill.

---

[14]John Spanier, *Games Nations Play,* 7th ed. (Washington, DC: The Congressional Quarterly Press, 1990), p. 392.

When Gorbachev became General Secretary of the Soviet Communist Party in 1985, he quickly learned the severity of the economic crisis that the Soviet Union faced. He immediately began a series of economic reforms known as *perestroika* or a "restructuring" toward a market system. His reforms included the introduction of civil liberties knows as *glasnost* ("openness") within the Soviet society. He encouraged the removal of the privileged position of the Communist Party and allowed competition in elections. He even permitted the Supreme Soviet to initiate actions rather than merely act as a rubber stamp to the Communist Party leadership's decisions.

To accomplish his political and economic reforms, Gorbachev needed to shift spending from the military to the civilian sector of the Soviet economy. His actions unleashed a pent-up demand for more political and economic freedom, while hardline communists tried desperately to maintain control. His emphasis on the priority of domestic affairs required pursuit of a conciliatory foreign policy, especially in reducing strategic military forces. The burden of the Cold War spending had caused the Soviet Union to divert so many resources to military spending that its economy was falling further behind the West.

Gorbachev changed several long-held doctrinaire foreign policy positions of the Soviet Union. For example, he indicated that the value of peace would take precedence over the class struggle, and repudiated the Brezhnev Doctrine by stating that socialist countries had no right to intervene in one another's affairs. "Sufficiency" would be the basis for determining the level of Soviet military preparedness. Soviet forces in Eastern Europe would be reorganized into a defense posture that would preclude the possibility of offensive military moves against the West to reassure NATO. To this end, he promised to withdraw six tank divisions and bridging units and their equipment from Warsaw Pact countries.

Gorbachev wanted to slow down the arms race in order to divert more resources to domestic Soviet economic policy. He proposed a strategic arms treaty to slow Reagan's Strategic Defense Initiative (SDI) and limit intermediate nuclear forces (INF) to include nuclear missiles based in the United States and Europe and strategic bombers. Gorbachev believed that if Reagan signed such a treaty, his strongly anticommunist record would make it very difficult for conservative senators in the president's own Republican Party to continue their opposition, as would be likely if the president were a Democrat. The Senate ultimately gave its consent to the treaty negotiated under Reagan and Gorbachev by a vote of 93–4 as conservative opposition to it crumbled. In 1988 Gorbachev committed the Soviet Union to a unilateral 10 percent reduction in its military budget.

The Reagan administration, which began by characterizing the conflict between the United States and the Soviet Union as one between good and evil, by 1988 espoused detente and warmly supported Gorbachev's attempts at domestic reform. By the end of the Reagan administration, American-Soviet relations were closer than under any other President since World War II. The Cold War effectively ended the year after Reagan left office.

Gorbachev's reforms gave a great deal of freedom to the peoples of Russia and the Eastern Bloc countries. His limited democratization and the restraint he placed on the Communist Party led to shifts in power both in Russia and elsewhere in the Soviet sphere of control. Communist governments in Eastern Europe, which had been maintained only by the threat of bayonets, were quickly swept away. The Baltic states which had been incorporated into the Soviet Union during World War II, regained their independence in1990. Mikhail Gorbachev refused to use force to suppress the fragmentation of the Soviet empire as his predecessor Leonid Brezhnev surely would have. Gorbachev was himself a victim of the revolution he started. Overtaken by the tide of change, he was forced to resign in December 1991 and with that the Soviet Union essentially collapsed.

The Cold War thus came to an end with the Soviet empire collapsing in upon itself. Rather than a violent battle between communists and counter revolutionaries in which the losing forces vowed to continue the struggle, the change was surprisingly swift and peaceful. Most of the inhabitants of the communist countries celebrated the victory of the values of the West over communism.

In place of the Soviet Union there is now the Commonwealth of Independent States (CIS), which facilitates cooperation among the independent republics that formerly made up the Soviet Union. Russia, led by President Boris Yeltsin, is merely the largest of the former Soviet Republics.

Although George Bush was in the White House at the time, he was unable to claim credit for the unraveling of the Soviet Union. The containment policy initiated by President Truman in 1948 and pursued on a bipartisan basis by the United States was an important ingredient in the West's victory over communism. But the failure of Soviet domestic policy and the corruption of the Soviet system was a greater ingredient.

FOREIGN POLICY AFTER THE COLD WAR

The policy of containment that became an integral part of the Cold War began as a pragmatic reaction to a very real threat. Over time, this anticommunist sentiment defined a major value in the outlook of Americans. The Cold War provided a reaffirmation of the values of freedom and democracy over the antithetical system represented by communism, as well as the need to guarantee the peace through military power. The East-West struggle led most Americans to identify themselves as strongly anticommunist. Winning the Cold War suddenly deprived American foreign policy of the galvanizing sense of purpose that had been its fixed star since the Truman administration. In the late 1990s Americans no longer shared a need to unite to oppose a common enemy. There is little likelihood that another common enemy will emerge to equal the potential threat of international communism and to concentrate our will and spirit in defense of "the American way."

The lack of a unifying foreign threat means that American foreign policy will become more partisan. Presidents will no longer be conceded the right to take almost whatever action they deem necessary on behalf of the nation's interests as they were during the extraordinary circumstances of the Cold War. American foreign policy issues will be more controversial than in the past. This will reduce support for defense programs, economic or military aid, or any other proposal that may be perceived as excessive concern for foreign affairs at the expense of American taxpayers. The end of the Cold War means that there will be greater attention paid to domestic policies at the expense of foreign and military policies.

The collapse of the Soviet Union left the United States as the only legitimate super-power. This does not mean the end of international conflict. On the contrary, the decline of Soviet power breathed new life into nationalistic rivalries in Eastern Europe.

The end of the Cold War will result in greater congressional challenges to presidential leadership in foreign policy. For decades the preeminence of the role of the president in conducting foreign policy was aided by the tensions of the Cold War. It allowed presidents to exercise leadership in foreign affairs with far less interference than could usually be done in domestic policy. This was especially true when Republican Presidents occupied the White House, and Democrats controlled Congress.

It should be noted that President Eisenhower had warned of the growing alliance between military and industrial interests, a military-industrial complex, influencing Congress to fund the military and defense industries quite apart from national security needs. Cold War logic justified and even required huge expenditures for exotic and expensive military weapons systems. These expenditures overwhelmingly reward affluent business interests engaged in military production. Many conservatives found this "higher" policy of national defense also proved to be an effective justification to keep social welfare spending low. Liberals wanted to show that they were patriotic pragmatic realists and also supported the diversion of funds for national security.

Traditionally Democrats have had a more activist foreign policy than Republicans. In fact, Republicans have frequently accused the Democrats of recklessness in foreign policy, noting that Democrats were in the White House when the nation became involved in both world wars, Korea and Vietnam. However, the Democrats' convention in Chicago in 1968 revealed serious divisions between the party's anticommunist hawks and its doves. For the next twenty-five years Democrats have, to their disadvantage with voting Americans, generally been perceived as weaker on foreign and defense issues.

Prior to World War II, Republicans and conservatives tended to be the most isolationist in opposition to Roosevelt's activist foreign policy. But after the war, the menacing specter of communism united the Republican Party in a demand to counter communism wherever it appeared. The most damning charge against a political opponent during the postwar period was that he or she was "soft on communism."

Postwar Republican presidents, while inclined to deemphasize the role of government in domestic policy in favor of market solutions, emphasized the need for a "strong" leadership role by the U.S. government in foreign policy. Richard Nixon, who was forced to resign the presidency in disgrace after Watergate, salvaged his reputation to some extent later on and made a modest comeback in some circles based on his reputation as a foreign policy expert. Reagan's willingness to switch from an oppositional stance to accepting arms control agreements resulted in solid advances in the condition of world peace. George Bush, who wanted to be known as the "foreign policy president," gained high marks for his foreign policy efforts. His interest in foreign policy was so great that after the collapse of the Soviet Union and the conclusion of the Gulf War in early 1991, he was perceived to have no domestic policy, and this went a long way toward costing him the 1992 election.

However, the unexpectedly swift end to communism in the early 1990s shattered Republican Party unity concerning an interventionist foreign policy. Opposition to communism had been perceived to be in our vital national interests, but current problems in Somalia, Bosnia, or Haiti are not. Many Republicans had long been uncomfortable with the contradiction of supporting "big government" intervention abroad in the form of major international political and military actions while arguing that "big government" at home is incapable of solving domestic problems and solutions should be left to the marketplace. A new consensus has yet to be reached.

FUTURE CHALLENGES AND FOREIGN POLICY

The end of the Cold War has reduced the threat of a global nuclear catastrophe. However, without the international bipolar competition, and the discipline it imposed, the world is reverting to greater anarchy that characterized the pre–World War II period. The Cold War provided a simple test to distinguish allies from adversaries, or good guys from bad guys. It was based upon which camp a nation or its leaders leaned toward, capitalism or communism. But such simplistic distinctions, which aroused strong support for decades, are now obsolete.

In the post–Cold War world, it is far more difficult to determine exactly what an American national policy interest is, as well as to distinguish allies from adversaries. For this reason alone, it is much more difficult to obtain steadfast support for foreign policy. This is especially true since so few trouble spots are or will be perceived as a threat to America's vital interests.

Starting with the Clinton administration, America must begin the complicated task of redefining its role in the international community. The basic foreign policy questions are: What are the new goals of U.S. foreign policy? What are the obstacles to realizing these goals? How can the United States best achieve its interests?

With the collapse of communism, Americans clearly want more attention paid to long-neglected domestic problems. Foreign policy challenges must be perceived in the national interest in order to receive broad public support. But the American public also believes that the United States has great responsibilities and cannot withdraw from world affairs. And while it is important to maintain military strength in an unstable world, the country cannot go it alone without friends and allies.[15] There is clear support for an active involvement with the UN to expand peacekeeping efforts, to eliminate chemical and nuclear weapons around the world, to clean up the environment, and to suppress illegal international drug trafficking.[16] Emphasizing domestic priorities and supporting a major proactive foreign policy are not mutually exclusive positions. Nor is an activist international role inherently liberal or conservative. Recently, the U.S. Information Agency reported that, "Americans usually prefer non-military measures (e.g., aid cutoff, trade sanctions) to counter a foreign threat. Willingness to intervene depends largely on the U.S. interests at stake. . . ."[17]

---

[15]Daniel Yankelovich, "Foreign Policy after the Election," *Foreign Affairs,* vol. 71, no. 4 (1992), pp. 6–7.

[16]Norman J. Ornstein, "Foreign Policy and the Elections," *Foreign Affairs,* vol. 71, no. 3 (1992), p. 14.

[17]USIA Office of Research and Media Reaction, "Opinion Analysis M-66-98," Washington DC, May 5, 1998.

ETHICAL CONCERNS AND FOREIGN POLICY

The U.S. emphasis on supporting democratic governments is related to the goal of encouraging human rights and social justice. The United States prefers to support constructive change through the ballot box rather than change brought by bullets. During the Cold War, when policy makers perceived our national security or economic needs diverging from the goals of encouraging democracy and justice, they swallowed their scruples. This was unfortunate because support for human rights can be an effective tool of foreign policy that strengthens democratic principles and American leadership.

Promoting democratic principles is both morally right and in accordance with our national heritage. Oftentimes the national interest and morality support the same policy decision, such as the goal of defeating Nazi Germany. The choice is more difficult when moral principles appear to diverge from political reality. For example, in Operation Desert Storm, the United States used force to dislodge Iraqi forces from Kuwait. We restored a nondemocratic government to power without pressing for democratic reforms. In Saudi Arabia, we have supported the monarchy of King Fahd against the threat of Iraqi invasion. The Islamic world denies the basic principle of gender equality. To pressure countries in that region of the world to change, however, would undoubtedly result in greater instability and political turmoil than in supporting the status quo. President Clinton's June 1998 trip to China renewed the human rights debate. Clinton's goal to guide China toward democracy by offering "most favored nation" status angered many who want some vindication for the human rights violations in Tiennamen Square.

Many are disappointed that the moral principles enunciated by the Founding Fathers in the Declaration of Independence have not been taken as a firmer guiding principle in America's foreign ventures. It is clear, however, that democracy requires favorable conditions to take root. It is easy to forget that the evolution of self-government has a longer pre- than post-revolutionary history even in the United States.

A current major policy problem for the United States is how to ensure that democratic principles and free market reforms are cultivated in Russia and Eastern Europe. Democratic nation building in the former Soviet republics and in Eastern Europe would permit even lower levels of U.S. defense expenditures. It would also provide a major investment opportunity for business firms if those countries developed stable democratic processes. But the success of democratic governments is far from certain in the fifteen independent states that formerly made up the Soviet Union.

It has proven far easier to pressure friendly states to undertake democratic reforms and secure human rights than states with whom relations are strained. It is easier to foster democratic reforms in states that are dependent on the United States like the Philippines than in more hostile states like the People's Republic of China.

The tools available range from quiet diplomacy to the withholding of military and economic aid. Many critics believe that now that Third-World leaders are unable to seek communist support, the United States should encourage democracy and human rights more forcefully than in the past. The difficulty is that supporting democracy and human rights in ambiguous circumstances is not in itself a guide to effective policy. If not done carefully, pressuring nondemocratic states too hard may inadvertently result in a more repressive regime gaining power.

President Clinton stated in a speech in Milwaukee in October 1992 that the United States should pursue a "pro democracy foreign policy." However, he did not advocate a foreign policy focusing narrowly on that principle. He said, "We know there may be times when other security needs or economic interests will diverge from our commitment to democracy and human rights." Idealistic goals must be tempered with the pragmatism of the realist. However, a foreign policy that tries to nurture democratic development should place a priority on economic and political methods rather than military means.

NATIONALISM AND ETHNIC CONFLICT

Unfortunately, the disintegration of the Soviet Union did not result in an international surge in favor of peaceful democratic forms of government. Instead, the breakdown of the East-West conflict has facilitated a resurgence of older conflicts reined in for decades by Cold War rivalries. In some former communist countries where the authority of the nation-state itself is weak, many people have reverted to precommunist nationals, racial, ethnic, and religious identifications. The oppressive communist regimes in the former Soviet Union and Yugoslavia, whatever else their failures, did repress the fratricidal ethnic and religious rivalries now raging in Georgia and Bosnia.

During the Cold War the superpowers could also control client states on the periphery of their blocs. While Moscow's leverage to coerce client states has vanished, the ability of Washington to force compliance has also tapered off. In the Middle East and sub-Saharan Africa, in particular, imperialistic European nations earlier in this century created colonies by drawing lines on maps in disregard for ethnic, linguistic, or economic factors. The peace in these areas was often maintained only out of necessities imposed by the Cold War. Without the discipline of superpower rivalry to suppress regional and border conflicts, such problems are becoming much more numerous. The result is frequently the creation of millions of refugees and mass migrations on a scale previously unknown, as in Rwanda. North Korea's unwillingness to allow inspection of its nuclear arsenal in the mid 1990s is an example of the post–Cold War "independence" of former Soviet satellites.

Many of the problems appear all but insoluble even with superpower intervention. For example, Iraq has made territorial claims on Kuwait since London created the Kuwaiti protectorate in the 1920s. Most Iraqis do not regard the border with Kuwait as either just or permanent. The inability of Saddam Hussein to enforce Iraq's claim over the area in the Gulf War does not lessen the righteousness of the cause in the eyes of Iraq's citizens. The United States has merely replaced British imperialism as the enemy. This impression is reinforced by America returning a nondemocratic government to power in Kuwait, which has led to cynicism regarding how important democracies are to the United States even in a post–Cold War world.

Territorial disputes, civil wars, ethnic conflicts (several of which have spilled across international borders) as well as the collapse of governmental authority in some states threaten world peace. While such conflicts, like Northern Ireland, may not threaten American national security, others like India and Pakistan's nuclear competition cannot be ignored. The United Nations has tried to play a constructive role by mediating disputes and the use of neutral peacekeeping troops interposed between warring factions. The Clinton administration has tried to prod the UN to take action to prevent governments from destroying its own citizens. Sovereignty does not include the right to commit genocide against one's own nationals. The Nuremberg Trials settled that issue. The UN has cooperated in the gathering of evidence to be used to prosecute individuals who have committed atrocities in Bosnia and Serbia. It is the obligation of the international community, not of the United States or any other states, to prevent genocidal policies.

The U.S. policy may be most effective when prodding the UN to take action. The United States can provide logistical and material support for such operations. The use of U.S. troops for peacekeeping operations presents a unique set of problems. Canada, Sweden, and Ireland among others have long experience in peacekeeping operations and are not as likely to be targeted by a faction seeking notoriety as are American troops.

The Clinton administration announced a policy of considering U.S. personnel participation in a given peace operation if it advances American interests and if the unique risks to American personnel have been weighed and are considered acceptable. American participation must be considered essential for the operation's success, and there must be clear objectives and an identifiable endpoint for U.S. participation.

ECONOMIC THEMES

Military Spending and Economic Power

There is an unusual relationship between military power and economic power. A nation that would be a military superpower must make significant investments in military production and spending. This must ordinarily be done at the expense of investment in consumer goods. The United States can have the status of a military and economic superpower only if its citizenry exercises a greater propensity to save and invest in civilian research and development (R&D). Historically there is a tendency for economic powers to invest heavily in military spending. Exorbitant military spending undermines economic power. But in the long run, as Gorbachev found out, military power requires a sound economic structure.

During the Cold War the United States diverted about 6 percent of GDP from consumer production to military spending. This is one reason the American economy has lagged behind those of Japan and Germany for the last couple of decades. About 70 percent of R&D money in the United States was spent on the military. Most of the best engineers and scientists in America during that time worked in military rather than consumer goods research. In Japan the emphasis was the reverse.

International Trade

International trade has become a significant part of the U.S. economy only in the last half of the century. Sales of goods and services abroad, or exports, now amount to 10 percent of what the American economy produces. **Exports** are goods produced domestically but sold in foreign markets. The goods and services purchased in the United States but produced abroad, or imports, have increased dramatically in the last 20 years.

Imports are goods produced in foreign countries but purchased in the United States. Imports have exceeded exports consistently since 1975.

Whenever nations engage in international trade, there are potential problems. International trade differs from domestic trade in that a foreign entrepreneur's right to sell in another country's domestic market can be limited by **tariffs,** or taxes on imports. Tariffs result in higher prices for consumers. Other regulatory restrictions on imports, such as requirements that a percentage of the products must be assembled within the host state, called nontariff barriers, may also limit trade. Foreign producers may also find countries impose quotas, or absolute limits on the amounts of goods that can be imported.

COMPARATIVE ADVANTAGE

Why do people engage in international trade, which has so many potential difficulties? Would it not be easier if each country relied on the productive capacity of its own economy? The answer is that Adam Smith's reasoning that applied to a domestic economy was shown by David Ricardo to also apply to international trade. National economies differ because they have different comparative advantages. **A comparative advantage exists when a country can produce a good at a lower opportunity cost (give up less production of other goods) than another country.** For example, suppose that in the United States it costs $150 to produce a leather jacket but only $100 to produce a portable disc player. In the United States, the opportunity cost of producing a leather jacket is equal to that of producing one disc player. Since the cost is the same, the United States must reduce its production of leather coats by one to get one more disc player. Japan has a comparative advantage in producing disc players because its opportunity cost is only two-thirds of a leather jacket. This gives the United States a comparative advantage in the production of leather jackets. Notice that if one country has a comparative advantage in one good, the other nations must have a comparative advantage in the production of another good. Comparative advantage is based on the opportunity cost, not total costs.

Free trade between nations results in situations where a nation as a whole is better off, but some workers are worse off. Industries with a comparative advantage will expand and new workers will be hired as products are produced for the export market. Consumers will also be better off, as they can buy imported products at lower prices. Workers in industries without a comparative advantage will face a downward pressure on wages, and may face layoffs.

The areas of comparative advantage for the American economy have been shifting for a number of years, and there have been job losses as some kinds of industry have moved abroad. The Clinton administration has pledged to provide retraining programs for Americans who lose jobs to help them find employment in the job areas where the United States still enjoys a comparative advantage over foreign competitors. It also supported NAFTA on the basis that free trade should result in a net benefit to the American economy since the overall gains it produces exceed any losses.

Since nations are not self-sufficient they must obtain through trading the goods they are unable to produce or find too expensive to produce themselves, or they must accept a lower standard of living.

Trade barriers result in higher prices for consumers, governments impose them because they are frequently more responsive to business interests than to consumer interests.

One reason policy makers today must be concerned with international trade issues is because of America's current balance of trade situation, or the gap between the value of goods it exports and imports. When the value of exports exceeds the value of imports, a country runs a **trade surplus.** When the value of imports exceeds that of exports, a country runs a **trade deficit**. From the end of World War II until the early 1980s, the United States consistently exported more than it imported. Then is the early 1980s persistent and massive trade deficits emerged. The United States has been running a trade deficit which increased to $170 billion in 1987. Since then the level has declined, but it still runs at about $100 billion annually.

Why Worry About Trade Deficits?

Running a trade deficit has similarities to running a budget deficit. It allows a nation to consume (import) more than it produces (exports) by spending past savings, or by borrowing. When the United States runs a trade deficit, the country must make up the difference by selling assets like real estate, stocks, bonds, and even whole corporations. In the more than half a century from World War I until the 1980s, the United States was the major creditor nation of the world. It ran large trade surpluses with other countries, lending large sums abroad and acquiring large amounts of foreign assets in the process. Net American foreign investment reached a peak of $141 billion at the end of 1981. Then, in just four years, the total accumulated investments of over sixty years were undone. By the end of 1985, foreign assets in the United States exceeded American-held assets abroad by $112 billion.[18] Since then, the United States has become the world's biggest debtor nation and instead of receiving interest income, we must pay out interest every year while getting nothing in return.

An important factor in determining whether a country runs a trade deficit or surplus is its ability to produce goods more cheaply than other countries. Through the 1950s and 1960s, American workers were highly competitive even though their wages were higher than most foreign workers. American productivity was so great that American goods were of higher quality and lower price, and therefore more desirable than foreign goods. That began to change by the late 1970s as Japan and Third-World countries invested heavily in developing their industrial bases. Foreign governments were not about to allow natural market forces to determine outcomes with so much at stake. Governments intervened to subsidize much of the research and development necessary for business development and manufacturing. In the process, they proved that governmental intervention can strengthen national markets. Foreign manufacturers with new and modern industrial facilities and lower wages began with increasing frequency to compete effectively with American manufacturers.

Other trade pressures magnify a trade deficit. When a trade deficit occurs, imports rise and exports fall. A fall in exports means that domestic production falls, which means that domestic workers have less income and consequently demand for goods falls and

---

[18]Paul Krugman, *The Age of Diminished Expectations* (Cambridge, MA: MIT Press, 1992), p. 40.

unemployment rises. Higher unemployment means that workers spend less and incomes fall more. Conversely, in a nation like Japan that exports more than it imports, as production rises, Japanese citizens have more income to spend on consumer goods or investments, resulting in high employment levels so that ultimately Japanese incomes rise even further. The effect of Japan's exports on income creates export-led economic growth. That is, Japan's trade surplus stimulates higher incomes.

Pleas for Protectionism

Free trade has its critics who argue that trade restrictions would directly reduce the deficit. It is often claimed that trade is unfair because of low foreign wages, or government subsidies. However, if U.S. producers would benefit from tariffs, consumers would lose. Consumer prices would rise with tariffs while quality of domestic products would fall, lowering the standard of living. Trade restrictions also invite retaliation. If one country erects trade barriers, other countries respond with restrictions of their own.

The economic arguments in favor of free trade are forceful, but have been challenged by those who argue that it may be in the public interest to restrict or suspend free trade. There are several arguments advanced in favor of trade restrictions.[19]

The **national defense argument** contends that it would be foolhardy to rely on imports for items necessary to our national defense. Combat ships and aircraft, along with munitions, are critical to national defense. It would be too risky to leave weapons production to commercial trading partners. Although the argument undoubtedly may have some legitimacy, it is often misapplied. The national defense argument has been stretched to include agriculture, the fishing industry, and other tangentially related industries.

The **antidumping argument** in which dumping is defined as the sale of goods abroad at a price lower than their sale in the domestic market, or below their average cost, claims that dumping is an unfair trade practice because it is done to drive out domestic producers and then raise prices. However, this is a questionable market strategy because once dumpers have driven out the competition and raised their prices, the domestic competition will return. Meanwhile the dumping nations would have only a string of losses to show for their effort of selling below cost to drive out the competition. During this period domestic consumers would have been the beneficiaries of buying products at very low prices.

The **infant-industry argument** is probably the most blatant appeal for special interest protection. The argument is that new or "infant" industries may need protection until they have grown and become competitive with more "mature" foreign competitors. Critics point out that an infant industry grown to maturity is more powerful and even more insistent that benefits not be taken away.

The **saving domestic jobs argument** masquerades in different guises. One form of the argument is that domestic producers cannot compete with foreign producers because of the higher wages received by American workers relative to those paid by foreign producers. Without protection, domestic producers will be forced to shut down and

---

[19]Arguments adapted from Roger A. Arnold, *Economics,* 3d edition. St. Paul: West Publishing Company, 1996, pp. 752–58.

domestic jobs will be lost. However, the argument ignores the point that the higher productivity of domestic workers is why the American worker earns more compared to the low wage of a less productive foreign worker. If an American worker working with capital goods earns $25 per hour with benefits and produces 100 widgets, the labor costs per unit will be lower than that of a foreign worker who receives $3 per hour but produces only 4 units of widgets per hour with minimal assistance from machinery. That is, a high wage disadvantage may be offset by a productivity advantage. Conversely a country's advantage of low wages can be negated by its low productivity disadvantage.

Another variation on this saving domestic jobs argument is that foreign governments subsidize foreign exports. When government subsidies lower the costs to foreign producrs, the result is that domestic producers cannot compete, leading to failure and the loss of domestic jobs.

The Politics of Protectionism

Since protectionism imposes higher costs on consumers and reduces their standard of living, why would governments respond to producer lobbying efforts? To understand why, let us assume that there are twenty American firms producing a consumer good we will call X. Suppose also that there are 40 million American consumers of good X. If the producers, fearing foreign competition, lobby for a tariff on foreign imports that would compete with their product, the consumers will end up paying higher prices. If the producers are successful in their lobbying effort, the consumers end up paying $40 million more in higher prices, and the producers receive $40 more for the protected product than if there were no tariff.

If the $40 million were divided equally between the twenty producrs, each would receive $2 million more as the result of the tariff. If the $40 million dollar higher costs were divided equally between the 40 million consumers, each would pay $1 more because of the tariff.

Producers are likely to consider the possibilities and decide to lobby for the tariff because if they are successful they will receive $2 million. Consumers may not be aware that anyone is lobbying for tariffs on X. If the consumer is aware he may conclude that it would be foolish to lobby against the tariff. If he wins, he will only save $1 which is not worth the time or expense that lobbying would take.

The **benefits of tariffs are highly concentrated** on only a few producers, while the costs are spread over millions of consumers. Therefore each producer stands to gain much more than each individual consumer stands to lose. Public choise theory would predict that producers will lobby vigorously to obtain the relatively large gains from protection from foreign competition, while consumers will not be inclined to mount significant opposition to keep from paying the small individual increase. Politicians are inclined to respond to the few producers intensely involved in lobbying on behalf of tariffs (or a variety of other subsidies), especially since campaign contributions emphasize the importance of the subsidy. Politicians may mistake the relative silence of the opposition as a lack of opposition.

The decade of the 1980s saw a surge in protectionism in the United States. Some blamed the weak American economy on unfair trade barriers that prevented the sale of

American goods in international markets, thereby costing American jobs. Protectionism, it was argued, would save American jobs from such unfair practices and strengthen the economy. While President Reagan talked about the virtues of unfettered market forces, protectionism spiraled. In 1980 about one-eighth of all imports into the United States were affected by protectionism; by 1990 that figure was 25 percent. By the end of the 1980s, about 40 percent of Japan's exports to the United States were limited by some form of protectionism. Japan was persuaded to "voluntarily" limit its export of cars to the United States or face the possibility of quotas.

President Clinton has committed himself to the reduction of all trade barriers. His commitment to win congressional approval of NAFTA over sharp opposition by labor is significant in this regard. He has also indicated his commitment to support a reduction in trade barriers at the Uruguay round of the General Agreement on Tariffs and Trade (GATT) negotiations. In addition, he has announced the goal of reforming domestic institutions to improve the competitive performance of the U.S. economy, including its international trade and financial position. Reducing the federal budget deficit, he has indicated, is one component in reducing the trade deficit.

The issue is no longer a zero-sum attempt to combat communist enemies, but a non-zero-sum economic competition among international partners to achieve domestic and international economic growth. There is an important link between domestic economic policy and foreign policy. A robust American economy based upon principles of justice provides a better opportunity for the United States to encourage human rights and democratic approaches along with open market systems. Any effective foreign policy must be based on an improvement in the international competitiveness of the American economy.

CONCLUSION

1 Foreign policy making by the American government is characterized by a unique set of political actors and processes. The Constitution ultimately provides that the president and Congress share responsibility in foreign policy. Actors involved in crisis situations in foreign policy tend to be limited to the president, leading members of Congress, and heads of executive agencies such as the Departments of State and Defense and the Central Intelligence Agency. Long-term national security issues, while generally formulated by the president, traditionally involve congressional involvement and bipartisan support through the need for funding. Such issues have not typically required major involvement by the American public. A decline in the consensus that the policy in Vietnam was either wise or necessary in opposing communism resulted in a more independent-minded Congress in regard to foreign policy.

2 From 1945 until the collapse of the Soviet Union in 1990, American foreign policy was based on the policy of containing communist expansion. This bipolar rivalry with the Soviet Union provided discipline and restricted foreign policy options for over forty years. It also reduced funding available for domestic needs such as housing, education, and poverty programs.

3 With the end of the Cold War many nations, particularly in Europe, have been freed from the constraints of superpower rivalry and have more freedom to pursue their national interests. The drive for further European integration has been slowed by the end of the Cold War.

4 The international system is in a state of transition. While international integration is occurring in some areas, nationalism, political turmoil, and even civil war have reemerged in others. Workable foreign policy tools for handling these situations have yet to be developed.

5 Economic and technical changes in international economic systems are eroding some of the sovereign political authority traditionally enjoyed by nation-states. Ideological confrontations between capitalism and communism are being replaced by competition between different models of market economies. Nations are competing to create favorable conditions for economic prosperity. Some governments play a far more active role as coordinators of their domestic economics than others.

QUESTIONS FOR DISCUSSION

1 Is the United States in decline as a superpower despite the collapse of the Soviet Union? Why?
2 Is there evidence that declining hegemonic powers like the Soviet Union create political instability and economic disarray?
3 Is the U.S. economy in disarray because the United States is the largest debtor nation in the world? Why or why not?
4 Why do most political scientists oppose trade restrictions?
5 Why is all voluntary international trade mutually beneficial?

KEY CONCEPTS

antidumping argument	intergovernmental organizations (IGOs)
comparative advantage	national defense argument
containment policy	National Security Council (NSC)
covert action	nongovernmental organizations (NGOs)
European Community (EC)	saving domestic jobs argument
exports	sovereignty
global village	trade deficit
imports	trade surplus
infant-industry argument	

SUGGESTED READINGS

C. Fred Bergsten, "The Primacy of Economics," *Foreign Policy* (Summer 1992), pp. 3–25.

Peter Drucker, *Post-Capitalist Society* (New York: Harper Collins, 1993).

Paul Krugman, *The Age of Diminished Expectations: U.S. Economic Policy in the 1990s* (Cambridge, MA: MIT Press, 1992).

Edward J. Lincoln, *Japan's Unequal Trade* (Washington DC: The Brookings Institution, 1990).

Thomas E. Mann (ed.), *A Question of Balance: The President, the Congress and Foreign Policy* (Washington DC: The Brookings Institution, 1990).

Jerel A. Rosati, *The Politics of United States Foreign Policy* (New York: Harcourt, Brace, Jovanovich, 1993).

Theodore Rueter (ed.), *The United States in the World Political Economy* (New York: McGraw Hill, 1994).

John W. Spanier and Eric M. Uslaner, *American Foreign Policy Making and the Democratic Dilemmas,* 6th ed. (New York: Macmillan, 1994).

John D. Steinbruner (ed.), *Restructuring American Foreign Policy* (Washington D.C.: The Brookings Institution, 1989).

Lester Thurow, *Head to Head* (New York: William Morrow, 1992).

Alvin Toffler and Heidi Toffler, *War and Anti-War: Survival at the Dawn of the 21st Century* (Boston: Little, Brown 1993).

Martin Tolchin and Susan Tolchin, *Buying into America* (New York: Times Books, 1988).

Martin Tolchin and Susan Tolchin, *Selling Our Security* (New York: Alfred A. Knopf, 1992).

INDEX